hermeneia

**Hermeneia
—A Critical
and Historical
Commentary
on the Bible**

Qoheleth

A Commentary

by Thomas Krüger

Translated by
O. C. Dean Jr.

Edited by
Klaus Baltzer

Fortress Press   Minneapolis

Qoheleth
A Commentary

Cover and interior design by Kenneth Hiebert
Typesetting and page composition by
The HK Scriptorium

ISBN 0-8006-6036-6 (alk. paper)

The paper used in this publication meets the minimum requirements of American National Standard for Information Sciences—Permanence of paper for Printed Library Materials, ANSI Z329.48–1984.

Manufactured in the U.S.A.

08   07   06   05   04   1   2   3   4   5   6   7   8   9   10

Contents
Qoheleth

Foreword	vii
Preface	ix
Endpapers	x
Abbreviations	xi

■ **Introduction** 1

Themes	1
Structure	5
Genres	8
Tensions and Contradictions	14
Origin and Historical Context	19
History of Influence and Reception	27
Language	34
Text	36

■ **Commentary** 39

1:1	Title	39
1:2	Motto	42
1:3—4:12	**The King and the Wise Man**	45
1:3-11	Prelude: Is There Any Gain with Regard to Eternity?	47
1:12—2:26	Reflections of King Qoheleth: The Devaluation of Happiness Not at One's Disposal	56
3:1-9	Interlude: Is There Any Gain with Regard to Time?	75
3:10—4:12	Reflections of the Wise Man Qoheleth: Happiness as the Highest Good Is Not at Our Disposal	80
4:13—5:8 [5:9]	**The King and the Deity**	101
4:13-16	Critique of Expecting Too Much from a King	102
4:17—5:6[5:1-7]	Exhortation to the Proper Attitude before the Deity	106
5:7-8[8-9]	Critique of Expecting Too Much from a King	113
5:9[10]—6:9	**Poverty and Wealth**	116
5:9-11[10-12]	Proverbs	119
5:12-16[13-17]	Negative Cases	120
5:17-19[18-20]	Positive Cases	122
6:1-6	Negative Cases	124
6:7-9	Proverbs	127
6:10—8:17	**Critical Discussion of Conventional Wisdom**	131
6:10-12	Human Limitations	132
7:1-14	Critique of Wise Advice	134
7:15-22	Limits of Righteousness and Wisdom	139
7:23-29	Limits of Wisdom	143
8:1-9	Knowledge and Power	150
8:10-15	The Righteous and the Wicked	158
8:16-17	Limits of Wisdom	163

9:1—12:7	**Life in View of Chance and Transitoriness**	165
9:1-12	Exhortation to Pleasure and Vigorous Action in View of Death and Chance	166
9:13—10:20	Strengths and Weaknesses of Wisdom	176
11:1—12:7	Advice for Life in View of the Uncertainty of the Future and the Certainty of Death	190
12:8	Motto	206
12:9-14	Epilogue	207

■ Endmatter

Bibliography	217
Indexes	273
Designer's Notes	305

The name *Hermeneia,* Greek ἑρμηνεία, has been chosen as the title of the commentary series to which this volume belongs. The word *Hermeneia* has a rich background in the history of biblical interpretation as a term used in the ancient Greek-speaking world for the detailed, systematic exposition of a scriptural work. It is hoped that the series, like its name, will carry forward this old and venerable tradition. A second, entirely practical reason for selecting the name lies in the desire to avoid a long descriptive title and its inevitable acronym, or worse, an unpronounceable abbreviation.

The series is designed to be a critical and historical commentary to the Bible without arbitrary limits in size or scope. It will utilize the full range of philological and historical tools, including textual criticism (often slighted in modern commentaries), the methods of the history of tradition (including genre and prosodic analysis), and the history of religion.

Hermeneia is designed for the serious student of the Bible. It will make full use of ancient Semitic and classical languages; at the same time, English translations of all comparative materials—Greek, Latin, Canaanite, or Akkadian—will be supplied alongside the citation of the source in its original language. Insofar as possible, the aim is to provide the student or scholar with full critical discussion of each problem of interpretation and with the primary data upon which the discussion is based.

Hermeneia is designed to be international and interconfessional in the selection of authors; its editorial boards were formed with this end in view. Occasionally the series will offer translations of distinguished commentaries which originally appeared in languages other than English. Published volumes of the series will be revised continually, and eventually, new commentaries will replace older works in order to preserve the currency of the series. Commentaries are also being assigned for important literary works in the categories of apocryphal and pseudepigraphical works relating to the Old and New Testaments, including some of Essene or Gnostic authorship.

The editors of *Hermeneia* impose no systematic-theological perspective upon the series (directly, or indirectly by selection of authors). It is expected that authors will struggle to lay bare the ancient meaning of a biblical work or pericope. In this way the text's human relevance should become transparent, as is always the case in competent historical discourse. However, the series eschews for itself homiletical translation of the Bible.

The editors are heavily indebted to Fortress Press for its energy and courage in taking up an expensive, long-term project, the rewards of which will accrue chiefly to the field of biblical scholarship.

The editor responsible for this volume is Klaus Baltzer of the University of Munich.

Frank Moore Cross　　　*Helmut Koester*
For the Old Testament　For the New Testament
Editorial Board　　　　Editorial Board

The German manuscript of the present commentary was completed in October 1999. Literature on the book of Qoheleth that appeared later could not be considered in the commentary, but it has been added to the bibliography.

I would like to express my appreciation to those who have helped me in the production of this commentary. They include, first, my teachers, colleagues, and friends in Munich and Zurich: Klaus Baltzer (who also supported me as volume editor), Rüdiger Bartelmus, and the late Odil Hannes Steck, to whom I am indebted for many valuable suggestions. With Martin Rose and Béatrice Perregaux Allison in Neuchâtel I was able to exchange not only ideas but also extensive bibliographical references. To the German scholar Johannes Anderegg, my colleague in the translation of the book of Qoheleth for the newly revised edition of the *Zürcher Bibel*, I am grateful for many enlightening insights. For help in the production of the manuscript and especially the bibliography, I must also express my gratitude to Peter Schwagmeier, Christine Forster Wenger, Markus Giger, Trix Gretler, Annette Schellenberg, and Susanne Weiss. Finally, I want to thank O. C. Dean for his good work in translating my complicated German into clear English and K. C. Hanson and Beth Wright, along with their colleagues at Fortress Press, for their careful editorial work.

Thomas Krüger
Zurich

The endpapers of this volume display manuscript fragments of Qoheleth designated 4QQoh^a (4Q109) and
4QQoh^b (4Q110), found in Qumran Cave 4. The first set
of fragments pictured include portions of Qoh 5:13-17;
6:1?, 3-8; 6:12—7:6; 7:7-10, 19-20. The second set of fragments include portions of Qoh 1:10-13 and 13-14. The
photographs (PAM 43.092 and PAM 43.090) are reproduced with the permission of the Israel Antiquities
Authority and provided by the Ancient Biblical Manuscript Center for Preservation and Research, Claremont,
California.

Abbreviations

α′	Aquila	BAT	Die Botschaft des Alten Testaments
ÄA	Ägyptologische Abhandlungen	BAW.AO	Bibliothek der Alten Welt. Der Alte Orient
ÄAT	Ägypten und Altes Testament		
AB	Anchor Bible	BBB	Bonner biblische Beiträge
ABD	Anchor Bible Dictionary, ed. D. N. Freedman, 6 vols. (New York: Doubleday, 1992)	BEAT	Beiträge des Erforschung des Alten Testaments
		BeO	Bibbia e oriente
AbrN	Abr-Nahrain	BethM	Beth Miqra
ACra	Analecta Cracoviensia	BEThL	Bibliotheca ephemeridum theologicarum lovaniensium
AF	Archivia di filosofia		
AGJU	Arbeiten zur Geschichte des Spätjudentums und Urchristentums	BEvTh	Beiträge zur evangelischen Theologie
		BHK	R. Kittel, ed., Biblia Hebraica (16th ed.; Stuttgart: Württembergische Bibelanstalt, 1971)
AION	Annali dell'Istituto Orientale di Napoli		
AJBI	Annual of the Japanese Biblical Institute		
AJSL	American Journal of Semitic Languages and Literature	BHS	K. Elliger and W. Rudolph, eds., Biblia Hebraica Stuttgartensia (5th ed.; Stuttgart: Deutsche Bibelgesellschaft, 1997)
AnBib	Analecta biblica		
ANET	James B. Pritchard, ed., Ancient Near Eastern Texts Relating to the Old Testament (3d ed.; Princeton: Princeton Univ. Press, 1969)	BHT	Beiträge zur historischen Theologie
		Bib	Biblica
		BibInt	Biblical Interpretation
		BIFAO	Bullétin de l'Institut français d'archéologie orientale
ANETS	Ancient Near Eastern Texts and Studies		
		BiHe	Bibel heute
ANRW	Aufstieg und Niedergang der römischen Welt	Bijdr	Bijdragen
		BiSe	Biblical Seminar
AOAT	Alter Orient und Altes Testament	BK	Bibel und Kirche
AOT	Hugo Gressmann, ed., Altorientalische Texte zum Alten Testament (2d ed. 1926; repr. Berlin: de Gruyter, 1970)	BKAT	Biblischer Kommentar, Altes Testament
		BL	Bibel und Liturgie
Arab.	Arabic	BN	Biblische Notizen
ARG	Archiv für Reformationsgeschichte	BOT	De Boeken van het Oude Testament
Aristotle		BRev	Bible Review
Eth. nic.	Ethica Nicomachea	BSac	Bibliotheca sacra
ASEs	Annali di storia dell'esegesi	BT	The Bible Translator
AsSeign	Assemblées du Seigneur	BTB	Biblical Theology Bulletin
ASTI	Annual of the Swedish Theological Institute	BThSt	Biblisch-theologische Studien
		BV	Biblical Viewpoint
ATD	Das Alte Testament Deutsch	BVC	Bible et vie chrétienne
ATSAT	Arbeiten zu Text und Sprache im Alten Testament	BWANT	Beiträge zur Wissenschaft vom Alten Testament
Aug	Augustinianum	Byz.	Byzantion
AUSS	Andrews University Seminary Studies	BZ	Biblische Zeitschrift
AUU, SSU	Acta Universitatis Upsaliensis, Studia Semitica Upsaliensia	BZAW	Beihefte zur Zeitschrift für die alttestamentliche Wissenschaft
AV	Authorized (King James) Version	BZNW	Beihefte zur Zeitschrift für die neutestamentliche Wissenschaft
AzTh	Arbeiten zur Theologie		
b.	Babylonian Talmud	ℭ	Hebrew fragments from the Cairo Genizah
'Abod. Zar.	'Aboda Zara		
B. Batra	Baba Batra	CBC	Cambridge Bible Commentary
Git.	Gittin	CBQ	Catholic Biblical Quarterly
Ned.	Nedarim	CBQMS	Catholic Biblical Quarterly Monograph Series
Sanh.	Sanhedrin		
Shab.	Shabbat	CC	Continental Commentary
BA	Biblical Archaeologist	CChrSG	Corpus Christianorum: Series graeca
BASOR	Bulletin of the American Schools of Oriental Research	CChrSL	Corpus Christianorum: Series latina

CChrCM	Corpus Christianorum: Continuatio mediaevalis	HAR	Hebrew Annual Review
		HAT	Handbuch zum Alten Testament
CEv	Cahiers évangile	Heb.	Hebrew
ChrCent	Christian Century	HBS	Herders biblische Studien
CJT	Canadian Journal of Theology	Hen	Henoch
comm.(s).	commentary(ies)	Her.	Hermanthena
ConBOT	Coniectanea biblica: Old Testament Series	HeyJ	Heythrop Journal
		HKAT	Handkommentar zum Alten Testament
corr.	correction		
CoTh	Collectanea theologica	HNT	Handbuch zum Neuen Testament
CTM	Concordia Theological Monthly	HS	Hebrew Studies
CuBi	Cultura bíblica	HSAT	Die heilige Schrift des Alten Testaments
DJD	Discoveries in the Judaean Desert		
ECarm	Ephemerides Carmeliticae	HSM	Harvard Semitic Monographs
EdF	Erträge der Forschung	HUCA	Hebrew Union College Annual
Ep. Arist.	Epistle of Aristeas	HvTSt	Hervormde teologiese studies
ErIsr	Eretz-Israel	ICC	International Critical Commentary
EstBib	Estudios bíblicos	Int	Interpretation
EtAug	Études augustiennes	IRT	Issues in Religion and Theology
EtB	Études bibliques	ITC	International Theological Commentary
EThL	Ephemerides theologicae lovanienses		
EThR	Études théologiques et religieuses	ITQ	Irish Theological Quarterly
EÜ	Die Bibel: Einheitsübersetzung	ITS	Indian Theological Studies
EvQ	Evangelical Quarterly	ITSSup	Indian Theological Studies Supplement
EvTh	Evangelische Theologie		
Exp.	Expositor	JB	Die Bibel: Deutsche Ausgabe mit den Erläuterungen der Jerusalemer Bibel
ExpT	Expository Times		
FB	Forschung zur Bibel	JBL	Journal of Biblical Literature
FCB	Feminist Companion to the Bible	JBQ	Jewish Bible Quarterly
FGLP	Forschungen zur Geschichte und Lehre des Protestantismus	JBR	Journal of Bible and Religion
		JCS	Journal of Cuneiform Studies
FGrHist	Die Fragmente der Griechischen Historiker, ed. F. Jacoby (Leiden: Brill, 1954)	Jer.	Jerome
		JETS	Journal of the Evangelical Theological Society
FOTL	Forms of the Old Testament Literature	JJS	Journal of Jewish Studies
		JNES	Journal of Near Eastern Studies
frg(s).	fragment(s)	JNSL	Journal of Northwest Semitic Languages
FS	Festschrift	Josephus	
GAT	Grundriss zum Alten Testament	Ant.	Antiquities
GB	Wilhelm Gesenius, Hebräisches und Aramäisches Handwörterbuch über das Alte Testament . . . bearbeitet von Dr. Frants Buhl (17th ed. 1915; repr. Berlin: Springer, 1962)	Bell.	Bellum Judaicum
		JQR	Jewish Quarterly Review
		JSHRZ	Jüdische Schriften aus hellenistisch-römischer Zeit
		JSOT	Journal for the Study of the Old Testament
GKC	Wilhelm Gesenius, Hebrew Grammar, ed. E. Kautzsch, trans. A. E. Cowley (2d ed.; Oxford: Oxford Univ. Press, 1910)	JSOTSup	Journal for the Study of the Old Testament Supplement Series
		JSQ	Jewish Studies Quarterly
GLECS	Comptes rendus du Groupe Linguistique d'Études Chamito-Sémitiques	JSS	Journal of Semitic Studies
		JTS	Journal of Theological Studies
		JudUm	Judentum und Umwelt
GOF.S	Göttinger Orientforschung: Syriaca	K	Ketib
GTJ	Grace Theological Journal	ℜ	Coptic translation
GuL	Geist und Leben	KAT	Kommentar zum Alten Testament
Habil.	Habilitationschrift	KatBl	Katechetische Blätter
HALOT	Ludwig Koehler, Walter Baumgartner, Johann Jakob Stamm, and Benedikt Hartmann, Hebrew and Aramaic Lexicon of the Old Testament, ed. and trans. M. E. J. Richardson et al. (5 vols.; Leiden: Brill, 1994–1999)	Kath.	Der Katholik
		KBL	Ludwig Koehler and Walter Baumgartner, Lexicon in Veteris Testamenti Libros (2d ed.; Leiden: Brill, 1958)
		KEH	Kurzgefasstes exegetisches Handbuch

KHC	Kurzer Hand-Commentar zum Alten Testament	OTMes	Old Testament Message
KT	Kaiser Taschenbücher	OTS	Oudtestamentische Studiën
𝔏	Old Latin	OTWSA	*Ou testamentiese weerkgemeenskap in Suid-Afrika*
Laur.	*Laurentianum*	PAAJR	*Proceedings of the American Academy of Jewish Research*
LD	Lectio divina		
Leš	*Lešonénu*	*PaVi*	*Parole di vita*
LiBi	Lire la Bible	PEQ	*Palestine Exploration Quarterly*
LiSa	Libros Sagrados	*PhilipSac*	*Philippiana sacra*
lit.	literally	PIBA	*Proceedings of the Irish Biblical Association*
LM	*Lutherische Monatshefte*		
LoB.AT	Leggere oggi la Bibbia. Antico Testamento	POT	De Prediking van het Oude Testament
		Protest	*Protestantesimo*
LTP	*Laval théologique et philosophique*	PSB	*Princeton Seminary Bulletin*
LumVie	*Lumière et Vie*	PSV	*Parola spirito e vita*
m.	Mishnah	PTA	Papyrologische Texte und Abhandlungen
MARG	*Mitteilungen für Anthropologie und Religionsgeschichte*		
		PW	Pauly-Wissowa, *Real-encyclopädie der classischen Altertumswissenschaft*
MEAH	*Miscelánea de estudios arabes y hebraicos*		
MGWJ	*Monatschrift für Geschichte und Wissenschaft des Judentums*	Q	Qere
		QD	Quaestiones disputatae
MLBS	Mercer Library of Biblical Studies	*RasIsr*	*Rasegna mensile di Israel*
MoBi	Monde de la Bible	RB	*Revue biblique*
MT	Masoretic text	*REJ*	*Revue des études juives*
MUN	Mémoires de l'Université de Neuchâtel	RevExp	*Review and Expositor*
		RevistB	*Revista bíblica*
Mus	*Muséon*	*RHPhR*	*Revue d'histoire et de philosophie religieuses*
NASB	*New American Standard Bible*		
NC	*Nouvelle Clio*	RIBLA	*Revista de interpretación bíblica latino-americana*
NCB	New Century Bible		
NEB	*New English Bible*	*RivB*	*Rivista biblica*
NEchtB	Neue Echter Bibel	*RStB*	*Ricerche storico bibliche*
NedThT	*Nederlands theologisch tijdschrift*	*RSV*	*Revised Standard Version*
NGTT	*Nederduitse gereformeerde teologiese tydskrif*	RTAT	Walter Beyerlin, ed., *Religions-geschichtliches Textbuch zum Alten Testament* (GAT 1; Göttingen: Vandenhoeck & Ruprecht, 1975)
NIBCOT	New International Biblical Commentary on the Old Testament		
NICOT	New International Commentary on the Old Testament	*RThPh*	*Revue de théologie et de philosophie*
		RV	Religionsgeschichtliche Volksbücher
NIV	*New International Version*	σ′	Symmachus
NJPSV	*New Jewish Publication Society Version*	SAT	Die Schriften des Alten Testaments in Auswahl
NRSV	*New Revised Standard Version*		
NRTh	*La nouvelle revue théologique*	SB [J]	Sainte Bible [Jerusalem]
n.s.	new series	SBAB	Stuttgarter biblische Aufsatzbände
NTOA	Novum Testamentum et Orbis Antiquus	SBBS	Soncino Books of the Bible Series
		SBFLA	*Studii biblici Franciscani liber annus*
NVB	Nuovissima versione della bibbia dai testi originali	SBLDS	Society of Biblical Literature Dissertation Series
NZSTh	*Neue Zeitschrift für systematische Theologie*	SBLHS	SBL Homage Series
		SBLSCS	SBL Septuagint and Cognate Studies
OBO	Orbis biblicus et orientalis	*SBLSP*	*SBL Seminar Papers*
OLA	Orientalia lovaniensia analecta	SBLTT	SBL Texts and Translations
OLP	*Orientalia Lovaniensia periodica*	SBS	Stuttgarter Bibelstudien
OLZ	*Orientalische Literaturzeitung*	*SBTh*	*Studia biblica et theologica*
Or	*Orientalia*	SC	Sources chrétiennes
Orph.	*Orpheus*	*ScC*	*La scuola cattolica*
OT	Old Testament	*ScEs*	*Science et esprit*
OTE	*Old Testament Essays*	*ScrC*	*Scripture in Church*
OTG	Old Testament Guides	*ScrTh*	*Scripta theologica*
OTL	Old Testament Library	SDM	Scripta et documenta Montserrat

Abbreviation	Expansion
Sef	*Sefarad*
SémBib	*Sémiotique et bible*
SESJ	Suomen Eksegeettisen Seuran julkaisuja
SJ	Studia judaica
SJOT	*Scandinavian Journal of the Old Testament*
SJT	*Scottish Journal of Theology*
SK	*Skrif en Kerk*
SKK	Stuttgarter kleine Kommentar
SMDSA	Series Minor Dipartimento di Studi Asiatici
SPAW	Sitzungsberichte der preussischen Akademie der Wissenschaften
SPIB	Scripta Pontificii Instituti Biblici
SpTo	*Spirituality Today*
SR	*Studies in Religion/Sciences religieuses*
SRivB	Supplementi alla Rivista biblica
St. Eph. Aug.	Studia ephemerides 'Augustinianum'
StIr	Studia Iranica
STLI	Studies and Texts, Lown Institute
StPatr	Studia Patristica
StZ	*Stimmen der Zeit*
SUNT	Studien zur Umwelt des Neuen Testaments
Sup	Supplement
SVF	*Stoicorum veterum fragmenta*
ϑ'	Theodotion
TANZ	Texte und Arbeiten zu neutestamentlichen Zeitalter
TBC	Torch Bible Commentaries
TBT	*The Bible Today*
TD	*Theology Digest*
TDOT	*Theological Dictionary of the Old Testament,* ed. G. J. Botterweck et al. (Grand Rapids: Eerdmans, 1974–)
TECC	Textos y estudios 'Cardinal Cisneros'
TeKo	*Texte und Kontexte*
Teol(Br)	*Teologia (Brescia)*
TGUOS	*Transactions of the Glasgow University Oriental Society*
ThGl	*Theologie und Glaube*
ThLZ	*Theologische Literaturzeitung*
ThQ	*Theologische Quartalschrift*
ThR	*Theologische Rundschau*
ThStK	*Theologische Studien und Kritiken*
ThT	*Theologisch Tijdschrift*
ThV	*Theologische Versuche*
ThViat	*Theologia viatorum*
ThW	Theologische Wissenschaft
ThZ	*Theologische Zeitschrift*
TJ	*Trinity Journal*
TLOT	*Theological Lexicon of the Old Testament,* ed. E. Jenni and C. Westermann (3 vols.; Peabody, Mass.: Hendrickson, 1997)
TOTC	Tyndale Old Testament Commentaries
TRE	*Theologische Realenzyklopädie,* ed. G. Krause and G. Müller (Berlin: de Gruyter, 1977–)
TRev	*Theologische Revue*
TSAJ	Texte und Studien zum antiken Judentum
TSJTSA	Texts and Studies of the Jewish Theological Seminary of America
TThZ	*Trier theologische Zeitschrift*
TUAT	Otto Kaiser et al., eds., *Texte aus der Umwelt des Alten Testaments* (3 vols.; Gütersloh: Gütersloher Verlagshaus, 1982–1997)
TynBul	*Tyndale Bulletin*
UF	*Ugarit-Forschungen*
Ugar.	Ugaritic
UTB	Uni-Taschenbücher
VC	*Vigiliae christianae*
VD	*Verbum domini*
VetChr	*Vetera Christianorum*
VF	*Verkündigung und Forschung*
Vg	Vulgate
VT	*Vetus Testamentum*
VTSup	Vetus Testamentum Supplements
WBC	Word Biblical Commentary
WB.KK	Die Welt der Bibel. Kleinkommentare zur Heiligen Schrift
WMANT	Wissenschaftliche Monographien zum Alten und Neuen Testament
WO	*Die Welt des Orients*
WTJ	*Westminster Theological Journal*
WUNT	Wissenschaftliche Untersuchungen zum Neuen Testament
WZKM	*Wiener Zeitschrift für die Kunde des Morgenlandes*
WZ(L).GS	*Wissenschaftliche Zeitschrift der Karl-Marx-Universität (Leipzig). Gesellschafts- und sprachwissenschaftliche Reihe*
y.	Jerusalem Talmud
Sanh.	*Sanhedrin*
ZAH	*Zeitschrift für Althebräistik*
ZAW	*Zeitschrift für die alttestamentliche Wissenschaft*
ZB	*Zürcher Bibel: Die Heilige Schrift des Alten und des Neuen Testaments* (1931; Zurich: Verlag der Zwingli-Bibel, 1954): *Das Buch Hiob, Das Buch Kohelet, Das Hohelied (Fassung 1998)* (Zurich: Verlag der Zürcher Bibel, 1998)
ZBK	Zürcher Bibelkommentar
ZDMG	*Zeitschrift der deutschen morgenländischen Gesellschaft*
ZDMGSup	Zeitschrift der deutschen morgenländischen Gesellschaft Supplements
ZDPV	*Zeitschrift des deutschen Palästina-Vereins*
ZThK	*Zeitschrift für Theologie und Kirche*
ZWTh	*Zeitschrift für wissenschaftliche Theologie*
ZZ	*Zwischen den Zeiten*

The book of Qoheleth presents a special challenge not only for professional commentators[1] but also for "normal" readers of the Hebrew text (or a modern translation). The themes treated by the book still address even modern readers directly—or in any case more directly than large portions of the historical sections and prophetic books of the OT. Even if most people in modern "Western" industrial societies no longer work in fields or are subjects of a king, they can relate without great difficulty to the reflections of the book of Qoheleth on work and rest or on behavior vis-à-vis those in power, and they can understand these reflections in terms of their own experiences. Nonetheless, the way in which these and other themes are handled in Qoheleth is a little puzzling. The fact that the book—at least at first glance—reveals no clear organization and no overall progression of ideas may be accepted as a literary peculiarity and perhaps even strike one as interesting. Yet when one finds on various themes many statements that are highly contradictory in both the broad and the narrow context, one begins to ask what could be the point of this book and what is the purpose expressed in it.

The present commentary seeks to help answer these questions. The introduction is intended as a first overview of the themes and problems in Qoheleth and of the clarifications developed in this commentary. First, I will briefly sketch the most important themes of the book of Qoheleth and their relationship to one another.

Themes

Eating, Drinking, and Pleasure as the Highest Good

Qoheleth 2:3 raises the question about "what is good for people to do under heaven as long as they live." Then in what follows this question is answered repeatedly to the effect that eating, drinking, and pleasure represent the highest and ultimately the only good worth striving for.[2] With this Qoheleth seems to represent not only a eudaemonist "ethic that regards happiness as the motive and aim of all striving," as was largely the case in early oriental wisdom and ancient Greek philosophy, but also a hedonism that "regards sensual desire, pleasure, and enjoyment as the motive, aim, or proof of all moral action."[3] It rejects any devaluation of sensual enjoyment when compared with presumed higher goods such as wealth, wisdom, and fame.[4] Human beings should seize the possibilities and opportunities to eat, drink, and enjoy themselves in the present[5] and not postpone pleasure—whether out of concern for the future, envy, greed, or miserliness, in the hope of increased possibilities of enjoyment in the future, or in the expectation that one's present behavior will later be rewarded (in life or after death).[6]

The "hedonism" of Qoheleth is not accompanied by a renunciation of the active shaping of life and the world; rather, this is expressly encouraged.[7] Nor does it simply legitimize an egocentric and egotistical attitude. Instead, the emphasis is on the right of every person to the possibility of enjoying life and on the fact that the awareness of the suffering of others restricts one's own enjoyment of life.[8] Instead of thinking only of oneself, one should get together with companions and turn over to the needy a portion of one's means of nourishment and enjoyment.[9] The determination of the highest good as eating, drinking, and pleasure is justified on the one hand through the criticism of alternative assumptions (see above) and on the other through the statement that it is a gift of God.[10]

1   For an overview see the literature listed in the bibliography under "Research Reports."

2   See (2:24-26?); 3:12-13, 22; 5:17-19; 7:14-15; 8:15; 9:7-10; 11:7-10.

3   Quotations are from Georgi Schischkoff., ed., *Philosophisches Wörterbuch; Begründet von Heinrich Schmidt* (Stuttgart: Kröner, 1974), s.v. "Eudämonismus" and "Hedonismus."

4   On wealth see 6:1-5. On wisdom see 7:1-14. On fame see 9:1-10.

5   See 3:12: "as long as they live"; 3:13: "in all their toil"; 3:22: "enjoy their work"; 5:17: "the few days of the life God gives us"; 7:14: "in the day of prosperity"; 8:15: "this will go with them in their toil

through the days of life that God gives them"; 9:8: "always"; 9:9: "all the days of your futile life . . . in life and in your toil"; 11:9: "while you are young . . . in the days of your youth."

6   On concern for the future see 5:12-14. On miserliness see 4:4-8. On future hope see 11:7-10. On later reward see 3:16-22; 8:10-15; 9:1-10.

7   See 3:12 ("be happy and enjoy themselves"); 9:7-9+10; 11:1-6+7-10.

8   For the former see esp. 5:17. For the latter see 4:1-3.

9   See 4:9-12; 11:1-2.

10   See (2:24, 26); 3:13; 5:18-19; 6:2.

God and Human Beings

In the book of Qoheleth God is regarded as the creator of human beings and their experience of reality.[11] In this respect God's creative activity (עשה *ʿśh*, מַעֲשֶׂה *maʿăseh*)[12] is not limited to a temporal beginning of the world. Rather, the passage of time in the world of experience also goes back to God.[13] Yet with the passing of time nothing really new happens; the same kinds of things repeat themselves over and over again—at least in the long view.[14] In this sense, however, creation can be regarded as finished.[15] Through the guidelines of God's creative work, human activity and enjoyment are equally enabled and restricted. Pleasure and enjoyment are, like life itself, a gift of God (נתן *ntn*, מַתַּת *mattat*) to human beings (see above).[16] By contrast, the contingency of time (עֵת *ʿēt*), fate (מִקְרֶה *miqreh*), and chance (פֶּגַע *pegaʿ*), as well as death, represent the judgment of God (שפט *špt*, מִשְׁפָּט *mišpāṭ*) over human beings—a judgment that ultimately all people meet in like manner, since none of them is completely innocent.[17]

This view of God as creator of the world and human beings, as giver of life and happiness, and as judge of human beings makes it possible to think of God as the maker of everything in a way that does not exclude human freedom ("deterministically") but rather makes it possible. From the human point of view, God's activity has agreeable and disagreeable, good and bad sides[18] and is experienced as gift or as judgment. In the context of the overall creative activity of God, however, everything is beautiful and appropriate in its time.[19] Thus the sides of reality experienced by people as negative must be neither (optimistically) negated nor (dualistically) separated from God. Human beings experience themselves just as ambivalently as they experience God: they can act correctly and still not completely avoid guilt;

they can experience happiness and still also be confronted with suffering. Doing good and happiness, guilt and suffering, cannot be calculated here in the sense of a strict "cause and effect" relationship, for contingency itself represents the judgment of God over human beings.

The outlined statements about God's activity show that in the view of Qoheleth this activity is not completely unknowable and incomprehensible for human beings. Yet at the same time, it is also not completely knowable and understandable—if for no other reason, because human beings cannot survey it "from beginning to end."[20] In particular, God has denied human beings knowledge of the future.[21]

The appropriate attitude of human beings toward God is the fear of God (ירא *yrʾ*, יִרְאָה *yirʾâ*).[22] It is not simply identical with the usual practice of religion but leads rather to critical participation in this practice: listening to God and confessing one's guilt before God, as expressions of fear and respect before God, are religiously more valuable than sacrifices and prayers, vows and dreams.[23] Because people who fear God know their shortcomings and accept the contingency of time as God's judgment, they expect no reward from God: the fear of God has its own value.[24]

The relationship between God and humanity in Qoheleth is seen as more distant than in other parts of the OT: "The Deity is in heaven, and you are upon earth."[25] Yet even here God is by no means a *Deus otiosus,* who largely leaves creation to itself and has no part in it. Rather, it pleases God when human beings can

---

11 אֱלֹהִים *ʾĕlōhîm*: 1:13; 3:10, 13; 5:3, 18; 7:18; 8:2, 13. הָאֱלֹהִים *hāʾĕlōhîm*: 2:24, 26; 3:11, 14, 15, 17, 18; 4:17; 5:1 (2x), 5, 6, 17, 18, 19; 6:2 (2x); 7:13, 14, 26, 29; 8:12, 15, 17; 9:1, 7; 11:5, 9; 12:7, 13, 14. For God as creator see 3:11, 14-15; 7:13-14, 29; 8:17; 11:5; 12:7.
12 3:11, 14; 7:13, 14, 29; 8:17; 11:5.
13 Cf. 3:11, 15; 7:13-14.
14 Cf. 1:9; 3:15; 6:10.
15 3:14.
16 On life see 5:17; 8:15; 9:9; 12:7. On God "giving" see 1:13; 2:26; 3:10, 11, 13; 5:17, 18; 6:2; 8:15; 9:9; 12:7; cf. also 2:24: מִיַּד הָאֱלֹהִים *mîyad hāʾĕlōhîm.*

17 On judgment see 3:17; 8:5-6; 11:9; 12:14; cf. also 5:1; 9:1. On lack of innocence see 3:18; 7:20, 29; 8:6, 11; 9:3.
18 See 7:14.
19 3:11.
20 3:11; cf. 8:17; 11:5.
21 3:21-22; 6:12; 7:14; 8:7; 9:12; 10:14; 11:1-6.
22 3:14; 5:6; 7:18; 8:12; 12:13.
23 See 4:17—5:6; 9:2.
24 See 7:18 and 8:12 in their respective contexts.
25 5:1; cf. the repeated "under the sun" (1:3, 9, 14; 2:11, 17, 18, 19, 20, 22; 3:16; 4:1, 3, 7, 15; 5:12, 17;

enjoy their lives.[26] Fools, by contrast, do not please God, and when people try to play down their guilt before him, God becomes angry.[27]

Futility and Fleetingness

The word הֶבֶל hebel—used repeatedly in 1:2 and 12:8—forms an impressive framework around the book of Qoheleth. Within this framework it designates, on the one hand, the "futility" and "absurdity" of certain human convictions and wishes and, on the other, the "fleetingness" and "transitoriness" of human life, which for the individual finds its definitive and irreversible end in death.[28] The two are related in the sense that all convictions and wishes prove to be futile and absurd when they do not do adequate justice to the fleeting and transitory nature of human life (and also its limitations in other respects). For human beings, the knowledge of life's fleetingness and transitoriness in the form of chance and death bestows additional worth upon pleasure and enjoyment in the present.[29]

Time and Chance

Time places limits on human beings in more than one way. In regard to "distant time" (עוֹלָם ʿôlām / עֹלָמִים ʿōlāmîm),[30] the limited life span of human beings, as well as the limits of their knowledge of the past and the future, becomes clear, as does the continued repetition of similar events and actions that define the range of human possibilities. In the short-term changing of the "times" (עֵת ʿēt) and "days" (יוֹם yôm) people learn that the success of their actions is affected by favorable or unfavorable circumstances that are not at their disposal.[31] Since human beings can foresee the future only in a very limited way, they experience the changing of the times

as chance (פֶּגַע pegaʿ) and fate (מִקְרֶה miqreh).[32] Thus the human experience of time as chance and as limitation on action and the enjoyment of life reflects the ambivalence of God's gift and judgment.

Gain and Portion

In the book of Qoheleth eating, drinking, and pleasure are repeatedly designated as the "portion" (or "right": חֵלֶק ḥēleq) of human beings.[33] Since חֵלֶק ḥēleq can also designate a legacy or benevolent gift, the word underlines the fact that the enjoyment of life, as a gift of God, is not at the disposal of human beings.[34] Where pleasure is more closely defined as one's share in (or of) work or in the property of a human being,[35] this calls attention to the fact that work and property have only a relative value for human beings as a means to the goal of pleasure (see below). Moreover, the designation of pleasure as "portion" reminds one that human beings live in relationship to other people[36] and that the goods that they use for themselves are no longer available to other people.

As the reflection in 2:10-11 shows (pleasure is a "portion" but not a "gain"), in the book of Qoheleth "gain" (יִתְרוֹן yitrôn) means something different from "portion" (חֵלֶק ḥēleq), namely, a lasting result of human action that remains at one's disposal.[37] Because of chance and transitoriness, there can be no such "gain" for human beings. Nevertheless, this does not obviate the fact that in certain respects wisdom offers a (relative) "advantage" (יִתְרוֹן yitrôn or יוֹתֵר yôtēr or מוֹתָר môtār) over folly.[38] In this connection then, there is also the possibility of a "gain" or "reward" (שָׂכָר śākār) for human beings for their toil—though it is, to be sure, not one that is reliably at their disposal.[39]

6:1, 12; 8:9, 15, 17; 9:3, 6, 9, 11, 13; 10:5) or "under heaven" (1:13; 2:3; 3:1).

26 9:7.

27 On fools see 5:3. On God becoming angry see 5:5.

28 See the commentary on 1:2. See also 1:4, 11; 2:16; 3:2, 19-21; 6:6; 8:8; 9:3-6, 10; 12:7.

29 See 3:19-22; 5:12–6:6; 9:1-11; 11:1–12:7.

30 1:4, 10; 2:16; 3:11, 14; 9:6; 12:9.

31 On עֵת ʿēt see 3:1-8, 11, 17; 7:17; 8:5, 6, 9; 9:8, 11, 12; 10:17. On יוֹם yôm see 2:3, 16, 23; 5:16, 17, 19; 6:3, 12; 7:1, 10, 14, 15; 8:8, 13, 15, 16; 9:9; 11:1, 8, 9; 12:1, 3.

32 On פֶּגַע pegaʿ see 9:11. On מִקְרֶה miqreh see 2:14, 15;

3:19; 9:2, 3.

33 2:10; 3:22; 5:17, 18; 9:9. On חֵלֶק ḥēleq see also 2:21; 9:6; 11:2.

34 See 3:22; 5:17; 9:9. Cf. 2:21 (legacy); 11:2 (gift).

35 2:10; 5:18.

36 See 9:6: the dead no longer have a "portion" in life.

37 See 1:3; 2:11; 3:9; 5:15. On יִתְרוֹן yitrôn see 1:3; 2:11, 13; 3:9; 5:8, 15; 7:12; 10:10, 11. Cf. מוֹתָר môtār: 3:19, as well as יוֹתֵר yôtēr: 6:8, 11; 7:11 (and, in another sense, 2:15; 7:16; 12:9, 12).

38 Cf. 2:13; 3:19; 5:8; 6:8, 11; 7:11, 12; 10:10.

39 Cf. 10:11 (יִתְרוֹן yitrôn); 4:9 (שָׂכָר śākār).

Work and Toil

Work and toil (עָמָל ʿāmāl/עמל ʿml or עִנְיָן ʿinyān/ענה ʿnh[40]) are a part of human life. They can be judged positively or negatively according to the circumstances, and determining factors include, above all, whether the impetus to work is formed by envy, greed, and miserliness or by interest in common success, and whether work is connected with rest breaks, as well as eating, drinking, and pleasure.[41] Work and toil cannot produce happiness in the form of pleasure and enjoyment, but pleasure and enjoyment can be part of work and toil.[42] The prospect of success can be increased through the application of "wisdom" in the sense of professional know-how in one's work or through the common effort of a team.[43] When possible unfortunate events are considered, however, the success of human efforts is not guaranteed.[44] Work and toil are a necessary[45] but not a sufficient condition of happiness. Thus their value is relative.

Wealth and Poverty

Like eating, drinking, and pleasure, wealth is also a gift of God, and as such it is not reliably at human disposal.[46] For its part, wealth does not guarantee that one can partake of eating, drinking, and pleasure. This can be prevented by various factors, for example, by contrary economic and political circumstances, sudden impoverishment, renunciation of enjoyment out of greed and concern about the future, as well as by excessive demands that make the available possibilities of enjoyment seem worthless.[47] Poverty, by contrast, usually goes hand in hand with oppression and contempt and makes it impossible for a person to enjoy life.[48] At best, poor people may have the opportunity, through political upheavals, to be liberated from their situation.[49] Yet this only confirms and underlines that poverty is to be judged in purely negative terms. Thus we see that human beings must have at their disposal a certain amount of personal property (and not necessarily wealth) in order to have the possibility of becoming happy. To this "portion" every person has a "right"—just as all rich people have a right to the enjoyment of their possessions.[50]

Power and Dominion

For a writing that is supposed to go back to a king, Qoheleth develops an astonishingly critical view of power and dominion. To expect from a king social justice and the abolishment of poverty is illusory, for rulers are interested above all in their own pleasure.[51] Occasionally a king may listen to a poor wise man, but he often prefers fools and makes wrong decisions.[52] On the basis of their relative power, rulers tend to overestimate their own worth.[53] In dealing with them, therefore, caution is advised, but also "civil courage."[54] Basically, the dominion of people over people is to be judged negatively.[55] It would be best if every man was his own master.[56] (With all the radicalness of its criticism of dominion, Qoheleth does not, of course, go so far as to also question slavery and patriarchy.[57])

---

40 For the former see 1:3; 2:10, 11, 18, 19, 20, 21, 22, 24; 3:9, 13; 4:4, 6, 8, 9; 5:14, 15, 17, 18; 6:7; 8:15, 17; 9:9; 10:15. For the latter see 1:13; 2:23, 26; 3:10; 4:8; 5:2, 13, 19; 8:16; (10:19?).

41 Cf., e.g., 4:6 vs. 4:4-5; 4:9-12 vs. 4:7-8; 5:17-19 vs. 5:12-16.

42 8:15; cf. 3:13, 22; 5:18; 9:9.

43 Cf. 4:9-12; 10:8-11.

44 See 10:11; 11:1-6.

45 See 4:5.

46 See 9:11. For wealth as a gift of God see 5:18; 6:2.

47 On economic and political circumstances see 6:2; 10:5-7. On sudden impoverishment see 5:12-14. On greed see 4:7-8. On concern for the future see 5:12. On excessive demands see 1:12–2:26.

48 See 5:15-16; 6:6, 8. On poverty see 5:7 (cf. 4:1); 9:15-16.

49 See 4:13-14; 10:5-7.

50 See 5:17-18.

51 See 4:13-16; 5:7-8; 10:16-19.

52 Cf. 9:13-18; 10:5-7.

53 See 1:12–2:26; 8:1-9.

54 See 8:1-9; 10:4, 20.

55 8:9.

56 5:8.

57 On slavery see 7:21; 2:7. Even if, under the interpretation developed below, 7:23-29 is not to be understood as a misogynist utterance, 9:9 still shows in exemplary fashion the androcentric perspective of the whole book (cf. also 2:8).

Wisdom and Folly

In spite of all its critical statements about "wisdom" and "the wise," the book of Qoheleth does not reject them completely. By contrast, "folly" and "fools" are judged completely negatively, and readers are admonished not to behave like fools.[58] In regard to wisdom and the wise, however, the book of Qoheleth is above all critical of excessive claims: not even the wise can fully comprehend the workings of God.[59] And wisdom can no more guarantee human happiness than can work and possessions. In this respect the wise have no advantage over fools; on the contrary, many alleged "wisdoms" prevent people from enjoying life, and the insights of the wise only allow them to see more clearly human limitations and the painful aspects of life.[60] In addition, the wisdom of the wise can only have an effect when it is recognized and acknowledged in its social environment, and it is always endangered by the wrong decisions of the mighty and the foolish.[61] A realistic wisdom, the kind the book of Qoheleth tries to convey to its readers, is aware of these limitations. In view of death and the uncertainties of life, wisdom leads people to seize possibilities for pleasure and enjoyment in the present, as well as opportunities to act, and to do what one does as "professionally" as possible, in order to protect oneself from possible dangers and to avoid unnecessary exertion while working.[62]

Structure

The book of Qoheleth shows a clear framework in the sayings of Qoheleth in the third person in 1:1 (title) and 12:9-14 (epilogue), as well as in 1:2 and 12:8, which quote Qoheleth's statements as a kind of motto:

- 1:1 Title
- 1:2 Motto
- 1:3–12:7 Corpus of the book
- 12:8 Motto
- 12:9-11 Epilogue

Whether and to what extent the corpus of the book in 1:3–12:7 also exhibits a planned structure is a question disputed by commentators.[63] It is clear that here we have a series of (more of less) short argumentatively and rhetorically cohesive units, which in any case comprise more than one verse and whose exact boundaries are admittedly subject to considerable debate. Kurt Galling, for example, divides the book of Qoheleth into 36 (1st ed.) or 26 (2d ed.) units that he calls "sentences." Moreover, in regard to the sequence of such small units "it is hard to overlook the fact that in certain parts of the book of Qoheleth an issue is pursued over lengthy stretches and through a majority of Galling's sentences, and it is further developed–certainly not in straight-line thought but in an associative continuation."[64] Thus in 5:9–6:9, for example, there are several relatively complete units on the theme of poverty and wealth that in their sequence develop a coherent train of reflection and argumentation. And 1:12–2:26 forms a coherent self-report on a series of experiences and reflections.

If we now look further for a possible framework for larger sections, we soon notice that often formally similar and/or thematically related units seem to form a bracket around larger text complexes.[65] Thus 5:9–6:9 is framed by three proverbs in 5:9-11 and three in 6:7-9. Before and after 1:12–2:26 there are poetic sections (1:3-11 and 3:1-9), which each begins (1:3) or ends (3:9) with the question of a possible "gain" for human beings. The

---

58 For the former see 4:5; 10:1, 12-15. For the latter see 4:17; 5:2, 3; 7:17.
59 8:16-17.
60 On the wise and fools see 2:13-16; 6:8; 9:11-12. On the alleged "wisdoms" see 6:10–7:14; 7:17. On insights of the wise see 1:18.
61 Cf. 9:13–10:20.
62 See 10:8-11. On wise actions see 9:1-12; 11:1–12:7.
63 See, e.g., Ludger Schwienhorst-Schönberger, "Kohelet: Stand und Perspektiven der Forschung," in idem, ed., *Das Buch Kohelet* (BZAW 254; Berlin: de Gruyter, 1997) 7–14.
64 W. Zimmerli, "Das Buch Kohelet," 226–27.
65 On the analysis of large-scale forward and backward references in the book of Qoheleth cf. esp. the studies of F. J. Backhaus, *"Denn Zeit und Zufall trifft sie alle"* (BBB 83; Frankfurt am Main: Anton Hain, 1993); and L. Schwienhorst-Schönberger, *"Nicht im Menschen gründet das Blück"* (HBS 2; Freiburg: Herder, 1994).

advice for religious behavior in 4:17–5:6 is enclosed by texts in which the topic is one's relationship to rulers (4:13-16 and 5:6-7). The themes of 9:1-12 (vv. 1-6: death; vv. 7-10: pleasure; vv. 11-12: contingency) are taken up again in reverse order in 11:1–12:7 (vv. 11:1-6: contingency; vv. 11:7-10: pleasure; 12:1-7: death). And 8:16-17, like 6:10-12, speaks against claims of a special knowledge of ethical orientation. On the basis of these observations, 1:3–3:9; 4:13–5:8; 5:9–6:9; 6:10–8:17; and 9:1–12:7 can be regarded as compositional units within the book of Qoheleth, which (like the book as a whole) are structured according to a pattern of A–B–A'.

Yet 3:10–4:12 does not fit into this structural scheme. First, this section does not reveal a framework of its own. Second, in terms of content it seems to be closely related to what precedes it.[66] Therefore, more recent scholarship often recognizes a unified "treatise" that introduces the book of Qoheleth and runs from 1:3 or 1:12 to at least 3:15.[67] The observations sketched on the division of 4:13–12:7 suggest delineating 1:3–4:12 as the first compositional unit (pattern: A–B–A'-B'). The structure of the whole book of Qoheleth can then be outlined as follows:

1:1	Title	
1:2	Motto	
1:3–4:12	The king and the wise man	
	1:3-11	Prelude: Is there any gain with regard to eternity?
	1:12–2:26	Reflections of King Qoheleth: The devaluation of happiness not at one's disposal
	3:1-9	Interlude: Is there any gain with regard to time?
	3:10–4:12	Reflections of the wise man Qoheleth: Happiness not at one's disposal as the highest good
4:13–5:8	The king and God	

	4:13-16	Critique of expecting too much of a king
	4:17–5:6	Call to the proper attitude toward God
	5:7-8	Critique of expecting too much of a king
5:9–6:9	Poverty and wealth	
	5:9-11	Proverbs
	5:12-16	Negative cases
	5:17-19	Positive cases
	6:1-6	Negative cases
	6:7-9	Proverbs
6:10–8:17	Critical discussion of conventional wisdom	
	6:10-12	Limits of human beings
	7:1-14	Critique of wise sayings
	7:15-22	Limits of righteousness and wisdom
	7:23-29	Limits of wisdom
	8:1-9	Knowledge and power
	8:10-15	The righteous and evildoers
	8:16-17	Limits of wisdom
9:1–12:7	Life in regard to chance and transitoriness	
	9:1-12	Call to pleasure and to vigorous action in view of death and chance
	9:13–10:20	Strengths and weaknesses of wisdom
	11:1–12:7	Advice for life in view of the uncertainty of the future and the certainty of death
12:8	Motto	
12:9-14	Epilogue	

This structural sketch by no means makes the claim of giving the "correct" and only appropriate division of Qoheleth; for this, the structural signals in the text are too vague and ambiguous.[68] Therefore, I will also men-

---

66 Cf., e.g., the clear backward references to 3:1-9 and 1:3-11 in 3:11 and 3:15 (pattern A-B-B'-A'). In its formulation 3:10 harks back to 1:13, and 4:9-12 ("two are better than one") forms a contrast to 2:25 ("who . . . except for me?"–pattern A-B-A'-B').

67 See N. Lohfink, "Das Koheletbuch: Strukturen und Struktur," in L. Schwienhorst-Schöberger, ed., *Das*

Buch Kohelet, 78ff.

68 Thus, correctly, José Vilchez (review of Schwienhorst-Schönberger, *Nicht im Menschen*) in *Bib* 76 (1995) 562–65.

tion at least briefly some other structural schemes proposed in more recent times.

A. G. Wright takes his orientation from the division of the judgments that all this is futility and chasing after the wind (only in chaps. 1–6) and the statements that call into question or dispute human abilities to learn about or comprehend (מצא *mṣ'*: mainly in chaps. 7–8) anything or know (ידע *ydʿ*: primarily in chaps 9–11) anything. (In addition, Wright has a number of rather questionable number speculations.) Based on Wright, Rolf Rendtorff, for example, sketches the structure of Qoheleth as follows:

1:1	Title
1:2-11	Poems about vain toil
I. 1:12—6:9	Critical investigation of human life. Overriding tenor: "all is vanity and a striving after wind"
II. 6:10—11:6	Consequences
6:10-12	Introduction
A. 7:1—8:17	Man cannot discover what is good for him to do.
B. 9:1—11:6	Man does not know what will come after him.
11:7—12:8	Poem on youth and old age
12:9-14	Epilogue[69]

This proposed division, however, does not do justice to the inclusion relationships sketched above (for example, 1:3-11/3:1-9 and 9:1-12/11:1—12:7). Moreover, the characterization of the subject matter of the individual sections (above all for 1:12—6:9) seems too wholesale and problematic in terms of content. The same is also true of C. L. Seow's structural sketch[70] (which for 6:10ff. at least falls more closely into the rough division of the structure recommended here):

1:1	Superscription

Part I

I.A. Reflection: Everything Is Ephemeral and Unreliable

I.A.1.	1:2-11	Preface
I.A.2.	1:12—2:26	Nothing is Ultimately Reliable
I.A.3.	3:1-22	Everything Is in the Hand of God
I.A.4.	4:1-16	Relative Good Is Not Good Enough

I.B. Ethics: Coping with Uncertainty

I.B.1.	5:1-7 (Heb. 4:17—5:6)	Attitude Before God
I.B.2.	5:8—6:9 (Heb. 5:7—6:9)	Enjoyment, Not Greed

Part II

II.A. Reflection: Everything Is Elusive

II.A.1.	6:10—7:14	No One Knows What Is Good
II.A.2.	7:15-29	Righteousness and Wisdom Are Elusive
II.A.3.	8:1-17	It's an Arbitrary World

II.B. Ethics: Coping with Risks and Death

II.B.1.	9:1-10	*Carpe Diem*
II.B.2.	9:11—10:15	The World Is Full of Risks
II.B.3.	10:16—11:6	Living with Risks
II.B.4.	11:7—12:8	Conclusion
12:9-13a	Epilogue	
12:13b-14	Additional Material	

Norbert Lohfink sees in Qoheleth both a "linear" structure, which guides the development of the material dynamically, and a "palistrophic structure," which is determined above all thematically and after the end of the reading reveals itself in looking back over the book.[71] The "linear-dynamic arrangement" can be summarized as follows:[72]

69 Rolf Rendtorff, *The Old Testament: An Introduction* (Philadelphia: Fortress Press, 1986) 265. Cf. also J. Mulder, "Qoheleth's Division and Also Its Main Point," in W. Cl Delsman and J. T. Nelis, eds., *Von Kanaan bis Kerala* (AOAT 211; Kevelaer: Butzon & Bercker; Neukirchen-Vluyn: Neukirchener Verlag, 1982) 149–59; R. Murphy, *Ecclesiastes* (WBC 23A; Dallas: Word, 1992) xxxix–xli.

70 C.-L. Seow, *Ecclesiastes* (AB 18C; New York: Doubleday, 1997) 46–47.

71 N. Lohfink, *Qoheleth* (CC; Minneapolis: Fortress Press, 2003) 7–8. Cf. L. Schwienhorst-Schönberger,

"Kohelet: Stand und Perspektiven der Forschung," in idem, ed., *Das Buch Kohelet*, 10.

72 According to Schwienhorst-Schönberger, "Kohelet," 10.

1:2-11	Opening (theses, questions, underlying cosmology)
1:12—3:15	Narrative introduction to the primarily anthropological central thesis
3:16—6:10	Deepening through many glimpses of social experience
6:11—9:6	*Refutation* of contrary positions, especially of older wisdom
9:7—12:8	*Application* through proposals about human behavior

The "palistrophic structure" results from this linear structure above all through consideration of the "critique of religion" in 4:17—5:6 as a separate unit, which at the same time then becomes the center of the whole book:[73]

1:2-3	Frame
1:4-11	Cosmology (poem)
1:12—3:15	Anthropology
3:16—4:16	Social critique I
4:17—5:6	Religious critique
5:7—6:10	Social critique II
6:11—9:6	Deconstruction
9:7—12:7	Ethics (concludes with a poem)
12:8	Frame

Apart from the fact that Lohfink's overall construction is "palistrophic" only in 3:16—6:10, it seems questionable above all because it assumes, without convincing justification, a caesura between 3:15 and 3:16.[74] At the same time his structural analysis fails to consider the obvious inclusion 1:3-11/3:1-9, as well as the likewise hardly disputable separation of 1:12—2:26 and 3:10ff. by 3:1-9 (likewise a "poem"!).[75]

Finally, Schwienhorst-Schöberger, following Backhaus, proposes a division of 1:3—12:7 into four parts, which show, in his view, "correspondences to the four parts of the classical ancient speech":[76]

1:3—3:22	Proposition (*proposito*): presentation and answering of the question of the content and conditions of the possibility of human happiness
4:1—6:9	Development (*explicatio*): discussion of a prephilosophical understanding of happiness: devaluation of traditional values in view of the determination of the highest good
6:10—8:17	Defense (*refutatio*): discussion of alternative determinations of happiness
9:1—12:7	Application (*applicatio*): exhortation to pleasure and to energetic action

Yet here too it seems questionable whether the characterizations of the four parts really delineate them from each other and aptly describe their content and function.

The question of the overall structure of Qoheleth is of limited relevance for its interpretation. In any case, a relatively self-contained small unit is to be interpreted both for itself and in the larger context. And in some passages the boundary between successive sections in the text seems by intention to be unclearly marked (cf., e.g., under 4:13—5:8 below).

Genres

In Qoheleth there are numerous examples of the characteristic genres of the OT and ancient Near Eastern—Egyptian wisdom literature.[77] They give the book as a whole a stamp of "wisdom."

---

73 Lohfink, 8.

74 Lohfink, "Koheletbuch," 78ff.

75 Lohfink's main objection to the division of 1:3—4:12 proposed here is "that the block 3:10—4:12 cannot be integrated into the assumed concentric main structure" (Lohfink, "Koheletbuch," 105). The division presented here, however, assumes no "concentric main structure" (A-B-A') at all for 1:3—4:12, but rather a structure following the pattern A-B-A'-B'. If with Lohfink one regards 1:3/4-11 as a section in itself, one can without difficulty construct a further section 1:12—4:12 with "concentric main structure"

(A: 1:12—2:26—B: 3:1-9—A': 3:10—4:12).

76 Schwienhorst-Schönberger, "Kohelet," 11-12 (cf. *Nicht im Menschen*) with reference to H. Lausberg, *Handbuch der literarischen Rhetorik,* 3d ed. (Stuttgart: Steiner, 1990) 147—49. Cf. also A. A. Fischer, *Skepsis oder Furcht Gottes?* (BZAW 247; Berlin: de Gruyter, 1997) 252, who delineates the following four "book parts": I: 1:2—3:15; II: 3:16—6:9; III: 6:11—8:17; IV: 9:1—12:8.

77 Cf., e.g., Otto Kaiser, *Introduction to the Old Testament* (Minneapolis: Augsburg, 1975) 366—77; idem, *Grundriß der Einleitung in die kanonischen und*

Many statements can be formally regarded as proverbs. They stand out from the context through their form (for example, through the parallelism of members), and their content formulates an assertion that is understandable in and of itself. Since they are mostly embedded in more comprehensive argumentative contexts, the identification of proverbs is in individual cases often unclear and debated among commentators.[78] As special forms of the proverb we find the comparison saying and the numerical saying, as well as the relatively frequent comparative טוֹב *ṭôb* saying ("better . . . than . . .") and (formally developed from it?) אֵין־טוֹב *ʾên-ṭôb* sayings ("there is nothing better than . . .").[79] There are occasionally examples of a woe saying or a beatitude.[80] Besides the proverbs in the book of Qoheleth we find

numerous (substantiated) admonitions in the imperative, jussive, or vetitive, which can also be placed together with longer admonitory speeches.[81] Frequently there are questions (not all of which are rhetorical).[82] Finally there are example stories and texts that can perhaps be called "didactic poems."[83]

Large sections of Qoheleth with statements in the first-person singular are stylized "autobiographically":[84] Qoheleth reports as narrator on his own experiences and reflections. This form of presentation makes it possible to integrate statements on a theme that are in tension with one another into a coherent train of thought. Thus, for example, in 2:13-15 an advantage of wisdom over folly (in a certain respect) is at first conceded (a), but then an advantage of wisdom over folly (in another

---

deuterokanonischen Schriften des Alten Testaments, vol. 3: *Die poetischen und weisheitlichen Werke* (Gütersloh: Gütersloher, 1994) 49-62; Roland E. Murphy, *Wisdom Literature* (FOTL 13; Grand Rapids: Eerdmans, 1981). On the wisdom genres in Qoheleth see, in addition to Kaiser, *Grundriss,* 3:88-91, also, e.g., F. Ellermeier, *Qohelet, I/1: Untersuchungen zum Buche Qohelet* (Hertzberg: Jungfer, 1967); J. A. Loader, *Polar Structures in the Book of Qohelet* (BZAW 152; Berlin: de Gruyter, 1979) 18ff.

78 R. F. Johnson, "A Form-Critical Analysis of the Sayings in the Book of Ecclesiastes" (Th.D. diss., Emory University, 1973) (following D. Michel, *Qohelet* [EdF 258; Darmstadt: Wissenschaftliche Buchgesellschaft, 1988] 30) identifies "sayings" (which also include admonitions) in the following verses: 1:15, 18; 2:14a; 3:20b; 4:5-6, 9, 12b, 13a, 17; 5:2, 6, 9-11; 6:7, 9; 7:1-4, 5-7, 8-9, 10-12, 19-21; 8:1a, 1b, 5; 9:4b, 17, 18; 10:1, 2-3, 4, 8-9, 10, 11, 12-15, 16-20; 11:1-2, 3-4, 7. According to Loader's classification (*Polar Structures,* 18ff.), the proverbs would include—apart from the special cases named below—the "true sayings" in 1:18; 5:9; 11:3 (synonymous parallelism); 5:11 (antithetical parallelism); 7:19 (synthetic parallelism); 5:10; 10:11 (simple construction) as well as the maxims in 1:15; 2:14a; 4:5, 12; 5:2; 7:4, 19; 8:4, 8; 9:4; 10:1, 2, 3, 8, 9, 11, 12, 18; 11:3, 4. Ellermeier names as examples of the "true sayings in reflection" 6:7; 7:19, 28; 11:3, as "true sayings in aphorism" 5:9a, 10a, 11; 9:17; 10:1, 2, 8, 9, 10, 11, 12, 18?, 19, and as "proverbs" 1:15?, 18?; 2:14a; 4:5, 12b; 5:2; 7:4, 6a?, 12a; 9:4b; 11:4. One could also see, however, proverbs (at least in part) in the statements classified by Ellermeier (*Qohelet,* I/1, 55–57, 60) as "observation without verb" (1:4-7; 2:12bβ, 21abα; 5:16), "recognition without verb"

(1:13b; 2:18b; 3:19bα; 4:6; 5:15a; 7:6b-7, 11b, 18, 23bβ; 8:14a; 9:3; 11:5), and "thesis as starting point" (2:24a; 3:1; 6:7, 10; 11:7).

79 Comparison saying: 2:13; 7:6a, 12a; 9:12; 11:5 (see Loader, *Polar Structures,* 22, who also points to 8:13; this verse *contains* a comparison but is not a comparison saying). Numerical saying: 4:12 ("1-2-3"). Comparative טוֹב *ṭôb* saying: 4:(2-3) 6, 9, 13; 5:4; 6:3b, (5b,) 9a; 7:1, 2a, 3a, 5, 8a, 8b, 11a, 18aα; 9:4b, 16, (17,) 18a; cf. G. S. Ogden, "The 'Better'-Proverb (Ṭob-Spruch), Rhetorical Criticism, and Qoheleth," *JBL* 96 (1977) 489–505. Comparative אֵין טוֹב *ʾên ṭôb* saying: 2:24; 3:12, 22; 8:15; cf. Ogden, "Qoheleth's Use of the 'Nothing is Better' Form," *JBL* 98 (1979) 339–50.

80 See 2:16bβ(?); 4:10b; 10:16, 17.

81 Imperative: 4:17a; 5:3b, 6b; 7:13a, 14a; 8:2(?); 9:7a, 9a, 10a; 11:1a, 2a, 6a, 9a, 10a; 12:1a, 12a, 13b. Jussive: (5:1bβ); 8:3a; (9:8; 11:9a). Vetitive: 5:1a, 3a, 5a, 7aβ; 7:9a, 10a, 16a, 17a, 18aβ, 21a; 8:3a; 10:4a, 20a; 11:6a. Admonitory speeches: 4:17–5:6; 9:7-10; 11:1–12:1(7).

82 1:3; 2:2bβ, 12bα, 15aβ, 19a, 22, 25; 3:9, 21, 22b; 4:8bα, 11b; 5:5b, 9aβ, 10b, 15b; 6:6b, 8a, 8b, 11b, 12a, 12b; 7:10a, 13b, 16b, 17b, 24bβ; 8:1, 4b, 7b; 10:14bβ.

83 Example story: 9:14-15. Didactic poems: 1:4-11; 3:1-8; 12:2-7.

84 See 1:12–2:26; 3:10–4:16; 5:12–6:6; 7:15–10:7. Cf. O. Loretz, "Zur Darbietungsform der 'Ich-Erzählung' im Buche Qohelet," *CBQ* 25 (1963) 46–59; P. Höffken, "Das EGO des Weisen," *ThZ* 41 (1985) 121–34; M. Schubert, "Die Selbstbetrachtungen Kohelets," *ThV* 17 (1989) 23–34; T. Longman, *Fictional Akkadian Autobiography* (Winona Lake, Ind.: Eisenbrauns, 1991) 118–29. Ellermeier (*Qohelet,*

respect) is denied (b), and from this the (excessive) striving for wisdom is fundamentally called into question (c) (for details see the commentary):

(a) And I saw
> that wisdom has an advantage over folly, as light has an advantage over darkness: The wise man has eyes in his head, but the fool walks in darkness.

(b) Yet I understood (also)
> that the same fate befalls all of them.

(c) And I thought:
> "What can happen to the fool can also happen to me; why then have I been so exceedingly wise?"
>
> And I thought
> that this also was futile.

While the value of wisdom here is (at least) limited by further insights, in 8:10-13, for example, the value of the fear of God (b) is maintained even in light of experiences that seem to contradict it (a) (for details see the commentary):

(a) Then I saw
> how the wicked people were buried and went in to rest; but those who had done right had to leave a holy place and were forgotten in the city. That also is futile. Because the sentence against the evil deed is not executed immediately, the desire to do evil grows within people. For a sinner does evil a hundred times and still lives a long time.

(b) I know, however,
> that it is good for the God-fearers that they fear God. And it is not good for the wicked man, and like a shadow he will not live long when he does not fear God.

Similar complex and tension-filled trains of thought can also be developed without an "autobiographical" narrative framework, by directly juxtaposing various observations or convictions. Thus 4:4-6 (after an introduction in the first person) first expresses a point of view that makes work appear basically questionable (a), and then an insight that speaks against a total renunciation of work (b), in order to draw the conclusion that for humans work and rest should be in a sensible balance (c) (for details see the commentary):

(a) And I saw
> that all labor and all skillful work are affected by one person's envy of another. This also is futile and a striving after wind.

(b)
> The fool folds his hands and consumes his (own) flesh.

(c)
> A handful of rest is better than two handfuls of labor and a striving after wind.

More than with the reflections that are presented in "autobiographical" form, here the reader is challenged to connect the opposing and at first seemingly contradictory statements of the text into a coherent train of thought (cf., e.g., 7:1-14; 8:1-9).

For both forms of reflection, which appear more than once in the book of Qoheleth,[85] there are models in the OT and ancient Near Eastern–Egyptian wisdom litera-

---

I/1, 66–79) assigns these statements to the following types: "reflection" (1:16-17a; 2:1a, 15a, 15b; 3:17ff.), "intention" (1:13a, 17a; 2:1aβ, 3, 12a; 7:23abα, 25; 8:9, 16), "observation with verb" (1:14a; 2:14b, 24b; 3:10, 16; 4:1, 4aα, 7-8a, 15-16a; 5:12; 6:1-2aα; 7:15; 8:9, 10a; 9:11a, 13; 10:5, 7), "recognition with verb" (1:17b; 2:13, 15b; 3:12, 14a, 22a; 5:17; 6:3b; 7:26, 27-28, 29; 8:14b, 17; 9:1, 16), "survey that leads to recognition" (2:11a), "consequence at the end" (2:17a; 4:2-3a; 8:15), "consequence as starting point" (2:18a, 20), "self-presentation" (1:12), and "enterprise" (2:4-8).

85 In terms of content Ellermeier, *Qohelet*, I/1 53ff., distinguishes three "models of reflection" in the book of Qoheleth: (1) "The *unified critical reflection*" ("The train of thought begins with the negative and is thus a unified expression of the critique of an optimistic understanding of existence": 2:18-19, 20-23; 3:16-22; 4:1-3; 6:1-6, 10-12; 7:15-22; 7:23–8:1; 8:2-8; 9:11f; 10:5-7; 11:1-6); (2) "The *critical broken reflection*" ("It begins with a seemingly positive or neutral point and pushes forward to a critique . . .": 1:4-11; 1:12–2:11; 2:12-17, 24-26; 3:1-15; 4:13-16; 7:5-7, 11-14; 9:13-16; 10:12-15; 11:7–12:7); (3) "The *critical reverse broken reflection*" ("Here the train of thought starts out with the negative and leads to a relative value, without being able to remove the basic sting of the critique": 4:4-6, 7-12; 5:12-19; 6:7-9; 8:9-15; 8:16–9:10). Cf. also R. Braun, *Kohelet und die frühhellenistische Popularphilosophie* (BZAW 130; Berlin: de Gruyter, 1973), 153ff.

ture. In the OT and early Jewish wisdom literature we find many relatively short reports on experiences and reflections of a speaker or on his career as a "wise man."[86] More broadly presented "autobiographical" stylizations are found in Wisdom 6–9, but also in texts such as Daniel 7–12; *1 Enoch* 17–36; 72–82; and the *Testaments of the Twelve Patriarchs*.[87] Yet even the collections and compositions of individual sayings in Proverbs 10ff. seem to be well thought out and intended as a stimulus to further reflection.[88]

The book of Qoheleth as a whole can be best characterized formally as a wisdom teaching. The title in 1:1 and the epilogue in 12:9-14 have corresponding forms in Egyptian wisdom instructions.[89] In addition to examples of information about the author in the third person at the beginning (e.g., Khety and esp. Ankh-Sheshonq) or at the end (e.g., Kagemni) of an instruction, there are also examples of an opening of the instruction with an "autobiographical" report (e.g., Ptahhotep, with a change from a third- to a first-person report; cf. Qoheleth 1–2).[90] The latter is also found in the Proverbs of Ahiqar, in the book of Tobit, and in the *Testaments of the Twelve Patriarchs*.[91] In the framing of a teaching in the third person, one may also compare not only Deuteronomy and especially the narrative framework of Job, but also the preface to the Greek Book of Sirach, Daniel 1–6 as introduction to Daniel 7–12, and the introductions to

Daniel 7; 8; 9; 10–12; and *1 Enoch* 1; 12; 13 (in each case with a change from third to first person). As information about the author (in third person) at (or toward) the end of a book, Qoh 12:9ff. corresponds above all to Sir 50:27-29.

The expectations of readers awakened by the form of the book of Qoheleth as a work of instructive wisdom literature are, however, systematically disappointed by its content. The teaching authority of King Solomon is "deconstructed" and repudiated already in the first chapters of the book. In chapter 3, at the latest, the reader notices that regarding the tensions between the statements of the king in 1:12–2:26 and their "revision" in 3:10–4:12, the book conveys no clear teaching, but instead carries on a "debate" between different teachings: "Qoheleth does not present the rounded whole of a teaching but rather develops what he has to say in the form of an ongoing dialogue that bears strong polemical traits."[92] While the book of Qoheleth presents itself in the form of a didactically oriented wisdom text (like, for example, Proverbs and Sirach), its content, by contrast, belongs to a "reflective, problem-oriented" wisdom tradition (like, for example, Job), which is to be judged more as an expression of a "critical wisdom" than as the

---

86   For the former see Prov 7:6ff.; 24:30ff.; Job 4:8ff.; 5:3ff.; Ps 37:25ff., 35-36; 73. For the latter, Prov 4:3-4; Sir 24:30ff.; 33:16ff.; 51:13ff.

87   Cf. also the examples named by K. Berger, "Hellenistische Gattungen im Neuen Testament," *ANRW* 25.2 (1984) 1272–73, of first-person reports on the relationship to philosophy in Greek autobiographical letters.

88   See, e.g., Thomas Krüger, "Komposition und Diskussion in Proverbia 10," *ZThK* 89 (1995) 413–33, repr. in idem, *Kritische Weisheit* (Zurich: Pano, 1997) 195-214.

89   See H. Brunner, *Altägyptische Weisheit* (BAW.AO; Zurich: Artemis, 1988) 75: "The title of the teachings brings, after the genus designation *sebâjet* . . . the name of the author. This shortest possible form of the title is often expanded by the name of the son, to whom the teaching is imparted, by the official title of the father and the son, if he carries one, and finally sometimes also by a few lines that extol the usefulness of the teaching. . . . Then follows, in

some of the more important works, a description of the circumstances under which the book came into being."

90   Cf. Qoh 1:12–2:26; see also M. V. Fox, "Frame Narrative and Composition in the Book of Qohelet," *HUCA* 48 (1977) 83–106; idem, *Qohelet,* 312ff.

91   Cf. also Longman, *Fictional Akkadian Autobiography*; idem, *The Book of Ecclesiastes* (NICOT; Grand Rapids: Eerdmans, 1998) 15–20; he defines the genre of the book of Qoheleth as "framed wisdom autobiography."

92   W. Zimmerli, "Das Buch der Predigers Salomo," in H. Ringgren and W. Zimmerli, *Sprüche/Prediger* (3d ed.; ATD 16/1; Göttingen: Vandenhoeck & Ruprecht, 1980) 128. Cf. the analogous characterization of the Teaching for Merikare in Hellmut Brunner, *Grundzüge einer Geschichte der altägyptischen Literatur,* 4th ed. (Darmstadt: Wissenschaftliche Buchgesellschaft, 1986) 27: "In terms of content, the Teaching for Merikare belongs in the circle of 'debate literature,' in that it deals with problems of

symptom of a "crisis of wisdom."[93] Since the form of wisdom teaching in the book of Qoheleth is adopted critically and ironically (see the commentary to 12:9-14), it allows no direct conclusions regarding the social and institutional context in which and for which it was written.

From the realm of Greek-Hellenistic literature the "specifically popular philosophical genre of the diatribe, which arose at the time of Qoheleth," is frequently introduced as a comparison to the book of Qoheleth.[94] It was developed by Bion of Borysthenes in the first half of the third century, that is, "at about the same time [as the] philosophical polemic form of satire" of Menippos of Gadara, and like it "exercised a strong influence on later Hellenistic and Roman literature," including "Jewish and Christian preaching."[95]

"From the older diatribes we have only some larger fragments from a certain Teles of Megara, who lived around the middle of the third century B.C.E."[96] With the exception of no. 6, in which a conclusion (ll. 3-4) is drawn from an introductory thesis (1-2) and then further developed (4ff.), they reveal a discursive structure. In each case it is already evident at the beginning of the

texts: often a thesis is introduced or "quoted" and then immediately refuted. Thus no. 1 begins with a quotation (ll. 1-2: $\kappa\rho\epsilon\hat{\iota}\tau\tau\acute{o}\nu$ $\varphi\alpha\sigma\iota$ $\tau\grave{o}$ $\delta o\kappa\epsilon\hat{\iota}\nu$ $\delta\acute{\iota}\kappa\alpha\iota o\nu$ $\epsilon\hat{\iota}\nu\alpha\iota$ $\tau o\hat{\nu}$ $\epsilon\hat{\iota}\nu\alpha\iota$, "People say that seeming to be just is better than being so"). Then a "dialogue" is introduced that develops the refutation of the quoted thesis (2-3: "Seeming to be good isn't better than being so, is it?"). Number 4A introduces the thesis to be disputed with $\delta o\kappa\epsilon\hat{\iota}$ $\mu o\iota$: "It seems to me that the acquisition of money frees one from scarcity and want" (1-2). This is again followed with a question (l. 3: $\kappa\alpha\grave{\iota}$ $\pi\hat{\omega}\varsigma$, "and just how?"). Without introduction, no. 4B presents a thesis for discussion: "Poverty is a deterrent to being a philosopher, but wealth is a useful thing for this" (1-2). Line 3 opens its refutation with $o\grave{\nu}\kappa$ $\epsilon\hat{\nu}$ ("not well spoken"). Number 7 introduces the thesis to be refuted in the form of a question: "Perhaps ($\mu\acute{\eta}\pi o\vartheta$') in the same way that a pomegranate is called 'seedless,' and people 'neckless' and 'chestless,' people are called 'painless' and 'fearless'?" (1ff.). Number 3 presents the thesis to be discussed and the strategy for refuting it in one introductory sentence: "Perhaps ($\mu\acute{\eta}\pi o\tau\epsilon$) in response to the man who thinks that exile makes people less competent could aptly be brought up

world order and theodicy, but in terms of form belongs to teachings about life." (Cf. also ibid., 29–30, on the "wisdom" character of Egyptian autobiographies and harp songs, with which the book of Qoheleth likewise shows connections [see below].)

93 On this distinction between "didactic" and "reflective" wisdom literature, cf. M. Küchler, *Frühjüdische Weisheitstraditionen* (OBO 26; Freiburg: Universitätsverlag; Göttingen: Vandenhoeck & Ruprecht, 1979) 25; and Hermann von Lips, *Weisheitliche Traditionen im Neuen Testament* (WMANT 64; Neukirchen-Vluyn: Neukirchener Verlag, 1990) 97, 100. Von Lips's intention with this (tradition-historical) distinction is to name "different genres of wisdom writings" (ibid., 97). Yet one point of the book of Qoheleth seems to lie in the tension between form and content, when in the form of a wisdom teaching (genre) it's content develops a critical reflection on wisdom teachings (tradition). Cf. Krüger, *Kritische Weisheit*, v–viii; and also, e.g., von Lips, *Weisheitliche Traditionen*, 92–100 ("Exkurs 3: Krise der Weisheit?").

94 Braun, *Kohelet*, 165; cf., e.g., Lohfink, 10; see M. Hengel, *Judaism and Hellenism* (2 vols. in 1; Philadelphia: Fortress Press, 1974) 1:115; 2:77 n. 52; Schwienhorst-Schönberger, "Kohelet," 21–24. Braun (*Kohêlet*, 165) names as traits common to the book

of Qoheleth and the diatribe: "the correspondence of the epilogue 12:8 and the title 1:2," "the disparate positioning of reflective and didactic sections," and "the frequent use of expressions and catch phrases." Here and in the following section cf. F. J. Backhaus, "Kohelet und die 'Diatribe': Hermeneutische und methodologische Überlegungen zu einem nach ausstehenden Stilvergleich," *BZ* 42 (1998) 248–56.

95 Hengel, *Judaism and Hellenism*, 1:84.

96 Rainer Nickel, ed., *Epiktet, Teles und Musonius; Wege zum Glück* (Zurich and Munich: Artemis, 1987) 202; cf. the German translation of Teles 2 and 3, ibid., 203ff.; and in Reiner Nickel, ed., *Epiktet–Teles–Musonius; Ausgewählte Schriften* (Sammlung Tusculum; Zurich: Artemis, 1994) 370ff. The translation and line numbers in the following are according to E. N. O'Neil, ed., *Teles (The Cynic Teacher)* (SBLTT 11; Graeco-Roman Religion 3; Missoula, Mont.: Scholars Press, 1977).

as a comparison the matter of skills" (1ff.). And no. 5 offers thesis and refutation in the form of a quotation: "If it is necessary to measure the happy life from an excess of pleasure, no one, says Crates ($\varphi\eta\sigma\grave{\iota}\nu$ $\acute{o}$ $K\rho\acute{\alpha}\tau\eta\varsigma$), can really be happy" (1ff.). By contrast, no. 2, along with no. 6, begins with an assertion that is the foundation for the following discussion (1ff.).

In the course of the argumentation that follows, in which Teles repeatedly operates with questions, examples, and quotations from literature, a "dialogue" can develop, in which the addressee also gets to speak.[97] With the exception of nos. 5 and 6, the course of the argumentation regularly includes objections, which are immediately refuted.[98] As in the introductory discussion theses, we also have here a variety of introduction possibilities: an objection can be cited (for example, no. 3, l. 37: $\varphi\alpha\sigma\acute{\iota}\nu$; no. 4B, l. 46: $\varphi\alpha\sigma\grave{\iota}$ $\delta\grave{\epsilon}$; no. 7, l. 52: $\varphi\eta\sigma\grave{\iota}\nu$ $\acute{\eta}$ $\delta\acute{o}\xi\alpha$); it can be formulated by a dialogue partner in the form of an assertion (in part with an introductory $\grave{\alpha}\lambda\lambda\grave{\alpha}$: no. 1, l. 29; cf. no. 7, l. 121) or as a question (e.g., no. 4A, l. 47), and in the last named reference, as well as in no. 2, ll. 124ff. ($\delta o\kappa\epsilon\hat{\iota}$ $\mu o\iota$), it is not entirely clear whether Teles himself or his dialogue partner is speaking. In regard to the model of an argument with "quotation" and "commentary," which is recommended for the interpretation of the book of Qoheleth (see below), no. 3 is of special interest: here the first objection is explicitly quoted (ll. 37-38: $\varphi\alpha\sigma\acute{\iota}\nu$) and commented upon. Then come a series of objections that are obviously likewise "quoted" by the speaker but not explicitly marked as quotations (ll. 52-53, 69-70, 105ff., 116-17, 146-47

introduced with $\grave{\alpha}\lambda\lambda\grave{\alpha}$; in addition, ll. 116-17, $\delta o\kappa\epsilon\hat{\iota}$ $\mu o\iota$; ll. 91-92, 97-98, 105ff., 146-47, in interrogatory form). That these objections are also "quotations" can be inferred from lines 130-31: "But many use it as a reproach that . . . , saying. . . ." The diatribes of Teles show that the boundaries are rather fluid between a genuine dialogue, a monologue that with quotations makes reference to counterpositions, and reflections in which the speaker himself considers possible objections ("it seems to me . . .").

"S. K. Stowers (1981) has shown that the phenomenon of the diatribe does not rest on street preaching or speaking to the masses or on polemics vis-à-vis opponents of philosophy (as one has assumed since J. Weiss, Deissmann, and especially R. Bultmann). Rather, the diatribe goes back to the relationship between student and teacher in a lecture in school."[99] "Its purpose is to point out error, to convince and to convict and then to lead one to truth, to a righter way of life."[100] Here the "fictitious opposition" of the student as dialogue partner in no way excludes "the real opposition of concrete groups."[101] Above all, the beginning of Teles 3 (see above) shows an interest in conveying to the reader competence for independent argumentation with counterpositions. Precisely this also seems to be the intention of the book of Qoheleth: the reader is not supposed to learn (by heart) prepared "wisdoms" but to become capable of forming independent judgments.[102]

In addition to genuine wisdom (or philosophical) genres and argumentation forms, however, the book of Qoheleth also contains texts and text sections whose

---

97 E.g., no. 1, ll. 2ff.; no. 7, ll. 121ff.
98 See no. 1, ll. 29ff.; no. 2, ll. 124ff.; no. 3, ll. 37ff.; no. 4A, ll. 47ff.; no. 4B, ll. 46ff.; no. 7, ll. 52ff.
99 K. Berger, "Hellenistische Gattunge," 1125–26; cf. S. K. Stowers, *The Diatribe and Paul's Letter to the Romans* (SBLDS 57; Chico, Calif.: Scholars Press, 1981); Thomas Schmeller, *Paulus und die "Diatribe": Eine vergleichende Stilinterpretation* (NTA n.s. 19; Münster: Aschendorff, 1987).
100 Stowers, *Diatribe,* 58; quoted in Berger, "Hellenistische Gattungen," 1126.
101 Berger, "Hellenistische Gattungen," 1129.
102 On diatribe cf. also ibid., 1124ff. (who recommends as a genre designation "Dialexis" or "Diatribe/ Dialexis"). Of the characteristics of the "Diatribe/ Dialexis" named by Berger, ibid., 1129ff., the follow-

ing are of special interest in comparison with the book of Qoheleth: "reworking of smaller genres" ("examples," "parables," "catalogs," "quotations": 1130), "juxtaposition of admonitions and argumentation," "emphasis on the 'I' of the speaking teacher," "themes: pain, enjoyment, desire, honor, wealth, poverty, age, death" (1131), "forms of argumentation: thesis, counterthesis . . . conclusion by analogy, comparison, examples; exclusion process; syllogisms; equatings; transitions; introduction of new criteria; conclusions; conclusions a fortiori" (1132).

topic and style have models in other realms of literature. Thus the report of "King Qoheleth" on his "great works" reminds one of royal inscriptions and poetic glorifications of rulers.[103] "The evocation of such forms in the framework of aristocratic drinking sprees and love plays probably portrays the background for the royal travesty of Qoh 2 [or 1:12–2:26–T.K.], where it is taken into the service of a specifically 'wisdom' or philosophical-experimental question."[104] The same is true of the exhortation to joy and the enjoyment of life (*carpe diem*) in view of the death facing all people (*memento mori*) in Qoh 9:1-10; 11:7–12:7 and elsewhere, which recalls in particular the Egyptian "songs of the harper."[105]

On the basis of these affinities, Christoph Uehlinger has proposed the "hypothesis" that "in terms of cultural history the book of Qoheleth can best be understood as symposiastic philosophy." For "the juxtaposition of various small genres in the book of Qoheleth (proverbial genres from the wisdom tradition, self-reported royal travesty, didactic speeches, reflections, quotations, poems, and songs) and the occasional, quite abrupt transition from one to another (for example, from reflection to song in 9:7), are best understood against the background of the symposium (as the real *Sitz im Leben* and/or as a fictive-ideal constellation). Such symposiastic events apparently took place in the early Hellenistic Judah of the third and second centuries B.C.E. Teaching and song played an important role here. In those days, wisdom and/or philosophy were not only presented in the schools and in the marketplaces; they were not only present as public diatribes. They were also—and for the upper class perhaps above all—cultivated as private discussions in the context of symposia" (cf. Proverbs 9).[106] Here also, to be sure, it seems problematic to draw from the genres used in the book a direct inference back to

the social and institutional context in which and for which the book as a whole was written. (See below on the origin and history of influence of the book of Qoheleth.)

Tensions and Contradictions

Since Abraham ibn Ezra and Spinoza, interpreters have constantly pointed to the occurrence of contradictions in the book of Qoheleth. They are mentioned already in *Shabbat* 30b; cf. *Megillah* 7a. . . . In 2:13-14; 7:19; 8:1; 10:10, 12 wisdom is praised, but it is faulted in 1:18; 2:15, 16; 6:8; 10:1; wealth is called good in 5:8 [5:9]; 6:8; 7:11; 9:16 but evil in 5:9-14 [5:10-15]; one set of sayings calls the enjoyment of life good, another calls it evil. Qoheleth contradicts himself in evaluating each of the goods of this world. . . . In consequence of these many contradictions, one cannot—even with frequent attentive reading of the book—easily come to a clear knowledge of what it actually teaches and requires; and therefore no two interpreters fully agree in their conceptions of the content and basic thought of this puzzling book.[107]

In the history of interpretation of the book of Qoheleth, various basic approaches have been developed in order to explain and understand its inner tensions and contradictions.

A *biographical* explanatory model traces them back to the idea that the book of Qoheleth is composed of texts that were written by one and the same author at different times in different "moods" and from different "points of view": "the unity lies behind the statements in the mind of the writer."[108] If one and the same author at

---

103 Cf. O. Loretz, *Qohelet und der Alte Orient* (Freiburg: Herder, 1964) 62-63; H.-P. Müller, "Kohelet und Amminadab," in Diesel et al., eds., *Jedes Ding*, 149–65; C. Uehlinger, "Qohelet im Horizont mesopotamischer, levantinischer und ägyptischer Weisheitliteratur der persischen und hellenistischen Zeit," in Schwienhorst-Schönberger, ed., *Das Buch Kohelet,** 203–7. See also the references to Egyptian biographical inscriptions of the late period in Uehlinger, "Qohelet," 207–10.

104 Uehlinger, "Qohelet," 205–6. Cf. the travesties "upward" ("king") and "downward" ("shepherds") in

Canticles and in Greek pastoral poetry; see Bernd Effe, ed., *Theokrit und die griechische Bukolik* (Wege der Forschung 580; Darmstadt: Wissenschaftliche Buchgesellschaft, 1986); idem, *Die Genese einer literarischen Gattung: Die Bukolik* (Konstanzer Universitätsreden 95; Konstanz: Universitätsverlag, 1977).

105 Ibid., 210–22.

106 Ibid., 234–35.

107 Gerson, 16–17.

108 G. Wildeboer, "Der Prediger," in *Die Fünf Megillot* (KHC 17; Tübingen: Mohr, 1898) 111. Cf. Michel, *Qohelet*, 10ff. On "moods" see, e.g., S. R. Driver, *An*

different times expressed different views, however, one must still ask what he (or an editor) was trying to say with the compilation of these different views.[109] Moreover, the boundary between *one* author, who expressed different views at different times (and in different moods), and *several* different authors (or editors) is fluid, and so is the boundary between a "biographical" and a redaction-historical explanatory model. Finally, while a "biographical" explanatory model can make the tensions and contradictions between different, relatively self-contained textual units in the book of Qoheleth plausible, it is less able to explain tensions and contradictions within such text units.

Here lie the strengths of the *literary-critical* or *redaction-historical* approaches that do not operate merely with more or less mechanical rearrangements and revisions of the text.[110] They assume either (1) a redactional compilation (and glossing) of individual texts going back to Qoheleth by one or more editors of the book, or (2) a substantial updating of a basic text going back to Qoheleth by one or more redactors.

1. The more recent research mostly assumes relatively few glosses beyond the framework in 1:1(2) and 12:(8)9-14, which is usually regarded as redactional. "11:9b is now almost universally treated as an addition, while 2:26, 3:17, 7:26, 8:5, 8:12-13a, which are treated by all or most scholars as secondary, are generally regarded as a corollary of Qoheleth's own thought."[111] Along this line, A. Fischer has recently attempted to reconstruct the origin of the book of Qoheleth as follows: a (first) editor gathered "notes from a Qoheleth school" (in the form of "original compositions" and "individual texts") in four "book sections," which he bound together with his own "transitions" and provided with a title (1:1*) and an epilogue (12:9-11a).[112] This "first epilogist" designated Qoheleth as a "wise man," whereas Qoheleth himself could "hardly have understood himself as such because of his critical stance with regard to wisdom."[113] A later

Introduction to the Literature of the Old Testament (9th ed.; Edinburgh: Clark, 1913) 466: "evidently [the book] reflects the author's changing moods and these, for some reason, he has presented side by side without always bringing them into logical connexion with each other." On "points of view" see, e.g., V. Zapletal, *Das Buch Kohelet* (Freiburg: Gschwend, 1905, 2d ed. 1911) 31: Qoheleth "recorded his thoughts as they came to him. Thus we have here a kind of chronological order. The result may be in part that apparently quite contradictory judgments are given in regard to the same object, just as we often judge the same thing differently at different times. In Qoheleth, nonetheless, this difference can be explained primarily by the different points of view from which he regards things."

109 Cf., e.g., J. L. Crenshaw, *Ecclesiastes* (OTL; Philadelphia: Westminster, 1987) 48–49: he sketches first the beginnings of a "biographical" explanatory model: "I believe the tensions of the book represent for the most part the fruit of a lifetime's research. Changing circumstances evoke different responses to conventional wisdom and to one's former thoughts. Differences in societal concerns also dictate a variety of literary expressions. Qohelet bears his soul in all its twistings and turnings, ups and downs, and he invites readers to accompany him in pursuit of fresh discovery." Following this he indicates a possible interpretation of the resulting tensions and contradictions in the book of Qoheleth:

"But the contradictions suggest more than the result of time's passage. They express the ambiguities of daily existence and the absurdity of human efforts to understand it. As in a kaleidoscope, apparently incongruent features of the text come together almost magically, framing many different but meaningful configurations."

110 See Michel, *Qohelet*, 17ff. "Bickell derives the present form of the book's text from a manuscript whose pages were put together incorrectly. Another way of removing contradictions is the idea of text modifications; Grätz, Bickell and Siegfried make use of them rather arbitrarily. Bickell supports his accident hypothesis through such a large number of text modifications that almost thirteen pages of his writing are filled with them" (Gerson, 18; cf. Michel, *Qohelet*, 17).

111 Kaiser, *Introduction*, 400. On the older research cf. the overview in Ellermeier, *Qohelet I/1*, 131ff. (who excludes even 3:17a$\beta\gamma$, 18aα; 5:6a; 6:2aβ; 8:12-13; 9:3bα; 11:9b, 10b; and 12:1a as secondary).

112 Fischer, *Skepsis;* see his summary on p. 252. For original compositions see 1:3–3:15; (3:16–4:16a?) 4:17–5:6; 5:9–6:9a; 7:1-22; 9:1-12; 9:13–10:13; 11:1–12:7. For individual texts see 3:16–4:3; 4:4-12, 13-16a (?); 5:7-8; 7:25-29; 8:1-8, 9 (?), 10-15; 10:15, 16-17, 18, 19, 20. The book sections are I: 1:2–3:15; II: 3:16–6:9; III: 6:11–8:17; IV: 9:1–12:8. The transitions are 1:2; 4:16b; 6:9b, 11-12; 7:23-24; 8:16-17; 10:14; 12:8.

113 Ibid., 25.

editor identified Qoheleth with Solomon through the glosses in 1:1aβb and 12:11b. Finally, a "second epilogist," "who received the scroll already as a Solomonic writing," "attempted to establish the interpretation of the teachings of Qoheleth along the lines of traditional legal piety through the second epilogue in 12:12-14 and his corrections undertaken in 3:17; 6:10; 9:3b; 11:9b."[114]

(2) At the beginning of the twentieth century, there were a number of attempts to explain the tensions and contradictions in the book of Qoheleth as redactional expansions.[115] Whereas Siegfried distinguished (at least) nine literary strata, McNeile, Barton, Podechard, and Buzy (with variations in detail) posited, in addition to the basic stratum of the book going back to Qoheleth, three more successive redactional strata, which go back to a "Hasid" ("pious one"), a "Hakam" ("wise one"), and an "editor."[116] Recently, Martin Rose has developed a similar model.[117] He assumes that a basic text from the Persian period going back to Qoheleth (I: "le maître" or "le sage") was reworked and updated first in the Ptolemaic period (early third century) by a student (II: "le disciple") and then (late third century) by a further editor (III: "le théologien-rédacteur").[118] While Qoheleth rec-

ommends pleasure as an alternative to wisdom, which he criticizes, his student is critical of this choice; the editor then attempts to balance the ambivalences and contradictions produced by his predecessors.

3. In addition to glosses and expansions, one must basically also reckon with the possibility that the author of the book incorporated into his work individual pieces of text of greater or smaller length that came from other hands, as well as reworking some of his own drafts.[119]

The plausibility of literary-critical and redaction-historical reconstructions can ultimately be tested only with the help of an examination of the texts in question. In the process it will be seen that the book of Qoheleth in its present form can be fully understood as a coherent text, if one takes into account its discursive character and considers the possibility of an ironic playing around with the traditional genres and themes (see, for example, the commentary on 1:1 and 12:9-14; 7:1-14; 8:1-9, 10-15). In any case, the task of interpretation of a particular text is not finished with only the reconstruction of the history of its origin.[120] This task, however, will be the special focus of the present commentary.

---

114 Ibid., 35.

115 Cf. already Johann Gottfried Herder, *Briefe, das Studium der Theologie betreffend* (2d ed.; Frankfurt, 1790), letter 11, pp. 180–82 (see Michel, *Qohelet*, 24–25), who perceives in the texts that address the reader in the second person singular the voice of a "teacher" that is different from the voice of the "researcher" and "seeker," to whom the basic content of the book of Qoheleth goes back.

116 Michel, *Qohelet*, 18, 20.

117 Rose, "Qohéleth, le maître: Compréhension de l'univers et compréhension de soi," *Variations herméneutiques* 3 (1995) 3–22. Cf. also the contributions of O. Loretz on various individual texts ("Anfänge jüdischer Philosophie nach Qohelet 1,1-11 und 3,1-15," *UF* 23 [1991] 223–44; "'Frau' und griechisch-jüdische Philosophie im Buch Qohelet [Qoh 7,23–8,1 und 9,6-10]," *UF* 23 [1991] 245–64; "Poetry and Prose in the Book of Qoheleth [1:1–3:22; 7:23–8:1; 9:6-10; 12:8-14]," in J. C. de Moor and W. G. E. Watson, eds., *Verse in Ancient Near Eastern Prose* [AOAT 42; Kevelaer: Butzon & Bercker; Neukirchen-Vluyn: Neukirchener Verlag, 1993] 155–89), as well as Backhaus, "Widersprüche."

118 I: 1:4-7, 9a, 14aα, 17aα, bα, 18; 2:12a, 13-14, 16bβ,

20a; 3:9-10, 11bα, 12; 8:9a, 15. Going back to II, for example, are 1:1* (דִּבְרֵי קֹהֶלֶת *dibrê qōhelet*) and 12:9-10; 1:2 and 12:8; 2:1-3, 11, 17; 3:18-22; 4:2-4; 9:1-3, 11-12. Going back to III, for example, are 12:13-14; 2:18-19 (20-23?), 24; 3:1-4 (16?), 17; 8:(12?)13.

119 Other hands are often suggested, for example, for (parts of) 1:3-11; 3:1-9; 9:7-10; 11:7–12:7 or for individual sayings such as 1:15 and 1:18. "According to some older interpretations, the book of Qoheleth contains nothing but notes and excerpts from other books; it is, according to Luther, 'assembled like a Talmud from many books, perhaps from the library of King Ptolemy Euergetes in Egypt' (similarly, Grotius, Cheyne)" (Gerson, 18). On reworking see J. Coppens, "La structure de l'Ecclésiaste," in M. Gilbert, ed., *La Sagesse de l'Ancien Testament* (2d ed.; BEThL 51; Leuven: Leuven Univ. Press and Peeters, 1990) 288–92, who proposes that Qoheleth himself could have later expanded "un livret fondamental" and finally added sayings with a wisdom provenance (see Michel, *Qohelet*, 40).

120 Cf., e.g., Odil Hannes Steck, *Die Prophetenbücher und ihr theologisches Zeugnis* (Tübingen: Mohr, 1996). ET=*The Prophetic Books and Their Theological Witness*, trans. J. D. Nogalski (St. Louis: Chalice, 2000).

In contrast to text-genetic explanatory approaches, J. A. Loader tries to make the tensions and contradictions in the book of Qoheleth understandable as intentional and meaningful *"polar structures"*: "Excepting the epilogue, not a single palpable contradiction can be found in the book. The 'contradictions' that caused the rabbis so much brain-racking and that can be eliminated so skillfully by critics are nothing other than intended polar structures" (in addition to 12:9-14, Loader also excludes 1:1-11 from his consideration).[121] Within the framework of such "polar structures," according to Loader, mutually contradictory statements A and B are related to each other within a textual unit in such a way that both A and B are valid. Since both cannot be true at the same time, the result is a tension that on the "theoretical" level is consciously maintained with the repeated הֶבֶל *hebel* statements, while in the repeated exhortations to pleasure and enjoyment, the possibility of overcoming this tension in a "practical" way is demonstrated. This basic argumentative structure of the text in the book of Qoheleth can be sketched in the following way, according to Loader:[122]

Pole A ————— *hebel*-tension ————— B Pole
|
carpe diem

Nevertheless, we must ask here whether and in what way the texts really make clear that in the case of mutually contradictory statements within a text unit, both are to be regarded as equally valid. On close examination the texts of the book of Qoheleth show a far greater breadth of variation of possible relationships between mutually contradictory statements and between statements that are mutually in tension. "Actually, Koheleth approaches the subject of opposites with a simple logic in which both options may be desirable, one may be preferable to the other, or one may cancel the other."[123] Moreover, tensions and contradictions between larger text units (e.g., 1:12–2:26 and 3:10–4:12) remain unexplainable in Loader's model.[124]

According to many older interpreters, the book contains a *dialogue* between religious wisdom and antireligious pseudowisdom or between a teacher and his student or between a Pharisee and a Sadducee or between an Israelite Hakam and a Greek sophist, and so forth (Herder, Eichhorn, Döderlein, Nachtigall, Schenkel, and others). The dialogue hypothesis is, to be sure, considered by almost all recent interpreters as an outdated point of view; some of them, however, quietly reintroduce it, trying to explain some of the contradictions by saying that *Qoheleth quotes his intellectual opponents* in order then to fight their teachings as false teachings. This is especially true of Leimdörffer, who lets Sadducees, Essenes, and the Pharisaic author speak one after another, and Tyler, according to whom Qoheleth presents the philosophical and religious teachings of his contemporaries and weighs them against each other.[125]

In recent times Perry in particular has taken up the approach of interpreting the book of Qoheleth as a dialogue, whereas especially Lohfink and Michel have attempted to explain the tensions and contradictions in individual texts through the assumption that Qoheleth "quotes foreign opinions in order to discuss them."[126] The problem with this explanatory model is that the texts explicitly reveal neither a change of speakers nor a sequence of "quotes" and "commentaries." Thus one

---

121 Loader, *Polar Structures,* 133; see also his commentary.

122 Loader, *Polar Structures,* 111.

123 E. Horton, "Koheleth's Concept of Opposites as Compared to Samples of Greek Philosophy and Near and Far Eastern Wisdom Classics," *Numen* 19 (1972) 21.

124 Cf. also the review by N. Lohfink in *BZ* 25 (1981) 112–13.

125 Gerson, 18, emphasis added. On more recent research cf. Michel, *Qohelet,* 21–33; L. Schwienhorst-Schönberger, "Kohelet," 18–19.

126 Michel, *Qohelet,* 32. N. Lohfink ("War Kohelet ein Frauenfeind? Ein Versuch die Logik und den Gegenstand von Koh. 7, 23-8, 1a herauszufinden," in Gilbert, ed., *Sagesse,* 259–87, 417–20; also in his comm.) sees quotations that are commented on in the following text in 7:1a, 5-6, 8-9, 11-12, 19, 26; 8:1b, 5, 12b-13. D. Michel (*Untersuchungen zur Eigenart des Buches Qohelet* [BZAW 183; Berlin: de Gruyter, 1989]) assumes foreign opinions quoted and criticized by Qoheleth in 3:16; 4:5, 13-14; 5:7-8, 10-11; 6:7; 7:1-6, 11-12, 19, 26, 28; 8:1-5; 9:1, 17; 10:1a, 2, 4, 8-10, 12-13, 16-20.

must ask: "What does the author seek to achieve by *not* using the means at his disposal to indicate that the words and opinions expressed do not belong to the speaker?"[127]

The most likely possibility of explaining tensions and contradictions remains, in any case, the attempt to interpret these as intended and meaningful elements of larger *trains of thought and argumentation*—even going beyond individual texts (see the commentary on 1:3–4:12; see also the examples introduced above under "Genres"). "Much of what the author says is only momentarily valid . . . as one link in the chain of deductions. It does its duty and is vanquished; the later assertion abolishes the earlier one. And Qoheleth teaches definitively only what in the end remains uncontradicted."[128] Moreover, in the sense of a "reception-oriented interpretive approach," we must recognize that the text operates with allusions to contemporary texts and concepts, as well as with intended ambiguities, in order to provoke readers to a repeated reading and to the formation of their own judgment.[129]

As already noted above (under "Genres"), the proverbial compositions in Proverbs 10ff. also seem to count on readers who have the ability and will to read attentively and reflect critically on a web of ambiguous and tension-filled assertions, admonitions, and warnings. Yet, as Gerhard von Rad has shown, even a wise saying often exhibits a high degree of ambiguity. The stylistic means of the *parallelismus membrorum* serves here, on the one hand, the refinement of the assertion: "The striving here is not for precision in the concept but for precision in the portrayal of the object, if possible, in its entire breadth." On the other hand and at the same time, however, it also bestows on the saying a relatively large openness with regard to its meaning: "The ['paral-

lelistically halved'] single line often enough makes higher claims and demands a greater degree of intellectual participation than a developed didactic poem. The single line is much more dense and affords more room for manoeuvre from the point of view of meaning and application than the didactic poem, the content of which is much less ambiguous as to its meaning."[130] If it is within a "wise" man's competence "to understand a proverb and a figure, the words of the wise and their riddles" (Prov 1:6; cf. Sir 29:2-3; Wis 8:8; Qoh 8:1), they formulate at the same time a demand that the "wise" texts make on their readers.

Comparable demands on the assistance of readers are also made by large parts of contemporary Greek-Hellenistic literature, which are marked by an "elite exclusivity" and "address themselves to a very limited circle of literarily educated addressees: the Greek upper class in the ambiance of the court. . . . Authors like Callimachus, Theocritus, and Arat placed their poetic output under the motto of radical innovation and thereby founded a new literary aesthetic. . . . By thus constantly keeping in mind the whole repertoire of pre-Hellenistic 'classical' writing as foil and frame of reference, they assumed a public that had the necessary literary qualifications to comprehend the interplay of tradition and innovation and to do justice to the exclusive aesthetic of these authors."[131]

In the commentary on the texts of the book of Qoheleth, therefore, we must take into account the possibility that in their argumentation they demand a high degree of interpretive cooperation from their readers.[132] A sign of this could be, above all, the gaps and ambiguities in the texts that challenge the reader to interpretation, but also allusions to traditional texts and concepts, as well as possible positions in the context of the con-

127 M. V. Fox, "The Identification of Quotations in Biblical Literature," *ZAW* 92 (1980) 427.

128 F. Hitzig, "Der Prediger Salomo's," in E. Bertheau und F. Hitzig, *Die Sprüche Salomo's–Der Prediger Salomo's* (KEH 7; Leipzig: Hirzel, 1847) 125.

129 Schwienhorst-Schönberger, "Kohelet," 19–20; Backhaus, "Widersprüche," 147–48.

130 Gerhard von Rad, *Wisdom in Israel* (Nashville: Abingdon, 1972) 27. Cf. ibid., 28 on antithetical parallelism: "The endless possibility of variation in this literary form consists in the fact that these contrasts are not, in fact, precise opposites. . . . In each

case we have simply one possible opposite among many. In this way it stimulates thoughtful people to let its ideas play to and fro in their minds."

131 B. Effe, ed., *Hellenismus* (Die griechische Literatur in Text und Darstellung 4; Stuttrgart: Reclam, 1985) 13.

132 Cf. here, e.g., Umberto Eco, *Lector in fabula: La Cooporazione interpretiva nei testi narrativi* (Milan: Bompiani, 1979); and idem, *The Limits of Interpretation* (Advances in Semiotics; Bloomington: Indiana Univ. Press, 1990).

temporary discussion of themes that are treated in the texts. Thus it is possible, for example, that a "quotation" could be easily identified by contemporary readers even without explicit marking, because it was familiar to them as a self-explanatory part of their "knowledge of the world." In addition to such elements of the argumentation, through which most of the interpretive possibilities are opened, there are also elements to be considered that steer the interpretive cooperation of the readers in a certain direction and thereby limit its room to operate. Of particular importance here, in addition to the structure of individual text units, are also pervasive leitmotifs such as the high regard for pleasure and enjoyment as "highest good" and references to the human finitude, the contingency of time, and the unpredictability of the future (see above under "Themes").

Origin and Historical Context

Time of Origin
Even if one assumes that the book of Qoheleth does not go back to different authors, we must, nonetheless, reckon with a lengthy time of origin (several years or decades); whether it is a "work of old age," as is often assumed, cannot be determined. A terminus ad quem for the finishing of the book is given by the fragment of a Qoheleth manuscript found in Qumran (4QQoh[a]), which was written between 175 and 150 B.C.E. (see below: "Text"). The book of Sirach, composed around 175 B.C.E., seems to presuppose the book of Qoheleth, even if no direct literary references to Qoleleth can be demonstrated in Sirach.[133]

In recent research it is generally assumed that the book of Qoheleth was composed in Jerusalem in the sec-

ond half of the third century B.C.E., that is, about a generation before Sirach.[134] Some possible—yet by no means clear—historical allusions could point to the last years of the third century (after the accession of Ptolemy V in 204 B.C.E.).[135] This hypothesis on the time and place of origin of the book of Qoheleth, which the following commentary assumes, is supported by—in addition to a number of linguistic peculiarities of the text (see below)—its references to political and social circumstances, as well as the possibility of placing it easily in the context of the cultural conflicts and discussions of this era. The latter seems much more difficult in an earlier time period.[136]

Contemporary History
After the end of the wars of succession (321–301 B.C.E.), in the course of which Jerusalem was taken four times by Ptolemy I and a considerable number of Judeans were deported to Alexandria,[137] Jerusalem and Judea belonged for a century (301–200/198) to the Ptolemaic province of Syria and Phoenicia (Coele-Syria).

After the military conquest of their second great foreign possession after Cyrenaica, the first Ptolemies quickly and intensively opened up Coele-Syria for the economy and the administration of their empire. This is reflected literarily in the papyri of the Zenon archive in a decree of Ptolemy II Philadelphus from the year 260 on the declaration of livestock and slaves, as well as in the Tobiad story of Flavius Josephus. Archaeologically important is the demonstrated spread of Ptolemaic coins and, especially for the Jewish heartland, the series of local Yehud coins reaching into the time of Ptolemy II (282–246), which were pre-

---

133 Cf. J. Marböck, "Koheleth und Sirach: Eine vielschichtige Beziehung," in Schwienhorst-Schönberger, ed., *Das Buch Kohelet*, 175–301; F. J. Backhaus, "Qohelet und Sirach," *BN* 69 (1993) 32–55; idem, *Zeit und Zufall*, 412–20; see also below.

134 Cf., e.g., Schwienhorst-Schönberger, "Kohelet," 24–25.

135 Cf. Hitzig; L. Levy, *Das Buch Qoheleth* (Leipzig: Hinrichs, 1912) 30–32; and the comm. on 4:13 and 10:16-17.

136 On the basis of linguistic characteristics (see below) Seow (11–21; idem, "Linguistic Evidence and the Dating of Qohelet," *JBL* 115 [1996] 643–66) dates

the book of Qoheleth "in the Persian period . . . specifically between the second half of the fifth and the first half of the fourth centuries B.C.E." (comm. 21). D. C. Fredericks (*Qoheleth's Language* [ANETS 3; Lewiston, N.Y.: Mellen, 1988]) wants to go back even into the 8th or 7th century before Christ.

137 Powerful Alexandrian Diaspora Judaism apparently cultivated good relations with the Ptolemaic rulers. According to legend (cf. *Epistle of Aristeas*), the Pentateuch was supposed to have been translated into Greek here (by Jerusalem scribes!) under Ptolemy II (285–246).

sumably given out by the Jerusalem high priest at the behest of the government in Alexandria. Ptolemy I Soter (306/304–283/282) had already created a unified coin system for the core countries Egypt, Cyrenaica, Cyprus, and Coele-Syria, in which royal Ptolemaic money was the only permitted legal tender. Thus were the Judeans also very quickly incorporated into two realms of the Hellenistic world: administration and commerce.[138]

In addition to this, in the third century the five so-called Syrian wars fought between Ptolemies and Seleucids (274–271, 260–253, 246–241, 221–217, and 201–200/198) brought familiarity with the Hellenistic military establishment.

As a hyparchy incorporated into and subordinated to the province of Syria and Phoenicia (along with Samaria, Galilee, Idumea, and Ashdod), Judea seems to have enjoyed a kind of partial autonomy, which in addition to extensive political self-administration (through the high priest, the priesthood, and the elders) also included the validity of its own "paternal laws" ($\pi\acute{\alpha}\tau\rho\iota o\iota$ $\nu\acute{o}\mu o\iota$).[139] The Ptolemies seem to have forgone the installation of a governor in Jerusalem and recognized the high priest as political representative of the area to the king ($\pi\rho o\sigma\tau\acute{\alpha}\tau\eta\varsigma$). After the pro-Seleucid high priest Onias II, in the course of the third Syrian war, suspended the payment of taxes to the Ptolemies, with Joseph ben Tobiah ca. 240–218, a "private man" could acquire, in addition to the tax lease, also the $\pi\rho o\sigma\tau\alpha\sigma\acute{\iota}\alpha$ for Judea vis-à-vis the king. After an increasing weakness of the Ptolemies in comparison with the Seleucids became evident in the fourth Syrian war, Joseph turned to the Seleucids. That led to a split in the Tobiad family;

Joseph's son Hyrcanus, who remained loyal to the Ptolemies, withdrew into a comfortable residence in the east Jordanian 'Arāq el-Emîr. "The high priests, inclined to be pro-Seleucid since Onias II, did not stand out politically during the second half of the third century before Christ."[140]

With the (quite critically drawn) picture of a "king over Israel in Jerusalem," Qoh 1:12–2:26 perhaps also brings to mind contemporary local potentates like the Tobiads or the high priests. Qoheleth 4:13 and 10:16-17 perhaps allude to the discussion between partisans of the Ptolemies and the Seleucids in Jerusalem. And 10:5-7 could reflect experiences of the ascent of the "nouveaux riches," which become graphic for us in an exemplary way in the presentation of the Tobiad Joseph in Josephus (cf. *Ant.* 12.4). In any case, in dealing with the king (and his local representatives),[141] 8:1-9 and 10:4 advise extreme caution. And when 9:14ff. tells of the siege of a little city by a great king, this can also awaken memories of the crusades of the Ptolemies against Jerusalem and through Jewish territory.

Economically, Judea seems to have greatly prospered in the third century. The Ptolemies contributed to an increase in agricultural output through the development of new plants and the promotion of contour farming and irrigation. Nevertheless, the "economic boom" (as in many ways also today) hardly benefited the broad masses of the population. For the Ptolemaic state mercantilism primarily served to increase royal income in the form of taxes from "land won by spear" ($\delta o\rho\acute{\iota}\kappa\tau\eta\tau o\varsigma$ $\chi\acute{\omega}\rho\alpha$), which was ultimately regarded as property of the king, even if it was not directly subject to him as "royal land" ($\gamma\tilde{\eta}$ $\beta\alpha\sigma\iota\lambda\iota\kappa\acute{\eta}$). In Judea direct taxes and imposts were leased to tax leaseholders ($\tau\epsilon\lambda\tilde{\omega}\nu\alpha\iota$). The one who

138 R. Bohlen, "Kohelet im Kontext hellenistischer Kultur," in Schwienhorst-Schönberger, ed., *Das Buch Kohelet,* 257–58 (lit.).

139 This is supported by the findings of archaeoloogical excavations, according to which in the 3rd century B.C.E. in Jerusalem and Judea—in contrast to the surrounding area—only a few traces of Greek-Hellenistic material culture are demonstrable (cf. C. R. Harrison, "Hellenization in Syria-Palestine: The Case of Judea in the Third Century BCE," *BA* 57 [1994] 94–108; A. M. Berlin, "Between Large Forces: Palestine in the Hellenistic Period," *BA* 60 [1997] 2–51).

140 H. Donner, *Geschichte des Volkes Israel und seiner Nachbarn in Grundzügen* (2d ed.; Göttingen: Vandenhoeck & Ruprecht, 1995) 2:479.

141 See N. Lohfink, "Das 'Poikilometron': Kohelet und Menippos von Gadara," *BK* 45 (1990) 19; idem, "Der Bibel skeptische Hintertür: Versuch, den Ort des Buchs Kohelet neu zu bestimmen," *StZ* 198 (1980) 17–31; repr. in idem, *Kohelet* (4th ed.), 5–17; repr. in idem, *Studien,* 11–30; idem, "*melek, šallîṭ* und *môšel* bei Kohelet und die Abfassungszeit des Buches," *Bib* 62 (1981) 535–43, repr. in idem, *Studien,* 71–82.

got the opportunity (as in the case of Joseph ben Tobiah) was the one who, without regard to his family and his social position, promised the king the highest income. Shortfalls in income had to be covered by the tax leaseholder from his own capital. In this way the Ptolemies could achieve the highest possible return from taxes and imposts and at the same time bind the indigenous upper class to themselves. The local tax leaseholders were controlled by royal officials. Here "three levels of administration" can be distinguished: "In the province the *oikonomoi* at the head of the hyparchies oversaw the state revenues. They were subordinate to the *dioiketes* for all of Syria and Phoenicia, who in turn were responsible to the *dioiketes* in Alexandria."[142] The "little man" could profit from this system at best insofar as the king was interested in his labor and his paying taxes and therefore opposed enslavement of the indigenous "free" population (σώματα λαϊκὰ ἐλεύθερα) through private indebtedness.

In Qoh 5:7-8 this system seems to be precisely described and criticized. Its victims could be intended by the "oppressed" in 4:1[143] but also by the rich in 6:2, whose "wealth, possessions, and honor" are consumed by strangers. Out of negative experiences with contemporary systems of government and economics, 4:9-12, 13-16; 5:7-8; and 8:9 seem to have drawn conclusions that are unusually sharp for OT criticism of power: only together can people stand up against the exploiters (4:12); no king will ever eliminate poverty (4:13-16); it would be best if every landowner were his own master (5:9) and no person had dominion over other people (8:9). The book of Qoheleth also indicates, however, that political and economic conditions in the Ptolemaic period could be experienced not only as restriction and threat, but also as an opportunity for the individual to achieve wealth and prosperity through work, business, and the joy of risk. The book of Qoheleth deals critically with such striving for gain and competitive thinking too (cf. 4:1-12; 5:9—6:9).

The experiences of foreign political and economic determination, the calling into question of traditional social orders and values, and an increased pressure for production were dealt with differently by different people. They could lead to a feeling of impotence and helplessness, but they could also be seized as a chance, through spirited and risky behavior, to achieve a "gain" that under more stable conditions would have remained unreachable.[144] And they can also lead to the individual clinging anxiously to traditional cultural traditions, or they can liberate him or her to critically test foreign traditions and form his or her own judgment. The latter is presented by the protagonist of the book of Qoheleth in exemplary fashion. That his "critical individuality" also owes (at least) the sketched *experiences* to Hellenistic culture in Judea in the third century B.C.E. is "widely accepted" in most recent research.[145] By contrast, whether we may, in addition to that, assume between "Qoheleth" and "Hellenistic culture" an "interaction on the *level of reflection*"[146] is open to dispute.

Greek Literature and Philosophy

On the one hand, C. R. Harrison, for example, questions a direct influence of Greek literature and philosophy on the book of Qoheleth.[147] On the other hand, Schwienhorst-Schönberger, for example, ascertains such close correspondences between the book of Qoheleth and contemporary Greek philosophy in form ("diatribe" [?]) and content (question of the happiness of the individual, "devaluation of what is not at one's disposal") that, in his opinion, we must accept at least a

---

142 Bohlen, "Kohelet," 259.

143 Ibid.

144 Cf. the summary of C. R. Harrison, "Qoheleth in Social-Historical Perspective" (diss., Duke, 1991) 199–279 in Bohlen, "Kohelet," 263–64: "The integration of Judea into the Ptolemaic economic structures led to the rise of a new class, the petite bourgeoisie, and modified norms of behavior. The new middle class was marked by striving for prosperity, craving for profit, speculation, accelerated tempo of life and work, and the materialization and commercialization of values. At the same time this class experienced how threatened every individual was by the vicissitudes of life and by economic failure."

145 Bohlen, "Kohelet," 255, in regard to Hengel, *Judaism and Hellenism,* 1:126–27.

146 Bohlen, "Kohelet," 262 (emphasis added).

147 See C. R. Harrison, "Hellenization in Syria-Palestine"; idem, "Qoheleth among the Sociologists," *BibInt* 5 (1997) 160–82; idem, "Qoheleth."

stimulus and probably also a far-reaching influence of Greek philosophy on the book of Qoheleth.[148]

Now, on the one hand, we must concede that Harrison is right in that concrete influences by (or references to) Greek literature and philosophy in the book of Qoheleth are not *demonstrable*.[149] On the other hand, however, we must also agree with Schwienhorst-Schönberger when he points to the *possibility* that the author of the book of Qoheleth was familiar with the realm of Greek philosophy—not least of all in view of possible contacts of Jerusalem scholars with the Jewish community in Alexandria. In any case, correspondences and differences between the book of Qoheleth and philosophical texts and concepts of the Hellenistic period are of interest for a cultural-historical understanding of the book—independent of whether they go back to an "interaction on the level of reflection" (Bohlen) or are to be interpreted as analogous approaches toward coping with analogous challenges in the world of experience.

Thus, for example, in contemporary Hellenistic philosophy the question of the happiness of the individual is as prominently of interest as in the book of Qoheleth (and as, say, in Proverbs 1–9 and Sirach). "What is actually at stake and what ultimately gives meaning to all our thought and action cannot be the happiness of the state or the community, but the happiness of the individual."[150] The basic approach, common to various directions within Hellenistic philosophy, of determining the happiness available to human beings through a devaluing and becoming indifferent to everything not at one's

disposal[151] is taken up in the book of Qoheleth and reflected on critically (see the concluding remarks to 1:12–2:26). And the criticism of power in the book of Qoheleth (see "Themes" above), which is relatively radical for the OT and early Jewish literature, perhaps has its roots not only in the experiences of suffering but also in familiarity with democratic traditions and concepts from the Greek world.

Regarding the much-discussed question of Greek-Hellenistic "influences" on the book of Qoheleth, not always is the complexity of the interaction processes between different cultures taken sufficiently into account.[152] The book of Qoheleth (like a number of other contemporary writings) shows how traditions and concepts of Israelite-Jewish culture could be received and transformed in view of new experiences and in accordance with new issues and interpretive perspectives in Hellenistic times.

Wisdom

What the book of Qoheleth says about the possibilities and limits of human wisdom (see above) corresponds basically to the view of wisdom in the older parts of the book of Proverbs (Proverbs 10ff.): wisdom can lead to a happy and fulfilled life, but it cannot reliably guarantee such a life—and, not least important, it subjects the usual conceptions of a good life to a critical examination.[153] Whereas the book of Job calls attention especially to the limits and ambivalences of wisdom, the newer introduction to the book of Proverbs (Proverbs 1–9), which was probably composed not very long before Qoheleth,

---

148 Schwienhorst-Schönberger, *Nicht im Menschen*, 274–332. See the presentation and discussion of both positions in Bohlen, "Kohelet," 262–68.
149 Cf. the corresponding statements of J. G. Eichhorn and O. Kaiser in Bohlen, "Kohelet," 267–68.
150 M. Hossenfelder, *Die Philosophie der Antike*, vol. 3: *Stoa, Epikureismus und Skepsis* (Munich: Beck, 1985) 32. This common premise of different directions in Hellenistic philosophy may go back not only to the theoretical insight into the primacy of the individual before the community (this factor is emphasized by Hossenfelder, *Philosophie*, 32), but also to cultural and social-historical changes (critical of this is Hossenfelder, ibid., 26–27)—and here a role is played not only by the fact that the traditional local elite (in part) forfeited their cultural and political

influence, but also by the fact that in the literary sources available to us we hear increasingly from people who do not belong to the elite.
151 Ibid., 32–34.
152 As notable exceptions, see, e.g., M. Lichtheim, *Late Egyptian Wisdom Literature in the International Context* (OBO 52; Freiburg: Universitätsverlag; Göttingen: Vandenhoeck & Ruprecht, 1983); Uehlinger, "Qohelet."
153 On the lack of guarantee see Prov 16:1, 9; 19:21; 20:24; 21:30-31; 24:21-22. On the critical examination see 15:16-17; 16:8; 17:1; 19:1; 28:6.

arouses clearly increased expectations of wisdom's power and, by contrast, allows its limits and ambivalences to recede into the background, if not disappear entirely.[154] The book of Qoheleth polemicizes against such an understanding of wisdom as the guarantee of a long, successful, and happy life. Thus it does not turn against the "wisdom tradition" of the OT as such but against a specific development and pointed emphasis of this tradition, as it becomes concrete in Proverbs 1–9 (and then similarly somewhat later in the book of Sirach[155]).

This development and focusing of the wisdom tradition seem in turn to be the reaction to a "crisis" of traditional wisdom. Proverbs 1–9 clearly reveals the competition between the traditional habits handed down by parents and alternative ways of life. Such alternatives are embodied here in "sinners" and "evildoers," as well as in the "strange woman."[156] By contrast, Proverbs 1–9 strengthens traditional values and norms and exhorts one to hold fast to what was learned from mother and father.[157] This traditional wisdom teaching is closely connected with the fear of God, imbued with the authority of the Torah and with prophecy, and bound to perspectives of salvation and disaster, blessing and curse, life and death that are likewise derived from Torah and prophecy (cf. Prov 8:35-36).[158] Since wisdom is identified with the order of creation and personified as a feminine, quasi-divine figure, it is provided with a religious nimbus that protects it from any critical examination or calling into question.[159] "The personification of wisdom, which makes it the first creature and playing companion of Yahweh during his works of creation, may already be under the influence of the Hellenistic Isis aretalogies."[160] That suggests a shaping of this wisdom concept in the (progressive) Ptolemaic period. It was then taken up in the book of Sirach and developed further.

If the book of Qoheleth turns against a concept of wisdom as it becomes concrete for us in Proverbs 1–9, and this concept of wisdom for its part already represents a reaction to the "crisis" of older concepts of wisdom, then the book of Qoheleth is not to be understood, as often happens in the literature, as a symptom or trigger of a "crisis of wisdom," but rather as an alternative attempt to overcome the "crisis" of traditional wisdom. In contrast to Proverbs 1–9, this attempt is based not on an emphatic enhancement and religious elevation of the traditional character of wisdom, its "dogmatic" aspect, but on an accentuation of its relationship to experience, its "empirical" dimension. Against a "dogmatic" hardening of wisdom, the book of Qoheleth brings experience critically into play. Assertions of the wisdom tradition are tested "empirically" and considered critically. Qoheleth "sees," "considers," and "knows." "He weighed and tested and corrected many proverbs" (Qoh 12:9). From the standpoint of tradition-oriented wisdom, such a procedure must appear extremely questionable, because it bestows on the short-term experiences of a single person too great a weight vis-à-vis venerable tradition (cf. Job 8:8-10). Therefore, only rarely does the traditional wisdom of the OT before Qoheleth make express reference to experience. And when that happens, it almost always serves the confirmation of traditional convictions (cf. Job 4:8-10).[161] Qoheleth, by contrast, measures wisdom teachings against his own experiences. They teach him that wisdom is by no means as easy to find as Proverbs 1–9 and then Sirach assert.[162]

---

154 Cf., e.g., Prov 3:13-26; 4:5-9.

155 For further comparison see also the book of Tobit, as well as texts of a wisdom character from Qumran.

156 For the former see Prov 1:10ff.; 2:12ff.; 3:31ff.; 4:14ff. For the latter see Prov 2:16ff.; 5:3ff.; 6:24ff.; 7:5ff.

157 Cf. Prov 1:8-9; 4:1ff.; 6:20ff.

158 The connection with the fear of God is programmatic in Prov 1:7 and 9:10. For Torah cf. Prov 3:3; 6:21; 7:3 with Deut 6:6-9. For prophecy see Prov 1:20ff.

159 On creation see Prov 3:19-20; 8:22ff. On the personification see Prov 1:20ff.; 8-9.

160 Otto Kaiser, *Grundriss der Einleitung in die kanonischen und deuterokanonischen Schriften des Alten Testaments* (Gütersloh: Gütersloher Verlag, 1994) 3:64-65.

161 Cf. Job 4:8ff.; 5:3ff.; Prov 24:30ff.; Ps 37:25; 73.

162 See Prov 2:4-5; 8:17; 14:6; Sir 4:12-13; 6:27; 51:13ff., 26-27 vs. Qoh 7:23 (and Job 28).

If "the woman" in Qoh 7:25-29 refers to wisdom, this section turns critically against the female personification of wisdom and a concomitant eroticization of the educational process,[163] and it points out in this connection that the "academic" pursuit of wisdom is fully dominated by men. The fear of God in the book of Qoheleth—as similarly in Job 28—is not, as in Proverbs 1–9 and Sirach, the beginning or fruit of wisdom; rather it preserves people from overestimating their wisdom (and their righteousness).[164] When the book of Qoheleth contests the claim of wise men to be able to comprehend the whole work of God, the close connection between wisdom and divine creation in Proverbs 1–9 and in Sirach must appear questionable.[165] Yet the polemic against the "wise" who claim for themselves such a comprehensive knowledge of God's activity seems primarily to turn against prophetically inspired, comprehensive concepts of history, as formulated, for example, in Isaiah 40–66, in Daniel 1–7, and in the Enoch literature (see below).

When the book of Qoheleth, vis-à-vis excessive expectations of wisdom and corresponding claims of the wise, sees a useful wisdom above all in the "know-how" of experts that helps them avoid dangers and unnecessary exertions without being able to guarantee them the success of their work (cf. Qoh 10:8-11), it is returning to the elementary meaning of "wisdom" in the OT:

Thus the Bezalel designated in Exod 31:3 as *ḥākām* is, as it were, the chief architect for the building and equipping of the tent shrine. Exodus 35:25 ascribes an *expert sense* (*ḥakmat lēb*) to the skillful women who know how to spin. In a similar way, one can speak of the wisdom of the bronze worker (1 Kgs 7:14), the goldsmith (Jer 10:9), the shipbuilder (Ezek 27:9), the skilled artisans building the temple (1 Chr 22:15), the mourning women (Jer 9:17), and naturally also the interpreter of dreams (Gen 41:8, cf. Gen 41:39), can be the topic.[166]

With this "redimensioning" of the concept of wisdom vis-à-vis its elevation in Proverbs 1–9 and in the book of Sirach, the book of Qoheleth accentuates again more strongly the ambivalence of wisdom and its limits, which are mentioned in Proverbs 10ff.

Torah

Texts like Deut 4:6-8; Josh 1:7-8; Psalms 1; 19; 119; and Sirach 24 document—each in its own way—a high estimation of the Torah. The requirement of a downright blind and legalistic obedience to the Torah, as it is raised in Num 15:37-41 (cf., e.g., Neh 13:1-3), could, however, by no means have been a majority—to say nothing of consensus—opinion in Judaism at the time of origin of the book of Qoheleth. The close connection between Torah and wisdom in Deuteronomy 4 and Sirach 24 aims less at a limitation of wisdom research and teaching through a binding with the Torah than at an understanding of the Torah as a rational foundation for an orientation to life that is capable of intercultural competition. The focus here is on the Torah as a whole with its basic lines of ethical orientation, not as a collection of individual commandments and prohibitions. Not until Bar 3:9–4:4 is the relationship of wisdom and Torah turned around— probably already under the influence of the Maccabean crisis—and wisdom limited to the Torah.

The composition of the Pentateuch still reveals traces of a conflict between tendencies toward completing and fixing the Torah and an understanding of it as a dynamic and historical entity. The instructions for writing and reading the Torah in Deut 30:9-13 and 31:24-29 regard the Torah as a completed corpus, present in written form (cf. Josh 1:7-8; Deut 17:18-20). And Deut 34:10-12 (vs. Deut 18:15ff.?) raises Moses (and thereby also the Torah passed on by him) above all later prophets (and their revelations) and delineates the time of Moses as the normative founding epoch of the history of Israel. By contrast, Deut 17:8-13 and 18:15-19 provide the possibility of a further development of the Torah by priests,

---

163 See, e.g., Prov 7:4; Sir 6:18-37.
164 See Qoh 7:15-18.
165 On comprehending the whole work of God see Qoh 8:16-17; cf. 3:11; 8:5-6. On wisdom and creation see Prov 3:19-20; 8:22-31; Sir 33:7-19; 42:15-25; cf. also Pss 104:24; 136:5; Jer 10:12.

166 Otto Kaiser, *Der Gott des Alten Testaments: Theologie des Alten Testaments,* part 1: *Grundlegung* (UTB 1747; Göttingen: Vandenhoeck & Ruprecht, 1993) 264 n. 3.

judges, and prophets. In Exodus–Numbers the Pentateuch documents a successive, in part ad hoc, revelation of the Torah, and in Deuteronomy Moses recapitulates the Torah for a new generation of Israelites (starting with the Decalogue in Deuteronomy 5 par. Exodus 20), without simply repeating its content literally.[167] Finally, according to Exod 18:13-27 (cf. Deut 1:9-18) the Torah (= "Moses") presents the main features of ethics and the law, but leaves some room for the administration of justice in the individual case. In this way the Pentateuch itself shows possibilities of a reception of the Torah that is essentially more "liberal" than that that seen in Num 15:37-41 (and Neh 13:1-3).

Qoheleth 12:13 deals ironically with a "legalistic" Torah piety. Qoheleth 11:9 contradicts perhaps consciously the corresponding demand in Num 15:39. Qoheleth 4:17—5:6 shows a varied reception of requirements of the Torah: 5:3-4 takes up the demand to fulfill a vow without delay from Deut 23:22-24 but substantiates it anew with a reference to its reasonableness; Qoh 5:5 speaks against a playing down of guilt as a "mistake," as could be suggested by the cultic requirements in Leviticus 4–5 and Num 15:22-31; and Qoh 4:17 suggests the total forgoing of sacrificial meals, which in the Torah are prescribed as a component of the regular sacrificial cult. With this reasonable critical reception of individual Torah requirements, the book of Qoheleth follows a "liberal" understanding of the Torah.

The main features of his view of the relationship of God and humankind seem, however, to be indebted to the essence of the Torah and more precisely to the so-called primal history in Genesis 1–11: God created the world beautiful and good (Qoh 3:11-15; cf. Genesis 1–2); he also bestowed a special position on human beings, who, however, did not do justice to it (Qoh 3:18; 7:29; cf. Genesis 3ff.); no one is free of guilt (Qoh 7:20, 29; 8:6, 11; 9:3; cf. Gen 6:5; 8:21); and death is God's definitive "judgment" on humankind (Qoh 3:16-21; 9:1-3; 11:9—12:7; cf. Gen 3:17-19; 6:3). For these statements the book

of Qoheleth does not appeal expressly to Genesis 1–11, nor does it substantiate them in a different way; rather, it presupposes them as commonly known and relevant. It receives the Torah not as a "canonical" text (in the sense, say, of later rabbinic Judaism), but as a "classical" work.[168]

Eschatology

When Qoh 3:11 speaks of a beginning and an end of God's activity, it suggests in addition to the creation of the world also an end to the world, in addition to a protology also an eschatology—a theme that was of some importance in contemporary Jewish literature. With the conviction that humankind can know little, if anything, about the end of the world and time (see above under "Themes: Time and Chance"), the book of Qoheleth makes skeptical and critical reference to the corresponding theological developments of its time.

The eschatology of OT prophetic writings, whose productive literary accretion had probably not come to an end by the time of origin of the book of Qoheleth, culminated in the announcement of the creation of a new heaven and a new earth by God in Isa 65:17ff. The concept of an eschatological new creation is not completely unproblematic theologically, for it raises the question, Why did God not create the world in the beginning as one expected it in the new creation? The angelological book of 1 Enoch seems to do justice to this problem. It assumes, namely, that God created places for the eschatological punishment of sinners and rewarding of the righteous at the same time as the familiar present world of experience. In his cosmic travels (1 Enoch 17–36) Enoch can already view them. Therefore, a new creation is not necessary for 1 Enoch 1–36 (versus 1 En. 72:1). The "end of the world" is limited to the present everyday earth (cf. 1 En. 1:6-7).

Qoheleth 1:9-11 can be understood as an ironic rereading of the expectation of an eschatological new creation that in its critique goes even further. The limita-

---

167   On the ad hoc revelation see Num 15:32ff.; 36. Regarding recapitulation see also references to the setting down of the law before Sinai and according to Moses in Exod 15:25 and Josh 24:25, as well as an ongoing writing of the Torah by Joshua in Josh 24:26.

168   On this distinction cf. Jan Assmann, *Das kulturelle*

Gedächtnis (C. H. Beck Kulturwissenschaft; Munich: Beck, 1992) 101ff.; David Tracy, *Theologie als Gespräch* (Mainz: Matthias-Grünewald, 1993) 24ff. Eng. ed., *Plurality and Ambiguity: Hermeneutics, Religion, Hope* (San Francisco: Harper & Row, 1987).

tion of the discussion to the realm "under the sun" leaves the possibility of an end of the world open—and out of consideration. For if there should be such an end of the world at all, it will, in any case, not happen for some time yet (on this kind of distant eschatological expectation see Psalm 102). And the earlier things that according to Isaiah 65 one will no longer think about in the new world also include, in any case, those who are presently alive—who are already subject to forgetfulness here below in this world. Accordingly, a possible end of the world is completely irrelevant for the conduct of their lives. Therefore, they should seize now, in their lives, the God-given possibilities of eating, drinking, and being happy (cf. Isa 65:13).

A comparable, ironically broken reception of late prophetic eschatology is found in the closing poem on (old age and?) death in Qoheleth 12 (cf. v. 2 with Isa 13:9-10; Joel 2:10-11). It presents the death of every individual as a kind of end of the world and last judgment, and thus it gives, on the one hand, a realistic measure to eschatological hopes (or fears): If the world comes to an end, human beings must die—no more, no less. On the other hand, however, the death of each individual is also interpreted as God's judgment on that person. Thus here we have the beginnings of an "existential interpretation" of prophetic eschatology. Here too—just as with the "distant eschatology" of Qoh 1:9-11—there are comparable concepts in late psalms. Thus, for example, Ps 104:27-30 can be interpreted as a "de-eschatologizing" rereading of the expectation of a new world in Isaiah 65: every day God creates a new earth. And he provides not only his servants but also all living beings with food and drink in due season—and human beings, moreover, with wine, which gladdens their hearts (Ps 104:15). This and other similar sayings in late psalms can be understood with Kratz as documents of a "cultic-wisdom reception of earlier salvation perspectives," in which "life" is provided with "traits of salvation" and acquires "theological dignity."[169] With their forgoing of eschatology, these psalms stand close to the book of Qoheleth. To what extent they are antecedents of the book of Qoheleth or have already received it would have to be discussed in detail. (A probably later revival of the expectation of an eschatological judgment over the nations is then documented by Psalm 149.)

In addition to a cosmic universal eschatology, the book of Qoheleth criticizes even more clearly hopes for a continued existence of the individual after death, that is, an individual eschatology (cf. Qoh 3:19-21; 9:4-6). Totally rejected here are individual otherworldly expectations as they are formulated probably in their clearest and most detailed form in extant contemporary Jewish literature in the report on the resting places of the "spirits (of the souls) of the dead" in *1 Enoch* 22. This occurs in Qoheleth 3 by all appearances with reference to the biblical primal history (see above). In this spirit, then, Sirach also encourages one to accept death as human destiny in accordance with the Torah (Sir 41:3-4).

Interestingly, the two OT psalms that come closest to being capable of interpretation as an expression of the hope for life after death, Psalms 49 and 73, make a comparison, as does Qoheleth 3, between humankind and animals. If one reads Psalm 49 without v. 15 (often regarded as an addition), which focuses on a ransoming of life from the power of the underworld, it formulates a view of death that is close to Qoheleth 3 (cf. esp. Ps 49:10-12). With the insight that all mortals must die, the speaker of this psalm consoles himself when he sees how evildoers become rich and even fall into boasting. By putting an end to injustice, death here has something like a judicial function—similar to that in the book of Qoheleth—even if in the end it affects all people (and animals). Now, if Psalm 49:15 (as a later addition?) formulates the hope of a rescue *from* death (and not *before* death), the general fate of death for humans and animals thereby becomes, at least in some exceptional cases, the transition stage into a life after death. The insight into this possibility then separates human beings from animals (v. 20). Nevertheless, Psalm 49 in its present form also holds fast, with Qoheleth 3, to the idea that all people and animals—at least initially—must go to one and the same place, to the underworld. In Psalm 73 this seems not (or no longer?) to be the case, for its speaker expects to remain with God even in death and to be taken up (like Enoch and Elijah?) into glory (vv. 23-24). With this hope (and even more with its fulfillment),

<hr/>

169 See Pss 132:15; 136:25; 145:15-16; 146:7; 147:8-9, 14; R. G. Kratz, "Die Gnade des täglichen Brots: Späte Psalmen auf dem Weg zum Vaterunser," *ZThK* 89 (1992) 36.

he believes he can lift himself above the animals (vv. 21-24).[170]

Temple and Cult

The book of Ezra-Nehemiah attaches to the Jerusalem temple and its cultus central importance for the restoration of "Israel" in its homeland after the Babylonian exile.[171] The books of Chronicles, in their rewriting of the history of Israel, again lay increased weight on the importance of the temple and the cult (cf. also Sirach 50). The importance that they can gain for the spirituality of the individual person is recognizable in numerous psalms.[172] The fact that various religious and theological conceptions can be connected with temple and cultus can be demonstrated, for example, by a comparison between the relevant regulations in the books of Leviticus and Deuteronomy. Whereas in the latter book, it is above all the social dimension of the celebrations at the central shrine that is emphasized, in which the socially weak members, widows, orphans, and strangers, should participate (cf. Deut 16:14; 26:11; etc.), in Leviticus the emphasis is on the function of purification and atonement (cf. Leviticus 1–7; 12–16).

By contrast, in wisdom statements the proper behavior of the individual person is placed above cultic performances.[173] In the prophetic realm this concern is broadened to the entire people and radicalized to the extent that ultimately righteousness can fully replace cultic actions.[174] In addition, "rational" considerations are also expressed that make the cultic adoration of God in the temple seem questionable: God needs no temple as a dwelling and no sacrifice as nourishment.[175] The book of Qoheleth takes up these traditions of temple and cult criticism in 4:17–5:6 and 9:2 and takes them further. It promotes not an abolition or reform of the cultus, but a "rational" interpretation of cultic acts or the renunciation of participation in them on the part of the individual. In so doing it makes—not without critical irony—the "fear of God" the criterion of the adoration of God (5:6). The temple is not needed for the atonement of guilt (5:5) but for the cultivation and transmission of religious traditions (4:17).

History of Influence and Reception

"Corpus Salomonicum" (Proverbs-Qoheleth-Canticles)

The inclusion of the book of Qoheleth (as the reading for the third day of the Feast of Tabernacles) in the five *Megillot* ("festival scrolls": Canticles, Ruth, Lamentations, Qoheleth, Esther) goes back to German manuscripts of the Middle Ages. According to older Palestinian tradition, the third part of the OT canon (*Ketubim*, "writings") was ordered in this way: Chronicles, Psalms, Job, Proverbs, Ruth, Canticles, Qoheleth, Lamentations, Esther, Daniel, Ezra-Nehemiah. The five *Megillot* already stand here side by side, though not yet in the chronological order of the festivals to which they are assigned as readings. In addition to these (and other) "liturgical" orderings, ancient Jewish and Christian witnesses also document "literary" and "chronological" arrangements in which, as a rule, the three "Solomonic" writings Proverbs, Qoheleth, and Canticles are cited in this order.[176] Accordingly, these three writings could be understood already at an early date as a kind of "Corpus Salomonicum." Redactional additions connecting the three "Solomonic" books cannot be demonstrated. Their juxtaposition, nonetheless, produces some threads of meaning that span the whole corpus.

---

170 Then should a Qoheleth therefore be declared "dumb as an animal" because he did not recognize the difference between the fates of evildoers on the one hand and the pure and innocent on the other?

171 For the Diaspora cf. 1 Kgs 8:46ff.; Dan 6:11.

172 Cf., in addition to the "pilgrimage songs" Psalms 120–34, esp. Psalm 84, as well as, e.g., 23:6; 26:8; 27:4; 42:2; 63:2; 65:4.

173 Cf. Prov 15:8; 21:3, 27; Sir 34:21ff.; 35:8ff., as well as Psalms 15; 24.

174 Cf., e.g., Amos 5:21ff.; Mic 6:6ff.; Isa 1:10ff.; 58; Jeremiah 7, as well as Psalms 40:7ff.; 50.

175 Cf. 1 Kgs 8:27; Isa 66:1ff.

176 See R. Beckwith, *The Old Testament Canon of the New Testament Church and Its Background in Early Judaism* (Grand Rapids: Eerdmans, 1985) 181–234, 449–68.

Thus all three books (Qoheleth at least suggestively) present themselves as "Solomonic" writings, without consistently holding to this fiction.[177] Like the book of Qoheleth, Canticles seems to play ironically and critically with the Solomon fiction. In the sequence of the three writings one reads the book of Qoheleth after the book of Proverbs as a critical reflection of the "wisdom" developed there (and then again Qoh 3:10ff. as a critical reflection of 1:12–2:26), just as Canticles is the realization of the exhortation to enjoy life in the book of Qoheleth (esp. Qoh 9:9: "Enjoy life with the wife whom you love"; cf. also Cant 8:6-7 with Qoh 7:26). The theme "seek (בקש biqqēš) and find (מצא māṣāʾ)"—related to wisdom (as woman) as if to a beloved person—plays an important role in all three writings.[178] If for the young man it is initially a question of seeking wisdom (as woman) and resisting the attempts at seduction of strange women (Proverbs 1–9), a happy life is possible in the end only with a wife (Proverbs 31; Canticles)—not least of all because the most important wisdom available to human beings consists in the insight that the enjoyment of life represents the highest good (Qoheleth).

The literary background of the "Corpus Salomonicum" remains elusive. (Was the book of Qoheleth written from the beginning as an expansion of the book of Proverbs—and Canticles as an expansion of the book of Qoheleth? Was there an older connection between Proverbs and Canticles?) In any case, however, the insertion of the book of Qoheleth into this corpus and the sequence Proverbs-Qoheleth-Canticles shows an early reception of the book of Qoheleth that takes its essential concerns seriously and agrees with them. The fact that even Qoh 12:9-14 in no way revokes the insights of the book of Qoheleth is without doubt made clear by the following book of Canticles.

Jesus Sirach

The book of Sirach was presumably completed about thirty years after the book of Qoheleth (ca. 175 B.C.E.) in Jerusalem. Its composition probably stretched over a longer period. In comparison to the book of Qoheleth it aims more at the preservation than the criticism of inherited wisdom and religious traditions. Thus with a comparative reading one can often get the impression that the book of Qoheleth deals with views that are formulated in the book of Sirach.[179] In some places in the book of Sirach, nonetheless, there seems to be already "a literary and in part critical echo" of the Qoheleth texts.[180]

Sirach agrees with Qoheleth that the lives of all people end definitively and unavoidably with death (cf. Sir 41:1-4). "Whether life lasts ten or a hundred or a thousand years, there are no questions asked in Hades" (Sir 41:4; cf. Qoh 6:3-6). With regard to eschatological or apocalyptic expectations for the individual person, as well as for the community, Sirach shows the same reserve as Qoheleth. In his prayer for deliverance from foreign domination (Sir 36:1-22), he asks not for anything new and different, but for the restoration of an earlier state beneficial to Israel (cf. Qoh 1:9). Yet whereas Qoheleth looks skeptically at any presumed knowledge of the future, Sirach appreciates the prophets precisely because of their predictions (cf. Sir 36:20-21; 48–49; and here esp. 48:24-25 on Isaiah). Sirach also gives the cultus a higher evaluation than does Qoheleth (cf. Sir 45:6ff.; 50). Ethically and religiously correct behavior is more important than the offering of sacrifices (Sir 34:21–35:26); yet since this is required in the Torah, it should be practiced (Sir 35:6-7). Here we see that the Torah as commandment, as well as a source of insight, knowledge, and wisdom (cf. Sir 17:11ff.; 24:23ff.), is of greater importance for Sirach than for

---

177 For "Solomonic" attribution see Prov 1:1; 10:1; 25:1; Qoh 1:1, 12; Cant 1:1. Cf. Prov 22:17 (see *BHS*); 24:23; 30:1; 31:1; Qoh 3:10ff.; 12:9ff.; Cant 8:11-12.

178 Cf. Prov 2:4-5; 3:13; 4:22; 7:15; 8:9, 12, 17, 35 up to 31:10; Qoh 7:24-29; 8:17; 12:10; Cant 3:1-4; 5:6-8; 6:1; 8:1.

179 On the assumption of a literary priority of Sirach before the book of Qoheleth cf. N. Peters, "Ecclesiastes und Ekklesiastikus," *BZ* 1 (1903) 47–54, 129–50; and Whitley, *Koheleth*. Cf. also the critique in Backhaus, *Zeit und Zufall*, 412–20.

180 J. Marböck, "Kohelet und Sirach: Eine vielschichtige

Beziehung," in Schwienhorst-Schönberger, ed., *Das Buch Kohelet,* 281. Marböck points, for example, to Sir 31:3-4 (cf. Qoh 5:14, 15, 17); Sir 30:22-23 (cf. Qoh 5:17-19); Sir 14:11-16 (cf. Qoh 9:7-10); Sir 11:4-6 (cf. Qoh 10:6); Sir 37:19-26 (cf. Qoh 12:9), as well as Sir 39:12-35 (cf. Qoh 3:11).

Qoheleth. In Qoheleth, by contrast, the viewpoints of a realistic anthropology that was received from primal history and is conscious of human limitations (cf. Genesis 3; 6:5; 8:21) play hardly any role in Sirach (cf. Sir 17:1ff., with a later addition in vv. 16-17a [𝔊 248] that is oriented toward Genesis 6/8).

In contrast to Qoheleth, wisdom according to Sirach can be found by anyone who earnestly seeks it—although its limits are named too.[181] As in Proverbs 1–9, wisdom in Sirach also serves as a signpost and aid for a happy life in accordance with and with the support of the "deed-result connection," which lets things go well for the righteous but bad for the evildoer. Sirach, in contrast to Qoheleth, holds that individuals have the freedom to act rightly (cf. Sir 15:11—16:23). Against the experiences cited by Qoheleth, which contradict a "deed-result connection," Sirach offers the consideration that in the hour of death God repays people for their deeds, and that this hour of death can cause all previous unjustified suffering or well-being to be forgotten (Sir 11:15-26 𝔥/17-28 𝔊). The so-called theodicy pericope, Sir 39:12-35, can be understood as an attempt, in a critical rereading of Qoheleth 3, not only to postulate the just ordering of the world by God as ultimately opaque and unknowable for human beings, but to demonstrate it through experiences and to make it understandable.[182] Whereas according to Qoheleth 3 the judgment of God over all people consists in the contingency and change of time, in Sirach 39 time brings the judgment of God, in which the "righteous" and "evildoers" will be distinguished. As a consequence of this view of wisdom and divine justice, the understanding of the "fear of God" in Sirach is much closer to Proverbs 1–9 than to Qoheleth (and Job 28) and the praise of God gains central importance for the wise.[183]

With Marböck we can summarily characterize the relationship of Sirach to Qoheleth as follows:

In the juxtaposition of the two sages, Qoheleth is indisputably the more brilliant writer and more radical thinker, who captured something of the immediate breath of his time: the loss of certainty. He fascinates in the unrelenting consequence of his questions and his critique of temporary traditional certainties and values, with his courage to concentrate on a few insights giving orientation for the homeless: on the reverent, awed facing of God's free action but, at the same time, on the call to accept the gifts of the Creator in the face of death. Probably only a short time afterward Sirach commends his broad literary and theological synthesis of the tradition of faith, cult, and ethos, of Torah, prophets, and writings, perhaps as an offer or repeated attempt to integrate all groups in Israel in the house of tradition, which still carries him and gives him shelter. He does this in the language of affirmation, of approval of the possibilities of knowledge given by the Creator to human beings (Sir 17:1-14), who encounter God's wisdom, in the defense and hymnic celebration of the goodness of God's works and, above all, the cultic-religious order of his day.[184]

Lohfink assumes that the book of Qoheleth was introduced into the Jerusalem temple school as a textbook at the beginning of the second century B.C.E. to expand the "Proverbs of Solomon."[185] In this connection Qoh 12:9-11 was added as an epilogue.

The book of Sirach was composed soon after. It may have been an attempt to bring a radical and completely new perspective to the textbook system, which had proved unsatisfactory even after Qoheleth was included. . . . It not only intended to replace Proverbs and Qoheleth in one stroke, but it also linked the normative culture of Israel directly to the Law and the Prophets. . . .

The second postscript of Qoheleth [Qoh 12:12-14] may well have come from the time of debate whether to create a new school text. It seems to try to arouse even the students (addressed as "my son") against the

181 On seeking see Sir 6:18ff.; 14:20—15:10; 24; 38:24—39:11; 51:13ff. On limits see Sir 1:2-6; 18:4-7; 43:27-32; Marböck, "Kohelet," 292–94.
182 Cf. Marböck, "Kohelet," 284ff.
183 Ibid., 295–96.
184 Ibid., 296.
185 N. Lohfink, "Les épilogues du livre de Qohélet et les débuts du Canon," in P. Borati and R. Meynet, eds., Ouvrir les écritures (LD 162; Paris: Cerf, 1995) 77–96; idem, comm., 11–12; Marböck, "Kohelet," 281ff.

plan to prepare new textbooks, since these would only increase their burden of class materials. At the same time it defended the orthodoxy of the book, which no doubt the protagonists of a more tradition-oriented curriculum reform had questioned, by attributing back to Qoheleth the proposed leading theme of Sirach's new textbook: "Fear God, and keep his commandments."[186]

Upon closer examination, nevertheless, Lohfink's interpretation of Qoh 12:9-14 proves doubtful (see commentary below on the passage). Statements such as Qoh 4:17–5:6; 8:10; or 9:2 would hardly be expected in a textbook for the temple school. With Uehlinger (see above under "Genres") one could see in the book of Qoheleth a document of "private" literary culture as well as a "school book." And Sir 51:23 and 29 invite the readers and hearers of the book of Sirach not into the "temple school" but into the (probably not identical) "teaching house" of Ben Sirach (which, to be sure, could also be interpreted as a consequence of the rejection of the book of Sirach as textbook for the temple school). From this point of view, Lohfink's hypothetical connection of the books of Qoheleth and Sirach with a (likewise purely hypothetical) "academic reform" of the Jerusalem temple school appears not impossible but, nonetheless, not very probable.

Wisdom of Solomon
Whereas the "Corpus Salomonicum" approvingly receives the book of Qoheleth and the book of Sirach partly agrees with it and partly leads into substantial discussion, the Wisdom of Solomon, which was probably written in Alexandria in the first century B.C.E., presents in its first part (chaps. 1–6) views that are diametrically opposed to those in the book of Qoheleth. The biblical primal history is reinterpreted in such a way that death in no way means the definitive end of all human beings: God did not create death (Wis 1:13-14). He created human beings to immortality; only through the envy of the devil did death come into the world (2:23-24). After death people are rewarded or punished by God for their righteous behavior or evildoing (3:1–12:5). Evildoers are not aware of this when they let themselves be led astray by the (presumed) transitoriness of human life (2:1-5) into craving for pleasure (2:2-9) and into unrighteousness (2:10-20). Even if it is a question here of a "critique of the skeptical worldview of a wisdom or philosophical kind but not directly of Qoheleth as a document,"[187] the whole argumentation of the book of Qoheleth is thereby placed in a light that makes it seem extremely questionable. The same is also true for the following parts of the book when they emphasize the accessibility of wisdom for human beings (Wisdom 7–10), and God's just governance in nature and history in the sense of the deed-result connection is pointed out (chaps. 11–19).

An argumentative interaction with the views of the book of Qoheleth is not to be found in the Wisdom of Solomon. Instead, it offers other convictions that it obviously presupposes as accepted by its readership. As a "Solomonic" writing (which, like the book of Qoheleth, it is not explicitly), the book of Wisdom forms in the Septuagint a counterweight and corrective to the book of Qoheleth. This raises the question, however, of whether and how the contrary views of the two writings can fit into a coherent whole as teachings of "Solomon." Various Jewish and Christian authors have tried to achieve such a synthesis by interpreting the book of Qoheleth with the presupposition of fundamental convictions that in essence correspond to those expressed in the Wisdom of Solomon (see below). From our present perspective, however, we must state that the book of Qoheleth shows that the renunciation of the expectation of repayment beyond death by no means necessarily has to lead to craving pleasure and to unrighteousness, as Wisdom 2 assumes.

Other Early Jewish Literature
If for the book of Qoheleth God's order of creation, which makes life possible (Qoh 3:11), and God's intervention into world events, which supports life ("judgment": 3:17), manifest themselves in an experienceable way and at the same time elude human comprehension (3:11; 1:8-11), the book is probably thereby already making critical reference to early "apocalyptic" texts and concepts.[188] It seems that the critical calling into ques-

---

186 Lohfink, 12–13.
187 Thus Dieter Georgi, *JSHRZ* III.4, on Wis 2:1.

188 As in Daniel 2–7; *1 Enoch* 1–36; 72–82; cf. the commentary on Qoh 1:3-11 and Qoheleth 3, as well as

tion of the knowability of the divine ordering of time in the book of Qoheleth led in turn to the time problem being thoroughly reworked in the wisdom and apocalyptically shaped literature of early Judaism and to insights being opened into the divine ordering of time by way of revelation.[189] Thus in the book of Sirach the theme "time" not only plays a central role in the "theodicy pericope" Sir 39:12-35 (see above). Sirach also emphasizes the necessity of knowing the "right time"[190] and regards the required wisdom as a gift of God (Sir 1:1-10).

The meaning of time for the individual conduct of life is developed narratively in the book of Tobit (Tobit 1–12), especially in the longer and presumably older text version of the Codex Sinaiticus. In the first chapters the events around Tobit in Nineveh are carefully synchronized with those around Sarah in Ecbatana: Tobit and Sarah turn to God in prayer at the same time (3:7, 10) and the two prayers simultaneously reach God (3:16), who then initiates events through which the problems of Sarah and Tobit are finally and simultaneously resolved.[191] In this way the narrator indicates to his readers time's order and structure of meaning, which are hidden from the actors but recognizable for the readers. Only with the happy ending of the story do the actors then understand that in the complex and multilayered events that they have experienced, everything had its time, its meaning, and its function for a good outcome. The story thereby evokes trust in the divine ordering of time, even if this is not always equally recognizable.

Within the context of the story, the theme "time" comes up in two more places. According to Tob 6:18 Sarah was destined already before creation to be the wife of Tobias. Thus the course of an individual person's life seems to be determined beforehand by God (cf. Ps 139:16). Qoheleth 6:10 perhaps alludes to such a concept and takes issue with it. According to Tob 12:14, Raphael was sent to Tobit at the same time to test him and to heal him. Thus is the ambivalence of the human experience of time addressed, and only later, in retro-

spection of a larger context of events, does clarity arise. In Qoheleth, this ambivalence of the experience of time is both more generally and more radically conceived: time is always and for everyone both the enabling of happiness and success and—in its aspects of contingency and transitoriness—God's judgment over human beings (and not only God's testing of human beings).

The closing chapters of the book of Tobit (13–14), which were presumably added around the time of the origin of the book of Sirach, go still a bit further. In his prayer in Tobit 13, Tobit mentions two continuities in the changes of time: God (v. 1) and—for the future, after its restoration—the holy city of Jerusalem (vv. 11, 16). With this he also emphatically places his individual lifetime in the context of the history of his people. This is then reinforced in the eschatological perspective of Tobit 14, which now also speaks explicitly of the temporal order of history when it expresses the conviction that the announcements of the prophets will come true *in their time* (vv. 4-5). Just as in the lives of Tobit and the other actors of Tobit 1–12, there is accordingly also a hidden order and temporal structure of meaning in history. If this order and meaning were recognizable by the readers earlier than the actors (apart from the angel Raphael), so it is in the history of the prophets, to whom God grants advance insight into the order of time—and indirectly also to the readers of their writings.

The expansion of the book of Tobit reveals exemplarily the attempt to take up and overcome the problems of the book of Qoheleth within the framework of apocalyptic concepts. The fact that vis-à-vis such undertakings the skeptical position of the book of Qoheleth could also be maintained is attested not only by its canonization but perhaps also by the book of Judith. Here in the context of Judith's prayer we find statements about God's determination of time, which Gerhard von Rad has correctly placed beside the "apocalyptic" "idea of the determination of times":[192] "For you [God] have done these things and those that went before and those

---

Rosso Ubigli, "Qohelet di fronte all'apocalittica," *Hen* 5 (1983) 209–34.

189   U. Luck, "Das Weltverständnis in der jüdischen Apokalyptik," *ZThK* 73 (1976) 283–305.

190   Cf. Sir 1:23-24; 2:2; 4:20, 23; 8:9; 18:21; 20:6-7, 20; 22:6, 16; 27:12; 29:2-3, 5; 31:28; 40:23.

191   On the "time" aspect cf. also Tob 2:11; 3:11; 4:1.

192   Von Rad, *Wisdom in Israel*, 277; see 270–77.

that followed. You have designed the things that are now, and those that are to come. What you had in mind has happened; the things you decided on presented themselves and said: "Here we are!" For all your ways are prepared in advance, and your judgment is with foreknowledge" (Jdt 9:5-6).

In the context of the book of Judith, however, this deterministic understanding of history is obstructed—and ultimately also neutralized—by a strong skepticism in regard to human possibilities of knowing: "You are putting the Lord Almighty to the test, but you will never learn anything! You cannot plumb the depths of the human heart or understand the workings of the human mind; how do you expect to search out God, who made all these things, and find out his mind or comprehend his thought?" (Jdt 8:13-14). Therefore, human beings can and must regard themselves in their actions de facto as free—and the success or failure of their actions as contingent (8:15-17). Only the consequence of guilt and punishment presents a sort of guideline (yet not a strict or even predictable regularity) to which God orients himself in his actions and which thus also makes possible a certain orientation for human beings (cf. Jud 8:18ff.). Judith acts accordingly in the story: she seizes the initiative and still holds to her piety.

By combining the ideas of God's radical determination of all events and of its total unknowability by human beings, the book of Judith regains for humankind a high degree of freedom of action and uncertainty of success. Thus it can be read as a reinforcement of the insight of Qoh 3:11 vis-à-vis apocalyptic attempts to overcome it.

New Testament
The list of "loci citati vel allegati ex Vetere Testamento" of Nestle-Aland indicates a literal Qoheleth quotation in the NT: in his letter to the Romans, Paul affirmingly cites Qoh 7:20 (in connection with Psalms 14; 53), according to which no one is righteous (Rom 3:10).[193] As in the book of Qoheleth, in Paul this insight is substantiated with a reference to primal history (which is admittedly interpreted somewhat differently than in Qoheleth;

cf. Romans 5). Yet whereas, in regard to the guilt of all people, the book of Qoheleth accepts the contingency of time and death as the "judgment" (and the opportunities for joy and pleasure as the "gift") of God, Paul deals with the possibility of this guilt being overcome, which is a gift bestowed by God in Christ and seized by human beings in faith (Rom 3:21-26). In this way the universal culpability of all people is relativized and overcome.

In a comparable way Paul adopts and relativizes in Rom 8:20 the transitoriness of all creatures, emphasized by Qoheleth, by placing it in an eschatological context: creation is subject to "futility" ($\mu\alpha\tau\alpha\iota\delta\tau\eta\varsigma$)—yet with the hope of a final liberation from decay (v. 21). If in 2 Cor 5:10 the expectation of an eschatological judgment is formulated with echoes of Qoh 12:14, from our present viewpoint this also gives rise to the question, to what extent the critical deconstruction and reconstruction of eschatological expectations in the book of Qoheleth are also to be made valid vis-à-vis the relevant NT conceptions.[194] If the NT often emphasizes that the day and hour of the eschatological event are not known to human beings and also not communicated to them by God (cf., e.g., Mark 13:32-33 par.; 1 Thess 5:1ff.), this opens the door to some of the skepticism of the book of Qoheleth regarding the possibilities of prognostication (see also Jas 4:13-14 and John 3:8 [cf. Qoh 11:3]).

Statements or bits of advice from the book of Qoheleth echo in a number of other NT passages. For example, Mark 2:18-20 par. (celebrating and fasting each in its time) recalls Qoh 3:1-8 (cf. also Matt 11:17: dancing and wailing). James 1:19, with Qoh 7:9, exhorts moderation in anger. And Matt 6:7, like Qoh 5:1, advocates reserve in prayer (vs., e.g., 1 Thess 5:17; Luke 8:1ff.). Likewise, the warning against greed and hoarding in Luke 12:13ff. corresponds to that in Qoh 5:9—6:9 on possessions and enjoyment, just as the encouragement to carefree enjoyment in the present and trust in God's provision of food in Matt 6:25ff. In this connection 1 Tim 6:7, along with Job 1:21 and Qoh 5:14, points out that at our birth we brought nothing into the world and, similarly, we can take nothing out of it at our death. As in the book of Qoheleth, here too this insight leads to satis-

---

193 Barbara Aland et al., eds., *Novum Testamentum Graece* (27th ed.; Stuttgart: Deutsche Bibelgesellschaft, 1993) 789.

194 On the presentation of the problem cf., e.g., Rudolf Bultmann, *The Presence of Eternity: History and Eschatology* (New York: Harper, 1957).

faction and the abandonment of striving for wealth (1 Tim 6:6ff.), as well as generosity toward those who have less (vv. 17ff.). In contrast to Qoheleth, however, these texts also reckon with the possibility of compensation or retribution beyond death.

The Further History of Qoheleth's Influence

The further history of the influence and reception of the book of Qoheleth up to the present time can be sketched here only with a few rough strokes.[195] As part of the "Corpus Salomonicum," the book of Qoheleth seems to have been counted among the Holy Scriptures in Judaism as in Christianity beginning (at the latest) in the second century C.E. The documented discussions on its canonicity, above all in the Jewish realm (as also regarding the likewise discussed books of Ezekiel, Proverbs, Canticles, and Esther) seem already to presuppose its factual canonical validity.[196] They show that the process of the origin of the canon is to be distinguished from its later (synagogal or ecclesiastical) reception. The origin of the canon apparently involved theological points of view that later—under appeal to the canon—seemed questionable. In the rabbinic discussions it was above all the "secular" character, the internal contradictions, and the "heretical" tendencies that made the book of Qoheleth (as well as the other two "Solomonic" writings, Proverbs and Canticles) appear problematic.[197]

For the "orthodoxy" of this writing, one could point to its (seemingly) "pious" conclusion in Qoh 12:13-14, in which are formulated both an exhortation to Torah observance and the expectation of an eschatological judgment. From that standpoint, then, 1:2-3 (and the whole following book) could be critically relativized: these statements on the "futility" of human "work and toil" relate only to the realm "under the sun," and therefore not to the Torah (which, because of its preexistence, belongs to the divine realm "above the sun") and its observance, not to eschatological expectations.[198] Other problematic statements and internal contradictions in the book of Qoheleth could be set aside with the assumption that Solomon was citing the views of others in order to controvert them.[199] Finally, one could point to Solomon as the inspired author.[200]

With regard to the "biography" of this presumed author of the book of Qoheleth, one could again make some of its peculiarities understandable. For example, the Targum holds that Solomon, in anticipation of the disintegration of his kingdom under his son and successor Rehoboam, designated his own work and toil as futile and fleeting (Qoh 1:2-3). According to a legend to which the Targum alludes in Qoh 1:12-13, Solomon was dethroned as punishment for his idolatry and replaced by a "doppelgänger," while he himself had to eke out his existence as a beggar (see commentary below on 1:12). In this situation, his views expressed in the book of Qoheleth become understandable.

Among the Christian church fathers we find the interpretation of the three "Solomonic" books of Proverbs, Qoheleth, and Canticles as didactic texts that build on one another for the spiritual life:

---

195 Cf. in detail Ginsburg, 27–243; concisely Murphy, xlviii–lvi; see also the information in the bibliography.

196 Here and on the following see Beckwith, *Canon*, 274–337 (who for comparison refers to the critical discussion of canonicity of certain NT writings in Luther).

197 If the school of Shammai, in contrast to the school of Hillel, called the canonicity of the book of Qoheleth into question, perhaps this happened because the latter could appeal to Qoheleth for its "liberal" views (cf. Beckwith, *Canon*, 301).

198 Cf. in this sense, e.g., the wisdom writing from the Cairo Geniza: "It is good to choose gain above all and to banish from the heart everything futile. This world is futile, and the coming world is gain. It is not worthwhile to busy oneself with anything that is not gain. . . . Whoever despises this world and its affairs and whoever honors the Torah and is occupied with it, is certain to reach the world to come" (1:3-5, 16-17; after the German translation of Klaus Berger: *Die Weisheitsschrift aus der Kairoer Geniza* [TANZ 1; Tübingen: Francke, 1989] 13).

199 This interpretive approach is found, e.g., in Gregory Thaumaturgus, Gregory of Nyssa, Gregory the Great, Jerome, Bonaventure, and Saadia Gaon.

200 Cf. R. L. Murphy, "Qohelet Interpreted: The Bearing of the Past on the Present," *VT* 32 (1982) 331–37.

The patristic tradition on "the books of Solomon" derived from Origen; it was transmitted by St. Jerome, and reproduced in the *Gloss*. Solomon wrote his three books, Proverbs, Ecclesiastes and the Canticle, in order to instruct mankind in the three states of the spiritual life. Proverbs taught men how to live virtuously in the world and was meant for beginners. Ecclesiastes taught them to despise the things of the world as futile and fleeting and was meant for *proficientes* [those who are progressing]. The Canticle told initiates of the love of God.[201]

Among the Reformers, Johannes Brenz (1528), Martin Luther (1532), and Philipp Melanchthon (1550) have addressed the book of Qoheleth with commentaries. They reject the tendency to read the book of Qoheleth as instructions for contempt of the world (*contemptus mundi*), which was predominant in older Christian and especially monastic receptions. Instead they interpret it as an introduction to the calm fulfillment of everyday "worldly" duties and activities. Theologically, they interpret the book of Qoheleth as a writing against free will (Luther), as a teaching about divine providence (Melanchthon), and as an illustration of the Pauline doctrine of justification (Brenz). Here traits of the text are brought to bear that remained hidden in the older history of reception because of the guiding presuppositions of an "orthodox" Jewish or Christian interpretation. This was due, naturally, not only to the Reformers' humanistic interests in what the biblical writings themselves had to say, but also to the Reformers' own theological convictions, which guided their readings.

The basic assumptions of modern historical-critical interpretation of the Bible have shaped the understanding of the book of Qoheleth by modern exegetes. The differences between a premodern interpretation and a scientific commentary are immediately obvious in a comparative reading. Historical-critical exegesis seeks in the first place to do justice not to contemporary convictions or needs but to the text itself as a historical document. That includes the effort to achieve as exactly as possible an understanding of the text with its specific characteristics and differences from other biblical and extrabiblical ancient texts, as well as from contemporary convictions; it also includes the critical reconstruction of historical conditions of its origin and tradition. A starting point for this approach was the calling into question of the "Solomonic" authorship by Hugo Grotius (1644; see below).

Today's readers are often inclined to interpret the book of Qoheleth either (negatively) as a dark foil before which the gospel stands out all the more radiantly or (positively) as a "skeptical backdoor" to the Bible, which opens wide to the questions and doubts of modern people.[202] The interpretation developed in the present commentary, which concentrates on the meaning of the text in its time of origin, offers reason for skepticism toward both approaches to understanding: the book of Qoheleth stands by no means as far from the other biblical writings of the Old and New Testaments as it may at first seem—and with its views about God, human beings, and the world, it seems rather strange to the basic convictions of most people in modern, "Western," industrial societies. Apart from the fact that in confrontation with this strangeness there is always the chance of gaining new insights, today the book of Qoheleth can perhaps above all serve as an example of an intellectually honest, both well-intentioned and critical, and, not least of all, also self-critical treatment of cultural and religious traditions that is itself not above criticism (nor does it claim to be).

Language

Hugo Grotius noted in the *Praefatio* to his *Annotationes ad Qohelet*: "Ego tamen Salomonis non puto sed scriptum ferius sub illius regis, tamquam poenitentia ducti nomine. Argumentum eius rei habeo multa vocabula, quae non alibi quam in Daniele, Ezra et Chaldaeis interpretibus reperias" ("I do not believe that [the book of Qoheleth] is from Solomon. Rather it is written under the name of that king, as if he were led to repentance. As a proof of this I take many words which are not found

---

201 Beryl Smalley, *Medieval Exegesis of Wisdom Literature: Essays* (ed. R. E. Murphy; Atlanta: Scholars Press, 1986) 40 (quoted according to Murphy xlix).

202 For examples see Michel, *Qohelet*, 122–26.

elsewhere except in Daniel, Ezra, and in the Aramaic translations").[203] More recent attempts to explain the linguistic peculiarities of the book through the assumption of an original Aramaic version, the hypothesis of a Canaanite-Phoenician influence on its author, or the genus of the text and the use of a popular dialect are just as unconvincing as the general calling into question of the indications of a late stage of linguistic development by Fredericks.[204] Thus, as the preliminary result of his detailed studies of the orthography, morphology, and syntax of the language of the book of Qoheleth, Schoors, for example, maintains: "The language of Qoh is definitely late in the development of BH [Biblical Hebrew] and belongs to what scholars recently have called Late Biblical Hebrew (LBH)."[205]

Schoors points to the following peculiarities of the language of the book of Qoheleth, which

are typical of LBH, although not all of them are equally cogent proof of a late date: the interchange between *śin* and *samekh*; the use of *matres lectionis*, showing a middle stage between BH and Qumran Hebrew; the form יהוא (Qoh 11:3); the exclusive use of אני; the feminine demonstrative pronoun זה; the frequency of the particle שׁ; the use of nouns ending in ־וּת; the plural שְׁפָתוֹת instead of the dual (10:12); the absence of imperfect consecutive in specific instan-

ces; the presence of an imperfect consecutive וְאֶקְטְלָה; the merging of ל"ה and ל"א roots; the participle הֹוֶה (2:22); the particle בכן; the adverb כְּבָר; the particles כל־עמת שׁ־/לְעֻמַּת; the use of בלא meaning "before"; the particle אֵלּוּ; the frequent use of שׁ/אשׁר as a conjunction; the combination of עד אשׁר with לא; the high concentration of composite conjunctions with שׁ/אשׁר; the interjection אי; the suffix ־הֵם instead of ־הֶן; the erratic use of the article; the phrase אִין + ל + infinitive; את before a noun in the nominative case; שׂבע construed with מן. Some features are less conclusive, but they corroborate the general picture: the use of the indefinite pronoun מַה/(שׁ) מִי; nouns of the type *qitlōn/ qitlān*; feminine nouns ending in -*t*; the composite preposition מלפני; the use of the infinitive absolute *pro verbo finito*; the frequent omission of the retrospective suffix in relative clauses.[206]

The language of the book of Qoheleth is older than that of the Mishnah. "But Qoh undoubtedly shows some Mishnaic traits together with some features that are close to Mishnaic."[207] Even if the identification of "Aramaisms" is not entirely unproblematic, "it seems that some of the later traits mentioned above can be accepted as Aramaisms, for example, a larger usage of nouns ending in ־וּת; nouns of the *qᵉtāl* type; the particle אֵלּוּ; the more frequent use of שׁ/אשׁר as a conjunction,

203 In *Annotationes in Vetus Testamentum*, part 1 (Paris, 1644), quoted according to F. Bianchi, "The Language of Qoheleth: A Bibliographical Survey," *ZAW* 105 (1993) 210–11. On the history of research see esp. Bianchi, "Language," 210–23; and A. Schoors, *The Preacher Sought to Find Pleasing Words: A Study of the Language of Qoheleth* (OLA 41; Leuven: Departement Orientalistiek and Peeters, 1992) 1–16.

204 For Aramaic see J. Burkitt, "Is Ecclesiastes a Translation?" *JTS* 23 (1922) 22–26; F. Zimmermann, "The Aramaic Provenance of Qohelet," *JQR* 36 (1945/46) 17–45; idem, "The Question of Hebrew in Qohelet," *JQR* 40 (1949/50) 79–102; C. C. Torrey, "The Question of the Original Language of Kohelet," *JQR* 39 (1948/49) 151–60; H. L. Ginsberg, *Studies in Koheleth* (TSJTSA 17; New York: Jewish Theological Seminary of America, 1950). For Canaanite-Phoenician see M. H. Dahood, "Canaanite-Phoenician Influence in Qoheleth," *Bib* 33 (1952) 30–52, 191–221; idem, "The Language of Qoheleth," *CBQ* 14 (1952) 227–32; idem, "The

Phoenician Background of Qoheleth," *Bib* 47 (1966) 264–82; idem, "Qoheleth and Northwest Semitic Philology," *Bib* 43 (1962) 349–65; idem, "Qoheleth and Recent Discoveries," *Bib* 39 (1958) 302–18. On popular dialect see Bo Isaksson, *Studies in the Language of Qohelet with Special Emphasis on the Verbal System* (AUU, SSU 10; Uppsala and Stockholm: Almqvist & Wiksell, 1987). Finally, see Fredericks, *Language;* cf. Schoors, *Preacher.*

205 Schoors, *Preacher,* 221, with reference to E. Y. Kutscher, *A History of the Hebrew Language* (Jerusalem: Magnes Press and Hebrew University, 1982) 81–85; and R. Polzin, *Late Biblical Hebrew* (HSM 12; Missoula, Mont.: Scholars Press, 1976).

206 Schoors, *Preacher,* 221–22.

207 Ibid., 222, contra Fredericks, *Language.*

which is a calque of Aramaic דִי; the high concentration of composite conjunctions, such as בְּשֶׁל אֲשֶׁר (Aram. בְּדִיל דִי) or שֶׁ עַל־דִּבְרַת (Aram. עַל דִּבְרַת דִי)."[208] As lexical Aramaisms or words that otherwise are not attested before the Persian period but appear in Egyptian Aramaic texts of the fifth century, we may note: יִתְרוֹן *yitrôn*, חֶסְרוֹן *ḥesrôn*, חֶשְׁבּוֹן *ḥešbôn*, נְכָסִים *nĕkāsîm*, זְמָן *zĕmān*, כְּאֶחָד *kĕʾeḥād*, טַחֲנָה *taḥănâ*, and לוה *lwh*; loanwords from Persian are פַּרְדֵּס *pardēs* and פִּתְגָם *pitgām*.[209]

On linguistic grounds, Seow would like to place the origin of the book of Qoheleth in the Persian period (5th/4th B.C.E.), since it contains no Greek loanwords and since the verb שׁלט *šlṭ* in the sense of "to have the right of disposal" (Qoh 2:19; 5:18; 6:2) and the nouns שַׁלִּיט *šallîṭ* and שִׁלְטוֹן *šilṭôn* in the sense of "proprietor" (7:19; 8:8-9) are otherwise used only in texts from the Persian period.[210] This *argumentum e silentio* is, nonetheless, not entirely unproblematic, especially since the named terms in 7:19 and 8:8-9 are probably not used in the sense of legal possession but in the sense of (political) power, which is regarded by Seow as later.

On the question of peculiarities of language in the book of Qoheleth that are conditioned by genre, dialect, or jargon, we may again cite Schoors:

Some features, which I have listed as late, could be due to a more vernacular dialect, as has been said also of MH [Mishnaic Hebrew]. But again, the general distribution of a large number of features taken together shows them to be late at the same time. A few features which I have listed as late can also betray a northern origin: for example the feminine demonstrative זֹו/זֹה, the particle שֶׁ, the singular feminine noun הוֹלֵלוֹת. Even the high frequency of Aramaisms

could be due to North-Israelite influence. As for literary genre, the sapiental, argumentative style dealing with abstract ideas may have favoured the use of abstract nouns ending in וֹן- or וּת-, the frequency of nominal clauses, the use of the imperfect tense with frequentative force, or the word order, in which the object often precedes the verb for the sake of emphasis. The relatively frequent lack of concord of subject and verb could be a trait of colloquial language, whereas the rather frequent use of גַּם with an emphatic meaning and the phrases of the type אֲנִי קָטַלְתִּי seem to betray Qoh's personal style. It is this personal style together, of course, with the contents so unusual for a biblical book, which renders Qoh at the same time so difficult and so puzzling.[211]

Text

The following interpretation is based on the Hebrew Masoretic text (𝔐) of the Leningrad/St. Petersburg B 19ᴬ manuscript completed in 1008 C.E., as it is printed in *BHK* and *BHS* and is now also accessible in a facsimile edition. (The somewhat older Aleppo Codex does not contain the book of Qoheleth.) 𝔐 is by and large in good condition. Corrections seem to be indicated only in relatively few places. They concern consonants and vowels (as well as punctuation).[212] Moreover, decisions are often required between Ketib (K) and Qere (Q).[213] In 3:19(?) and 3:21 the Masoretes seem to have interpreted the text through their vowel pointing in a way that is the opposite of its original meaning (see the notes on these passages).

Of the two Hebrew Qoheleth fragments discovered in Qumran (ℚ), 4QQohᵇ[214] with bits from Qoh 1:10-14(?) is dated between the mid-first century B.C.E. and the

---

208 Schoors, *Preacher*, 223.
209 Seow, 13.
210 Seow, "Linguistic Evidence"; idem, comm., 13–14. On this, Seow refers to D. M. Gropp, "The Origin and Development of the Aramaic *šallîṭ* Clause," *JNES* 52 (1993) 31–36.
211 Schoors, *Preacher*, 223–24.
212 On consonants see 4:10 (word division); 5:15 (?); 7:27 (word division); 8:2; 9:14; 10:1, 15, 18; 11:9; 12:1, 6 (2x). On vowels see 1:5; 3:19, 21; 4:2; 5:8, 11, 15; 8:10, 12 (?); 10:3, 10; 12:6, 7, 10, 12. On punctuation see, e.g., 1:5; 8:11.
213 See 4:8, 17; 5:8, 10; 6:10; 7:22; 9:4; 10:3, 10, 20; 11:9; 12:6. Cf. A. Schoors, "Kethib-Qere in Ecclesiastes," in J. Qaegebeur, ed., *Orientalia Antiqua* (OLA 13; Leuven: Peeters, 1982) 214–22.
214 = 4Q110, frgs. 1 and 2; see E. Ulrich, "Ezra and Qoheleth Manuscripts from Qumran (4QEzra, 4QQoh)," in Ulrich et al., eds., *Priests, Prophets and Scribes* (JSOTSup 149; Sheffield: JSOT Press, 1992) 148–50; G. W. Nebe, "Qumranica I: Zu unveröffentlichten Handschriften aus Höhle 4 von Qumran," *ZAW* 106 (1994) 313.

early first century C.E. The manuscript offers two orthographic and one lexical variant to 𝔐.[215] In line 8 it contains three letters (נבֹֿו gbŵ) that cannot be made to agree with 𝔐 (v.15).[216] Between v. 11 and v. 12 is a space that is probably supposed to mark a division between sections. The other fragment 4QQoh^a[217] contains parts of Qoh 5:13-17 (col. I); 6:3-8 and 6:12—7:6 (col. II), as well as 7:7-10, 19-20 (col. III), and is dated between 175 and 150 B.C.E. The manuscript offers a number of orthographic variants (above all, plene writings)[218] but also some that are text-critically relevant:

5:14: 𝔐 כאשר k'šr (cf. 𝔊 καϑώς) — 𝔔 כיא ky'.

5:15: 𝔐 וגם wgm (cf. 𝔊 καί γε) — 𝔔 גם gm.

5:16: 𝔐 . . . בחשך יאכל וכעס הרבה bḥšk y'kl wk's hrbh . . . — 𝔔 . . .]כעסX ok's[. . . ; before כעסX ok's there seems in 𝔔 to have been no ל l (cf. 𝔐 יאכל y'kl).[219]

6:3: 𝔐 ממנו הנפל mmnw hnpl — 𝔔 הנפל ממנו hnpl mmnw.

6:4: 𝔐 ילך ylk — 𝔔 הלך hlk.

6:6: 𝔐 ואלו w'lw — 𝔔 ואם לוא w'm lw'.

6:8: 𝔐 כי מה ky mh — 𝔔 כמה kmh.

6:8: "The tops of two clear *lamedhs* (the second possibly erased), about 2 cm apart, are clearly visible early in the line [l. 7 of 𝔔]; however, this configuration does not match 𝔐 (*lhlk ngd*) for these words. Line 7 may therefore contain the remains of a variant reading, part of which may have been erased."[220]

6:12: 𝔐 . . . ויעשם כצל אשר מי יגיד wy's'm kṣl 'šr my ygyd . . . — 𝔔 שם יגֹֿיד[. . .]X[. . . . . .]°[. . .]îm yĝ[yd. The letters contained in 𝔔 cannot be made to agree with 𝔐.

7:2: 𝔐 משתה mšth (cf. 𝔊) — 𝔔 [ש]מחה ś]mḥh.

7:2: 𝔐 הוא סוף כל האדם hw' swp kl h'dm — 𝔔 ה[וֹ]אה כול סוף[האדם h]w'h kwl swp [h'dm.

7:4: 𝔐 בבית (אבל) bbyt ('bl) — 𝔔 בית byt (2x?).

7:5: 𝔐 מאיש שמע m'yš šm' — 𝔔 * *mlmw^c corrected to מלשמוע mlšmw^c.

7:6: 𝔐 וגם wgm (cf. 𝔊 καί γε) — 𝔔 גם gm.

7:6: "Space for about 10 letters would have preceded *hbl*; this may signify a longer text than *gm zh*/*hbl*, an erasure (thus Muilenburg), or possibly a defect in the leather."[221]

7:6/7: "Several words were originally written but seem to have been erased."[222]

7:7: 𝔐 ויאבד wy'bd (cf. 𝔊 ἀπόλλυσι) — 𝔔 ויעוֿה wy'wh.

7:19: 𝔐 תעז t'z — 𝔔 תעזֹֿר t'z̊r (cf. 𝔊 βοηϑήσει).

7:19: 𝔐 אשר היו 'šr hyw — 𝔔 [ש]היו š[hyw.

7:20: 𝔐 אשר יעשה 'šr y'šh — 𝔔 ש[יע]שה š[y']šh.

In 6:4 the writer of 𝔔 seems to have noticed a parablepsis (ובחושך שמו wbḥwšk šmw) and corrected it himself (ובחושך הלך ובחושך שמו wbḥwšk hlk wbḥwšk šmw).

The variations in 𝔔 nowhere point conclusively to text versions that are older than 𝔐. They do, however, emphatically point out that the book of Qoheleth was apparently passed on soon after its creation in different text versions. Here we must also reckon with the possibility of interpretive "study manuscripts."[223] How 𝔐 is related to the original text of the book of Qoheleth is beyond our knowledge.

The Greek translation of the book of Qoheleth in the Septuagint (𝔊) exhibits a number of striking peculiari-

---

215 Orthographic: 1:10: 𝔐 לעולמים 𝔔 לעלמים l'lmym — lʿwlmym; 1:11: 𝔐 לא 𝔓 — לוא lw'. Lexical: 1:14: 𝔐 שנעשו 𝔔 אשר נעשו 'šr n'šw — šn'św.

216 Nebe, "Qumranica I," 313, reads נבֹֿר gbr̊ instead of נבֹֿו gbŵ and assumes "that v. 15 is erroneously forgotten and the scriptural remnants correspond to 1:16," where 𝔔 reads הגברתי hgbrty instead of הגדלתי hgdlty (𝔐).

217 = 4Q109, frgs. 1-6; see J. Muilenburg, "A Qoheleth Scroll from Qumran," *BASOR* 135 (1954) 20–28; repr. in Muilenburg, *Hearing and Speaking the Word* (Chico, Calif.: Scholars Press, 1984) 375–83; Ulrich, "Qoheleth Manuscripts," 142–47; Nebe, "Qumranica I," 312–13.

218 Orthographic variants: 6:4: 𝔐 בא b' — 𝔔 בה bh; 6:5: 𝔐 נחת nḥt — 𝔔 נוחת nwḥt; 7:5: 𝔐 גערת g'rt — 𝔔 גערות g'rwt?

g'rwt; 7:8: 𝔐 מראשיתו mr'šytw — 𝔔 מרשיתו mršytw. Plene: 5:17: 𝔐 בכול bkwl; 6:4: ובחושך wbḥwšk (2x); 6:5: לוא lw', ולוא wlw'; 6:6: לוא lw', הלוא hlw', הכול hkwl; 6:7: כול kwl, לוא lw'; 7:2: כול kwl; 7:3: משחוק mśḥwq; 7:5: לשמוע lšmw'; 7:6: שחוק śḥwq; also 6:5: נוחת nwḥt; 7:5: גערות g'rwt?

219 Ulrich, "Qoheleth Manuscripts," 144.

220 Ibid., 145–46.

221 Ibid., 146.

222 Ibid., 147.

223 Cf. Odil Hannes Steck, *Die erste Jesajarolle von Qumran (1QIs^a)* (SBS 173/1, 2; Stuttgart: Katholisches Bibelwerk, 1998) 17–19 on 1QIsa^a.

ties in which it agrees with the Aquila version (α'), which strives for a "literal" rendition.[224] Barthélemy has, therefore, held the view that the Septuagint version of the book of Qoheleth is in reality a work of Aquila, whereas the third column of Origen's Hexapla, which is designated as "Aquila" (α'), more strongly resembles the version of Symmachus (σ') than that of Aquila.[225] By contrast, Hyvärinen and Jarick have called attention to the comparatively greater "literalness" of α' vis-à-vis 𝔊.[226] Thus it seems possible that "LXX Ecclesiastes is merely Aquilanic" and "the third column of the *Hexapla*

is Aquilan."[227] "The theological standpoint of the Greek translation [𝔊] remains yet to be worked out."[228]

The Peshitta (𝔖)[229] and the Vulgate (𝔙) seem to translate the book of Qoheleth from the Hebrew—yet with the and occasional influence of 𝔊. In contrast to these versions, the translations into Coptic, Ethiopic, and Arabic are of less importance for text-critical reconstruction. The Aramaic Targums (𝔗 = ed. Sperber) mingle translation with Midrash and are interesting less for text criticism than for the history of reception of the book of Qoheleth (see above).

---

224 Thus the Hebrew *nota accusativi* אֵת *'et* is translated into Greek with σύν (e.g., 1:14: εἶδον σὺν πάντα τὰ ποιήματα), Heb. גַּם *gam*/וְגַם *wĕgam* with Gk. καί γε (e.g., 2:14: καὶ ἔγνων καί γε ἐγὼ), Heb. לְ *l* + inf. with Gk. τοῦ + inf. (e.g., 1:8: οὐ δυνήσεται ἀνὴρ τοῦ λαλεῖν), Heb. לְ *l* + noun with Greek article + noun (e.g., 4:11: καὶ ὁ εἷς πῶς θερμανθῇ) (Seow, 7).

225 D. Barthélemy, *Les devanciers d'Aquila* (VTSup 10; Leiden: Brill, 1963).

226 E.g., 𝔊 ἐκκλησιαστής – α' κωλεθ for 𝔐 קֹהֶלֶת *qōhelet*; 5:5: 𝔐 הַמַּלְאָךְ *hammal'āk*, "messenger" – 𝔊 τοῦ θεοῦ "God" – α' τοῦ ἀγγέλου, "messenger, angel"; 12:9: 𝔐 הָעָם *hā'ām*, "people" – 𝔊 ἄνθρωπον, "human being" – α' λαόν, "people" (Seow, 8).

227 Seow, 8. See K. Hyvärinen, *Die Übersetzung von Aquila* (ConBOT 10; Lund: Gleerup, 1977); J. Jarick, "Aquila's Kohelet," *Textus* 15 (1990) 131–39.

228 Murphy, xxv. Cf., e.g., G. Bertram, "Hebräischer und griechischer Qohelet," *ZAW* 64 (1952) 26–49; S. Holm-Nielsen, "On the Interpretation of Qoheleth in Early Christianity," *VT* 24 (1974) 170–71; R. B. Salters, "Observations on the Septuagint of Ecclesi-

astes," *OTE* 6 (1992/93) 163–74; J. Cook, "Aspects of the Relationship between the Septuagint Versions of Kohelet and Proverbs," in A. Schoors, ed., *Qohelet in the Context of Wisdom* (BEThL 136; Leuven: Leuven Univ. Press and Peeters, 1998) 481–92; F. Vinel, "Le livre de l'Ecclésiaste," in M. d'Harmonville et al., eds., *Autour des livres de la Septante: Proverbes, Ecclésiaste, Nombres, 3ème Livre des Regnes* (Le centre d'études du Saulchoir; Paris: Cerf, 1995) 27–45; idem, "Le texte grec de l'Ecclésiaste et ses caractéristiques," in Schoors, ed., *Qohelet in Context,* 283–302.

229 See A. S. Kamenetzky, "Die P'šita zu Koheleth," *ZAW* 24 (1904) 181–239; R. Gordis, *Koheleth: The Man and His World* (3d ed.; New York: Schocken, 1968) 140-43; A. Schoors, "The Peshitta of Koheleth and Its Relation to the Septuagint," in C. Laga, J. A. Munitiz, and L. van Rompay, eds., *After Chalcedon: Studies in Theology and Church History* (OLA 18; Leuven: Peeters, 1985) 347-57.

1

Translation

1   **The words of Qoheleth, the son of David, the king in Jerusalem.ᵃ**

    1a   𝔊 𝔏 Syh 𝔎 read: "the king of Israel in Jerusalem."

The title of the book of Qoheleth offers in concise form the information that was essential (in the contemporary understanding) about its author (name, lineage, office, and sphere of operation).[1] This information is not to be understood in the sense of the modern concept of author. It does not assert the authenticity of the "words of Qoheleth" but claims the authority of "Qoheleth" for the present book.[2] In this sense, in Prov 1:1 the book of Proverbs is placed under the authority of King Solomon, although it also contains the words of other wise men, who are named (30:1: Agur; 31:1: Lemuel) or anonymous (22:17 [see *BHS*]; 24:23), and points expressly to the process of its redaction (25:1). Kings or high officials also figure in Egyptian wisdom writings as the author or recipient of wisdom teachings.[3] In such authorizations, knowledge and power are closely linked.

The book of Qoheleth takes up the convention of the authorization of wisdom teachings but uses it in a way that thwarts and, as it were, "deconstructs" its intentions: Qoheleth is not an Israelite king who is known from OT traditions.[4] The designation "descendant" or "son of David" suggests his identification with Solomon, without expressly making that identification.[5] The first-person report of "King Qoheleth" in 1:12–2:26 is reminiscent of the biblical image of Solomon, which, however, often seems to be treated ironically. After chapter 2

---

1   In the OT cf. esp. Jer 1:1; Prov 1:1, also Amos 1:1; Neh 1:1; Prov 10:1; 30:1; 31:1, as well as the titles of Egyptian wisdom teachings; see Brunner, *Altägyptische Weisheit*, 75; cf. K. F. D. Römheld, *Die Weisheitslehre im Alten Orient: Elemente einer Formgeschichte* (BN Beihefte 4; Munich: Manfred Görg, 1989) 17ff.

2   Cf. D. G. Meade, *Pseudonymity and Canon: An Investigation into the Relationship of Authorship and Authority in Jewish and Earliest Christian Tradition* (WUNT 39; Tübingen: Mohr, 1986). The same is true of the OT prophetic writings, whose "naming is not to be understood in the modern, post-Greek sense as information on authors but on authority. . . . They were probably also understood thus by contemporaries, of whom at least a minority familiar with the traditional texts could identify the new editions as such" (Otto Kaiser, *Der Gott des Alten Testaments: Theologie des AT*, part 1: *Grundlegung* [UTB 1747; Göttingen: Vandenhoeck & Ruprecht, 1993] 243). The Babylonian Talmud (*B. Batra* 14b-15a) then distinguishes between "authorities" and "authors" of the biblical books: thus, for example, Hezekiah and his collegium (cf. Prov 25:1) "wrote" the books of Isaiah, Proverbs, Canticles, and Qoheleth; the "men of the great synagogue" "wrote" Ezekiel, the *Testaments of the Twelve Prophets*, Daniel, and Esther.

3   Cf., e.g., the teachings of King Amenemhet I (Brunner, *Altägyptische Weisheit*, no. 6), of Prince Djedefhor (ibid., no. 1), and for King Merikare (ibid., no. 4; in l. 256 they quote an otherwise unknown "Teaching of King Khety"). The "writers or authors" named in Egyptian wisdom teachings can, "apart from a very few exceptions, be relegated to literary fiction" (Heike Sternberg-el Hotabi, *TUAT* 3:191). P. Seibert (*Die Charakteristik: Untersuchungen zu einer altägyptischen Sprechsitte und zu ihren Ausprägungen in Folklore und Literatur,* part 1: *Philologische Bearbeitung der Bezeugungen* [ÄA 17; Wiesbaden: Harrassowitz, 1967] 69–70) has recommended that one distinguish between "teaching authority" and "teaching recorder" (cf. Römheld, *Weisheitslehre*, 18 n. 3).

4   Contra Lohfink: "the name Qoheleth may possibly evoke in the minds of readers of the Hebrew Bible that, according to 1 Kgs 8:1, Solomon assembled (*yaqhēl*) in Jerusalem all the ancients of Israel, and all the heads of the tribes"; similarly, Crenshaw, for example, and A. S. Kamenetzky ("Der Rätselname Kohelet," *ZAW* 34 [1914] 226), who in view of the occurrence of the root קהל *qhl* in 1 Chr 28:1, 8; 29:1; 2 Chr 1:3, 5; 5:2, 3; 6:3, 12; 7:8 holds that the name קֹהֶלֶת *qōhelet* characterizes Solomon "as the one in whose biography the stem *qhl* often appears." Yet that appears almost as erroneous as F. Zimmermann's ("The Aramaic Provenance of Qohelet," *JQR* 36 [1945/46] 43–44) interpretation of קֹהֶלֶת *qōhelet* as a cryptogram for Solomon, since the number value of the Aramaic equivalent(!) כנשה *knš* corresponds to that of שלמה *šlmh* (Solomon) (see Whitley, *Koheleth*, 5).

5   In addition to Solomon, any other, later member of the Davidic dynasty *can* be designated בֶּן־דָּוִד *ben-dāwid*, "descendant of David." And מֶלֶךְ בִּירוּשָׁלָם *melek bîrûšālāim*, "(a) king in Jerusalem," *can* refer back to both "Qoheleth" and "David." Contrary to Delitzsch, but with Ellermeier (*Qohelet*, I/1, 165),

"Qoheleth" no longer speaks as "king." The epilogue in 12:9-14 designates him as a "wise man" (12:9) and places his book on the level of the "sayings of wise men" (12:11). Moreover, in the continued reading of the book of Qoheleth, the identification of "Qoheleth" as "king (Solomon)" reveals itself more and more clearly as a fictive travesty. Moreover, what "Qoheleth" says as a "wise" man in chapters 3–12 contradicts in part his statements as "king" in 1:12–2:26. The "subtle playing with the identity" of the teaching authority thwarts the function of authorization and legitimization, and it leaves the reader free to compare his/her own life with its experiences, and to accept its logic only after critical examination."[6] Wisdom and power are not necessarily connected with each other (cf. 4:13).

In the book of Qoheleth the critique of the legitimation of wisdom teachings through a royal teaching authority is not absolutely against the "Solomonic" wisdom of the book of Proverbs as such. It makes clear, however, that in any case "Solomon" became an authority on wise thinking and living not as a king but as a wise man (cf. Wisdom 6–9)—and that his authority must prove itself ever anew with the readers of his teachings. Moreover, it throws a critical light on the claims of knowledge and education of contemporary Hellenistic rulers, as well as those of representatives of the "upper class" who live "like a king" (cf. Job 29:25).[7]

If one sees in the authorization of the book of Qoheleth through the title in 1:1 (and the epilogue in 12:9-14) a deliberate playing with literary conventions,[8] the "editorial framework" of the book as such still does not allow the conclusion that the "words of Qoheleth" were revised redactionally. More obvious at first is the assumption that the author of the book of Qoheleth put his reflections of fictive teaching authority into "Qoheleth's" mouth. In this way he reserved for himself the possibility of also distancing himself again from "Qoheleth" (cf. below on 12:9-14).

Morphologically, in קֹהֶלֶת *qōhelet* we have a feminine singular participle (qal) of the root קהל *qhl*, which in the reflexive stem (niphal) means "gather together," in the causative stem (hiphil), "gather (someone)"; "a singular participle of the basic stem also occurs occasionally with other verbs (e.g., דֹּבֵר *dōber*) and thus presents no difficulties linguistically."[9] The interchanging of indetermination (קֹהֶלֶת *qōhelet*: 1:1, 2, 12; 12:9) and determination (הַקֹּהֶלֶת *haqqōhelet*: 7:27 [corr.]; 12:8) indicates that in "Qoheleth" a designation of function became the name of its (according to 1:1-2; 12:8-9, male) bearer.[10] It could be a matter of a kind of nickname that by its particular nature characterizes its bearer.[11]

מֶלֶךְ *melek* is not determined by the following בִּירוּשָׁלָ͏ִם *bîrûšālāim*. Even if one understands מֶלֶךְ בִּירוּשָׁלָ͏ִם *melek bîrûšālāim* with Ellermeier (ibid., 166) as an "asyndetic attributive clause" ("who was [a] king in Jerusalem"), the reference back to both Qoheleth and David remains possible. And the conventions for book titles lead one to expect here an indication of the "author's" office.

6   Lohfink, 44.
7   In New Aramaic every village chief is designated מלך *mlk*. On this basis it is occasionally recommended that one understand מֶלֶךְ *melek* in Qoh 1:1, 12 not in the sense of "king" but rather as "councilor" (Kroeber), "property-holder" (Ginsberg, *Studies,* 12ff.), or "counselor" (W. F. Albright, "Some Canaanite-Phoenician Sources of Hebrew Wisdom," in M. Noth and D. Winton Thomas, eds., *Wisdom in Israel and in the Ancient Near East* [VTSup 3; Leiden: Brill, 1955] 15, n. 2).
8   Cf. here also Fox, *Qohelet;* idem, "Frame-Narrative."
9   Michel, *Qohelet,* 2.
10 Cf. the references to grammatically feminine designations for functions that are performed by men in Qumran and in the Mishnah in Whitley, *Koheleth,* 4–5 (and already in Delitzsch, 204–5; Loretz, *Qohelet,* 146–47). In Ezra 2:55-57 there are several "names of the kind a master can give to his slaves to describe their characteristics or something similar: Hassophereth (v. 55) = writer, teacher; Peruda or Perida (v. 55) = apart, alone; Giddel (v. 57) = great (. . .); Pochereth-hazzebaim (v. 57) = gazelle catcher" (A. H. J. Gunneweg, *Esra* [KAT 19.1; Gütersloh: Gütersloher Verlagshaus, 1985] 63). Here too indetermination and determination alternate just as in Qoheleth. From this standpoint Michel's (*Qohelet,* 4) statement that in Qoh "12:8 and perhaps also 7:27 the word *qohelet* is not used as a proper name but as an appellative," since "in Hebrew no article can stand before a proper name," must be critically relativized.
11 "At that time . . . in Alexandria the Cyrenaic Hegesias was named Peisithanatos, that is, 'suicide advisor'" (Lohfink 10).

Yet it is not entirely clear in what this consists: "The name Koheleth remains as enigmatic today as ever before."[12] 𝔊 translates קֹהֶלֶת *qōhelet* with ἐκκλησιαστής, "participant in a popular assembly" (Gk. ἐκκλησία = Heb. קָהָל *qāhāl*),[13] Jerome with *concionator*, "popular speaker" (cf. Luther: "preacher"). Thus there are two directions in which the designation קֹהֶלֶת *qōhelet* from the Hebrew verb קהל *qhl* can be understood:[14] (1) a function that is defined in some way that is over against and in relation to a popular assembly (however it might be more closely defined[15]), or (2) a representation of this popular assembly or its participants themselves (and the two possibilities do not have to be mutually exclusive).

In the first case the teaching authority of the book of Qoheleth would be characterized by the name קֹהֶלֶת *qōhelet* as a person who had in special measure devoted himself to "the people" (cf. 12:9) and rejoiced over the corresponding recognition and esteem.[16] Then one could imagine with Lohfink "that Qoheleth offered his

teaching publicly [= for the 'people'] in the marketplace, as did the Greek peripatetic philosophers. Now that must have been something new in Jerusalem, and it would have excited a lot of attention. A group of students gathered around him, and from this he acquired the name 'Qoheleth.' Either he, or his editor, flirted with this allusion in the book that later gatherd his teaching together."[17]

In the second case the designation קֹהֶלֶת *qōhelet* could indicate that in the book of Qoheleth the "voice of the (simple) people" is brought to expression: "I, the patient, silent public, bored by archaic teaching—I now speak for myself, in order to say what all the world down below ultimately thinks."[18]

If one reads the book of Qoheleth as a continuation of the book of Proverbs,[19] the title in Qoh 1:1 fits into a series of (sub)titles in Proverbs (Prov 1:1; 10:1; 22:17 [see *BHS*]; 24:23; 25:1; 30:1; 31:1).

---

12 Gordis, 193.

13 σ': παροιμιαστής, i.e., one who speaks in proverbs or parables.

14 Other derivations are found, for example, in Ginsberg, *Studies*, 33–35 ("the Convoker," from Syr. *qhl*), E. Ullendorf, "The Meaning of קהלת," *VT* 12 (1962) 215 ("the arguer," from Aram.-Syr. *qhl*), and Whitley, *Koheleth*, 6 ("the Sceptic," from Syr. *qhl*, "to consider").

15 קָהָל *qāhāl* "can designate a team gathered for war, a judicial community, a cultic group, and the full assembly of the Jewish cultic community, but . . . also more limitedly, a 'company of evildoers' (Ps 26:5)" (Michel, *Qohelet*, 5). H.-P. Müller (קָהָל *qāhāl* assembly," *TLOT* 3:1132) wonders "whether there was a wisdom *qāhāl* which may also be envisioned in Sir 15:5," and he points to *b. ʿAbod. Zar.* 18a, where *mqhyl qhlwt* means "the gathering of students by a rabbi."

16 For the former see P. Joüon, "Sur le nom de Qohelet," *Bib* 2 (1921) 53–54; for the latter see Loretz, *Qohelet*, 146–48.

17 Lohfink, 10–11.

18 "Moi, le Public, le patient, le muet, lassé d'un enseignement périmé, voici que je parle à mon tour, pour dire ce que tout le monde a fini par penser tout bas" (Pautrel, 9–10, quotation according to Michel, *Qohelet*, 3). In Michel's view (ibid.), Pautrel's "interpretation was not adopted by anyone, although it is grammatically closer than the one previously sketched." Cf. also the recommendation of A. S. Kamenetzky ("Die ursprünglich beabsichtigte Aussprache des pseudonyms קהלת," *OLZ* 34 [1921] 11–15) to read *qhlt* as *qĕhillōt* as "popular assembly."

19 Cf. the introduction above under the heading "Corpus Salomonicum."

2 **Futile and fleeting,[a] said Qoheleth,** **futile and fleeting! All (that) is futile.**	**2a** Or: "Futility of futilities," "futilest futility"; "fleetingness of fleetingnesses," "fleetingest fleetingness."

This "motto" in the form of a quotation of the "teaching" of Qoheleth is repeated almost exactly at the conclusion of the book in 12:8.[1] At the beginning of the book, it is highly ambiguous.

First, it is unclear in what sense we are to understand the predicate הֶבֶל *hebel,* which is elevated to the superlative in the compound הֲבֵל הֲבָלִים *hăbēl hăbālîm.*[2] The term הֶבֶל *hebel* can (a) mean concretely "breath (of wind)," (b) be abstracted to "nothing, illusion, delusion" or "transitoriness, futility," and in this abstract sense is (c) often used as a (derogatory) designation for "idols" and "idolatry."[3]

𝕲 (ματαιότης, "vanity, foolishness, transitoriness") and 𝕭 (*vanitas,* "futility, empty appearance, fantasy, failure, boastfulness, mendacity") accentuate more strongly the negative connotations of the Hebrew expression, whereas α' (ἀτμός or ἀτμίς, "steam, mist, smoke") remains closer to its concrete background. Many scholars assume *one* special meaning of הֶבֶל *hebel* throughout the book of Qoheleth, for example, "Eitelkeit" ("vanity"),

"enigma, mystery," "incomprehensible," "irony," and "absurd."[4] Yet even here the meaning of הֶבֶל *hebel* seems to vary according to context between the negative: "worthless, futile," and the neutral: "transitory, fleeting." The translation with "futile and fleeting" attempts to keep this range of meaning open at the beginning of the book.

Second, it is not clear to what הַכֹּל *hakkōl* refers. Does it mean "the entirety" of the world, "the universe" as a whole with all its parts?[5] Or does the expression point (cataphorically) to what follows in the sense of "all *that* (about which we are going to talk)"?[6]

In view of these ambiguities, the motto at the beginning of the book leaves open a number of possible meanings:

■ Everything (that people do) is meaningless and worthless (cf. 1:3).[7]

1   On the sequence of title and motto in the form of a quotation of the book's author or the teaching authority, cf. Amos 1:1-2 (v. 1: דִּבְרֵי עָמוֹס *dibrê ʿāmôs,* "the words of Amos . . ."; v. 2: וַיֹּאמַר *wayyōmar,* "And he said . . ."), as well as Egyptian wisdom teachings (see Brunner, *Altägyptische Weisheit,* nos. 1, 2, 5, 6, 7, 8, 13, 14, 24). Cf. the framing of Proverbs 1–9 by 1:7 and 9:10 (and Proverbs 1–31 by 1:7 and 31:30).

2   See GKC § 133: On the irregular compound form (הֲבֵל *hăbēl* instead of הֶבֶל *hebel*), cf. Schoors, *Preacher,* 75.

3   Cf. R. Albertz, "הֶבֶל *hebel* breath," *TLOT* 1:351–53; K. Seybold, "הֶבֶל *hebhel,*" *TDOT* 3:313–20.

4   See, respectively, A. Lauha, "Omnia Vanitas: Die Bedeutung von *hbl* bei Kohelet," in J. Kiilunen, V. Riekkinen, and H. Räisänen, eds., *Glaube und Gerechtichkeit* (SESJ 38; Helsinki: Suomen eksegeettise seura, 1983) 19–25; G. S. Ogden, "'Vanity' It Certainly Is Not," *BT* 38 (1987) 301–7; W. E. Staples, "The 'Vanity' of Ecclesiastes," *JNES* 2 (1943) 95–104; idem, "Vanity of Vanities," *CJT* 1 (1955) 141–56; T. Polk, "The Wisdom of Irony: A Study of *hebel* and Its Relation to Joy and the Fear of God in Ecclesiastes," *SBTh* 6 (1976) 3–17; finally,

M. V. Fox, "The Meaning of *hebel* for Qohelet," *JBL* 105 (1986) 409–27; idem, *Qohelet,* 29–51; D. Michel, *Qohelet,* 84–86; idem, *Untersuchungen,* 40–51.

5   Cf. Jer 10:16; 51:19; Pss 103:19; 119:91; 145:9; 1 Chr 29:12, as well as Sir 36:1; 39:21, 34; 43:27, 33; 51:12d (cf. 18:1; 24:8); 11QPsᵃ 151: 28:7-8; 1QApGen 20:12-13; *m. Abot* 4:22. See Hengel, *Judaism and Hellenism,* 2:94 n. 259; Lohfink, "Koh 1,2 'alles ist Windhauch'—universale und anthropologische Aussage?" in R. Mosis and L. Ruppert, eds., *Der Weg zum Menschen* (Freiburg im Breisgau: Herder, 1989) 202–6.

6   Lohfink, "Koh 1,2 'alles ist Windhauch'—universale und anthropologische Aussage?" in R. Mosis and L. Ruppert, eds., *Der Weg zum Menschen* (Freiburg im Breisgau: Herder, 1989) 201–16 (repr. in Lohfink, *Studien zu Kohelet,* 125–42).

7   Cf. the paraphrase in Gregory Thaumaturgus (ca. 213–70 C.E.): "How empty and useless human activities and all human pursuits are" (ὡς κενὰ καὶ ἀνόνητα τὰ ἀνθρώπων πράγματά τε καὶ σπουδάσματα, ὅσα ἀνθρώπινα). S. John Jarick, *Gregory Thaumaturgos' Paraphrase of Ecclesiastes* (SBLSCS; Atlanta: Scholars Press, 1990) 8.

- Everything (that people assert) rests on illusion or error (cf. 1:10).[8]
- Everything (people? [cf. 1:4]—the world?) is transitory.[9]

In regard to the use of the expression הֶבֶל *hebel*,[10] 1:12–2:26 and 3:10–12:7 can be read as different "interpretations" of the motto in 1:2 (and 12:8): whereas 1:12–2:26 illustrates the possibility of understanding it as a derogatory judgment on the whole of living reality (הֶבֶל *hebel* = "futile"), the following text beginning with 3:10 suggests an understanding as a statement about the transitoriness of all creatures (and humans in particular: הֶבֶל *hebel* = "fleeting"—which does not exclude limited negative judgments about certain phenomena). That indicates that 1:3–12:7 not only develops variations on one and the same basic thought formulated in 1:2 and 12:8[11] but also points to an overall argumentative inclination.

In 1:3–12:7 there are numerous qualifying nominal clauses with the predicate הֶבֶל *hebel* with comprehensive or limited reference that are comparable to 1:2.[12] In addition to such stereotypical formulations, הֶבֶל *hebel* occurs several times, starting with 4:7 (cf. 5:7; 6:4, 11; 8:14), especially as a qualification of human lifetime (יְמֵי [חַיֵּי] *yĕmê [ḥayyê] hebel*: 6:12; 7:15; 9:9 [2x]; in terms of content 11:8, 10 also belong here). With regard to the distribution and sequence of the הֶבֶל *hebel* statements in the book, it is notable that in 1:3-11, the section immediately after the motto in 1:2, and in the corresponding section 3:1-9, the expression הֶבֶל *hebel* does not occur.

In 1:12—2:26 הֶבֶל *hebel* occurs exclusively in qualifying nominal clauses, in which הֶבֶל *hebel* has a pervasive (negatively) judging sense and refers to human action and human concepts of value (cf. the parallel "striving after wind," רְעוּת / רַעְיוֹן רוּחַ *rĕ'ût / ra'yôn rûaḥ*: 1:14, 17; 2:11, 17, 26). The comprehensive judgments in 1:14; 2:11, 17 (הַכֹּל הֶבֶל *hakkōl hebel*) are confirmed and reinforced by the limited judgments in 2:1, 15, 19, 21, 23, 26 (גַּם הוּא / זֶה הֶבֶל *gam-hû' / zeh hebel*).

Beginning with 3:10 the stereotypical use of הֶבֶל *hebel* is overcome. Qualifying nominal clauses with הֶבֶל *hebel* in a (critically) judging sense now refer not only to definite, limited phenomena; הֶבֶל *hebel* is also used increasingly in the value-neutral sense of "transitory, fleeting." In order to make the motto of 1:2 (and 12:8) more precise, we can look here particularly at statements from the opening and closing parts of 3:10–12:7. When 3:11 asserts that the Divinity "has made everything [or 'the universe': הַכֹּל *hakkōl*] so that it is beautiful in its time," this stands over against a devaluation of the whole world. The general judgment הַכֹּל הֶבֶל *hakkōl hebel* in 3:19 clearly refers in its context to the transitoriness of all living beings. Correspondingly, the only further הֶבֶל *hebel* statement in the book of Qoheleth formed with כֹּל *kōl*, 11:8, points to the transitoriness of human future life (כָּל־שֶׁבָּא הֶבֶל *kol-šebbā' hebel*) in old age, where life is as fleeting as "youth and black hair" (11:10).

---

8   Cf. the quotation of the Cynic Monimos (ca. 340 B.C.E.) in Menander (frg. 215, Z, 7; cf. Diogenes Laertius 6.82-83): "He said, namely, that that which is assumed [as existing] is all mist" (τὸ γὰρ ὑπο-ληφθὲν τῦφον εἶναι πᾶν ἔφη). See Y. Amir, "Doch ein griechischer Einfluss auf das Buch Kohelet?" in idem, *Studien zum antiken Judentum* (BEAT 2; Frankfurt am Main: Lang, 1985) 35–50.

9   For people see, e.g., Job 7:16; Pss 39:6-7, 12; 62:10; 94:11; 144:4. For the world see Isa 51:6; 65:17, as well as the "eschatological" interpretation of Qoh 1:2-3 in the wisdom writing of the Cairo Geniza (1:4): "This world is transitory, but the coming world is gain" עולם הזה הבל הוא ועולם הבא יתרון הוא ('wlm hzh hbl hw' w'wlm hb' ytrwn hw').

10   Cf. here also N. Lohfink, "Ist Kohelets הבל—Aussage erkenntnis theoretisch gemeint?" in Schoors, ed., *Qohelet in Context*, 41–59; idem, "Koh 1,2 'alles

ist Windhauch'—universale und anthropologische Aussage?" in R. Mosis and L. Ruppert, eds., *Der Weg zum Menschen: FS Alfons Deissler* (Freiburg in Breisgau: Herder, 1989) 201–16, repr. in Lohfink, *Studien zu Kohelet*, 125–42; idem, "Zu הבל im Buch Kohelet," in Lohfink, *Studien*, 215–18; M. V. Fox, "The Meaning of *hebel* for Qohelet," *JBL* 105 (1986) 409–27; idem, *Qohelet*, 29–51; Backhaus, *Zeit und Zufall*, 332–44.

11   Thus Loader, *Polar Structures*, 9.

12   Comprehensive: הַכֹּל הֶבֶל *hakkōl hebel* (1:14; 2:11, 17; 3:19; cf. 11:8: כָּל־שֶׁבָּא הֶבֶל *kol-šebbā' hebel*); limited: (גַּם)זֶה הֶבֶל *(gam) zeh hebel* (2:15, 19, 21, 23, 26; 4:4, 8, 16; 5:9; 6:2, 9; 7:6; 8:10, 14; cf. 2:1: גַּם־הוּא *gam-hû' hebel*; 11:10: הַיַּלְדוּת וְהַשַּׁחֲרוּת הֶבֶל *hayyaldût wĕhaššaḥărût hebel*).

The motto of the book of Qoheleth is indeed "misunderstandable in the highest degree."[13] Its point in regard to what follows seems to lie, however, in its very openness and ambiguity. With the assumption of a subsequent collection and revising of the words of a "historical Qoheleth" (see above on 1:1), the interpretation of 1:2 and 12:8 as a "secondary" redaction framework of these "words"[14] also becomes questionable.

13   Ellermeier, *Qohelet* I/1, 100.
14   Thus, e.g., Ellermeier (*Qohelet* I/1, 96ff.); Galling; Lauha; Whybray; contra, e.g., Barton; Gordis; Kroeber; Lohfink, "Koh 1,2," 211 n. 16.

It is often assumed that the first three or four chapters of the book of Qoheleth comprise a larger literarily and argumentatively coherent composition.[1] A number of observations suggest that 1:3—4:12 can be regarded as the first major division, whose structure can be sketched as follows:

- 1:3   The question of "gain" in view of the totality of human toil
- 1:4-11   Poem: human activity on the horizon of distant times (עוֹלָם *ʿôlām*)

- 1:12—2:26   Reflections of "King Qoheleth"

- 3:1-8   Poem: human activity on the horizon of changing times (עֵת *ʿēt*)
- 3:9   The "gain" question in view of the special effort in one's activity

- 3:10—4:12   Reflections of the "wise man Qoheleth"

At the same time, 4:13 ("Better a child, needy and wise, than a king, old and foolish . . ."), which opens the next major division (4:13—5:9), suggests that the reader, in retrospect, critically examine the comments made by Qoheleth in the guise of a "king" in 1:12—2:26. Section 3:10—4:12, in which Qoheleth speaks without this disguise (and thus as a "wise man," according to 12:9), can be read as a critical commentary on 1:12—2:26, as already signaled by the revisiting of 1:13 in 3:10. The poetic sections 1:3-11 and 3:1-9 bracket the reflections of "King Qoheleth" and name basic experiences of human life that are variously interpreted in 1:12—2:26 and 3:10—4:12.

As a leitmotif, 1:3 and 3:9 formulate the question of a possible "gain" (יִתְרוֹן *yitrôn*) that a man can achieve from all his "work and toil" (עָמָל *ʿāmāl*). Verse 1:3 raises this question concerning the totality of human efforts (בְּכָל-עֲמָלוֹ *běkol-ʿămālô*) with regard to the finitude of the individual person on the horizon of distant time(s) (עֹלָמִים / עוֹלָם *ʿôlāmîm/ʿôlām* 1:4-11). And 3:9 asks about the worker's "gain" from the effort he has applied (בַּאֲשֶׁר הוּא עָמֵל *baʾăšer hûʾ ʿāmēl*), in view of the time-bound nature and contingency of human activity within the individual life (עֵת *ʿēt*: 3:1-8). Thus "gain" (יִתְרוֹן *yitrôn*) designates both what remains in the end from all human

---

1   The following divisions are recommended in recent research: 1:12—3:15 (Lohfink, "Das Koheletbuch: Strukturen und Struktur," in Schwienhorst-Schönberger, ed., *Das Buch Kohelet,* 39–121; H.-P. Müller, "Theonome Skepsis und Lebensfreude: Zu Koh 1,12–3,15," *BZ* 30 [1986] 1–19); 1:2/3–3:15 (D. Michel, "Humintät angesichts des Absurden: Qohelet [Prediger] 1,2–3,15," in H. Foerster, ed., *Humintät Heute* [Berlin: Lutherisches Verlagshaus, 1970] 22–36; A. A. Fischer, "Beobachtungen zur Komposition von Kohelet 1,3–3,15," *ZAW* 103 [1991] 72–86; idem, *Skepsis,* 183–250); 1:2/3–3:22 (Eaton; Backhaus, *Zeit und Zufall,* 87–158; Schwienhorst-Schönberger, *Nicht im Menschen,* 12–125); 1:4–4:3 (D. Lys, "L'Etre et le Temps: Communication de Qohèleth," in Gilbert, eds., *Sagessse,* 249–58; idem, *L'Ecclésiaste ou Que vaut la vie? Traduction, Introduction générale, Commentaire de 1,1 à 4,3* [Paris: Letouzey et Ané, 1977]); 1:2/3–4:16 (G. R. Castellino, "Qohelet and His Wisdom," *CBQ* 30 [1968] 15–28; S. de Jong, "A Book on Labour: The Structuring Principles and the Main Themes of the Book of Qohelet," *JSOT* 54 [1992] 107–16, repr. in D. J. A. Clines, ed., *The Poetical Books: A Sheffield Reader* [BiSe 41; Sheffield: Sheffield Academic Press, 1997] 222–30; Seow); 1:12–6:9 (A. G. Wright, "The Riddle of the Sphinx: The Structure of the Book of Qoheleth," *CBQ* 30 [1968] 313–34, repr. in J. L. Crenshaw, ed., *Studies in Ancient Israelite Wisdom* [New York: Ktav, 1976] 245–66, repr. in R. B. Zuck, ed., *Reflecting with Solomon: Selected Studies on the Book of Ecclesiastes* [Grand Rapids: Baker, 1994] 45–65; idem, "The Riddle of the Sphinx Revisited: Numerical Patterns in the Book of Qoheleth," *CBQ* 42 [1980] 38–51; similarly J. S. M. Mulder, "Qoheleth's Division and Also Its Main Point," in W. C. Delsman and J. T. Nelis, eds., *Von Kanaan bis Kerala* [AOAT 211; Kevelaer: Butzon & Bercker; Neukirchen-Vluyn: Neukirchener Verlag, 1982] 149–59; S. G. Brown, "The Structure of Ecclesiastes," *Evangelical Quarterly Review* 14 [1990] 195–208). Cf. the concept and discussion of some recommendations in V. D'Alario, *Il libro del Qohelet: Struttura letteraria e retorica* (SRivB 27; Bologna: Dehoniane, 1992), 35–58; and Lohfink, "Koheletbuch." On the division proposed used here (1:3–4:12) cf. also T. Krüger, "Qoh 2,24-26 und die Frage nach dem 'Guten' im Qohelet-Buch," *BN* 72 (1994) 79ff., and most recently N. Kamano, "Character and Cosmology: Rhetoric of Qoh 1,3–3,9," in Schoors, ed., *Qohelet in Context,* 419–24 (1:3–3:9).

toil (1:3) and the return available to one through one's own efforts (3:9; cf. 2:11). In either case, 1:4-11 and 3:1-8 show that the human possibilities of "gain" vis-à-vis the experience of finitude and contingency are in both respects limited. The reflections of "King Qoheleth" in 1:12—2:26 and the reflections of the "wise man Qoheleth" in 3:10—4:12 present two possibilities for interpreting and overcoming these basic experiences:[2]

For "King Qoheleth" the possibility of being able to achieve a lasting and available "gain" is the criterion for the judgment of his experiences (cf. 1:3 before 1:4-11): if there is no gain, everything is meaningless and worthless (2:11). Then there is nothing good that a person could and should realize through his or her activity (2:24; cf. 2:3). Tangential to his reflections (1:13; 2:24, 26), "King Qoheleth" also draws God into his considerations—and makes God responsible for the bad (1:13) and nonsensical (2:24-26) sides of human life.

For the "wise man Qoheleth," by contrast, the experience of finitude and contingency is the criterion for answering the "gain" question (cf. 3:9 after 3:1-8). It is constitutive for his judgment of the experience of reality that it—together with the possibilities and limits of human activity contained in finitude and contingency—goes back to God, who made everything beautiful (3:11, 14-15). While "King Qoheleth" regards work and possessions (2:22-23), as well as pleasure and enjoyment (2:24-26), as worthless, for the "wise man Qoheleth" pleasure and enjoyment represent the highest and only good

(3:12-13). Since they can be bestowed on people only by God, they do not constitute a lasting "gain" (יִתְרוֹן yitrôn) at one's disposal, but are one's "portion" (חֵלֶק ḥēleq, 3:22), which is not at one's disposal. Work (4:4-6) and possessions (4:7-8) have a relative value when and to the extent that they enable a person to have pleasure and enjoyment. Different from the "king," the "wise man Qoheleth" regards human life not only from the egocentric perspective of the individual but also on the level of social life in community (3:16-21; 4:1-12). In this context, a common effort for a "good reward" (שָׂכָר טוֹב śākār ṭôb, 4:9) is better than egotistical striving for individual "gain."

If one understands "ethics" as a "theory of the human conduct of life,"[3] 1:3—4:12 can be characterized as a *discursive laying of the foundations of ethics*. Here it is specifically a matter of a "generally insightful answer to the question, in what does the good life or the highest good that human beings can realize through their actions actually consist"[4] (cf. 2:3, 24; 3:12-13, 22; 4:9). In the refinement of the ethical question to the problem of the achievability of *self*-determined goals and purposes of the *individual* person (the "gain" question), the book of Qoheleth adopts the basic initiative of contemporary Hellenistic philosophy.[5] In the critique of its development by the "king" (1:12—2:26) in 3:10—4:12, this individualistic narrowing of ethics in the sense of the Hellenistic zeitgeist is overcome in the critical reception of Old Testament traditions.

---

2   Cf. esp. 1:3 with 2:11; 1:10 with 2:12; 1:11 with 2:16, as well as 3:1-8 with 3:11a; then 1:8 with 3:11b; 1:9-10 with 3:15, as well as 3:9 with 4:6, 8-9 (with a significant terminological difference between "gain" [יִתְרוֹן yitrôn] and "wage" [שָׂכָר śākār]!).

3   Thus the definition of "ethics" in Trutz Rendtorff, *Ethik: Grundelemente, Methodologie und Konkretionen einer ethischen Theologie,* vol. 1 (ThW 13/1; Stuttgart: Kohlhammer, 1980) 11. ET=*Ethics,* trans. K. Crim (Philadelphia: Fortress Press, 1986).

4   This is a characteristic of "ethics as a philosophical discipline," according to Jan Rohls, *Geschichte der Ethik* (Tübingen: Mohr, 1991) 2.

5   Cf. Hossenfelder, *Philosophie,* 23ff., and below on 1:12—2:26.

1

Is There Any Gain with Regard to Eternity?

3   What does a man gain from[a] all his work and toil[b] under the sun?

4   A generation goes, and a generation comes,
and the earth remains constant into distant time.

5   The sun comes up[a] and the sun goes down,
and hurries to the[b] place[c] where it comes up (again).

6   It blows to the south, and turns to the north;
it turns, it turns, it blows, the wind,
and because it turns, it returns,[a] the wind.

7   All streams run to the sea,
and the sea is not full;[a]
to the place where the streams flow,
there they flow again and again.[b]

8   All words[a] are wearisome,[b]
no one is able to speak;[c]
the eye is not satisfied with seeing,[d]
and the ear is not full with hearing.

9   What has happened[a] (once) is what will happen (again),
and what has been done (once) is what will be done (again).
And there is nothing fully new[b] under the sun.

10   One may well say,[a]
"Look at this! This is something new!"
It has long since already existed,
in the distant times
that were before us.[b]

11   There is no remembrance of people of long ago,
nor will there be any remembrance
of people yet to come
by those who come last.[a]

3a   Thus with interpretation of the preposition בְּ *b-* in בְּכָל־עֲמָלוֹ *bĕkol-ʿămālô* as *beth pretii;* cf. E. Jenni, *Die hebräischen Präpositionen,* vol. 1: *Die Präposition Beth* (Stuttgart: Kohlhammer, 1992) 150ff., esp. 156, no. 1856 on Qoh 2:22; 3:9; 4:9; 9:9. Other possible translations: "what gain has a man (achieved) *in* all his work and toil" (thus Jenni, ibid. 345, no. 442, on Qoh 1:3), or: "what gain has a man (achieved) *through* all his work and toil" (*beth constitutionis;* cf. Jenni, ibid., 90ff., esp. 93; on the syntactic structure cf. Prov 15:23 [Jenni, ibid., 93, no. 1395]).

3b   Literally: "from all his work/toil with which he toils."

5a   In view of the participles predominant in vv. 4-7 a correction of the vocalization of the verb וזרח *wzrḥ* from וְזָרַח *wĕzāraḥ* to וְזֹרֵחַ *wĕzōrēaḥ* is suggested (see *BHK*); the assumption of a consonant metathesis (וזרח *wzrḥ* < זורח* *zwrḥ, thus *BHS*) is unnecessary. If, however, one vocalizes וזרח *wzrḥ* with 𝔐 as *wĕqātal* (with perfect meaning, as often in the book of Qoheleth), the following verb ובא *wbʾ* should also be read as *wĕqātal* (thus Lohfink, "Die Wiederkehr des immer Gleichen," *AF* 53 [1985] 128) and translated: "the sun came up and the sun went down . . ."

5b   Literally: "its."

5c   Contra the Masoretic accents, שׁוֹאֵף *šôʾēp* could be bound to the preceding וְאֶל־מְקוֹמוֹ *wĕʾel-mĕqômô* (see *BHK; BHS*).

6a   Or: "and returns to its turning" (cf. 𝔙: et in circulos suos revertitur); cf. Schoors, *Preacher,* 201.

7a   Or: "is not (yet) full."

7b   Or: "continually." The understanding of v. 7b is disputed; cf., e.g., Ellermeier, *Qohelet,* I/1, 195ff.; P. J. Holzer, "Die Mensch und das Weltgeschehen nach Koh. 1,4-11: Eine Textanalyse" (Th.D. diss., Univ. of Regensburg, 1981) 263ff.; Y.-J. Min, "How Do the Rivers Flow? (Ecclesiastes 1.7)," *BT* 42 (1991) 226–31. The above recommended translation assumes that שׁוב *šwb* + לְ *l-* + inf. cs. here means "do something again" (cf. GKC §120 and Qoh 5:14). Other possible translations: "to the place where the streams rise, there they return again in order to rise again" (= circulating water system; cf. 𝔙) or: "to the place where the streams flow, there they return to flow (anew)" (= intermittently flowing waters; cf. 𝔊).

8a   Or: "things," but see the commentary below.

8b   Or: "are exhausted."

8c   The conjecture לֹא־יְכַלֶּה *lōʾ-yĕkalleh* for לֹא־יוּכַל *lōʾ-yûkal* is arbitrary (see *BHS*; cf. Galling: "no one can 'definitively say' something"; lit.: "no one stops [or finishes] talking").

8d   On the problems of the usual German translation of the OT singular usage שָׂבַע *śbʿ* + לְ *l-* + inf. cs. (רָאָה *rʾh*) with "satt werden *zu* sehen" see Backhaus, *Zeit und Zufall,* 15.

9a   On the construction see, e.g., GKC §137c; Schoors, *Preacher,* 59–60; cf. 3:15, 22; 6:10; 7:24; 8:7; 10:14.

9b   The expression אֵין כָּל־חָדָשׁ *ʾên kol-ḥādāš* is ambiguous: depending on whether one combines כָּל *kol* more closely with אֵין *ʾên* or with חָדָשׁ *ḥādāš,* one can translate: "there is *absolutely* nothing new" or "there is nothing *completely* new." The Masoretic accents point more to the second understanding, which better corresponds to the context. That there is something like "new" grain (Lev 26:10), a "new" house (Deut 20:5), a "new" king (Exod 1:8), or even a "new" wife (Deut 24:5) is hardly to be disputed (further examples in C. Westermann, "חָדָשׁ ḥādāš new," *TLOT* 1:394–95; R. North, "חָדָשׁ ḥādāš," *TDOT* 4:243; 778). All of that, however, is nothing *fully* (of a) new (kind)"—as would be, say, a "new" covenant (Jer 31:31).

10a Literally: "There is a case in which someone says" or "a matter about which one says," or "There is a word that says."

10b On the incongruence between עֹלָמִים ʿōlāmîm (pl.) and הָיָה hāyâ (sg.) that results from this understanding of the sentence, cf. GKC §145a; Schoors, *Preacher*, 22–23, 157–58. The emendation to הָיוּ hāyû following some mss. is not necessary. Against

the alternative translation ventured by Lohfink: "But for ages there has already existed what has happened before our eyes," is that מִלִּפְנֵי millipnê (מִלְּפָנֵנוּ millĕpānênû) seems to contain an element of distancing ("away from"). Michel's present-tense translation of הָיָה hāyâ ("what happens before our eyes") is hardly tenable.

11a The expressions (הָ)רִאשֹׁנִים (hā)riʾšōnîm and (הָ)אַחֲרֹנִים (hā)ʾaḥărōnîm can designate both "the earlier" and "the later" (things, people, generations) and "the first" and "the last." לָאַחֲרֹנָה lāʾaḥărōnâ is found elsewhere in the OT only in Num 2:31 in the sense of "last" (cf., however, also בָּאַחֲרֹנָה bāʾaḥărōnâ in Deut 13:10; 17:7; 1 Sam 29:2; 2 Sam 2:26; 1 Kgs 17:13; Dan 8:3). On the preposition עִם ʿim (translated here with "by") cf. Schoors, *Preacher*, 201–2.

The section 1:3-11 is a poetically stylized[1] prelude that, with the "gain" question in v. 3 and the following statements about the position of individual people in the world, calls attention to the statement of the problem in the first major division of the book of Qoheleth (1:3–4:12). The key word הֶבֶל *hebel* from the motto in 1:2 is not taken up here. Verses 3-11 clearly assert only the transitoriness of all human beings (but not of humankind: v. 4). Moreover, it becomes clear that any possible "gain" achieved by individual people is likewise transitory (v. 11). By contrast, it is still an open question here whether in view of these experiences "everything" becomes meaningless, or whether it is an attitude toward life primarily oriented toward achieving a "gain" that proves to be nonsensical. "King Qoheleth" will draw the first conclusion in 1:12–2:26, but the "wise man Qoheleth" will vote for the second one in 3:10–4:12.

Initially the text shows no clear disposition. Each verse contains a relatively closed unit of meaning.[2]

As a question, v. 3 is different from the following statements. Verses 4-7 are bound together by the almost totally pervasive formulation of participial clauses, as well as the recurrence of a series of key words:

- הלך *hlk* (v. 4: "go"; v. 6: "blow" [2x]; v. 7: "flow" [3x])
- בוא *bwʾ* (v. 4: "come"; v. 5: "go down")
- שוב *šwb* (v. 6: "returns"; v. 7: "doing something again/continually"; cf. the similar sounding verbs שָׁאַף *šʾp*, "long for, strive" [v. 5] and סבב *sbb*, "turn" [v. 6 (3x)])
- מָקוֹם *māqôm*, "place" (vv. 5, 7)
- שָׁם *šām*, "where" (vv. 5, 7)

In syntactical construction, v. 8 corresponds initially to v. 7 (כֹּל *kōl*, "all," + determinative m. sg. noun + m. pl. participle; cf. also וְלֹא־תִמָּלֵא *wĕlōʾ-timmālēʾ* "is not full," in v. 8 with אֵינֶנּוּ מָלֵא *ʾênennû mālēʾ*, "is not full," in v. 7) but

---

1 With the exception of v. 3 and v. 10, Qoh 1:3-11 contains more or less clear (synonymous, antithetical, or synthetical) parallelisms. On the "poetic analysis" of the text, see Backhaus, *Zeit und Zufall*, 8ff.

2 Yet at first glance the transitions are often not clearly marked. Thus, v. 6aα, for example, can be read at first as a continuation of v. 5bβ: the sun comes up and goes to the south. Only with v. 6aβ does it become clear that the topic can no longer be the sun (cf. S. Japhet, "Goes to the South and Turns to the North' [Ecclesiastes 1:6]: The Sources

and History of the Exegetical Traditions," *JSQ* 1 [1993/94] 289–322). Verse 8aα can be understood initially as a statement about "all things" that continues the preceding thought (cf. v. 7: "All streams . . ."). Only with v. 8aβ is it clear that the subject is not humankind and language. The end of the "quotation" in v. 10a is not expressly marked. The reader must recognize that it is contradicted in v. 10b. Cf. E. M. Good, "The Unfilled Sea: Style and Meaning in Ecclesiastes 1:2-11," in J. G. Gammie et al., eds., *Israelite Wisdom* (SBLHS 3; Missoula, Mont.: Scholars Press, 1978) 59–73.

then changes over to formulations with negated *yiqtōl* forms. In terms of content, the descriptive statements about experienced reality are replaced, beginning in v. 8, by statements about their knowability and nameability . With three statements, v. 9 draws a conclusion from what has gone before. Here the beginning (מַה *mah*, "what") and end (תַּחַת הַשֶּׁמֶשׁ *taḥat haššemeš*, "under the sun") of this verse correspond to the beginning and end of v. 3. Verse 10a formulates both an objection to v. 9 (taking up the key word חָדָשׁ *ḥādāš*, "new"; יֵשׁ *yēš*, "there is" vs. אֵין *ʾên*, "there is not") and an illustration of v. 8 (picking up the key words דָּבָר *dābār*, "word," and ראה *rʾh*, "see"; cf. also אמר *ʾmr*, "say," in v. 10a with דבר *dbr*, "speak," in v. 8). By contrast, v. 10b reinforces the assertion of v. 9 (each twice הָיָה *hyh*, "to be"). Verse 11 makes clear both the reason for the objection formulated in v. 10a and—referring back to v. 8 and v. 9—its questionableness. (Syntactically v. 11, with אֵין זִכְרוֹן *ʾên zikrôn*, "there is no remembrance," refers back to v. 9 [אֵין כָּל־חָדָשׁ *ʾên kol-ḥādāš*, "there is nothing fully new"] and with לֹא־יִהְיֶה *lōʾ-yihyeh*, "there will be no," back to v. 8 לֹא־יוּכַל *lōʾ-yûkal* . . . לֹא־תִשְׂבַּע *lōʾ-tiśbaʿ* . . . וְלֹא־תִמָּלֵא *wĕlōʾ-timmāleh* . . . , "cannot . . . is not satisfied . . . is not full . . .") In the sequence of "people of long ago," "people yet to come," and "those who come last," v. 11 recalls the passing of generations mentioned in v. 4a. Verse 11a (אֵין זִכְרוֹן לָרִאשֹׁנִים *ʾên zikrôn lāriʾšōnîm*, "there is no remembrance of people of long ago") brings to mind the beginning of v. 3 (מַה־יִּתְרוֹן לָאָדָם *mah-yitrôn lāʾādām*, "what does a man gain").

The argumentative structure of 1:3-11 can be sketched as follows:

3   Question
4-8   Description of individual phenomena
9   General assertion (as summary or conclusion)
10-11 Discussion (objection and refutation)

■ **3** The question formulated in v. 3 regarding a possible "gain" (יִתְרוֹן *yitrôn*)[3] for human beings in view of the totality of their toil[4] "under the sun" is not expressly answered in vv. 4-11. (The noun יִתְרוֹן *yitrôn* does not reappear until 2:11.) Nonetheless, a partial answer to this question can be derived a fortiori from v. 11: if in the long view there will no longer be any remembrance (זִכְרוֹן / זִכָּרוֹן *zikrôn/zikkārôn*[5]) of a person,[6] then the duration of any possible other gain from human endeavors must, in any case, be all the more limited (מַה־יִּתְרוֹן *ma-yitrôn?* – אֵין זִכְרוֹן *ʾên zikrôn!*). The end of the remembrance of a man also brings the end of any other gain that he can achieve through work and toil (as long as one does not include the possibility of an "otherworldly" or "eschatological gain"—against such expectations, cf. 3:16-22).

■ **4** Verse 4a names a basic presupposition of this train of thought: in the sequence of generations[7] the individual person is transitory. Therefore, one can ask about gain in regard to the *totality* of his toil under the sun (when he "goes," that is, dies; cf. 5:15; 6:4). Against the transitoriness of individual human generations v. 4b sets

---

3   In the OT the noun יִתְרוֹן *yitrôn*, "gain," is attested only in Qoheleth. As a nominal formation of the verb יתר *ytr* (niphal: "be left over, remain left over"; hiphil: "leave over, have left, have a surplus, have an advantage"), it means, say, "gain, yield, advantage" (cf. יֶתֶר *yeter* II, "what is left over, remainder, surplus," and יוֹתֵר *yôtēr*, "what is left over, what is too much"). יִתְרוֹן *yitrôn* "is possibly an expression of mercantile language (Gordis according to Plumptre) and designates the 'surplus, gain' of a business" (Zimmerli). On the difference between יִתְרוֹן *yitrôn*, "gain," and חֵלֶק *ḥēleq*, "portion," see below on 2:11.

4   "The basic meaning of ʿāmāl can be summarized as follows: ʿāmāl indicates primarily the process of work . . . and the trouble that it causes . . . then the result of work: either the gain, property for which one has worked . . . or the distress, the suffering

one causes others . . ." (S. Schwertner, עָמָל *ʿāmāl* toil," *TLOT* 2:925).

5   In view of the following זִכָּרוֹן *zikkārôn* in v. 11b, זִכְרוֹן *zikrôn* in v. 11a (and 2:16) could be a construct form. In view of the numerous nouns of the formation *qitlōn* in the book of Qoheleth, however, we seem to have here, instead, alternate vocalizations of the absolute state. Cf. Schoors, *Preacher*, 63.

6   Cf., by contrast, the evaluation of posthumous reputation, e.g., in Prov 10:7; 22:1; Ps 112:6; Sir 37:26; 41:11, as well as Isa 56:5.

7   On the critique of the interpretation of דּוֹר *dôr* as the "circular motion" of nature (G. S. Ogden, "The Interpretation of *dwr* in Ecclesiastes 1.4," *JSOT* 34 [1986] 91–92), see M. V. Fox, "Qoheleth 1.4," *JSOT* 40 (1988) 109.

the constancy of the earth "into distant time" (לְעוֹלָם *lĕʿôlām*). The juxtaposition of human generations and the earth in v. 4a and b shows two ways of viewing the immeasurable duration of time (which in Hebrew can be indicated both by דוֹר . . . וְדוֹר *dôr . . . wĕdôr* and by עוֹלָם *ʿôlām*[8]): while humankind endures through the change of generations, the earth remains the same.

■ **5** A third way is demonstrated by v. 5, which probably has an underlying conception of an orbit of the sun. It travels half the time (during the day) over the earth and half (at night) under it:[9] the constant, uniform movement of an identical entity.

■ **6** In contrast to this, the wind is in (constant?) irregular motion.[10] Here there is "nothing permanent but the fluctuation" (Delitzsch). Since the wind turns again and again, it also blows repeatedly in the same direction (and one may ask whether it is always the same wind that blows to the south or to the north).[11]

■ **7** Like v. 4, v. 7a also formulates a contrast: the rivers, which like human generations are in constant movement (cf. the use of the verb הלך *hlk* in both cases), contrasts with the sea as a tranquil point of reference (in correspondence to the earth in v. 4).[12] If the translation of v. 7b preferred above is correct, the rivers also agree with human generations in that they (in contrast to the sun and the wind) do not "return" but constantly flow off in the same direction.[13]

■ **4-7** The comment that the sea does not get full(er), in spite of the rivers emptying into it, makes clear that the flowing of rivers into the sea is a goal-directed process but not one that aims at "efficiency." In retrospect, the reader can also make the same comment on the processes described in vv. 4-6: through their various behaviors, the earth, the sun, the wind, and the rivers produce no gain (and do not even seem to be trying to do so).[14] Precisely this—along with the constant repetition of the same things in the world (cf. vv. 9-10)—seems to be the point of vv. 4-7. From the text we may draw neither the assertion of the unchanging (and unchangeable) nature of the world (so Lauha: "Everything is and

8   On דוֹר *dôr* as a time concept, cf. G. Gerleman, "דוֹר *dōr* generation," *TLOT* 1:334; on עוֹלָם *ʿôlām* E. Jenni, "עוֹלָם *ʿôlām* eternity," *TLOT* 2:852–62; H. D. Preuss, "עוֹלָם *ʿôlām*," *TDOT* 10:530–45.

9   On ancient Near Eastern conceptions of the sun's path, cf. Bernd Janowski, *Rettungsgewissheit und Epiphanie des Heils,* vol. 1 (WMANT 59; Neukirchen-Vluyn: Neukirchener Verlag, 1989) (see index, 207, s.v. "Sonnenlauf"). Cf., e.g., the Egyptian picture in Othmar Keel, *The Symbolism of the Biblical World: Ancient Near Eastern Iconography and the Book of Psalms* (New York: Seabury, 1978) 32 no. 26, with the statement: "The majesty of this god [the sun god] enters the world of the dead through her [the goddess of heaven Nut's] mouth. The world of the dead is open when he enters into it. The stars follow him into her and come out again after him, and they hasten to their place."

10   Contra, e.g., Lohfink, "Wiederkehr," 137, and R. N. Whybray, "Ecclesiastes 1.5-7 and the Wonders of Nature," *JSOT* 41 (1988) 108, who also assume a circulation orbit here. According to Qoh 11:5, however, the turning of the wind is unpredictable and incalculable.

11   "South" and "north" here do not have to be the only possible or discernible wind directions. They complete the four cardinal directions after the course of the sun from east to west represented in v. 5. Thus the attempts by Paul Humbert, *Recherches sur les sources égyptiennes de la littérature sapientiale d'Israël*

(Neuchâtel: Secrétariat de l'Université, 1929) 113, on the one hand, and by Hertzberg, 71, on the other, to reconstruct a place of origin of the book of Qoheleth based on this passage are problematic.

12   Corresponding points of reference for the movements of the sun and the wind in vv. 5-6 were the "place" of the sun's rising and the cardinal directions "south" and "north."

13   Here the identity of the rivers does not seem to be problematic in the same way as in the famous dictum of Heraclitus (DK 22, B 91): "It is impossible to step into the same river twice" (ποταμῷ γὰρ οὐκ ἔστιν ἐμβῆναι δὶς τῷ αὐτῷ): Jaap Mansfeld, ed., *Die Vorsokratiker* I (Stuttgart: Reclam, 1983) 272–73, no. 96.

14   See the comparison of the "flow of capital" with the flow of rivers in Aristophanes' *Clouds*: The debtor Strepsiades says to a creditor: "And how can the sea not grow at all, you moron, in spite of all the streams that empty into it; but you demand that your capital increase?" (1293ff.). Cf. Dialogue 1279ff.: "(Strepsiades:) What do you think? Does it always rain new water whenever it rains, or does the sun repeatedly scoop up the same water? (Amynias:) I don't know. It's all the same to me. (Strepsiades:) And you have the audacity to demand your money back, yet you have no inkling about heavenly things?" (based on Aristophanes, *Die Wolken* [trans. Otto Seel; Stuttgart: Reclam, 1963] 80–81) (cf. Braun, *Kohelet,* 59).

remains as before . . .") nor the assumption of eternal nature of everything that is[15] or a "cyclic theory" of the cosmos (Lohfink). The commonalities and differences between human generations, earth, sun, wind, and rivers make clear that the text "assumes a structural but not an individual sameness in the passage of time."[16]

■ **8** Accordingly, v. 8 returns to the "gain" question of v. 3 (יְגֵעִים yĕgēʿîm, "are wearisome,"[17] takes up עָמָל ʿāmāl / עמל ʿml, "work/toil," again; אִישׁ ʾîš, "human being, man," takes up אָדָם ʾādām, "human being") and, after consideration of the cosmological entities earth, sun, wind, and rivers/sea (vv. 4b-7), focuses attention again on humankind (v. 4a).[18] Its position in the cosmos is most comparable to that of rivers.[19] The fact that neither people nor rivers ever achieve a final goal or result is demonstrated by v. 8 in an area in which human beings would seem at first glance to be different from the rest of the world: their ability to speak and know. Because the words of human language cannot do justice to the complexity of experienced reality (that may be meant by the metaphorical way of saying that they are "wearisome" or "exhausted"),[20] no one can successfully speak[21] (v. 8a). And because the human perception of reality can never be finally "satisfied" or "filled," the empirical possibilities of human knowledge are limited[22] (v. 8b). Thus even when people seem to stand over against the world, there too they are part of the world (cf. v. 3: "under the sun").

■ **9** That observation allows an extrapolation from the ongoing repetition of like things that can be experi-

---

15 Lohfink, "Wiederkehr," 143.

16 Otto Kaiser, "Schicksal, Leid und Gott: Ein Gespräch mit dem Kohelet, Prediger Salomo," in M. Oeming and A. Graupner, eds., *Altes Testament und christliche Verkündigung: FS Antonius H. J. Gunneweg* (Stuttgart: Kohlhammer, 1987) 30–51, here 38.

17 The verbal adjective יָגֵעַ yāgēaʿ (cf. Deut 25:18; 2 Sam 17:2; Sir 11:11) is intransitive. That makes it difficult to translate: "all things are wearisome" (i.e., for human beings; thus Backhaus, *Zeit und Zufall*, 426). Backhaus's auxilliary construction, that in terms of content יְגֵעִים yĕgēʿîm in Qoh 1:8 "in intransitive use expresses an effect on a person in a qualifying way" (ibid., 38), is hardly convincing.

18 Initially, כָּל־הַדְּבָרִים kol-haddĕbārim could be understood as a comprehensive expression for the phenomena described in vv. 4-7: "all things" (thus 𝔅 and, e.g., Whybray, "Ecclesiastes 1.5-7," 107). Yet vv. 4-7 contain no indication that they are "wearisome" or "exhausted" (יְגֵעִים yĕgēʿîm). Moreover, as v. 8 continues, it is clear that the topic here is human beings and their speaking and knowing capabilities. This suggests interpreting כָּל־הַדְּבָרִים kol-haddĕbārîm as "all words" of which people make use in "speaking" (לְדַבֵּר lĕdabbēr).

19 Cf. v. 8aα (כָּל־הַדְּבָרִים יְגֵעִים kol-haddĕbārim yĕgēʿîm) with v. 7aα (כָּל־הַנְּחָלִים הֹלְכִים kol-hannĕḥālîm hōlĕkîm) and v. 8bβ (לֹא־תִמָּלֵא lōʾ-timmālēʾ) with v. 7aβ (אֵינֶנּוּ מָלֵא ʾênennû mālēʾ).

20 These limits on the possibilities of human speech are vividly illustrated by vv. 4-7: here we see the variational breadth of meaning of identical expressions, which comes to light in the translation. Thus בוא bwʾ in v. 4 means "come" in the sense of "appear, be born," but in v. 5 "go down." In v. 4 הלך hlk means the "going" (= "dying") of a human gener-

ation; in v. 6 it means the "blowing" of the wind and in v. 7 the "flowing" of the river. In v. 6 שוב šwb means "turn around, return," but in v. 7 "do something again." The variety of meanings in the language is further illustrated in v. 7 and in v. 8 itself by the ambiguous expression כָּל־הַדְּבָרִים kol-haddĕbārîm. The ambiguity of "words" is reflected in Stoic language theory; cf. the discourse in Diogenes Laertius 7.62: "Ambiguous is an expression that means two or more things, taken literally and actually and according to linguistic usage. Hence we may understand more than one thing by this expression. Thus the words Αὐλητρὶς πέπτωκε mean, first, 'the farm has fallen three times' and, second, 'the flute player has fallen.'" (The understanding varies according to the separation of the words: Αὐλη τρὶς πέπτωκε or Αὐλητρὶς πέπτωκε.) Cf. John G. Gammie, "Stoicism and Anti-Stoicism in Qoheleth," *HAR* 9 (1985) 178.

21 The verb יכל ykl "be able" can be used in the sense "be able to do something successfully," "be equal or superior to someone," and "be able to grasp or understand something" (cf. Ps 139:6). Verse 8aβ recalls the "catchword" of "incapability of speech" (ἀφασία) in Pyrrhonist skepticism (cf. Hossenfelder, *Philosophie*, 147ff.). Verse 10 shows, however, that this incapability of speech here is not meant to be absolute, as with the Pyrrhonists, but *relative*.

22 The problem of the origin of knowledge from the perceptions of the senses is especially considered in Stoic epistemological theory; cf. Hossenfelder, *Philosophie*, 69ff. Qoheleth 1:8 speaks against the assumption that the book of Qoheleth represents an "essentially empirical methodology" (thus Fox, *Qohelet*, 80; cf. 79ff. and idem, "Qohelet's Epistemology," *HUCA* 58 [1987] 137–55).

enced in the cosmological realm of events (היה *hyh*) to a corresponding repetition of like things in the anthropological realm of human activities (עשה *ʿśh*), which we find in v. 9. In both cases, therefore, there can be "nothing fully new" (חָדָשׁ *ḥādāš*). In any case, this places limits on the possibilities of human "gain": there is no way that a man, through his own efforts, can produce something that has never existed. Thus when "King Qoheleth," nonetheless, asserts this of himself (cf. 1:16; 2:9), he is deceiving himself. How such deceptions occur is shown by vv. 10-11.

■ **10** Verse 10a formulates an objection to the assertion in v. 9b: over and over, there are still events, conditions, and actions that are regarded and designated as "something new"! Verse 10b questions the correctness of such assertions by harking back to v. 9a and also indicating how such erroneous views come about: now and then similar things repeat themselves after long periods of time (לְעֹלָמִים *lĕʿōlāmîm*, "in distant times"). Such spans of time, however, cannot be surveyed by an individual generation (to say nothing of an individual person) in its own experience (cf. v. 4). It is dependent on remembering its predecessors[23] and their experiences.

■ **11** The next verse shows that this remembering has its limits.[24] Therefore, one can have the illusion of something "fully new." Here the knowledge-critical line of argumentation in v. 8 is resumed and taken further. The

questioning of any remembrance of "people of long ago" is perhaps just as extremely formulated as the assertion in v. 8 that no person is able to speak. Yet (הָ)רִאשֹׁנִים *(hā)riʾšōnîm* can also mean "the first ones." Then v. 11 would not question that there are memories of ancestors, but rather that such memories reach back to the beginning of history (cf. 3:11b). Likewise, just as in the present there is no remembrance of the (distant) past ("people of long ago") or the beginning of history ("the first ones"), at the end of history there will be no remembrance of "people yet to come" (from the standpoint of the present) "by those who come last" (עִם שֶׁיִּהְיוּ לָאַחֲרֹנָה *ʿim šeyyihyû lāʾaḥărōnâ*). In the present, one may well imagine a beginning and end of history, yet one can no longer remember a beginning, and an end is not expected in the foreseeable future. (The future between now and the "end" will last at least two generations!)[25] Qoheleth 3:11 will bring this state of affairs into focus (and substantiate it theologically). That in the end there will be no remembrance of those now living can be inferred all the more strongly from the lack of remembrance of "people yet to come." In the text it is highly effective that v. 11 does not mention the present, living generation at all. When, however, there is no remembrance (at least in the long term) of an individual, then there can, in any case, be no question of remembrance (זִכָּרוֹן / זִכְרוֹן *zikrôn/zikkārôn*) as a possible gain (יִתְרוֹן

---

23   Basically, the expressions רִאשֹׁנִים *riʾšōnîm* and אַחֲרֹנִים *ʾaḥărōnîm* in v. 11 can designate both "earlier" and "later" *people* (or generations) (thus, e.g., Gordis, Lohfink), as well as *things*, events, or times (thus, e.g., Galling, Lauha; Galling relates v. 11bβ again to people ["who will exist later"], whereas Lauha also interprets this expression in the sense of events ["There remains no memory of what was earlier, nor of what happened later. One does not remember it—nor what will happen last."]). Speaking for the translation preferred here is the fact that then "the content of v. 11 links back to v. 4, and in this way forms a frame" (Lohfink, 40), and that אַחֲרֹנִים *ʾaḥărōnîm* in 4:16 likewise designates people.

24   זִכָּרוֹן *zikkārôn*, like the Eng. "remembrance," can designate both something that reminds one of something or someone and the process of remembering (cf. W. Schottroff, "זכר *zkr* to remember," *TLOT* 1:383–84). Thus "remembrance" has an "objective" and a "subjective" dimension. Hence the text leaves open whether the lack of remembrance

results (only) from the later ones not being *able* to remember or (also) from their not *wanting* to remember.

25   Cf. the "eschatological *distant* expectation" in Psalm 102 and, on this text, Odil Hannes Steck, "Zu Eigenart und Herkunft von Psalm 102," *ZAW* 102 (1990) 357–72. (According to Steck, the text is to be dated in the beginning years of the Seleucid hegemony between 200/198 and 194 B.C.E.) Cf. also J. C. H. Lebram, "The Piety of the Jewish Apocalyptists," in David Hellholm, ed., *Apocalypticism in the Mediterranean World and the Near East* (Tübingen: Mohr, 1983) 173: "If . . . we wish to calculate the date when the Kingdom of God is expected to begin from the chronological indications in 4 Ezra, for example, we come up with dates which are generations away from the probable time at which the book was composed."

yitrôn) of human work and toil (v. 3; cf. 2:13-17; 9:5).

Verse 11 provides a first answer to the "gain" question of v. 3: in view of the transitoriness of the individual person, his or her "gain" possibilities "under the sun" are, in any case, limited. *If,* moreover, the world as a whole is also transitory, which v. 11 leaves open as a conceptual possibility (cf. 1:2), this would reduce human possibilities of "gain" all the more. The question of eternity or the finitude of the cosmos is, therefore, ethically irrelevant. In this sense 1:3-11 can be understood as a countermodel to contemporary, early Jewish conceptions of an "eschatological ethic."

■ **1:3-11** In the interpretation of 1:3-11 we must note that this is the prelude of a larger argumentative section (1:3–4:12). Thus at this stage we must leave open the question of how the states of affairs named here are to be evaluated and what consequences are to be drawn for the human conduct of life. In 1:12–2:26 and 3:10–4:12 various possibilities are presented for working through the experiences mentioned in 1:3-11 (and 3:1-9). Likewise left open in 1:3-11 is the question of how the experiences named here are to be presented in theological perspective. (Until now the discussion has still not mentioned God!) For example, can the limits of possible human knowledge named in v. 8 be overcome (at least a little bit) with divine help? And are there perhaps "over the sun," in the beyond or the eschaton (in spite of v. 11?), still possibilities of "gain" for human beings? These questions will be addressed and answered (negatively) by the theological reflections in 3:10-22.

In this connection, a deficit in substantiation that relates to the argumentation in 1:3-11, read for itself alone, is then also removed: the idea that not only in the cosmological but also in the anthropological realm there is "nothing fully new" (v. 9) is based here only on the fact that human beings are part of the world and not fundamentally different from the rest of the world (vv. 4-8). The limits of memory noted in v. 11 show how the illusion of something fully new can come about. In view of these limits, however, we also cannot exclude the possibility that one day there may actually have been something new (that is simply not remembered). This argumentative aporia is set aside in the theological argumentation of 3:10-15, in that both the repetition of the same kinds of things in the world (3:14-15) and the limits of the possibilities of human knowledge (3:11) are traced back to God.

The questioning of the experience of something "fully new under the sun" in 1:9 is often interpreted as "a mirror of the hopeless political and spiritual stagnation in Palestine in the Ptolemaic period" (Kroeber). As an assertion against appearance (v. 10), however, it seems to have time-critical dimensions.[26] It is more the reflection than the reflex of its time of origin. Hellenist rule and culture could be experienced as "something fully new" in the Palestine of the Ptolemaic period[27] and presented themselves as something "new" (and better than the "old"[28]). The quarrel over the proper reaction to these novelties ultimately led in Palestinian Judaism to civil war.[29] When on the level of "distant times" there is

---

26 Ptolemy V (204–180 B.C.E.) has himself worshiped as "a king like the Sun (or the sun god Re)" (Austin, *Hellenistic World,* 374 [no. 227]) and his image put on coins with a sun crown. Could a contemporary reader thus also associate "under the sun" with "under the rule of the Ptolemies"?

27 Cf. Otto Kaiser, "Die Sinnkrise bei Kohelet," in Kaiser, *Der Mensch unter dem Schicksal: Studien zur Geschichte, Theologie und Gegenwartsbedeutung der Weisheit* (BZAW 161; Berlin: de Gruyter, 1985) 101: "If one considers the time in which Qoheleth lived, one must wonder whether news especially of the military but also of the other accomplishments of Hellenistic civilization had not reached him in Jerusalem."

28 So reads, for example, a Ptolemy "service instruction" to an οἰκονόμος from the late 3d century B.C.E. (Austin, *Hellenistic World,* 429–34 [no. 256]: 432

[ll. 223ff.]): "Take especial care that no act of extortion or any other misdeed is committed. For everyone who lives in the country must clearly know and believe that all such acts have come to an end and that they have been delivered from the previous bad state of affairs, and that [nobody] is allowed to do what he wishes, [but] everything is arranged for the best." It is a question here of a "recurring profession by the royal administration" (Austin, ibid., 434 n. 20)!

29 In 2 Macc 4:10-11 the establishment of the "Greek way of life" (τὸν Ἑλληνικὸν χαρακτῆρα) in Jerusalem under Jason is characterized as the abolishing of the "traditional constitution" and the introduction of "new, unlawful practices" (καὶ τὰς μὲν νομίμους καταλύων πολιτείας παρανόμους ἐθισμοὺς ἐκαίνιζεν).

nothing "fully new" under the sun (v. 9b), then a view of the present as "progress" must appear just as questionable as its interpretation as "decline."[30] By contrast, the concept of an ongoing repetition of the same kinds of things in world history by no means excludes the possibility of the perception, as well as the expectation, of fundamental historical changes; it limits only the range of possible changes (v. 9a). Here lies a critical potential of the text both with regard to an attitude that adapts itself to the Hellenistic normality and in relation to positions that expect a fundamental change in the world.[31]

It is indeed "hardly conceivable that a Jewish theologian of the third century B.C.E. could support this thesis [Qoh 1:9] without a side glance at the contemporaneous historical ideas of postprophetic eschatology and apocalypticism."[32] Qoheleth 1:3-11 does not basically exclude the possibility of an end of the world (v. 11!—cf. esp. Isaiah 65–66) but rather an eschatological imminent expectation or expectations of something "fully new" *in* the world.[33] Above all, however, the text reveals strong reservations concerning the assumption that a person can still achieve some "gain" beyond the realm "under the sun": this may perhaps be possible for those who will be there at the end—yet those presently alive will already be long forgotten (v. 11).

The eschatology of Isaiah 65–66 is thus ethically neutralized by being pushed into the distant future.[34] The eschatological holy gifts given to the presently living "servants of Yahweh" under the presupposition of the near expectation of the end of the world (cf. Isa 65:20-25)— circumscribed in Isa 65:13 with the catchwords "eat," "drink," and "rejoice"!—become in the book of Qoheleth the highest and only good *in* life, *under* the sun, in view of the distance to a possible eschaton (cf. 3:12-13, 22; 5:17-19; 8:15; 9:7-10; 11:7-10). Therefore, the book of Qoheleth can forgo helpful constructions like a resurrection of the dead and a retribution in the beyond that make the longer time until the eschaton bearable (cf., e.g., Dan 12:1-3; *1 Enoch* 22).

---

30 The objection in v. 10a is meaningful against the background of both conceptions. It does not necessarily have to be an "objection of those who hold that the times are getting worse" (thus Lohfink with a view to 7:10). As conceptions of a world historical decline (to the "eschatological turning point"), cf., e.g., Dan 2; 7 and *1 Enoch* 80.

31 The former is contra Frank Crüsemann, "The Unchangeable World: The 'Crisis of Wisdom' in Koheleth," in Willy Schottroff and Wolfgang Stegemann, eds., *God of the Lowly: Socio-Historical Interpretations of the Bible* (Maryknoll, N.Y.: Orbis, 1984) 64. The latter is with Crüsemann, ibid.

32 Kaiser, "Sinnkrise," 100. Cf. T. Krüger, "Dekonstruktion und Rekonstruktion prophetischer Eschatologie in Qohelet-Buch," in A. A. Diesel et al., eds., *"Jedes Ding hat seine Zeit . . .": Studien zur israelitischen und altorientalischen Weisheit* (BZAW 241; Berlin: de Gruyter, 1996) 107–29, repr. in Krüger, *Kritische Weisheit,* 151–72.

33 On the former expectation see Isa 65:17, where the creation of "a new heaven and a new earth" (cf. 66:22) is announced by the ptc. בּוֹרֵא *bôrēʾ* as "immediate or very imminent" ("futurum instans"); see GKC §116p. Does Qoh 1:11 (אֵין זִכְרוֹן לָרִאשֹׁנִים *ʾên zikrôn lāriʾšônîm,* "there is no remembrance of the people of long ago") refer (ironically) to the terminology of Isa 65:17 (וְלֹא תִזָּכַרְנָה הָרִאשֹׁנוֹת *wĕlōʾ tizzākarnâ hāriʾšōnôt,* "the former things [heaven and earth] shall not be remembered")? Cf. also Isa 41:22-23, 26; 42:9; 43:9, 18-19; 44:7-8; 46:9-10; 48:1-11. On the latter expectation see, e.g., Ezek 11:19-20; 36:26-27 ("new heart," "new spirit"); Jer 31:31 ("new covenant"); Isa 62:2 ("new name"). In these passages the new does *not* "repeat the old . . . ancient pattern" (contra Lohfink, "Wiederkehr," 144).

34 If Isaiah 65–66 originated in the first third of the 3d century B.C.E., as Odil Hannes Steck assumes (*Der Abschluß der Prophetie im Alten Testament* [BThSt 17; Neukirchen-Vluyn: Neukirchener Verlag, 1991] 91ff., 197; cf. idem, *Studien zu Tritojesaja* [BZAW 203; Berlin: de Gruyter, 1991] 217ff., 248ff.), its eschatological near expectation had, at the time of the origination of the book of Qoheleth, already been taken *ad absurdum* by the progression of history; cf. the roughly contemporaneous *distant* expectation in Psalm 102 (see above), as well as the cultic-wisdom reception of prophetic-eschatological perspectives on salvation in the late psalms, which interpret everyday providence as the experience of the salvific presence of divine governance; see Pss 104:14-15, 27-28; 132:15; 136:25; 145:15-16; 146:7; 147:8-9, 14; and also Reinhard Gregor Kratz, "Die Gnade des täglichen Brots: Späte Psalmen auf dem Weg zum Vaterunser," *ZThK* 89 (1992) 1–40.

In its critical reservations against tendencies toward an eschatological re(!)orientation in contemporary Judaism, Qoh 1:3-11 has important traditions of the OT on its side. A comparable conception of the return of the same things in the cosmos is formulated in Gen 8:22:[35] "As long as the earth endures, cold and heat, summer and winter, day and night, shall not cease." A view of *history* as the repetition of similar processes is found especially in the so-called Deuteronomistic history (Deuteronomy–2 Kings), whose view of history remained effective into the time of origin of the book of Qoheleth and beyond.[36] In view of these tradition-historical relationships, one can hardly maintain that the book of Qoheleth shows "an unbridgeable distance from all the basic Yahwist traditions."[37]

Qoheleth 1:3-11 adds cosmological observations to the answering of the basic ethical question of a person's possibilities of "gain." This corresponds to the "common conviction of the Hellenistic age that the wise individual who understands the true structure of the universe is also the righteous."[38] Unlike, for example, Sir 16:24–17:14 and *1 Enoch* 2–5,[39] however, the cosmos does not function here basically as an ethical model for humankind. The view of earth, sun, wind, and rivers shows human beings not primarily how they should act, but what they as part of the cosmos can or cannot achieve through their actions. (In this way, then, the cosmos is again also a "model" for human beings as it takes their striving for "gain" *ad absurdum*.) In this ordering of "cosmology" and "ethics" one may forgo cosmological speculations that go beyond daily experience, as they are documented for contemporary Judaism, for example, in *1 Enoch* 17–36 and 72–82 (cf. Qoh 1:8).[40]

---

35 This text is compared with Qoh 1:3-11 by, e.g., C. C. Forman, "Koheleth's Use of Genesis," *JSS* 5 (1960) 256–57; and Kaiser, "Sinnkrise," 101. Cf. further Psalm 104, which, after the creation of the ordered cosmos by Yahweh (vv. 1-9), describes the return of similar things *in* this cosmos (vv. 10-30) and in v. 30b possibly translates (and thereby neutralizes) expectations of an "eschatological" re-creation into everyday experience; cf. Thomas Krüger, "'Kosmotheologie' zwischen Mythos und Erfahrung," *BN* 68 (1993) 72–73, repr. in Krüger, *Kritische Weisheit*, 118.

36 Cf. Klaus Koch, "Geschichte II: Altes Testament," *TRE* 12:580–81. "The principles according to which Yahweh shapes history through his word and subsequent reaction to human activity remain the same for all times [in the Deuteronomistic History]" (581). Cf. esp. Nehemiah 9; Dan 9:4-19; Bar 1:15–3:8; Tobit 13, and also Odil Hannes Steck, *Israel und das gewaltsame Geschick der Propheten: Untersuchungen zur Überlieferung des deuteronomistischen Geschichtsbildes im Alten Testament, Frühjudentum und Urchristentum* (WMANT 23; Neukirchen-Vluyn: Neukirchener Verlag, 1967) 113ff.

37 Thus Crüsemann, "Unchangeable World," 90.

38 J. J. Collins, "Cosmos and Salvation: Jewish Wisdom and Apocalyptic in the Hellenistic Age," *History of Religions* 17 (1977) 137.

39 Cf. here Lebram, "Piety," 188ff.

40 These Enochic texts show "that there existed in the third century B.C.E. broad areas of speculation of a pseudo-scientific kind in Judah and in Jewish circles . . . a rather sophisticated and rich realm of speculation and 'sacred science' within Judaism" (Michael E. Stone, *Scriptures, Sects, and Visions: A Profile of Judaism from Ezra to the Jewish Revolts* [Philadelphia: Fortress Press, 1980] 35; cf. 27ff.; idem, "The Book of Enoch and Judaism in the Third Century B.C.E.," *CBQ* 40 [1978] 479–92; idem, "Lists of Revealed Things in the Apocalyptic Literature," in Frank Moore Cross, Werner E. Lemke, and Patrick D. Miller, eds., *Magnalia Dei: The Mighty Acts of God: Essays on the Bible and Archaeology in Memory of G. E. Wright* [Garden City, N.Y.: Doubleday, 1976] 414–52).

1

The Devaluation of Happiness Not at One's Disposal

12 I, Qoheleth, became[a] king[b] over Israel in Jerusalem.

13 Then I intended[a] to research and find out[b] by wisdom all that was done[c] under heaven.[d] This is a bad business; God has left[e] it to people to be busy with. 14 I considered all the works that were done under the sun; and look, all this was futile and a striving after wind.

15 What is crooked cannot become straight,[a]
  and what is missing cannot be counted.

16 I thought:[a] look, now I am[b] greater and wiser than anyone who was (ruler) over[c] Jerusalem before me, and my heart has seen much wisdom and knowledge. 17 So I intended[a] to understand what wisdom is and to understand what blindness is and folly.[b] I understood that this also was a striving after wind.

18 For with much wisdom comes much vexation,
  and one who understands more has more to suffer.[a]

2:1 I thought:[a] Make a test of pleasure and enjoy something good! And see: this also was futile.

2 Of laughter I said: Foolish!
  And of pleasure: What can it accomplish?[a]

3 I tried[a] bathing[b] my body in wine—my mind still guiding me in[c] wisdom—and laying hold of folly, until I might see what[d] is good for people to do[e] under heaven[f] as long as they live.[g] 4 I accomplished great works:[a] I built myself houses; I planted vineyards for myself. 5 I made myself gardens and parks, and planted in them all kinds of fruit trees. 6 I made myself pools from which to water the forest full of sprouting trees. 7 I bought[a] male and female slaves, and had[b] [slaves] who were born in my house; I also had herds, cattle, and smaller stock, more than all who were before me in Jerusalem.[c] 8 I also gathered for myself silver and gold and the property of kings and of the provinces. I got singers, both men and women, and the highest desire of men: women and more women.[a] 9 So I became greater and richer than anyone

1:12a Or: "was" (הָיִיתִי *hāyîtî*); cf. 1 Sam 15:26; 2 Sam 2:11; 1 Kgs 11:37. Müller, "Skepsis," 3 assumes that the perfect here is "timeless ('am,' not 'was')," though one may also hear "a note of performatory meaning ('am now/herewith a king')"; cf. also Schoors, *Preacher*, 172–73.

12b Or (with the Masoretic accents): "I am Qoheleth. I was/became king."

13a Literally: "I devoted my heart/my mind to . . ."

13b Or: "to inquire about and to research wisdom in regard to everything . . ."? On the problem of the understanding of the prepositions בּ *b* and עַל *ʿal* cf. Schoors, *Preacher*, 198–99; Müller, "Skepsis," 3–4. In view of the performance report in v. 14, in which "all deeds that are done under the sun" are the object of investigation, the instrumental understanding of בְּחָכְמָה *baḥokmâ* in v. 13, which the textual variants in 𝔠 (where עַל *ʿal* is missing) and Or (אֶל *ʾel* instead of עַל *ʿal*) also presuppose, is to be preferred (cf. also Jenni, *Präpositionen*, 1:147, no. 1788).

13c The time reference of נַעֲשָׂה *naʿăśâ* depends on whether one interprets the form as participle or as perfect and whether, in the latter case (and with שֶׁנַּעֲשׂוּ *šennaʿăśû* in v. 14), one assumes as the point of reference of the anteriority the present time of the speech ("all the deeds that *were* done") or the time of the seeking and searching out ("all the deeds that *had been* done"). Cf. Schoors, *Preacher*, 96–97, 185–86.

13d Numerous Hebrew mss. and 𝔠 𝔖 𝔗 𝔙 read "under the sun."

13e Or: "allowed" or "commissioned" (lit.: "given"). On the construction (נתן *ntn* with לְ *l-* of the person and לְ *l-* with infinitive) cf. Esth 3:11; 8:11; 2 Chr 20:10. It would also be possible to connect נָתַן אֱלֹהִים *nātan ʾĕlōhîm* as an asyndetic relative clause with הוּא עִנְיַן רָע *hûʾ ʿinyan rāʿ* (cf. Qoh 2:26; 3:10): "It is a bad business that God has given human beings . . ." (cf. Schoors, *Preacher*, 210). By contrast, the translation in Lohfink (= *EÜ*: "to examine and to explore . . . whether all that is carried out under the heavens is really a bad business") is, from the standpoint of syntax, rather improbable.

15a A correction of לִתְקֹן *litqōn* ("be/become straight") to לְהִתָּקֵן *lĕhittāqēn* ("be made straight"[?], thus *BHS*) is not necessary.

16a Literally: "I said, I with my heart/mind."

16b The emphatically preposed אֲנִי *ʾănî* ("I") is lacking in 𝔠.

16c Numerous Hebrew mss., along with 𝔊 𝔖 Syh 𝔗 𝔏 𝔙, read "in Jerusalem" (cf. 2:7).

17a Literally: "I applied my mind." וָאֶתְּנָה *wāʾettĕnâ* is one of the rare narrative forms in the book of Qoheleth (cf. also 4:1, 7). See Schoors, *Preacher*, 86–88.

17b Thus according to the Masoretic accents. Another translation possibility: "to know (what) wisdom (is) and knowledge, blindness and folly" (thus 𝔊 𝔖 𝔙 𝔗). In contrast to this, the translation recommended by

who had been before me in Jerusalem. Also my wisdom remained with me. 10 Whatever my eyes desired I did not keep from them. I kept my heart from no pleasure. My heart rejoiced over all my possessions.[a] And this was my portion of all my possessions. 11 Yet when I considered all my works that my hands had done and the possessions that I had acquired through toil,[a] look: all this was futile and a striving after wind and no gain[b] under the sun.

12 So I turned to consider wisdom and blindness and folly. What (can) the man (still do) who comes after the king? What has already been done long ago![a]

13 And I saw that wisdom has an advantage over folly, as light has an advantage over darkness:

14 The wise man has eyes in his head,
　　but the fool walks in darkness.

Yet I understood (also) that the same fate befalls all of them. 15 And I thought: "What can happen to the fool can also happen to me; why then have I been so exceedingly wise? And I thought[a] that this also was futile.

16 For in the distant future the wise man will be remembered as little[a] as the fool. For in the days to come[b] both will be already forgotten. Alas, the wise man must die just like the fool! 17 So I[a] hated life, for the work that was done[b] under the sun seemed evil to me: it was all futile and a striving after wind.

18 And I hated all my possessions for which I had toiled under the sun, for I must leave it to the[a] man who comes after me. 19 And who knows whether he will be a wise man or a fool? And yet he will have at his command all of my possessions, for which I toiled and used my wisdom under the sun. This also is futile.

20 So I came to despair[a] over all my possessions, for which I had toiled under the sun.[b] 21 For a man comes to possessions with wisdom and insight and skill,[a] and then must leave it as inheritance to another man who has not worked for it. This also is futile and a great evil.

22 What then does a man have from all his work and the striving of his mind, with

Gordis and ventured by Michel as an alternative, "to know that wisdom and insight are folly and lack of understanding," is rather improbable. שִׂכְלוּת *siklût* here may be regarded as an orthographic variant of סִכְלוּת *siklût*, "folly" (cf. 2:3, 12, 13; 7:25; 10:1, 13) (thus numerous mss.; cf. Schoors, *Preacher*, 19). Contra 𝔊 (ἐπιστήμην) and, e.g., Galling ("understanding").

18a Literally: "for in a lot of wisdom (lies) much vexation, and if one increases knowledge, one increases suffering." 𝔊 reads "knowledge" (γνώσεως) instead of "vexation."

2:1a Literally: "I said, I in my heart/mind."

2a The book of Qoheleth uses as the feminine form of the demonstrative pronoun זֹה (זֹה *zōh*) instead of זֹאת *zōʾt* (זֹאת *zʾt*); cf. 2:24; 5:15, 18; 7:23; 9:13; and Schoors, *Preacher*, 52–53.

3a Literally: "I searched in/with my mind/heart" or "I searched my mind/heart."

3b Literally: "to draw my flesh through wine." The verb משׁךְ *mšk* is often understood in the sense of "refresh, give refreshment to." Yet here it may be a question of a drastic expression for excessive enjoyment, which is relativized by the following circumstantial clause; cf. Müller, "Skepsis," 6.

3c On the modalizing function of the preposition בּ *b-* cf. Jenni, *Präpositionen*, 1:329ff. (on Qoh 2:3: 336, no. 413).

3d On אֵי־זֶה *ʾê-zeh* as interrogative pronoun (in the sense of מָה *mâ*) cf. 11:6 and Schoors, *Preacher*, 57–58.

3e It would also be possible to interpret the אֲשֶׁר *ʾăšer* clause as a refinement of לִבְנֵי הָאָדָם *libnê hāʾādām*: ". . . for the people who do something. . . ."

3f Two Hebrew mss., as well as 𝔊 𝔖 Syh ℜ 𝔙, read "under the sun."

3g Literally: "the number of the days of their life."

4a Literally: "I made my works/deeds great."

7a Numerous Hebrew mss. and 𝔖 also read here "myself" (לִי *lî*).

7b Some Hebrew mss., 𝔊 and 𝔖 read instead of the sg. הָיָה *hāyâ* the pl. הָיוּ *hāyû*.

7c Numerous mss. and the versions read (in assimilation to 1:16 and 2:9) "than anyone who was before me in Jerusalem."

8a Literally: "a woman and women." The interpretation of the *hapax legomenon* שִׁדָּה וְשִׁדּוֹת *šiddâ wěšiddôt* is in dispute (cf. Whitley, *Koheleth*, 21–22; F. Ellermeier, "Der Harem Qohelet/Salomos—vorläufiges Warnsignal zu Qoh. 2,8," in Ellermeier, *Sibyllen-Musikanten-Haremsfrauen* [Theologische und orientalische Arbeiten 2; Herzberg: Jungfer, 1970] 22–27; E. Bons, "*šidda w[e]šiddōt*: Überlegungen zum Verständnis eines Hapaxlegomenons," *BN* 36 [1987] 12–16). The translation "woman (women)" is suggested by the context ("the greatest desire [lit.: "desires," probably an intensive plural] of men"), as well as by the Akk. *šaditum*,

57

which he toils under the sun, 23 if his whole life[a] consists only of suffering, and his toil only brings him vexation, and his heart cannot rest even at night? This also is futile.

24   Nothing good comes about through a man.[a] That he can eat and drink and allow himself something good[b] in all his toil—that also comes, as I saw, from the hand of the Deity.[c] 25 For who can eat and who must worry[a] except me[b]? 26 To a man who pleases him,[a] he gives wisdom and insight and pleasure, but the one whose life is a failure[b] he busies with gathering and heaping, in order to give it to a man who pleases the Deity.[c] This also is futile and a striving after wind.

Ugar. *št*, and Arab. *šitt*, "lady, woman" (cf. also Heb. שַׁד *šad*/שֹׁד *šōd*, "breast"). The ancient versions tone down the text (𝔊 "a cupbearer and female cupbearers" [οἰνοχόον καὶ οἰνοχόας], 𝔖 "cupbearers and female cupbearers" [ܐ̈ܩ̈ܬܫ ܘܐ̈ܩܬܫ *šqwtʾ wšqytʾ*], α' "a cup and cups" [κυλίκιον καὶ κυλίκια], 𝔙 "siphons and water pots" [*scyphos et urceros*], 𝔗 "baths and bathhouses with tubes that poured forth tepid water and tubes that poured forth warm water"; see Whitley, *Koheleth*, 21–22).

10a   On the construction (שׂמח *śmḥ* + מן *min*) cf. Prov 5:18. Or: "*after* all my toil" (cf. Jer 31:13)? עָמָל *ʿāmāl* can designate both the *process* and the *result* of the work (the latter meaning is clear in vv. 18ff.). The joining of "pleasure" and "work/possessions" through the preposition מן *min* is unique in the book of Qoheleth; otherwise it always talks of the pleasure and enjoyment of people *in* their work (בַּעֲמָלוֹ *baʿămālô*: 2:24; 5:18; 8:15; בְּכָל־עֲמָלוֹ *bĕkol-ʿămālô*: 3:13; 5:17; בְּמַעֲשָׂיו *bĕmaʿăśāyw*: 3:22). Some Hebrew mss. and ℭ also read here בְּכָל־עֲמָלִי *bĕkol-ʿămālî*.

11a   Literally: "that I had toiled to achieve," or "the work I expended in implementation."

11b   Or: "and there is no gain."

12a   Or (with numerous Hebrew mss.): "what the latter has already done long ago" (עָשָׂהוּ *ʿāśāhû* instead of עָשׂוּהוּ *ʿāśûhû*). Verse 12b is a *crux interpretum*. Cf., e.g., Schoors, *Preacher*, 156–57; D. Lys, *L'Ecclésiaste*, 230–37; Backhaus, *Zeit und Zufall*, 101–5; K. A. D. Smelik, "A Re-Interpretation of Ecclesiastes 2, 12b," in Schoors, ed., *Qohelet in Context*, 385–89. The versions already seem to be concerned with an interpretation of the MT. The interpretation recommended here and frequently found elsewhere assumes that between מֶה *meh* and הָאָדָם *hāʾādām* the verb יַעֲשֶׂה *yaʿăśeh* is tacitly to be added ("aposiopesis"; cf. GKC §167a). Other recommended translations include the following: "What kind of person will that be who comes after the king that they have already made [= instituted] long ago?" (where the last relative clause could refer to the king or his successor). "How is it with the person who will come after the king in regard to what one has already done long ago?" (Aalders) or ". . . compared with the one who was previously elected [= his predecessor]" (Elster).

15a   Literally: "I said in my heart/mind."

16a   On עִם *ʿim* = "like" cf. Schoors, *Preacher*, 201–2.

16b   On בְּ *b-* + שׁ *š-* = בְּ *b-* + אֲשֶׁר *ʾăšer* = "for, because," cf. Schoors, *Preacher*, 144; on כְּבָר *kĕbār* = "already" cf. ibid., 116–17. הַיָּמִים הַבָּאִים *hayyāmîm habbāʾîm* should be interpreted as temporal accusative (cf. ibid., 189).

17a   Several Hebrew mss., as well as 𝔊 and 𝔗, place after the verb an emphatic "I" (אֲנִי *ʾānî*).

17b   Literally: "the doing that was done."

18a   ₵ reads: "a."

20a   Literally: "and I (myself) turned and gave my heart/mind to despair. . . ."

20b   Numerous mss. and � add: "and had been wise" (cf. v. 19).

21a   Literally: "for there is a man whose possessions have come about through wisdom. . . ."

23a   Literally: "all his days."

24a   Thus with interpretation of the preposition בּ *b-* in בָּאָדָם *bāʾādām* as *beth constitutionis* for the announcement of the "cause in a statement of existence" (see Jenni, *Präpositionen*, 1:90ff., cf. Schoors, *Preacher*, 197; Krüger, "Qoh 2,24-26"). Other possible translations: "It does not come about through a man as something good that he eats and drinks and allows himself something good in all his work. Even that comes, as I myself saw, from the hand of the Deity." Or: "There is nothing good in a man who eats and drinks. . . ." Or: "It is not good for a man if [or: that] he eats and drinks. . . ." The versions try to eliminate the contradiction between 2:24 and the following positive statements in the book of Qoheleth about eating, drinking, and pleasure (cf. 3:12, 22; 5:17; 8:15). ℭ "There is nothing good for a man except that he eats and drinks . . ." (. . . ܐܠܐ ܐܝܬ ܠܓܒܪ *lyt dṭb lgbrʾ ʾlʾ dnʾkwl wdnštʾ*. . . ; cf. �). 𝔙 "Is it not better to eat and drink . . . ?!" ("nonne melius est comedere et bibere . . ."). ᵹ "There is nothing good in a man; what he eats and what he drinks and what he shows of his soul is something good in his toil," that is, good does not come out of a man but is given to him from outside [?] (οὐκ ἔστιν ἀγαθὸν ἐν ἀνθρώπῳ· ὃ φάγεται καὶ ὃ πίεται καὶ ὃ δείξει τῇ ψυχῇ αὐτοῦ, ἀγαθὸν ἐν μόχθῳ αὐτοῦ). ᵹ and 𝔙 advise against the usual correction of שֶׁיֹּאכַל *šeyyōʾkal* to מִשֶׁיֹּאכַל *miššeyyōʾkal* according to ᵹ and � (see *BHS*): "There is nothing 'better' with (or: 'for') a man, 'than' that he eats and drinks. . . ."

24b   Literally: "let his soul see/enjoy something good."

24c   Literally: "that also—I myself have seen that it comes from the hand of God."

25a   Or: "and who can enjoy . . ."? On the meaning of the verb חוש *ḥwš* cf. F. Ellermeier, "Das Verbum חוש in Koh. 2,25," *ZAW* 75 (1963) 197–217; idem, *Qohelet*, I/1, *Einzelfrage Nr. 7: Das Verbum חוש in Qoh. 2,25* (2d ed.; Herzberg: Juingfer, 1970); and, e.g., Murphy; Backhaus, *Zeit und Zufall*, 108ff. In view of the ancient versions (ᵹ, ϑʹ· πίεται; ℭ ܢܫܬܐ *nšth* = "drink"—𝔙 *deliciis affluet*—ᵹᴼ αʹ σʹ φείσεται; Jerome *parcet* = Heb. יָחוּס *yāḥûs* [or יָחֻש *yāḥuš*] "have worries"?) and the linguistic usage of the Mishnah (חוש *ḥwš* = "be worried, consider"), the translations "enjoy" or (better, in my view) "worry" are possible. In the former case v. 25 would pick up the theme "eating and drinking and allowing oneself something good" from v. 24a; in the latter case, this *and* the themes of "suffering" and "vexation" from vv. 22-23 would be taken up.

25b   Or: "without me"? Yet the term חוּץ מִן *ḥûṣ min,* which is attested only here in the OT but more often in the Mishnah, seems to mean not "without" but "except"; see GB, KBL, and *HALOT* s.v., contra, however, J. de Waard, "The Translator and Textual Criticism (with Particular Reference to Eccl 2,25)," *Bib* 60 (1979) 515–16 n. 16. Cf. the versions: ᵹ (πάρεξ αὐτοῦ = "except" or "contrary to"), Jerome (*sine illo*), 𝔙 (*ut ego*), ℭ (ܠܒܪ ܡܢܗ *lbr mnh = extra* or *praeter*), Syh (ܣܛܪ ܡܢܗ *str mnh = sine* or *praeter*), � (בר מנה *br mnh* = "without" or "except"), � ("without him"), see de Waard, "Translator," 513 and 515–16 n. 16. The suffix of the first-person sg. (מִמֶּנִּי *mimmenni*) is often (with some Hebrew mss., ᵹ � ℭ Syh Jer) corrected to third-person masc. sg. and related to God: "without him." Or holding to the MT as the word of God, the sentence is interpreted: "Who then can eat . . . without me."

26a   Or: "who is good before him."

26b   Or: "to the sinner."

26c   Or: "who is good before the Deity."

The section 1:12—2:26 has Qoheleth appear in the role of a "king over Israel in Jerusalem" (1:12). He reports in retrospect on a series of experiences and reflections that have brought him to the conviction that all striving for accomplishment, possessions, wisdom, and happiness are absurd, since human beings can achieve no "gain" through their actions (2:11). Work and rational reflection bring one only vexation and unrest (2:22-23). A "good life" is not achievable through one's own planned efforts; it can be given only by God (2:24). God, however, distributes happiness among people in a totally arbitrary manner, as it pleases him (2:26). So for individuals who want to shape their lives themselves with the cleverly calculated application of their powers, there is only despair (2:20) and hatred toward a life that does not fulfill their wishes (2:17).

The king's comments in 1:12—2:26 can be divided into three parts:

- In 1:12—2:11 he demonstrates the absurdity of striving for achievement, possessions, wisdom, and happiness in the context of human life. In so doing he repeatedly measures his own accomplishments against those of his predecessors (1:16; 2:7, 9).

- In 2:12-21 he includes death and its consequences in his reflections, and he now speaks often of his successors (2:12, 18-19, 21).
- In 2:22-26 he formulates the results of the foregoing comments: here the king generalizes his own experiences and reflections into statements about all people.

The conclusions of smaller sections of the text are marked by the stereotyped judgment "this also [or: all] is futile (and a striving after wind)" (1:14, 17; 2:1, 11, 15, 17, 19, 21, 23, 26), which is followed in 1:15, 18, and 2:1 by a proverbial sentence and in 2:11 by the statement that there is "no gain under the sun." In terms of content, in each of these sections one of the three following dimensions stands in the foreground:[1]

- Activity-work-possessions:[2] 1:13-15; 2:18-19, 20-21, 22-23
- Wisdom-knowledge[3] versus folly-blindness:[4] 1:16-18; 2:13-15, 16-17
- Pleasure-enjoyment:[5] 2:1-2, 24-26.

In 2:3-11 all three fields of activity are combined programmatically (cf. 2:3).

For the further argumentation of the book of Qoheleth, the conclusions of 1:12—2:26 remain as a demonstration of the fundamental limits of a person's power of disposition over his or her own life. Verses 3:10ff. show that these limits by no means necessarily have to drive one to despair.

1:12—2:11 Happiness in Life Is Not at One's Disposal

After his self-introduction in 1:12 the king reports in 1:13—2:11 on a series of undertakings and reflections that he had initiated and in which he repeatedly compares himself with his predecessors. In this process, activity (1:13-15), wisdom (1:16-18), and pleasure (2:1-2) prove equally to be "futile" and "a striving after wind." Thus, taken by themselves, they do not represent goals and purposes in life worth striving for. The following attempt to join together activity, wisdom, and pleasure (2:3-11) seems initially to lead to success (2:9-10). Yet the closing reflection shows that here too no "gain" was achieved (2:11).

Closer examination reveals that the king's argumentation is built on presuppositions that are not expressly formulated in the text but form the basis of his argumentative stringency. As soon as one exposes these—thoroughly questionable—presuppositions, it becomes clear that the king's conclusions are valid only in relation to certain basic assumptions. In this respect the king's comments reveal to a critical reader something more and different from what the king actually says.

The section 1:13-15 devalues human *activity*, because it is dependent on conditions that it can change only in limited ways, if at all (v. 15). Here it is presupposed that human beings will regard only the goals and purposes that they can achieve through their own efforts, reliably and without limitation, as worth striving for.

Unlike activity, *wisdom* in 1:16-18 does not seem to the king "a striving after wind" because its goals cannot be reached. According to 1:16, the king has achieved wisdom and knowledge in abundance and to a greater degree than all his predecessors. If he nonetheless excludes them from his life as goals worth striving for, it is because they are connected with vexation and suffering (1:18). Here it is presupposed that the only goals

---

1   Fischer, *Skepsis*, 208–9 points, by way of comparison, to the distinction of three ways of life in Aristotle (*Eth. nic.* 1095b–96a and elsewhere): the basing of life on enjoyment, on practical activity, or on knowledge and philosophy.

2   Key words: עשׂה *ʿśh* (qal: 2:2, 3, 5, 6, 8, 11[2x], 12; niphal: 1:13, 14; 2:27), מַעֲשֶׂה *maʿăśê* (1:14; 2:4, 11, 17), ענה *ʿnh* (1:13), עִנְיָן *ʿinyan* (1:13; 2:23, 26), עמל *ʿml* (2:11, 18, 19, 20, 21, 22), עָמָל *ʿāmāl* (2:10[2x], 11, 18, 19, 20, 21, 22, 24).

3   Key words: חָכְמָה *ḥokmâ* (1:13, 16[2x], 17, 18; 2:3, 9, 12, 13, 21, 26), חָכָם *ḥākām* (2:14, 16[2x], 29), חכם

4   Key words: הוֹלֵלוֹת *hôlēlôt* (1:17; 2:12), הלל *hll* pual (2:1), שׂ/סִכְלוּת *ś/siklût* (1:17; 2:3, 12, 13), סָכָל *sākāl* (2:19), כְּסִיל *kĕsîl* (2:14, 15, 16[2x]).

5   Key words: שִׂמְחָה *śimḥâ* (2:1, 2, 10, 26), שׂמח *śmḥ* (2:10), ראה *rʾh* (qal/hiphil) + טוֹב *ṭôb* (2:1, 24), שׂחק *śḥq* (2:2), אכל *ʾkl* (2:24, 25), שׁתה *śth* (2:24). Antitheses: כָּעַס *kāʿas* (1:18; 2:23), מַכְאוֹב *makʾôb* (1:18; 2:22), שׂנא *śnʾ* (2:17, 18), יאשׁ *yʾš* (2:20), חוש *ḥwš* [?] (2:25).

(2:15, 19), דַּעַת *daʿat* (1:16, 17[2x], 18; 2:21, 26), ידע *ydʿ* (1:17; 2:14), רַעְיוֹן לֵב *raʿyôn-lēb* (2:22).

60

and purposes worthy of human striving are those connected with—or at least not restrictive of—pleasure and enjoyment.

In this sense it is logical when in 2:1-2 the king turns to direct striving for *pleasure and enjoyment*. Regarding their devaluation, here too it is not, say, because pleasure and enjoyment are unachievable for the king. Rather, according to 2:2, the decisive point is that pleasure and enjoyment are unwise and unproductive: laughter is folly, and pleasure accomplishes nothing. With this the discussion here harks back to the two previous investigations. At the same time, we realize that for the king, only the connection of activity, wisdom, and pleasure can represent a life goal worth striving for.

After activity, wisdom, and pleasure have each proved themselves to the king to be meaningless, in 2:3-11 the king tries to connect these three goals with one another: he strives for *enjoyment* ("bathing my body in wine"), without giving up his *wisdom* ("my mind still guiding me in wisdom"), and at the same time accomplishing "great *works*" (2:3-4). Contrary to what might be expected according to 1:13—2:2, this undertaking succeeds: the activity of the king is successful (2:4-8), his wisdom remained with him (2:9), and he can allow himself every conceivable pleasure (2:10). When he, nevertheless, ultimately comes to the devaluating judgment that here too "all this was futile and a striving after wind," this results from his closing thought in 2:11: with all the successes, his efforts have still led to no "gain" (יִתְרוֹן *yitrôn*). Presupposed here is the idea that for human beings, the only goals that are worth striving for are those that represent a "gain" from one's own efforts. If someone cannot achieve such a gain, then in that person's life there are no goals and purposes worth striving for.

Thus in the course of the king's comments in 1:12—2:11 we can recognize various aspects of the conception of a "good life" that underlie his value judgments. The only goals and purposes that seem to him worth striving for are

- those that are at one's disposal reliably and without limitation (1:13-15),
- those that do not restrict pleasure and enjoyment (1:16-18),
- those that connect pleasure and enjoyment with wisdom and activity (2:1-2), and

- those in which he can achieve a "gain" through his actions (2:3-11).

The argumentation is propelled by, among other things, the fact that the reason for the devaluation of certain goals and purposes is in each case removed by what follows:

- Whereas according to 1:13-15 human activity is devalued because of limitations on what is achievable through it, according to 1:16-18 wisdom is achievable in unlimited abundance.
- If according to 1:16-18 wisdom's shortcoming consists in its being connected with vexation and suffering, 2:1-2 shows, by contrast, the possibility of experiencing pleasure and enjoyment.
- The reason for the devaluation of pleasure and enjoyment in 2:1-2, its incompatibility with wisdom and activity, is eliminated in 2:3-11, since the king succeeds here in joining together activity, wisdom, and pleasure.
- Thus the last decisive criterion by which the king can judge possible goals and purposes in life proves to be his "gain" orientation (2:11; cf. 1:3; 3:9). Then in 2:12-21 it is still further refined and radicalized: even if within life there is a (relative) "gain" (v. 13), it still loses any possible value at the latest when faced with death (vv. 16ff.).

The development of the king's argumentation in 1:12—2:11 thus makes clear that it is not (only) the unavailability of the "good" that leads him to the devaluation of activity, wisdom, and enjoyment, but (also and first of all) his conception of a "good life": if a good life consists in individuals realizing their self-selected goals through their own efforts in striving for accomplishment and possessions, wisdom and happiness, then its failure is unavoidable—even for a king. Yet who should have such exalted expectations of a good life if not a king?

1:12 Introduction
■ **12** The formulation of Qoheleth's self-introduction as king in 1:12 (הָיִיתִי מֶלֶךְ *hāyîtî melek*) leaves open whether he is presenting himself to the reader as ex-king or as

head of state.[6] In either case, the undertakings and reflections mentioned in 1:12–2:26 were carried out by him as king. According to the OT, only David and Solomon were "king over Israel in Jerusalem." Thus, according to 1:1, "Qoheleth" would have to have been Solomon. Naturally, even the difference in names lets any impartial reader see through this identification as a fictive travesty.

This royal travesty has a double rhetorical and argumentative function in what follows. First, it makes possible the "travesty at the top," "to base an anthropology not on the experiences of people who fail to grow or to achieve anything in life, but rather on the experiences of the highest human possibility, in the most fortunate world situations, joyfully lived" (Lohfink).[7] Second, anyone familiar with OT traditions knows that a king, more than the "little man," runs the risk of overestimating himself and his possibilities for shaping life and the world—and that such hubris is often followed by a great fall.[8]

If 1:12–2:26 demonstrates the failure of the overdrawn expectations of a "successful life" using the example of a king, it also calls into question the assumption that the high and mighty have special wisdom at their disposal.[9] Corresponding claims and self-representations are caricatured in the royal travesty. Many aspects of the text can be seen as a parody of OT stories of Solomon's wisdom and wealth. In addition, certainly for the first readers the text also addressed experiences with the Hellenistic rulers of its time, as well as with contemporaries who, on a smaller scale, could afford or wanted to live "like a king" (Job 29:25).

1:13-15 Limits of Activity

■ **13a** Right at the beginning of his rule, as his first act, as it were, King Qoheleth undertakes, with the help of his wisdom, the researching of all (human) deeds and works under heaven.[10] If one understands נַעֲשָׂה *naʿăśâ* as a participle, it is a question of all action in general; if one reads it as perfect, then the king is concerned here with the deeds of his predecessors. When the king decisively traces his undertaking back to his own decision ("I applied my mind," וְנָתַתִּי אֶת־לִבִּי *wĕnātattî ʾet-libbî*),[11] this

---

6   "The formula 'I, [name], am king of . . .' belongs (typologically) to the usual forms in West Semitic inscriptions of 'self-introduction'" of a king (Loretz, *Qohelet*, 62–63; cf. idem, "Darbietungsform," 55–56; Isaksson, *Studies*, 50). Going in the direction of ex-king later was "the narrative imagination of the Haggadists. . . . Thus *y. Sanh.* 2.7 recounts that Solomon was pushed from his throne because of his sins, and an angel with the same appearance took his place. Solomon went begging from one teaching house to the next. And everywhere he presented himself as king of Jerusalem, he was beaten with a shepherd's staff or at best received reproaches and a portion of groats" (R. Lux, "'Ich, Kohelet, bin König . . .': Die Fiktion als Schlüssel zur Wirklichkeit in Kohelet 1, 12–2, 26," *EvTh* 50 [1990] 336; cf. also 𝔗; *b. Sanh.* 2.6b; *b. Giṭ.* 68b).

7   Cf. Midrash *Qohelet Rabbah* (on 3:11): "If anyone else [besides Solomon] were to say *hbl hblym* [1:2; 12:8], I would answer: 'This one, who does not (even) have two cents of his own, despises all the world's possessions!'" (see Michel, *Qohelet*, 77; Gordis, 211).

8   Cf., e.g., Judges 9; Isa 10:5-15; 14:5-21; Ezekiel 28; Daniel 4. Song of Songs describes the erotically intensified form of life with a juxtaposition of travesty at the top ("royal play") and travesty at the bottom ("pastoral play").

9   Cf. here L. Kalugila, *The Wise King* (ConBOT 15; Lund: Gleerup, 1980), as well as H.-J. Gehrke, *Geschichte des Hellenismus* (Oldenbourg Grundriss der Geschichte 1A; Munich: Oldenbourg, 1990) 8:31, on the education and philosophical interests of Alexander and his successors. The fact that the king's knowledge perspective is a ruler's perspective is already indicated by the (chiastic) adoption of the prepositions עַל *ʿal* and בְּ *b-* from v. 12 (עַל־יִשְׂרָאֵל בִּירוּשָׁלָ͏ִם *ʿal-yiśrāʾēl bîrûšālāim*) in v. 13 (בַּחָכְמָה *bahokmâ ʿal kol* . . .).

10   Contra, e.g., Murphy: "The reference is to 'all that *happens* in life' (thus Fox, *Qohelet*, 175), not to everything that human beings do." Müller, "Skepsis," 4 with n. 5, assumes that כָּל־אֲשֶׁר נַעֲשָׂה *kol-ʾăšer naʿăśâ* designates here "total reality," and חָכְמָה *hokmâ* its "moral order."

11   Cf. 1:17; 7:21; 8:9, 16; Prov 23:26; Ezek 28:2, 6; 1 Chr 22:19; 2 Chr 11:16; Dan 10:12. Such power of a human being over the "heart" or "mind" seems by no means to be taken for granted in the OT (and was inconceivable until relatively late).

seems like a parody of the tradition of Solomon in Gibeon in 1 Kgs 3:4-15; 2 Chr 1:1-12, according to which King Solomon asked for and received from God his mind (לֵב *lēb*: 1 Kgs 3:9, 12) and his wisdom (חָכְמָה *ḥokmâ*: 2 Chr 1:10, 12).

■ **13b** Even King Qoheleth brings his endeavor to examine all human deeds and works with the help of wisdom into relationship with God. Nonetheless, he sees there "a tiresome effort" (עִנְיַן רָע *ʿinyan rāʿ*, cf. 4:8; 5:13).[12] That God has "given" (נָתַן *nātan*) this to people to busy themselves with can be understood in different ways. Most assume the meaning of this sentence to be that God commissioned human beings with the exploring of all activity under heaven. Then the king would trace his undertaking here both back to his own initiative (v. 13a) and to the initiative of God (v. 13b). In all the following undertakings, however, he brings only his own decision to bear. (God is not mentioned again until 2:24, 26.) Thus the statement is better understood to mean that God leaves it to human beings to investigate (דרש *drš*) all that is done under heaven, but God himself "is not concerned about it" (cf. Ps 10:4: בַּל־יִדְרֹשׁ *bal-yidrōš*)—a view against which the OT often polemicizes.[13] It would be completely in line with the king's comments on the arbitrariness of God's actions in 2:26. He would then document here at the beginning of his comments his

"secular" view of life.[14] In any case, v. 13b (like 2:24, 26) reveals that the king connects God more with the (in his view) bad aspects of life than with the good.

■ **14** Astonishingly, the king has no difficulty at all carrying out his investigatory plans, which have as their object no less than *all* human deeds and works (cf., however, 7:24; 8:16-17). The result is as clear as it is devastating: "All this was futile and a striving[15] after wind."

■ **15** This judgment is reinforced and substantiated by the proverbial sentences in v. 15: human actions must be connected with preexisting conditions (v. 15b) and can change them only in limited ways, if at all (v. 15a).[16] The notion that nothing crooked can "become straight" (תקן *tqn*) can, of course, hardly be accepted in such a wholesale sense (cf. the report on the "great works" of the king in 2:4-8). According to 7:13, one cannot make straight (תקן *tqn* piel), what *God* "has made crooked" (עות *ʿwt* piel); according to 12:9, the "wise man Qoheleth" has, nonetheless, "made straight" = "corrected" (תקן *tqn* piel; cf. also Dan 4:33) many proverbs. Yet a king who claims to be able to do "whatever he pleases" (Qoh 8:3) can accept no boundaries *whatever* on his possible actions. Only with the presupposition of this claim is the argumentation of 1:13-15 conclusive; it is formulated from the perspective of a king and bound to that perspective.

---

12 Based on the syntax, it would also be possible to understand v. 13 in the sense that the king judged "all that was done under heaven" as "a tiresome effort" (thus, e.g., Fischer, "Beobachtungen zur Komposition von Kohelet 1,3–3,15," *ZAW* 103 [1991] 76–77). Speaking against this, nevertheless, is the fact that—in contrast to the following sections—the result of the examination is stated before the report on its execution (v. 14a).

13 Cf. Pss 10:11; 64:7; 73:11; 94:7; Job 22:13-14; Isa 29:15-16; Ezek 8:12; 9:9, as well as Mal 3:14-15; Zeph 1:12; Pss 14:1; 53:2.

14 On the "secularism" of 1:12–2:26, cf. Eaton, 55ff. (in Eaton, however, related to 1:2–2:23), but also his critical comments on the application of this interpretive concept (ibid., 157).

15 רְעוּת *rěʿût* (1:14; 2:11, 17, 26; 4:4, 6; 6:9), just like רַעְיוֹן *raʿyôn* (1:17; 2:22; 4:16), probably derives from the root רעה *rʿh* III, as its meaning can then be assumed to be "graze, tend," "occupy oneself with something," or "desire, want." Cf. 𝔊 προαίρεσις, versus 𝔙 *adflictio*.

16 Klein, *Kohelet*, 90, regards v. 15 as a "double proverb." In the present context, v. 15 concerns the general fact that the external world is not at human disposal (Lohfink), and this defines the limits of human possibilities for action and shaping that world. It is variously assumed that v. 15 adopts proverbs that "originally" had a special meaning. According to Galling, for example, v. 15a and b originally referred to the crooked back and the shrinking body size of an old person. Lohfink agrees with this reflection for v. 15a, whereas v. 15b, in his view, comes "from the merchant's table," yet it "can just as well be applied to farmers who, because of a meager harvest in the autumn, cannot manage to deliver their dues to the lords and to the government." Michel assumes (following Hertzberg and Zimmerli) that "the sentences come from the pedagogical practice of wise men and pronounce judgment on unteachable fools" (*Untersuchungen*, 11). Cf. in this sense, for example, the Egyptian admonition (Brunner, *Altägyptische Weisheit*, no. 11): "You shall not make what is

1:16-18 Limits of Wisdom: Wisdom without Pleasure

■ **16** Through his investigations and reflections on human possibilities of action and accomplishment in vv 13-15, King Qoheleth has, according to his own estimation, acquired greater wisdom than all his predecessors.[17] For Solomon one could, in addition to his father David, also think of pre-Israelite rulers over Jerusalem (for example, the legendary Melchizedek: Gen 14:18-20; Ps 110:4). The king's claim that he towers above his predecessors corresponds to the ruler ideology of the ancient Near East.[18] If here he regards his previously unattained wisdom as the result of his own efforts, this again has the effect of a parody of the OT Solomon traditions according to which it was God who equipped Solomon with a mind (1 Kgs 3:12) and wisdom (2 Chr 1:12) and let him surpass every predecessor and successor (cf. Qoh 2:12).[19]

■ **17** Whereas the attempt to actively shape the world proved to be "a striving after wind" (v. 14), striving for wisdom seems to promise success (but cf. 7:23-24; 8:16-17).[20] Nevertheless, the reflection on wisdom and folly shows that "striving for spirit" (רוּחַ *rûaḥ*) is also only "a striving after wind" (רוּחַ *rûaḥ*).

■ **18** The closing proverbs show why and in what sense that is true: with education and knowledge, human beings get themselves only more vexation and suffering.[21] With this the king contradicts the view that wisdom and education help people to a long and happy life. With such promises, wisdom teachers could recruit pupils.[22] They presuppose that wisdom is not sought for its own sake but as a means to the end of a happy life. The king also begins with this presupposition in his judgment on wisdom in vv. 17-18. As in vv. 14-15, one can also ask here whether the king's sweeping judgment holds up against experience (cf., by contrast, 2:3, 9-10, 26).

2:1-2 Limits of Pleasure: Pleasure without Wisdom and Activity

■ **1** Since wisdom and knowledge bring one only vexation and suffering (1:18), it is logical when King Qoheleth now strives directly for pleasure and enjoyment. Like wisdom, they seem for him to be entirely attainable, even if the carrying out of the plan of v. 1a is not expressly noted here. Yet even pleasure and enjoyment now seem to the king, upon closer examination, to be without meaning or value (הֶבֶל *hebel*).

■ **2** Again, this judgment is subsequently reinforced and explained, this time not with proverbs but with self-quotations of the king ("I said," אָמַרְתִּי *ʾāmartî*): Laughter is uneducated[23] and pleasure unproductive. Here the argumentation of the king becomes circular and contradic-

---

crooked straight. . . . Everyone is drawn by his character . . ." (ll. 10-11), but also the Teaching of Ani (Brunner, no. 10): "The workman fetches the crooked limb, bends it straight, and makes a staff of it; he makes the straight limb, however, into a collar. You, heart that cannot know: are you now ready to let us instruct you, or have you failed?" (ll. 405ff.; cf. further Ankh-Sheshonq [Brunner, no. 15], l. 127 and P. Chester Beatty IV [Brunner, no. 12], ll. 202ff.).

17 Proverbs 3:7 and Isa 5:21 arouse skepticism toward people who hold themselves to be wise ("who are wise in their own eyes").

18 Cf. Loretz, "Darbietungsform," 55; idem, *Qohelet*, 160; T. Ishida, "Solomon Who Is Greater Than David," in J. A. Emerton, ed., *Congress Volume, Salamanca 1983* (VTSup 36; Leiden: Brill, 1985) 145–53.

19 Cf. further 1 Kgs 1:37, 47; 3:13; 10:23.

20 By contrast, according to Job 28, in the active shaping of the world human beings can expand their limits farther and farther (vv. 1-11), but not thereby find wisdom (vv. 12ff.).

21 It is occasionally assumed that v. 18 takes up traditional proverbs that "originally" asserted "that learning and being educated require effort and pain" (Lauha; cf., e.g., Michel, *Untersuchungen*, 14). Speaking against this, however, is the point that v. 18 calls aggravation and suffering concomitant phenomena of wisdom and knowledge, not the price of their acquisition. Yet v. 18 could ironically refer to unpleasantnesses such as whippings and beatings that are usually connected with being educated in wisdom (cf., e.g., Prov 3:11-12; 13:1, 24; 19:18; 22:15; 23:13-14; 29:15, 17; Sir 4:17; 6:18ff.). C. Klein, *Kohelet und die Weisheit Israels: Eine formgeschichtliche Studie* (BWANT 132; Stuttgart: Kohlhammer, 1994), 90–91, holds: "The proverbs in 1:18 may have originally been the words of pupils who complained about the arduousness of learning."

22 Cf. esp. Prov 3:13-26; 4; Sir 6:18-31; 51:13-29; further, e.g., Prov 9:11-12; Sir 1:20; 4:12-13.

23 Cf. 7:6; Prov 29:9; Sir 21:1, 15, 20.

tory: if he just evaluated wisdom negatively, because it restricts pleasure and enjoyment (1:17-18), he now speaks against pleasure because it is "foolish, blind" (מְהוֹלָל *mĕhôlāl*), and thus not "wise" (cf. the opposition of "wisdom" and "blindness" [הוֹלֵלוֹת *hôlēlôt*] in 1:17). And if in 1:14-15 he judges all human "works and deeds" (הַמַּעֲשִׂים שֶׁנַּעֲשׂוּ *hammaʿăśîm šennaʿăśû*) as without meaning or value, here he devalues pleasure because it "accomplishes" nothing (מַה־זֹּה עֹשָׂה *mah-zōh ʿōśâ*). That shows that the king is by no means ready, as a consequence of his investigations and reflections, to revise his concept of a "good life." For him it is and remains imaginable only as a combination of activity, wisdom, and enjoyment.

2:3-11 Limits of Activity, Wisdom, and Pleasure: No Gain

■ **3** After the three previous investigations have shown that activity, wisdom, and pleasure are each in themselves without meaning or value, King Qoheleth now tries a combination of these three attitudes toward life. Here, according to 2:2, he must enter a compromise; thus enjoyment and wisdom can be joined with each other only in such a way that folly also gets a chance.[24] The aim of this undertaking is to find out what "good" can be realized by human beings for themselves in their lives through their actions.

A comparison with Mic 6:8, "It is told to you, O mortal, what is good [מַה־טּוֹב *mah-ṭôb*], and what does Yahweh require of you: nothing but to do justice, and to love goodness ['solidarity': חֶסֶד *ḥesed*], and to walk humbly with your God," makes clear which prior decisions have already been made in this specific formulation of the basic ethical question. What is "good" must be discovered by mortals themselves; they no longer let it be "told" to them or even "required" of them by God. (But the king makes the claim of being able to determine the "good" for the rest of humankind!) "Good" now involves only what is good for the individual and no longer the

well-being of the community, which is the aim of the concepts of "justice" and "solidarity" in Mic 6:8. Finally, the formulation of the question about the "good" here already indicates that what is "good" can only be what human beings can realize through their own actions in accordance with their own goals.

Corresponding changes in the basic approach to ethics are also shown in Hellenistic philosophy, which on the question about the good and happy life is likewise oriented toward the individual: "What is really important . . . cannot be the happiness of the state or of the community, but only the happiness of the individual." The eudaemonia of a "successful life" consists for the individual "in the attainment of all preset goals. If the happy individual is the ultimate goal, then all goals must be set for its sake, and that means they must be set by the individual himself." Accordingly, "happiness consists in the attainment of all *self-chosen* goals." It can no longer be "defined as Aristotle does when he sees in it 'an activeness of the soul in the sense of its essential competence' and understands by this the complete realization of the role given to human beings within a teleologically ordered world on the basis of their nature" (*Eth. nic.* 1098a).[25]

■ **4-8** In order to find out what "good" can be realized by human beings for themselves in their lives through their actions, the king details his great works and deeds. The fact that in this process he understands himself as the "creator" of his own happiness is revealed by several echoes of Genesis 1–2 in his presentation.[26] In reports on their great deeds, rulers of the ancient Near East and the Hellenistic period boasted not only of their wisdom and wealth but also about the promotion of religious cults and the welfare of their subjects (through assurance of the productivity of the land and defense against enemies in war).[27] King Qoheleth, by contrast, reports exclusively on works and deeds that he has done for himself (note the repeated "myself," לִי *lî*). Here too he gives

---

24 One may certainly ask whether wisdom and excessive indulgence in wine can really be united; cf. Prov 20:1; 21:17; 23:20-21, 29-35; 31:4.

25 Hossenfelder, *Philosophie*, 32–33.

26 Cf. v. 5 ("I planted all kinds of fruit trees") to Gen 1:11; 2:8; v. 6 ("to water") to Gen 2:6, 10; v. 6 ("trees") to Gen 2:9; see Müller, "Skepsis," 7, with n. 32; A. J. C. Verheij, "Paradise Retried: On

Qohelet 2:4-6," *JSOT* 50 (1991) 113–15.

27 For the ancient Near East see Keel, *Symbolism*, 269ff.; Loretz, *Qohelet*, 154ff.; for Hellenistic rulers cf. Gehrke, *Geschichte des Hellenismus*, 46ff., 165ff., 238ff. (lit.), and, e.g., the texts no. 217 (Ptolemy II), 222 (Ptolemy III), 227 (Ptolemy V) in Austin, *Hellenistic World*.

the impression of a caricature of Solomon, who according to OT traditions not only had at his disposal wisdom, wealth, and possibilities of enjoyment, but also, among other things, built a temple and achieved prosperity for his people (and whose "harem" is not evaluated positively by tradition).[28] If according to 1 Kgs 1:37 and 47 *God* made Solomon's throne great (גדל *gdl* piel), here King Qoheleth *himself* makes his works great (גדל *gdl* hiphil: v. 4).

In the critical portrayal of the text, however, the first readers could recognize, in addition to Solomon, the Hellenistic rulers of their own time, as well as lower-ranking representatives of political and economic power in Jerusalem and Judea—for example, the Tobiad Joseph, a "self-made man," who "thought it smart and advantageous to base his happiness on his wealth" (Josephus, *Ant.* 12.4.5) and who between 182 and 175 B.C.E. in present-day ʿArāq el-Emîr built his son Hyrcanus a palace with a park and an irrigation system (*Ant.* 12.4.11; cf. Qoh 2:4-6).[29] A testimony to "the private enslavement that was rampant at the time in Palestine" (cf. v. 7) is found in the decree of Ptolemy II from the year 261/260 B.C.E., in which the topic is the purchase and acquisition by force of "native free individuals" (σῶμα λαικὸν ἐλεύθερον), as well as those who were already slaves (ὄντα οἰκετικά; cf. those "born in my house," בְּנֵי־בָיִת *běnê-bayit*, in v. 7).[30] It is indicative of King Qoheleth's perspective that in his striving for his own happiness, he wastes no thought on the happiness or unhappiness of the people who contribute to his happiness and carry out his "great works" for him (cf. 4:1-3).

■ **9-11** This time, the king's undertaking seems, at first glance, to have been a complete success. With his great works he has now exceeded all his predecessors (vv. 7, 9; cf. 1:16), he has retained his wisdom (v. 9), and he can permit himself every conceivable pleasure (v. 10). With this he seems to have overcome the limits of activity, wisdom, and pleasure that the previous investigations have uncovered: a person can really change reality (contra 1:13-15), wisdom does not exclude pleasure (contra 1:16-18), and enjoyment can very likely be combined with activity and wisdom (contra 2:1-2). Nonetheless, the closing reflection shows that even here the king has come up against a limit to his possibilities that leads to the devaluation of his accomplishments as "futile [meaningless and worthless] and a striving after wind": with all the success of his actions, he has still achieved no "gain" (יִתְרוֹן *yitrôn*, v. 11).

■ **10** The sudden reversal from (apparent) success to its reflective devaluation is foreshadowed already in the king's statements on the pleasure he has experienced (v. 10). For if this represents his "portion" (חֵלֶק *ḥēleq*) of all his efforts, then the value of his wisdom and his "great works" is thereby relativized: it consists ultimately only in making pleasure and enjoyment possible. Verses 1-2, however, show that this goal could also have been achieved without the cost of "great works"—and that pleasure and enjoyment by themselves seem to the king not at all worth striving for! Therefore, pleasure is not a "gain" (יִתְרוֹן *yitrôn*) of his efforts (v. 11), but only his "portion" (חֵלֶק *ḥēleq*).[31] A further distinction between "portion" and "gain" is revealed by the designation of

---

28 On the wisdom of Solomon cf. 1 Kings 3; 4:29ff.; 10; 2 Chronicles 1; 9; on his wealth, 1 Kgs 4:21ff.; 10; 2 Chr 1:13ff.; 9; on his numerous wives, 1 Kgs 11:1ff.; on his building activity, 1 Kings 5–7; 9:15ff.; 2 Chronicles 2–4; 8:1ff.; on the prosperity of the people, 1 Kgs 4:20, 25. According to 1 Chronicles 25; 27:27ff. Solomon inherited vineyards, cattle, and musicians from his father David.

29 R. Michaud, *Qohélet et l'hellénisme: La littérature de sagesse: Histoire et théologie II* (LiBi 77; Paris: Cerf, 1987), 143–44, sees in Qoh 2:8a an allusion to the economic reform of Ptolemy I (cf. ibid., 90–91). On lower ranks see Norbert Lohfink, "*melek, šallîṭ* und *môšēl* bei Kohelet und die Abfassungszeit des Buches," *Bib* 62 (1982) 535–43. On Joseph see Josephus, *Ant.* 12.4. According to Michaud, *Qohélet*, 144,

Qoh 2:8b could be an allusion to his amorous adventures at the court of Alexandria (cf. ibid. 103ff.).

30 H. G. Kippenberg, *Religion und Klassenbildung in antiken Judäa* (2d ed.; SUNT 14; Göttingen: Vandenhoeck & Ruprecht, 1982), 79.

31 By contrast, Hans Heinrich Schmid, *Wesen und Geschichte der Weisheit* (BZAW 101; Berlin: de Gruyter, 1966) 187–88 and Müller, "Skepsis," 8 n. 35, for example, assume that חֵלֶק *ḥēleq*, like יִתְרוֹן *yitrôn*, designates a "gain"; cf., however, J. G. Williams, "What Does It Profit a Man? The Wisdom of Koheleth," *Judaism* 20 (1971) 179–93, repr. in Crenshaw, ed., *Studies,* 375–89; Michel, *Untersuchungen,* 119–20; T. Kronholm, "יתר *yātar* I," *TDOT* 6:489–90: 1087.

inheritance as "portion" in v. 21: in contrast to a "gain," the "portion" of an individual is neither necessarily earned by that person himself (he receives it as inheritance),[32] nor does he keep it in the long run (at his death he will in turn pass it on as inheritance). The designation of pleasure as "portion" also means that it is not totally at one's disposal (cf. v. 24).[33] This means for the king, however, that it is meaningless and worthless (cf. v. 26, versus then 3:22; 5:18-19; 9:9).[34]

■ **11** The closing reflection of the king in v. 11 can be understood in two ways. If one interprets עָמָל ʿāmāl as "work, toil," he is comparing here his application of effort with the outcome, and he reaches the conclusion that no "gain" or "surplus" (יִתְרוֹן yitrôn) has been achieved. For the desired yield (pleasure), the effort has not been worth it (though one may well ask here how much "work and toil" a king *himself* actually expended for his "great works"). If, however, one interprets עָמָל ʿāmāl as "possession," the king notes in v. 11 that in the long run none of this remains (cf. vv. 12ff.). Thus a "good life" may be humanly achievable, yet represents no "gain" for one's efforts. Verse 11 shows that one can nullify the joy in and of life through one's own "gain" orientation (cf. v. 2 and then vv. 12-21). "The title of Harold Kushner's book about Ecclesiastes (*When All You've Ever Wanted Isn't Enough*) is an accurate summary of the contents of this chapter."[35]

2:12-21 Happiness Not at One's Disposal in View of Death

If the investigations and reflections of King Qoheleth in 1:12—2:11 move within the framework of his life (with a look back at his predecessors), in 2:12-21 he now takes into consideration the fact that he must die one day and leave his possessions to a successor. From this viewpoint he comes here to further insights about his wisdom (vv. 13-17) and the possessions he has worked to acquire (vv. 18-21). The transition in v. 12 can be read as "disposition information" for what follows (Lohfink): v. 12a announces the investigation of wisdom and folly in vv. 13-17; the theme "successor" (v. 12b) is taken up and discussed in vv. 18-21.

As in 1:13—2:11, we can also delineate four smaller sections in 2:13-21 by means of the closing *hebel* judgments (vv. 15, 17, 19, 21):

■ Verses 13-15 connect with v. 11: although one can achieve no "gain" (יִתְרוֹן yitrôn) through one's work,

---

32 חֵלֶק ḥēleq often stands as a parallel idea to נַחֲלָה naḥălâ ("[portion of] possession, inheritance"), גּוֹרָל gôrāl ("lot [portion], destiny"), or חֶבֶל ḥebel ("[measuring] string" > "piece of field") "for the 'portion of the land'" (H. H. Schmid, "חלק ḥlq to divide," *TLOT* 1:432), which for the farmer is the foundation and presupposition of his work, but not its product. The fact that חֵלֶק ḥēleq can also mean "fate" (ibid.) shows that the concept contains an element of not being at one's disposal.

33 This is also indicated when the king speaks here of his heart's pleasure, which he has not hindered: here the "heart" (לֵב lēb), which the king has previously had at his sovereign disposal (see above on 1:13a), gains a certain dynamic of its own vis-à-vis the "self."

34 On the difference between the view of "pleasure" in 2:1-11 (and 2:24-26) and the statements on it starting in chap. 3, cf. also R. Bartelmus, "Haben oder Sein: Anmerkungen zur Anthropologie des Buches Kohelet," *BN* 53 (1990) 56-57: "The false king Qoheleth speaks only of pleasures that he himself has undertaken, which he himself has 'tried,' which

he himself wanted to 'do,' buy, even compel. . . . Where Qoheleth, by contrast, first comes to speak positively of the enjoyment of life [according to Bartelmus starting at 2:24; according to the interpretation presented here, not until 3:12], it is clear that the pleasure he values positively presupposes an attitude quite different from that caricatured in the second section [i.e., 2:1-11], namely, the readiness to accept what God has given to human beings." Bartelmus stimulates one "to recall the Frommian distinction of pleasure and enjoyment, which is based on the idea that externally similar experiences can be evaluated differently, depending on the attitude of the individual toward them" (ibid., 57, cf. Erich Fromm, *To Have or to Be?* [New York: Harper & Row, 1976]).

35 K. A. Farmer, *Who Knows What Is Good? A Commentary on the Books of Proverbs and Ecclesiastes* (ITC; Grand Rapids: Eerdmans, 1991) 157; cf. also Bartelmus, "Haben oder Sein."

wisdom offers the wise person a definite "advantage" (יִתְרוֹן *yitrôn*). Nevertheless, for the king this immediately loses its value, since even wisdom does not protect a person from the "fate" (or: "chance": מִקְרֶה *miqreh*) that can thwart one's plans and limit one's power of disposal over one's life.

■ Verses 16-17 negate the "advantage" of wisdom even further in view of the fact that the wise man must die one day, just like the fool. In the long view, not even the "remembrance" (זִכְרוֹן *zikrôn*) of the wise man will represent a lasting "gain" (יִתְרוֹן *yitrôn*) for him (cf. 1:3, 11).

■ The resulting hatred of the king for life (v. 17) is directed in vv. 18-19 especially at the possessions he has worked for. With death his power of disposition over his property comes to an end and is passed on to his successor—without regard to whether the latter is a wise man or a fool.

■ The king is finally brought to despair in vv. 20-21 by the thought that his heir will, in any case, have at his disposal property that he has not worked for himself. That flagrantly contradicts his "work ethic," according to which one must work for one's own good life.

In 2:12-21 the king's reflections about his experiences move into the foreground. Just as 2:2 and 11 lead to the subsequent devaluation of the pleasure first experienced by him, the reflections in 2:13-17 and 18-21 now cause his wisdom (cf. 1:16; 2:9) and his acquired possessions (cf. 2:4-9) to seem worthless in retrospect. If in 1:12—2:11 he is spurred on to his undertakings by the desire to surpass his predecessors, his life is now soured in 2:12-21 by envy of his successors (cf. 4:4). The king's comments in 2:12-21 again make clear that he can imagine a "good life" only as the realization of his own goals through his own efforts. As soon as he encounters the limits of his power of disposition, he loses every "good" he has striven for, even the ones he has already attained.

2:12 Transition

Verse 12 announces the theme of the following reflections: the comparison between "wisdom" and "folly" (v. 12a, cf. vv. 13-17) and the question of the king's successors[36] (v. 12b, cf. vv. 18-21).

■ **12a** Already in 1:16-18, after the king had recognized the limits of human activity (1:13-15), he turned to the investigation of "wisdom" and "blindness and folly" (1:17). So here too the knowledge that he has not achieved any gain with his great works (2:11) leads him to the question of whether wisdom could open for him the possibility of "gain" (v. 13).

■ **12b** If the understanding of the half verse recommended in the translation above is correct, the comment on the king's successors in v. 12b, just like the comparison with his predecessors earlier (1:16; 2:7, 9), emphasizes the uniqueness of the accomplishments of King Qoheleth. It reminds us again of King Solomon, to whom God had promised that with his reason, his wisdom, and his wealth, he would tower over all his predecessors and successors (1 Kgs 3:12; 2 Chr 1:12; see above on 1:16). According to 1 Kgs 12:14 and 2 Chr 10:14, his son Rehoboam did nothing different from what King Qoheleth in 1:12—2:11 had also done: he tried to surpass his father and predecessors—and in doing so squandered the greater part of his inheritance.[37]

2:13-15 Limits of Wisdom: Contingency

■ **13-14** Some assume that here the king is critical of the view that wisdom has an "advantage" (יִתְרוֹן *yitrôn*) over folly and rejects this view while appealing to his own insight. The introductory verb וְרָאִיתִי (*wĕ*)*rā'îtî* would then be understood in the sense, "I considered (the assertion). . . ."[38] Yet vv. 13-14 can be easily interpreted

---

36 It is most simply understandable if one assumes that in what follows "Qoheleth" is still speaking in the role of a "king over Israel in Jerusalem." Also speaking against the assumption of an end of the royal parody in 2:11 (thus, e.g., Gordis; Galling; Michel) are the references back to 1:12–2:11 in 2:15, 18, and 20.

37 The same can be said of the successors (διάδοχοι) of Alexander; see Gehrke, *Geschichte des Hellenismus*, 31.

38 Cf., e.g., Michel, *Untersuchungen*, 24ff.; Backhaus, *Zeit und Zufall*, 105–6; Klein, *Kohelet*, 70; and already Galling; Gordis.

as conceding an "advantage" of wisdom ("I saw . . ."), which, nonetheless, is immediately relativized again ("I recognized/knew . . ."): it is true that through wisdom the wise man is better oriented in reality than the fool, but in spite of his wisdom, the wise man—just like the fool—is not reliably protected from the vagaries of fate as the fool.[39] That means, however, that wisdom—despite its "advantage" over folly—can offer a person no prospect of a "gain" that is reliably at one's disposal.

■ **13-14a** The idea that wisdom improves one's ability to orient oneself in the experience of reality is a fundamental conviction of the wisdom tradition.[40] A Sumerian puzzle speaks of the education of a wise scribe in the tablet house opening a man's eyes or giving him eyes in the first place.[41] The modern "Enlightenment" stylized and legitimized itself with the help of a similar metaphor.

■ **14b** The wisdom tradition, however, also points to the limits of wisdom: even the wise man sees himself confronted with chance and accidents that can frustrate his plans and reflections.[42] Verse 14b expresses this experience of "contingency" with the catchword מִקְרֶה *miqreh*.[43] This term designates "what happens by itself, without the will of the concerned or any known author" (KBL), and it can be translated, say, with "chance," "fate," or "happenstance" (GB).[44] The fact that in the book of Qoheleth מִקְרֶה *miqreh* always appears in the context of

statements about death (besides 2:13-17, see also 3:19 and 9:2-3) does not show that the expression is used here "always with the meaning of the fate of death" (thus Lauha). Rather, death is the example par excellence for everything "contingent" and "not at one's disposal" that a person can "encounter" (קרה *qrh*, see 9:11-12). The reference to the "contingent" as the limit of the wise shaping of life in vv. 14b-15 reflects a "defining basic trait" of Hellenistic culture: the feeling of being at the mercy of forces and events beyond one's control.

One felt like a victim of events, completely passive in the sense of suffering. The powers to which one was subject seemed just as insuperable as they were inscrutable. Significantly, one now "discovered" the infinite power of the goddess of fate Tyche that was expressed precisely in the incalculability and unpredictability of blind chance. One had a lively sensitivity for vicissitude, and especially for the unexpected and unlikely; the paradoxical—as it was called—had almost become the normal.[45]

■ **15** Since wisdom, even where it is present "in excess" (יוֹתֵר *yôtēr*; see 1:16; 7:16), also cannot completely exclude the element of contingency in life, it becomes totally worthless for King Qoheleth. Here we see again

---

39 Cf., e.g., Hertzberg; Zimmerli; and Lauha, who understand vv. 13-14 as an "it-is-true-but" statement, and Ellermeier, *Qohelet,* I/1, 67, who interprets vv. 12-17 as a "reflection with a critical turn" ("kritische gebrochene Reflexion") that concedes to wisdom a "relative value."

40 On the metaphors of "light-darkness" and "eye," cf. Job 12:24-25; Sir 3:25 (G 248); 22:11; Wis 7:10, 26, 29, as well as Prov 4:18-19; 6:23; 13:9; 24:20; Job 18:5-6, where, however, not "wisdom" and "folly" but the "righteous" and the "wicked" are compared with light and darkness.

41 "A house . . . one without open eyes [vl. 'one who has no eyes'] went inside it; one with open eyes [vl. 'one who has eyes'] came out of it. The solution: it is a tablet house" (*TUAT* 3:44).

42 The future is basically unpredictable (Prov 27:1). Human actions can have unexpected consequences ("paradoxical" in the original sense of "against expectations") (11:24; 14:12; 16:25). The working of God (in mysterious ways!) sets limits on human

beings' power of disposition over their own lives (10:22; 16:1-2, 9, 33; 19:14, 21; 20:24; 21:1, 30—critical of this is 19:3). Last but not least, the problem of "contingency" is a central theme of the book of Job.

43 In addition to Qoh 2:14-15; 3:19(3x); 9:2-3, the word is found in the OT only in 1 Sam 6:9; 20:26; Ruth 2:3.

44 Ruth 2:3 shows that מִקְרֶה *miqreh* can certainly also designate a "happy happenstance" (contra Galling; Lauha).

45 Gehrke, *Geschichte des Hellenismus,* 72. On the "special adoration and consideration" of the "goddess Tyche (fate and chance in one)," cf. ibid., 75; on the thematization of fate, chance, and paradox in literature, ibid., 88–89 (tragedy and comedy), 94–95 (history writing), 95–96 (novel). Yet 𝕲 translates מִקְרֶה *miqreh* in the book of Qoheleth not with τύχη but with συνάντημα ("meeting"). The reinforced perception of contingency as the boundary of wisdom's shaping of life in Hellenistic times is illustrated by

69

that the king is not ready to be satisfied with relative values and goods. For him, anything that is not reliably at his disposal or does not support his power of disposition is not worth striving for.

2:16-17 Limits of Wisdom: Death and Oblivion

■ **16** Since the wise man, just like the fool, must one day die (cf. Ps 49:11), and in the long view (לְעוֹלָם *lĕ'ôlām*) no remembrance (זִכְרוֹן *zikrôn*) of him will remain (cf. 1:11), the advantage (יִתְרוֹן *yitrôn*) of wisdom for the king completely loses any value.[46] With v. 16 the king contradicts the assumption that a wise man can count on an "eternal remembrance" (cf. Sir 37:26; 39:9; 41:11) or perhaps a life beyond the boundary of death (cf. Pss 49:16; 73:23ff.). This seems regrettable to him (cf. the lamenting אֵיךְ *'êk*, "like").

■ **17** The insight into the impossibility of achieving any kind of lasting gain leads the king to hate life. Even if one considers that the "semantic scope of *śn'* . . . reaches from the strongly affective 'to hate' . . . to a somewhat diluted 'to feel aversion for, not want, avoid,'"[47] we have here "an outrageous statement" not only "in the context of wisdom" (Zimmerli). The nearest comparison is Job's "revulsion" (קוט *qwt* niphal) over his life (Job 10:1), which is based, to be sure, on entirely different experiences from those evoking the king's hatred of life (cf. Qoh 4:1-3).[48] By contrast, 9:4ff. and 11:7ff. emphasize the value of life precisely in view of the prospect of death. As in the foregoing, in v. 17 the things done "under the sun" (cf. 1:14) do not have to designate "world events" but can refer especially to human activity, if one assumes that here we have a *casus pendens* construction: "It seemed to me grievous that all activity that is carried out under the sun is futile and a striving after wind." Verse 17 then already leads, by way

of the following reflections of the king, beyond the limits of human activity. Their products are indeed "futile" and "fleeting" (הֶבֶל *hebel*) in the quite literal sense that one cannot in the long run hold on to them.

2:18-19 Limits of Activity: Inheritance without Wisdom

■ **18** Since after his death the king must leave to his successor everything that he has produced for himself (see vv. 4-8: לִי *lî*; cf. Ps 49:11; Sir 11:19; 14:15), his work and his possessions (עָמָל *'āmāl*) lose any value for him and indeed appear to him just as worthy of hate as his life (v. 17). Playing a role here, in addition to his own loss, is perhaps his envy of his successor. It is noteworthy that just the very thought of his future loss makes the king's present possessions seem worthless to him. According to 9:4ff., however, future loss is precisely what enhances the value of present goods and opportunities to act (cf. also Sir 14:11ff.).

■ **19** Death marks a limit to the human power of disposition over one's possessions not only in the sense that afterward one can no longer enjoy them oneself. One cannot even reliably determine who, after one's death, will have disposition over the fruits of one's labor. Obviously the king—regardless of his previous reflections on the theme "wisdom and folly"—would prefer his successor to be wise. For a fool to have disposition over property would contradict his postulate that one can and must oneself work for a good life with wisdom (cf. v. 21). Until now, the king has held to this postulate in spite of all contradictory experiences and considerations. Verse 19 can again be read as an ironic allusion to the OT Solomon traditions: according to 1 Kings 12 and 2 Chronicles 10, Solomon's son and successor Rehoboam listened to false advisers. Sirach 47:23 characterizes him as "broad in folly and lacking in sense"

---

the Egyptian Papyrus Insinger (ca. 300 B.C.E.), which ascertains each time at the end of a chapter (with small variations in language): "Destiny and happiness: they come—it is God who sends them" (see Brunner, *Altägyptische Weisheit*, 297–98). According to Lichtheim (*Late Egyptian Wisdom Literature*, 140) the Egyptian expressions used here, *šзy* and *šḥne*, correspond to the Greek terms ἀνάγκη and τύχη.

46   Yet court ritual ascribed to the king "eternal life": cf. 1 Kgs 1:31; Neh 2:3; Dan 2:4; 3:9; 5:10; 6:7, 22. Note that the formulation of v. 16a in the Hebrew (כִּי אֵין זִכְרוֹן לֶחָכָם עִם־הַכְּסִיל *kî 'ên zikrôn leḥākām 'im-*

hakkĕsîl) recalls v. 13a (שֶׁיֵּשׁ יִתְרוֹן לַחָכְמָה מִן־הַסִּכְלוּת *šeyyēš yitrôn laḥokmâ min-hassiklût*).

47   E. Jenni, שׂנא *śn'* hate," *TLOT* 3:1278.

48   Cf. further Job 3:11ff.; 6:8ff.; 7:15ff.; 10:18ff., also Num 11:15 (Moses); 1 Kgs 19:4 (Elijah); Jer 20:14ff. (Jeremiah); Jon 4:3, 8 (Jonah); Tob 3:6 (Tobit).

(רחב אולת וחסר בינה *rḥb ʾwlt wḥsr bynh*). Through his behavior, he lost his power of disposition over all the possessions of his father—and thereby exceeded the worst fears of King Qoheleth.[49]

2:20-21 Limits of Activity: Inheritance without Work

■ **20-21** If v. 19 takes into consideration the possibility that the successor of the king could be a foolish person, vv. 20-21 now mention a state of affairs that will necessarily result at the king's death: his successor will have disposition of property that he himself has not earned. This is true in any case of inheritance. Therefore, in v. 21 the king is no longer speaking of himself but quite generally of a "person." What drives him to despair (יאש *yʾš* piel) is the knowledge that the phenomenon of property transfer through inheritance is not compatible with his "achievement" thinking. According to him, a person can and must work out a good life for himself by coming "to possessions with wisdom and insight and skill." Yet in the very process of doing this, he accumulates possessions that after his death will become the "portion" (חֵלֶק *ḥēleq*) of another person and for the latter represent no "gain" (יתרון *yitrôn*) from his own efforts. Thus in view of death, the king's "achievement" thinking itself leads *ad absurdum*. At this point a critical reader can ask in retrospect whether the "great deeds" of the king (vv. 4-8) were possible only because of what he had inherited from *his* father. In contrast to King Qoheleth, 4:8 will argue that the prospect of one day leaving one's possessions to an heir could, nonetheless, make a person's efforts seem meaningful and understandable.

2:22-26 Result: The Devaluation of Happiness Not at One's Disposal

In 2:3 King Qoheleth set himself the goal of finding out "what is good for people to do under heaven as long as they live." In 2:22-26 he formulates the outcome of the resulting investigations and reflections: "Nothing good comes about through a man" (2:24). Wise activity does not necessarily lead to a happy life (vv. 22-23). Conversely, a happy life is not necessarily the fruit of a person's own efforts; rather, God can grant or withhold a "good life" from a person without regard to that person's accomplishments (vv. 24-26). Both strike the king as meaningless and "futile" (הֶבֶל *hebel*, vv. 23, 26), for this contradicts his requirement for the "doability" of a "good life": for him a happy life is worth striving for only if it represents the "gain" from wise activity that is reliably at one's disposal. If a "good life" is not at one's disposal in this sense, then it is not worth striving for—even if it should be possible as a gift of God.

2:22-23 Work without Pleasure

■ **22** Verse 22 asks first about the yield of the work and toil that a person does with the application of his mind "under the sun": "What does a man have from [that] (מֶה־הֹוֶה לָאָדָם *meh-hōweh lāʾādām*)?" The answer is clear, according to vv. 10-11: no "gain" (v. 11) and, at best, pleasure as one's "portion" (v. 10).

■ **23** Verse 23 reinforces this with the example of a life rich in work but poor in pleasure: looking back,[50] it must seem ultimately "meaningless and worthless" (הֶבֶל *hebel*; cf. 4:8). The key words "suffering" (מַכְאֹבִים *makʾōbîm*) and "vexation" (כַּעַס *kaʿas*) recall 1:18, where vexation and suffering are designated as the concomitant phenomena of increased wisdom; "toil" (עִנְיָן *ʿinyān*) refers back to the "bad business" in 1:13b. If, however, work alone—like wisdom—brings a person only aggravation, it is pleasure that makes a "successful life." Yet this is not only foolish and unproductive (v. 2); it is also, and above all, not reliably at one's disposal (v. 10).

2:24-26 Pleasure without Work

■ **24** Verse 24 is usually corrected to the effect that there is nothing better for human beings than to eat, drink, and enjoy something good (cf. ⅁ and ⅀). According to everything that King Qoheleth has had to say up to this point,[51] however, this would hardly be understood as an expression of the value of pleasure and enjoyment as in

---

49   The fall of the Alexandrian empire may well have been also remembered by the first readers of this text.

50   Cf. the perfect שָׁכַב *šākab*. Perhaps v. 23 parodies an obituary of a hard-working person.

51   The tension between the common understanding of v. 24 and what precedes it was perceived by Zimmerli: "The radical change can be surprising. Qoheleth has just confessed in the foregoing sentence that he hated life and he was driven to the

3:12, 22; 5:17; and 8:15 (cf. 9:7ff.), but rather as a reinforcement of his devaluation of all conceivable goods: pleasure and enjoyment are meaningless and worthless (cf. 2:1-2, 10-11, 26), and there is nothing better (v. 24)! If, however, we stay with the MT, as recommended above, v. 24 expresses the fact that the good is not at the disposal of human beings: "Nothing good comes about through a man."[52] The possibility of eating, drinking,[53] and enjoying life is not a "gain" of human efforts but is at best a person's "portion" (cf. 2:10-11); it is not within the human power of disposition; it comes, rather, from the hand of God. The term "God" here seems to be only another expression for the impotence and contingency (מִקְרֶה miqreh: 2:14) with which people see themselves confronted in their lives (cf. v. 26).[54] That the king expects nothing good from God was already apparent in 1:13b and becomes completely clear in 2:26.[55]

■ **25** If one interprets v. 25 as a statement about God's sole power of disposition over human happiness and unhappiness (cf. 𝔊 𝔖 Jer), it reinforces v. 24b and anticipates v. 26. If, however, one understands the verse in the sense of the translation recommended above, we have here "the last grammatical trace of the royal fiction" (Lohfink): if not even the king can create his own happiness, what chance does an ordinary mortal have? Once again, we may have here an ironic allusion to the OT Solomon traditions: under Solomon's rule, his people also "ate and drank and were happy" (1 Kgs 4:20; cf. also v. 25 and Psalm 72)! By contrast, it does not occur to King Qoheleth that as ruler he could contribute to the happiness of his subjects. Here at the end of his reflections, however, the idea seems to come to him that he is perhaps not the only person "who can eat and who must worry."

■ **26** Indeed, v. 26 raises a possibility that the king has

not yet considered at all: in addition to people who like himself try to achieve a "good life" through their own efforts and the gathering and accumulation of possessions (cf. 2:8), there are also those to whom God (in contradiction to 1:18!) gives "wisdom and insight and pleasure." In addition, the latter can enjoy the goods that the former have accumulated. Thus God grants some people their happiness at the expense of others. That contradicts (just as in the case of "inheritance without work" in vv. 20-21) quite strikingly the king's way of thinking, which accords all "goods" a value only when they are earned by oneself for oneself. For the king, such a distribution of human happiness and unhappiness by God, therefore, can only seem "meaningless" and "futile" (הֶבֶל hebel).

The terms with which the king describes those who in his eyes are favored or disadvantaged by God are ambiguous. "One who pleases God" (טוֹב לִפְנֵי הָאֱלֹהִים ṭôb lipnê hāʾĕlōhîm) can be a person who is in accord with God's will or with the cultic or moral norm set by God—or someone who, without personal effort, is granted the favor of the Godhead.[56] And a person "whose life is a failure" (חוֹטֵא ḥôṭēʾ) can be a "sinner"—or someone who (for whatever reasons) has not achieved his goals,[57] because without God's favor, he had "bad luck." If one assumes (with the majority of commentators) that in v. 26 the king is using terms of the "religious" tradition in a "secular" way, the verse is to be understood as a statement on the "arbitrariness of divine determination."[58] If, however, one assumes that the "religious" or "moral" meaning of the expressions can also be heard here, in v. 26 the king is also expressly referring back to

---

52 Cf. the translation in Lohfink (= EÜ): "That happy disposition . . . is not a given in human nature."

53 On "eating and drinking" as the epitome of a "good life" in the OT, cf. R. Smend, "Essen und Trinken—ein Stück Weltlichkeit des Alten Testaments," in *Die Mitte des Alten Testaments: Gesammelte Studien,* vol. 1 (Munich: Kaiser, 1986) 200–211.

54 Cf. also the passages in the book of Proverbs given above in reference to 2:14a.

(from footnote column, top:) edge of despair. And now comes the admonition [?] to enjoy what the day has to offer in eating and drinking and the possibilities of things going well."

55 As an "orthodox" gloss (thus, e.g., Lauha and Oswald Loretz, "Altorientalische und kanaanäische Topoi im Buche Kohelet," *UF* 12 [1980] 271–72), vv. 24b–26bα would be rather unskillfully placed *before* the הֶבֶל hebel judgment in v. 26bβ.

56 For the former see H. J. Stoebe, "טוֹב ṭôb good," *TLOT* 2:490. For the latter see Gk. θεοφιλός (Braun, *Kohelet,* 53).

57 Cf. R. Knierim, "חטא ḥṭʾ to miss," *TLOT* 1:406.

58 Müller, "Skepsis," 11–12. Cf., e.g., Gordis, 87ff.

72

a divine distribution of happiness and unhappiness to people according to the standards of a "righteous distributive repayment" (Lauha[59]) (cf. Prov 13:22; 28:8; Job 27:16-17): in his "secular" conception of a "good life," religious and ethical points of view can only seem "meaningless" and "futile"; what counts is solely one's own "accomplishment." This, however, is not taken into consideration by God—one way or the other.

In the characteristic style of the foregoing comments of the king, it is easy to understand the closing הֶבֶל *hebel* judgment in v. 26 as an evaluation of the whole activity of God portrayed in (v)v. (24-)26.[60] Syntactically, however, it would also be possible to relate this judgment only to the attitude of "gathering (אָסַף *'sp*) and heaping (כָּנַס *kns*)," which was the subject of the immediately preceding section. Then the king would, here at the end of his reflections, come to the insight that his "gain" orientation, which manifested itself in the "gathering and heaping" of property (2:8: כָּנַס *kns*), wisdom (1:16: יָסַף *ysp* hiphil), and possibilities for enjoyment, and which led him to the devaluation of all presumed goods as הֶבֶל *hebel*, is itself "futile" (הֶבֶל *hebel*). At the same time, to be sure, he would reject the possibility of changing his attitude toward life: indeed, he did not choose it for himself; rather, God "gave" it to him.

In this "tragic" (or, according to point of view, even "cynical") self-understanding, King Qoheleth would then meet with his Alexandrine "colleague" Ptolemy II ("Philadelphos," 285–246 B.C.E.), of whom the historian Phylarchos, who was still living in the third century B.C.E., reports the following "anecdote":

Ptolemy, the second king of this name in Egypt, despite the fact that he was the most brilliant of all rulers and devoted to education (παιδεία) beyond others, was nevertheless so deceived in his power of judgment and seduced by immoderate luxury that he believed that he would live for ever and asserted that he alone was immortal. When he felt better after an attack of gout which lasted for several days and watched through some windows how the Egyptians were enjoying their simple meal lying in groups on the sand of the river bank, he exclaimed: "Unhappy man I am, that I cannot become like one of these."[61]

1:12—2:26 and the Program of a "Devaluation of What Is Not at One's Disposal"

In his presentation of Hellenistic philosophy as the common basis of Stoicism, Epicureanism, and Pyrrhonist skepticism, the three defining philosophical directions in the Hellenistic period, Malte Hossenfelder has reconstructed a "program for the devaluation of everything not at one's disposal":[62]

[If] happiness lies in the fulfillment of goals, unhappiness in their nonfulfillment, and goal setting with the individual [see above on 2:3], then he must only make sure that he sets no unattainable goals, harbors no wishes that cannot be fulfilled, but directs all his striving toward things that he knows can become reality. Yet this can be realized with the certainty and endurance necessary for happiness only if he considers exclusively those things to be of value and worth striving for that he himself has completely at his disposal at any time and without any foreign help or influence, and if he considers everything not available in this sense to be pointless.[63]

In 1:12—2:26, King Qoheleth proceeds exactly in the sense of this program when he regards everything that represents no certain and disposable "gain" as meaningless and worthless ("futile and a striving after wind").[64] The king carries out this program so radically that in the end there is absolutely no "good" left that is worth striving for and at one's disposal: human beings cannot work out their happiness through their own efforts; a "good life" is not reliably at their disposal; thus every experienceable happiness is meaningless and worthless (2:22-26)!

---

59   Lauha regards [v]v. [24b-]26abα as an "orthodox" gloss (see above); cf. for v. 26abα, e.g., McNeile, Barton, and Podechard.

60   Thus, e.g., Lohfink, Murphy.

61   FGrHist 81 F 40 (Athens 12, 536e), quoted according to Hengel, *Judaism and Hellenism*, 1:130.

62   Hossenfelder, *Philosophie*, 201.

63   Ibid., 34.

64   Cf. Krüger, "Qoh 2,24-26," 82–83.

Whereas the Stoics perceive an available happiness in harmony with "nature" and the Epicureans in a moderate "desire," the Pyrrhonist skeptics—like King Qoheleth—were of the opinion "that even happiness is not at one's disposal."[65] As a result, they set themselves the goal of "excluding any zeal in the pursuance of any matter or any involvement whatever, in order to let every event in the world and in themselves pass over them with the greatest possible equanimity."[66] In 1:12–2:26 (cf. 2:17, 18, 20), King Qoheleth is, to be sure, a long way from such equanimity. With his "contempt for theory" (1:16-18; 2:13-17) and "criticism of property" (2:18-21), he is, on the contrary, close to the Cynics.[67] Yet contempt for theory and criticism of property do not lead the Cynics—in contrast to King Qoheleth—to despair and hatred of life. For, according to Diogenes, "contempt of desire produces the greatest desire of all, when one has previously adapted oneself to it through practice" (Diogenes Laertius 6.71).[68]

In the radicality of his carrying out the program of "devaluation of what is not at one's disposal," King Qoheleth came close to Hegesias, called *Peisithanatos* ("recommender of suicide") (ca. 320–280 B.C.E.), "who—because of his activity in Alexandria, where, as his name asserts, he is supposed to have persuaded many to commit suicide—was forbidden by Ptolemy Lagi to stay any longer." Hegesias "was probably the first and only ancient philosopher who developed an expressly pessimistic system."[69] As teaching of the "Hegesiasts," Diogenes Laertius (2.94) reports: "Happiness is clearly impossible, for the body is haunted by all kinds of ailments; the soul, however, is the companion of the body and shares its ailments and traumas; and as for our hopes, many are shattered by fate. All of this excludes the real presence of happiness." By contrast, King Qoheleth seems not to question the *possibility* of happiness, but only whether it is *at our disposal* (cf. 2:24-26).

Even if the reflections of King Qoheleth in 1:12–2:26 do not correspond completely to any philosophical "school" in the Hellenistic period, they still seem to reflect a "zeitgeist analogous to or identical with" that of contemporary Greek philosophy, by whose discussions the author of the book of Qoheleth could scarcely remain untouched.[70] The following section, 3:1–4:12, will take up and expand the critical interaction with this "zeitgeist" of Hellenism and develop a theological alternative to the program of a "devaluation of what is not at one's disposal."

65 Hossenfelder, *Philosophie*, 149.

66 Ibid., 154.

67 Cf. ibid., 184. Thus, according to Crates, "the goods of happiness are futile and fleeting" (Diogenes Laertius 6.86—whereas the "gain" of philosophy for him still consists in "a daily measure of beans and a worry-free mind" [contra Qoh 1:18!]). And Diogenes answered (according to Diogenes Laertius 6.63) "the question, what gain had philosophy brought him . . . : even if nothing else, then at least this: to be ready for any turn of fate" (cf. Qoh 2:13-14). (Quotations are according to *Diogenes Laertios, Leben und Meinungen berühmter Philosophen*, German translation by O. Apelt, ed. K. Reich [2d ed.; Philosophische Bibliothek 53/54; Hamburg: Meiner, 1967].)

68 Contrary to the Cynics, "King Qoheleth" does not draw from his insights the conclusion that he should "throw his money away," as the Cynic Anacharsis in a letter "to the son of the king" demands (A. J. Malherbe, *The Cynic Epistles; A Study Edition* [SBLSBS 12; Missoula, Mont.: Scholars Press, 1977] 43; cf. also his letter to Kroisos, ibid., 47ff.). According to Diogenes Laertius 6.87, Krates, in his devotion to Cynicism, sold his property and divided the proceeds among his fellow citizens.

69 Braun, *Kohelet*, 29; cf. Diogenes Laertius 2.86.

70 Quotation from Otto Kaiser, "Judentum und Hellenismus," *VF* 27 (1982) 73. Beginning in the 3d cent. B.C.E., there is abundant evidence of a "*higher, literary Greek education*" in Palestine; see Hengel, *Judaism and Hellenism*, 1:65ff.; idem, *Jews, Greeks and Barbarians: Aspects of the Hellenization of Judaism in the Pre-Christian Period* (Philadelphia: Fortress Press, 1980) 117ff.; in the 2d–1st century B.C.E. "all the philosophical schools were represented in Palestine and Phoenicia," with a certain "preponderance of the *Stoa*" (Hengel, *Judaism and Hellenism*, 1:87; cf. 1:83ff.; cf. also John G. Gammie, "Stoicism and Anti-Stoicism in Qoheleth," *HAR* 9 [1985] 184). From this standpoint, one can hardly justify limiting the level of comparison in advance to "early Hellenistic *popular* philosophy" (and here even further to the "*pessimistic*" tradition) (thus Braun, *Kohelet*).

3 **Is There Any Gain with Regard to Time?**

1   For everything there is a (certain) season,
     and there is a (favorable) time for every matter
       under heaven:

2   a time to bear[a] and a time to die;
     a time to plant, and a time to pluck up what is
       planted;

3   a time to kill, and a time to heal;
     a time to tear down, and a time to build up;

4   a time to weep, and a time to laugh;
     a time of mourning, and a time of dancing;

5   a time to throw away stones, and a time to gather
       stones together;

6   a time to seek, and a time to leave lost;
     a time to embrace, and a time to refrain from
       embracing;
     a time to keep, and a time to throw away;

7   a time to tear up, and a time to sew together;
     a time to keep silent, and a time to speak;

8   a time to love, and a time to hate;
     a time of war, and a time of peace.

9   **What gain does the one who works have from making a special effort?[a]**

2a   Or: "to procreate." לָדֶת *ledet* (qal) is often understood passively in the sense of הֻלֶּדֶת *hulledet* (hophal) or הוּלַד *hiwwāled* (niphal, cf. 7:1) and translated "to be born" (cf. 𝔙 *nascendi*, contra, however, 𝔊 τεκεῖν, 𝔖 ܐܬܝܠܕ *m'ld*, 𝔗 מיליד *myld*). Against this interpretation, nonetheless, is the fact that active verbs are used exclusively in what follows.

9a   Or: "from that for which he is toiling."

The section 3:1-9 is the mirror image, in its structure, of 1:3-9:

- general assertion   3:1   1:9
- illustration through
  individual phenomena   3:2-8   1:4-8
- concluding question   3:9   1:3

In the course of reading, one may understand this section as a continuation of the comments of King Qoheleth in 1:12—2:26.[1] Verse 9 would then (as a rhetorical question) reinforce his assertion in 2:11 that there is no gain under the sun, and vv. 1-8 could be read as an illustration of his remarks on fate (מִקְרֶה *miqreh*) in 2:14-15.[2] The king would then be pondering here, in retrospect, the time-bound nature of his undertakings and reflections:[3] Just like the contingencies of fate, death, and God, time also limits his power of disposition over his own life. From the king's perspective, this state of affairs would without doubt be judged negatively (הֶבֶל *hebel*).

As in 1:3-11, however, 3:1-9 also lacks any evaluation of the described state of affairs. Then 3:11 lets the time-bound nature of all events appear in a positive light: God "has made everything *beautiful* in its time"! Since 3:10 begins a critical revision of the king's reflections in 1:12—2:26, it is perhaps more appropriate in the greater compositional context to understand 3:1-9 (in a second reading) as a poetic interlude corresponding to 1:3-11, "a sort of meditative pause" (Lohfink) between the reflections of "King Qoheleth" in 1:12—2:26 and those of the "wise man Qoheleth" in 3:10—4:12. May one perhaps also see in the closing of the "catalog of the times" (vv. 2-8) with "a time for peace" (עֵת שָׁלוֹם *'ēt šālôm*) an indication of the end of the "Solomonic" royal travesty?

In terms of content, 3:1-9 can be understood as a continuation and expansion of 1:3-11: if it was a question there of the possibilities and limits of human activity on

---

1   Thus, e.g., Lohfink, who regards 2:24—3:15 as a unit, in which the royal fiction is taken up in 2:25.

2   Cf. Hengel, *Judaism and Hellenism*, 1:125, on καιρός and χρόνος as "concepts of fate" in the Greek-Hellenistic world.

3   Of the activities named in 3:2-8, the following can be related back to 1:12—2:26: "dying" (מות *mwt*:

3:2a/2:16), "planting" (נטע *nt'*: 3:2b/2:4-5), "building" (בנה *bnh*: 3:3b/2:4), "laughing" (שחק *śḥq*: 3:4a/2:2), "gathering" (כנס *kns*: 3:5a/2:8, 26), "speaking" (דבר *dbr*: 3:7b/1:16; 2:15), "hating" (שנא *śn'*: 3:8a/2:17-18).

the horizon of "distant ages" (עֹלָם/עֹלָמִים ʿôlām/ʿôlāmîm), here we now see the smaller changes of "time" (עֵת ʿēt) within human life. There is also here a repetition of similar things, as expressed in 1:9: "What has been done (once) is what will be done (again)."[4] If in regard to distant time the question was raised as to what gain people could have from *all* their efforts (1:3), now, in view of the changing of the times, the focus is on the question of what gain can be secured for people through their *toil* (3:9).

■ **1** The introductory thesis is formulated in an artful parallelism of synonyms; its members are related to each other chiastically, and the second line contains an element that goes beyond the first:

(a) לַכֹּל	(b) זְמָן	
(b') וְעֵת	(a') לְכָל־חֵפֶץ	(c) תַּחַת הַשָּׁמָיִם

(a) *lakkōl*	(b) *zĕmān*
(b') *wĕʿēt*	(a') *lĕkol-ḥēpeṣ*
(c) *taḥat haššāmāyim*	

"Everything" (הכֹּל [hak]kōl) in v. 1a is further defined by "every matter under heaven" (כָּל־חֵפֶץ תַּחַת הַשָּׁמָיִם *kol-ḥēpeṣ taḥat haššāmāyim*) in v. 1b: it is not a question here of "world events" in general, but rather, and especially, of "intentional" human activity (חֵפֶץ *ḥēpeṣ* = "pleasure, concern, interest, wish, desire, goal, purpose, matter, business"). Through the preposition לְ *l*, the "most gen-

eral relationship marker" in the system of Hebrew prepositions,[5] this is connected with its "predetermined" or "appropriate" or "favorable time" (זְמָן *zĕmān* or עֵת *ʿēt*).[6] Syntactically, in v. 1a and b we have existential statements with prepositionally added precision.[7] They can be read in a double sense. If one accentuates more strongly the *relationship* between the two components (nominal group and prepositional group), the stress is on the fact that the *realizability* of every plan is *limited* because it requires a favorable time (cf. the frequent translation: "Everything has *its* time"). If, however, one lays the emphasis more strongly on the element of the *existential* statement (as is clear in vv. 4b, 5aβ, 8b), v. 1 means that in the changing of the times, the realization of *every* plan is *possible,* in spite of one's limited lifetime ("for *everything* there is a favorable time").

Thus v. 1 first names in a very open way the possibilities and limits of human activity in time. Then the general statements formulated here are illustrated and made more precise in the following vv. 2-8.

■ **2-8** These verses name 28 (4 x 7) "matters" in 14 (2 x 7) pairs. This could indicate that here "seven, the number of completion, perfection," is supposed to be developed into "four, the cardinal points of the heavens," in order that "the fullness of the time at human's disposal" can be described as ordered "cosmos."[7] The enumerated "matters" cannot be understood throughout as examples

---

4   Cf., e.g., Siegfried; Gordis; Lohfink.

5   "In later Jewish literature, ʿēt is replaced by zᵉmān" (E. Jenni, "עֵת ʿēt time," *TLOT* 2:961). On לְ *l* see Jenni, *Präpositionen,* 1:20–21.

6   Cf. R. Bartelmus, *Einführung in das biblische Hebräisch* (Zurich: Theologischer Verlag, 1994), 45–46.

7   N. Lohfink, "The Present and Eternity: Time in Qoheleth," *TD* 34 (1987) 237. Cf. Hengel, *Judaism and Hellenism,* 1:165, on the "sevenfold structure" of the cosmos in Aristobulus. With Levy, we may ask whether the text alludes to astrological number speculations (Gordis argues against this). Loader (*comm.*; *Polar Structures,* 11ff.; "Qohelet 3,2-8: A Sonnet in the Old Testament," *ZAW* 81 [1969] 240–42) recommends a division of vv. 2-8 into four "strophes" that are distinguished from one another through the model of the sequence of "favourable" [f] and "unfavourable" [u] (or "desirable" and "undesirable") actions: (I) vv. 2-3 (2x fu, 2x uf), (II) vv. 4-5 (2x uf, 2x fu), (III) vv. 6-7 (2x fu, 2x uf), (IV) v. 8

(fu - uf). Yet such a qualification is neither suggested by the text nor clearly preferable in every passage. Just as questionable is A. G. Wright's ("'For Everything There Is a Season.' The Structure and Meaning of the Fourteen Opposites [Ecclesiasates 3,2-8]," in M. Carrez, J. Doré, and P. Grelot, eds., *De la Tôra au Messie: Mélanges Henri Cazelles* [Paris: Desclée, 1981] 321–28) assumption that v. 4 and v. 7, which are concerned with joy and sorrow, mark the close of two strophes, the first of which in vv. 2-3 names "constructive" and "destructive" actions, whereas the second in vv. 5-6 juxtaposes "union" and "separation." This is supposed to show "that the joys and sorrows of life come from constructive/destructive actions and from separations and unions caused by love and hate on the individual and social levels" (idem, "Ecclesiastes [Qoheleth]," in R. E. Brown et al., eds., *The New Jerome Biblical Commentary* [Englewood Cliffs, N.J.: Prentice-Hall, 1990] 492).

of "advantages and disadvantages, good and bad sides" of life.[8] Not all of the paired actions are mutually exclusive.[9] The (in part) downright trivial character of the named "matters" does not so much reinforce the assumption of a complete "determination" of human life as to make it ironic.[10] By contrast, the aspect of the constant changing of the "times"[11] could play a role in the context as a limit on the durability of a possible "gain" (v. 9). The common denominator of the phenomena named in vv. 2-8 seems, nonetheless, to consist above all in the fact that favorable or unfavorable temporal circumstances both allow and limit the success of human actions. Yet the fulfillment of one's plans are, in any case, not reliably at one's disposal solely through one's own efforts. According to 2:11, however, only such results can be credited as "gain" (v. 9). Yet at the same time, the adduced examples also show that the time-bound nature of human action exhibits wide variations in specific cases, and thus the degree of human freedom to decide and act is defined anew in each individual case.[12]

■ **2a** With "to bear" (or "to procreate") and "to die," the first pair of "matters" juxtaposes the highest human possibilities, collaborating in the creation of new life, with human transitoriness. For humankind, procreation and birth are, naturally, not always plannable and at one's disposal, but they are considerably more so than death

(cf. 8:8).[13] In the world of the first readers of the text, the "time to bear" was, at the same time, for women not infrequently also the "time to die." As a matter of fact, reproduction and death are closely related; one requires the other: "A generation goes, and a generation comes" (1:4).

■ **2b** By contrast, the plucking up of what is planted annihilates in a meaningless way the result of planting. The reference here is probably to hostile actions (perhaps in war?), but hardly to the harvest, which one does not "pluck up," or the pulling up of weeds that are not "planted."[14] Even if the "times" of planting and the plucking up of what is planted are not at one's disposal, they doubtless still leave one a considerably greater margin for decision and action than, say, the "time to die" (cf., e.g., Deut 20:19-20).

■ **3** Whereas "to kill" and "to heal" (on the latter cf. Sir 38:13), just like "to plant" and "to pluck up," are opposite actions in intention and effect, "to break down" and "to build up" can be parts of a comprehensive course of action (say, the building or remodeling of a house), which are meaningfully carried out in succession.[15]

■ **4** "To weep" and "to laugh," "to mourn" and "to dance" are to a high degree motivated and provoked by corresponding "causes." The corresponding "times," however, do not *force* people to behave in accordance with them (cf. 2:2; 7:2-4, as well as 7:14; 9:8-9).

---

8   Thus Loretz, *Qohelet*, 252; and, e.g., Loader.

9   Thus, e.g., K. Galling, "Die Rätsel der Zeit im Urteil Kohelets (Koh. 3,1-15)," *ZThK* 58 (1061) 2.

10 Thus, e.g., Lauha; Murphy.

11 Cf. O. Eissfeldt, "Alles Ding währt seine Zeit," in *Kleine Schriften,* vol. 5 (ed. R. Sellheim and F. Maass; Tübingen: Mohr, 1973) 174.

12 The fact that there are commonalities *and* differences between the situations named in vv. 2-8 is already signalized by the syntactic variants on the surface level of the text: the pattern עֵת *ʿēt* + ל *l* + inf. (20x) is broken in vv. 4b, 5aβ (עֵת *ʿēt* + inf.) and v. 8b (עֵת *ʿēt* + noun). Verses 2bβ and 5a also add an object, and v. 5bβ a prepositional modification. The repetition of the verb שׁלך *šlk* hiphil ("throw away," v. 5a, 6b) shows that we are dealing with different counterparts. The literary-critical elimination of these differences (cf., e.g., O. Loretz, "Anfänge jüdischer Philosophie nach Qohelet 1,1-11 und 3,1-15," *UF* 23 [1991] 233ff.) trims the text according to the standard of the expected "statement" itself.

13 With J. Blenkinsopp, "Ecclesiastes 3,1-15: Another Interpretation," *JSOT* 66 (1995) 55–64, we may indeed wonder, whether the "time to die" could also be intended to include the right time for suicide.

14 The qal of עקר *ʿqr* is not attested elsewhere in the OT. The niphal in Zeph 2:4 refers to the destruction of a city; the piel to the laming of horses or steers through the cutting of the tendons of their hind feet (Gen 49:6; Josh 11:6, 9; 2 Sam 8:4; 1 Chr 18:4). For the harvest, see, e.g., Whitley, *Koheleth,* 31. For pulling weeds see, e.g., G. Sauter, *Was heisst: nach Sinn fragen? Eine theologisch-philosophische Orientierung* (KT 53; Munich: Kaiser, 1982) 28.

15 Cf. Crenshaw.

■ **5a** In line with the *Midrash Rabbah,* the throwing away or gathering of stones is often interpreted as a metaphor for indulgence or nonindulgence in sexual activity.[16] Here, however, one could also think just as well (if not better) of the cultivation and protection of a field (through throwing away stones from the field and then gathering them again for the building of a wall) or its ruining in war and later restoration (cf. 2 Kgs 3:19, 25), of the placing of losing and winning of stones in a board game, or the giving out and gathering in of counting stones by a trader in the buying and selling of wares.[17]

■ **5b** The opposition of "to embrace" and "to refrain from embracing" may express, on the one hand, the trivial state of affairs that one can always do only one of the two things at the same time (but also always does one or the other, whereas one can easily at any given time neither "procreate" [or "bear"] nor "die," etc.). Or, on the other hand, the idea here is that there are situations in which it is indeed *possible* for a person "to embrace," but it is *appropriate* "to refrain from embracing" (cf. 2 Sam 11:6ff.). Then here too it would be clear that the time-bound nature of human action does not fully exclude human freedom of decision, but rather challenges it.

■ **6** The two pairs of actions in v. 6 formulate genuine alternatives: one must either "seek" something or "leave [it] lost," either "keep" it or "throw [it] away"—*tertium non datur* (whereas one does not necessarily have to either "throw away" or "gather": v. 5a). The first pair refers to lost objects; the second to those present. Taken together, the two pairs of actions describe all the possibilities of dealing with objects of personal possession. For each of these possibilities, there are favorable or appropriate situations.

■ **7** Tearing up (clothes) and remaining silent are sometimes interpreted as a signs of mourning (in accordance with the *Midrash Rabbah*).[18] Yet "tearing up" and "sewing together" can simply refer to a process "out of everyday

domestic life."[19] The idea that there is an appropriate and favorable time for "keeping silent" and "speaking" is a theme often treated in the wisdom tradition.[20]

■ **8** Whereas "love" and "hate" are largely withheld from human powers of disposition (and "love" can in time turn into "hate"), certainly for the "little people," "war" and "peace" are conditions of their lives that are not at their disposal (cf. 8:8). For kings, however, there is a "time" in which they "go out to battle" (2 Sam 11:1), that is, a time (of year) favorable for waging war, in which, however, they are by no means compelled to wage war.

■ **9** The time-bound nature of human activity described in vv. 2-8 limits the possibilities of gain (יִתְרוֹן *yitrôn*) for human beings (cf. 1:3; 2:11) in two respects. First, the changing of the times sets a limit on the *duration* of any possible gain—and not just in regard to "eternity" (cf. 1:3-11) but already within the limited human life span (cf. Sir 11:19; 18:25-26): "From morning to evening conditions [that is, time ($\kappa\alpha\iota\rho\acute{o}\varsigma$)] change; all things move swiftly before the Lord" (18:26). Second, the *accessibility* of any possible gain is limited when the success of human activity depends on the favor or lack of favor of time and circumstance, against which the effort (עמל *ʿml*) expended in the action cannot (or in any case cannot reliably) prevail.

■ **1-9** When read for itself, Qoh 3:1-9, like 1:3-11, leaves many questions open. The text, for example, still says nothing about whether and to what extent a person is in a position to know if there is or is not a favorable time for a particular project and to predict the changing of the times.[21] Moreover, 3:1-9 reveals nothing about whether and to what degree chance, fate, or the Deity rules in the changing of the times.[22] Finally, the text contains no evaluation of the described states of affairs. In the eyes of the king in 1:12—2:26, they are without doubt a further example of the "futility" (הֶבֶל *hebel*) of all human activity and striving. Then, however, 3:10—4:12

---

16   Cf. the parallels "embrace" and "refrain from embracing"; against this, however, is Galling, "Rätsel," 9–10.

17   Cf. ibid., 7ff.

18   Thus, e.g., Delitzsch; Loader.

19   Lauha.

20   Cf. Prov 15:23; Sir 1:23-24; 4:23; 20:6-7, 20; and Walter Bühlmann, *Vom rechten Reden und Schweigen: Studien zu Proverbien 10–31* (OBO 12; Fribourg,

Switzerland: Universitätsverlag; Göttingen: Vandenhoeck & Ruprecht, 1976).

21   Cf. also 3:11, 22; 6:12; 7:14; 8:5-7; 9:11-12; 10:14; 11:2, 6.

22   Cf. also 3:11-15, 17; 7:13-14; 8:17; 11:5.

shows them in a different light. As a "result" of 1:3—3:9, one can ascertain that in view of time, on both the large and the small scale, it must seem (at the very least) questionable whether human beings alone, through their own efforts, can through careful management achieve a reliably available gain of unlimited duration (1:3; 2:11; 3:9).

The statements of 3:1-8 correspond completely in their still "by no means fatalistic or deterministic in form . . . to the wisdom tradition; for both ancient Near Eastern and OT wisdom teachers, a concern for the recognition of the right moment is fundamental."[23] It is not only of fundamental importance for agriculture and ships but also for the feast calendar.[24] Here the boundaries between meteorology and prophecy, astronomy and astrology are (by our present-day understanding) completely fluid.[25]

The "time" theme seems to have had a special virulence in the Hellenistic period as an expression of the feeling of dependence on uncontrollable "fate" or "chance."[26] Moving against this feeling, it seems, are statements in early Jewish literature close to the time of the book of Qoheleth that point to the ordering of

"time" and its determination by God. Thus, for example, Pss 104:27 and 145:15 emphasize the "timeliness" of God's provisioning of creation with necessary food. Sirach 39:16-35 takes up this idea (cf. vv. 16, 33) and builds it up into a conception of a proper *temporal* order (cf. vv. 28-29: מִשְׁפָּט *mišpāt*) of the world, in which everything has importance in its time (v. 21). According to Sirach, this order is revealed both in the realm of daily life[27] and in the area of historical changes (cf. Sir 10:4) and also "eschatology" (cf. 48:10; 51:30 𝔊). *1 Enoch* 1–36 and 72–82 emphasize for cosmological processes that they all appear "in their time."[28] And according to Daniel 2 and 7, God "gives" (יהב *yhb*) the kingdoms of the world "a season and a time" (זְמָן וְעִדָּן *zĕman wĕʿiddān*) of their end (7:12) and God "changes" (שנה *šnh* haphel) the "times and seasons" (עִדָּנַיָּא וְזִמְנַיָּא *ʿiddānayyâ wĕzimnayyâ*), as well as their rulers (2:21).[29]

On this level, Qoh 3:1-8 can be read both as an expression of Hellenistic "contingency consciousness" and as an assertion of a "temporal ordering" of reality in the sense of the named early Jewish conceptions. Independent of this, however, according to v. 9 "time" limits, in any case, a person's chances of "gain"!

23   E. Jenni, "עֵת *ʿēt* time," *TLOT* 2:959–60. Jenni refers here to Loretz, *Qohelet*, 200, and Gerhard von Rad, *Wisdom in Israel*, 140–41, as well as "the pedagogical poem concerning the farmer's activities in Isa 28:23-29; also Jer 8:7; Ezek 16:8; Amos 5:13; Job 5:26; Prov 15:23; 25:11 . . . ; one could also include here the 'wise who know the times' in Esth 1:13 and 'the sons of Issachar who understand the times so that they know what Israel must do' in 1 Chron 12:32" (ibid., 960).

24   Cf. זְמָן *zĕmān* in Esth 9:27, 31, as well as Dan 7:25. For agriculture, in addition to Isa 28:23-29, cf. here also, e.g., the Gezer calendar, as well as Hesiod, *Works and Days*, 383ff. For ships see Hesiod, ibid., 618ff.

25   Cf. *TUAT* 2:46ff., 76ff., 94ff., 132ff.; Hesiod, *Works and Days*, 765ff. That "it was Hesiod's treatment of the theme which prompted Koheleth's composi-

tion" (Whitley, *Koheleth*, 175) can hardly be asserted, in spite of the partially agreeing themes and statements.

26   Cf. Hengel, *Judaism and Hellenism*, 1:125, and above on 2:14-15.

27   Cf. Sir 1:23-24; 4:20, 23; 6:8; 11:9, 20; 18:25-26; 20:1, 6-7, 19-20; 22:6; 26:4; 27:12; 29:2, 8; 30:24; 31:28; 32:4; 38:13.

28   Cf. *1 Enoch* 2:1; 18:15; 72:1, 7; 75:3-4; 78:15-16; 79:2, 4-5; 80:1; 82:10.

29   Cf. further Dan 7:22, 25; 8:17; 9:25; 11:6, 13, 14, 24, 35, 40; 12:1, 4, 9, 11. Cf. also the historical periods in Tob 14:4-5: "for a time" (*RSV*) (μέχρι χρόνου) or "until the times of the age are completed" (*RSV*) (ἕως πληρωθῶσιν καιροὶ τοῦ αἰῶνος).

3

Happiness as the Highest Good Is Not at Our Disposal

3:10 I considered the business that God has left[a] the sons of men to be busy with.[b] **11** He has made[a] everything so that it is beautiful in its time. He has put distant time[b] into their minds,[c] yet[d] man cannot comprehend[e] the work that the Deity has done from beginning to end.[f] **12** I understood that they bring about nothing better than[a] to be happy and do good[b] as long as they live. **13** And if a man in all his toil eats and drinks and enjoys what is good, this is also a gift of God![a] **14** I understood that whatever the Deity does is definitive:[a] nothing is to be added to it, nor anything taken from it.[b] The Deity has made it so that man will fear him.[c]

15 What happened (once before) has long since happened (again),[a] and what will happen[b] has long since already happened (once before). And the Deity seeks what has been driven away.[c]

16 And, furthermore,[a] I saw under the sun: to the place of justice, wickedness (has penetrated), and to the place of righteousness, wickedness![b] **17** I thought:[a] The Deity will judge the righteous and the wicked. For there is a time for every matter and (so also) for[b] everything that is done there.[c] **18** I thought[a] about[b] human beings: the Deity wanted to set them apart and had to see[c] that they are, for each other, (only) animals.[d] **19** The fate of humans[a] is indeed the same as the[b] fate of animals, and[c] they have one and the same fate. Both must die,[d] and all have one and the same life spirit; and humans have no advantage over animals, for they are all fleeting: **20** they are all going to the same place. They all come from dust, and they all return to dust. **21** Who knows then whether[a] the life spirit of humans goes upward, and the life spirit of animals goes downward into the earth?

22 So I saw that there is nothing better than for a man to enjoy his work. For that is his portion. For who can bring him to see what will be in the future?[a]

4:1 And again I[a] considered the full extent of oppression that is practiced under the sun,[b] and look: the tears of the oppressed—and they have no one who comforts them. And from the hand of

---

3:10a Or: "given" (cf. above on 1:13).

10b Instead of לַעֲנוֹת *laʿănôt* (𝔐), 𝔊 vocalizes לְעֲנּוֹת *lĕʿannôt*: "in order to depress [or humiliate?] them."

11a On occasional proposals to interpret the perfect עָשָׂה *ʿāśâ* in the present (Isaksson) or to vocalize it as a participle (Joüon), cf. Schoors, *Preacher*, 175, 185–86.

11b On the numerous recommendations on the interpretation (say, as "eternity," "world," "duration of time," "passing of time") or emendation of הָעֹלָם *hāʿōlām* (say, to עָמָל *ʿāmāl*, "effort" [see BHK], עֶלֶם *ʿēlem*, "knowledge" [Hitzig], or "ignorance" [Graetz]), cf. Ellermeier, *Qohelet*, I/1, 309ff.; Braun, *Kohelet*, 111ff.; Whitley, *Koheleth*, 31ff.; J. L. Crenshaw, "The Eternal Gospel (Eccl. 3:11)," in Crenshaw and T. Willis, eds., *Essays in Old Testament Ethics: FS J. P. Hyatt* (New York: Ktav, 1974) 39ff. In the context (cf. the following "from the beginning to the end"), as well as in view of 1:3-11, the interpretation of הָעֹלָם *hāʿōlām* as a time concept has the greatest probability (cf. E. Jenni, "עוֹלָם *ʿôlām* eternity," *TLOT* 2:861). It is also supported by the versions (𝔊 τὸν αἰῶνα, 𝔖 ܠܥܠܡ *ʿlmʾ*, 𝔙 *mundum* [עֹלָם *ʿôlām* = "world"] *tradidit disputationi eorum*).

11c Contra, e.g., Lauha, who relates בְּלִבָּם *bĕlibbām* back to הַכֹּל *hakkōl*: "he also put duration into everything" (cf. Ellermeier, *Qohelet*, I/1, 320; Lohfink; see also Schoors, *Preacher*, 163–64). Yet the continuation here leads us to think more of the human "heart" or "mind" (v. 10). מִבְּלִי *mibbĕlî* picks up the last three consonants of בְּלִבָּם *bĕlibbām* palindromically. Here there seems to be an intentional play on words, which speaks against a correction to בּוֹ *bô* or בָּם *bām* (thus *BHS*; cf. Galling).

11d On the linking of מִבְּלִי *mibbĕlî* and אֲשֶׁר *ʾăšer*, attested only in this place, cf. Schoors, *Preacher*, 147–48. A final or consecutive understanding ("so that not"; cf. 𝔊 𝔙 𝔗 𝔖) seems very unlikely, both in view of the context (to the extent that one interprets הָעֹלָם *hāʿōlām* in the way suggested above) and in view of the usage of מִבְּלִי *mibbĕlî* in the OT (in the sense of "unless" or "because not"; see the lexica).

11e Literally: "find out." On מצא *mṣʾ* in the sense of "grasp, comprehend," cf. 8:17 (par. ידע *ydʿ*, "know"); see also Anthony R. Ceresko, "The Function of Antanaclasis (*mṣʾ* 'to find' // *mṣʾ* 'to reach, overtake, grasp') in Hebrew Poetry, Especially in the Book of Qoheleth," *CBQ* 44 (1982) 551–69.

11f Or: "from the beginning to the end they cannot comprehend/find out"—yet cf. the commentary.

12a Or: "that nothing good comes about through them except . . ." (*beth constitutionis*; cf. note on the translation of 2:24) or "that with them there is nothing good except. . . ." In the context, בָּם *bām* is to be related to "the people" (v. 11: הָאָדָם *hāʾādām*; cf. v. 12 end: בְּחַיָּיו *bĕḥayyāyw*) (*constructio ad sensum* with incongruity of number). A correction to בָּאָדָם *bāʾādām* (cf. *BHS*) or

their oppressors violence (goes out)—and they have no one who comforts them. 2 And I counted[a] the dead, who have already died, as more fortunate than the living, who are still[b] alive. 3 But better than both[a] is he who has not yet existed, who[b] has not (yet) seen the evil deeds that are done under the sun.

4 And I saw that all labor and all skillful work are affected by one person's envy of another.[a] This also is futile and a striving after wind. 5 The fool folds his hands and consumes his (own) flesh.[a] 6 A handful of rest is better than two handfuls of labor[a] and a striving after wind.

7 And again I[a] saw something futile under the sun: 8 someone all alone, without anyone else, who has neither a son nor a brother. And all his toil has no end. Also "his eye"[a] cannot see enough riches. And for whom am I toiling and depriving myself of the enjoyment of my goods[b]? This also is futile and a bad business. 9 Two (have it) better than one alone, for[a] they have a good wage for their toil. 10 For if they fall, one can help his companion up. But woe[a] to one who is alone and falls, and no one else is there to help him up. 11 Also, two are warm if they lie together (to sleep). Yet one alone—how can he keep warm? 12 And if someone overpowers one who is alone,[a] two can withstand him. And a threefold cord is not quickly broken.

---

deletion (Gordis) does not seem necessary; cf. Schoors, *Preacher*, 197.

12b לַעֲשׂוֹת טוֹב *laʿăśôt ṭôb* is frequently interpreted—in the sense of εὖ πράττειν (thus, e.g., Müller, "Skepsis," 16) or εὖ δρᾶν (thus, e.g., Braun, *Kohelet*, 53–54)—as "enjoy good," "enjoy oneself." Yet this meaning is attested neither in the book of Qoheleth nor elsewhere in the OT; cf. 7:20 (עשה טוֹב *ʿśh ṭôb* vs. חטא *ḥṭʾ*); 4:17; 8:11-12 (רָעָה / עשה רָע *ʿśh rāʿ*[*â*] = "do [something] bad"), as well as 7:14 ("be joyful" = הָיָה בְּטוֹב *hyh bĕṭôb*).

13a Or (with the assumption of a double *pendens* construction): "it is also a gift of God that [or: if?] everyone can eat and drink and enjoy something good in all their toil."

14a Literally: "will remain to (the most) distant time" (יִהְיֶה לְעוֹלָם *yihyeh lĕʿôlām*). לְעוֹלָם "Verbal and nom. clauses use *lĕʿôlām* to indicate a (preserved, produced, unalterable) constant status and also frequently the qualitative significance of durability, finality, unalterability" (E. Jenni, "עוֹלָם *ʿôlām* eternity," *TLOT* 2:856).

14b On the construction אֵין *ʾên* + ל *l* + inf., cf. Schoors, *Preacher*, 183; Seow, 18–19.

14c Or: "that they [the people] will fear him" (on the construction cf. Ezek 36:27), or: "and the Deity acted (thus), so that one will fear him" (cf. 𝔊 𝔙), or: "the Deity made (it thus), so that they will fear him" (cf. GKC §166b). Also possible is the translation: "the Deity made that which one fears" (cf. GKC §157c). By contrast, the translation possibility proposed by Bartelmus, "Haben oder Sein," 59–60, appears rather improbable: "and the Deity made (everything beautiful) before which one (inexplicably) is afraid" (cf. also Backhaus, *Zeit und Zufall*, 127ff.).

15a Or: "what happened had long since happened (once before)."

15b Or: "what is happening (right now)" (אֲשֶׁר לִהְיוֹת *ʾăšer lihyôt*)? ל *l* + inf. cs. seems here to replace a finite verb in the impf. (יִהְיֶה *yihyeh*); cf. GKC §114i and the note below on 3:18c.

15c The context suggests understanding נִרְדָּף *nirdāp* (Lam 5:5: "be driven") here as a metaphorical expression for the past or past events (cf. 𝔙 *et Deus instaurat quod abiit*). On the missing determination after אֵת *ʾet*, cf. 4:4; 7:7, 14; 8:9; 9:1; 12:14 (see Schoors, *Preacher*, 164–65).

16a Or: "constantly" (Galling), "continually" (Murphy). Yet after v. 10, v. 16 seems to introduce a "further" observation or reflection, as then also in 4:1, 4, 7.

16b Literally: "the place of justice—there [or: to there] wickedness; the place of righteousness—there [or: to there] wickedness." As a rule, שָׁמָּה *šammâ* has a local-terminative meaning ("to there") but can also be used locatively ("there") (cf. Schoors, *Preacher*, 101–2). The locative שָׁם *šam* in the following v. 17 suggests interpreting שָׁמָּה *šammâ* in v. 16 in a local-terminative sense. Based on the consonantal text, one could read in the second case, instead of the repeated "wickedness" (הָרֶשַׁע *hāreša'*), "the wicked one" (הָרָשָׁע *hārāšā'*) (cf. 𝕲 𝕿); nonetheless, cf. the repeated "with no one to comfort them" in 4:1.

17a Literally: "I said, I in my heart/mind."

17b The preposition עַל *'al* seems here to be synonymous with לְ *l*; cf. Schoors, *Preacher*, 200–201.

17c The reading שָׁם *šām* ("there") is supported by the versions (cf. 𝕲 𝕾; it is probably also presupposed in 𝔙 [*tunc*]). A correction to שָׂם *śām* ("a time . . . he has determined"; thus, e.g., Delitzsch; Barton), שֹׁמֵר *šōmēr* ("over all doing he watches"; see BHK), or מֵשִׂים *mēśîm* "watching" (cf. Job 4:20; see BHS) seems as little warranted as the assumption that שָׁם *šām* has here "an asseverative force" ("indeed, also": C. F. Whitley, "Has the Particle שׁם an Asseverative Force?" *Bib* 55 [1974] 394–98; cf. idem, *Koheleth*, 34–36); cf. Schoors, *Preacher*, 100–101.

18a Literally: "I said, I in my heart/mind."

18b Here (as in 8:2) עַל־דִּבְרַת *'al-dibrat* is usually interpreted causally ("because of human beings"), whereas in 7:14 an intentional sense is assumed ("so that"); cf. Schoors, *Preacher*, 147. In the translation, then, "it is true" or something similar must be added; cf., e.g., Zimmerli: "Because of human beings (it is true) . . . ." Nevertheless, the train of thought in vv. 17-18 remains unclear. Thus it seems simpler to understand עַל־דִּבְרַת *'al-dibrat* here (in analogy to עַל־דְּבַר *'al-děbar* or עַל־דִּבְרֵי *'al-dibrê*) as "about, regarding" (cf. 𝔙 *dixi . . . de filiis hominum*).

18c לְ *l* + inf. cs. (וְלִרְאוֹת . . . . לְבָרָם . . . *lěbārām . . . wělir'ôt*) seems here, as in v. 15 (see n. 15b above on the translation), in each case to replace a finite verb in the impf. (or perf.?—cf. 4:2); cf. GKC §114i and Geier: "futurum est ut purget eos Deus" (quotation according to Schoors, *Preacher*, 184). An interpretation of the idioms as a complement to אָמַרְתִּי *'āmartî* ("I said to myself . . . that God sets them apart . . ."; cf. 𝕲 ὅτι διακρινεῖ) or of לְ *l* as *lamed emphaticum* ("in truth, God sets them apart [or set them apart] . . ."; thus Gordis) would not change anything essential in the meaning of the sentence. If one understands עַל־דִּבְרַת *'al-dibrat* in the sense of "because of," an intentional sense could also be assumed for לְ *l* + inf. cs. (cf. 𝔙 *ut probaret*). The idea that וְלִרְאוֹת *wělir'ôt* is connected with אָמַרְתִּי *'āmartî* (thus Whitley, *Koheleth*, 37; Backhaus, *Zeit und Zufall*, 136: "I said to myself: 'As far as human beings are concerned—God has set them apart.' But I recognized that they are animals . . .") suggests itself neither syntactically nor semantically (cf. Schoors, *Preacher*, 180–81). On the discussion of the syntactic problems in v. 18, see Schoors, *Preacher*, 112–13. The verb בָּרַר *brr* ("set apart, sort out"; cf. 𝕲 διακρινεῖ, Jer *separat*) is often understood here as "examine, test" (cf. 𝔙 *probaret*). 𝕾 derives the verb from the root בָּרָא *br'*, "create." וְלִרְאוֹת *wlr'wt* can also be vocalized as hiphil inf. ("show"; thus 𝕲 𝕾 𝔙 Jer) (וְלַרְאוֹת *wělar'ôt*).

18d שֶׁהֶם־בְּהֵמָה הֵמָּה לָהֶם *šehem-běhēmâ hēmmâ lāhem* may be an intentional pun. To strike הֵמָּה *hēmmâ* or לָהֶם *lāhem*, as is occasionally recommended, would be arbitrary. לָהֶם *lāhem*

can be understood as intensification (*lamed emphaticum*) or in the sense of a *dativus ethicus* (cf. Schoors, *Preacher*, 113–14; Murphy assumes a *dativus commodi*). In the context, however, the point of the statement seems to be that *God* sets human beings apart (from the animals), but they *themselves* behave like animals and treat *each other* like animals. On the ambiguity of לָהֶם *lāhem* ("with respect to themselves" or "with respect to each other") cf. Delitzsch; see also Schoors, *Preacher*, 153.

19a With the versions, מִקְרֶה בְנֵי־הָאָדָם *miqrēh běnê-hā'ādām* and מִקְרֵה הַבְּהֵמָה *miqrēh habběhēmâ* may be interpreted as construct connections. מקרה *mqrh* would then be vocalized with *sere* (מִקְרֵה) instead of with *segol* (מִקְרֶה); cf. 2:15. 𝔐 seems to interpret both idioms as nominal clauses: "Human beings are (determined by) fate/chance . . .", cf. 4:4 and GKC §141c-d.

19b Thus with the assumption of a comparative ו *w*; cf. GKC §161a. It would also be possible to assume two coordinated existential statements: "There is a fate of human beings and there is a fate of animals, yet both have the same fate."

19c "And" is lacking in numerous Hebrew mss., 𝕲 Syh 𝕾 𝕿 Jer. If one follows that reading, v. 19aα can be interpreted as a *pendens* construction: "The fate of human beings and the fate of animals—they have one and the same fate"; cf. Schoors, *Preacher*, 125.

19d Literally: "Like this one's death, so (is) this one's death."

21a With the versions הַעֹלָה *ha'ōlâ* and הַיֹּרֶדֶת *hăyōredet* may be thus read. 𝔐 (probably on dogmatic grounds) reads the article (הָעֹלָה *hā'ōlâ* and הַיֹּרֶדֶת *hayyōredet*): "Who knows the life spirit of human beings, which goes upward and the life spirit of animals, which descends to the earth?" This turns the assertion of the text on its head.

22a Literally: "after/behind him." On the temporal sense of אַחֲרֵי *'aḥărê* cf. 6:12 and E. Jenni, "אחר *'ḥr* after," *TLOT* 1:83–88.

4:1a וָאֶרְאֶה *wā'er'eh* is one of the rare *wayyiqtol* forms in the book of Qoheleth (cf. 1:17; 4:7).

1b Literally: "all the oppressions that are done."

2a The inf. abs. (וְ)שַׁבֵּחַ *(wě)šabbēaḥ* ("count as fortunate") obviously represents a finite verb here; cf. 8:9 and GKC §113gg, Schoors, *Preacher*, 178.

2b The *hapax legomenon* עֲדֶנָה *'ădēnâ* (like עֶדֶן *'āden* in the following verse) is probably a contraction of עַד *'ad* ("until") and הֵנָּה *hēnnâ* ("here, now") (and perhaps better pointed as עֲדֶנָּה *'ădennâ*; see BHK); cf. Schoors, *Preacher*, 117.

3a Thus under the presupposition that . . . אֵת אֲשֶׁר *'ēt 'ăšer* . . . is the subject of an independent clause (cf. 𝕲 𝕾). It would perhaps also be possible to interpret . . . אֵת אֲשֶׁר *'ēt 'ăšer* . . . as the object of וְשַׁבֵּחַ אֲנִי *wěšabbēaḥ 'ănî* ("still more than both of them, I count those fortunate . . .") or before . . . אֵת אֲשֶׁר *'ēt 'ăšer* . . . to tacitly expand "a verb like *I consider* or *I call*" (GKC §117l; cf. 𝔙 *iudicavi*). Cf. Schoors, *Preacher*, 191–92.

3b Or: "because he. . . ."

4a Literally: "are the one's envy of the other" (cf. note on 3:19a above and GKC §141c-d). On the construction (. . . רָאִיתִי . . . כִּי . . . אֶת . . . *rāʾîtî . . . ʾet . . . kî . . . = "I saw that . . ."), cf. Gen 1:4 and Schoors, *Preacher*, 214.

5a 𝔙 adds *dicens* at the end of v. 5 and with it interprets v. 6 as the utterance of the "fool" (thus also Ibn Ezra).

6a מְלֹא כַף נָחַת *mĕlōʾ kap nāḥat* and מְלֹא חָפְנַיִם עָמָל *mĕlōʾ ḥop-nayim ʿāmāl* are to be understood as appositional connections of *"measure and content"* (GKC §131d); cf. Exod 9:8; Lev 16:12; Schoors, *Preacher*, 120–21, 190. The assumption of an "adverbial accusative" (cf. Gordis: "one handful achieved through ease"; Murphy: "one handful with rest") is problematic, since v. 6 contains no verb. σ' and 𝔗 add an "and" before "rest": "Better one hand full and rest than both hands full of toil/property and a striving after wind" (see *BHK*, *BHS*).

7a Cf. 4:1 (with n. 1a).

8a Instead of "his eyes" (K, thus also 𝔙), it is better to read the singular with Q and numerous mss. and versions.

8b Literally: "and let me/my soul lack in goods." On the mean-ing of טוֹבָה *tôbâ* in distinction from טוֹב *tôb*, see Thomas Krüger, "Erwägungen zur Bedeutung von טוב und טובה im Qoheletbuch," *ThZ* 53 (1997) 53–63 (= FS Ernst Jenni).

9a A conditional function of אֲשֶׁר *ʾăšer* ("if/in case they have a good wage . . ."; thus Lohfink; Schwienhorst-Schönberger, *Nicht im Menschen*, 132; similarly Michel, *Qohelet*, 140: "it happens, namely, that . . .") is not to be excluded grammatically (cf. Joüon, §167j), but it makes little sense in view of the substantiation of v. 9 (כִּי *kî*) in the following vv. 10-12 through conditional clause constructions (3x אִם *ʾim*).

10a וְאִילוֹ *wĕ*ʾîlô is to be read with numerous mss. and versions as וְאִי לוֹ *wĕ*ʾî lô; cf. 10:16: אִי־לָךְ *ʾî-lāk*. אִי *ʾî*, "although absent from other biblical writings, occurs in MH and in Jewish Aramaic (e.g., MYeb 13:7; MEd 4:8; RHash 19a; Ber 6b; Sanh 11a)" and is "definitely late" (Schoors, *Preacher*, 149, contra Fredericks, *Language*, 177, 192, 260). 𝔗 reads וְאִלּוּ *wĕ*ʾillû ("and if"; cf. 6:6).

12a On the syntactic peculiarities of this clause, cf. Schoors, *Preacher*, 154, 162, 190.

The section 3:10—4:12 offers a "re-vision" (3:10) of the comments of "King Qoheleth" in 1:12—2:26. His thoughts are corrected here above all through two viewpoints that broaden and thereby critically relativize his knowledge perspective:

First, in the investigation of the possibilities and limits of human activity, it is not sufficient to include God only tangentially in one's view (cf. 1:13; 2:24, 26). Rather, his directives must be considered fundamentally and continually (3:10-22). This provides a critical correction to the *secularism* of the king.

Second, human happiness and unhappiness depend not only on a person's own efforts (and on God) but also on relations with other people and on the social structures in which one lives (4:1-12). That they are included in the reflections here calls into question the *individualism* of the king.

This double expansion of one's horizon leads to a new answering of the question, what good can people attain and what are they to strive for in their lives (cf. 2:3)? Pleasure and enjoyment are the highest (3:22), indeed, the only good (3:12), even if they are not reliably attainable by human beings through their own efforts (3:13) and thus represent no "gain" (יִתְרוֹן *yitrôn*), but rather a "portion" (חֵלֶק *ḥēleq*; 3:22). Therefore, instead of chasing after individual gain, people should, in addition to their work, also afford themselves rest (4:6) and enjoyment (4:8) and, together with others, strive for a "good wage" (שָׂכָר טוֹב *śākār tôb*; 4:9).

3:10-22 God and the "Good": Happiness as "Portion"

The reflections in 3:10-22 form a thematic unit, in that they bring into view the God-given conditions for human life and activity (vv. 10-11, 14-15, 17-18) and, in consideration of these conditions, answer the question of the "good" (vv. 12-13, 22). In regard to the expressions in first person singular, which in each case introduce a new step in the train of thought, three reflections or observations or insights (ראה *r*ʾh) can be distinguished from one another, the first two of which lead to two further recognitions (ידע *yd*ʿ) or considerations (אמר *ʾmr* + בְּלֵב *bēlēb*):

v. 10: "I have seen (רָאִיתִי *rāʾîtî*) . . ."
    v. 12: "I know (יָדַעְתִּי *yādaʿtî*) . . ."
    v. 14: "I know (יָדַעְתִּי *yādaʿtî*) . . ."
v. 16: "And, furthermore, I saw (וְעֹוד רָאִיתִי *wĕ*ʿôd rāʾîtî*) . . ."
    v. 17: "I said to myself (אָמַרְתִּי אֲנִי בְלִבִּי *ʾāmartî ʾănî bĕlibbî*) . . ."
    v. 18: "I said to myself (אָמַרְתִּי אֲנִי בְלִבִּי *ʾāmartî ʾănî bĕlibbî*) . . ."
v. 22: "So I saw (וְרָאִיתִי *wĕrāʾîtî*) . . ."

From the presupposition that God has made everything beautiful in its time but granted human beings only a limited understanding of his activity (v. 11), 3:10-15 derives two insights. (1) The only "good" that for humans is attainable and worth striving for consists in pleasure and enjoyment. As God's "gift" to humankind, these are not fully within the human power of disposition (vv. 12-13). (2) At the same time, God's work of creation limits their possibilities of changing reality through their own activity. In addition to joy over the possibilities of enjoyment, therefore, the human attitude toward life that is appropriate to creation also includes awe or fear of God, who made everything so definitively beautiful that a profound changing of reality is neither possible nor necessary (vv. 14-15).

Verses 16-21 confront the assertion of a world that is in every respect beautiful and not in need of change with the experience of pervasive injustice that penetrates the core of a righteous order (v. 16). This experience gives rise to two considerations. (1) The changing of the times also gives injustice its place *and* its limit in reality; it represents at the same time God's judgment over the righteous and the wicked (v. 17). (2) Wickedness in the world comes from the fact that humans are not equal to the task for which God has "set them apart." They behave like animals—and thus things do not go for them any different than for animals. A judgment of God over human beings beyond death is, therefore, not necessary and not to be expected (vv. 19-21).

Verse 22 can thus reinforce in closing the insight of vv. 12-13: enjoyment is the "highest good" and the "portion" that people can attain and are to strive for at any given time in their lives.

3:10-15 God and Time

This section revisits and relates several ideas that were developed or suggested in the foregoing text.[1] Then, in several argumentatively decisive places in the course of the book of Qoheleth, there are references to statements in 3:10-15.[2] That shows that this section is of central and fundamental importance for the whole book.[3]

■ **10** Verse 10 quotes 1:13b almost word for word (the differences transliterated in roman type):

1:13b הוּא עִנְיַן רָע נָתַן אֱלֹהִים לִבְנֵי הָאָדָם לַעֲנוֹת בּוֹ

3:10 רָאִיתִי אֶת־הָעִנְיָן אֲשֶׁר נָתַן אֱלֹהִים לִבְנֵי הָאָדָם לַעֲנוֹת בּוֹ

1:13b hû *ʿinyān* rāʿ *nātan ʾĕlōhîm libnê hāʾādām laʿănôt bô*

3:10 rāʾîtî *ʾet-hā*ʿinyān *ʾăšer nātan ʾĕlōhîm libnê hāʾādām laʿănôt bô*

A "bad business" (עִנְיַן רָע *ʿinyān rāʿ*) that "God has left . . . to people to be busy with" is what the "king" in 1:13, at the beginning of his reflections, calls his project "by wisdom to research and to find out all that is done under heaven." At the end of his comments in 2:26 the "king" then spoke of people whose "life is a failure" and whom God "busies (נָתַן עִנְיָן *nātan ʿinyān*) with gathering and heaping"—and judged not only this business but also, at least implicitly, the behavior of God as meaningless (הֶבֶל *hebel*). When now in 3:10 "the business (הָעִנְיָן *hāʿinyān*) that God has left [or: given] the sons of men" is again made the object of "consideration" (רָאִיתִי *rāʾîtî*) and at the same time leaves open whether this business is bad or good, meaningless or meaningful, this already signals that what follows concerns a critical revision of the reflections of the "king" in 1:12—2:26.

---

1   Cf. 3:10 with 1:13b (and 2:26b); 3:11a with 3:1-8; 3:12-13 with 2:24-26; 3:14 with 1:15; 3:15 with 1:9.

2   Cf. 3:11b with 3:22b; 6:12b; 7:14b, 24; 8:7; 9:1b, 12a; 10:14b; 11:2b, 5-6; cf. 3:12-13 with 3:22; 5:18-20; 8:15; 9:7-10; 11:8-9; cf. 3:14 with 7:13–14; and cf. 3:15 with 6:10; 7:10.

3   Cf. Crenshaw, "Eternal Gospel," 25–26.

■ **11a** The statement that God "has made everything so that it is beautiful in its time" (אֶת־הַכֹּל עָשָׂה יָפֶה בְעִתּוֹ *et-hakkōl ʿāśâ yāpê bĕ ʿittô*) contains two assertions: (1) God made everything,[4] and (2) everything is beautiful in its time.[5]

1. The idea that God "makes everything" (present tense) is also asserted by Isa 44:24 (אָנֹכִי יְהוָה עֹשֶׂה כֹּל *ʾānōkî yhwh ʿōśeh kōl*; cf. Isa 45:7: עֹשֶׂה כָל־אֵלֶּה *ʿōśeh kol-ʾēlleh*). Here, as in Qoh 3:11a, the "divine process of creation is . . . removed from a mere speaking of creation in the beginning. Just as Deutero-Isaiah . . . can speak of the creation of all things in his own time and even of things to come with the word בָּרָא *bārāʾ* 'create,' Qoheleth speaks with the more general word עָשָׂה *ʿāśâh* 'make' of what God also creates and makes happen over the course of time."[6] In this very spirit then, the Jewish wise men in the "symposium" of the *Letter of Aristeas* (*Ep. Arist.* 187-294) hold the view "that God constantly effects everything" (210) and "everything is prepared and managed by God according to his will" (234[7]). In contrast to the opinion of Epicurus "that the gods do not concern themselves with the world," this was also the view of the Stoics: "The world . . . is ruled by divine providence, and there is only one god, and that is reason, which is working and shaping in all things."[8] This was the view, for example, of Cleanthes in his hymn to Zeus: "No work takes place on earth without you, Deity (οὐδέ τι γίγνεται ἔργον ἐπὶ χθονὶ σοῦ δίχα, δαῖμον), neither in the divine ethereal sphere nor in the sea" (ll. 15-16).[9] "Cleanthes' Hymn to Zeus could also have come from the hand of Ben Sira, with some minor alterations,"[10] who is likewise convinced that God has "made all things" (Sir 43:33: את הכל [עשה יײ] *ʾt hkl [ʿśh yyy]*, πάντα γὰρ ἐποίησεν ὁ κύριος), indeed, that God *is* "all" (Sir 43:27: הוא הכל *hwʾ hkl*, τὸ πᾶν ἐστιν αὐτός).[11]

2. The assertion that everything created by God "is beautiful [or appropriate][12] in its time" takes up the judgment of the original works of creation as "good" from Genesis 1 (cf. Gen 1:4, 10, 12, 18, 21, 25, and especially v. 31) and expands its frame of reference to creation in its entire temporal extent. The predicate "beautiful" (יָפֶה *yāpeh*) here is by no means "more detached" than "good" (טוֹב *tôb*), making Qoh 3:11 "fall short of the positive judgment of Gen 1:31."[13] Perhaps it

---

4   הַכֹּל *hakkōl* here probably means simply "all (of that)" (with the article perhaps referring back to 3:1-8; cf. 1:14; 2:11, 17) and not "the universe" or "the whole thing" (thus, e.g., Müller, "Skepsis," 14; contra, e.g., Galling). Also speaking against the difference in meaning, assumed by Müller (ibid.), between הַכֹּל *hakkōl* as "universal concept" in Qoh 3:11 and כָּל־אֲשֶׁר עָשָׂה *kol-ʾăšer ʿāśâ* ("everything that he [God] [had] made") in Gen 1:31 is that אֶת־הַכֹּל עָשָׂה *ʾet-hakkōl ʿāśâ* from Qoh 3:11a is taken up in v. 14a with כָּל־אֲשֶׁר יַעֲשֶׂה הָאֱלֹהִים *kol-ʾăšer yaʿăśê hāʾĕlōhîm*.

5   Syntactically the third m. sg. suffix in בְּעִתּוֹ *bĕ ʿittô* can also refer back to God (as subject of the verb עָשָׂה *ʿāśâ*). In this sense Müller, "Skepsis," 13, for example, understands בְּעִתּוֹ *bĕ ʿittô* as a "designation of the mythical primeval time of God" and interprets v. 11a as follows: "what may have been good in the primeval time of creation now appears problematic in the time of human experience (3:1-9)" (ibid., 14; similarly, e.g., Lauha). Yet according to v. 14 (impf.: יַעֲשֶׂה *yaʿăśeh*!) the creative work of God is by no means limited to a "mythical primeval time." Verse 11b also seems to comprehend the world in its entire temporal extent ("from beginning to end") as "the work that the Deity has done."

6   Zimmerli; cf. Isa 40:26, 28; 41:20; 42:5; 45:7-8, 12, 18.

7   Cf. also the comments in N. Meisner, *JSHRZ* II.1, 75 (on the passage).

8   Hossenfelder, *Philosophie*, 115, 85.

9   Effe, ed., *Hellenismus*, 158–59.

10   Hengel, *Judaism and Hellenism*, 1:148.

11   Cf. the summary of Sirach's "creation theology" in Patrick W. Skehan and Alexander A. Di Lella, *The Wisdom of Ben Sira* (AB 39; New York: Doubleday, 1987) 80: "God is the Creator of all, including wisdom (24:8; cf. 42:15—43:33). He creates by simply uttering his all-powerful word (39:17-18; 42:15c); cf. Gen 1:3-24. He knows all things, including the deepest mysteries of the universe, and sees all things, even before they come to be (15:18-19; 23:19-20; 39:19-20a; 42:18-20). The marvelous order and dazzling beauty of the heavens as well as all the ordinary and awesome elements of nature are due to God's all-embracing wisdom and might (43:1-26)."

12   יָפֶה *yāpeh* in Middle Hebrew often means "appropriate, proper" (Fox, with reference to Jastrow, *Dictionary*).

13   Thus Müller, "Skepsis," 14; similarly, e.g., Michel, *Untersuchungen*, 60–61; cf., however, H. J. Stoebe, "טוֹב *tôb* good," *TLOT* 2:489; H. Ringgren, "יָפֶה *yāpâ*," *TDOT* 6:220.

is supposed to interpret the "good" from Genesis 1 in the sense of the "Greek-cosmological καλός."[14] Moreover, perhaps the terminological deviation from Genesis 1 is also supposed to do justice to the fact that according to the primeval biblical story (Genesis 1–11), the original creation, which was "very good" (Gen 1:31) in every respect, became in the course of time "corrupt" (6:11-12) and now also contained "evil" (6:5; 8:21). By contrast, Sirach wants to maintain that even in the present experience, the works of God are all "good" (טובים twbym: Sir 39:16 [𝔊: καλὰ σφόδρα], 33 [𝔊: ἀγαθά]) and "desirable" ([נחמד]ים nḥmd[ym], ἐπιθυμητά: 42:22)[15] but must himself concede elsewhere that ("because of evildoers") evil was also created (40:10: על רשע נבראה רעה ʿl ršʿ nbrʾh rʿh).

Thus, with reference back to Genesis 1, Qoh 3:11a offers a theological interpretation of the time-contingent nature of all human actions and suffering, as presented in 3:1-8. Neither this statement nor the corresponding assertions in the book of Sirach[16] exclude the idea that in the framework of what God has made beautiful in its time (1) there is room for human action and (2) for human beings not everything is "good" in the same way. That is clearly to be inferred from the broader context.

1. Qoheleth 3:1-8 shows that the works of God do not deprive human beings of every freedom but rather make available the *relative freedom* to act in changing times and circumstances. With what God creates "in its time" God gives human beings the opportunity to act ("time *for* . . ."), without forcing them to act. The repeated admonitions and warnings in the book of Qoheleth presuppose that human beings have at their disposal a certain amount of freedom to decide and to act. On the basis of their behavior they may die "before [their] time" (בְּלֹא עִתֶּךָ bĕlōʾ ʿittekā) (7:17), but also enjoy their lives "always" (בְּכָל־עֵת bĕkol-ʿēt, 9:8). Accordingly, in spite of its time-contingent nature, which is based on the work of God, human action is not fully "determined."[17]

2. God makes—for human sensitivity—both "good" and "bad" days (7:14). Within the framework of everything that God has made so that it is *beautiful* in its time (3:11), there is "nothing better than" (3:12, 22) for a man to rejoice and enjoy his life. Thus, if from God's perspective "everything . . . is beautiful in its time," from the human perspective, nonetheless, not everything is "good" in its time. Qoheleth 7:14 shows how a man can overcome "bad" experiences by becoming aware of the limits of his own perspective.

When read in connection with 3:1-8, v. 11a asserts that God made the world in such a way that at any given time a certain human action is "beautiful" and "appropriate." Thus, even what from the human viewpoint is "bad" appears on the horizon of God's whole creation activity in a "beautiful" light. And when human beings

---

14   Otto Kaiser, "Die Sinnkrise bei Kohelet," in idem, *Der Mensch unter dem Schicksal; Studien zur Geschichte, Theologie und Gegenwartsbedeutung der Weisheit* (BZAW 161; Berlin: de Gruyter, 1985) 101.

15   Sir 39:16: "All the works of the Lord are good, and he supplies every need in its time (מעשי] אל כלם טובים וכל צורך בעתו יספיק [mʿśy] ʾl klm ṭwbym wkl ṣwrk bʿtw yspyq)"; Sir 39:33-34: "All the works of the Lord are good, and he will supply every need in its time (מעשה אל כלם טובים לכל צורך בעתו יספוק mʿśh ʾl klm ṭwbym lkl ṣwrk bʿtw yspwq). No one may say, 'This is bad! What (does) that (mean)?' For he will give meaning to everything in its time (אל לאמר זה רע מה זה כי הכל בעתו ינבור ʾl lʾmr zh rʿ mh zh ky hkl bʿtw ygbyr)" [my trans.]. Müller ("Skepsis," 14 n. 60) sees here an "orthodox" correction of the "heterodox" statement of Qoh 3:11a (similarly Hertzberg, 48).

16   Cf. (1) with Sir 15:11: "Do not say, 'It was the Lord's doing that I fell away'; for he does not do what he hates (or: he did not do: אל תאמר מאל פשעי כי את אשר שנא לא עשה ʾl tʾmr mʾl pšʿy ky ʾt ʾšr śnʾ lʾ ʿśh; thus

𝔖^A; 𝔖^B has a different text)." On (2) cf. with Sir 39:25: "From the beginning good things were handed out to (or: created for? [חלק ḥlq]) the good, but to sinners good things and bad"; Sir 39:27: "All[?] these are good for the godly, but for sinners they turn into evils"; Sir 40:10: "Because of the wicked, bad things were created (על רשע נבראה רעה ʿl ršʿ nbrʾh rʿh) . . . [my trans.]."

17   Galling, Kroeber, and Loader, for example, assume that according to Qoheleth 3 human action is "determined" by the activity of God. According to Lohfink, "The Present and Eternity," 239 (cf. comm.) the text even asserts that "every human action is at the same time divine action."

act "appropriately," they reproduce in their own actions the "beauty" of God's creation.

■ **11b** The difference between the divine and human perspectives on perceiving reality is substantiated in v. 11b. On the one hand, God has "put distant time (הָעֹלָם hāʿōlām) into their minds." In view of the use of עוֹלָם ʿōlām in the preceding context (cf. 1:4, 10; 2:16; then also 3:14; 9:6; 12:5), the term may refer here to a concept or idea of a "distant time" that extends far beyond the life of an individual human being in the direction of either the past or the future or both.[18] On the other hand, humankind cannot find out "the work that God has done from beginning to end," that is, "grasp" and "comprehend" it (cf. 8:16-17; 11:5 and already 1:8-11). Thus human beings can understand the idea that God made everything beautiful in its time, and they can also experience this fragmentarily and at certain points, if they are happy and enjoy their lives (vv. 12-13; cf. 5:17: טוֹב אֲשֶׁר־יָפֶה ṭôb ʾăšer-yāpeh). But they cannot grasp and comprehend in every individual case how and in what sense that which God has made is "beautiful."

Since God, according to v. 11a, made "everything," v. 11b hardly means that human beings cannot "find out" *what* God made. Furthermore, since statements about the work of God are possible, according to v. 11a,[19] then v. 11b is also not to be understood in the sense that human beings can know nothing at all about God's work. Rather, it may mean that people cannot completely comprehend the work of God—if only because, first of all, it goes way beyond the temporal horizon of their possibilities of experience (cf. 1:10-11).

Verse 11b traces the possibilities and limits of human knowledge back to God. According to v. 11a, both are "beautiful" and "appropriate" for human beings. On this basis we cannot expect that God will make it possible for human beings to go beyond the limits of their creaturely knowledge.[20]

If v. 11a can be understood as the reception of Genesis 1 on the level of Hellenistic philosophical thinking, the same could be said for v. 11b in regard to Genesis 2–3. The paradise story would then be understood here in the sense that people *cannot* go beyond the boundaries of knowledge set for them by God: the transgression of the prohibition of eating from the "tree of knowledge" (2:17; 3:3) leads them only to knowledge of their own nakedness (3:7; God's statement in Gen 3:22 would then be understood as ironic).[21]

In that Qoh 3:11b sets the limits of human knowledge of the work of God in terms of "creation theology," it at least forms the basis for a strong skepticism about conceptions that assert that God conveys to human beings knowledge of God's past and future activity in its total temporal extent. Such conceptions were represented at the time of origin of the book of Qoheleth in the realm of prophetic literature and the continuing formation of tradition. According to Isa 46:10 Yahweh declares "the end from the beginning (מֵרֵאשִׁית אַחֲרִית mērēʾšît ʾaḥărît) and from ancient times (מִקֶּדֶם miqqedem) things not yet done."[22] Accordingly, prophetic texts could claim a knowledge of the future activity of God until the "end of time" (אַחֲרִית הַיָּמִים ʾaḥărît hayyāmîm).[23] Qoheleth 3:11 makes such claims seem at least questionable. Just as questionable from this standpoint, however, is any attempt to develop a "rational *theodicy*" by showing the "doctrine of the *purposefulness of creation*," as Sirach, for example, claims for itself.[24] Questionable in the light of

---

18　By contrast, it is rather improbable that עֹלָם ʿōlām here means the "corso dei tempi" (F. Piotti, "Osservazioni su alcuni problemi esegetici nel libro dell' Ecclesiaste: Studio I," *BeO* 20 [1978] 172) or the "connection of all things in their proper time" (Sauter, *Was heisst*, 31).

19　Cf. further 3:13-15, 17-18; 5:5, 17-19; 6:2; 7:13-14, 29; 8:15; 9:1, 7, 9; 11:9; 12:14.

20　Cf. 3:22; 6:12; 7:14, 24; 8:7; 9:12; 10:14; 11:2, 6.

21　Cf., however, the interpretation of Genesis 2–3 in Sir 17:6-10: "6 Discretion and tongue and eyes, / ears and a mind for thinking he [God] gave them [human beings]. / 7 He filled them with knowledge and understanding, / and showed them good and

evil. / 8 He put the fear of him into their hearts / to show them the majesty of his works. / 10 And they will praise his holy name, / 9 to proclaim the grandeur of his works."

22　Cf. also Isa 41:22-23, 26; 42:9; 43:9; 44:7-8; 48:3.

23　Cf. Isa 2:2; Jer 23:20; 48:47; 49:39; Ezek 38:16; Hos 3:5; Dan 10:14; further, e.g., Dan 2:28-29, 45; *1 En.* 81:2; *Jubilees* 1 (on Jubilees), and 4:18-19; 10:17 (on *1 Enoch*); Sir 48:24-25 (on Isaiah), as well as the claim of knowledge about "the beginning and end and middle of times" in Wis 7:18.

24　Hengel, *Judaism and Hellenism,* 1:145; cf. esp. Sir 39:12-35; 40:8-10; 42:15-25.

Qoh 3:11, finally, is the claim of the "king" in 1:12–2:26 that he had "considered all the works that were done under the sun" (1:13-14) and could allow himself a (negative) judgment on God's activity (2:24-26). With this claim, however, the results of his investigations also become problematic. They are appropriately revised in 3:12-13.

If human beings cannot fully comprehend the work of God (v. 11b), the statement that God "has made everything so that it is beautiful in its time" (v. 11a) cannot be "empirically verified." It cannot be derived from experience but rather formulates a perspective—taken from tradition (Genesis 1)—that makes the interpretation of experience possible. In this respect there is no qualitative difference between Qoh 3:11 and the eschatological-apocalyptic perspectives of OT prophetic writings or the wisdom-cosmological perspective of the book of Sirach. In comparison with these, however, Qoh 3:11 clearly remains closer to everyday and generally accessible experiences.

■ **12-13** That it is "good" to "be happy and do good" (v. 12) and to eat, drink, and enjoy what is good (v. 13) is self-evident. When the "king" in 1:12–2:26, nevertheless, comes to a devaluation of this (presumed) good, he does so because, first, it was for him not reliably at his disposal (as "gain") through his own efforts (2:10-11) but came "from the hand of God" (2:24-26), and because, second, it did not survive his death (2:12-23). Under the presuppositions formulated in 3:11, however, this state of affairs no longer offers any cause for a subsequent devaluation of what at first glance seems good, for if every human action and suffering depends on God's preconditions (vv. 1-8, 11), then the value of a good thing cannot by diminished by the fact that it is not fully and freely at one's disposal (v. 13). And if God grants a man "his life" as "his time," then the man can experience and realize something good only in this time; what

happens after his death is irrelevant to his happiness (v. 12).

■ **12** Not everything that God made "beautiful" (יָפֶה, *yāpeh*) (v. 11a) is regarded by human beings as "good" (טוֹב *ṭôb*). For them "something good" can only mean "to be happy" (לִשְׂמוֹחַ *lismôaḥ*), that is, *passive* enjoyment, and "to do good" (לַעֲשׂוֹת טוֹב *laʿăśôt ṭôb*), the *productive* realization of something good. Because of its tautological sentence structure (there is nothing good except to do [or enjoy] something good), vv. 12-13 offer no real definition of the "good" but presuppose that what is "good" for a human being is self-evident. Yet this contradicts the argumentation of the "king" in 1:12–2:26, the point of which is that what at first seems good to a person proves, after later reflection, to be "futile" (הֶבֶל *hebel*) (cf. 2:24: . . . אֵין־טוֹב בָּאָדָם *ʾên-ṭôb bāʾādām* . . . with 3:12: . . . אֵין טוֹב בָּם כִּי אִם *ʾên ṭôb bām kî ʾim* . . .). The argumentation of the "king" is critically relativized further by the fact that according to 3:12 something "good" for a man is achievable exclusively "in his life" (בְּחַיָּיו *bĕḥay-yāyw*). With this presupposition, the fact that for a man neither posthumous fame nor the products of his work are reliably and continually at his disposal after his death presents no problem and gives no cause to also devalue good things achieved in life (cf. 2:12-21). Likewise, however, 3:12 also rejects positive expectations of something "good" after death on the basis of which the good things achievable by human beings in their lives could be relativized (cf. 3:21-22). When God made everything in its time (בְּעִתּוֹ *bĕʿittô*) beautiful or appropriate (v. 11a), it is also beautiful and appropriate for people in their striving for something good to limit themselves to the time of their life (בְּחַיָּיו *bĕḥayyāyw*; cf. also 3:2), and *in* their life to take advantage, without delay, of any present opportunities for pleasure and action. Access to the "tree of (eternal) life" is and remains barred for human beings, according to the will of God (cf. Gen 3:22-24).

■ **13** No more than by death, however, is the good achievable by human beings devalued by the fact that all human action is dependent on God-given conditions. For these conditions are to be regarded as beautiful and appropriate (v. 11a). In this sense 2:24 is critically corrected in 3:13:

2:24	אֵין־טוֹב בָּאָדָם	שֶׁיֹּאכַל וְשָׁתָה	וְהֶרְאָה אֶת־נַפְשׁוֹ טוֹב		בַּעֲמָלוֹ	. . . מִיַּד הָאֱלֹהִים הִיא
3:13	וְגַם כָּל־הָאָדָם	שֶׁיֹּאכַל וְשָׁתָה	וְרָאָה	טוֹב	בְּכָל־עֲמָלוֹ	מַתַּת אֱלֹהִים הִיא

2:24	*ʾên-ṭôb bāʾādām*	*šeyyōʾkal wĕšātâ*	*wĕherʾâ ʾet-napšô ṭôb*		*baʿămālô*	*mîyad hāʾĕlōhîm hîʾ*
3:13	*wĕgam kol-hāʾādām*	*šeyyōʾkal wĕšātâ*	*wĕrāʾâ*	*ṭôb*	*bĕkol-ʿămālô*	*mattat ʾĕlōhîm hîʾ*

The fact that a man is not in a position "to let *himself* enjoy something good" (הֶרְאָה אֶת־נַפְשׁוֹ *herʾâ ʾet-napšô ṭôb*, 2:24), but can only "enjoy something good" (רָאָה טוֹב *rāʾâ ṭôb*, 3:13) that *God* gives him, is according to 3:11 (in contrast to 2:26) no longer any reason for the man to devalue achievable good as "futile." For one thing, God-given conditions are, according to 3:11a, "beautiful" and "appropriate," and, for another, they make the man's own efforts (עָמָל *ʿāmāl*) by no means totally meaningless and worthless; rather, they make such efforts possible and set limits to their success (cf. 3:1-9, 11b). Thus the good achievable in life in the form of enjoyment and the realization of good (in the sense of a "gain") is, to be sure, not completely and reliably at the disposal of human beings, but nonetheless to a greater degree than other goals and purposes.

Both points become noticeable in later statements of the book on enjoyment and the realization of the "good" by human beings. On the one hand, the limits of the availability of the good are recognizable when we read that it may be that God does *not* enable people to enjoy their possessions (6:2), that he makes good and bad days (7:13-14), that in their youth people are possibly in a better position to enjoy their lives than in old age (11:7ff.), and that the success of human activity always remains uncertain (11:6). On the other hand, pleasure and enjoyment can be almost excepted from the time-bound nature of all human activity stated in 3:1-8 (cf. 8:15: "that can *accompany* them . . . in the time of their lives"; 9:8-9: "*always*," "*all* the days of your fleeting life").

If, according to 3:13, *every* person who has opportunities for enjoyment owes these to God, this rejects not only a devaluation of the possession of goods in the sense of the "king" (cf. 2:18ff.) but also any idealization of being without property (cf. 5:11—6:9). Perhaps v. 13

also indicates that actually, according to the conditions resulting from God's work of creation, *every* person should have the opportunity to eat and to drink and to enjoy something good in all his work and toil.[25]

■ **14** Verse 14 takes up the statements on God's work (עשה *ʿśh*) in v. 11. Whereas v. 11 speaks of what God "has done" (perfect), v. 14 speaks of what God "does" (imperfect: general state of affairs). This makes clear that God's work is not finished, but rather includes past, present, and future. Yet at the same time it is "enduring," "definitive," and—at least for human beings—"unchangeable" (לְעוֹלָם *lĕʿôlām*). This is underlined by the statement that regarding what God does, "nothing is to be added to it, nor anything taken from it."[26] Read in the light of v. 11a, this statement has a thoroughly positive overtone: God's work is unchangeable because it needs no change (in the sense of improvement). Thus the "awe" of human beings before God, which is evoked by God, in addition to fear of the power and superiority of God (*tremendum*), also includes reverent recognition of the perfection of God's work (*fascinosum*).[27]

In the context it is clear that this "fear of God" is not the "*beginning*" of a "wisdom" that leads further,[28] but rather consists precisely in the fact that human beings accept the *limits* of their "wisdom" (cf. Job 28 with v. 28): if the fear of God is the consequence or aim of God's work, through which human knowledge is both enabled and limited (v. 11), it cannot at the same time be the "beginning" of a "wisdom" that goes beyond these limits of knowledge.[29]

In a way similar to Qoh 3:14, Sirach also speaks of the endurance and unchangeableness of God's works: "When the Lord created his works from the beginning, and, in making them, determined their boundaries, he arranged his works in an eternal order (εἰς αἰῶνα) and

25   See the note on the translation; cf. Gen 1:29; 2:16-17; 3:17-19; and, e.g., Ps 104:14-15.

26   This assertion adopts a set formulation that served "perhaps already in Egypt, certainly in Mesopotamia, to assure the intact state of an important, but above all, holy text" (Müller, "Skepsis," 16 n. 68); cf. Deut 4:2; 13:1; Sir 18:6; 42:21; as well as W. Herrmann, "Zu Kohelet 3,14," *WZ(L)GS* 3 (1953/54) 293–95, repr. in W. F. Albright, ed., *Geschichte und Altes Testament: FS Albrecht Alt* (BHT 16; Tübingen: Mohr/Siebeck, 1955) 163–65; E. Reuter, "Nimm nichts davon hinweg und füge nichts hinzu! Dtn

13,1 seine alttestamentlichen Parallelen und seine altorientalischen Vorbilder," *BN* 47 (1989) 107–14.

27   Contra, e.g., Backhaus, *Zeit und Zufall*, 361–66.

28   Cf. Prov 1:7; 9:10; 15:33; Ps 111:10; Sir 1:10, 14.

29   Whereas according to Sir 17:8 God has given human beings "the fear of him into their hearts to show them the majesty of his works," in Qoh 3:14 the fear of God results from the fact that for human beings God's works are not changeable or comprehensible (v. 11).

their dominion for all generations (εἰς γενεὰς αὐτῶν)" (Sir 16:26-27 ᴳ). "He has set in order the splendors of his wisdom; he is from all eternity one and the same. Nothing can be added or taken away (לֹא נֶאֱסָף וְלֹא נֶאֱצָל *lᵒ nᵒsp wlᵒ nᵒṣl*). . . . How desirable are all his works. . . . All things live and remain forever (לָעַד *lᶜd*) . . ." (Sir 42:21-23 ᴴ; cf. 18:6).

If Sirach reveals here the conception of a stable and essentially unchangeable cosmos, texts like Daniel 2; 7 and Tobit 14, by contrast, develop a "universal-historical, eschatological" view of the time-related nature of God's activity (cf. above on 3:1-9). Already pointing in this direction is the development of the use of לְעוֹלָם *lᵉôlām* in the realm of prophetic tradition. Whereas in Psalms, for example, the predicate לְעוֹלָם *lᵉôlām* is mainly applied to the activity of God experienceable in the present,[30] in Deutero-Isaiah עוֹלָם *ᶜôlām* becomes "the code word for God's world and God's activity that will survive as solely determinative in the eschaton."[31] "The impact of Deutero-Isaiah is most noticeable in Isa 60:15, 19–21; 61:7f.; also in 35:10; 51:11": עוֹלָם *ᶜôlām* "indicates the finality of the coming salvation or judgment."[32] "With the increasing development of eschatological concepts in apocalypticism, *ᶜôlām* became a constant attribute of the world beyond (cf. Dan 12:2)."[33] By contrast, Qoh 3:14 (like Sirach) holds fast to the endurance and finality of *this* world as the creation of God.

■ **15** The idea that God's work is enduring, definitive, and unchangeable does not mean, however, that there can be no changes in the world. This is made clear by v. 15, which takes up the concept of a constant repetition of similar things from 1:4-11 and interprets it theologically (cf. Gen 8:22). If v. 15b is to be understood in the sense of the translation recommended above, that God

"seeks what has been driven away" (יְבַקֵּשׁ אֶת־נִרְדָּף *yᵉbaqqēš ᵓet-nirdāp*)—that is, repeatedly makes sure that what has happened once happens again and again (1:9)—then this sentence summarizes and combines the statements about God's work in v. 11a and v. 14a: everything that God does is related both to "its time" (בְּעִתּוֹ *bᵉᶜittô*) and to "eternity" (לְעוֹלָם *lᵉôlām*), because, and in the sense that, God repeatedly creates the same things. Also quite sensible in the context, however, would be the interpretation of Levy (cf. Delitzsch), who regards the verbs בקש *bqš* and רדף *rdp* as synonyms here and translates: "God strives again for what has (already once) been striven for," that is, "he brings about nothing new." Finally, with an eye to the following section, we may also hear in v. 15b the quite concrete meaning that "God seeks what is pursued" (thus ᴳ). This could then be understood in the sense that in the changing of the times effected by God, something like a "balance of justice" is realized.[34]

3:16-21 God and the Law

■ **16** After the comments on God's activity in vv. 10-15, v. 16 directs attention to a happening "under the sun" that seems to sharply contradict the assertion that God has "made everything so that it is beautiful in its time" (v. 11): wickedness has penetrated to the "place of justice" and "righteousness," that is, to where justice is actually administered and righteousness is supposed to be reestablished. If, however, the administration of justice itself is infected by wickedness, this means the failure of society's judicial venue, through which wickedness could be eliminated or at least kept in check. Wickedness can then spread unhindered.[35]

---

30 Cf. E. Jenni, "עוֹלָם *ᶜôlām* eternity," *TLOT* 2:860.
31 Ibid.; cf. Isa 40:8; 45:17; 51:6, 8; 54:8; 55:3, 13.
32 Jenni, ibid.; cf., e.g., Dan 2:44; 7:18; 12:3.
33 Jenni, ibid.
34 In this sense Qoh 3:15b seems to have been adopted in Sir 5:3 ᴴᴬ: "Do not say, 'Who can have power over him [read with ᴳ: me]?' For the Lord seeks (the) pursued" (כי ייי מבקש נרדפים *ky yyy mbqš nrdpym*). ᴳ reads instead: "For the Lord will surely punish . . ." (ὁ γὰρ κύριος ἐκδικῶν ἐκδικήσει). According to Skehan and Di Lella, *Wisdom of Ben Sira*, ᴴᴬ offers here "a reworked text" (180) "based on Qoh 3:15" (182).

35 "The topos of breaking the law appears often in the Near Eastern realm. In early Greece this problem is treated above all by Hesiod and Theognis" (Braun, *Kohelet*, 93; cf. Hesiod, *Works and Days* 220ff.; Theognis 53ff.).

■ **17** By contrast, v. 17a asserts that God "will judge [or: judges] the righteous and the evildoer." Here the "judging" of God should be understood in the sense that God brings justice to the "righteous" and condemns the "evildoer" (cf. Deut 25:1; 1 Kgs 8:31-32). Thus miscarriages in the administration of justice (v. 16) are eliminated, and "just order" is reestablished. At first glance, this concept of a divine judgment seems rather "conventional" and "orthodox"; later comments in the book of Qoheleth seem to directly contradict it (cf. 7:15; 8:10-14; 9:1-3). Therefore, a number of exegetes exclude v. 17 as a secondary, "orthodox" gloss (cf. 12:14).[36] Nevertheless, the second half verse gives a highly unconventional turn to the idea of a divine judgment. It allows two possible understandings that do not mutually exclude, but rather complement, each other:

1. If God brings about justice at a certain time, this implies that up to this point he tolerates injustice (cf. 8:11). If in the world "there is time for every matter" (cf. 3:1-8), then that includes the miscarriages of justice named in v. 16 ("for everything that is done there," that is, in the "place of justice" and "righteousness"). The concept of a divine judgment is thus integrated into the understanding of God's activity that is developed in 3:1-15b and at the same time thereby relativized: if everything that God makes is beautiful and appropriate in its time (v. 11), this is true both for his tolerance of wickedness and for his intervention against it.

2. Yet one can also understand v. 17 to mean that here the concept of a divine judgment is being reinterpreted in the sense of the understanding of divine activity that was previously developed: the changing of the times (cf. 3:1-8) not only allows wickedness but also limits its duration. In this way the changing of the times also implements something like a "divine judgment"—

even if in a somewhat different sense than is commonly assumed.[37] Along this line, 11:9b then seems to interpret the mortality of a man as God's "judgment" over him.

The comments that follow in vv. 18-20 on "fate" and death, which affect all people (as well as both people and animals), tend to support the second interpretation of v. 17. The expectation of a special intervention of God in the sense of the first interpretation is, in any case, called into question by v. 21 for the time after the death of a human being.

The understanding of vv. 16-17 is disputed among scholars.[38] Michel and Schwienhorst-Schönberger understand v. 16 as a statement about the future judgment of God in the world beyond, before which (or to which) wickedness will be sent.[39] This statement is quoted by Qoheleth here and "considered" (רָאִיתִי *rāʾîtî*) in the following text. Whereas Michel excludes v. 17 as "a secondary expansion of the second epilogist" and recognizes only in vv. 18-22 Qoheleth's critique of the expectation of a divine judgment after death, Schwienhorst-Schönberger understands v. 17 as Qoheleth's critique of the view cited in v. 16: "'If, as you say, there is a place of judgment for the evildoer, then also for the righteous man, for his activity—like all activity (כָּל־הַמַּעֲשֶׂה *kol-hammaʿăśeh*)—will be judged by God (cf. 11:9b; 12:14).' This statement is substantiated again with a reference to 3:1. Then שָׁם *šām* at the end of 3:17, with reference to 3:16 (שָׁמָּה *šāmmâ*), would be a circumlocution for the last judgment."[40]

In my opinion, however, Schwienhorst-Schönberger's interpretation of v. 17 is difficult to comprehend philologically (unfortunately he offers no translation of this verse). "Against the thesis that 3:16b represents a quotation related to the last judgment" is—as Schwienhorst-Schönberger himself concedes[41]—the point "that we have

---

36   Cf., e.g., Siegfried; Galling; Lauha; Crenshaw; Michel, *Untersuchungen*, 250.

37   According to Sirach 39, *behind* the (only seemingly contingent) experience of "time" (cf. the time concepts in vv. 16, 20, 21, 28, 30, 33, 34) God's order of "law" is perceivable (cf. v. 29: משׁפט *lmšpṭ*). According to Qoh 3:17, by contrast, the (at least for human beings) contingent changing of the "times" *is* God's "judgment."

38   See the review of some proposed interpretations in

Michel, *Untersuchungen*, 248–50.

39   Ibid., 250–51; Schwienhorst-Schönberger, *Nicht im Menschen*, 115–16.

40   Schwienhorst-Schönberger, *Nicht im Menschen*, 117.

41   Ibid., 116.

here an observation that Qoheleth made 'under the sun'"; one could at best "avoid this difficulty by relating 'under the sun' not to the event in 3:16b but to the assertion. Thus one would have to translate as follows: 'Furthermore, I encountered under the sun the following opinion.'"[42] Speaking against this interpretation, nonetheless, is the fact that the statement that Qoheleth "saw" or "observed" (רָאִיתִי rāʾîtî) something "under the sun" seems always in other places to introduce observations and not "quotations" (cf. 1:14; 4:1, 7; 5:12; 6:1; 9:11, 13; 10:5).

■ **18** The linguistic form of v. 18 raises a number of problems of understanding.[43] In any case it is clear that the distinction between the "righteous" and "evildoers" (v. 17) is abolished here in speaking of "human beings." The concept of a divine judgment is thereby anthropologically relativized. If the translation of v. 18 recommended above is correct, we now find here—after v. 11 took up the topic of Genesis 1–3—the further development of "the primeval story" in Genesis 1–9 briefly summarized:[44] God wanted to "set them [human beings] apart"[45] (for dominion over the animals: 1:26-28), yet their behavior was no different from "all flesh" (6:12-13).[46] For the injustice experienced in the world (Qoh 3:16), accordingly, their Creator is not responsible: human beings are (cf. 7:29). Humankind is, in general and as a whole, "bad" (cf. Gen 6:5; 8:21 and Qoh 7:20,

29; 8:6, 11; 9:3), even if *within* it there may be *relatively* "righteous" individuals (cf. Gen 6:9; 7:1: Noah; Gen 5:22, 24: Enoch).[47] Therefore, it is absolutely "just" if all human beings are subjected in the same way to "time" (v. 17), that is, to contingency and death (vv. 19-20).

If we follow the usual understanding of v. 18, however, God set human beings apart, so that they can "see" (or in order to "show" them) that they are animals. Then we would ascertain here—not without a certain irony—that the sole difference between humans and animals consists in the fact that human beings know (or should know) that they are not essentially different from animals. This could then be formulated likewise with a view to the primeval story and in particular to the creation story in Genesis 2, which regards people, like animals, as "living beings" (נֶפֶשׁ חַיָּה nepeš ḥayyâ: Gen 2:7) that were formed by God out of the "ground" (אֲדָמָה ʾădāmâ: 2:19; cf. Qoh 3:20). According to Gen 2:18-19 God sees no essential difference between the man and the animals: for him they are "a helper as partner"[48] (עֵזֶר כְּנֶגְדּוֹ ʿēzer kĕnegdô). It is the man who "does not want to recognize the beings corresponding to him and brought to him by the Creator as a partner"[49] (Gen 2:20).

Perhaps the syntactically complicated formulation in Qoh 3:18 is supposed to keep open the two possible understandings, both of which can be regarded as interpretations of the primeval story.

---

42 Ibid.

43 See the notes on the translation, as well as Backhaus, *Zeit und Zufall*, 137–38.

44 Cf. Krüger, "Rezeption."

45 The verb ברר *brr* I designates in qal "with the exception of Ezek 20:38 in Neh 5:18; 1 Chr 7:40; 9:22; 16:41 a setting apart or selection in the positive sense . . . (a special position is given)" (Backhaus, *Zeit und Zufall*, 138); cf. the meanings in niphal: "keep oneself pure," piel: "purify"; hithpael: "prove to be pure," hiphil: "purify."

46 By contrast, Sir 17:2-4 (as well as Psalm 8) speaks without qualification also for the present-day experiential reality of the dominion of humankind over the world of animals.

47 In this sense the book of Qoheleth seems to *interpret* the primeval story, in which the tension between the opinion that *all* human beings are bad and the view that there are righteous *individuals* (cf., in addition to Enoch and Noah, also Seth, innocent of Cain's fratricide, and his son Enosh [=

"human being"!] in Gen 4:25-26) seems to be understood, rather, in the sense that the general badness of humankind does not exclude the righteousness of individuals (cf. Gen 4:7, which presupposes that human beings are basically capable of overcoming sin).

48 Jenni, *Präpositionen*, 2:44.

49 Rüdiger Bartelmus, "Die Tierwelt in der Bibel I," in Bernd Janowski, Ute Neumann-Gorsolke, and Uwe Glessmer, eds., *Gefährten und Feinde des Menschen: Das Tier in der Lebenswelt des alten Israel* (Neukirchen-Vluyn: Neukirchener Verlag, 1993) 264.

■ **19-20** What the "king" ascertains in 2:14-16 in the comparison of the wise man and the fool is taken up here and radicalized in the comparison of humans and animals; at the same time, however, it is also relativized in its consequences: people and animals are subject in the same way to contingency (מִקְרֶה *miqreh;* see above on 2:14) and death. The two have one and the same life spirit (רוּחַ *rûaḥ;* cf. Gen 6:3, 17; 7:15, 22; Ps 104:29-30); both came from dust (cf. Gen 2:7, 19) and return again to dust (cf. Qoh 12:7; Gen 3:19; Ps 104:29; also, e.g., Job 34:14-15; Pss 90:3; 146:4). If both are transitory (הֶבֶל *hebel;* see above on 1:2), there is no advantage (מוֹתַר *môtar*) of human beings over the animals; in death they both go to the same "place" (cf. 6:6): into the "dust." Whether the transitory nature of human beings (vv. 19-20) is the consequence of their not doing justice to their role, for which God set them apart (v. 18), or whether human beings were created from the beginning as transitory beings remains open here—as in the primeval story.

■ **21** The assumption that the difference between people and animals will be revealed after death when the life spirit (רוּחַ *rûaḥ*) of people goes upward, whereas the life spirit of animals goes down into the earth, is at the very least questionable, because it cannot be verified by human beings. Experience (vv. 19-20) clearly speaks against it. Verse 21 does not stand in contradiction to 12:7, according to which after the death of a person, the "dust" returns to the earth, but the "life spirit" returns to God (that is, "upward"; cf. Sir 40:11[50]). What is called into question here is not "that the life spirit of people rises upward," but that in distinction thereto "the life spirit of the animals goes down to the earth." That is, if humans and animals have one and the same life spirit (v. 19), which comes from God (12:7), we may assume that the life spirit of animals also returns to God at their death (cf. Ps 104:29-30; Job 34:14-15).[51]

Verse 21 is often understood as a polemic "against a popular idea—which perhaps arose under Greek-Hellenistic influence—of the continued life of individuals after death."[52] Yet the verse seems to call into question not so much the "assertion of the *rising* of the souls (spirits) of humans to God"[53] as the assumption presupposed therein that human beings, in distinction from animals, have something like a personal "life spirit" whose individuality is maintained after death.[54]

"Both in Euripides and in Greek epitaphs there often appears the conception that after death the human soul mounts to its dwelling place, the *aether,* the seat of the gods."[55] "Among the central themes of Plato's philosophy and Platonism is the fate of the soul after death.

50 See Skehan and Di Lella, *Wisdom of Ben Sira,* 471.

51 By contrast, behind Gen 1:24 ("Let the earth bring forth living creatures . . .") stands the idea that "land animals are brought forth from the earth, as are the plants," according to Gen 1:11 (Hermann Gunkel, *Genesis* [Macon, Ga.: Mercer Univ. Press, 1997] 111, with reference to "similar statements . . . in other cosmogonies"; cf. also Gen 1:20 on the water creatures [and birds]; according to Gunkel this marked the "difference between animal and human": "God himself made humans [vv. 26ff.] [ibid., 112]; the latter is also true, however, for animals according to Gen 1:25 [cf. v. 21]). This idea would support the assumption that the life spirit of animals returns to the earth at their death. The Masoretes reinforce this assumption through their vocalization (see above the note on the translation).

52 Schwienhorst-Schönberger, *Nicht im Menschen,* 120; cf., e.g., Backhaus, *Zeit und Zufall,* 140; Michel, *Untersuchungen,* 117–18; Hengel, *Judaism and Hellenism,* 1:124–25; Ulrich Kellermann, "Überwin-

dung des Todesgeschicks in der alttestamentlichen Frömmigkeit vor und neben dem Auferstehungsglauben," *ZThK* 73 (1976) 279ff.; critical of this view is A. A. Fischer, "Kohelet und die frühe Apokalyptik: Ein Auslegung von Koh 3,16-21," in Schoors, ed., *Qohelet in Context,* 339–56.

53 Thus Michel, *Untersuchungen,* 118 (emphasis added), who holds 12:7 to be an "orthodox gloss" (ibid., 117).

54 Cf. Kellermann, "Überwindung des Todesgeschicks," 280. On the difference between the "souls" of plants (ψυχὴ ϑρεπτική), animals (ψυχὴ αἰσϑητική), and human beings (ψυχὴ λογική or νοητική) in Aristotle see, e.g., Karl Vorländer, *Philosophie des Altertums* (Geschichte der Philosophie 1; Reinbek: Rowohlt Taschenbuch, 1963) 127. Whether in Aristotle "a personal immortality is asserted or denied is not absolutely certain, although the scales seem to tilt in the latter direction" (ibid., 128).

55 Hengel, *Judaism and Hellenism,* 1:124.

Menon (81a–86b), *Politeia* (608c–11a), *Phaidros* (245c–46a), and above all *Phaidon* offer reflections on the immortality of the human soul."[56] Whereas the Stoics assumed an "ascension" of the human soul after death, yet without believing it to be "immortal," it was an essential "presupposition of the Epicurean attitude toward death . . . that with it existence actually ends, which means, in particular, that the soul is also mortal."[57]

In the Jewish world around the time of origin of the book of Qoheleth, a tendency toward identification of the "breath of life" (רוּחַ *rûah*) of human beings with their individual "(death-)soul" (נֶפֶשׁ *nepeš*) is evident in *1 Enoch* 1–36: "Enoch 9:3 speaks of the 'souls [of the dead]' of all the children of men (*naphshoth bene 'anasha'*), and 13:6 of the 'souls [of the dead]' (*naphshot*) of the fallen angels. The author of the 'Book of Watchmen' himself, on the other hand, in his portrayal of the intermediate state after death and before the last judgment, speaks, with respect to the individual, of the 'spirit of the dead man' (*ruach-'enash met*, Enoch 22:5), and with respect to all the dead of the 'souls of all the children of men' (*naphshoth kol bene 'anasha'*, Enoch 22:3). In later Judaism the divine breath and the dead soul were no longer distinguished; this is shown by . . . [*4 Ezra* 7:78ff.].[58]

According to Psalm 49 "a man . . . without understanding is like the beasts that perish" (v. 20, NIV; cf. v. 12), whereas for himself, the wise speaker of the psalm (cf. vv. 3-4) expects that God will rescue him from the underworld (v. 15; cf. also Ps 73:22ff.). If the idea here is not only deliverance from threatening death, the continued individual existence of a part of human beings beyond death is expressly juxtaposed to the annihilation of animals in death. It is precisely these differentiations that are called into question in Qoh 2:14-16 (wise man–fool) and 3:19-21 (human–animal).

3:22 Pleasure as the "Highest Good"

■ **22** Whereas "King Qoheleth," through the insight that he as "wise man" is subject to contingency and death just like the "fool" (2:14-16), comes to the point of hating life (2:17), for the "wise man Qoheleth" the knowledge that as a human being he will fare no better than the animals (3:19-21) only confirms his estimation of pleasure as the "highest" and "only good" (cf. vv. 12-13). Even if the special effort in his work does not lead reliably to a "gain" (3:9), a person can still receive pleasure in his work as his "portion" (cf. v. 13). For the "king" this was too little (2:10-11); for the "wise man" there is nothing better (3:22). Nor can the insight into the unpredictability of the future, which brought the "king" to despair in regard to his successor (2:12, 18), change anything, for human beings are referred by God to the present time as an opportunity for action and for enjoyment (3:1-8, 11). Therefore, they should seize the available possibilities for pleasure and not push enjoyment into an uncertain future—whether in or after life.[59]

4:1-12 The "Good" and Human Beings: Happiness as "Wage"

The previous section, 3:10-22, defined the highest and only "good" for human beings in view of the God-given conditions that make it possible for people to have a happy life but do not guarantee it. The question discussed in 3:15-21 as to how God relates to the "wickedness" that people inflict upon each other already leads

---

56 Ricken, *Philosophie*, 91–92.

57 Cf. Hossenfelder, *Philosophie*, 84, 115.

58 Otto Kaiser and Eduard Lohse, *Death and Life* (Biblical Encounters; Nashville: Abingdon, 1981) 41. On the ascension of the "spirits" after death cf. (in addition to Dan 12:3), e.g., *Jub.* 23:31; *1 En.* 103:4; 104:2, 4, as well as Josephus, *Bell.* 2.8.11 and *Ant.* 18.1.5 on the Essenes.

59 Michel (*Untersuchungen*, 121–22) assumes that Qoh 3:22 "argues against people who . . . expect to receive 'their portion' from Yahweh only after death." According to Schwienhorst-Schönberger (*Nicht im Menschen*, 121) this verse refers beyond 3:16-21 "back to the views of life, criticized in 2:12-

23, that aim at an enduring gain. . . . For all of them it is a question of an 'afterward': for the rich man in the passing on of his possessions to his heirs, for the wise man in the praiseworthy remembrance of the following generations, for the godly man in ongoing life after death." By contrast, Backhaus (*Zeit und Zufall*, 141–42) tries to show that v. 22bβ can relate only to the future of the "world within" before death. Nevertheless, the various possibilities of interpretation are not necessarily mutually exclusive.

to the section 4:1-12, which reflects on the importance of interpersonal relations for the happiness or unhappiness of the individual. As in 3:10-22, we can also distinguish in 4:1-12 three "reflections," "observations," or "insights" (ראה *rʾh*). In each case they lead to the recognition that a condition or mode of behavior is "futile" (הֶבֶל *hebel*; the term does not appear in vv. 1-2) and offer a (relatively) "better" alternative (טוֹב מִן *ṭôb min*):

v. 1: "And again I considered . . ."
    (v)v. (2-)3: "better . . . than . . ."
v. 4: "And I saw . . ."
    v. 4: "This also is futile and a striving after wind!"
    v. 6: "better . . . than . . ."
v. 7: "And again I saw something futile . . ."
    v. 8: "This also is futile and a bad business!"
    v. 9: "better . . . than . . ."

Verses 1-3 show that there can be circumstances in which death is preferable to life. Yet even such conditions—"made" by people!—cannot call into question the fundamental preference of life over death. This critically corrects the "king's" "hatred of life" in principle (2:17).

Verses 4-6 relativize the value of work in view of its motivation through envy and recommend a sensible balance of work and rest. Here too is a critical correction of the comments of the "king," who completes his accomplishments in an effort to surpass his predecessors (1:16; 2:7, 9) and whose devaluation in principle of work was ultimately motivated by envy of his successor and heir (2:18-23).

Verses 7-12 criticize the endless work of a man in striving for riches for himself alone and contrast this with the value of cooperative work. Thereby, at the same time, the individualism and egocentrism of the "king" are criticized, for he acquires only good for himself (2:4-8), and his thinking and acting are directed exclusively toward his own wishes (2:25: "For who can eat and who must worry except me?").

4:1-3 Oppression

■ **1** Verse 1 is often claimed as a testimony to the "pessimism of Qoheleth": in contrast to the prophetic protest against injustice and oppression, he learns to live with present conditions in the world in "resigned" (if not "cynical") fashion.[60] In the clarity with which oppression and its consequences are named, the text is in no way inferior to comparable statements in the prophetic writings.[61] The repeated indication that no one intervenes against oppression ("and they have no one who comforts them") shows here as in Ezek 22:29-30 and Isa 59:13, 16 that not only the "oppressors" are responsible for unjust conditions, but also all the members of the community who could render help but do not do so (cf. also Lam 1:2, 9, 17, 21). For everyone who is in a position to "comfort" (נחם *nhm* piel), which "if necessary and possible includes real assistance,"[62] is obligated to act. Concrete "oppression" could also include here the system of debtor slavery (Lohfink).

---

60 Cf., e.g., Michel, *Qohelet*, 140: "Without the hope of compensation after death (cf. 3:16-22), inconsolable oppressions make life not worth living"; Crenshaw: "Qohelet juxtaposes the situations of oppressor . . . and oppressed . . . lending force to the refrain about the helpless victims. Such misery pained Qohelet, but he suggests no way to comfort the unfortunate persons nor does he urge hearers to correct injustice"; Frank Crüsemann, "The Unchangeable World: The 'Crisis of Wisdom' in Koheleth," in Willy Schottroff and Wolfgang Stegemann, eds., *God of the Lowly: Socio-Historical Interpretations of the Bible* (Maryknoll, N.Y.: Orbis, 1984) 72: "When confronted with the concrete suffering in society Koheleth knows of no comforter. He is sure that he himself is not called upon to fill this role—a possibility that had been viewed far differently in

the earlier caritative wisdom (see Prov. 24:11ff.!").

61 According to Crüsemann ("Unchangeable World," 57) the "universality of suffering as well as the power that causes suffering," is recognized and named in the book of Qoheleth even "with a bluntness greater than that of the prophets." On the theme of "oppression" (root עשק *ʿšq* and derivatives) in the prophetic writings cf. Isa 30:12; 33:15; 52:4; 54:14; 59:13; Jer 6:6; 7:6; 21:12; 22:3, 12, 17; 50:33; Ezek 18:18; 22:7, 12, 29; Hos 5:11; 12:8; Amos 3:9; 4:1; Mic 2:2; Zech 7:10; in the wisdom literature: Prov 14:31; 22:26; 28:3, 16-17; Job 35:9; Pss 62:11; 73:8.

62 H. J. Stoebe, "נחם *nhm* piel to comfort," *TLOT* 2:736.

■ 2 In view of the evils named in v. 1, v. 2 formulates "a lament disguised as its opposite, namely the praises of the dead and of those not born" (Lohfink). It recalls the "king's" hatred, expressed in 2:17, of life (or the living: הַחַיִּים *haḥayyîm*).[63] Nonetheless, whereas the "king" came to hate life because he recognized the unfulfillability of his own wishes, in 4:2 "the exploitation begets the lamentation of the exploited" (Lohfink): here it is not one's own suffering but the perception of the suffering of others (vv. 1, 3: רָאָה *rʾh*) that gives rise to the lament. In this 4:1-2 also sets itself apart from texts like Jer 20:14-18 and Job 3. Sirach's distinction, according to which death for the poor and suffering is better than life but bitter for the prosperous (Sir 30:17; 40:28-29; 41:1-2; cf. Job 3:17ff.), cannot be shared by Qoh 4:1-2 out of "sym-pathy" with the oppressed. Thus the radical devaluation of life by the "king" in 2:17 seems to be confirmed here—even if for quite different reasons.

■ 3 Nevertheless, in the continuation in v. 3 the train of thought takes an ironic turn: how much better still than for the dead, who have their experiences of suffering behind them, must it be—according to the logic of v. 2— for those who have never experienced "the evil deeds that are done under the sun." Yet that can only be those who have "not *yet*(!) existed," that is, those who still have their life—with all its experiences of suffering—before them. In this way, the thought of v. 2 is continued *ad absurdum* by following its own logic to its conclusion: in the end, then, "a living dog [still] has it better than a dead lion" (9:4).

4:4-6 Envy

■ 4 "Labor" and "skillful work" (כִּשְׁרוֹן *kišrôn*, cf. 2:21) in v. 4 are plainly identified with "envy" and "jealousy" (קִנְאָה *qinʾâ*) (see the note on the translation). Even if the term קִנְאָה *qinʾâ* is not necessarily used in a derogatory way,[64] it still has here (as also in, e.g., Prov 14:30; Job 5:2; Sir 40:5) a clearly negative connotation. "In the interpersonal realm" קִנְאָה *qinʾâ* "indicates the attitude, often accompanied by strong emotional component, of one partner toward the other regular partner."[65] "Envy" and "jealousy" disturb interpersonal solidarity, whose lack is lamented in v. 1. So here not only is the "oppression of the lower classes . . . is based on the fact that every transaction and business operation no less than every public service employment within the Ptolemaic system was characterized by rivalry" (Lohfink). Even on the part of the "oppressed" themselves, envy and jealousy stand in the way of a solidarity that could enable them to defend themselves against the pressure exerted on them (cf. v. 12).[66]

Verse 4 is illustrated by the behavior of the "king" in chaps. 1-2: he wants to surpass all his predecessors with his wisdom and his works (1:16; 2:7, 9). As a "wise man," he wants to have an "advantage" over the "fool" (2:13-16). And in 2:18-23, "clearly it is envy of his successor that turns life bitter for him."[67] Whereas the "king," on the basis of this attitude determined by envy, devalues all presumed goods as "futile" and "a striving after wind," here in 4:4 envy itself is criticized as "futile and a striving after wind."

In this critical attitude toward "envy" and "jealousy" v. 4 agrees with OT and early Jewish wisdom traditions,[68] but also, for example, with the statements of the Cynics. Thus Diogenes, for instance, is supposed to have said: "People . . . compete in order to bring each other down and step on each other. . . ."[69] By contrast, there

---

63 Cf. also 2:17: "for the work that was done under the sun seemed evil to me," with 4:3: "who has not (yet) seen the evil deeds that are done under the sun." On comparable statements in Greek and Egyptian literature, cf. Braun, *Kohelet*, 94–95; Whitley, *Koheleth*, 173–74; Schwienhorst-Schönberger, *Nicht im Menschen*, 129; Lichtheim, *Late Egyptian Wisdom Literature*, 167.

64 See G. Sauer, "קִנְאָה *qinʾā* fervor," *TLOT* 3:1146.

65 Ibid. Here one can think of both the "competition between various economic subjects" and the "disturbances ('jealousy') within an economic unit consist-

ing of *several* persons" (Schwienhorst-Schönberger, *Nicht im Menschen*, 130 n. 9, who himself supports the latter).

66 On the lower social strata's "envy" of the upper strata, cf. the warnings in Pss 37:1; 73:3; Prov 3:31; 23:17; 24:1, 19; Sir 9:11-12; on the lack of solidarity among the "poor," cf., e.g., Prov 14:20; 19:4, 7; Sir 13:20.

67 Crüsemann, "Unchangeable World," 68.

68 See n. 66 above.

69 According to Diogenes Laertius 6.27; Braun, *Kohelet*, 81 n. 224.

is a more positive evaluation of competition in Hesiod.[70] Whereas according to his *Theogony* (226–27) "the gloomy *eris* ['strife'] bore painful tribulation, hunger, also forgetfulness, and tearful worry,"[71] in his *Works and Days* he brings out more strongly the ambivalence of the *eris*: "There is not just *one* species of *eris*; indeed, two reign on earth" (11-12). Whereas the one causes discord and enmity, the other "even encourages casual men to work" (20): "thus neighbor strives with neighbor for the better profit. *This eris* is useful to the mortal" (23-24). If competition is evaluated here positively as an incentive to work and to striving for profit, the very opposite seems to be the case in Qoh 4:4: work is questionable because and to the extent that it is motivated by "envy" and "jealousy."

■ **5** Nevertheless, it is necessary for a man to work. Only "the fool folds his hands" (cf. Prov 6:10; 24:33), that is, is lazy—and thereby destroys himself ("consumes his [own] flesh"). This insight corresponds to traditional wisdom teaching.[72] Therefore, it is excluded by some commentators as "a corrective marginal gloss" to v. 4 or understood as a "quotation" that is commented on critically in v. 6.[73] In the train of thought of vv. 4-6, nonetheless, in my opinion v. 5 presents no problem in understanding:[74] work has negative aspects (v. 4), but total inactivity would also be ruinous (v. 5); therefore, it behooves one in life to maintain a sensible balance between work and rest (v. 6).

The statement that the fool "consumes his flesh" is occasionally interpreted in the sense that in spite of his laziness, he "still has his flesh to eat."[75] Verse 5 would then formulate an observation "that implicitly contradicts the traditional warning against laziness": "against all the rules, it can happen that also the unskilled and not so industrious people can have enough to eat."[76]

Verse 5, however, would then hold fast to the idea that it is "foolish" not to work at all. Speaking against this interpretation, nonetheless, is that only in one place in the OT does בָּשָׂר *bāśār* with a suffix designate the "flesh" (of an animal) that is available to a human being as food (Job 31:31 *RSV*: "if the men of my tent have not said, 'Who is there that has not been filled with his meat?'"; cf., by contrast, e.g., Job 19:22: "Why do you, like God, pursue me, never satisfied with my flesh?"). Otherwise בָּשָׂר *bāśār* with suffix always refers to the "flesh" of an animal or a human being's (*own*) "flesh" (thus also Qoh 2:3; 5:5; 11:10). When Yahweh makes the oppressors of Zion "eat their own flesh" (Isa 49:26), he is not providing them with food: he is letting them consume *themselves*.

■ **6** If work is as problematic (v. 4) as it is unavoidable (v. 5), it behooves one to make room in life for "rest" (נַחַת *nāḥat*; cf. 6:5; 9:17) along with work (cf. the Sabbath commandment). That it is better not "to have all hands (חָפְנַיִם *ḥopnayim*) full of work" (and thus ultimately only to "strive after wind"), but to allow oneself "one hand (כַּף *kap*) full of rest" (and accomplish one's work with the other hand), is by no means "self-evident to the point of absurdity," as Gordis holds; this is shown by the example cited in vv. 7-8 (as also by the interpretation of v. 6 as the speech of the "fool" of v. 5 in 𝕲 and in Ibn Ezra; see note above on the translation).

That less is sometimes more is often stated in traditional wisdom: "Better is a dry morsel with quiet (שַׁלְוָה *šalwâ*) than a house full of feasting with strife (רִיב *rîb*)" (Prov 17:1). "Better is little with the fear of the Lord than great treasure and trouble (מְהוּמָה *mĕhûmâ*) with it" (15:16). "Better is a dinner of vegetables where love is than a fatted ox and hatred with it" (15:17). "Better is a little with righteousness than large income with injus-

70 Cf. Braun, ibid.

71 In addition to this clearly negative judgment of *eris*, however, cf. the more positive view of *zēlos* ("zeal, jealousy, rivalry") and *nikē* ("victory") in *Theogony* 383ff.

72 Cf. Prov 6:9-11; 24:30-34, as well as Prov 10:4-5; 12:11, 24, 27; 18:9; 19:15, 24; 20:13; 23:20-21; 26:14-15. Cf. also Schwienhorst-Schönberger, *Nicht im Menschen*, 130 n. 11: "The value of work represents the main theme in Hesiod's *Works and Days*: work saves one from hunger (298-301) and bestows riches (305-7), esteem, and honor (311-12). The gods hate

the lazy man (308-9)."

73 For the former see Lauha; cf. McNeile; Barton; Podechard. For the latter see Gordis; Hertzberg; Michel, *Qohelet*, 140.

74 Cf., e.g., Loader; Eaton; Fox.

75 Thus *EÜ* and Lohfink; cf. Crenshaw; Schwienhorst-Schönberger, *Nicht im Menschen*, 130; Murphy leaves this possible understanding open.

76 The former quotation is from Schwienhorst-Schönberger, *Nicht im Menschen*, 130; the latter from Lohfink.

tice" (Prov 16:8). "Better is a little that the righteous person has than the abundance of many wicked" (Ps 37:16; cf. also Prov 21:9, 19; 25:24). In each of these sayings two values are weighed against each other: a fatted ox is better than a dinner of vegetables, and love is more pleasing than hate; yet love has a higher value than a fatted ox, and thus in case of doubt, a dinner of vegetables with love is preferable to a fatted ox with hate (Prov 15:17). In Qoh 4:6 this argumentation schema—"non-A plus B is better than A plus non-B"—is transformed ironically: rest and work are opposites and are, as v. 5 and v. 4 showed, not in themselves values to strive for; their combination does not lead to a conflict of values but rather form a goal worth striving for: "A plus non-A is better than *only* A [or *only* non-A])".

4:7-12 Greed

■ **7-8** Verses 7-8 are initially understandable in themselves as a closed "observation" or "reflection": a solitary individual, who—probably out of greed (cf. 5:9 and Prov 27:20)—works unceasingly, would actually have to come to the insight himself that his behavior is senseless (הֶבֶל *hebel*), as soon as he asks himself for whom he is actually working. (This reflection is put in his own mouth here as direct address in the first person.) For neither he himself, who lacks enjoyment in his goods, nor an inheriting son or brother[77] will enjoy the fruits of his labor. For such a person, "a handful of rest" would doubtless be better than "two handfuls of labor" (v. 6).

Verse 8 presupposes that the behavior of this man would be not quite so senseless if he at least had an heir for whom he could work. With this the argumentation of the "king" in 2:18-23 is in retrospect critically corrected. It is not the fact that *everyone* must one day leave behind the fruit of his labors to another person that robs his work of its meaning and worth (2:18-21); rather, it is the

special circumstance that one has *no heir* that his work could benefit. And if a man does not allow himself some pleasure and rest in his work, this is not an unavoidable "disaster," as the "king" suggests in 2:22-23, but rather a mode of behavior for which he himself is responsible—and which is ultimately motivated by his greed. (That it is ultimately also senseless to deny oneself the enjoyment of one's goods for the sake of an heir will be shown in 5:12-14.)

■ **9** Verse 9 offers a positive alternative to the nonsensical behavior of the solitary individual in v. 8. The advantage of "two" over the loner lies in the fact that they can expect a good "wage" (שָׂכָר *śākār*) from their work. The nature of this "wage" (and how it is different from a lasting "gain" [יִתְרוֹן *yitrôn*] at one's disposal) is demonstrated in vv. 10-12 with three examples (v. 10: . . . כִּי אִם *kî ʾim* . . . , v. 11: . . . גַּם אִם *gam ʾim* . . . , v. 12: . . . וְאִם *wĕʾim* . . .).

■ **10-12** The three examples named here for the superiority of the "two" over the "one" could have in mind "situations in traveling": a tired traveler stumbles (v. 10), the cold at night (v. 11), ambush (v. 12)."[78] That in such situations two are superior to one is as obvious as the extrapolation of two to three (and more) in v. 12b.

For comparison Hertzberg points to the speech of Diomedes in Homer's *Iliad* (10.222ff.): "Yet if another man wants to follow me, then the confidence would be greater and the courage more fearless. If two men go together, the one notices something helpful before the other; the individual, no matter how attentive, never sees as sharply and is also weaker in common sense."[79] Cf. further, e.g., the Egyptian Teaching of Ankh-Sheshonq 345: "No one leaves his traveling companion without God calling him to account." Ibid. 449–50: "In battle the man finds a brother; on the road, the man finds a companion." Sirach 13:21: "When the rich per-

---

77 Schwienhorst-Schönberger's thesis—that it is a question "not of the fact that he *has* no son and no brother . . . but rather that he keeps them out of his successful work, that is, he forgoes a traditional family business for the sake of the effectiveness of the work" (*Nicht im Menschen*, 131 n. 17)—is not supported by the wording of the text: "he has neither a son nor a brother" (בֵּן וָאָח אֵין־לוֹ *bēn wāʾāḥ ʾēn-lô*)!

78 Lohfink. Less likely, by contrast, is the idea that vv. 10-12 "allude to the theme of age and death in

highly subtle form," since "above all older people need the help of someone else in order to get up again after a fall," and "4:11 refers to old King David" (1 Kgs 1:1-4) (Schwienhorst-Schönberger, *Nicht im Menschen*, 132–33).

79 Braun, *Kohelet*, 81 n. 228.

son totters, he is supported by friends . . ."; 37:5: "A good friend fights with an enemy, and against an adversary he takes the shield." "On the theme of friendship cf. also Aristotle, *Nicomachean Ethics* 9.9 (1169b-70b), where he takes up the question, Does the happy man need friends? (1169b). Ibid., 1170a: 'Now life is difficult, however, for a person who lives alone.' Books 8 and 9 are completely devoted to the theme of friendship."[80]

Especially close to Qoh 4:10-12 is the series of sayings in the "canonical" version of the Gilgamesh Epic:[81]

3 // 23 A slippery floor cannot [endanger two who help each other.]

4 // 24 Two triplets (by contrast) [. . .]

5 // 25 A threefold cord [cannot be broken.]

6 // 26 A strong lion (and) his two cubs [are invincible.]

Whereas here it is a matter of the united strength of attackers, Qoh 4:12 has in view people who must defend themselves against a stronger person.

■ **9-12** With the sketch of a model of human work in the context of elementary interpersonal solidarity, vv. 9-12 exhibit, first of all, an alternative to the case, demonstrated in vv. 7-8, of a questionable individualism: a "comrade" or "companion" (חָבֵר *ḥābēr*: v. 10) can also be sought by someone who has no son or brother. In view of the meaninglessness of his work, he should not only allow himself some rest (v. 6) but also work together with one or more comrades (vv. 9-12). Beyond that, however, vv. 9-12 also present possibilities for confronting the evils named in vv. 1-6: envy and jealousy (v. 4), oppression and denial of comfort (v. 1) have no place in mutual "cooperation," as it is described by vv. 9-12. Here the work is done together and its reward enjoyed together (v. 9). The closing statement that the "two" can better resist violent aggression than one alone, and that a "threefold cord" is not so quickly broken (v. 12), also suggests one possibility as to how one could effectively

deal with the power of oppressors mentioned in v. 1. Here we not only have a "small correction" of the "very individualistic focus" of the comments of the "king" in 1:12—2:26 (Lohfink)—they are radically called into question: "It is not good that man should be alone" (Gen 2:18).

Numerous and diverse comments on the theme "friends and associates" can be found in the near vicinity of the book of Qoheleth in Sirach.[82] In addition to the praise of "faithful friends" (cf. Sir 6:13-15) and the exhortation to remain true to "old friends" (9:10), the discussions here about true and false friends (cf. 6:7-12; 12:8-9; 37:1-6) and the admonition to caution in the making of friendships (cf. 6:5-6; 12:10—13:22) take in a broad area. In comparison to this, Qoh 4:9-12 speaks astonishingly unconditionally of the value of "comradeship"—without ignoring the negative aspects of interpersonal relations (cf. 4:1, 4).

■ **3:10—4:12** The comments of the "king" in 1:12—2:26 should demonstrate that the common point of departure of various directions in Hellenistic philosophy, the program of a "devaluation of what is not at one's disposal," leaves people no good worth striving for, if it is consistently carried out. This insight drove the "king" to despair and hatred of life (2:17, 20). In critical dispute with the comments of the "king," 3:10—4:12 overcomes this descent into despair—and thus at the same time the point of departure of the philosophical ethics of Hellenism—without falling back from the point of reflection reached in 1:12—2:26: in contradiction to the teaching of the Stoics and Epicureans, happiness is not at human disposal, and yet—in contrast to the view of the Pyrrhonist skeptics—it is worth striving for.

Whereas the various directions of Hellenistic philosophy recommend holding "as worth striving for and valuable exclusively that which one has at one's own disposal at any time and without any foreign help or exertion of

---

80 Schwienhorst-Schönberger, *Nicht im Menschen*, 133 n. 30.

81 Gilgamesh Epic IV vi 3-6/11-14 // V ii 23-26; quoted according to Uehlinger, "Qohelet," 181–82; cf. 180–83; S. N. Kramer, "Gilgamesh and the Land of the Living," *JCS* 1 (1947) 40; A. Shaffer, "The Mesopotamian Background on Qohelet 4:9-12," *ErIsr* 8 (1967) 246–50 (Heb.) 75*; J. Y. S. Pahk, *Il canto della gioia in Dio: L'intinerario sapienzale espresso*

dall'unità litteraria in Qohelet 8,16–9,10 e il parallelo di Gilgameš Me. iii (SMDSA 52; Naples: Istituto Universitario Orientale, 1996).

82 Skehan and Di Lella, *Wisdom of Ben Sira*, 5, point to the following passages on this theme: Sir 6:5-17; 7:18; 9:10; 11:29-34; 12:8—13:23; 22:19-26; 27:16-21; 33:6; 36:23-25; 37:1-15.

influence, and by contrast everything not available in this sense [is classified] as pointless,"[83] Qoh 3:12-13, 22 maintains that what seems to people worth striving for, is worth striving for: "to be happy and do good as long as they live." As a "gift of God," however, this happiness is not reliably at one's disposal. Nor can one attain it totally independently of the particular time-conditioned circumstances of the outside world; rather, one must at least have at one's disposal the necessary means to be able to "eat, drink, and enjoy something good." This contradicts the "radical internalization of eudemonia" in Hellenistic ethics.[84] Finally, a person has a better chance of attaining happiness not at one's disposal if one does not attempt to reach it for oneself alone and "without any foreign help" but rather in solidarity and "friendly" cooperation with others (4:9-12). With this the concentration of Hellenistic philosophy on "the happiness of the individual" in "consequence of the discovery of the individual as the more fundamental entity vis-à-vis society" is critically overcome.[85]

The fresh approach to ethics in 3:10–4:12 is decidedly theologically grounded with a creative reception of the "primeval story" in Genesis 1–11: the human being, as a being with limited capabilities for knowledge (cf. Genesis 3), is, according to the will of God, subjected to contingency and death. Since humankind as a whole does not do justice to the special position in the world accorded to it by God (cf. Genesis 1–6), no human being has a legal claim on God to a successful life. The contingent change of the times put into operation by God, however, sets limits to the wickedness that people perpetrate on each other and at the same time offers them the opportunity to change unjust conditions. In the process they can make use of the fact that God has not left human beings alone (Gen 2:18). As a religious attitude, this theological conception involves the fear of God

(Qoh 3:14), in which human beings can seize the possibilities for happiness granted to them and respect their human limitations.

Humankind is thus neither consoled in the sense of a wisdom "theodicy" (cf. Sirach) with the idea that in the world God has ultimately ordered everything in a just way, nor in the sense of an individual (cf., e.g., Psalms 49; 73) or universal (cf., e.g., Isaiah 65–66) eschatology put off until beyond the presently experienced reality, when God will take care of justice and order. Instead, human beings are left to so arrange their lives and common living conditions that while they cannot achieve an enduring gain that is at their disposal, they can still—in a common effort with their fellows—receive a "good wage" (4:9).

Here Qoh 4:9-12 in no way tries to reestablish the "feeling of the unity of the individual with environment and world," which in Hellenistic culture gave way to "the awareness of opposition, independence and self-hood."[86] That can already be clearly recognized in the reference to oppression and envy as negative aspects of common social life in 4:1, 4. Anyone who is no longer rooted in a "natural" community, who has no "son or brother" (4:8), can and should enter into a connection with a "comrade" or "companion" (4:10: חָבֵר *ḥābēr*). In the background is perhaps the model of a nonnatural community formed on a free-will basis, as cultivated in Hellenistic associations.[87] Here, in addition to school and cultural associations, as well as purely social organizations, "professional associations were particularly important in view of the great mobility of the population; they offered accommodations and lodging to traveling colleagues and helped them find work and settle in a foreign city."[88] In the Jewish realm the Essenes, for example, formed a "community" (יַחַד *yaḥad*) and the Pharisees "associations" (חֲבוּרוֹת *ḥăbûrôt*) in a more or less close analogy to Hellenistic associations.[89]

---

83   Hossenfelder, *Philosophie*, 34; see above on 1:12–2:26.
84   Hossenfelder, *Philosophie*, 39.
85   Ibid. 32, 39.
86   P. Wendland, *Die hellenistisch-römische Kultur in ihren Beziehungen zum Judentum und Christentum* (3d ed.; HNT I, 2-3; Tübingen: Mohr [Siebeck], 1912) 47–48, quoted according to Hengel, *Judaism and Hellenism*, 1:117.
87   Cf. F. W. Walbank, *Die hellenistische Welt* (3d ed.;

Munich: Deutscher Taschenbuch, 1989) 65ff.; Koester, *Introduction*, 67ff.; Frederick W. Danker, "Associations, Clubs, Thiasoi," *ABD* 1:501–3.
88   Koester, *Introduction*, 69.
89   See Hengel, *Judaism and Hellenism*, 1:243ff.; Moshe Weinfeld, *The Organizational Pattern and the Penal Code of the Qumran Sect: A Comparison with Guilds and Religious Associations of the Hellenistic-Roman Period* (NTOA 2; Fribourg: Editions Universitaires; Göttingen: Vandenhoeck & Ruprecht, 1986).

Qoheleth 4:13–5:8[1] can be delineated as a second partial composition following 1:3–4:12. Thematically, its form is circular:

- 4:13-16   Critique of expecting too much from a king
- 4:17–5:6   Exhortation to a proper attitude toward the Deity
- 5:7-8   Critique of expecting too much from a king

As a relatively delineated composition, 4:13–5:8 is at the same time, nonetheless, part of the more comprehensive development of the text. The section is closely connected with the preceding and following contexts, and this must be kept in mind in its interpretation.

In the beginning and end of the section, as well as between its three parts, the transitions are smooth. This suggests a planned sequence of text units, whether intended from the beginning or produced by a redactional reworking.

Formally, 4:13-16 continues the reflections of 3:10–4:12. In its formulation, 4:13 connects especially with 4:9 ("better . . . than . . .") and at the same time can be read as a resumé of 1:3–4:12 (cf. above on the composition of 1:3–4:12).

The beginning of 4:17 ("Watch your feet when you go . . .") can also be understood as an admonition to the reader, bringing 4:13-16 to a close and advising the reader not to become a supporter of the new ruler (cf. הלך *hlk*, "go," in 4:15). Only with the continuation of 4:17 (". . . to the house of God") does it become clear that thematically something new has begun.

Formally, 5:7-8 continues the admonitions of 4:17–5:6. In terms of content, experiences are now addressed that the reader makes when leaving the "house of God" (in Jerusalem, 4:17) and going into the "province" (Judea, 5:7).

Then the beginning of 5:9 can again be read initially as a statement about the "king" named in 5:7-8: "Whoever loves money will never have enough money."

The compositional connection of statements about the king with statements about the Deity[2] evokes the discussion about a theological legitimation and/or critique of monarchical rule as it was practiced in OT traditions at various times and with different options (cf., e.g., in 1 Samuel 8–12). In view of experiences with rulers in the past (4:13-16) and in the present (Qoh 5:7-8), Qoh 4:13–5:8 is critical of the expectation that a king can provide a perfect world (cf. here, e.g., Psalm 72). Qoheleth 4:17–5:6 reveals clearly enough that the limits of the possibilities of human politics are not compensated for by God or by the temple (cf., e.g., Haggai). In this sense 4:13–5:8 confronts overdrawn expectations of the given political conditions (or emerging changes) as well as messianic-eschatological hopes or a theocratic celebration of God's salvific presence in the temple.

---

1   The English versification varies from the Hebrew: Qoh 4:17–5:19 Hebrew = Qoh 5:1-20 English.
2   Schwienhorst-Schönberger, *Nicht im Menschen*, 141–42, suggests comparison with Prov 15:33–16:15, as well as Prov 21:1; 24:21; 25:2; and Exod 22:28.

13
> Better a child,[a] needy and wise,
> than a king, old and foolish,
> who no longer has the insight to let
> himself be warned.

14
> Even if someone came out of prison[a] and
> onto the throne,[b] poor people[c] would
> still be born under his rule.[d] 15 I saw all
> the living who moved under the sun
> (already) following the next[a] child that
> was to take his place. 16 There was no
> end to all the people with each one
> who placed himself at their head.[a] Yet
> the later ones no longer rejoiced in
> them.[b] This also is futile and chasing
> after the wind!

13a Or: "young man."

14a Literally: "house of the prisoners"; cf. the variant reading הָאֲסוּרִים *hāʾăsûrîm* in some Hebrew mss. "Most of the critics agree that the form *hāsûrîm* is the equivalent of *hāʾăsûrîm* and thus implies the elision of the *aleph*. . . . To understand the word in the sense of 'prisoners' certainly is the best solution. It is the oldest known interpretation, viz. that of the LXX, and it has remained traditional ever since, as may appear from the Vg, Syr, Gregorius Thaumaturgus, Ibn Ezra up to the modern commentators" (Schoors, *Preacher*, 40–41).

14b Literally: "came out of prison in order to become king."

14c Or: "a poor man."

14d On the syntax see the commentary.

15a Literally: "second."

16a Literally: "who was before them." "Before them" (לִפְנֵיהֶם *lipnêhem*) can be understood both temporally and in the sense of social status (of the ruler). In the first case "each one who was before them" refers to rulers earlier than those named in vv. 13-15; in the second case, to any previous rulers of the people. It would also be possible syntactically to relate the suffix of the third person m. pl. to the various rulers and interpret לְכֹל אֲשֶׁר־הָיָה לִפְנֵיהֶם *lĕkōl ʾăšer-hāyâ lipnêhem* as an asyndetic explication of לְכָל־הָעָם *lĕkol-hāʿām*; the following בּוֹ *bô* would then refer back to the "people": "There was no end to all [the people] that were before them [each new ruler]. Yet the later ones [rulers] could no longer rejoice over them [the people]." Opposed to this interpretation, however, is the fact that according to v. 15, all the people followed each new ruler. If one corrects לְכֹל אֲשֶׁר־הָיָה לִפְנֵיהֶם *lĕkōl ʾăšer-hāyâ lipnêhem* to לְכֹל אֲשֶׁר־הָיוּ לְפָנָיו *lĕkol ʾăšer-hāyû* (cf. 𝔊 𝔅 𝔖) *lĕpānāyw* (cf. 𝔅 𝔖), v. 16a can be interpreted as a statement about the "next child" of v. 15: "There was no end to all the people who were before him. Yet the later ones could no longer rejoice in him."

16b On the syntax of v. 16a see Backhaus, *Zeit und Zufall*, 169–70.

■ **13** Verse 13abα, as a proverb, is understandable on its own terms. It values wisdom higher than wealth, power, and age.[1] The juxtaposition of "wise child" and "foolish king" relativizes the close connection between wisdom and power in ancient Near Eastern and Hellenistic royal ideology (see above on 1:12) that is still at work in the placing of OT wisdom writings under the teaching authority of "King Solomon" (see above on 1:1). In the context of the book of Qoheleth, 4:13abα can then be understood as the closing critique of the comments of

---

1 Cf., e.g., Sir 10:23-25, 30-31; Job 32, as well as the Euripides fragment 264N cited in Braun, *Kohelet*, 95 n. 277.

the "king" in 1:12–2:26 and as a "reader's introduction" to 1:3–4:12. The conclusion in v. 13bβ, however, then gives the proverb a new twist: if the old king "*no longer has [or had] the insight to let himself be warned,*" he apparently lost his wisdom only with increasing age. Then the poor child, because of its wisdom, is better qualified than the old king for royal rule. Thus v. 13, through its last clause, is a vote for the replacement of an "old king" with a new, "young" ruler. This understanding of v. 13 is confirmed by the continuation of the text in vv. 14-16, which concerns "the fickleness of popular favor and the insecurity at the top of the political ladder" (Lohfink).

From the text it is not clear whether v. 13 (1) refers to an event in the (more recent) past, (2) expects a change of ruler in the (near or distant) future, or (3) discusses the question of the replacement of a no longer competent king in a more theoretical fashion, apart from a concrete situation. In any case, however, vv. 14-16 then criticize false expectations of "salvation" from a recent or anticipated change of ruler.

1. The perfect יָדַע *yādaʿ* in v. 13bβ could indicate that v. 13 has in view a concrete case in the more recent past. In particular, this could be (as then also in 10:16-17) the transition of power in the Ptolemaic kingdom around the middle of the year 204 B.C.E. from Ptolemy IV ("Philopator," 222-204, born after 240) to Ptolemy V ("Epiphanes," 204-180). Already coregent soon after his birth on 9 October 210, Ptolemy V became the new king soon after his sixth birthday.[2] Under the terms of a (forged) will of Ptolemy IV and after the murder of his wife Arsinoe III, the guardianship was assumed by "the two most powerful men in the kingdom, Sosibios and Agathocles, who had already been the de facto administrators of the government's affairs."[3]

As for Ptolemy IV,

the tradition in Polybius (5.34; 14.12) conveys the picture of a king who, through his neglect of governmental affairs and through a life lived in the exhilaration of unending feasts, led to the fall of the kingdom. This judgment underlies the "histories" of Phylarchos (FGrHist. 81), the "Stories about Philopator" by Megalopolis (FGrHist. 161), and the Arsinoe biography of the old Eratosthenes (FGrHist. 241 F 16). Evident here is a negative attitude toward a courtly life that to an increasing extent was ruled by the ruler ideal of Tryphe and by opulent life in connection with the veneration of Dionysos.[4]

In this sense, Ptolemy IV could certainly be regarded as a foolish ruler. With his death at age forty, he was, to be sure, not very old—and the child Ptolemy V was not necessarily needy.[5]

2. The image of a needy and wise child (or young man) could likewise express the hope for a usurper from the lower social strata. In this connection messianic promises (or promises interpreted in that sense) from the prophetic traditions of the OT could also play a role. (On יֶלֶד *yeled* or ילד *yld*, cf. Isa 9:5; Mic 5:2; on the wisdom of the messianic ruler, Isa 11:2; Jer 23:5; on his lowly origins, Zech 9:9.)

3. Finally, v. 13 can also be read as a more theoretical position on the question that, for example, the Ptolemy king formulated in the *Letter of Aristeas* (288): "What is better for the people: if their ruler is of low birth or if he is of royal blood?" Here a Jewish wise man answers this question as follows:

If it is the best on the basis of nature! (289) For even rulers of royal birth are at times inconsiderate and harsh against their subjects; more often, however, those of lowly origins, who (themselves) have known

---

2   Hölbl, *Geschichte des Ptolemäerreiches*, 118.
3   Ibid. 119.
4   Ibid. 118.
5   S. K.-D. Schunck, "Drei Seleukiden im Buche Kohelet?" *VT* 9 [1959] 192–201, repr. in Schunck, *Altes Testament und Heiliges Land: Gesammelte Studien*, vol. 1 [Frankfurt am Main: Lang, 1989] 9–18) sees in 4:13-14 an allusion to the transition of power in the Seleucid kingdom from Antiochus II ("Theos," 261–246) to Seleucid II ("Kallinikos," 246–225, b. ca. 265). In his opinion, v. 15 refers then to Antiochus III ("the Great," 223–187, b.

241). Hitzig "sees in the old, foolish king the spiritually contracted but so much the more covetous, high priest Onias, under Ptolemy Euergetes; and in the poor but wise youth, Joseph (the son of Tobias), who robbed Onias of his place in the state, and raised himself to the office of general farmer of taxes" (Delitzsch, 214). These and further attempts to relate vv. 13ff. to concrete events (cf. Gordis) show that the text is capable—precisely because of its ambiguity—of interpreting various experiences and giving them a common denominator.

misery and poverty, prove to be more cruel than the godless tyrants. (290) As already said, however: a good and educated character qualifies one for power. Thus you are also a great king and tower over everyone less through the reputation of your rule and wealth than through the moderation and goodness that God has given you.[6]

Whereas Qoh 4:13 can be initially understood, contrary to these considerations, as a vote for a ruler of lowly origins, the continuation in vv. 14-16 shares the skepticism of the Jewish wise man in the *Letter of Aristeas*. That these reservations concerning a ruler of low birth must by no means lead to an approval of the dynastic rule of the Ptolemies is made clear in Qoh 5:7-8 [8-9].

■ **14** Since v. 14 names no new subject, it is usually understood as a continuation of v. 13. It can then be read as either a report on the rise of the "child" (or "young man") or as the prehistory of the "old king."[7] The latter seems rather improbable, since the "next child" named in v. 15 would then have to be identical with the "child" of v. 13.[8] In the interpretation of v. 14 as the report on the rise of the "child," it is usually assumed that in v. 14b כִּי גַם *kî gam* introduces a conces-

sive clause ("although he . . . was born poor"). That cannot be excluded syntactically, but it seems, nonetheless, by no means unproblematic.[9] If, by contrast, one understands כִּי גַם *kî gam* adversatively—as in the translation recommended above—v. 14 not only tells of the rise of the "child" of v. 13 (14a) but also of its consequences (14b): even under his rule another poor child is born.[10] A change at the political top cannot eliminate the problem of poverty even when the new ruler himself comes from lowly origins.

■ **15** Therefore the disappointed subjects turn away from him and direct their expectations toward a "new child who [as the new bearer of hope] takes his place" or "[as the new ruler] is supposed to take his place."

■ **16** Thus the result is a constant repetition of expectations, disappointments, and new expectations. One learns from history how meaningless and unpromising this cycle is: every previous ruler has failed to live up to the hopes placed in him.[11]

■ **13–16** If the interpretation of 4:13-16 proposed here (for which the understanding of v. 14b is important) is correct, the point of this section lies less in the lament over "the transitoriness of fame" (Gordis), "the worth-

---

6 Based on the translation of N. Meisner, *JSHRZ* II.1.

7 For the former see, e.g., the translation of the *ZB*: "For out of prison the former [the 'youth' of v. 13] went forth to become king, although he was born poor when the latter [the 'king' of v. 13] was king" ("Denn aus dem Gefängnis ging jener hervor, um König zu werden, ob er gleich arm geboren wurde, als dieser König war"; in this sense see also the *Luther Bibel*, the *JB*, and *EÜ*). In the context of this interpretation, the suffix in בְּמַלְכוּתוֹ *běmalkûtô* can also be related to the "young man": "although in his [own later] kingdom he had been born poor." For the latter see, e.g., *RSV*: "(13) Better is a poor and wise youth than an old and foolish king, who will no longer take advice, (14) even though he had gone from prison to the throne or in his own kingdom had been born poor."

8 The *RSV* has to correct the text in v. 15: "I saw all the living who move about under the sun, as well as that [Heb.: 'the second'] youth, who was to stand in his place."

9 Schoors, *Preacher*, 130, 134–36, assumes for כִּי גַם *kî gam* in Qoh 4:14; 7:22 and 8:12 a concessive meaning (yet not in 4:16; 8:16; and 9:12). Against this, however, cf. Backhaus, *Zeit und Zufall*, 168 with n. 21. Outside the book of Qoheleth כִּי *kî* + גַם *gam*

seems never to have a concessive meaning in the OT (cf. Gen 35:17; Deut 12:31; 1 Sam 21:9; 22:17; 2 Sam 4:2; Isa 26:12; Jer 6:11; 12:6; 14:5, 18; 23:11; 46:21; 48:34; 51:12; Ezek 18:11; Hos 9:12). The construction of Hos 9:12 (. . . כִּי גַם . . . כִּי אִם *kî ʾim* . . . *kî-gam* . . . = "even if . . . then still . . .") could perhaps support the interpretation of the syntax of Qoh 4:14 proposed here.

10 Cf., e.g., also Reichert and Cohen, 135 (cited in Schoors, *Preacher*, 130 n. 599): "for even in his (own) kingdom one has become poor"; Backhaus, *Zeit und Zufall*, 435: "for even under his rule a poor one was born." Whereas Backhaus (ibid.) assumes an indefinite subject for v. 14a ("Indeed, someone came out of prison to [then] become king . . ."), he interprets (ibid., 168) v. 14a as a presentation of the "social rise" of the "young man" of v. 13 and v. 14b as a statement "that under the rule of the now reigning young and wise parvenu a *rš* ('poor one') is born." Supporting this latter interpretation is the fact that v. 15 seems with the "next (or 'second') child" to presuppose the rise of the "first child" of v. 13.

11 This is also true for Joseph, David, and Solomon, to which, according to Ogden and Schwienhorst-Schönberger (*Nicht im Menschen*, 134–35), individ-

lessness of wisdom" (Loader), or "the fickleness of popular favor" (Lohfink) than in a fundamental critique of the system of monarchical rule: within the framework of this system—as experience teaches—the problem of poverty will not be eliminated. Therefore, the hope for a new king—be it a new Ptolemaic ruler or a Jewish-Israelite "messiah"—does not go far enough. Indeed, ultimately this hope only stabilizes the monarchical system, whose shortcomings are the source of the problem.

By criticizing any expectation of salvation from a change of ruler, the text exhorts its readers to assume a reserved, sober attitude toward the political conditions and changes of its time. The beginning of 4:17 [5:1] ("Watch your feet when you go . . .") can be understood as a closing admonition not to become fellow travelers of new or aspiring rulers (cf. vv. 15-16). Messianic-eschatological expectations also fall short, since they remain within the framework of the monarchical system of rule. The text develops no alternative to this system, yet the literary connections between 4:9-12 and 4:13-16 (cf. "better . . . than . . ." in vv. 9 and 13, as well as the key words שְׁנַיִם šěnayim, "two," and שֵׁנִי šēnî, "second/next," in vv. [7,] 9-12, and 15), at least suggest such an alternative system: instead of expecting an improvement of conditions "from above," from a new ("second") king, one should rather endeavor to bring about an improvement in living conditions "from below"—together with one's fellow human being ("second") and "comrade"—through mutual help and support.

---

ual statements of the text allude. Associations of this kind in the reading of Qoh 4:13-16 are quite possible. Nonetheless, the text does not allude *throughout* to *one* of these figures; cf. Schwienhorst-Schönberger, ibid.: v. 13 = "allusion to David, Joseph, and Solomon," v. 14a = "allusion to Joseph in Egypt," v. 14b = "allusion to David" (who under the rule of Saul was born as a "poor man"[?]), vv. 15-16a = "allusion to the story of the rise and fall of Solomon."

4:17[5:1] Watch your feet[a] when you go to the
house of the Deity. And draw near in
order to hear, and not in order to make
a sacrificial offering, as the fools do.[b]
They do not understand that they are
doing something bad.[c]

5:1[2] Do not be rash with your mouth, and let
your heart not be too hasty to bring
something[a] before the Deity. For the
Deity is in heaven, and you are on
earth. Therefore, do not make many
words.[b] 2[3] For whoever has much toil
begins to dream, and whoever speaks
a lot begins to talk like a fool.[a]

3[4] When you make a vow to the Deity,
fulfill it without delay. For fools do not
please (him). What you vow,[a] you are
to fulfill! 4[5] It is better for you not to
vow at all than to vow (something) and
not fulfill (your vow).

5[6] Do not let your mouth lead your flesh
into a sin,[a] and do not say to the messenger:[b] it was a mistake. Why should
the Deity become angry over your
speech[c] and destroy the work[d] of your
hands?

6[7] When dreams multiply, and futilities and
many words:[a] fear the Deity![b]

4:17a[5:1a] Thus K, Q, and the versions read the singular
("your foot").

17b[5:1b] On the interpretation of the inf. abs. קָרוֹב *qārôb* as
imperative cf. 𝔊 and, e.g., Rashi. Other possible
interpretations: "and coming near in order to hear
(is better) than if the fools offer a sacrifice" (cf.
𝔅); "and to hear (brings a person) nearer (to God)
than if . . ." (cf. Ibn Ezra). Cf. Schoors, *Preacher*,
171, 179. It would also be possible to correct מִתֵּת
mittēt to (הַכְּסִילִים זֶבַח) מַתַּת *mattat* (*hakkĕsîlîm zābaḥ*)
(cf. 𝔖 𝔊): "A gift of the fools is a sacrifice." 𝔐 and
the versions would then have corrected this fundamental critique of sacrifice for "dogmatic" reasons. 𝔊 reads: ὑπὲρ δόμα τῶν ἀφρόνων θυσία σου
("your sacrifice stands higher than the gift of the
fools"). Backhaus (*Zeit und Zufall*, 176 n. 36)
points out that the expression נתן זֶבַח *ntn zebaḥ*
("give a sacrifice") is otherwise attested in the OT
only in Exod 10:25 (Pharaoh could give sacrifices
to the Israelites, who can then present them to
God in the wilderness). For this reason, perhaps
the focus here is less on the *presentation* than on
the *donation* of sacrifices (and the related meals)
by "the fools."

17c[5:1c] Cf. 𝔅 (*qui nesciunt quid faciant mali*). Or: "They do
not know to do something bad" (cf. Lohfink; cf.
also 4:13; 10:15; somewhat different is 6:8). 𝔊 and
𝔖 understand the constructions in this sense but
instead of רָע *rāʿ* ("something bad") read καλόν
("something beautiful") or טב *tb* ("something
good"). More problematic, by contrast, is the frequent interpretation: "They do not understand, so
they act badly" (cf. Delitzsch and others). Cf. the
discussion in Schoors, *Preacher*, 182; Backhaus,
Zeit und Zufall, 176. The conjecture "they do not
know how to keep from doing evil" (*NRSV*; cf.
BHS) has no basis in the text tradition.

5:1a[2a] Or: "a word."

1b[2b] Literally: "therefore your words are to be few."

2a[3a] Literally: "for the dream comes with much effort,
and the voice of a fool with many words."

3a[4a] Instead of the accusative particle אֵת *ʾēt* some 𝔊
mss. read the personal pronoun אַתְ *ʾattā*: "you, fulfill what you have vowed" (cf. α' 𝔊 𝔗).

5a[6a] Literally: "Do not let your flesh lead into sin." On
the unusual form of the hiphil infinitive from חטא
ḥṭʾ (לַחֲטִיא *laḥăṭîʾ*) cf. GKC §53q.

5b[6b] 𝔊 reads: "before the Deity" (cf. 𝔖).

5c[6c] Literally: "your voice."

5d[6d] Some Hebrew mss. and the versions read here the
plural ("the works").

6a[7a] It would also be possible to understand v. 6a as an
independent clause: "in many dreams (there are)
also futilities and words in excess," or "in many
words and futilities (there are) also words in

excess" (cf. GKC §143d, and, e.g., Crenshaw; Why-bray).

6b[7b]   Here again, instead of the accusative particle אֶת ʾēt some 𝔊 and 𝔖 mss. read the personal pronoun אַתָּ ʾattā: "you, fear the Deity" (cf. v. 3 [4]).

■ **4:17—5:6** In this section the reader is addressed directly for the first time in the book of Qoheleth. Various instructions for action (imperative, vetitive, and jussive) are connected with statements (or in v. 5b a question) that substantiate, motivate, or more clearly define them. Thematically, five subsections can be distinguished:

- ■ Behavior in the Temple: "hearing" and "sacrifice" (4:17)
- ■ Behavior in prayer: "words" (5:1-2)
- ■ Fulfillment of "vows" (5:3-4)
- ■ Dealing with guilt (5:5)
- ■ Summary: exhortation to "fear the Deity" (5:6)

■ **4:17** This verse does not warn "against thoughtless rushing to the temple" (thus Crenshaw; the passages cited by him for comparison, Prov 1:15; 25:17 [cf. also 4:27], are formulated differently). Rather, it advises readers "to be careful when they go to the Temple" (Why-bray). *That* they will do so, he takes for granted. *How* they are supposed to conduct themselves there is clarified and substantiated in what follows. First, they are to go into the temple "in order to hear" (cf. קרב *qrb* + לִשְׁמֹעַ *lišmōaʿ*; cf. Deut 5:27 and Isa 34:1). This presupposes that in the temple there is something to hear (e.g., hymns or readings from sacred writings). In any case, in relation to the "hearing," the "sacrifice" is of less value—if it is not rejected entirely.[1] The "sacrifice" (זֶבַח *zebaḥ*) is distinguished, on the one hand, from the bloodless sacrificial gift (מִנְחָה *minḥâ*) and, on the other, from the

burnt offering (עוֹלָה *ʿôlâ*), which is offered completely. It is in part consumed by those participating in the sacrificial celebration (cf., e.g., Exod 18:12; Deut 12:6-7). Thus the critique of Qoh 4:17 is probably not aimed at every kind of sacrifice but rather especially at "sacrificial celebrations that degenerated into festive banquets" (Lohfink). When the text holds up "the fools" before readers' eyes as a negative example, it reveals the ideal of "reasonable worship." The closing remark that the fools "do not know to do something bad" or "do not notice that they are doing something bad"[2] expresses, in addition to "contempt and irony" (Crenshaw), a certain forbearance toward "the fools": they do not know any better.[3] It is noteworthy that the text exhorts one neither to put an end to "foolish" practices in the sanctuary nor to distance oneself from the temple on the basis of such "foolish" practices. To the *individual* it recommends conducting one's temple visit in a "reasonable" manner and to tolerate the "unreasonable" cult practices of others.

In the spectrum of OT and early Jewish discussion on the meaning and significance of the cult of sacrifice, Qoh 4:17 represents an independent but by no means extreme position. In the wisdom tradition[4] the value of sacrifices is often measured by the moral behavior of the one making the sacrifice (cf. Prov 15:8; 21:27; Sir 34:21ff.; 35:8ff.): "To do righteousness and justice is more acceptable to the Lord than sacrifice" (Prov 21:3). According to Sir 35:2-5 behavior that is faithful to the Torah is worth as much as the offering of sacrifices and in principle can replace the latter: "One who heeds the commandments makes an offering of well-being. The

---

1   Cf. the note on the translation of 4:17b, as well as 9:2.
2   Cf. the note on the translation.
3   Cf., however, also below on 5:5.
4   Cf. here L. G. Perdue, *Wisdom and Cult* (SBLDS 30; Missoula, Mont.: Scholars Press, 1977); A. B. Ernst, *Weisheitliche Kultkritik: Zu Theologie und Ethik des* *Sprüchebuchs und der Prophetie des 8. Jahrhunderts* (BThSt 23; Neukirchen-Vluyn: Neukirchener Verlag, 1994).

one who returns a kindness offers choice flour, and one who gives alms sacrifices a thank offering. To keep from wickedness is pleasing to the Lord, and to forsake unrighteousness is an atonement." It is nonetheless precisely loyalty to the Torah (and only this!) that requires that sacrifices be offered: "The one who keeps the law makes many offerings. . . . Do not appear before the Lord empty-handed, for all these things are to be done because of the commandment" (Sir 35:1, 6-7; cf. Exod 23:15; 34:20; Deut 16:16). In the prophetic tradition, in addition to the critique of concrete sacrificial practices in certain historical situations there are also statements that reveal a more fundamental critique of sacrifice.[5] Here the—prophetically inspired—juxtaposition of "sacrifice" and "hearing" in 1 Sam 15:22 comes especially close to Qoh 4:17: "Has the Lord as great delight in burnt offerings and sacrifices, as in obeying the voice of the Lord? Surely, to obey is better than sacrifice, and to heed than the fat of rams." (Cf. also Isa 1:19; Jer 7:23; Ezek 20:39, as well as Mic 6:8; Ps 40:7-9). In the Psalter, finally, Pss 40:7-9; 50:7-15; and 51:18-19, as well as Isa 66:3, could document a "'pietism' free of temple and sacrifice" (Zimmerli on Qoh 9:2).

Whereas Qoh 4:17 agrees with the passages in Proverbs mentioned above in shining a critical light on sacrifice, the fundamental nature of the critique expressed here, as well as the juxtaposition of sacrifice and hearing, corresponds rather to the prophetic tradition. It is especially striking that the critique of sacrificial practice here is based not on "morality" but on "reason" (cf. here also Isa 66:1ff. and Ps 50:10ff.). The ideal conception of the temple cult perceivable behind Qoh 4:17 seems to correspond largely to the presentation in the *Epistle of Aristeas* (92ff.): regarding animal sacrifice, only burnt offerings are mentioned here. There is (just as in Sir 45:6ff. and 50:1ff.) no mention of sacrificial meals. *Epistle of Aristeas* 95 emphasizes as particularly impressive the "silence" that reigns in the temple (cf. Qoh 5:1-2), as well as the "reverence" (cf. Qoh 5:6) and the "wise manner worthy of a great Deity" of cultic practice.[6]

■ **5:1-2** These verses advise restraint with regard to prayer: one should pray neither too much nor in too much detail. This advice is based first (v. 1) on the distance between God ("in heaven") and human beings ("on earth"): respect for God's superiority forbids people to practice a relationship that is "in some way collegial with God" (Lohfink). Second (v. 2), the traditional wisdom ideal of restraint in speech[7] in the interpersonal realm is carried over into the relationship with God: also in dialogue with God, the "fool" betrays himself by making many words. Verse 2 perhaps quotes an already coined proverb that regards dreams critically (v. 2a) in addition to wordy speech (v. 3b; cf. v. 6).[8] Since v. 2b, however, clearly refers (in a substantiating way) back to v. 1(bβ), v. 2 does not seem to introduce an independently important new theme ("dreams") (thus Lohfink).

The value of frequent and long prayers was very much in dispute in Judaism as well as later in Christianity.[9] Sirach 7:10 (in contrast to Qoh 5:1) admonishes: "Do not grow weary when you pray," whereas Sir 7:14 (in agreement with Qoh 5:1) advises: "Do not repeat

---

5   In the former sense see Jer 6:19-20; 14:11-12; Ezek 20:25ff.; Hos 8:1ff.; Mal 1:7ff.; 2:13-14. In the latter see Isa 1:10ff.; 66:3; Jer 7:22; Amos 5:21-22 (where the perhaps later inserted v. 22aα seems to make burnt offerings an exception to the critique); Hos 6:6; Mic 6:6ff.

6   Cf. to this John J. Collins, *Between Athens and Jerusalem; Jewish Identity in the Hellenistic Diaspora* (New York: Crossroad, 1983) 182–83.

7   Cf. Walter Bühlmann, *Vom rechten Reden und Schweigen* (OBO 12; Fribourg: Universitätsverlag; Göttingen: Vandenhoeck & Ruprecht, 1976); Emma Brunner-Traut, "Weiterleben der ägyptischen Lebenslehren in den koptischen Apophthegmata am Beispiel des Schweigens," in Erik Hornung and Othmar Keel, eds., *Studien zu altägyptischen Lebenslehren*

(OBO 28; Fribourg: Universitätsverlag; Göttingen: Vandenhoeck & Ruprecht, 1979) 173–216.

8   It is not entirely clear from the Hebrew word order of v. 2a whether dreams arise *through* much "occupation" or whether they are accompanied *by* much "occupation" (i.e., occupy a person). The assumption that v. 2a polemicizes against the activities of temple personnel, who—on the basis of dreams—give oracles to prayers (Kroeber), is just as speculative as the hypothesis that the statement is directed toward "terrifying dreams" (cf. Job 4:12ff.; 33:14ff.) that give rise to prayers in the temple (Perdue, *Wisdom and Cult*, 184).

9   Cf., e.g., Mt 6:7 vs. 1 Thess 5:17 and elsewhere; on this see Ulrich Luz, *Matthew 1–7* (CC; Minneapolis: Fortress Press, 1989) 364–66; H. L. Strack and P.

yourself when you pray." According to Sir 39:5-6 prayer is among the duties of the "wise," whereas the prayer of artisans consists in "the exercise of their trade" (38:34).

Whereas Job 33:14ff., for example—in accordance with the Hellenistic "zeitgeist"[10]—gives dreams a high value as a means of "revelation" (cf. also, e.g., Job 4:12-13; Genesis 40–41; Daniel 2; 4; 7), Sir 34:1-7 expresses skeptical reservations in regard to dreams: "Divinations and omens and dreams are unreal. . . . Unless they are sent by intervention from the Most High, pay no attention to them" (vv. 5-6).

In ancient Near Eastern religious history, the withdrawal of the gods from the earth into heaven begins already in the third millennium B.C.E.[11] "Since the Pers[ian] period, Yahweh is indicated by the title 'God of heaven.'"[12] "Heaven is the Lord's heaven, but the earth he has given to human beings" (Ps 115:16). According to 1 Kgs 8:27-30, Yahweh also hears from heaven prayer addressed to him in the temple. The fact that the Deity is in heaven (Qoh 5:1)[13] does not make him into a "distant despot who has no contact with human beings" (thus Lauha; cf., however, v. 5b). Knowledge of the *distance* between God and humankind by no means excludes a *relationship* between them.

■ **3-4** Like sacrifice and prayer, a vow can also be regarded as a constitutive element of worship (cf., e.g., Isa 19:21; Jonah 1:16). Verse 3 exhorts one to take vows seriously. The "reasonable" approach to vows with respect before God should itself, according to v. 4, lead to a certain restraint here as in the case of prayer, if not to forgoing completely the making of vows. Here the text

agrees with Deut 23:22-24: "If you make a vow to the Lord your God, do not postpone fulfilling it; for the Lord your God will surely require it of you, and you would incur guilt. But if you refrain from vowing, you will not incur guilt." Proverbs 20:25 and Sir 18:22-23, for example, also warn against ill-considered vows.

■ **5** Many regard this verse as the continuation of vv. 3-4. Then we would have here a warning against hasty vows that are excused to the "messenger" (i.e., probably the priest; cf. Mal 2:7), who demands their fulfillment, as "a slip of the tongue" (שְׁגָגָה šĕgāgâ [inadvertent mistake]).[14] Since, however, in OT law שְׁגָגָה šĕgāgâ is used without special reference to vows, one may assume rather that v. 5 turns to a new theme.[15] The text warns not only against "sins of haste" (Zimmerli) but likewise against guilt *and* "cultic trivialization" of incurred guilt;[16] "the first part of the prohibition warns one not to commit a willful sin, and the second warns one not to compound one's guilt by lying to the 'priestly official' by saying that it was a šĕgāgâ, that is, an inadvertent or unconscious sin"[17]—wherein the "concealment of real guilt in the šĕgāgâ-sacrifice"[18] itself would be a new, deliberate guilt and would lead to new guilt.

In the background of the text we can recognize the question of the relationship of "theoretical" legitimation and "practical" execution of the Jerusalem temple cult (cf. Whybray): according to Num 15:30-31, transgressions that are carried out "high-handedly"—that is, deliberately and knowingly—cannot be atoned and forgiven; they lead to exclusion from the cultic community. Cultic atonement is possible only for "unintentional" sins (שְׁגָגָה

Billerbeck, *Kommentar zum Neuen Testament aus Talmud und Midrasch* (9th ed.; Munich: Beck, 1986) 1:403ff.

10 Cf. Hengel, *Judaism and Hellenism*, 1:202ff., 210ff.

11 Cf., e.g., Ernst Axel Knauf, *Die Umwelt des Alten Testaments* (Neue Stuttgarter Kommentar: Altes Testament 29; Stuttgart: Katholisches Bibelwerk, 1994) 252.

12 J. A. Soggin, "שָׁמַיִם šāmayim heaven," *TLOT* 3:1371; cf., e.g., 2 Chr 36:23; Ezra 1:2; Neh 1:4; Dan 2:18-19; Jonah 1:9; Ps 136:26.

13 Cf. also Whybray: "This lapidary statement has been interpreted in quite different ways: as being entirely in accordance with the main Old Testament tradition (so Hertzberg) and as completely 'heretical' (Gordis) and a deliberate denial of Dt. 4:39's

'Yahweh is God in heaven above and on the earth beneath' (e.g. Loader). The former view is nearer to the truth."

14 Thus, e.g., Crenshaw; cf. R. B. Salters, "Notes on the History of Interpretation of Koh 5,5," *ZAW* 90 (1978) 95–101.

15 Thus, e.g., also Perdue, *Wisdom and Cult*, 186; N. Lohfink, "Warum ist der Tor unfähig, böse zu handeln? (Koh 4,17)," in F. Steppat, ed., *XXI. Deutscher Orientalistentag vom 24. bis 29. März 1980 in Berlin: Ausgewählte Vorträge* (ZDMGSup 5; Wiesbaden: Steiner, 1983) 119. On שְׁגָגָה šĕgāgâ see Leviticus 4–5; 22:14; Num 15:22ff.; 35:11, 15; Josh 20:3, 9.

16 Lohfink, "Warum," 119 n. 39.

17 Perdue, *Wisdom and Cult*, 186.

18 Lohfink, "Warum," 119 n. 39.

šĕgāgâ, vv. 22ff.). In practice, such a claim on cult participants (cf. here also Psalms 15 and 24) could probably have been maintained only if factual "sins" were declared to be "unintentional." What in Leviticus 4–5; Num 15:22ff.; 35:9ff. "are named as concrete transgressions are all such that with a little casuistry one can subsume everything possible under šĕgāgâ."[19] Against this kind of practice Qoh 5:5 exhorts one to confess guilt[20]—and apparently presupposes that this absolutely does not make participation in the temple cult impossible (cf. Psalm 51).

In the wider context v. 5 contains another point to which Lohfink has drawn attention. Different from the preceding sections, v. 5 lacks a reference to the behavior of "fools" as a contrast to the recommended "reasonable worship." Such would be superfluous here, because those who declare their transgressions before the priest as "unintentional"—if one takes them at their word— reveal themselves as "fools": they themselves

> declare to a certain extent through their šĕgāgâ-practice that they live only half-consciously. On their own, they assert thereby, on the one hand, that they are not really conscious individuals who are clearly responsible for what they do and, on the other hand, that they actually do not act badly, either. Here Qoheleth skewers them in advance in 4:17b by saying that they are incapable of doing evil. He takes seriously, as it were, the self-assertion implicit in their practice of sacrifice.[21]

Qoheleth 5:5, by contrast, demands a "reasonable"—and also, precisely in the cultic realm, honest—dealing with guilt.

Verse 5b gives this demand emphasis with a reference to the danger of a punishing intervention of God. After 3:17ff., this expectation seems at first somewhat strange. Therefore, v. 5b is sometimes excluded as an "orthodox expansion."[22] Yet what is said in 3:17ff. by no means excludes the possibility that beyond his "judicial" action in the form of contingency and death, God also, in the course of events, intercedes *in individual cases* with his

punishing wrath. In addition, there is a certain irony of 5:5 in that God's wrath is offered as a prospect precisely for the one who seeks to conceal his guilt. (That no one is completely without guilt will then be made clear in 7:20.)

■ **6a** In terms of content, v. 6a reaches back to v. 2. In addition to "words" and "dreams," here we find "absurdities" or "futilities" (הֲבָלִים *hăbālîm*) named that also occur in the context of the cultic adoration of God—not only in the temple, but there also. No doubt intended here are "meaningless" and "nonsensical" words (cf. 6:11), dreams and other cult practices (such as sacrifice, hasty and wordy prayers, unfulfilled vows, and שְׁגָגָה *šĕgāgâ* declarations"; cf. 4:17–5:5). In the context of instructions for the proper worship of God, however, we can also hear the meaning of הֲבָלִים *hăbālîm*, otherwise predominant in the OT, as "nothings" = "idols" (see above on 1:2; cf. then by contrast "the Deity" in v. 6b). The formulation of v. 6a, in comparison with the הֶבֶל *hebel* judgments in the preceding sections ("all that" or "this [also] is futile"), reveals that here (and in 4:17–5:6 in general) it is not *all* of the usual practice of worshiping God that is regarded as "nonsense"; it is only asserted (or presupposed) that here also many things happen that are "futile" and "nonsensical."

■ **6b** Correspondingly, v. 6b does not ask readers to withdraw from traditional worship but *in that context* to "fear the Deity" (אֶת־הָאֱלֹהִים יְרָא *ʾet-hāʾĕlōhîm yĕrāʾ*). Unlike in 3:14 and 8:12-13, the topic here is not "fear *before* (מִלִּפְנֵי *millipnê*) God" but, in the usual terminology, "fear of God" (cf. with אֵת *ʾet* 12:13; without אֵת *ʾet* 7:18; 8:12). After what has been said before (cf. esp. 5:5b), it is clear that this "fear of God" also includes here the numinous element of "fear *before* God." A point of the exhortation to "fear God" at the close of 4:17–5:6 lies in the fact that in the view of the text the (temple) cult is apparently not *eo ipso* already an expression of the "fear of God"; rather, the "fear of God" functions here as a *criterion* for judging cultic practices and a *guideline* of behavior *in the cultic realm: "The only correct basis for cultic religion is

---

19 Ibid., 119 n. 40.

20 In this sense also Prov 28:13; Sir 4:26 (cf. 17:25ff.; 39:5); Pss 25:11, 18; 32:3ff.; 51; 130:3-4, as well as Job 5:8ff.; 8:5-6; 11:13ff.; 22:23ff.; 33:18ff. (cf. Perdue, *Wisdom and Cult*, 171ff.). Cf. also the prayers in the "Deuteronomic" tradition in Ezra 9; Neh 1:5ff.;

9; Daniel 9; Bar 1:15–3:8; Tob 3:1-6, which include the confession of guilt.

21 Lohfink, "Warum," 119–20.

22 Cf., e.g., Michel, *Untersuchungen*, 257.

the feeling of awe occasioned by the mysterious majesty of the divine."[23] In this sense v. 6b is by no means so "orthodox" that it would have to be regarded as a later expansion.[24]

■ **4:17—5:6** With "sacrifice," "prayer," and "vow," this section addresses themes that are also treated in the books of Proverbs and Sirach.[25] Within the context of these traditional "wisdom" themes, the text places its own accents. Thus its relativization of the value of sacrifice through "hearing" corresponds to prophetic traditions and their "Deuteronomic" reception, and it fits in perhaps with contemporary piety movements criticizing temple and sacrifice. The critique of the שְׁגָגָה šĕgāgâ practice in 5:5 takes up the requirement of the recognition of guilt in the "Deuteronomic" tradition (cf. also the position of the "friends" in the book of Job, as well as Sir 17:25ff.; 39:5; and, e.g., Psalm 32) and turns it critically against current cult practice, as it was apparently exercised in the Jerusalem temple on the basis of the Torah. In contrast to the polemic against "foreign" religions and their cultic practices (which is perhaps heard in v. 6a with the key word הֲבָלִים hăbālîm), in Qoh 4:17—5:6 the dominant theme is the critical testing of one's own religion regarding problematic elements: "fear of God" and "idolatry" cannot be neatly and cleanly divided between one's own and foreign religions.

The independent position of the text is especially recognizable in the way in which it substantiates and motivates the recommended behavior in the cultic realm. While 5:5b formulates something like a threat of punishment, there is no promise of salvation for those who venerate God in the "proper" way (by contrast, cf., e.g., Prov 3:9-10; Sir 35:10-11). While 5:3-4 alludes to the Torah (Deut 23:22-24), the text does not expressly refer to it (as does, e.g., Sir 35:7). Repeatedly serving as motivation for the "proper" adoration of God is the distancing of one-

self from the behavior of "fools" (not, as in Proverbs, of the "unrighteous"). Here we can perceive the ideal of a "reasonable worship of God" that is marked—in the words of *Ep. Aris.* 95—with "silence," "reverence," and practicing of the cult in a "manner worthy of a great Deity."

Thus 4:17—5:6 proves to be a pointed and prominent statement in the context of the contemporary *internal* Jewish discussion on the theme "cult." Themes like circumcision, purity laws, separation, and monotheism, which in the consideration of Judaism *from the outside* and its self-representation *for outsiders* were prominent in the Hellenistic period,[26] do not come into view here. The "reasonable worship of God" recommended by the text could also be practiced by "pagans" toward their deity. The text, however, addresses (Hebrew-speaking) Judeans who attend the Jerusalem temple (4:17). The lack of explicit polemics against foreign religions is hardly an indication of a lax attitude in regard to religious questions, such as that displayed in the second half of the third century B.C.E., for example, by the Tobiads; indeed, the text specifically calls one to treat prayer, vows, and sins with religious seriousness. On this basis it is very questionable whether its author had stood on the side of the "Hellenists" in Jerusalem at the time of the Maccabean revolt, as Crüsemann holds.[27] Neither, however, is it to be assumed that he—like the community of Qumran—distanced himself from the Jerusalem temple because of questions of cultic practice.

The difficulties of fitting Qoh 4:17—5:6 into the discussion of cult and religion in contemporary Hellenistic philosophy become easily recognizable in the comment of Braun on this section.[28] He finds here

a skepticism toward certain religious activities that is not known in wisdom[?], but that conforms to certain expressions of the surrounding world. Thus contem-

---

23 Thus Perdue, *Wisdom and Cult,* 177—but with reference to Job 38–42.
24 Cf., e.g., Michel, *Untersuchungen,* 257.
25 Cf. the overview of "cultic" themes in OT wisdom literature in Perdue, *Wisdom and Cult,* 350–51; on "sacrifice" and "prayer" cf. Prov 15:8, 29; 17:1; 21:3, 27; 28:9; Sir 7:10, 14; 17:25ff.; 34:21—35:26; 39:5-6; on "vows" cf. Prov 20:25; 31:2; Sir 18:22-23.
26 Cf. Hengel, *Judaism and Hellenism,* 1:255ff.
27 Frank Crüsemann, "The Unchangeable World: The

'Crisis of Wisdom' in Koheleth," in Willy Schottroff and Wolfgang Stegemann, eds., *God of the Lowly: Socio-Historical Interpretations of the Bible* (Maryknoll, N.Y.: Orbis, 1984) 68–69.
28 Braun, *Kohelet,* 126–27. Cf. here also Schwienhorst-Schönberger, *Nicht im Menschen,* 138 n. 60.

porary thinkers of early Hellenism, in agreement with the gnomic and popular philosophical tradition, condemn mistakes in religious practice; in addition, caution with prayer and vows is especially emphasized, but there is also implicit and explicit criticism of the value of religious activity. Accordingly, one can determine that for the Greeks as well as for Qoheleth, religious activity happens only out of fear of a negative intervention of the deity. This in no way corresponds to more traditional belief, but to enlightened religiosity that is by nature based on pragmatism and must be understood more as formal, obligatory fulfillment of traditional norms, since for this thinking, a personal relationship with the numinous no longer needs to be assumed.

Braun's comments reveal the breadth of the discussion in the Greek world but hardly do justice to the position of Qoh 4:17–5:6. When the text exhorts one to practice prayer and vows with religious seriousness, the "value of religious activity" is thereby basically accepted. Qoheleth 4:17–5:6 in no way asserts that the veneration of the gods is of no use because they help the evil ones.[29] If the text contains no *explicit* reference to any commandment, this shows that it does not understand the worship of God "as the formal fulfillment of duty in regard to traditional norms," but rather as "reasonable" action in critical reception of such norms. In its attitude toward the (temple) cult, 4:17–5:6 clearly stands closer

to OT and early Jewish texts such as Psalm 50 and Sirach 34–35—in spite of all the differences—than to the Greek positions cited by Braun.

This can also be demonstrated by a comparison with the judgment of religious practice in the contemporary directions of Hellenistic philosophy. With the Cynics, the "rejection in principle of existing law, state and civilisation"[30] was also extended to religion: "One should, according to Diogenes, not feel bound by ritual or sacral regulations. One may with impunity take away things from sacral precincts, and there is no reason to fear ritual impurity caused by the eating of any animal (Diog. Laert. 6.73)."[31] Qoheleth 5:5b stands in clear contradiction to Epicurus's conviction that while the gods exist, they do not intervene in what happens in the world.[32] The attitude of the Pyrrhonist skeptics, who (like the priest Pyrrho of Elis) worship the gods in traditional fashion without being convinced of their existence,[33] can hardly be reconciled with Qoh 5:6b. And in contrast to Qoh 5:2, 6a "the Stoics were convinced that by means of interpreting omens, oracles, and dreams, the future could be discovered."[34] Whereas the Stoics endeavored "to integrate popular religion into their philosophical system" and to this end developed their "teaching of the 'tripartite theology' (*SVF* II 1009),"[35] Qoh 4:17–5:6 knows only "reasonable" and "foolish" cult practices.

---

29   Menander, *Kolax*, 25ff.; quoted in Braun, *Kohelet*, 127 n. 398; cf. also Hengel, *Judaism and Hellenism*, 1:122ff.

30   Aalders, *Political Thought*, 56.

31   Ibid., 59.

32   See Hossenfelder, *Philosophie*, 115–16.

33   See ibid., 171.

34   Otto Kaiser, "Determination und Freiheit beim Kohelet / Prediger Salomo und in der frühen Stoa," *NZSTh* 31 (1989) 266.

35   Ricken, *Philosophie*, 168. "The mythical theology is that of the poets; the political, that of the public

cultus; and the physical (natural), that of the philosophers. The distinction shows that according to the stoic view, popular religion is necessary for the survival of the state and morality. It accords natural theology the highest position and the task of criticism. The etymological explanation of the names of the gods and the allegorical interpretation of myths serve the communication of popular religion and of philosophical theology" (ibid., 168–69).

7[8]   When you see how the poor are
            oppressed in the province, and law and
            justice are denied, do not be frightened
            (or: surprised) about this.ᵃ For a higher
            (official) watches over a high one, and
            over them are (even) higher ones. **8[9]**
            And it is an advantage for a land in all
            this,ᵃ when every plowed field has a
            (or: its own) king.ᵇ

7a[8a] Literally: "about the/this matter" (חֵפֶץ *ḥēpeṣ*); cf. 3:1, 17 (5:3).

8a[9a] Thus with correction of the vocalization for בְּכֹל הִיא *běkol hî²* (cf. K) and reference of הִיא *hî²* back to the conditions described in v. 7. If, however, one reads בְּכֹל הוּא *bakkōl hû²* with the Masoretes (cf. Q), one could interpret בְּכֹל *bakkōl* in the sense of "in every respect" (cf. Gen 24:1) and translate "an advantage of a land is, in every respect, a king . . ." (cf. Murphy).

8b[9b] The interpretation of v. 8 is vigorously disputed among commentators. "Gordis's opinion about the impenetrable obscurity of this verse has much to be said for it" (Whybray). The following recommendations for interpretation presented by Eaton do not by any means exhaust the discussion on the interpretation of v. 8:

> The beginning of the verse may be translated: *And an advantage to* (or *for*, or *of*) *a land is.* . . Then the Hebrew becomes difficult. Should it be translated "for all" (*AV, JB*), "in all" (*RSV*), "on the whole" (Barton, Leupold), "over everything" (Gordis), "after all" (*NASV,* Moffatt) or "always" (Delitzsch)? Is the word "served" (Heb. *ne²ĕbād*) to be attached to "king" or (as the Masoretic pointing suggests) to "land," and does it have a simple adjectival sense ("served," "cultivated") or a permissive sense ("allowed to be cultivated")? This in turn leads to numerous possibilities of translation. Is the advantage "a king whose own lands are well tilled" (*NEB*)? Or that "even a king is subject to the soil" (Gordis; *cf. AV*)? Or is the advantage "a king for a field under tillage" (Plumptre)? Or "a king who has control" (Moffatt)? Or "that a cultivated land has a king" (as a counterweight to bureaucratic corruption; so Lauha, *cf.* also Barton)?

> Also to be mentioned here are the translations recommended by Harold Fisch (*The Holy Scriptures* [Jerusalem: Koren, 1992]): "Moreover, land has an advantage for everyone: he who tills a field is a king," and Zlotowitz: "The advantage of land is supreme; even a king is indebted to the soil."

■ **7-8** This section continues the direct address to the reader in 4:17—5:6. Thematically the section brings to mind 4:13-16 (key words: "king" and "the poor"); moreover, "oppression" recalls 4:1-3 and the denial of "law and justice" recalls 3:16-21. Verse 9aα can be read initially as a continuation of v. 8. Only with continued reading does it become clear that v. 9 (then also) begins a new theme.

■ **7** Like the preceding sections in 4:17—5:6, v. 7 formulates a well-reasoned request. The introductory circumstantial clause ("when you see. . .") directs one's view away from the Jerusalem temple (4:17) and toward the surrounding "province" Judea. In view of what is to be seen in this "province," its Hebrew designation, מְדִינָה *mědînâ* ("judicial district," from the root דִּין *dyn*: "do justice, maintain justice, hold judgment") gains an ironic undertone. Since the verbs תמה *tmh* ("be frightened" or "be surprised") and שמר *šmr* ("pay attention to . . ."—in the sense of "guard, watch over"—or "protect") are ambiguous in the present context (cf., e.g., Murphy and Gerson), request and reason in v. 7 can be read and interpreted in two ways:

(1) ". . . do not *be frightened*. For a higher one *watches* over a high one . . ."

(2) ". . . do not *be surprised*. For a higher one *protects* a high one . . ."

If one follows the first reading, v. 7 downplays the experience of oppression and injustice in Judea with a reference to the functioning of the Ptolemaic system of governance and administration:[1] individual evils are no reason to be disturbed; they are bound to be discovered and eliminated by a cleverly devised system of hierarchical controls.

The extant "official" documents from the Ptolemaic empire are by no means silent about evils resulting from "maladministration." "The evidence is unusually abundant and explicit compared to the other monarchies."[2] In a "memorandum" from the late third century, in which the duties of an οἰκονόμος are described—probably by a διοικητής[3]—we read, for example: "During your tour of inspection try as you [go] about to encourage everybody and make them feel happier; you should do this not only by words, but also should any of them have a complaint against the village-scribes or the village-

chiefs (κώμαρχαι) about anything to do with agriculture, you should investigate the matter and as far as possible put an end to such incidents" (ll. 42ff.). "Take especial care that no act of extortion or any other misdeed is committed. For everyone who lives in the country must clearly know and believe that all such acts have come to an end and that they have been delivered from the previous bad state of affairs, and that [nobody] is allowed to do what he wishes, [but] everything is arranged for the best. And (so) you will make the countryside safe and (sc. will increase) the revenues in no small way" (ll. 224ff.). This text reveals the control system of the Ptolemaic administration, the related claim (propagated by officials) that "everything is arranged for the best," and the underlying interest in the assurance of incomes for the crown.[4]

If, however, one follows the second reading of v. 7, the verse forms a radical critique of the Ptolemaic governmental organization, in which "the authorities that check each other at the same time protect each other" (Galling): that this repeatedly resulted in evils is no wonder in view of the "corruption of the administration" (Lauha). "They mutually protect their advantage: no crow is going to peck out the eye of another" (Hitzig).[5] As in 4:13-16, so here also it is not a question of evils that are to be eliminated within the system; rather, this system produces the very evils that it claims to eliminate.

1   Cf., e.g., Hengel, *Judaism and Hellenism*, 1:6–7, 18ff., 39ff., 50ff.; P. Schäfer, *Geschichte der Juden in der Antike* (Neukirchen-Vluyn: Neukirchener Verlag, 1983) 31ff.; Michaud, *Qohélet*, 90ff., 165; Michael Rostovtzeff, *A Social and Economic History of the Hellenistic World* (Oxford: Clarendon, 1941) 1:279–80, 349; R. S. Bagnall, *The Administration of the Ptolemaic Possessions outside Egypt* (Columbia Studies in the Classical Tradition 4; Leiden: Brill, 1976). The interpretation of v. 7 as a statement about the dominion of God and the angels ("there is one higher than the high who watches and there are high ones above them"; see Zlotowitz) is not as likely in the context (cf. Delitzsch).

2   Austin, *Hellenistic World*, 382.

3   Ibid., no. 256.

4   Also instructive for the first point is Austin, no. 260b: The royal scribe of the νομή turns over to a τοπογραμματεύς the naming of a κωμογραμματεύς through the διοικητής and charges him: "Take care

5   that he carries out what he has promised." For the second see Austin, no. 258, where a διοικητής writes to a ὑποδιοικητής: "The king and the queen attach great importance to justice being done to all their subjects in the kingdom." For the third see Austin, no. 236, 238 (l. 35), 259.
In this reading of the text one can also interpret גָּבֹהַּ *gābōah* ("high one, highly placed one") as "arrogant one" (cf. in this sense 7:8). According to J. L. Kugel ("Qohelet and Money," *CBQ* 51 [1989] 35–38) גָּבֹהַּ *gābōah* here would designate a "bribed one." Delitzsch would like to understand שמר *šmr* "in the sense of hostile lurking": "Over the one who is high, who oppresses the poor and is a robber in respect of right and justice, there stands a higher, who on his part watches how he can plunder him to his own aggrandisement; and over both there are again other high ones, who in their own interest oppress these, as these do over such as are under them."

■ **8** This verse seems to see an advantage in the existence of the king—and thus the top of the hierarchy of the highly and more highly placed—and therefore to express an antirevolutionary, skeptical conservatism (Kroeber), which still holds the monarchy to be relatively better than anarchy (Zimmerli).[6] More specifically, v. 8 could see the "advantage" of the monarchy in the idea that the king is there "for a cultivated field"; that is, he is concerned about agriculture.

In fact, the Ptolemaic rulers had a special interest in the "cultivated field," a prime source of their revenues. The increase in proceeds from taxes in Ptolemaic Judea was "only possible as a result of more intensive cultivation and the consequent increase in the fertility of the country."[7] One stimulus in this direction came, for example, from (temporary) tax exemptions for newly cultivated land.[8] In this way, the interest of the king in the "tilled field" could also be of "advantage" for the small farmer.[9]

After the ambiguous v. 7, nonetheless, v. 8—understood as a statement about the advantage of the monarchy—can hardly be read other than as an ironic "quotation" of "official" Ptolemaic power ideology.[10] According to v. 7 there is no doubt as to what should be thought about that: the king is only the "culmination" of a system in which each "more highly placed one" strives solely for his own advantage (cf. Neh 5:4; 9:36-37). "Whoever loves money will never have enough money" (v. 9).[11]

Yet v. 8, like v. 7 before it, also seems to be readable in two ways. The expression מֶלֶךְ לְשָׂדֶה נֶעֱבָד *melek lĕśādeh neʿĕbād* can also be understood in the sense of "one king for every cultivated field," that is, "for every cultivated field its own king." The advantage for a country would then consist in the fact that everyone (at least every landowner?) is his own master (cf. 8:9).

---

6   Lauha regards v. 9, therefore, as a "marginal note that a supporter of the existing social order added in order, with reference to the order-bestowing court of the monarch, to correct the one-sidedness of Qoheleth's critique of authority." At the beginning of the verse Galling adds מַה *mah*: "'What an advantage' it is for the land in all this, when a king is there only for the tilled field."

7   Hengel, *Judaism and Hellenism,* 1:28–29.

8   Cf. Austin, *Hellenistic World,* no. 231, ll. 93ff.; 259; 260b.

9   Lohfink assumes that in view of the fact that the (ancient Israelite) agricultural system of free farmers on their own land must have driven them into indebted slavery because of the pressure of taxes in the Ptolemaic period, v. 8 supports the idea of turning the land into "land of the king" that—circumventing the hierarchies described in v. 7—was placed directly under the king. This is also the view of Schwienhorst-Schönberger, *Nicht im Menschen,* 139–40, who interprets vv. 8-9 in toto as a critique

of the assertions of vv. 8b and 9. On "Land of the king" (γῆ βασιλική) cf. Rostovtzeff, *Social and Economic History,* 1:277ff.; Hengel, *Judaism and Hellenism,* 2:20 n. 170.

10   Cf. the commentary of the *Jerusalem Bible*: "It is a question of the usual pretexts with which infringements and violations of the law were covered." In this spirit, A. T. Varela ("A New Approach to Eccle 5:8-9," *BT* 27 [1976] 240–41) recommends the following translation: "(And they will tell you that) all of this means progress for the country, (and that) the king is the servant of the land."

11   Michel (*Untersuchungen,* 110) assumes that v. 9 juxtaposes "the conditions described in v. 8" in Palestine under Ptolemy rule with "a national-monarchist ideal as counterprogram." On this, v. 10 then offers a critical commentary that—just like 4:13-16—is closed with a הֶבֶל *hebel* judgment. In my view, however, v. 10aα can at best be understood in this sense as a critical commentary on v. 9. Then with the continuation of v. 10 a new theme is clearly introduced.

5

5:9[10] Whoever loves money will never have enough money. And who[a] loves wealth[b] without gain[c]? This also is futile.

10[11] When goods[a] increase, those who consume them do also And what gain does the owner[b] have, other than to look on[c]?

11[12] Sweet is the sleep of the laborer,[a] whether he has little or much to eat. Yet the surfeit[b] of the rich man does not let him sleep.[c]

12[13] There is a grievous[a] evil that I have seen under the sun: wealth was set aside by its owner[b] in case of misfortune.[c] **13[14]** Yet this wealth was lost through a misfortune.[a] But he had fathered a son[b]—and (now) had nothing more in hand. **14[15]** As[a] he came out of his mother's womb, naked, he must go again, as he came. And he has nothing from it for[b] his toil that he could pass on.[c]

15[16] Yet[a] this too is a grievous[b] evil: just as[c] one[d] came, he must go (again). And what gain does he have, if he[e] toils for the wind **16[17]** and yet must[a] eke out all his days in darkness and has much vexation, is sick and angry?[b]

17[18] See what I have seen as something good: it is beautiful[a] to eat and drink and see goods things[b] for all the work one has done under the sun in the whole time of one's life,[c] which the Deity has given one. (Every)one is entitled to that as one's portion.[d] **18[19]** And if the Deity has given someone wealth and possessions and enabled him to eat from it and carry away his portion and rejoice over all his property,[a] that is a gift of God. **19[20]** For he does not think much about the (limited) time of his life,[a] if the Deity busies him[b] with pleasure.[c]

6:1 There is an evil[a] that I have seen under the sun, and it lies heavy[b] on humankind: **2** There is a man to whom the Deity gives wealth, possessions, and honor, and he[a] lacks nothing of all that he desires; yet the Deity does not enable him to eat from it; rather a stranger consumes it. This is futile and a grievous ill.

5:9a[10a] The interrogative pronoun מִי *mî* is usually interpreted as an indefinite pronoun: "And whoever loves wealth . . ."; cf. Schoors, *Preacher*, 59, and 𝔅 𝔖. On the interpretation of v. 9aβ as a question cf., e.g., Hitzig and 𝔊, as well as the corresponding clause in v. 10b [11b].

9b[10b] On the use—unique in the OT—of the preposition ב *b* after אהב *ʾhb* (which could also go back to a dittograph) cf. Schoors, *Preacher*, 193; Jenni, *Präpositionen*, 1:253-55.

9c[10c] That is, "that brings no gain." On the understanding of לֹא תְבוּאָה *lōʾ tĕbûʾâ* as in apposition to הָמוֹן *hāmôn* cf. GKC §152u. If one interprets מִי *mî* as an indefinite pronoun (see n. 9a above), one would have to translate: "And whoever loves wealth will (have) no gain" (or: "[will not have enough] gain"); cf. 𝔅 𝔗. According to Gordis, "the form should be revocalized תְבוֹאֵהוּ לֹא [*lōʾ tĕbôʾēhu*] = תְבוֹאֵהוּ לֹא [*lōʾ tĕbôʾēhû*], 'it will not come to him'" (cf. 𝔖).

10a[11a] "The goods" (טוֹבָה *ṭôbâ*, cf. 5:17; 6:3, 6, in distinction to the "good" or "better" (טוֹב *ṭôb*) in 5:17; 6:3, 9. Cf. T. Krüger, "Das Gute und die Güter: Erwägungen zur Bedeutung von טוב und טובה im Qoheletbuch," *ThZ* 53 (1997) 53-63.

10b[11b] Literally: "their [the goods'] owners" (pl.; cf. v. 12), taken up again in the following with a singular suffix ("his eyes"; see n. 10c). According to GKC §124i it is a question here of a "majestic" or "royal" plural.

10c[11c] Literally: "except the seeing [K רְאִית *rĕʾît*, Q רְאוּת *rĕʾût*, 𝔊ᵠ Or רְאוֹת *rĕʾôt*] of his eyes."

11a[12a] 𝔊 σ' ϑ' read τοῦ δούλου, "of the slave" (הָעֶבֶד *hāʿebed* instead of הָעֹבֵד *hāʿōbēd*).

11b[12b] Or: "abundance."

11c[12c] In analogy to v. 9b and v. 10b, instead of the article (הַשָּׂבָע *haśśābāʿ*) one could also read here the interrogative (הֲשָׂבָע *hăśābāʿ*) and interpret the sentence as a question: "And does the surfeit of the rich man not let him sleep?" (On וְ *wĕ-* before הֲ *hă-* cf. 1 Sam 15:35; Prov 24:28.)

12a[13a] Literally: "sick."

12b[13b] Or: "for its owner" (lit.: "its owners"; cf. n. 10b above); thus Lohfink, "Kohelet und die Banken: Zur Übersetzung von Kohelet V,12-16," *VT* 39 (1989) 491, 494-95 n. 16.

12c[13c] Literally: "for his misfortune/illness," which one could also understand in the sense of "to his misfortune."

13a[14a] Or: "a bad business."

13b[14b] Or: "fathered a son."

14a[15a] 𝔏 reads כִּי *ky* instead of כַּאֲשֶׁר *kaʾăšer*.

14b[15b] On the meaning of the preposition ב *b* in the present context see Jenni, *Präpositionen*, 1:152-53.

3 If a man were to beget a hundred children and live a long time[a] and reach a great age,[b] but could not satisfy himself from his goods[c]—and even were to have no burial,[d] I would say: a stillborn child has it better than he.[e] **4** For it came in futility and goes[a] away in darkness, and its name remains hidden in darkness. **5** Also it has not seen the sun or come to know it. The sun has more peace[a] than he.

6 And if one should have lived two times a thousand years and seen no good things[a]—do not all go to the same place?

7 All of a man's toil is for his mouth.

And yet his appetite is never satisfied.

8 For what[a] advantage does the wise man have over the fool?

Of what use is it to the poor man if he knows how to live?[b]

9 It is better to enjoy what one has in sight[a]

than to give appetite free reign.[b]

This too is futile and a striving after wind.

14c[15c] Literally: "that he will [or can] let go through his hand" or "in his hand" or "in his [= the son's] hand." Lohfink assumes that the expressions נשא nś², הלך *hlk* hiphil, and בְּיָד *bĕyād* here have a "bank-technical" meaning and translates: "He can withdraw absolutely no more of his wealth, which he deposited into his account" ("Kohelet und die Banken," 493).

15a[16a] ℒ has no copula before גַם *gam*.

15b[16b] Literally: "sick" (cf. v. 12).

15c[16c] Instead of כָּל־עֻמַּת *kol-ʿummat* one should probably read כִּלְעֻמַּת *kilʿummat* (BHS), כִּי לְעֻמַּת *kî lĕʿummat* (cf. 𝔊 𝔖 Jer), or כֹל לְעֻמַּת *kol lĕʿummat* (BHK); cf. Schoors, *Preacher*, 146–47.

15d[16d] Or: "he"; then the subject here would still be the same man as in v. 14.

15e[16e] Or: "what gain has the one who. . . ."

16a[17a] 𝔊 reads ἐν σκότει καὶ πένθει, "in darkness and sadness" (בְחֹשֶׁךְ וָאֵבֶל *bĕḥōšek wā²ēbel* instead of בַחֹשֶׁךְ יֹאכֵל *baḥōšek yōkēl*).

16b[17b] Literally: "and his sickness and anger." 𝔊 𝔖 𝔗 𝔙 read: "and (in) much vexation and sickness and anger."

17a[18a] Or: "See what I have seen: it is good, that is, beautiful" (cf. Lohfink); or "See what I have seen as something good, that is, beautiful" (cf. Gordis). The Masoretic accents support the interpretation recommended above.

17b[18b] Literally: "a good (thing)" (טוֹבָה *ṭôbâ* in distinction from טוֹב *ṭôb*); see above on v. 10.

17c[18c] Literally: "the number of the days of his life."

17d[18d] Literally: "for that is his [someone's] portion."

18a[19a] Or: "in his whole work."

19a[20a] Literally: "the days of his life."

19b[20b] Literally: "his heart, his mind."

19c[20c] 𝔊 𝔖 𝔗 read: "if the Deity busies him with the pleasure of his heart." Some propose that מַעֲנֵה *maʿăneh* (or מַעֲנֵהוּ *maʿănēhû*) be translated not with "busies" (ענה *ʿnh* III) but with "answers" (ענה *ʿnh* I) or "oppresses" (ענה *ʿnh* II) (see Backhaus, *Zeit und Zufall*, 194–95; Schwienhorst-Schönberger, *Nicht im Menschen*, 149); yet cf. 1:13; 3:10.

6:1a Some Hebrew mss. read here "a bad [lit.: sick] evil" (as in 5:12, 15]).

1b Or: "in multiple ways."

2a Or: "his desire" (נַפְשׁוֹ *napšô*).

3a Literally: "many years."

3b Literally: "and [if] many were the days of his years" (cf. Delitzsch). Or: "and as many [years] as are the days of his years"? See the commentary on this verse.

3c Literally: "but he/his desire (נַפְשׁוֹ *napšô*) would not be satisfied by the good (טוֹבָה *ṭôbâ*)."

3d Literally: "even (if) he had/had had no burial."

3e Literally: "better than he is the stillborn child" (cf. 4:3).

4a Instead of יֵלֵךְ *yēlēk*, ℒ reads הלך *hlk*, which can be interpreted as participle (הֹלֵךְ *hōlēk*, "goes"; cf. 𝔊) or as perfect (הָלַךְ *hālak*, "went").

5a ℒ reads נוחת *nwḥt* instead of נַחַת *naḥat*.

6a   Literally: "no good" (טוֹבָה *ṭôbâ* in distinction from טוֹב *ṭôb*); see above on 5:10.

8a   𝔏 reads כמה *kmh* instead of כי מה *kî mah*.

8b   Literally: "to walk with the living." On the construction cf. Gordis; Schoors, *Preacher*, 165–66 (as well as 𝔊 𝔖). Other possible translations: "What [kind of advantage] does a poor man [לְעָנִי *lĕʿānî* instead of לְעָנִי *leʿānî*] have who knows how. . . ?" Or: "What [kind of advantage] does the poor man have? He knows how to live" (cf. 𝔙).

9a   Literally: "better (is) the view of the eyes." מַרְאֵה עֵינַיִם *marʾēh ʿênayim* (cf. 11:9) can mean both "the seeing of the eyes" (subj. gen.; thus, e.g., Delitzsch) and "that which the eyes see" (thus, e.g., Galling). "Seeing" (ראה *rʾh*) includes "enjoying" in 2:1, 24; 3:13; 5:17; 6:6; 8:16; 9:9; 11:7.

9b   Literally: "than the wandering of the soul/of desire (נֶפֶשׁ *nepeš*)" (cf. Wis 4:12: ῥεμβασμὸς ἐπιθυμίας) or "than going around with desire" (cf. GKC §118q).

■ **5:9—6:9** This section, in which the theme "wealth and poverty" is prominent, reveals a concentric structure:

    5:9-11: proverbs
       5:12-16: negative cases ("evil")
          5:17-19: positive cases ("something good")
       6:1-6: negative cases ("evil")
    6:7-9: proverbs

In 5:9-11 we already hear themes that will be treated in the following verses in reverse order and in part with different accents (cf. Lohfink):

    5:9: "Whoever loves money will never have enough money" (לֹא־יִשְׂבַּע *lōʾ-yiśbaʿ*)
       5:10: "When goods increase, those who consume them do also" (אכל *ʾkl*)
          5:11: laborer—rich man
          5:12-16: rich man—laborer
       6:1-2: ". . . a stranger consumes it" (אכל *ʾkl*)
    6:3-6: a man "cannot satisfy himself from his goods" (נפְשׁוֹ לֹא־תִשְׂבַּע *napšô lōʾ-tiśbaʿ*)

The section 5:12—6:6 discusses by example the value of wealth and poverty (as well as long life) in light of the concomitant possibilities for the enjoyment of life ("eating, drinking, and pleasure").

| 5:12-14 | wealth | without enjoyment |
5:15-16	*poverty*	without enjoyment
5:17	*poverty*	*with enjoyment*
5:18-19	wealth	*with enjoyment*
6:1-5	wealth	without enjoyment
6:6	*poverty*	without enjoyment

The thematic development of the text can be sketched as follows:

Verses 5:9-11 formulates three proverbial sayings about wealth that diminish its value—if not completely call it into question. In vv. 9 and 10, nonetheless, the second half of each verse raises reservations about a complete devaluation of wealth. Verse 11 is critically illuminated by the continuation in vv. 12-16.

The example in 5:12-14 shows that the loss of wealth is a "grievous evil." This is all the more true when the owner has not already enjoyed his wealth because he wanted to save it "for bad times." Thus the "evil" in this case arises basically not through the loss of wealth but through the fact that a rich man does not enjoy his possessions.

Verses 5:15-16 can be read both as a continuation of vv. 12-14 and as a new example. A "grievous evil" like the loss of wealth occurs when a man "toils for the wind" all his life; that is, in spite of all his work, he never reaches a point where he can enjoy his life. If vv. 12-14 show that wealth has a value only to the extent that it enables one to enjoy one's life, vv. 15-16, by contrast, make it clear that as a rule, poverty makes the enjoyment of life an impossibility.

Verses 5:17-19 draw from the foregoing examples the following conclusions. Even in view of the problems of wealth and poverty, "eating and drinking" prove to be the "good" really worth striving for (cf. 3:12–13, 22). The examples in 5:12-16, however, have made clear that only those who have at their disposal a certain minimum of "(their own property and) good things" (ראה טוֹבָה *rʾh ṭôbâ*: 5:17) can "see [or: enjoy] something good" (ראה טוֹב *rʾh ṭôb*: 3:13). For the rich man, the crucial "gift of God" (not at one's disposal) consists not only in his possessions but also and above all in the possibility of enjoying life with the help of these possessions (v. 18). With life span, verse 19 brings into play, in addition to wealth and poverty, yet another presumed value, which is then discussed in 6:3-6.

Verses 6:1-2 reinforce 5:18 with a counterexample. If a man has "wealth, possessions, and honor," whose fruits, however, he cannot consume and enjoy, this is an "evil" and a "grievous ill."

Verses 6:3-6 show, in connection with 5:19, that not even a long life can make up for the lack of possibilities for enjoyment. This is true both for the rich man, who "cannot satisfy himself from his goods" (vv. 3-5; cf. 6:1-2; 5:18, and 5:12-14), and for a man who all his life has "seen no good things" (v. 6; cf. 5:17 and 5:15-16).

Verses 6:7-9 close the unit with three proverbial sayings that, just like the introductory figures of speech in 5:9-11, are clarified and refined by the argumentation in 5:12—6:6.

In the wider context of the book of Qoheleth, 5:9—6:9 takes up from 1:12—4:12 the determination of "eating, drinking, and pleasure" as the highest and only "good" (3:12-13, 22). It is confirmed here, on the one hand, in the discussion of the problem of poverty and wealth: the criterion for the judgment of poverty and wealth is the degree to which they enable one to eat, drink, and enjoy oneself. On the other hand, however, in this context the determination also undergoes a refinement. In order to achieve the highest "good" (טוֹב *ṭôb*) in his life, a man must have at his disposal at least a minimal amount of material "goods" (טוֹבָה *ṭôbâ*), which allow him to eat,

drink, and enjoy himself. (Cf. to 5:9—6:9 as a whole the summary after 6:9.)

5:9-11[10-12] Proverbs

With three proverbially formulated, ambiguous figures of speech, 5:9-11 draws attention to the theme "wealth and poverty," which is developed in what follows.[1]

■ **9** The first sentence in v. 9 (aα) is ambiguous. It can be understood both in the sense that one who loves money (or silver) cannot, in his insatiability, get enough of it (cf. 4:8), and in the sense that (because one cannot eat money) one cannot be sated with money (or silver).[2] If one understands the following sentence (v. 9aβ) as it is normally read, as a statement ("whoever loves wealth [will not be satisfied with] gain" or something similar), v. 9a as a whole would be read as a proverb about the insatiability of greed for money and wealth.[3] The closing הֶבֶל *hebel* judgment (v. 9b) would then qualify striving for wealth as meaningless. If, however, one interprets v. 9aβ as a question ("Who loves wealth that brings no gain?"), then the wholesale devaluation of striving for wealth, which could be derived from v. 9aα, is critically called into question: if wealth basically and in every case "brings no return," hardly anyone would strive for it. In this case a fundamental and wholesale devaluation of striving for wealth is "untenable" (v. 9b). At the same time, however, we can also recognize that wealth, upon close examination, is sought as a means to an end ("gain"). The following analyses will show that ultimately this end can consist only in the enjoyment made possible by wealth.[4]

1 Michel, *Untersuchungen*, 188, assumes that in 5:10-11 "a naively popular critique of wealth" is expressed and is critically corrected in vv. 12ff. (According to Michel, v. 9 belongs to 5:7-8.) Yet, in my view, he thereby overlooks the critical aspects that are already recognizable in the ambiguous formulation of vv. 9-11.

2 In this sense Prov 12:11 and 28:19 perhaps juxtapose agriculture and economics. Hengel (*Judaism and Hellenism*, 1:54; 2:41 n. 413) sees in Prov 24:30-34; 27:23-27; Sir 7:15; 20:28; and Qoh 2:4-5; 5:8 evidence of an "agricultural ideal" that could have developed as a "reaction against the predominance of city life."

3 On the critique of the "love" of gold and money, wealth and luxury, cf. Prov 21:17 (as well as 13:11;

15:27; 20:21; 21:5; 23:4-5; 28:20, 22) and Sir 31:5. Cf. also the polemic of the Cynics against the type of the *philargyros* or *philoploutos* (see, e.g., Diogenes Laertius 6.50; cf. Braun, *Kohelet*, 96; G. J. D. Aalders, *Political Thought in Hellenistic Times* [Amsterdam: Hakkert, 1975] 53ff.).

4 Schwienhorst-Schönberger (*Nicht im Menschen*, 143 n. 74) refers for comparison to Plato, *Euthydemos* 280d; and Sophocles, *Antigone* 1168–71. Cf. also Euripides, frg. 198N (Braun, *Kohelet*, 117 n. 369); Menander, frg. 509; Sir 14:13ff.

■ **10** If one understands v. 9 in the sense that striving for money and wealth never leads to success, v. 10 can be read as justification for this point of view: the more a man owns, the more people share in his wealth, and thus in the end he can only look on, as others consume his possessions.[5] This interpretation of v(v). (9 and) 10 presupposes that v. 10b is a rhetorical question, as is usually the case. If, however, one reads v. 10b as a genuine question, then here—similar to v. 9a—a statement that tends to derogate the value of wealth (v. 10a) is critically called into question. No rich man will only look on as others consume his possessions. A further possible understanding of v. 10b results when one interprets the expression עֵינָיו (or רְאוּת) רְאִית rĕʾît (or rĕʾût) ʿênāyw not in the sense of "(merely) looking on" (or even "overlook"[6]) but in the sense of "enjoy" (cf. מַרְאֵה עֵינַיִם marʾeh ʿênayim: 6:9; 11:9; רָאה טוב/טובָה / רְאֵה טוֹב rᵉh ṭôb/ṭôbâ: 3:13; 5:17; רָאה חַיִּים rᵉh ḥayyîm: 9:9). Then even v. 10b (as a rhetorical question) would indicate that the only meaningful purpose of wealth consists in making enjoyment possible for its owner.

■ **11** This verse now seems to formulate in a quite undiminished way an advantage of poverty over wealth: the "laborer" can sleep well, in any case, whereas the "surfeit" of the rich man robs him of sleep (or at least cannot guarantee him peaceful sleep).[7] The intention here may be both his "oversatisfaction" and his striving for the

"satiation" of his acquisitiveness (cf. v. 9). That the life of a propertyless laborer is, naturally, by no means as "sweet" as v. 11a suggests is shown in what follows (cf. v. 16).[8] And if one reads v. 11b in analogy to v. 9aβ and v. 10b as a question ("can a rich man not sleep because he is satiated?"), v. 11 itself would call the devaluation of wealth critically into question.

5:12-16[13-17] Negative Cases

■ **12-14** These verses show with an example that the *relative value* of wealth consists in making pleasure and enjoyment possible for its owner. The described case is to be judged a "grievous evil," both because a man has lost his wealth (vv. 13-14)—which shows the relative *value* of wealth—and because this man has "set aside" his wealth instead of enjoying it (v. 12), which shows that the *relative* value of wealth consists in being the means of enjoyment.

■ **12** From the formulation of v. 12b in the Hebrew, it is not entirely clear whether the wealth is set aside *by* its owner or was kept safe *for* him (say, by a bank) (see n. 12b on the translation). Even in the latter case, however, the owner would have forgone the immediate enjoyment of his wealth. Nor can one clearly deduce from the text that the owner laid aside his wealth "in case of misfortune" (cf. n. 12c on the translation). If one understands

5   Cf., e.g., Crenshaw: "Increased possessions require many people to watch over the wealth and to see that it continues to yield dividends. Slaves must be fed and clothed, employees reimbursed, and an ever-increasing band of dependents arrive at the door of the person with riches." Cf. further Prov 14:20; 19:4, 6, as well as Euripides, *Hecuba* 1227 (Schwienhorst-Schönberger, *Nicht im Menschen*, 143 n. 76).

6   Thus, e.g., Zimmerli; contra Ellermeier, *Qohelet*, I/1, 217.

7   On this view cf. Pythagoras (in Stobaeus, *Ecl.* 5.68); Axiochus 368c; Menander, frgs. 641, 612, 281 (Braun, *Kohelet*, 96 nn. 284–85). Comparable notions are to be found in Hellenistic bucolic poetry, which developed in connection with the poet Theocritus working in Alexandria in the third century B.C.E.; they are reflected in the OT in Canticles (cf. Hans-Josef Heinevetter, *"Komm nun, mein Liebster, Dein Garten ruft Dich!": Das Hohelied als programmatische Komposition* [BBB 69; Frankfurt am

Main: Athenäum, 1988] 213ff.). Whereas Theocritus himself assumed an "ironic attitude" toward the life of the "shepherds" and through the "accentuation of certain characteristics of the appearing shepherds," namely, their "unbridled aggressivity" and "uninhibited sexuality," emphasized the "raw primitive nature of such strata," there emerged "already in the immediate post-Theocratan bucolic poetry of Hellenism" a "tendency toward an idealization and sentimentalization of the pastoral world that was far from reality" (Effe, *Hellenismus*, 50–51).

8   Cf. also the more differentiated observations in Sir 31:1-4.

לְרָעָתוֹ *lĕrāʿātô* in this sense, the following sentence makes an ironic point: the "misfortune" against which this man wanted to protect himself through "saving" then consists precisely in the loss of his "savings."

■ **13-14** In vv. 13-14 one ambiguity of the Hebrew text lies in the fact that it is not clear which statements relate to the impoverished father and which to his son.[9] Perhaps the text here is "purposefully ambiguous" in order to underline "the common lot of the once-rich father and the poor son" (Crenshaw). Verse 14a agrees almost literally with Job 1:21a.[10]

■ **15-16** These verses are usually read as the continuation of vv. 12-14. Then these verses would describe the further destiny of the impoverished rich man or his son.[11] Yet the introduction in v. 15 (cf. v. 12) supports rather the idea that the topic here is a new case that expands and relativizes vv. 12-14: there are not only people who deny themselves the enjoyment of their possessions (cf. 4:7ff.), but also people who, under miserable conditions, toil their whole lives "for the wind,"[12] without ever acquiring even modest property of their own (cf. 4:1ff.). In any case, v. 16 shows that (contrary to v. 11) there is nothing "sweet" about a life without personal possessions.

A possible counterposition to vv. 12-16 in the OT is the "piety of the poor" to be observed in the Psalter, in which "poverty" is understood "in a theological sense as a positive entity."[13] The social-historical background of this phenomenon is a controversial topic in the literature.[14] It may be said with some certainty that the "piety

9   Verse 13bβ can be read both as a statement about the father, who now no longer possesses anything (thus, e.g., Lohfink), and as a statement about the son, who inherits nothing (thus, e.g., Galling). Verse 14a could be related to the father or the son, or it could be understood as a general statement about the "coming" and "going" of a man, about his birth and his death. (Lohfink assumes that "here 'going' is not to be seen as his death" but as the ongoing life of the impoverished rich man.) The continuation in v. 14bα seems rather to support the idea that throughout v. 14 the father is the subject of the verbs (thus, e.g., Crenshaw), yet v. 14a could also speak of the son and v. 14b of the father (thus, e.g., Gordis). It would also be possible to understand v. 14bα in the sense that the son will have nothing left from the property of his father. In v. 14bβ, finally, "*his* hand" can be the subject of the preceding verb; i.e., the father or the son does not (any longer) have any property at his disposal. Or one assumes as subject of the verb (and then also of v. 14bα) the father, who now carries nothing in his hands that he could give to his son (thus, e.g., Michel, *Untersuchungen*, 189).

10   Cf. also, e.g., Ps 49:18 and Solon 13.76: "No one goes into Hades together with his monetary possessions" (Braun, *Kohelet*, 96 n. 268).

11   Verse 15b could then be interpreted, say, as a retrospective on the life of the father before or after the loss of his wealth. The first is assumed, e.g., by Lauha and Michel: "The fact that this formerly rich man must depart from life like he came shows that he has toiled 'for the wind' and thus uselessly" (Michel, *Untersuchungen*, 189). While Michel relates v. 16 to the life of the impoverished rich man,

Lauha also sees his life before his impoverishment described in this verse. Against this interpretation, however, are the imperfects in v. 15b and v. 16a. Thus it seems better to understand vv. 15-16 as statements about the "subsequent life of the impoverished rich man." "He has to pay his debts, probably in debtors' servitude, if he is not sold into slavery. The text . . . will no more than suggest this" (Lohfink). Finally, it would also be possible to relate vv. 15-16 to the son named in v. 13, who, without an inheritance, must now work "for the wind."

12   The expression עָמָל לָרוּחַ *ʿml lārûaḥ* is found only here in the book of Qoheleth. Whereas רְעוּת רוּחַ *rĕʿût rûaḥ* (1:14; 2:11, 17, 26; 4:4, 6; 6:9) and רַעְיוֹן רוּחַ *raʿyôn rûaḥ* (1:17; 4:16) designate a "striving" that is meaningless because it is predestined to failure, עָמָל לָרוּחַ *ʿml lārûaḥ* refers to "work and toil" that remain without success because of external and, in principle, unavoidable reasons; cf. Ps 127:1 (עָמָל *ʿml* + שָׁוְא *šāw*); Isa 49:4; 65:23 (יָגַע *ygʿ* + לָרִיק *lĕrîq*). Cf. also Menander, frg. 580: "Why are you a good servant all to no purpose (τί διακενῆς εἶ χρηστός)? If your master is throwing away everything and you are not acquiring, you wear yourself out (σαυτὸν ἐπιτριβεῖς *sauton epitribeis*); you don't help him" (trans. F. G. Allinson).

13   Diethelm Michel, s.v. "Armut," *TRE* (1979) 4:72–76; cf., e.g., Frank-Lothar Hossfeld and Erich Zenger, *Die Psalmen I: Psalm 1–50* (NEchtB 29; Würzburg: Echter, 1993) 14–15.

14   Cf., e.g., Rainer Albertz, *A History of Israelite Religion in the Old Testament Period* (OTL; Louisville: Westminster John Knox, 1994) 518–22.

of the poor" reflects a "*social contrast*" between the (or parts of the) "lower classes" and the (or parts of the) "rich and powerful," which on the part of (some of) the poor was interpreted as a "*religious*" antithesis.[15] Now, against this background, the case in which a rich man loses his possessions can be judged to be something positive, desirable, and comforting for "the poor."[16] By contrast, Qoh 5:12-14 insists that this case is to be regarded as an "evil" and a "misfortune."

With this, however, the text—probably in reaction to reproaches from the side of "the poor"—also turns against an attitude of indifference vis-à-vis wealth and loss of property as it was perhaps propagated in certain circles "of the rich."[17] Job 1:21a (cf. Qoh 5:14a) documents such an attitude of calm indifference toward the loss of property on the part of the rich, which corresponds to the dominant stance toward poverty and wealth in Hellenistic philosophy: the Stoics regarded wealth as an—admittedly "preferred" ($\pi\rho o\eta\gamma\mu\acute{e}\nu o\nu$)— "adiaphoron."[18] "Thus the Stoic will seek the preferred things like health, prosperity, and the like and avoid their opposites, the disadvantageous things. But in the process, he will not endanger his inner peace, his apathy, because he will accept both the success and the failure of his longing."[19] Epicurus was "of the conviction that 'natural wealth'—that is, everything that is required for true happiness, for being free from the lack of desire—'is both limited and easily at one's disposal'; so that everything necessary is always abundantly available, but all unrestricted and unfulfillable wishes spring from empty delusion."[20] Sextus Empiricus explained the indifferent attitude of the Pyrrhonist skeptic to all goods "with the example of wealth. Whoever believes it is good will be disturbed in two ways as long as he does not have it: both because he does not share in this good and because

he torments himself to acquire it. As soon as he achieves wealth, however, he will be tormented in three ways: by unbounded joy, by the plague of maintaining it, and by the fear of losing it."[21] And the Cynic Teles judged wealth and poverty on the premise that one must "not attempt to alter conditions but adapt oneself to one's circumstances." Then, however, it is true that "whoever uses wealth appropriately also deals with its opposite" (Teles II).

■ **12-16** These verses turn against an idealization of poverty and against making wealth a matter of indifference: wealth cannot guarantee a person happiness (vv. 12-14), but total poverty makes a happy life impossible (vv. 15-16). Therefore, a certain minimum of personal property is required for a successful life (v. 17).

5:17-19[18-20] Positive Cases

■Verses 17-19 exhibit a "good" alternative to the "evils" described in vv. 12-16. Here v. 17 refers back to vv. 15-16 (work without property) and v. 18 to vv. 12-14 (wealth without enjoyment). With "length of life," v. 19 brings a new viewpoint into play, which is then taken up and discussed in 6:3-6.

■ **17-18** These verses refer back to the comments in 3:10-22 (cf. esp. vv. 12-13, 22). The determination of the highest and only "good" developed there is applied here to the problem of poverty and wealth and at the same time further developed and refined. Also taken up in vv. 17-18 is the antithesis of "laborer" and "rich man," which was presented in v. 11 and developed in vv. 12-16. If 3:12-13, 22 spoke generally of the same "good" for all people, to eat, drink, and enjoy oneself, here—in view of the existing class antitheses[22]—this "good" is now defined more precisely for "laborer" and "rich man."

15 Hermann Gunkel and Joachim Begrich, *Introduction to Psalms* (MLBS; Macon, Ga.: Mercer Univ. Press, 1998) 149-50.

16 Cf. Psalms 10; 34:11; 37:16ff., 35-36; 49:6ff., 17ff.; 73:16ff.; cf. Prov 13:22; 15:6; 1 Sam 2:5; Luke 1:53.

17 Cf. Prov 11:28; 23:4-5; Job 31:24ff.; Ps 62:11; Sir 31:6; 11:10ff. Ps 49:7 [49:6] criticizes "those who trust in their wealth"; 62:11b warns the rich not to set their hearts on their wealth.

18 Hossenfelder, *Philosophie*, 58–59.

19 Ibid., 60.

20 Ibid., 114, with reference to *Ratae Sententiae* 15.21;

Men. 130, 133; Usener 168:9ff.; frgs. 468ff.

21 Ibid., 152, with reference to *Math.* 11.112ff., 146; *Pyr.* 3.238.

22 Cf., e.g., Hengel, *Judaism and Hellenism*, 1:47ff.; Hans G. Kippenberg, *Religion und Klassenbildung im antiken Judäa* (2d ed.; SUNT 14; Göttingen: Vandenhoeck & Ruprecht, 1982) 78ff.

■ **17** For a man who does not have at his disposal "wealth and possessions" (v. 18), it is not only "good" (טוֹב *ṭôb*) but also "beautiful" and "appropriate" (יָפֶה *yāpeh*; see above on 3:11a), if he can enjoy his life: this corresponds to the preconditions and will of the Creator-God (cf. 3:11a). In order, however, to be able "in all his work to enjoy something *good*" (3:13: וְרָאָה טוֹב בְּכָל־ עֲמָלוֹ *wĕrāʾâ ṭôb bĕkol-ʿămālô*), he must see (his own property and) *good* for all his work (5:17: וְלִרְאוֹת טוֹבָה בְּכָל־ עֲמָלוֹ *wĕlirʾôt ṭôbâ bĕkol-ʿămālô*), for without a minimum of personal property, the enjoyment of life is not possible, as 5:15-16 shows.[23] To this "portion" (חֵלֶק *ḥēleq*) everyone has a "claim" (כִּי־הוּא חֶלְקוֹ *kî-hûʾ ḥelqô*; cf. 3:22).[24]

■ **18** Corresponding to this is the situation of the man to whom God has given not only his life (v. 17) but also "wealth and possessions" (v. 18). Also for him the "portion" (חֵלֶק *ḥēleq*) of his property to which he has a "claim" consists in the enjoyment of eating from it. Yet this enjoyment is not already guaranteed to him by his wealth; God must give him the possibility (cf. 6:1-2), and he himself must realize this possibility (cf. 5:12-14 and 4:7-8). Verse 18 speaks against a general devaluation of wealth or an indifferent attitude toward it: wealth is a "gift of God." At the same time, however, the value of wealth is relativized: it is only a means to the end of enjoyment. The rich man has a "claim" to this "portion" of his wealth (cf. 2:10). Thus the "claim" of the rich man to his possessions is both confirmed and restricted: when he has "eaten from it[25] and carried away his portion," he can also give to others their "portion" from what is left over (cf. 5:10; 11:2).

Thus, from the determination of the "highest good" in 3:10-22 and the analysis of social relationships in chaps. 4 and 5, vv. 17-18 develop the beginnings of a "sociopolitical" program, according to which rich *and* poor have a "claim" to the goods at their disposal.[26]

This program is to be distinguished from making the question of possessions a matter of indifference, as was the predominant view in contemporary Hellenistic philosophy (see above on vv. 15-16), as well as from a flight into the utopia of a classless society.[27] Nor does it aim toward a revolutionary redistribution of property.[28] Its initiative corresponds rather to measures such as the establishment of public assistance funds or state-owned factories, with which some Hellenistic poleis sought to battle poverty.[29]

A view of wealth that largely corresponds to 5:17-18 is developed in Sir 13:24—14:19: The prosperous should allow something from their possessions for themselves and for others equally. In addition to the "needy" (14:8), beneficiaries include above all the "friend" (14:13) and the "brother" (14:16). And there is no mention here of a "claim" of the needy on their "portion" of the available goods. In this regard, Qoh 5:17-18 [5:18-19] corresponds rather to the "social legislation" in Deuteronomy, which grants to those without possessions a legal claim to their portion of the goods available in Israel through the tithe in every third year (Deut 14:22-29; 24:12), participation in the sacrificial feasts (16:14; 26:11; and elsewhere), and the right of the petty theft of food (23:24-25) and gleaning (24:19-22): they "may come and eat their fill" (14:29 and elsewhere).

In the broader context of the book of Qoheleth, 5:17-18 can also be read as a critique of the judgment of wealth and enjoyment by the "king" in 1:12—2:26: wealth is not something that a man acquires completely by himself (cf. 2:4-9), nor is it a divine disaster that excludes pleasure (cf. 2:26), but rather a "gift of God." That a

---

23   Cf. on טוֹבָה *ṭôbâ* as "[material] good" 5:10, as well as 4:8; 6:3, 6; 9:18; Krüger, "Gute."

24   On חֵלֶק *ḥēleq* "in the sense of that which comes to one," see, e.g., H. H. Schmid, "חלק *ḥlq* to divide," *TLOT* 1:432. Michel (*Untersuchungen*, 191) holds that the term כִּי־הוּא חֶלְקוֹ *kî-hû ḥelqô* is directed here (as well as in 3:22) "against contemporaries who assert that the 'portion' (חֵלֶק [*ḥēleq*]) of a man is something else, and who connect this assertion with a negative estimation of wealth."

25   Cf. Fox: "*mimmennu* is partitive, a nuance ignored by most translations. In Qohelet's view you need not consume all you own."

26   On the social dimension of the use of חלק *ḥlq* / חֵלֶק *ḥēleq* in the OT, cf. M. Tsevat, "חלק *ḥālaq* II," *TLOT* 4:448-49.

27   On corresponding Hellenistic social utopias cf. Aalders, *Political Thought*, 64ff.; Kippenberg, *Religion und Klassenbildung*, 97ff.

28   On corresponding—and generally unsuccessful—attempts in the Hellenistic period, cf. Walbank, *Hellenistische Welt*, 172ff.

29   Cf. ibid., 166-67; Austin, *Hellenistic World*, no. 97; 113-16.

man's property represents no lasting "gain" (יִתְרוֹן yitrôn) that is at his disposal (2:11), but can at best afford him "pleasure" as his "portion" (חֵלֶק ḥēleq) (2:10), is no reason for despair (2:20). One who enjoys his wealth in the sense of 5:18 [5:19] does not—like the "king" (2:12ff.)—have to think about the (limited) length of his life and thereby spoil his joy in living (5:19).

■ **19** This verse seems at first glance enigmatic. Not until 6:3-6 does it become clear that with length of life, a new viewpoint has been introduced into the reflection. In view of the preceding, 5:19 can be understood, on the one hand, as a critique of the attitude of the "king" in 2:12ff. (see above) or, on the other hand, as an indication that the enjoyment of riches can free a rich man from setting aside his resources out of fear of future misfortune (cf. 5:12ff. [5:13ff.]).

By contrast, Sir 18:25-26 𝕲 recommends: "In the time of plenty think of the time of hunger; in the days of wealth think of poverty and need. From morning to evening the time can change completely; all things move away swiftly before the Lord." Cf. 11:23, 25 [25, 27] 𝕾: "In the day of prosperity, adversity is forgotten, and in the day of adversity, prosperity is not remembered. And a man's end will come over him. In bad times the good life is forgotten, and a man's end is made known to him." In view of this uncertainty of the future, only at a man's death can one decide whether he was happy: "Before you know a man, do not call him happy. For a man can be called happy (only) at his end. Before death, call no one happy. For (only) at his end is a man known" (11:26[28]). Because of the uncertainty of all external good living, a rich man should never feel too secure: "Do not say: '[What do I need?] Truly, I have acted as I pleased, and of what am I now still deprived?' Do not say: 'I have enough; what [evil] can [now still] happen to me?'" (11:21-22[23-24]). From this insecurity the propertyless derive a certain hope that their situation will improve one day: "Good things and bad, life and death, poverty and wealth, come from the Lord" (11:14). Thus, as Yahweh can deny a man the enjoyment of his hard-earned wealth through death (11:16-17), Yahweh can, conversely, let a "righteous man" come into possessions: "Do not [wonder] about the [evildoer], [trust] in the Lord and hope in his light, for it is easy in the eyes of the Lord, in an instant, suddenly [to make the poor man rich]. The blessing of God is the portion (גרל grl) of the righteous man, and at the right time (בעת bᶜt) [his] hope will flourish" (11:19-20[21-22]). For the propertyless the result is this conclusion: "My son, stand by your agreement [or what is apportioned to you], [reflect] on it, and grow old in your work!" (11:18).[30]

In antithesis to Sir 11:23, 25 the accent in Qoh 5:19 lies completely on pleasure, which naturally does not completely suppress the idea of worse times, yet is not spoiled by it. In contrast to Sir 11:25-26, Qoh 5:17-19 judges the situation of the rich and the propertyless not only in view of their death but in view of their present possibilities of enjoyment. Compared to Sir 11:21-22, Qoh 5:18-19 shows a far more positive evaluation of the enjoyment of the rich man. Whereas Sir 11:18, 19-20 encourages the man without property to accept his situation and hope for his "portion" (גרל grl) from God, Qoh 5:17 validates his "claim" (חֵלֶק ḥēleq) to something good. In comparison to Qoh 5:17-19, Sir 11:14-26 shows on the whole a more critical position toward wealth and property. Linked with this is a putting off of the poor until an intervention of God "at the right time." In contrast to this, Qoh 5:17-19 names in sober fashion the relative worth of wealth and its advantage over poverty and advocates that the rich let the poor participate in their possessions.

6:1-6 Negative Cases

■ **6:1-2** These verses reinforce 5:18 with a negative counterexample. It happens that someone is rich but cannot enjoy his wealth—not because he denies himself the enjoyment (as in 5:12 and 4:8) but because "the Deity does not enable him to eat from it." Instead of the rich man himself, "a stranger" enjoys his possessions.[31] This

---

30   Based on the German trans. of G. Sauer, *JSHRZ* III.5.

31   The assumption that the rich man cannot enjoy his possessions because he is hindered by death (thus, e.g., Siegfried), the loss of his property (thus, e.g., Zapletal), an illness (thus, e.g., Galling), or his lack

of the "inner readiness . . . to accept his wealth as the gift of God and rejoice in it" (Michel, *Untersuchungen*, 192) hardly does justice to the text. The exclusion of v. 2aβ ("a stranger consumes it") as a gloss (cf. Volz; Budde; Ellermeier, *Qohelet*, I/1, 295) seems arbitrary.

"evil" shows clearly once again that wealth is not valuable in itself but only as a means to the end of enjoyment.

Although the term נָכְרִי *nokrî* can "be applied to any stranger or nonrelative . . . (Ps 69:9; Prov 27:2; Isa 28:21)," as a rule it designates "a stranger to the people, that is, a foreigner, a non-Jew."[32] "Non-Jews from neighboring regions, such as Ammonites in the east or Idumeans in the south (some of whom were Phoenicians in origin), had settled in Judah. Moreover, Greeks from the highest social classes in Alexandria had rights to fees in the province of Syria and Phoenicia, to which Judah also belonged and these they later received as private property" (Lohfink). The case described here does not rest, to be sure, on a Jew losing his *property* to a stranger. Only the *enjoyment* of his wealth goes to the stranger. Involved here apparently are the conditions of the Ptolemaic tax system in Judea, in which tax revenues flow to the Greek king in Alexandria by way of a foreign tax leaseholder.[33]

Toward the end of the third century B.C.E., the lease for Ptolemaic state revenues went from indigenous aristocrats to the Tobiad Joseph, whose membership in "Israel" was at least doubtful, according to Ezra 2:59-60. Josephus (*Ant.* 12.4.4) reports "that the Tobiads had doubled the monetary value of the tribute of the province Syria-Phoenicia."[34] For a Jewish landowner, that meant an immense increase in the already substantial burden of taxes. Under these economic circumstances, it is quite conceivable that a rich man—as measured by his property in land and the means of agricultural production—would still hardly have at his disposal the means for his own enjoyment, especially if he shifted his business from the growing of grain to the production of oil, which "achieved a higher monetary value in the marketplace" but at the same time restricted the possibility of providing for oneself through one's own products.[35] The beneficiary of his wealth was then indeed a "stranger": first the Tobiad as tax leaseholder and then the Ptolemy king in Alexandria.[36]

Qoheleth 6:1-2 regards these conditions as "evil" and a "grievous ill" but at the same time traces them back to God's activity. That these conditions were not thereby also already approved and established theologically is demonstrated by a look at texts such as Deut 28:30-33 and Neh 9:36-37: there are also "evils" brought about by God that people must ascribe to themselves but whose elimination they can expect only from God.

■ **3-6** Whereas the examples in 5:12-16 and 6:1-2 introduced with יֵשׁ *yēš* were realistic and concretely conceivable, the examples with אִם *'im* and וְאִלּוּ *wĕ'illû* offered for discussion in 6:3-5, 6 are clearly fictitious and fabricated: no man sires one hundred children or lives two thousand years. The fictitious exaggeration serves to prove that even numerous progeny and a long life do not make up for the lack of possibilities for enjoyment. Verse 3 seems to have in view the case in which a man has goods at his disposal (הַטּוֹבָה *haṭṭôbâ*: determinate) but cannot enjoy them (cf. 6:1-2; 5:12-14 vs. 5:18), whereas v. 6 seems to have a man in mind who does not have personal property at his disposal (טוֹבָה *ṭôbâ*: indeterminate; cf. 5:15-16 vs. 5:17).

■ **3a** An abundance of children and a long life have traditionally been regarded as having a high value.[37] In Proverbs 1–9 (long) "life is offered as a gift of salvation, and, indeed, is linked to attention to the exhortations of the wisdom teacher or the call to follow personified wisdom."[38] In Isa 65:20, 22-23, and Zech 8:4-5, great age

---

32   Lauha; cf. R. Martin-Achard, "נֵכָר *nēkār* stranger," *TLOT* 2:740.

33   Cf. Kippenberg, *Religion und Klassenbildung*, 78ff., 9ff.

34   Ibid., 81

35   Ibid., 82; cf. 45ff. on the shift of agricultural production in Palestine in the second century.

36   The idea that the latter is also in view here could be indicated by the fact that the term אִישׁ נָכְרִי *'îš nokrî* occurs elsewhere in the OT only in Deut 17:15, in the prohibition against installing a "foreigner" as king in Israel.

37   On abundance of children as a blessing cf. Gen 15:5; 22:17; 26:4; Ruth 4:11-12; Job 29:5; Prov 17:4; Pss 127:3-5; 128:3; on childlessness as a curse and a disgrace, Gen 30:1, 23; 1 Sam 1:1-20; 2 Sam 6:13-23; 2 Kgs 4:8-17; Isa 47:8-9; Hos 9:11-12, 14, 16; *1 En.* 98:5; Luke 1:25; on long life as a blessing, Gen 5; 11:10-26; 25:8; 35:29; Judg 8:32; 1 Chr 29:28; 2 Chr 24:15; Job 42:17; Prov 10:27; 19:16; Isa 65:20; Zech 8:4; on early death as a disaster Gen 6:3; 38:7, 10; Job 36:6, 13-14; Pss 90:9-10; 102:24-25; Prov 22:23; Isa 38:10.

38   G. Gerleman, "חיה *ḥyh* to live," *TLOT* 1:417; cf. Prov 3:1-2; 4:10, 13, 22-23; 7:2; 8:35.

and numerous children are signs of the expected "eschatological" age of salvation (which, according to Isa 65:22, also includes enjoyment of the fruits of work!). By contrast, Sir 16:1-3 relativizes the value of a large progeny: "Better is the death of the childless man than that of one who has many children full of deception." Wisdom 3:13–4:6 argues very similarly. In the following verses, a new conception of a fulfilled life is developed: "But the righteous, though they die early, will be at rest (ἐν ἀναπαύσει ἔσται; cf. Qoh 6:5b). For old age is not honored for length of time (τὸ πολυχρόνιον) or measured by number of years (ἀριθμῷ ἐτῶν); but understanding (φρόνησις) is gray hair for anyone, and a blameless life is ripe old age" (Wis 4:7-9). In the discussion of the corresponding conceptions,[39] the emphasis that Qoh 6:3aα lays on the length of life according to years would become understandable. (Delitzsch assumes here an allusion to Genesis 5.)

Perhaps, however, v. 3aα can also be understood in the sense that a man lives as many years "as are the days of his years," that is—under the presupposition of a solar calendar[40]—364 years, which would correspond, say, to the age of Enoch (Gen 5:23: 365 years). If one might thus recognize in Qoh 6:3aα an allusion to Enoch, the reference to the lack of a burial in v. 3aβ would be explained. For according to Gen 5:24 Enoch did not die a natural death and was not buried, but—like Elijah later on (2 Kgs 2:3, 5)—was taken alive to God. Verse 3a would then declare not only an abundance of children and a long life but also a life at whose end one goes directly into a new existence with God (on corresponding hopes

cf., e.g., Ps 73:23; Wis 3:1ff.; 4:10ff.) to be of no value if the man has no possibility of enjoyment *in* this life (or himself renounces this possibility—say, in the sense of Ps 73:25).[41]

The reference to the lack of a burial in v. 3aβ could also be understood as a polemical sideswipe against the proviso formulated in Sir 11:26 that one can appropriately judge a man only at and after his death (see above on 5:19; cf. also Psalms 37; 49; 73): a long life without any enjoyment can certainly be judged—negatively—even before its end.[42]

■ **3b-5** These verses formulate this negative judgment through a comparison with a stillborn child, which perhaps, like 5:14a (cf. Job 1:21), alludes to statements in the book of Job (cf. Job 3:11-16; 10:18-22). The key word "rest" (נַחַת *naḥat*) refers back to Qoh 4:6.

■ **3-5** These verses expand and refine the example of 5:12-14 in the sense that for a rich man to deny himself the enjoyment of his wealth is senseless, *even if* he does not lose the wealth he has "set aside." In the broader context 6:3-5 corresponds to the case, presented in 4:8, of the rich man who allows himself no enjoyment, *although* he has no heir. Here it now becomes clear: *even if* a rich man has a hundred heirs, it would be senseless to allow himself no enjoyment.

■ **6** This verse seems to place the case of a rich man who cannot enjoy his goods (vv. 1-2, 3-5) alongside that of a man who has no goods at his disposal, that is, who is poor (cf. 5:15-16, 17). For such a man also, a long life cannot make up for the lack of possibilities for enjoyment. The closing rhetorical question (cf. 3:20 and then

39 Cf. Armin Schmitt, *Das Buch der Weisheit* (Würzburg: Echter, 1986) 66.

40 Cf. James C. Vanderkam, "Calendars: Ancient Israelite and Early Jewish," *ABD* 1:818–20.

41 Interpreting v. 3aβ in this direction is Michel (*Untersuchungen*, 146–47). The interpretation of v. 3aβ as a statement about "a life without death ('even if a grave would never await him')" (Schwienhorst-Schönberger, *Nicht im Menschen*, 152; cf. Levy) seems problematic in view of the perfect הָיְתָה *hāyĕtâ*, which hardly points to a future state of affairs.

42 Delitzsch sees in the missing burial a deficit that is added to the lack of enjoyment: "in an honourable burial and an honourable remembrance, good fortue, albeit shaded with sadness, might be seen"

(similarly, e.g., Hertzberg; Lauha). Gordis rightly objects to this: "But would Koheleth regard a joyless existence, even if followed by elaborate funeral rites, as worthwhile? Obviously not." Therefore, Gordis proposes in v. 3aβ to read לוֹ *lû* instead of the negation לֹא *lō*: "even if he have an elaborate funeral (on which men lay such great stress)" (cf., e.g., Galling; Kroeber). This interpretation would be meaningful in the context, but it has no basis in the text tradition. Finally, the proposals to connect v. 3aβ, as a statement about a stillbirth, with v. 3b (thus, e.g., Crenshaw; Murphy) or to place it after v. 5a (thus, e.g., Zimmerli; Whitley, *Koheleth*, 57) also seem problematic.

9:4-6) recalls that even such a long life will one day end with death, and afterward the man can no longer expect anything positive. Therefore, pleasure and enjoyment "as long as they live" (3:12) remain the highest and only good for human beings.

■ **1-6** The hard judgments in vv. 1-6 (cf. 4:1-3) are not intended to disparage people who must spend their lives under harsh conditions. Rather, in connection with 5:17-19 they underline the relative value of material possessions ("goods") and ward off as illusory any glossing over of the situation of the propertyless through reference to other values (such as long life and a "sweet sleep"; cf. 5:11).

6:7-9 Proverbs

The section 5:9—6:9 closes, as it began, with three proverbs on its theme. Just like the three introductory proverbs in 5:9-11, these also appear somewhat ambiguous and in need of interpretation. Here too this seems to result from the fact that they bring the argumentation developed in 5:12—6:6 into dialogue with other contemporary positions and concepts.

■ **7** This verse can be read first as an objection against what goes before it (cf. the key word נֶפֶשׁ *nepeš*, "desire," in vv. 2, 3). In 5:12—6:6 the possibility of being able to fulfill the desire for eating, drinking, and pleasure was the decisive criterion for judging various living conditions. When v. 7 now asserts that human appetite[43] remains unsatisfied in any case, this seems to turn the whole preceding argumentation upside down.[44]

If one takes v. 7 seriously as an objection in this sense, the consequence is that a man is not supposed to strive to satisfy the desire of his mouth—that is, to eat and to drink—but rather to free himself of this desire and thus

to orient his life toward other goals and values. In this sense Ps 73:25, for example, cancels all other wishes in view of fellowship with God: "And there is nothing on earth that I desire other than you" (וְעִמְּךָ לֹא־חָפַצְתִּי בָאָרֶץ *wĕʿimmĕkā lōʾ-ḥāpaṣtî bāʾāreṣ*). Comparable tendencies toward the devaluation of human desire are also shown, say, in the book of Sirach.[45] Thus Sir 23:4-6 𝔊 asks:

4 O Lord, Father and God of my life,
    do not give me the look of the eyes (μετεωρισμὸν ὀφθαλμῶν)!
5 And turn desire (ἐπιθυμίαν) away from me!
6 May gluttony (κοιλίας ὄρεξις)
    and lust (συνουσιασμὸς) not seize me,
    and do not give me over to shameful passion (ψυχῇ ἀναιδεῖ)![46]

Against the background of these statements from the book of Sirach on human "desire" (or related concepts), Qoh 6:7 would be understandable as a meaningful objection to the foregoing argumentation. This objection would then be aimed especially at the idea that in 5:12—6:6 the possibility of enjoyment as justified human "desire" or "need" (נֶפֶשׁ *nepeš*) is made the criterion for judging property and lack of property.

Verse 7 can also be understood, however, as the continuation of the preceding line of argumentation. If "eating and drinking" are the highest good for a person and one can never satisfy one's hunger and thirst for more than a limited time, human happiness at any given time is always attainable only in the present moment. Therefore, the experience of happiness in eating, drinking, and pleasure is, on the one hand, ephemeral for human beings; on the other hand, they can also have this experience again and again in their lives. The insight into this transitory character of happiness can keep people from developing unfulfillable wishes (cf. v. 9) and also from

---

43 Following P. R. Ackroyd, "Two Hebrew Notes," *ASTI* 5 (1966/67) 82–86; and M. Dahood, "Hebrew-Ugaritic Lexicogrpahy, VI," *Bib* 49 (1968) 368. Lauha and Lohfink relate the suffix of פִּיהוּ *pîhû*, "*his* mouth," to the "*one* place" (מָקוֹם אֶחָד *māqôm ʾeḥād*) named at the close of v. 6 and interpret v. 7 as a statement about the insatiability of the world below. Speaking against this, nonetheless, is the reference back to vv. 2 and 3 through the key word נֶפֶשׁ *nepeš*, which designates human desire there (cf. Michel, *Untersuchungen*, 149).

44 Michel, *Untersuchungen*, 150 assumes, therefore, that v. 7 does not reproduce the "opinion of Qoheleth" but rather is a "quotation of his dialogue partner" and is refuted by vv. 8-9.

45 Cf. also Hossenfelder, *Philosophie*, on the philosophical treatment of "desire" in the Stoics (48ff.) and Epicureans (110ff.) and in Pyrrhonist skepticism (169ff.).

46 After the translation of Sauer, *JSHRZ* III.5. Cf. also Sir 5:1-2; 6:1-3; 18:30—19:2.

denying themselves and others the enjoyment of their goods—in the erroneous view that they can thereby guarantee happiness over a period of time.

■ **8** This verse raises a number of problems of understanding.[47] If one follows the translation proposed above, this verse can also be understood as a continuation and refinement of the argumentation of 5:12[13]–6:6.

■ **8a** Verse 8a connects with the theme "wisdom and foolishness," which was not directly addressed in 5:9ff. but plays an important role in other texts of the book of Qoheleth. The question of the advantage of the wise man over the fool must be answered differently according to the preceding argumentation. On the one hand, the wise man has no advantage over the fool in that the former, like the latter, can find happiness only in the contingent and ephemeral enjoyment of goods. On the other hand, one advantage of the wise man may consist in the very fact that he knows this and does not seek, like a fool, to guarantee his happiness through his wealth or to seek his happiness in values other than the enjoyment of life.

The book of Sirach also warns against trusting in wealth, yet at the same time it also encourages the wise man not to strive for enjoyment but for wisdom. Thus, after the admonition in Sir 5:1-2 not to lean on wealth (חיל *ḥyl*) and income (כוח *kwḥ*) and not to follow one's desire (תעות נפש *tʿwt npš*) comes, in v. 10, the admonition: "Be supported by your knowledge (דעת *dʿt*)!" And the warning against the power of desire (נפש *npš*) in Sir 6:1-3 is followed in vv. 18ff. by an invitation to wisdom and the exhortation to direct one's desire toward it:

18 My son, from your youth on accept discipline,
   and into your gray years you will achieve wisdom (חכמה *ḥkmh*).

19 Approach her as one who plows and one who harvests,
   and wait for the bounty of her yield (לרב תבואתה *lrb tbwʾth*).
   Indeed, in her service you must toil (מעט תעבוד *mʿṭ tʿbwd*) but little,
   and already on the next day you will eat her fruit.

. . . .

26 With all your desire (ἐν πᾶσι ψυχῖ) approach her,
   and with all your power attend her ways.

Thus the wise man distinguishes himself in that he controls his desire with wisdom and knowledge. Instead of toward uncertain "goods" like wealth and enjoyment, he directs his desire toward wisdom, whose yield is at his disposal and to be achieved with little effort. This corresponds basically to the fundamental approach of Greek-Hellenistic philosophy:

> The Hellenistic schools are unanimous in the conviction that inner peace is threatened when one sets one's heart on what is unattainable, that is, when one imagines needs that one cannot satisfy with one's own power and at any time. Thus one may desire only that of which one is certain that one can also achieve it, but one must remain indifferent toward everything else. . . . For the interpretation of the world the result is the task of explaining it in such a way that what is of true value is that alone which is always at one's disposal, but everything not at one's disposal turns out to be without value and of no interest.[48]

The "advantage (יותר *yôtēr*) of the wise man over the fool" would then consist in the fact that he achieves everything he desires—because (and to the extent that!) he reasonably controls his desires and so interprets the world that what seems worthy of desire is only what he can also achieve.

Under the presuppositions of the ethic of the book of Qoheleth (cf. 3:10-15, 16-22; 5:17-19), however, this presumed "advantage" proves to be illusory. For if the good (טוב *ṭôb*) is not determined by the human setting of values but by the creative activity of God (יָפֶה *yāpeh*: 5:17; cf. 3:11), then the ethical interpretation of the world is not open to disposition by human beings. Unfulfilled desire for the (modest) enjoyment of life is not eliminated when a man suppresses it or directs his desire toward something else, but only when it is fulfilled (by modifying incursions into the outside world). Under these presuppositions, a "wise man" who redirects his desires from uncertain goods like property and enjoyment to the presumed "good" of wisdom and knowledge has no advantage over the "fool": his original desire remains unsatisfied.

47 In addition to the comms. cf. Michel, *Untersuchungen*, 151–55.

48 Hossenfelder, *Philosophie*, 24.

■ **8b** After what goes before it, v. 8b can hardly be understood other than as a rhetorical question that in a pregnant way summarizes the insight gained in 5:12–6:6, namely, that for a successful life a certain minimum of goods is required: the knowledge of a "poor man" (עָנִי ʿānî) does him no good if he has no chance to eat, drink, and enjoy himself. This also excludes any religious exaltation of poverty in the sense of a "piety of the poor" (see above on 5:15-16).

■ **9** Like v. 7, v. 9a can be read both as a critique of the argumentation of 5:12–6:6, which saw something basically positive in the fulfillment of "desire" (נֶפֶשׁ nepeš; 6:2, 3), and as a continuation of this argumentation. In the first case, the proverb speaks against the situation in which people harbor a desire for eating, drinking, and pleasure but do not have at their disposal the means to satisfy this desire (cf. Sir 11:18). In the latter case, by contrast, the proverb criticizes an attitude that demands more from life than an elementary and ephemeral enjoyment in the present moment (cf. 5:10; 11:9). According to the interpretation of v. 9a, the הֶבֶל hebel qualification following in v. 9b can then be related to v. 9a as a whole or to an excessive and unrealistic desire.

■ **5:9—6:9** In retrospect the argumentation of the section 5:9–6:9 can be summarized in the following way. It begins (in connection with 3:10-22) with the idea, first, that the possibility of an elementary enjoyment of life (eating, drinking, and pleasure) is an ethical "good" and, indeed, the only one, and, second, that the object of the ethical discussion can only be human life before death. Taken together with the experience that as a rule poverty also means the lack of opportunities for enjoyment (5:15-16; 6:6), whereas wealth makes enjoyment possible (5:18), without, of course, guaranteeing it (6:1-5), the result is different consequences: because property is no guarantee of enjoyment, it represents no positive "value in itself," but because poverty goes hand in hand with the lack of opportunities for enjoyment, it is an "evil." If wealth, nonetheless, is connected with possibilities of enjoyment, it is to be appraised positively as a "gift of God." Enjoyment represents the "portion" that a rich man can rightly claim from his property. At the same time, this points to limits on the meaningful (and ethically legitimizable!) claims of the rich man to his property. These limits are socioethically relevant when the equally justified claims of the propertyless are taken into consideration: they are also entitled to the possibility of enjoying life. Here we have the basic outline of a sociopolitical program for which one could cite as illustrations and possible concretizations on the level of traditional concepts the giving of the social law in Deuteronomy, and on the level of the historical situation the establishment of assistance funds, as well as measures for finding work in the Hellenistic poleis.

In the context of the contemporary discussion we may consider the following positions with which 5:9–6:9 deals critically:

■ a "piety of poverty," as exemplified in Psalm 73, under whose presuppositions a "voluntary" renunciation of the desire for wealth and enjoyment on earth could be propagated, combined with the hope of God's assistance and help for the "poor" in death;

■ an indifferent attitude toward wealth and poverty motivated by wisdom (for example, in the book of Sirach but also in Job 1) or by philosophy (in the various directions of Greek-Hellenistic philosophy)—in the context of which wealth and poverty were regarded as *adiaphora* and a rationally controlled adjustment of human wanting (the "desires") to the conditions of the outside world was required (along with the renunciation of attempts to change the conditions of the outside world);

■ an attitude of renouncing enjoyment on the part of the rich for the purpose of increasing their wealth (cf. 4:8 and the Tobiad Joseph, who, according to Josephus [*Ant.* 12.4.8] "assembled his riches through toil and doing without"), as well as the maudlin (and objectively cynical) laments of the rich over the "troubles" connected with their property (in 5:10-11?).

The argumentation developed in 5:9–6:9 yields a differentiated position in the context of the contemporary discussion:

■ Crucial to the discussion of a "piety of poverty" is the limitation of ethical argumentation to human life before death. Also, the "piety of poverty" begins with the position that poverty is experienced on the part of the "poor" as something negative. It then achieves, however, a new valuation of poverty and wealth *on earth* on the level of an individual eschatology. The

129

result of this revaluation is a renunciation of striving for a change of circumstances in the external world. Qoheleth 5:9–6:9 raises an objection to this orientation of desire toward the world beyond, which actually contributes to the stabilization of the status quo in this world. Thus the text turns not against "the poor" but against a religiously based idealization of poverty.

- Fundamental for the disagreement with a wisdom-philosophically based attitude of indifference and (inner) distance toward wealth and poverty is the maintaining of (material) enjoyment as an ethical good and, founded on it, the basically positive evaluation of the desire for possibilities of enjoyment. With this the text contradicts a steering of desire from the uncertainly available goods of the external world to goods at one's disposal, such as wisdom and peace of the soul. With the rejection of a judgment of wealth and poverty as *adiaphora,* the text, at the same time, challenges the wealthy to enjoy their riches as something good and takes from them the possibility of interpreting the situation of the poor (in objective cynicism) as something "ethically indifferent" and ultimately inconsequential for their (inner) happiness. Also for the rich the consequence of this conception produces the demand that the social and economic conditions of the external world be reshaped.

According to the Masoretes, between 6:9 and 6:10 lies the middle of the book of Qoheleth (calculated by verses). Also in terms of composition 6:9, as the end of the larger unit 5:9–6:9, marks the end of a section. Then, beginning with 6:10, one can more or less clearly delineate smaller, argumentatively relatively closed sections; larger compositions, by contrast, are not as clearly apparent as in the first half of the book. Following Backhaus and Schwienhorst-Schönberger we may regard 6:10—8:17 as another major section.[1] Its structure can be outlined as follows:

6:10-12	human limitations—critique of knowledge
7:1-14	critique of "wise" advice: enjoyment of the "good day"
7:15-22	limits of righteousness and wisdom
7:23-29	limits of wisdom—critique of knowledge
8:1-9	wisdom and power
8:10-15	the righteous and evildoers: fear of God and pleasure
8:16-17	limits of wisdom—critique of knowledge

The framing passages 6:10-12 and 8:16-17 turn explicitly against claims of a special knowledge that produces theoretical insights regarding ethics and action (knowing "what is good for human beings" [6:12]; comprehending "what is happening under the sun" [8:17]). Here 6:10-12 still formulates (rhetorical) questions ("who knows . . . ?"), whereas 8:16-17 closes in retrospect with clear statements (8:17: "human beings [or: the wise man] cannot comprehend").

Within 7:1—8:15, 7:1-14 and 8:10-15 correspond in that each ends with an exhortation to pleasure and the enjoyment of life (7:13-14; 8:15). Moreover, the הֶבֶל *hebel* qualification (גַם־זֶה הֶבֶל *gam-zeh hebel*) within 6:10—8:17 is

found only in these two sections (7:6; 8:10, 14). Thematically, however, 8:10-15 stands closer to 7:15-22 (no reliable "deed-result connection"; juxtaposition of "the righteous and the wicked"; recommendation of the "fear of God"). Also 8:1-9 shows links both with 7:1-14 (esp. 7:14/8:7: ignorance of the future) and with 7:15-22 (strength of wisdom vs. the weakness of human beings). With its critique of knowledge 7:23-29 (esp. v. 29) stands thematically close above all to the framing sections 6:10-12 and 8:16-17.[2]

In terms of content, 6:10—8:17 carries on a critical "discussion with alternative definitions of happiness"[3] that could call into question the view of eating, drinking, and pleasure as the highest good that was developed in 1:3–6:9. Here the text is apparently faced with various kinds of "experts" on the life and behavior of people ("wise men") who, based on their especially close contact with "wisdom" (7:23-29), claim to know better than Qoheleth what is "good" for people (6:10-12; 8:16-17). Qoheleth 7:1-14 rejects the postponement of pleasure and enjoyment in the present in the expectation of a still better future (before or after death). Then 7:15-22 and 8:10-15 show that righteousness and piety ("fear of God") cannot guarantee a person a successful life in the present or in the future (without therefore being ethically irrelevant!). And 8:1-9 demonstrates that even an opportunistic dependence on powerful people exposes a person to dangers that are at least as numerous as the possibilities for happiness it opens up. Hence pleasure and enjoyment in the present remain the highest and only good toward which people can and should orient themselves (7:14; 8:15; cf. 3:12-13, 22; 5:17-19).

1   Cf. Backhaus, *Zeit und Zufall*, 260–62; Schwienhorst-Schönberger, *Nicht im Menschen*, 157–58.

2   For the details of the content and linguistic relationships of the smaller units of 6:10—8:17 with each other and with the broader context in particular, cf. Backhaus, *Zeit und Zufall*, 214–59.

3   Schwienhorst-Schönberger, *Nicht im Menschen*, 157.

6

What was[a] has already been given names, and it is known what a human being is[b] and that humans cannot argue with the one who is more powerful[c] than they. 11 Yet there are many words that increase futility. What do humans gain from that? 12 For who knows what is good for human beings in life, in the time of their fleeting life, which they spend[a] like a shadow? Who could tell them what will be in the future[b] under the sun?

10a Though the translation of מַה־שֶּׁהָיָה *mah-šehāyâ* with "whatever has occurred" (Lohfink) would go well with the following context, it seems problematic in view of 1:9; 3:15; and 7:24.

10b Thus according to the Masoretic accents (*atnach* on אָדָם *ʾādām*; cf. 𝔊 (καὶ ἐγνώσθη ὅ ἐστιν ἄνθρωπος) and 𝔅 (*et scitur quod homo sit*). The assumption of a clause boundary between אֲשֶׁר־הוּא *ʾăšer-hûʾ* and אָדָם *ʾādām* (thus , e.g., Whitley, *Koheleth*, 61: "that which is, was already called by name, and it is known what it is"; "man cannot indeed argue with one that is stronger than himself"; similarly, e.g., Crenshaw) is syntactically less likely (cf. Schoors, *Preacher*, 126–27). A correction of the text (cf., e.g., Zimmerli: וְאָדָם לֹא־יוּכַל *wĕʾādām lōʾ-yûkal* . . . ; Fox: וְלֹא יוּכַל אָדָם *wĕlōʾ-yûkal ʾādām* . . . : "and a human being cannot argue . . .") does not seem necessary.

10c With Q, שהתקיף *štqyp* is to be interpreted in the sense of שֶׁתַּקִּיף *šettaqqîp*; cf. Schoors, *Preacher*, 35–36.

12a On עשה *ʿśh* in the sense of "spend (his life)," cf. Whitley, *Koheleth*, 61; Crenshaw.

12b Literally: "after him." Here we may consider not (only) the fate of a person after his death (cf. 3:19-21; 9:4-6, 10) but (also) what is yet to happen to him in his life ("under the sun") (cf. 7:14; 8:7; 9:12; 10:14; 11:2, 5-6, 10).

The section 6:10-12 can be read as an introduction to the critical discussion of various bits of advice for the conduct of life in 7:1-14 (but beyond that also through 10:20). It is a question here of "words that increase futility [or: transitoriness]" but bring humans no gain (v. 11), because they do not do justice to the fact that a person's life is at one's disposal only within a very restricted framework (v. 10), and one can never know exactly what the future will bring (v. 12). The section is framed by references to the past (מַה־שֶּׁהָיָה *mah-šehāyâ*, v. 10) and the future (מַה־יִּהְיֶה *mah-yihĕyeh*, v. 12) as the horizon and

limit of "transitory" (הֶבֶל *hebel*) human life. This recalls the basic comments in 1:3-11 (esp. vv. 9-10) and chap. 3 (esp. v. 15).

■ **10** This verse harks back to 1:9-10 and 3:15 (cf. the key words מַה־שֶּׁהָיָה *mah-šehāyâ*—taken up again in 7:24—and כְּבָר *kĕbār*): "What was has already been given names"; that is, there is nothing new for which one would have to invent a new "name," a new designation.[1] That is also true for human beings: their "nature" is known and will not change. The "nature" of humankind, which is already indicated in its "name" (אָדָם *ʾādām*; cf. אֲדָמָה

1   Verse 10 is frequently interpreted as a statement about the "determination" of human life by God; cf., e.g., Lauha: "The giving of names (v. 10) is, as it were, the call into existence (Gen 1:6, 8, 10; Isa 40:26). What exists and happens was predestined to come into being. Becoming known (נודע [*nwdʿ*] niphal) also occurs in the OT in the sense of predestination (Jer 1:5; cf. also Rom 8:29) [?]). The subject of predestination is not directly named, but in accordance with later Jewish understanding, the passive expression points to God, as the naming of the 'stronger one' at the end of the verse shows" (similarly, e.g., Galling; Zimmerli; Loader; Murphy).

In Genesis 1, however, "name giving" (vv. 5, 8, 10; cf. 2:19-20, 23; 3:20; 5:2) and "calling into existence" (vv. 3, 6, 9, etc.) are distinguished from each other. Naming marks the close of the related work of creation. The same also seems to be true of the name giving in Qoh 6:10 (cf. 1:9; 3:14-15): because the world is complete as the creation of God and not in need of change, then nothing totally new is to be expected in it—or from human beings.

ʾădāmâ, "earth"), includes being "bound to the earth" (cf. 5:1; Genesis 2–3): they "cannot argue (דִּין *dyn*) with the one who is more powerful than they." Who or what that is, is not said. Statements such as Isa 45:9 ("Woe to the one who strives [רִיב *ryb*] with his Maker, a vessel among earthen vessels [חַרְשֵׂי אֲדָמָה *ḥarśê ʾădāmâ*] . . .")[2] suggest, however, that one should think of God here. The following texts in chaps. 7–10 then discuss further (supposed) "powers" with which humans see themselves confronted in life: the king and other powerful people, women, chance, and death. That humans do not have to be helplessly subjected to each supposed greater power is shown already in 4:12 (where the verb תקף *tqp* likewise occurs).

■ **11** The numerous "words that increase futility" (דְּבָרִים הַרְבֵּה מַרְבִּים הָבֶל *dĕbārîm harbeh marbîm hābel*) may especially include, according to v. 10, assertions or bits of advice that suggest to human beings more possibilities of action and self-determination than they actually have (cf. 1:8, 10; 5:2, 6; 10:12-14). They mislead people into unrealistic expectations and wishes and into a mistaken way of life. Because such possibilities are thwarted by the realities of life, human beings can make no use (יֹתֵר *yōtēr*)[3] of them.

■ **12** What is "good" (טוֹב *ṭôb*) for human beings in their limited lifetime (cf. 2:3, 24-26) is, according to 3:12-13, 22 and 5:17-19, to do good and to enjoy good things—and to do this in the present time. What v. 12 is supposed to call into question is not this determination of the "good," which is reinforced in various ways in what follows (cf. 7:14; 8:15; 9:1-10; 11:1–12:7), but alternative and competing ethical concepts (cf. the critical discussion of טוֹב *ṭôb* . . . מִן *min* . . . ["better . . . than . . ."] statements in 7:1-14; 9:16-18).[4] The reference to the unpredictability of the future[5] leads to the conclusion that it is a matter of positions according to which human behavior in the present should be directed toward expectations for the future. The texts that follow in chaps. 7–10 offer a series of examples of corresponding advice, which, in view of the unpredictability of the future, prove to be "futile."

2 Cf. further Isa 29:16; Jer 18:6; Job 9:14ff., 30ff.; 13:3; 34:23, as well as statements from the Greek world mentioned in Braun, *Kohelet*, 119 n. 377 (esp. Menander, frg. 187: μή θεομάχει).

3 On the question of a possible "gain," "advantage," or "use" of human beings (יִתְרוֹן *yitrôn*, יֹתֵר *yōtēr*, מוֹתָר *môtar*) cf. already 1:3; 2:11, 13, 15; 3:9, 19; 5:8, 15; 6:8. The "advantage" of "wisdom" asserted in 7:11-12 is critically called into question by vv. 13-14. By contrast, 10:10-11 asserts a real "advantage" of "wisdom"—correctly understood.

4 Contra Michel, *Untersuchungen*, 163–64, who assumes that v. 12a does not reflect "the view of Qoheleth." Verse 12a does not have to be read from the start as a "rhetorical" question. With the background of primeval history (cf. v. 10), the question could be answered with "God" (cf. Gen 2:18) or "humanity" (cf. Gen 3:5, 22). The latter seems problematic in the present context (cf. v. 10). Thus v. 12a can be understood as a reference back to the basic comments in chaps. 1–3/4: what is "good" cannot be determined by human beings themselves (cf. 1:12–2:26); it is given to them in advance by God through God's creative activity (cf. 3:11-13).

5 Also the question who could "tell" (נגד *ngd* hiphil; cf. 8:7; 10:14) human beings the future could be answered initially with "God"; cf., e.g., Isa 41:26; 42:9; 44:7 (see *BHS*); 45:21; 46:10; 48:3, 5; Dan 2:28, 45; Gen 41:25, as well as Sir 48:25 on Isaiah: "He revealed what was to occur to the end of time" (עַד עוֹלָם הִגִּיד נִהְיוֹת *ʿd ʿwlm hgyd nhywt*). Yet according to 3:11 God has intentionally limited the ability of human beings to look beyond the present. Since everything that God has effected is "definitive" according to 3:14, God cannot be expected to grant humans further insights in the future. That even the "wise man" does not know more about the future than all other people (cf. 9:5) will be demonstrated again and again in what follows; cf. already 2:19; 3:21 and then 7:14; 8:7; 9:12; 10:14; 11:2, 5-6.

7

1 A good name is better than a good smell[a]—and the day of death than the day of birth.[b] **2** It is better to go to a house where people are mourning than to go to a house where people are celebrating,[a] for there one sees[b] the end of every person, and the living take it[c] to heart. **3** It is better to be vexed than to laugh, for a sad countenance does the heart good. **4** The heart of the wise is in a house where people are mourning, but the heart of fools is in the house where people are enjoying themselves.[a] **5** It is better to hear a wise man scolding than fools singing.[a] **6** For like the crackling of thorns under the pot is the laughing of fools. Yet[a] that also is futile. **7** For oppression makes a wise man foolish, and gifts[a] corrupt[b] the mind.[c]

8 Better is the outcome of a matter[a] than its beginning; better patient than proud. **9** Do not become too quickly vexed, for fools carry vexation within them.[a] **10** Do not say: Why is it[a] that the former times were better than the present? For you do not ask out of wisdom. **11** For wisdom is as good as property[a] and an advantage for those who see the sun; **12** for wisdom protects and money protects,[a] yet this is the advantage of knowledge: whoever has wisdom is kept alive by it.[b]

13 Consider the work of the Deity: Who can make straight what the Deity has made crooked? **14** On the day of happiness be joyful, and on the day of unhappiness reflect[a] on the fact that the Deity made the latter like the former. For[b] human beings cannot know what the future will be.[c]

1a   Literally: "Better a (good) name than good oil."

1b   Literally: "the day on which one was born."

2a   Literally: "a house of sadness . . . a house of feasting." Instead of בֵּית מִשְׁתֶּה *bêt mišteh* ("a house where one celebrates"), 4QQoh[a] seems to read בֵּית שִׂמְחָה *bêt śimḥâ* ("a house where one rejoices") (cf. v. 4).

2b   Literally: "that is."

2c   The object of "take it to heart" is lacking in the Hebrew text. Therefore, Ellermeier, *Qohelet*, I/1, 105ff. and Backhaus, *Zeit und Zufall*, 222, for example, recommend placing v. 4 before v. 3 and interpreting it as an object clause (". . . the living take to heart that the heart of the wise is . . .").

4a   Literally: "house of sadness . . . house of pleasure."

5a   Literally: "the scolding of a wise man . . . the singing of fools." Instead of נַּעֲרַת *gaʿărat* 4QQoh[a] reads נערות *gʿrwt* (= pl. נַעֲרֹות *gaʿărôt* or sg. נַעֲרוּת *gaʿărût?*).

6a   The conjunction ו *w* is missing in 4QQoh[a], where before הבל *hbl* (on the lower side margin) there is a gap. (Whether it was there in the original writing seems to be no longer determinable.)

7a   Literally: "a gift corrupts" (sg.).

7b   On the gender incongruence between וִיאַבֵּד *wîʾabbēd* (m.) and מַתָּנָה *mattānâ* (f.) cf. GKC §145o. Instead of ויאבד *wyʾbd* 4QQoh[a] reads ויעוה *wyʿwh*, "which appears to be a functional synonym used for the sake of greater specificity" (Fox).

7c   Thus 𝔐; cf. 𝔖 𝔗. By contrast, 𝔊 (καὶ ἀπόλλυσι τὴν καρδίαν εὐτονίας [vl. εὐγένειας] αὐτου; cf. α' ϑ' 𝔖[h]) and 𝔙 (*et perdet robur cordis illius*) see in "oppression" also the grammatical subject of v. 7a. Correspondingly, G. R. Driver, "Problems and Solutions," *VT* 4 (1954) 229–30—whom Whitley, *Koheleth*, 63, and Michel, *Untersuchungen*, 127, among others, follow—recommends that instead of מַתָּנָה *mattānâ* one read מְתָנָה *mětānâ* or מָתְנֹו *motnô* (from מֹתֶן* *mōten*, "strength"; cf. מָתְנַיִם *motnayim*, "loins, hips, small of the back"). Verse 7b would then be translated: "and destroys his strong heart" (Whitley) or "and ruins his certain ability to judge" (Michel). In the context, however, 𝔐 is quite sensible (see below).

8a   Or: "a word," "a talk."

9a   Literally: "Do not hurry to become vexed in your spirit, for vexation lies in the belly of fools."

10a   Or: "what has happened."

11a   Or: "wisdom is good with property."

12a   Literally: "in the shadow of wisdom, in the shadow of money [or: silver]." Instead of בצל *bṣl* . . . בצל *bṣl* . . . (𝔐), 𝔊 𝔖[h] 𝔎 presuppose בצל *bṣl* . . . כצל *kṣl* . . . and σ' 𝔖 𝔙 Jer, כצל *kṣl* . . . כצל *kṣl* . . .

12b   Literally: "wisdom keeps its owner [on the pl. cf. GKC §124i] alive."

14a   Literally: "see."

14b   The meaning of the conjunction עַל־דִּבְרַת שֶׁ *ʿal-dibrat še-* (cf. עַל־דִּבְרַת *ʿal-dibrat* in 3:18; 8:2) here is not entirely clear; cf. Schoors, *Preacher*, 147. Usually a final ("thus";

cf. Aram. עַל־דִּבְרַת דִּי *ʿal-dibrat dî* in Dan 2:30; 4:14) or consecutive ("so that") sense is assumed, which, however, makes v. 14bβ hard to understand in the context. If one assumes, as recommended above, a causal meaning ("because" or "for"; cf. עַל־דִּבְרַת *ʿal-dibrat* in 8:2?), then v. 14bβ is to be read as the substantiation of v. 14abα (with a critical sidelong glance at

vv. 1-12) (see above). It would perhaps also be possible to make v. 14bβ, in the sense of "with regard to the fact that . . ." (cf. עַל־דִּבְרַת *ʿal-dibrat* in 3:18?), a heading for what follows (vv. 15ff.).

14c Literally: "For human beings do not find [or: comprehend] anything behind (or after) themselves."

The section 7:1-14 offers in vv. 1-12 a number of problematic pieces of advice for the conduct of life that in vv. 13-14 are critically corrected in the sense of the determination of the "good" in 3:12-13, 22 and 5:17-19, as well as with reference back to 6:10-12. In vv. 1-12 the five maxims in vv. 1-6a and the five in vv. 8-12 clearly reveal different and mutually contradictory attitudes toward life: vv. 1-6a recommend that, in view of death (and the subsequent "better" life in the "beyond"?), one should stay away from pleasures. Verses 8-12, by contrast, advise against vexation and suggest that one look confidently to the future *in* life. In both positions a person's present behavior is determined by future expectations—negative or positive. Contrary to these positions, vv. 13-14 advise one to live entirely with one's eyes on the present, in view of a person's limited (by God) power of disposition over his or her life (v. 13, cf. 6:10: key word יוּכַל *yûkal*) and the unpredictability of the future (v. 14; cf. 6:12: key words אָדָם *ʾādām* and אַחֲרָיו *ʾaḥărāyw*).

When read after 6:10-12, the advice in 7:1-12 must appear highly questionable, for it promises human beings an "advantage" (7:11-12 vs. 6:11) and claims to know what is "good" for them (7:1-3, 5-6, 8, 11-12 vs.

6:12a) and what the future will bring them (7:1-2, 8 vs. 6:12b).[1] Here it is probably a question of a kind of "collage" of contemporary ethical maxims that illustrates what kind of "words" in 6:11 should come to mind. Whether present texts or proverbs are literally "quoted" and "commented on"[2] can hardly be decided, especially since we must take into account that the text offers its readers pointed caricatures of known positions. Verse 6b calls the preceding recommendations "futile." Verse 7 presents perhaps an "ideology-critical" explanation of various attitudes toward life: "oppression" can corrupt one's thinking just as much as "gifts." The former may lead to a negative attitude toward life, as comes to expression in vv. 1-6a, whereas the latter may elicit an optimistic trust in wisdom and money, as is voiced in vv. 8-12.

■ **1** The Hebrew text of v. 1a contains a play on words: טוֹב שֵׁם מִשֶּׁמֶן טוֹב *ṭôb šēm miššemen ṭôb*, literally: "better a [good] name than good [anointing] oil." Those who cannot afford an expensive perfume, which here no doubt stands *pars pro toto* for a certain level of luxury, can console themselves with the fact that their "(good) name" has a greater value (cf. Lohfink).[3] The continuation in

1   Moreover, the recommendations of 7:1-12 are in contradiction to the statements and admonitions that are often repeated in other passages in the book of Qoheleth; cf. 7:1a with 9:8; 7:1b with 9:5ff.; 7:2-6 with 3:12-13, 22; 5:17-19; 8:15; 9:7-10; 11:7ff.; and 7:11 with 6:8a; 9:11a. Cf. the attempts at a redaction-historical explanation of these tensions in McNeile; Barton; Podechard (see Michel, *Qohelet*, 20; cf. also Michel, *Untersuchungen*, 128ff.; Backhaus, *Zeit und Zufall*, 224).

2   Thus, e.g., N. D. Osborn, "A Guide for Balanced Living: An Exegetical Study of Ecclesiastes 7:1-4," *BT* 21 (1970) 185–96; Lohfink; Michel, "Qohelet Probleme: Überlegungen zu Qoh 8,2-9 und 7,1-14," *ThViat* 15 (1979/80) 81–103; idem, *Untersuchungen*, 81–105. Whereas Osborn and Lohfink assume a

manifold, rapid exchange of "quotation" and "commentary" in the text (Osborn: vv. 1a/1b, 2aα/2aβb, 3a/3b-4, 5/6-7 [with "quotation" in v. 7], 8/9-10, 11a/11b-12; Lohfink: vv. 1a/1b-4, 5-6a/6b-7, 8-9/10, 11-12/13-18 [similarly Backhaus, *Zeit und Zufall*, 221ff.]; contra J.-J. Lavoie, "La philosophie comme réflexion sur la mort: Étude de Qohélet 7,1-4," *LTP* 54 [1998] 91–107), Michel identifies vv. 1-6a (so also Levy) and vv. 11-12 as "quotations" that are commented on in vv. 6b-10 and vv. 13-14 (so also Schwienhorst-Schönberger, *Nicht im Menschen*, 160ff.).

3   Cf. Osborn, "Guide," 188: "The use of שֶׁמֶן *šemen* in the wisdom literature of the Old Testament frequently symbolizes luxury (Prov. 21:17) or plenty (Job 29:6)." On the value of a "name" cf., e.g., Prov

v. 1b ("and the day of death than the day of birth") could then be read as the ironic intensifiction of these maxims, which reveals their hostility to life: they play with the ambiguity of the term "name," which brings to mind both the "good reputation" during life as well as the "name" that survives death; the latter is established only with death.[4] Yet whether that name will last long after death must appear questionable according to 2:16 (cf. 1:11), and 6:10 raises doubts as to whether anyone can ever succeed in acquiring a special "name." Since v. 2 and v. 4 also show a strong orientation toward death, however, it also seems possible, if not probable, that v. 1 brings to expression an attitude toward life that is known to the readers of the book of Qoheleth from their contemporary environment, according to which people should forgo enjoyment in their "earthly" life in order to experience true happiness after death in the "beyond."[5] With this presupposition the day of death must indeed seem better than the day of birth.

■ **2-6a** As in v. 1, it also remains unclear in vv. 2-6a whether the readers of the book of Qoheleth could recognize here a position actually maintained in their time, or whether the text is caricaturing known ethical maxims.[6] Also, the two possibilities are not at all mutually exclusive. In any case, the connection between the forgoing of (or hostility toward: v. 1a) enjoyment represented in v. 1 and the conscious orientation of the conduct of life toward coming death (v. 1b) is maintained in vv. 2-6a.

■ **2-3** The idea that in view of the coming of death to all people one should mourn rather than celebrate (v. 2) seems by no means compelling.[7] On the contrary, in light of the transitoriness of human life, 9:7-10 and 11:7—12:7 exhort one to the enjoyment of life. It must also seem just as questionable whether things go better for the human "heart" when one is vexed than when one

laughs and enjoys oneself (v. 3; cf., however, 9:7; 11:9-10; Prov 14:13).

■ **4-6a** These verses strengthen, nonetheless, the recommendations of vv. 1-3 and also reinforce them by calling them the position of the "wise" who are thereby distinguished from "fools": while the wise mourn, fools devote themselves to pleasure (v. 4); while the wise are "scolding"[8]—that is, they exhort one to a serious and moral way of life—the fools are singing songs (v. 5). Yet their laughing is as short-lived as the crackling of thorns that burn under the pot (v. 6a): like them, the fools destroy themselves through their enjoyment.[9]

■ **6b** The *hebel* judgment in v. 6b ("that also is futile") can initially be related to the "laughing of fools" (v. 6a). The continuation of the text, however, makes clear that it also (and more likely) fits the whole attitude toward life described in vv. 1-6a, according to which a person should so orient one's life toward coming death that it is completely shaped by this end—which is understood as perhaps only a transition to a better life in the "beyond."

■ **7a** The statement that "oppression" (cf. 4:1; 5:7) can make a "wise man" foolish calls into question the stiff and static juxtaposition of "wise" and "foolish" in vv. 4-6. Qoheleth 4:1-3 shows how the experience of "oppression" can lead to a life-negating attitude. From that standpoint it seems possible to read v. 7a as an "ideology-critical" analysis of the attitude toward life formulated in vv. 1-6a: the factual impossibility of being able to enjoy one's life can make it seem "wise" to deny the value of enjoying life and completely renounce such enjoyment. Since, however, according to 3:12-13, 22, and 5:17-19 there is nothing better for a person than to enjoy his life, then this supposed "wisdom" is in reality "foolishness." It is understandable that "oppressed" people hold this "foolishness" to be "wisdom." Yet in the view of

22:1; Sir 41:1ff.; on the comparison of "name" and "oil" cf. Cant 1:3 (as well as Sir 49:1: "name"/"incense").

4   Cf. Sir 11:26 and above on 6:3. On "name" in the sense of "posthumous reputation" cf. Prov 10:7; Job 18:17.

5   Cf. Ps 73:25 on the forgoing of "earthly" needs, and Isa 56:5; 62:2; 65:15 on "name" in an "eschatological" context.

6   "According to Levy, 7:1-6a quotes an ascetic in the sense of Cynic-Stoic itinerant preaching" (Michel, *Untersuchungen*, 137 n. 23). On v. 1 Braun, *Kohelet*,

128 n. 401 refers to Diogenes (according to Diogenes Laertius 6.66): "To one who anoints himself with fragrant oil, he says: 'Take care that the good smell of your head does not cause you to smell bad in the world!'" Michel, *Untersuchungen*, 136–37, assumes that vv. 1-6a express the "pessimistic" view of life of "apocalypticism."

7   An example of a pious (and wise) man who prefers "mourning" to "feasting" is offered by Tobit 2.

8   Cf. Prov 9:8; 13:1, 18; 15:12, 32; 17:10.

9   Cf. Sir 27:13.

the book of Qoheleth, this "wisdom" helps them not to a better life but only to resignation to their bad living conditions.

■ **7b** Yet not only "oppression" but also "gifts" can corrupt the mind ("the heart").[10] This seems, according to the "wisdom" of the "oppressed" (vv. 1-6a), to focus attention on another form of "wisdom," whose representatives live from and are dependent on "gifts" of the prosperous and powerful. Verses 8-12 can be understood as an expression of the attitude toward life of such "wise" people, which is somewhat "more optimistic" than the "wisdom" of the "oppressed" of vv. 1-6, which it in part directly contradicts.

■ **8a** Whereas vv. 1-6 exhort one to a constant consideration of death as the—at least for the present, negative—"end of every person" (v. 2), v. 8a encourages confidence that the outcome of a matter will be better than its beginning.[11] Structurally, this repeats the argument of v. 1b with conditions reversed. Common to both attitudes toward life is the orientation of present actions toward the expected future—which must seem problematic after 6:12b (cf. 7:14bβ).

■ **8b** Above all in dealing with more powerful and more highly placed people, it behooves one to be patient and forbearing rather than to appear proud and arrogant (v. 8b; cf. 8:3; 10:4).[12] That could be an indication that ethical maxims, as formulated in vv. 8-12, thrive better under the protection of money (v. 12) and power than on the side of the "oppressed." In the present context, however, it would perhaps also be possible to read v. 8b as a judgment on the "proud" disparagement of life as it came to expression in vv. 1-6.

■ **9-10** Verse 9 stands in clear and direct contradiction to v. 3 and thus makes clear again that vv. 8-12 formulate an attitude toward life that diametrically opposes that in vv. 1-6. If in v. 9 we learn that "vexation" (or "displeasure") is a mark of "fools,"[13] v. 10, by contrast, qualifies the confidence in a positive future expressed in v. 8 as "wisdom": the times are not getting worse but better—or

at least they still remain just as good.[14] This does not entirely correspond to the view of 1:9-10; 3:15; and 6:10, according to which in the context of a comprehensive return of the same kinds of things, limited changes from better to worse are just as possible as those from worse to better.

■ **11-12** According to vv. 11-12a wisdom is as valuable as money and property, since a person who has wisdom at his disposal is as well "protected" by it as by money and property. Verse 12b even sees an advantage of wisdom over material goods in that its "owner" is kept alive by it.[15] The idea here may be that a person can lose material possessions, for example, through unfavorable circumstances (cf. 5:13), but not wisdom and education. In an unfortunate situation, however, they can help one to regain financial footing. Yet here we may also have an expression of the high self-confidence of "wise" men who with their wisdom earn their living "in the shadow of money" by being available to serve the rich and powerful and to receive "gifts" in return (v. 7b; cf. Sir 51:28). That this self-confidence does not always correspond to reality is revealed, for example, by 6:8 and 9:11-18. Not only "oppression" but also "gifts" can cloud one's clear view of reality.

■ **13-14** By contrast, vv. 13-14 exhort one to regard reality as the work of the Deity. As such they mark the boundary of possible human actions, as explained in chap. 3: "whatever the Deity does is definitive: nothing is to be added to it, nor anything taken from it" (3:14); "who can make straight what he has made crooked?" (7:13; cf. also 1:15). Likewise limited are the possibilities of human knowledge with regard to the future: "Human beings cannot know what the future will be" (v. 14bβ; cf. 3:11, 22; 6:12). Both points lead to the conclusion that it is best for human beings to orient themselves toward the present in their conduct of life and then enjoy what is good when the opportunity presents itself: "On the day [or: at the time] of happiness (טוֹבָה $\underline{t}\hat{o}\underline{b}\hat{a}$) be aware of good things (בְּטוֹב $b\breve{e}\underline{t}\hat{o}b$, v. 14a$\alpha$; cf. 3:12-13, 22; 5:17-

---

10 Cf. Exod 23:8; Deut 16:19; Sir 8:2; 20:29.
11 Cf. 1 Kgs 8:11; Sir 11:28.
12 Cf. Prov 14:29; 15:18; 16:32; 19:11; 25:15.
13 Cf. Prov 12:16; Job 5:2.
14 This interpretation of v. 10 is suggested in the context according to v. 8; cf. also Sir 39:16-17, 33-34. Read only for itself, v. 10 could also be understood

in the sense that the question, why do the times get worse, does not attest to wisdom either because its answering is obvious or because there is no reasonable answer to this question.

15 On vv. 11-12 cf. Prov 3:13ff.; 8:11ff.; 16:16; Sir 51:28.

19)."[16] Neither the prospect of death (vv. 1-6 with the key word יוֹם *yôm,* "day," in v. 1) nor the expectation of a better future (vv. 8-12 with the key word יָמִים *yāmîm,* "days," in v. 10) should hold one back from the enjoyment of the present, which God himself, through his works, has declared "good" (cf. 6:12).

If, however, the present as the "time [or: day] of unhappiness" offers one no opportunities for enjoyment, one should reflect on the fact that God has made both good and bad times (v. 14aβ, bα). According to chap. 3 this means that the changing of the times (cf. 3:1-9), regarded from God's standpoint, is beautiful (3:11), and it represents the "judgment" of God over human wickedness (3:16-17). These insights can help a person to accept and endure "times of unhappiness" in his life—especially since the openness and unpredictability of the future (v. 14bβ) always contain the *possibility* of an improvement in one's situation.

---

16 Cf. the "parallels" from the Greek world named in Braun, *Kohelet,* 120–21 n. 384, esp. Archilochus, frg. 670: "Rejoice over happy things, and do not be too hurt by unhappiness. Understand the rhythm that lifts and drops human beings."

15 In my fleeting days I have seen both: there is a righteous man who perishes in his righteousness, and there is an evildoer who lives a long time in his evil. 16 Do not be too righteous, and do not pretend to be too wise. Why do you want to be surprised?[a] 17 Do not be unjust too often, and do not be a fool. Why do you want to die before your time?[a] 18 It is good for you to hold fast to the one yet also do not let go of the other. The one who fears God does justice to both.[a]

19 For the wise man wisdom is stronger[a] than ten rulers in the city. 20 No man on earth is (so) just[a] that he does (only) good and never sins. 21 Do not give heed to all the words that people say, so that you will not hear how your slave reviles[a] you. 22 For you know[a] that often you yourself[b] have also reviled others.

16a The verb שׁמם *šmm* hitpolel (on the assimilation of ת *t* see GKC §54c) in this passage is usually translated something like "destroy yourself." Yet in all other OT occurrences (Isa 59:16; 63:5; Dan 8:27; Ps 143:4; cf. Sir 43:24) it means "be astonished, dismayed, stiffened." This sense can also be assumed with 𝕲 (ἐκπλαγῇς), 𝕾 (ܬܬܡܗ *ttmh*), and 𝖁 (*obstupescas*). In the context the "surprise" then consists in the fact that a person goes down in spite of his "righteousness" and "wisdom" (cf. v. 15). On this problem cf. R. N. Whybray, "Qoheleth the Immoralist? (Qoh. 7:16-17)," in Gammie et al., eds., *Israelite Wisdom*, 197ff.

17a Literally: "when your time has not (yet) come."

18a Or: "avoids all of that"?—יצא * yṣʾ* with accusative (אֶת *ʾet*) in the OT usually means "go out of something" (cf. Gen 44:4; Exod 9:29, 33, etc.); cf. 𝕲: ἐξελεύσεται and 𝕾, where ܢܩܦ *nqp* is probably miscopied from ܢܦܩ *npq*. In the Mishnah, however, יצא *yṣʾ* can also mean "fulfill the duty" (cf. Ehrlich; Podechard; Gordis; Galling; Whitley, *Koheleth*, 67; Whybray, "Qoheleth the Immoralist?" 200–201; Fox); cf. 𝖁: *nihil neglegit*. (In Dan 10:20 absolute יצא *yṣʾ* is perhaps used in the sense of "be finished with someone/something").

19a Since the verb עזז *ʿzz* seems to be intransitive ("be strong"; cf. Whitley, *Koheleth*, 67; contra Gordis; Murphy), the formulation (עזז *ʿzz* with the preposition ל *lĕ-*) is probably ambiguous: does wisdom prove its strength *for* the wise man, that is, in his favor (cf. 8:1ff. and 𝖁: *confortabit*), or *opposite* him, that is, *against* him (cf. 7:23ff.)? 4QQohᵃ (תעזר *tʿzr*) and 𝕲 (βοηθήσει) seem to set aside secondarily the intended ambiguity: "wisdom helps the wise man" (cf. Crenshaw; Murphy).

20a Or: "19 *This* wisdom . . . . 20 *that* no man on earth is (so) just. . . ."

21a The spectrum of meaning of קלל *qll* piel runs from "declare someone 'light,' i.e., despicable, insignificant, meaningless" "make the person despicable," to "curse, damn." "*qll* pi. is the most common verb for mocking and reviling speech by which one who feels uncertain or weak seeks to elevate oneself above another" (C. A. Keller, "קלל *qll* to be light," *TLOT* 3:1142–43).

22a Or: "21 . . . *For* you will never hear someone under you speak critically of you, 22 *and yet* you clearly perceive that you . . ." (so Lohfink; Michel)? In v. 22a 𝕲 apparently offers "duae interpretationes eiusdem textus" (Rahlfs, *Septuaginta*, on the passage).

22b Q reads plene written אַתָּה *ʾattâ* for אַתְּ *ʾattā* or אַתְּ *ʾattĕ* (K).

This section 7:15-22 begins with an observation ("I have seen") that connects the theme "wisdom and foolishness" from vv. 4-12 (cf. vv. 16, 19) with the viewpoint of "righteousness and unrighteousness" (vv. 15-17, 20). Righteousness and wisdom may raise a person's chances of a long and good life, but they cannot guarantee it, as shown by exceptional cases one can experience (v. 15). Therefore, in the conduct of one's life one should do justice to both the rule and the possibility of exceptions by avoiding injustice and foolishness, without displaying exaggerated wisdom and righteousness (vv. 16-18). Verses 19-22 expand and deepen the train of thought of vv. 15-18 in that they move the focus from the effects of just and wise behavior to the limited ability of a person: the opportunities to make wisdom (and righteousness) available to human beings (v. 19) are limited not only because they cannot guarantee a good, long life but also because no one is in a position to behave completely justly (and wisely) (v. 20). With this the advice of vv. 16-18 appears again in a new light: it recommends not simply an opportunistic "happy medium" between wisdom and foolishness, righteousness and unrighteousness, but a realistic insight into human beings in their possibilities and limits to behaving justly and wisely. Verses 21-22 expand the recommendations of vv. 16-18 to the end that people should admit mistakes not only to themselves but also to others—and especially to people dependent on them.

■ **15** The observation formulated in v. 15 deals critically with the conviction that a righteous man lives a long time, whereas an evildoer is quickly destroyed.[1] The reference to (more or less numerous?) individual cases[2] ("there is a righteous man/evildoer . . .") in which this is not true does not so much call into question the connection, assumed in this conviction, between behavior and result as such, as it points out that we have here at best a rule to which there are also exceptions and not an absolute and seamlessly valid conformity to a law. The formulation here that a righteous man is destroyed *in* his

righteousness, whereas an evildoer lives a long time *in* his evil, can be understood both in the sense that in certain circumstances a person may be destroyed *in spite of* his righteousness or, as the case may be, *in spite of* his evil, and in the sense that he is destroyed *because* of his righteousness or lives a long time *because* of his evil[3] (cf. 8:8, 10-14). The advice that follows in vv. 16-18 presupposes that the statements made in v. 15 about righteousness and evil are correspondingly true for wisdom and folly.

■ **16-17** Since one must always deal with "surprising" exceptions to the rule of the "deed-result connection," it seems to behoove one not to strive in exaggerated fashion for righteousness and wisdom (v. 16).[4] Yet all too frequently unrighteous behavior and foolishness can also lead to premature death and are therefore not to be recommended (v. 17). It is notable in v. 17 that foolish behavior, unlike unrighteousness (as well as righteousness and wisdom in v. 16), is not more precisely defined ("too often"). This may indicate that the text holds foolishness—as opposed to unrighteousness—to be fully avoidable.

Read only for itself, 7:16-17 seems like the purely opportunistic recommendation of a mediocre utilitarian ethic:[5] a person is supposed to behave righteously or unrighteously according to what is useful and expedient for him.[6] Following v. 15, however, vv. 16-17 could also be understood in the sense that people should not only

1 Cf., e.g., Prov 10:3, 24-25, 27-28, 30; 11:5, 8, 21; 12:3, 7, 12-13, 21; 13:6, 9, 21, 25; 14:11, 32; cf. also Prov 2:21-22; 3:33; 4:19-20; Job 4:7ff.; 8:8ff.; 11:13ff.; 15:20ff.; 18:5ff.; 20:4ff.; as well as Psalms 1; 37. On the so-called deed-result connection cf. Bernd Janowski, "Die Tat kehrt zum Täter zurück: Offene Fragen im Umkreis des 'Tun-Ergehen-Zusammenhangs,'" *ZThK* 91 (1994) 247-71.

2 Cf. Michel, *Untersuchungen*, 195.

3 Cf. Jenni, *Präpositionen*, 1:356-57.

4 According to Whybray, "Qoheleth the Immoralist?" 200, v. 16 only warns "against self-righteousness and against pretensions to wisdom" (cf. also G. R. Castellino, "Qohelet and His Wisdom," *CBQ* 30 [1968] 24). Fox objects to this with justification: "while *tithakkam* can mean 'pretend to wisdom,' it is doubtful that *těhi ṣaddiq* can mean 'claim to be righteous.' Moreover, this interpretation creates an awkward imbalance between a warning not to *pretend* to be something (v. 16a) and a warning not to *be* some-

thing (v. 17a)." "Pretensions to wisdom" are marked in Prov 3:7; 26:12, 16; 28:11 with the expression "to be wise in one's own eyes."

5 Qoh 7:16-17 is distinguished from the maxim of a "happy medium" (cf. Hesiod, *Works and Days* 693; or Aristotle, *Eth. nic.* 1106b-7a; cf. Schwienhorst-Schönberger, *Nicht im Menschen*, 171; further examples in Wölfel, *Luther und die Skepsis*, 71-72 n. 1; Braun, *Kohelet*, 129-30) in that here the "right measure" is not represented as "wisdom" and "virtue"; rather, "wisdom" and "righteousness" are themselves recommended only "in moderation."

6 Thus Eberhard Wölfel (*Luther und die Skepsis: Eine Studie zur Kohelet-Exegese Luthers* [FGLP X:12; Munich: Chr. Kaiser, 1958] 73), for example, calls Qoh 7:16-17 a "bankruptcy of ethics": the text recommends an "immorality that is so scrupulous as to place good and evil equally in one's own service" (similarly, e.g., Barton).

orient themselves toward the rule that righteousness and wisdom are necessary for a good, long life (v. 17), but should also take into consideration the fact that this rule is not true without exceptions (v. 16).[7]

■ **18** This verse is ambiguously formulated. If one understands by "the one" and "the other" righteousness or wisdom and unrighteousness or foolishness, then the result is the recommendation sometimes to be righteous but sometimes unrighteous (or sometimes wise but sometimes foolish)—according to which one at the moment promises the greatest usefulness. Against this, however, is the unqualified warning against foolishness in v. 17 ("do not be a fool," not: "do not behave foolishly too often" or something similar). From that standpoint "the one" and "the other" in v. 18 may refer rather to the two pieces of advice in v. 16 and v. 17: one should avoid both exaggerated righteousness and wisdom (v. 16) as well as too frequent unrighteousness and foolishness altogether (v. 17). To what extent the fear of God helps one do justice to both recommendations (v. 18b) is not clear at first glance.[8] Verse 20 (with a look back to chap. 3) suggests that for human beings the fear of God contains a realistic estimation of one's possibilities (cf. v. 17) and limits (cf. v. 16) in behaving "wisely" and "justly." The "fear of God" is then, in any case, to be distinguished from "righteousness" and "wisdom" and ranked above them. Thus the tendency to identify these three entities, which is also evident in, among other places, Proverbs 1–9 and in Sirach, must appear highly problematic.[9]

■ **19** According to v. 19 wisdom, unlike righteousness, seems to be able to reliably secure human life, because "for the wise man wisdom is stronger than ten rulers in the city." Like vv. 11-12, this assertion reveals the great self-confidence of "wise men" with regard to those in positions of power—but also a secret admiration of their "strength," which they seek to claim for themselves and even surpass (cf. 8:1ff.; 9:13ff.; Prov 21:22; 24:5). Verse 19 can, nonetheless, also be understood in the sense that wisdom proves to be "strong" not for the benefit of the wise man but vis-à-vis him and against him (cf. 7:23ff.). Through this ambiguity of v. 19 the self-confidence of the "wise man" is already critically called into question.

■ **20** This verse expressly contradicts this self-confidence: "Errare humanum est"; no one never makes a mistake.[10] (The verb חטא *ḥṭʾ* can be understood both in the ethical-religious sense of "to sin" and in the "profane" meaning of "to make a mistake"; see above on 2:26.) To such "mistakes," however, the "wise man" is also susceptible. Therefore, not even his (supposed) "strength" can protect him from unhappiness.

In the present section, what is said in vv. 15-18 is in retrospect critically called into question and relativized by vv. 19-20, as vv. 16-17 in 3:16-21 were by vv. 19-21: if no one is fully "righteous," then humankind cannot be divided as neatly and cleanly between the "just" and the "unjust" as is presupposed in v. 15 (cf. v. 20: אָדָם אֵין צַדִּיק . . . *ʾādām ʾên ṣaddîq, . . .* "no man is [so] just, . . ." with v. 15: . . . יֵשׁ צַדִּיק *yēš ṣaddîq, . . .* "there is a righteous man . . ."). In this way also, however, the observation that human behavior and its result do not always agree in a "just" way loses some of its offensiveness.[11]

Read with the hindsight of v. 20, the advice of vv. 16-

---

7   R. Lux, "Der 'Lebenskompromiss–ein Wesenszug im Denken Kohelets? Zur Auslegung von Koh 7,15-18," in J. Hausmann and H.-J. Zobel, eds., *Alttestamentlicher Glaube und biblische Theologie: FS H. D. Preuss* (Stuttgart: Kohlhammer, 1992) 267–78.

8   Verse 18b is often excluded as an "orthodox" addition that critically amends vv. 16-18a; cf., e.g., Volz; Budde; McNeile; Barton; Michel.

9   Cf. H.-P. Stähli, "ירא *yrʾ* to fear," *TLOT* 2:577: "Expressions for 'fear of God' . . . occur in wisdom texts variously in par. to *tām* 'right,' *yāšār* 'upright,' *ṣaddîq* 'righteous,' *sûr mēraʿ* 'to keep oneself from evil,' *śnʾ raʿ* 'to hate evil' (cf. Prov 3:7; 8:13; 10:27; Job 1:1, 8; 4:16; 28:28; also Psa 34:12, 15; 2 Sam 23:3; in opposition to *rāšāʿ* 'guilty' in Prov 10:27)." "*Yirʾat yhwh* parallels wisdom terms closely, esp. in the collection of sayings in Prov 1-9, and can also be used as a synonym of *dáʿat* 'knowledge' (cf. Prov 1:7, 29; 2:5; 9:10; 15:33; also Isa 11:2; 33:6; Job 28:28 . . .)" (ibid., 576). For Sirach cf. the programmatic introductory chaps. 1-2.

10   Cf. esp. 1 Kgs 8:46; Ps 14:1, 3; but also, e.g., Gen 6:5/8:21; Job 4:17ff.; 14:4; 15:14ff.; 25:4ff.; Prov 20:9; Sir 8:5; 19:16; Pss 51:7; 143:2; Mic 7:2; Isa 57:1; 59:4; Jer 5:1. On Greek analogies see Braun, *Kohelet*, 130 n. 416; on ancient Near Eastern parallels cf. Schwienhorst-Schönberger, *Nicht im Menschen*, 172–73 n. 73.

11   Thus, e.g., Eliphaz in Job 4–5 also points out that ultimately no one is "righteous" before God (4:17ff.), in order to be able to explain the fate of Job—whom at this stage of the dialogue he still holds to be "God-fearing" and "righteous" (4:6ff.; cf. 5:17ff.).

18 also now appears in a new light: for if a person in his conduct of life absolutely *cannot* avoid making mistakes and "sinning," he can only strive to be unjust as seldom as possible (v. 17). Being "too righteous" (v. 16) would then consist in closing one's eyes to one's own fallibility and in striving for a completely "sinless" way of life—or at least evoking the external appearance of a faultless and error-free conduct of life. Such excessive righteousness can then easily lead to mercilessness toward other people.

■ **21-22** In view of the foregoing, v. 21 recommends overlooking the mistakes of other people that concern oneself (!)—in the awareness that one has often enough made similar mistakes oneself (v. 22; cf. v. 20).[12] Such forbearance and tolerance of errors is demanded by the text especially of the master toward his slave. Instead of insisting on "righteousness" from him—a "righteousness" that in the present case would protect above all the master's position of power from attack—the master should simply overlook the invective of his slave and not hold himself to be morally superior to him.[13] The text does not say that, conversely, a slave is also supposed to be tolerant of his master's mistakes (as does 1 Pet 2:18-19).

---

12 In the basic structure of the ethical argumentation vv. 21-22 stands close to the NT parable of the unforgiving servant (Matt 18:21ff.; cf. Zimmerli).

13 It is tacitly presupposed that for the master there is no "existence-threatening effect" that comes from the reviling or cursing of the slave (cf. C. A. Keller, "קלל *qll* to be light," *TLOT* 3:1143), though cf. Prov 30:10. By contrast, the advice for the treatment of slaves in Sir 33:25-32, for example, has exclusively the interests of the master in view and presupposes his moral superiority.

7

23   **All this I tested with wisdom. I said, "I will achieve wisdom," but it remained far from me. 24 That which was, is far away, and deep, deep; who could comprehend it? 25 I undertook[a] to understand, to know, and to seek wisdom and knowledge, to understand that wickedness is folly, and lack of understanding is blindness.[b] 26 And now I find that the woman is[a] more bitter than death; she is[b] a snare,[c] her heart a net,[d] her hands fetters. The one who pleases the Deity[e] escapes her, but the sinner is caught by her. 27 See, this is what I found, said Qoheleth: all in all, the knowledge I found was[a] 28 that I was constantly seeking but not finding. Among a thousand I found one man, but I did not find a woman among all of these.[a] 29 See, this alone I found: the Deity made human beings right, but they sought great knowledge.[a]**

25a Literally: "I turned myself around, I and my heart/mind," or (with correction of וְלִבִּי *wĕlibbî* to בְּלִבִּי *bĕlibbî*, thus numerous mss.; see *BHS*): "I turned myself around in/with my heart/mind."

25b As object clauses or double accusatives, רֶשַׁע כֶּסֶל וְהַסִּכְלוּת הוֹלֵלוֹת *rešaʿ kesel wĕhassiklût hôlēlôt* can be connected with לָדַעַת *lādaʿat*; cf. Schoors, *Preacher*, 187–88.

26a On the syntax (מצא *mṣʾ* with a double accusative) cf. N. Lohfink, "War Kohelet ein Frauenfeind? Ein Versuch, die Logik und den Gegenstand von Koh. 7,23–8,1a herauszufinden," in Gilbert, ed., *Sagesse*, 278 n. 66; Schoors, *Preacher*, 188; and esp. Neh 9:8.

26b Or: "More bitter than death is the/that woman who is a snare . . ."; or ". . . the/that woman whose heart is a snare and a net, her hands are fetters"; cf. Schoors, *Preacher*, 48–49, 142.

26c Literally: "catching cord" (or "siege works"?–cf. 9:14 [?]; Lohfink, "War Kohelet," 285–86).

26d Literally: "trawling net."

26e Literally: "who is good before God."

27a Or: "see, this is what I found . . . (testing) one after the other in order to find knowledge (or a result) . . ." (cf. GKC §118q).

28a Or: "in all these [processes of seeking and (not) finding]"?

29a Lohfink, "War Kohelet," 284ff., and K. Baltzer, "Women and War in Qohelet 7:23—8:1a," *HTR* 80 (1987) 131, assume that חִשְּׁבֹנוֹת *ḥiššĕbōnôt* can be understood here (also) in the sense of "siege machines" (cf. 2 Chr 26:15).

The section 7:23-29 offers for the first time since 1:12—2:26 another coherent first-person report on a "test" of Qoheleth, its execution, and its outcome. It is held together above all by the catchwords "wisdom" and "knowledge," "seeking" and "finding/comprehending."[1] The rapid changing of statements about unsuccessful ("not find") and successful ("find") "seeking" processes makes the text seem on first glance highly confusing and contradictory. Yet its train of thought is revealed when one reads it as a critical and ironic discussion with the widespread view that "wisdom" is to be found by everyone who properly "seeks" it[2] and realizes that various concepts or aspects of "wisdom" are taken into consideration at the same time—even, among other things, the "personification" of wisdom as a woman (v. 26).

Verse 23a can be understood as a title for what follows: "All this I tested with wisdom." Verse 23bα ("I said, 'I will achieve wisdom'") then formulates the first test, whose result is stated in vv. 23bβ-24. A second course of investigation is opened up by v. 25. Verse 26, vv. 27-28, and v. 29 ascertain three results that are each introduced with "I find" or "I found" (in varied formulation). In vv. 27-28 two additional partial results can be distinguished with vv. 27b-28a ("all in all the knowledge I

---

1   "Wisdom" (חָכְמָה *ḥokmâ*): vv. 23, 25; "knowledge" (חֶשְׁבּוֹן *ḥešbôn* / חִשָּׁבוֹן *ḥiššābôn*): vv. 25, 27, 29; "seeking" (בקשׁ *bqš* piel): vv. 25, 28, 29; "finding/comprehending" (מצא *mṣʾ*): vv. 26, 27 [2x], 28 [3x], 29.

2   Cf., e.g., Sir 51:26: "She [wisdom] is close to those

who seek her, and those who give themselves to her will find her" (after the German translation of G. Sauer); cf. further, e.g., Prov 2:4-5; Sir 4:12-13; 6:27; 51:13ff., 26-27, as well as Prov 8:17; 14:6.

found . . .") and v. 28b ("Among a thousand I found only one man . . ."). Here vv. 27b-28a are connected via the key word "knowledge" with v. 29, and v. 28b via the key word "woman" with v. 26. In order to make clear the structure of the text and the key-word connections between its parts, I repeat the translation here in a presentation organized to emphasize some key words:

23 All this I tested with WISDOM.
I said, "I will achieve wisdom" ("become WISE").
but it remained far from me.
24 That which was, is far away, and deep, deep;
who could comprehend ("*find*") it?
25 I undertook to understand, to know, and to *seek* WISDOM and KNOWLEDGE,
to understand that wickedness is folly, and lack of understanding is blindness.
26 And now I *find* [or: comprehend]:
The *WOMAN* is more bitter than death;
she is a snare,
her heart a net, her hands fetters.
The one who pleases the Deity escapes her,
but the sinner is caught by her.
27 See, this is what I *found*, said Qoheleth:
all in all, the KNOWLEDGE I *found* was
28 that I was constantly *seeking* but not *finding*.
Among a thousand I *found* one *MAN* [or: *HUMAN BEING*],
but I did not *find* a *WOMAN* among all of these.
29 See, this alone I *found*:
the Deity made *HUMAN BEINGS* right,
but they *sought* great KNOWLEDGE.

■ **23** In v. 23 "wisdom" is both the instrument of the "test" (בְחָכְמָה *baḥokmâ*, "with wisdom")[3] and its object (אֶחְכָּמָה *ʾeḥkāmâ*, "I want to achieve wisdom" or "become wise"). As an instrument, "wisdom" is to be tested through its use. Yet the problem of this test consists in the fact that wisdom—as instrument and as object of the probe—evades one's grasp: "it (was and) remained far from me."

■ **24** This verse places beside this statement about the far away nature of wisdom the assertion—formulated as a rhetorical question—that past events or circumstances (מַה־שֶּׁהָיָה *mah-šehāyâ*, "what was"; cf. 1:9; 3:15; 6:10) are so "far" and "deep" that they can no longer be "found" or "comprehended" (מצא *mṣ*; cf. 3:11; 7:14; 8:17).[4] In terms of content, this takes up the argumentation of 1:11 and 3:11. The paralleling of wisdom's being far away (v. 23) with the past (v. 24) seems to presuppose that "wisdom," which is the topic in v. 23, has something to do with the (distant) past. This is true both of a "wisdom" that understands itself as knowledge of tradition that was taken over from the ancestors and of a "wisdom" that is defined through "creation" and/or "(salvation) history."[5] Both concepts or aspects of "wisdom" are critically called into question in 7:23-24 with reference back to 1:11 and 3:11: *such* "wisdom" is not to be found (cf. 8:16-17 and, e.g., Job 28).[6]

■ **25** Verse 25 introduces a "change of direction" in the investigation (סַבּוֹתִי *sabbôtî*; cf. 2:20) in which wisdom turns from instrument (and object) of the testing to object of the search for knowledge (cf. 1:13/17; 2:3/12). The identification of "wickedness" (רֶשַׁע *rešaʿ*) with "folly" (כֶּסֶל *kesel*) and "lack of understanding" (הַ[סִּכְלוּת] *[has]siklût*) with "blindness" (הוֹלֵלוֹת *hôlēlôt*) signals that we are now dealing with a different concept or a differ-

3 Cf. Jenni, *Präpositionen*, 1:146–47 (*beth instrumenti*), as well as 1:13 and 2:1.
4 See A. R. Ceresko, "The Function of Antanaclasis (מצא 'to find' // מצא 'to reach, overtake, grasp') in Hebrew Poetry, Especially in the Book of Qoheleth," *CBQ* 44 (1982) 551–69.
5 According to Sir 39:1 the wise man "seeks out the wisdom of all the ancients" (cf. the prologue to the Greek translation of the book of Sirach). Proverbs 1–9 understands "wisdom" as knowledge of tradition that is passed on by parents to their children (cf. esp. Prov 4:1ff.). And Job's dialogue partners also appeal repeatedly to the experiences and insights of the ancestors (cf. Job 8:9ff.; 15:17ff.; 20:4ff.; 22:15ff.). On the connection of "wisdom" and "creation" cf., e.g., Ps 104:24; Prov 8:22-31; Sir 1:1-10; 24; 42:15ff.; Wis 7:17ff.; on the connection of "wisdom" and "(salvation) history" cf. esp. Sirach 44ff.; Wisdom 10ff..
6 A contrast to Qoh 7:23-24 is found in Sir 4:15-19: "15 Whoever listens to me [wisdom] will judge righteously, and whoever pays attention to me will lodge in my chambers. 16 For while I pretend to be foreign, I walk with him. 17 In the beginning I test

ent aspect of "wisdom" from that in vv. 23-24, namely, the identification of (or at least very close connection between) "wisdom" and "righteousness" (cf. already 7:15-22).[7]

■ **26** This verse formulates a first result of the investigation announced in v. 25 (v. 25: "I undertook to understand, to know, and to seek . . ."; v. 26: "And now I find/comprehend . . ."). This result is, however, disturbing in two respects. First, it is by no means clear, on first glance, what the statements about "the woman" (הָאִשָּׁה *hāʾiššâ*) have to do with "wisdom" and "knowledge," "lack of understanding" and "blindness" or "wickedness." Second, based on the formulation of the text, it is not entirely clear whether it is speaking (1) of "woman as such," that is, of all women in general; (2) of a certain

subclass of women who are more closely defined through the statements introduced with אֲשֶׁר *ʾăšer* (". . . *that* woman *who* is a snare . . ."); or (3) of a "personification" of "folly" or "wisdom" as "woman."[8] We must accept that the text is intentionally ambiguous and is supposed to challenge its readers to work through the various possibilities of interpretation of v. 26 (cf. 8:1), keeping in mind the preceding and following contexts.

1. If one reads v. 26a as a statement about "the whole female sex" (Lauha), the result of this search for "wisdom and knowledge" (v. 25) is not without a certain irony (cf. Lauha; Fox): The effort toward a "wisdom education as the way to moral perfection" leads above all to the knowledge that for the man "the woman" is dangerous.[9] If one understands the expressions "the one who

him with temptations (נסיונות *nsywnwt*); afterward his heart [or: mind] will be filled with me. 18 I will let him walk again happily and reveal my secrets to him. 19 When he goes astray, I will disown him" (after the German translation of G. Sauer, *JSHRZ* III.5). In contrast to Qoh 7:23-24, here wisdom is not the means or object but the subject of the "testing" and the entire educational process (v. 17). During this process, the supposedly near wisdom does not prove to be "far away"; rather, the supposedly "foreign" wisdom proves to be near (v. 16). Cf. also the key words בקש *bqš* and מצא *mṣʾ* in context (Sir 4:12-13). Wisdom is "far" (רחוקה *rḥwqh*) "from mockers," according to 15:8; by contrast, according to 51:26 she is "near" (קרובה *qrwbh*) to those who seek (למבקשיה *lmbqšyh*) her, and she finds (מוצא *mwṣʾ*) those who give themselves to her."

7   Cf. also programmatically Prov 1:2-3 and, e.g., Proverbs 10, as well as Job 28:28; Sir 1:14ff.; Wisdom 1ff.; and Socrates' identification of "virtue" with "knowledge" (see also, e.g., Gernot Böhme, *Der Typ Sokrates* [Frankfurt am Main: Suhrkamp, 1988] 79–90). That in Qoh 7:25 "theses of the wisdom tradition are intended that assert wisdom education as the way to moral perfection" is also assumed, for example, by Lohfink, "War Kohelet ein Frauenfeind?" 275 n. 53.

8   Cf. on (1), e.g., Lauha; Hans-Peter Müller, "Neige der althebräischen 'Weisheit'; Zum Denken Qohäläts," *ZAW* 90 (1978) 238–64: 252; Lohfink, "War Kohelet ein Frauenfeind?"; Baltzer, "Women and War"; Michel, *Untersuchungen,* 225–38; Schwienhorst-Schönberger, *Nicht im Menschen,* 173–80; on (2) cf., among others, Zimmerli; Crenshaw; Murphy; Loretz, *Qohelet,* 115ff., 205; I. Riesener, "Frauenfeindschaft im Alten Testament? Zum Verständnis

von Qoh 7,25-29," in Diesel et al., eds., *Jedes Ding,* 193–207; on (3) cf., on the one hand, Allgeier ("Frau Torheit"; cf. Lohfink, "War Kohelet ein Frauenfeind?" 261–62), on the other, T. Krüger, "'Frau Weisheit' in Koh 7,26?" *Bib* 73 (1992) 394–403, repr. in Krüger, *Kritische Weisheit,* 121–30. The idea that "the woman" in v. 26 functions as "a figure of premature death" (Ogden) seems rather unlikely.

9   Lohfink, "War Kohelet ein Frauenfeind?" 274 n. 53. For corresponding misogynistic tendencies in contemporary early Jewish wisdom cf. Sir 25:24 ("From a woman sin had its beginning, and because of her we all die") or 42:13-14 ("From a garment comes a moth, and from a woman comes the wickedness of another woman. Better is the badness of a man than the friendliness of a woman; and a daughter makes more horror than all shame") (after the German translation of G. Sauer; cf. also Patrick W. Skehan and Alexander A. Di Lella, *The Wisdom of Ben Sira* [AB 39; Garden City, N.Y.: Doubleday, 1987] 90ff.). For early Hellenistic philosophy cf. Lohfink, "War Kohelet ein Frauenfeind?" 259 (with source references): "When the philosopher Diogenes was once asked what was the worst thing in life, he answered, 'a good-looking woman.' Once he saw women who were hanging on a tree. Then he cried out, 'Oh, if only all trees bore such fruit!' Of beautiful hetaerae he said that they are comparable to a deadly drink of honey." Cf. also Braun, *Kohelet,* 70–71 n. 180; Schwienhorst-Schönberger, *Nicht im Menschen,* 180 with n. 104.

pleases God" (טוב לפני הָאֱלֹהִים *ṭôb lipnê hāʾĕlōhîm*) and "sinner" (חוֹטֵא *ḥôṭēʾ*) in v. 26b in the "ethical" sense, then the "moral perfection" of the "wise man" consists in his not letting himself be caught by "the woman." If, however, one assumes that these expressions have no "ethical" meaning here ("to whom God is well disposed/who has good luck" or "whose life is a failure/who has bad luck"; see above on 2:26), v. 26b displays the limits of "moral perfection" through "wisdom education": only God can preserve a person (= a man) from the dangers of "the woman" (cf. Whybray); he himself has no control over this. In any case, as a statement about "the woman," v. 26 is plainly in tension with the exhortation of 9:9 to enjoy life with[10] a woman whom one loves (if one does not want to assume that "the love of women" belongs there "to the deceptive vanities of life" that were extolled with the bitter "irony" of the pessimist).[11] One can then either explain this tension redaction-historically by assigning 7:26 to a different "stratum" of the book of Qoheleth from that of 9:9.[12] Or one can attempt to interpret 7:26 as a "quotation" of a "foreign opinion" that in the continuation of the text is critically discussed and corrected.[13]

2. The interpretation of v. 26 as a statement about a certain class or certain type of woman is supported by a number of parallels to the formulations used here in the statements about the "strange woman" in the book of Proverbs (esp. in Proverbs 1–9).[14] Also in this understanding v. 26a can be read as the ironically formulated result of the search for "wisdom and knowledge" (v. 25), and v. 26b can be interpreted both as confirmation and as critique of the concept of a "moral perfection" through "wisdom education." Then the statement of 7:26 would, in any case, not contradict the exhortation of 9:9.

3. After "wisdom" and "folly" were named in (v. 23 and) v. 25 as the goal of Qoheleth's "search," it seems quite possible to see the "personification" of one of

---

10   In Qoh 9:9 the woman is not the means of enjoying life but a partner and sharer in this; thus here she is in no way "in a continuum with good food and sweet wine, with fresh laundry and fragrant hair oil" (thus Lohfink, "War Kohelet ein Frauenfeind?" 260).

11   Thus Lauha, 141; cf. 169.

12   Cf. O. Loretz, "Poetry and Prose in the Book of Qoheleth," in J. C. de Moor and W. G. E. Watson, eds., *Verse in Ancient Near Eastern Prose* (AOAT 42; Kevelaer: Butzon & Bercker; Neukirchen-Vluyn: Neukirchener Verlag, 1993) 155–89.

13   Cf. Lohfink, "War Kohelet ein Frauenfeind?"; Baltzer, "Women and War"; Michel, *Untersuchungen*, 225–38; Backhaus, *Zeit und Zufall*, 234–44; Schwienhorst-Schönberger, *Nicht im Menschen*, 173–80 (with a different delineation of "quotation[s]" and "commentar[ies]" in the text). Lohfink understands v. 26 as an assertion that the woman is "stronger than death" (מַר מִמָּוֶת *mar mimmāwet*). This assertion is tested "inductively" in vv. 27-28, according to Lohfink, and refuted with the proof that women are also mortal: "Of a thousand people (that I closely observed), I have found again (after a certain time) only a single one (all others had already been carried off by death)—and it was not a woman that I found again out of all of these" (thus the paraphrase of v. 28 in Lohfink, "War Kohelet ein Frauenfeind?" 281). Yet both Lohfink's interpretation of v. 28 and his understanding of מַר *mar* as "strong" seem problematic. (On the latter cf.

Mitchell Dahood, "Qohelet and Recent Discoveries," *Bib* 39 [1958] 308ff.; Whitley, *Koheleth*, 68–69; critical thereof is Fox; Backhaus, *Zeit und Zufall*, 240 n. 71.) Baltzer, "Women and War," interprets אֶלֶף *ʾelep* in v. 28 as a military term ("thousands"). Verses 27-29 would then juxtapose the dangerous nature of "the woman" asserted in v. 26 with the actual danger of the military with its "war machines" (חִשְּׁבֹנוֹת *ḥiššĕbōnôt*, v. 29), in which there are "only men" (= אָדָם אֶחָד *ʾādām ʾeḥād?*) but no woman (v. 28). Michel, *Untersuchungen*, 225–38, sees in v. 28b a second misogynistic "quotation," which, together with v. 26, is criticized and rejected by (v)v. 27(-28a) and v. 29 (similarly Backhaus, *Zeit und Zufall*, 234–44). According to Schwienhorst-Schönberger, v. 28a, "in allusion to Cant 3:1-2; 5:6 takes up a coined expression from the language of love," by which—from the perspective of a woman—v. 26 and v. 28b are criticized: "The (female) lover does not find a single man, of whom the men nevertheless assert that he can be found among a thousand" (*Nicht im Menschen*, 178).

14   On v. 26a cf. Prov 2:16-19; 5:3-6, 20-23; 6:24-26; 7:5-27; 22:14; 23:27-28 (as well as Sir 9:1-9; 26:22); on v. 26b cf. esp. Prov 5:22-23; 22:14 (as well as Sir 26:3, 23). Cf. among others Zimmerli; Crenshaw; Murphy; Loretz, *Qohelet*, 115ff., 205; Riesener, "Frauenfeindschaft," 197.

these two entities[15] in "the woman" that he "finds" according to v. 26. Here, after v. 25, the latter part of which speaks of "folly" (כֶּסֶל *kesel*), "lack of understanding" (הַסִּכְלוּת *hassiklût*, determined!), and "blindness" (הוֹלֵלוֹת *hôlēlôt*), "the woman" in v. 26 may initially lead one to think of the "foolish woman" (אֵשֶׁת כְּסִילוּת *ʾēšet kĕsîlût*), whose representation in Prov 9:13-18 coincides in a number of traits with the "strange woman."[16] If one also takes vv. 23-24 into consideration and interprets v. 23a ("all this I attempted with wisdom [בְחָכְמָה *baḥokmâ*, determined!]") as a title for vv. 23-29, it is, however, even more likely to see in "the woman" of v. 26 "(the woman) wisdom" that plays a prominent role in Proverbs 1–9 (cf. Prov 1:20-33; 8:1–9:6, as well as Sirach 24). In Sir 6:24ff. she comes with attributes quite similar to those of "the woman" of Qoh 7:26a:[17]

24 (𝔊) Squeeze your feet into *her fetters* (πέδας)
  and into her yoke your neck.
25 (𝔖) Bend your shoulders and carry her,
  and do not detest her advice
. . . .
27 Ask and research, seek and find,
  and when you get hold of her, do not let her go.
28 For at last you will find the rest she gives,
  and for you she will be changed into joy.
29 And for you *her net* (רשתה *ršth*) will become a strong
    defense (מכון עז *mkwn ʿz*),
  and *her bonds* (חבלתה *ḥblth*) a golden robe.
30 Her yoke is an ornament of gold,
  and *her cords* (מוסרתיה *mwsrtyh*) a purple band.
31 You will put her on like a robe of honor,
  and wear her like a splendid crown.[18]

The "pedagogical-didactic" component of the concept of a "personified" wisdom is easily recognizable

here.[19] The process of acquiring knowledge and education is "erotically" intensified; those who devote themselves to "wisdom" are "conquered" and "caught" by her as by a seductive woman. The real compulsions of the educational process ("yoke," "fetters," "cords," etc.) thus appear in a more pleasing light.[20] If one assumes that Qoh 7:26 describes such a picture of "the woman wisdom" as the result of the search for "wisdom and knowledge" (v. 25), this "wisdom" concept is already critically called into question in v. 26: *if* "wisdom" is a "woman" who is as seductive and dangerous as the "strange woman" against whom Proverbs 1–9 repeatedly warns, *then* she is "more bitter than death" (v. 26a). Those who escape her have been fortunate (v. 26b; cf. v. 23b); only a "sinner" lets himself by "caught" and "fettered" by her (v. 26b; cf. v. 29).

■ **27b-28a** In vv. 27-28 the further results of the search for "wisdom and knowledge" (v. 25) are recorded ("I found . . ."). If the translation recommended above is correct, vv. 27b-28a formulate a paradox similar to the Socratic dictum, "I know that I know nothing."[21] *What* Qoheleth "was constantly seeking but not finding" is left open by the text. According to vv. 23-24, one could think here of "wisdom"; according to v. 26, "the woman." If one understands v. 26 as a statement about women in general or a certain type of woman, vv. 27-28a can be read as an ironic relativization of this result of the search for "wisdom and knowledge" (v. 25): if the only result of this search consists in the insight that (certain) women are dangerous for men, this result is as good as no result—especially if one interprets v. 26b in the sense that it is totally beyond one's control whether one (or a man) is caught by "the woman." According to v. 26, however, vv. 27-28a can also be understood to mean that Qoheleth "was constantly seeking but not finding" the

15 Cf., e.g., Preuss, *Einführung*, 63ff. (lit.).
16 Cf. Arndt Meinhold, *Die Sprüche*, part 1: *Sprüche Kapitel 1–15* (ZBK 16, 1; Zurich: Theologischer Verlag, 1991) 158–59; Riesener, "Frauenfeindschaft," 205.
17 See Krüger, "Frau Weisheit," 402–3.
18 After the German translation of Sauer, *JSHRZ* III.5.
19 Cf. here also Meinhold, *Die Sprüche*, 44, as well as Sir 14:20–15:8; 51:13-21. Even today we can still speak of the university as *alma mater* ("fostering mother") and of the "scientific *eros*" (a desire for learning).
20 That the characterization of "the woman" in Qoh 7:26a (without the qualification "more bitter than death") can absolutely be understood as positive is shown by a comparison with Cant 4:4; 6:10; 7:5-6; 8:9-10 or with the Egyptian descriptive song, quoted by Baltzer, "Women and War," 129 n. 8, from Papyrus Harris 500: "My beloved's [mouth] is a bud, / Her breasts are apples of love, / Her arms are . . . / Her brow is a spring-snare of reeds, / And I am the wild goose. . . ."
21 Cf. Gernot Böhme, *Der Typ Sokrates*, 117–29.

woman described there. As a statement about women in general, v. 26 would thereby be negated: it does not stand up to empirical verification. As a statement about "the seductive ['strange'] woman" v. 26 would be ironically called into question by vv. 27-28a: such a woman would be quite desirable but not as easy to find as suggested, for example, by Proverbs 1–9. The same would be true for v. 26 as a statement about "the woman wisdom": she is represented as an erotic and seductive woman but as such is nowhere to be found (cf. vv. 23-24).

■ **28b** The statement that Qoheleth found among a thousand (people) only *one* man (or human being) but not a single woman (v. 28b) seems to reinforce the understanding of v. 26 as a negative statement about women in general: "Among a thousand there is perhaps one person who is as one should be, but that is not a woman" (Galling)—an assertion that is as misogynistic as it is misanthropic.[22] This interpretation of v. 28b is supported by the use of the expression "one in a thousand" in Sir 6:6: "May those whom you greet be many, but may your advising partner be one in a thousand."[23] Thus Qoh 7:28b can be paraphrased: "One finds one person among a thousand [sc. as true friend], but for this, a woman is out of the question."[24]

In the present context, however, v. 28b now becomes readable in a new way that almost changes the misogyny of this statement into its opposite: if Qoheleth found a man but not a woman, this can also be understood according to v. 26 (and vv. 27-28a), namely, in the sense that he found not a single woman who is "more bitter than death" or exhibits the other characteristics named there, but at most some men who fit this description.[25] Hence it seems conceivable that the text in v. 26 and v. 28 takes up two misogynistic topoi and combines them in such a fashion that they get into each other's way (without the text lending itself to an elegant division into "quotations" and "comments"). If, by contrast, one sees in v. 26 an allusion to the "personification" of wisdom as "woman," v. 28b can also be read as a further step in the ideology-critical deconstruction of this concept: the image of "the woman wisdom" is not only frightening and amoral (v. 26) and lacks any basis in reality (vv. 27-28a). It also veils the actual conditions of the professional educational establishment: in seeking after "wisdom" (v. 25), namely, one finds an elite circle ("one in a thousand"!) of "wise" men,[26] but not a single woman (v. 28b).

■ **27a** The ironically critical "play" with misogynistic statements in the text is perhaps also underlined by the

22 Even if v. 28b—in this interpretation—holds the great majority of men to be as bad as women (cf. Gordis; Crenshaw), the difference between men and women is not thereby completely eliminated (thus Whybray). Cf. here, e.g., the well-known anecdotes about Diogenes of Sinope in Diogenes Laertius: "Once he called out: 'Hey! People,' and when they ran up, he hit them with his stick and said: 'I called people, not filth'" (6.32). "By day he lit a light and said: 'I am looking for a person'" (6.41). "When he came home from Olympia and someone asked whether many people had been there, he answered: 'A lot of people, but few human beings'" (6.60; after the German translation of O. Apelt). Cf. also Braun, *Kohelet*, 71 with n. 184. The extent to which Qoh 7:28—thus understood—is supposed to be "a long way from the misanthropic and misogynistic utterances . . . of a Diogenes" (thus Riesener, "Frauenfeindschaft," 202) is not apparent to me.

23 After the German translation of Sauer, *JSHRZ*, III.5. Cf. also Job 9:3; 33:23.

24 Michel, *Untersuchungen*, 231; cf. Lauha. The attempt of V. P. Long to interpret v. 28 as an "expression of

his [Qohelet's] own experience" that "need not to be universalized" seems hardly plausible ("One Man among a Thousand, but Not a Woman among Them All: A Note on the Use of *maṣa* in Ecclesiastes vii 28," in K. D. Schunk and M. Augustin, eds., *"Lasset uns Brücken bauen . . .": Collected Communications to the XVth Congress of the International Organization for the Study of the Old Testament, Cambridge, 1995* [BEAT 42; Frankfurt am Main: Lang, 1998] 109).

25 With Baltzer ("Women and War") and in view of v. 26a one could think specifically of the military activity of men.

26 It is possible that מאלף *mʾlp* was readable in the consonantal text of v. 28b both in the sense of מֵאֶלֶף *mēʾelep* ("a [single] man *among a thousand*," thus 𝔐 and the versions) and in the sense of מְאַלֵּף* **mēʾallēp* ("a *teaching* man, a *teacher*"; cf. אלף *ʾlp* I piel in Job 15:5; 33:33; 35:11; the suffixed piel participle in Job 35:11, however, reads מְלַפֵּנוּ *mallēpēnû*). Then v. 28b would directly state that there are only male teachers of wisdom. In any case, it can hardly be doubted that books like Proverbs and Sirach were written by men for men.

expression "said Qoheleth" in v. 27a, which is unique in the book of Qoheleth (cf. 1:2 and 12:8 in the framework) and is excluded by most commentators as a redactional addition:[27] in 𝔐 "Qoheleth" is presented here, namely, through the feminine verb form (אָמְרָה קֹהֶלֶת *ʾāmĕrâ qōhelet*) clearly as a *woman*. But even if one corrects the text to אָמַר הַקֹּהֶלֶת *ʾāmar haqqōhelet* (cf. 𝔊 and 12:8), the feminine nominal formation קֹהֶלֶת *qōhelet* perhaps contains an indication that the statements, which are at first glance massively androcentric, are not to be taken very seriously in the context.[28]

■ **29** In any case, the result formulated in v. 29 ("this alone I found . . .") then closes the door on any devaluation of women vis-à-vis men: "The Deity made human beings right, but they sought great knowledge." That is, according to Gen 1:27 and 5:1-2 God made human beings "male and female." *To both,* according to Gen 5:3, God gave the name "human being" (אָדָם *ʾādām*; cf. Qoh 6:10). Both have lost their "straightforwardness" and integrity (יָשָׁר *yāšār*) through the search for "great knowledge (חֶשְׁבֹנוֹת *ḥiššĕbōnôt*)" (cf. Genesis 3; 4:17-22; 6:5: מַחְשֶׁבֶת *maḥšĕbōt*)—which, among other things, also led to the "rule" of the man over the woman (Gen 3:16). Thus in regard to primeval history (cf. Whybray), striving for "great knowledge" (cf. v. 25) appears in a questionable light: the search for "wisdom" spoils character—in this sense it definitely has its good side when it fails (vv. 23-24, 27-28).

---

27 Thus, e.g., Lauha, who interprets this (supposed) addition as the distancing of the editor from the misogynistic utterances of Qoheleth; by contrast, according to Michel (*Untersuchungen*, 236) the statement validates the "authority" of Qoheleth vis-à-vis the quotations in v. 26 and v. 28b.

28 Cf. Schwienhorst-Schönberger's interpretation of v. 28a as a "quotation" from the mouth of a woman and his reference to the terminological contacts between v. 28 and Cant 3:1-4; 5:6 (*Nicht im Menschen*, 173–80; cf. also Riesener, "Frauenfeindschaft," 201–2).

8

1 Who is like the wise man,[a] and who knows how to interpret a word?[b] The wisdom of a man lets his face shine, and his hard features are softened.[c]

2 Obey the command of a king,[a] for you have sworn him an oath before God.[b] **3** Do not hasten away from him; do not get involved in something bad,[a] for he can do anything he wants to. **4** For the word of a king has power, and who could say to him: What are you doing? **5** Whoever obeys the command[a] will meet no harm, and the heart of a wise man knows time and judgment.

6 For every matter there is time and judgment, for the evil[a] of a man weighs heavy[b] on him. **7** He does not know what will happen, for who could inform him of what will be?[a] **8** No man has power over the wind,[a] so that he could stop the wind,[b] and no man has power over the day of death. And in war there is no discharge, and injustice cannot save its doers.

9 All this I saw, and I gave attention[a] to everything that was done under the sun: when one man had power over another, it was bad for him.[b][c]

1a The lack of assimilation of the article in כְּהֶחָכָם *kĕheḥākām* is unusual but not impossible (cf. Schoors, *Preacher*, 43–44). A correction to מִי כֹה חָכָם *mî kōh ḥākām* (cf. α' and, e.g., Lohfink: "Who then is the one who knows") seems (as *lectio facilior*) inadvisable. The article here refers to a "generally known, clearly circumscribed, and—for that very reason—more closely defined category of people" (GKC §126l).

1b The verb form יוֹדֵעַ *ywdʿ* can be interpreted as qal (thus 𝔐 and the versions) ("who knows the interpretation of a word/thing") and also as hiphil ("who announces the interpretation").

1c Literally: "the hardness of his face is changed." Instead of the pual יְשֻׁנֶּא *yĕšunneʾ* one can also read piel יְשַׁנֶּא *yĕšanneʾ* (cf. 𝔙): "but power changes/distorts his face." 𝔊 and 𝔖 presuppose וְעַז־פָּנָיו *wĕʿaz-pānāyw* instead of וְעֹז פָּנָיו *wĕʿōz-pānāyw* and יִשָּׂנֵא *yiśśānē* instead of יְשֻׁנֶּא *yĕšunneʾ*: "but one with a hard/defiant/impudent face is hated."

2a Thus with the correction of אֲנִי *ʾănî* to אֶת *ʾet* according to 𝔊 𝔖 (cf. *BHS*). Also possible is a correction of אֲנִי פִּי *ʾănî pî* to אַנְפֵּי *ʾanpê* ("protect yourself before the face of" or "pay attention to the face of [a king]"; cf. Michel, *Untersuchungen*, 94 n. 25; Crenshaw). 𝔐 (אֲנִי פִּי־מֶלֶךְ שְׁמוֹר *ʾănî pî melek šĕmôr*) can be understood at best as an elliptical statement ("I [say]: obey the command of a king") (cf. Lohfink) or interpreted in the sense that אֲנִי *ʾănî*, "I," represents an independent utterance that answers the questions formulated in v. 1 (thus P. Beentjes, "'Who Is Like the Wise?' Some Notes on Qohelet 8,1-15," in Schoors, ed., *Qohelet in Context*, 303–15). In view of the following vetitives (cf. the sequence imperative-vetitive 4:17ff.), the correction of שְׁמוֹר *šĕmôr* to שֹׁמֵר *šômēr* ("I obey the order of a king"; cf. 𝔙) is, by contrast, less probable. The recommendation of *BHK* to read אַתָּה *ʾattâ* instead of אֲנִי *ʾănî* has no support in the textual tradition.

2b Or: "for God has sworn him an oath"; lit.: "and because of an oath of God." For a further possible understanding see the following note.

3a Or: "[v. 2] Obey the order of a king; yet if you are supposed to swear an oath before God, [v. 3] do not be frightened. Go away from him; do not get involved in something bad. . . ."

5a Or: "Whoever obeys the commandment. . . ."

6a Or: "the misfortune." 𝔊 ϑ' α' presuppose דַּעַת *daʿat*, "knowledge," instead of רָעַת *rāʿat*, which probably goes back to a mistaken exchange of ר *r* and ד *d* in the Hebrew original.

6b Literally: "is large."

7a Literally: "how it will be." σ' 𝔖 𝔙 seem to presuppose אֲשֶׁר *ʾăšer*, "what," instead of כַּאֲשֶׁר *kaʾăšer*.

8a Or: "(life) spirit."

8b Or: "(life) spirit."

9a Literally: "I gave my heart." The inf. abs. (וְ)נָתוֹן *(wĕ)nātôn* has here the function of a finite verb; cf. GKC §113z; Schoors, *Preacher*, 178.

9b The Hebrew text leaves open whether the ruler (cf. σ') or the one ruled is intended (cf. 𝔊 𝔖 𝔗, which, like one Hebrew ms., instead of לְרַע לֹו *lĕraʿ lô* read לְהָרַע לֹו *lĕhāraʿ lô*, "in order to harm him").

9c Other possible translations: "There was a time when man had power over man to his detriment [lit.: for the worse for him]";

cf. 𝔙. Or: "All this I saw . . . at a time when man has power over man to his detriment" (temporal accusative; cf. GKC §118i; Schoors, *Preacher*, 189). 𝔊 presupposes אֵת *ʾet* instead of עֵת *ʿēt*: "I gave attention to everything that was done under the sun: that. . . ."

On the delineation and internal structure of this section there is no agreement among commentators.[1] Yet the common themes of the two halves of v. 1 argue against a division between v. 1a and v. 1b (cf. the key words "wise man"–"wisdom"). With the theme "wisdom" v. 1 relates to 7:23, 25, but also contains a number of key words that are taken up again in vv. 2-9.[2] In the context v. 9, with its new formulation in the first person singular ("All this I saw . . ."), could mark a (relatively) new beginning.[3] But since in v. 10 another such new beginning immediately follows ("Then I saw . . ."), v. 9 could be understood rather (with a retrospective זֶה *zeh*, "this") as the closing summary of vv. 1-8.[4] This is also indicated by the repetition in v. 9b of significant key words from the preceding text.[5]

A number of key words from vv. 4-5 are repeated in vv. 6-8 in almost the exact reverse order:

v. 4a	שִׁלְטֹון *šilṭôn*		
v. 4b	מִי יֹאמַר־לֹו *mî yōmar-lô*		
v. 5a	רָע *rāʿ*	יֵדַע *ydʿ*	
v. 5b	עֵת וּמִשְׁפָּט *ʿēt ûmišpāṭ*	יֵדַע *ydʿ*	

v. 6a	עֵת וּמִשְׁפָּט *ʿēt ûmišpāṭ*	
v. 6b	רָעָה *rāʿâ*	
v. 7a	יֵדַע *ydʿ*	
v. 7b	מִי יַגִּיד לֹו *mî yaggîd lô*	
v. 8	שִׁלְטֹון *šilṭôn* / שַׁלִּיט *šallîṭ*	

Corresponding to this in terms of content is the fact that the comments of vv. 1-5 undergo a critical rereading in vv. 6-9 and are almost taken back. From the standpoint of content vv. 1-9 might be divided as follows:

v. 1 Introduction: Praise of the wise man and wisdom

vv. 2-5 The wise man and the king
    vv. 2-3a Admonition for behavior vis-à-vis the king
    vv. 3b-4 Reason 1: The power of the king
    v. 5 Reason 2: The ability of the wise man

vv. 6-8 Critique of vv. 3b-5: Human limits
    v. 6 Time as "judgment" of human evil (on v. 5)
    v. 7 The limits of human wisdom (on v. 5)
    v. 8 The limits of human power (on vv. 3b-4)

v. 9 Conclusion: critique of the rule of man over man

■ 1 This verse formulates a "praise of the wise man":[6] He distinguishes himself through his ability to "interpret" difficult statements or situations (v. 1a). And his wisdom gives him a self-assured and relaxed demeanor (v. 1b).

In the OT the "interpretive" competence of the wise man (v. 1a) plays an important role especially with Joseph (cf. Genesis 40–41) and Daniel (cf. Daniel 2; 4; 5; 7).[7] It is praised by the rulers with whom these men deal (cf. Gen 41:38-39; Dan 2:46ff.). With Joseph as well as

---

1 Cf., e.g., Gordis: vv. 1-9; Fox: vv. 1b-9; Lauha: vv. 2-9; Zimmerli: vv. 1-8; Galling: vv. 2-8; Lohfink: vv. 1b-12a (1b-4, 5-12a); Murphy: vv. 1-17 (1-4, 5-8, 9-15, 16-17).

2 Cf. מִי *mî*, "who": vv. 1a, 4b, 7b; חָכָם *ḥākām*, "wise man": vv. 1a, 5b; יָדַע *ydʿ*, "know": vv. 1a, 5a, b, 7a; דָּבָר *dābār*, "word, thing": vv. 1a, 3a, 4a, 5a; אָדָם *ʾādām*, "man": vv. 1b, 6b, 8a, 9b.

3 Cf. 7:15, 23, 25; 8:10, 16; 9:1, 11, 13.

4 Cf. 3:22; 5:17; 8:17.

5 Cf. on שׁלט *šlṭ*, "have power": vv. 4a, 8a (שִׁלְטֹון *šilṭôn*), 8a (שַׁלִּיט *šallîṭ*); on אָדָם *ʾādām*, "man": vv. 1b, 6b, 8a; on רַע *raʿ*, "bad": vv. 3a, 5a, as well as 6b (רָעַת הָאָדָם *rāʿat hāʾādām*).

6 For comparison, Braun, *Kohelet*, 131 n. 421, quotes from the Greek world Diogenes Laertius 6:12 (Antisthenes): "For the wise man nothing is strange or unfathomable."

7 In these texts we find key words corresponding to פֵּשֶׁר *pēšer* in Hebrew: פתר *ptr* ("interpret"): Gen 40:8, 16, 22; 41:8, 12-13, 15; פִּתְרֹון *pittārôn* ("interpretation"): Gen 40:5, 8, 12, 18; 41:11; and in Aramaic: פשר *pšr* ("interpret"): Dan 5:12, 16; פִּשְׁרָא *pišrāʾ* ("interpretation"): Dan 2:4-7, 9, 16, 24-26, 30, 36, 45; 4:3-4, 6, 15-16, 21; 5:7-8, 12, 15-17, 26; 7:16.

with Daniel, however, the text states emphatically that the "interpretations" conveyed by them go back to God (cf., in addition to Gen 41:38-39 and Dan 2:46ff., also Gen 40:8; 41:16; Dan 2:18-19, 21-23, 27-28, 47). On this basis Qoh 8:1a can also be read as a statement about the incomparable wisdom of God that is not at human disposal (cf. Dan 2:20ff.).[8] In the context, finally, v. 1a can also be understood as a suggestion to the reader that the following "word" requires an especially careful "interpretation."[9]

The idea that wisdom bestows on a person a self-confident and relaxed appearance (v. 1b)[10] is also found—with reference to "the heart" or "the mind"—in, for example, Sir 13:24-25[25-26]: "The heart of a person changes his face (לב אנוש ישנא פניו *lb ʾnwš yšnʾ pnyw*), both for good and for bad. The sign of a good heart is a radiant face (פנים אורים *pnym ʾwrym*), but brooding sorrows evoke arduous thoughts."[11]

The Hebrew consonantal text of Qoh 8:1b, however, is ambiguous (cf. n. 1c on the translation) and can also be read as a juxtaposition of wisdom and power: whereas wisdom can make a person's face "shine," through power it is "distorted." The connection of wisdom and power, which is totally unproblematic for Joseph and for Daniel, is thereby critically called into question.

Thus v. 1 as a whole can be read superficially as praise of the wise man who is able to interpret and is in a superior way relaxed. Below the surface, however, the text also points to the limits of wisdom. First, it raises the question of how human wisdom is related to God's wisdom; second, the connection of wisdom and power seems problematic.

■ **2-3a** Verses 2-3a turn in direct address (imperative, vetitive, and jussive) to the reader, who is confronted here with an admonition that is in several respects unclear and ambiguous:

1. Verse 2a can be understood both as a request to "observe" a king's command—that is, obey him in every case (cf., e.g., Prov 24:12)—and as an admonition to "pay attention to" the command (lit.: "the mouth") or, depending on the emendation of the text, the face of a king, in order to know, for example, the favorable time for the pursuit of one's own concerns or to be able to escape the ruler's dangerous moods (for such a rather "opportunistic" attitude toward the ruler, cf., e.g., Sir 8:1; 9:13). Both points of view are explicitly linked, for example, in the Aramaic Ahiqar sayings (10.6-10; cf. also Qoh 10:4):

6 Do not extinguish the word of the king;
  may it burn in your [heart]![12]
  Soft is the speech of the king (but at the same time) more cutting and powerful than a double-edg[ed] knife.

7 Look! Before you is something bristling [ag]ainst the ki[ng]: do not make an appearance! His rage] is more violent than lightning! Take care 8 that he does not make it fla[re] up over your me[mb]ers and you pass away before your time.

9 [Thus is the wra]th of the king: when something is ordered of you, it is a blazing [f]ire. Act quickly, [so t]hat it will not be ignited [o]ver you and make you hide your hands.[13]

---

8 "Apart from polemical statements like Isa. 31:2 and Job 9:4, the predicate 'wise' as applied to God is both rare and late. Hymnic passages such as Jer. 10:6f.; Job 12:13 . . . and Dnl. 2:10b praise the *chokhmāh* and *gᵉbhûrāh* of God. Dnl. bases the ascription on the inspiration Daniel has just received, through which God has shown himself to be the revealer of 'deep and mysterious things,' in this case an apocalyptic secret" (H.-P. Müller, "חכם *chākham*," *TDOT* 4:384).

9 Thus, e.g., Schwienhorst-Schönberger, *Nicht im Menschen*, 181.

10 By contrast, Lohfink assumes that v. 1b was "taken from a larger literary structure" in the context of

which "'his face' was not that of the knowing advisor, but rather that of the advice-seeking king"; cf. Prov 16:14-15. Yet in the present context, this understanding of v. 1b is unlikely.

11 Based on the translation of Georg Sauer, *JSHRZ* III.5.

12 "The expression means that the king's word is not supposed 'to leave one cold' but drive one to action" (Ingo Kottsieper, *TUAT* 3:336 note).

13 "The expression probably refers to a marking of the hands or arms of a disobedient servant" (Kottsieper, *TUAT* 3:337 note).

10 [Ful]fill the word of the king with all your heart.
[H]ow does wood argue with fire?
Meat with a knife? A person with a [king?][14]

2. In v. 2b שְׁבוּעַת אֱלֹהִים šĕbûʿat ʾĕlōhîm can designate both an oath of God (subj. gen.) and an oath before or with God (obj. gen.).[15] The first case could involve a sacred legitimation of the king through a divine oath; the second, an oath of allegiance to a king (cf. Josephus, *Ant.* 12:1), an oath in court, or the "ὅρκος βασιλικός, that, according to Egyptian custom, was to be sworn before the God-king at the beginning of a trial" (Lauha; cf. Galling).[16]

3. The relationship of v. 2b to v. 2a is syntactically ambiguous. Is v. 2b to be read as the basis of v. 2a (וְעַל דִּבְרַת wĕʿal dibrat = "and because of . . .")? Or does v. 2b begin a new admonition that extends to v. 3a (cf. *BHS*)? In the second case one must then also ask whether v. 2b follows v. 2a copulatively ("and because of/concerning[17] . . .") or adversatively ("but because of/concerning . . .").

4. In v. 3aα the verb בהל bhl niphal can be understood both in the sense of "take fright" and in the sense of "hurry" (cf. *HALOT* s.v.: "1. to be horrified, to be out of one's senses . . . 2. make haste . . .").[18] In the first case מִפָּנָיו mippānāyw can be connected both with אַל־תִּבָּהֵל ʾal-tibbāhēl ("Do not be frightened before his face! Go [away]!") and with תֵּלֵךְ tēlēk ("Do not be frightened! Go away from him!"). In the second case אַל־תִּבָּהֵל ʾal-tibbāhēl can be connected both with what precedes ("If it's a question of swearing an oath with God, do not hurry yourself!") and with what follows ("Do not be in a hurry to go away from him!").

5. עמד בְּדָבָר רָע ʿmd bĕdābār rāʿ (v. 3aβ) can mean both "stay with a bad word (of the king)" and "get involved in something bad" (cf. *HALOT* s.v. עמד ʿmd).

Thus, in sum, vv. 2-3a can be interpreted essentially in three ways: First, as a religiously based exhortation to render obedience to a king:

Obey the command of a king,
and because of the oath of God (that God has sworn
to him or that you have sworn to him).
Do not hasten away from him;
do not get involved in something bad . . .

Second, as an exhortation to render obedience to a king—even when he demands an oath:

Obey the command of a king,
and (even) concerning an oath with God [or: the
gods—which he demands from you]:
Do not hasten away from him;
do not get involved in something bad . . .

Third, as an exhortation to render obedience to a king—except when he demands an oath:

Obey the command of a king,
but concerning an oath with God [or: the gods—which
he demands from you]:
do not be frightened. Go away from him [or: do not
be frightened before him. Go away . . .];
do not get involved in something bad [or: do not stay
with something bad] . . .

---

14 After the translation of Kottsieper, *TUAT* 3:336–37.
15 In the latter sense cf. שְׁבוּעַת יהוה šĕbûʿat yhwh in Exod 22:10; 2 Sam 21:7; 1 Kgs 2:43 (see *HALOT* s.v.).
16 For the first see, e.g., Frank Crüsemann, "The Unchangeable World: The 'Crisis of Wisdom' in Koheleth," in Willy Schottroff and Wolfgang Stegemann, eds., *God of the Lowly: Socio-Historical Interpretations of the Bible* (Maryknoll, N.Y.: Orbis, 1984) 71; cf. Pss 89:4; 110:4 as well as Theognis 823–24 (Braun, *Kohelet*, 131 n. 422): "Do not promote a tyrant in the hope of personal advantage; also do not kill one, bearing in mind a divine oath." For the second see, e.g., Schwienhorst-Schönberger, *Nicht*
im Menschen, 182: "a kind of oath of office." Cf., e.g., the oath of soldiers ("the oath they were accustomed to swear at the proclamation of the kings": Austin, *Hellenistic World*, 373) in Polybius (15.25.3ff.) on the occasion of the ascent to power of Ptolemy V (204 B.C.E.).
17 On the meaning of עַל דִּבְרַת ʿal dibrat ("because of, concerning") see Whitley, *Koheleth*, 36; Schoors, *Preacher*, 123.
18 Only the second meaning could be assumed if one were to read the piel instead of the niphal (cf. *BHK*; *BHS*; Qoh 5:1; 7:9).

The semantic ambiguity of this admonition is in contradiction to its pragmatic function: the text does not make clear to its addressees how they are supposed to behave. The opportunism of a courtly wisdom is thereby caricatured and its internal contradictions exposed: the wise man sees himself as the sovereign master of the situation (cf. v. 1) and yet is only the king's plaything and the object of his moods. The wise man believes (or professes) that he can remain true to certain principles (especially regarding his religion), yet these principles are by no means clear and flexibly interpretable from the standpoint of opportunity.

If the "oath of God" is related to the oath of allegiance that was to be sworn to the ruler in Alexandria (personally or in the Jewish province before a Ptolemaic official), then the text possibly addresses a problem that in its time was ticklish and controversial (cf. also 9:2).[19] A refusal of the oath of allegiance could have been motivated both politically and religiously, the latter especially if the oath was to be sworn with the gods of the ruler.[20] With its ambiguity, Qoh 8:2-3a reflects perhaps the various contemporary attitudes toward the oath of allegiance.

■ **3b-4** In the form of several assertions and a rhetorical question, these verses substantiate the exhortations of vv. 2-3a.

It is not entirely clear whether the topic here is God or the king named in v. 2a. The latter could be supported by the fact that v. 4a takes up again the key word מֶלֶךְ *melek*; yet "king" can also be a predicate of God. Supporting the first view is the fact that vv. 3b and 4b

contain statements that in other places in early Jewish literature are found only in reference to God; yet we could also have here a reflection of the tendency toward the "deification" of the king in the Hellenistic ideology of sovereignty.[21] (This ambivalence of vv. 3b-4 corresponds to the ambiguity of the expression מִצְוָה *miṣwâ* in v. 5a: is the "command" of a king intended here, or the "commandment" of God? Or does מִצְוָה *miṣwâ* refer to the exhortation of vv. 2-3a itself?)

Read as a reference to the unlimited power of the king, vv. 3b-4 can support both an exhortation to obedience and an admonition of caution regarding him. If one relates the statements of this section to God, however, then its point may well lie in strengthening one's readiness to refuse obedience to the king in religious matters.

■ **5** Whereas vv. 3b-4 make statements about the king or God, v. 5 turns to the wise man who observes a command (of the king) or a commandment (of God). The behavior recommended in vv. 2-3a (cf. the taking up of the key words שׁמר *šmr* from v. 2a and דָּבָר רָע *dābār rāʿ* from v. 3aβ) is now placed into the context of a certain ethical attitude and motivated by it.

It is not quite clear in v. 5a whether ידע דָּבָר רָע *ydʿ dābār rāʿ* means "to know a bad thing" or "to get to know/experience a bad thing"; that is, whether the sentence is aimed at the presuppositions of the recommended behavior or at its consequences. In v. 5b the expression עֵת וּמִשְׁפָּט *ʿēt ûmišpāṭ* is ambiguous. Does מִשְׁפָּט *mišpāṭ* here have a juridical meaning ("law," "judgment," "trial"), or does it aim more generally at the (temporal)

---

19 If, moreover, the the book of Qoheleth came into being around 204 B.C.E., shortly after the coming to power of Ptolemy V, then it was dealing with a current problem, since the oath of allegiance to the king was to be sworn at the beginning of his reign.

20 For Herod's time, see Josephus, *Ant.* 15.10.4. On the basic religiously or philosophically motivated skepticism concerning the swearing of oaths, cf., e.g., the references in Ulrich Luz, *Matthew 1–7* (CC; Minneapolis: Fortress Press, 1989) 314–15. From the immediate environment of the book of Qoheleth cf. Sir 23:9-11; 27:14. On the various possible conflicts between religious and political loyalty into which a Jewish "wise man" could fall in service to a foreign king, cf., e.g., Daniel 1; 3; 6.

21 On v. 3b cf. Pss 115:3; 135:6; Dan 4:17 𝔊; on v. 4b cf. Sir 36:10; Job 36:22-23; cf. further v. 4a with Ps 33:6-9. In view of the "theological" dimension of the statements in vv. 3b-4 one can hardly interpret them—related to the king—in the sense of a "demythologizing of Ptolemaic divine kingship" (thus Lohfink). Regarding (at least the tendency toward) the divination of the king in court ceremony, cf., e.g., the wish "May the king live forever!" in 1 Kgs 1:31; Neh 2:3; Dan 2:4; 3:9; 5:10; 6:7, 22. On the Hellenistic ruler cult see, e.g., Gehrke, *Geschichte des Hellenismus*, 80–81, 167, 191; F. W. Walbank, "Könige als Götter: Überlegungen zum Herrscherkult von Alexander bis Augustus," *Chiron* 17 (1987) 365ff.

"order" of experienced reality?[22] It would also be possible to understand עֵת וּמִשְׁפָּט ʿēt ûmišpāṭ as a hendiadys in the sense of "the proper time" or "the proper time and manner of procedure" (Gordis). Perhaps the text consciously uses מִשְׁפָּט mišpāṭ in v. 5 in the faded sense of "order" so as to activate the possible meaning "judgment in v. 6." A wisdom concept in which the knowledge of the "right time" is a constitutive element of "wisdom" is presented especially in the book of Sirach; cf., e.g., Sir 20:7: "A wise man remains silent until the (right) time, but the fool does not pay attention to the (right) time."[23]

If one understands vv. 2-3a as an admonition to adopt an opportunistic attitude toward the ruler, v. 5 can be read as a final substantiation: through his obedience the wise man remains protected from harm (v. 5a), but through his knowledge of the right time he can also attain his own goals (v. 5b). If, however, one understands vv. 2-3a as an exhortation, if need be, to refuse the ruler obedience in cases of religious conflict (get involved in something bad: v. 2), v. 5 can also be related as substantiation: whoever, in a case of doubt, follows the religious commandment and wants to have nothing to do with something bad (v. 5a) can rely on the fact that evil has its time and will be subject to the (divine) judgment (v. 5b).

■ 1-5 The image of the (more or less) opportunistic wise man at a (foreign) royal court, which is ironically taken up in vv. 1-5, can be expanded and further shaped by the Joseph story, the Daniel stories, the Aramaic Ahiqar story, and also by texts like Ezra 7 and Nehemiah 2, the book of Esther, the prayer of Nabonidus, the Tobiad novel (Josephus, *Ant.* 12.4), the page story of 3 Ezra 3–5, and the book of Tobit. They let us infer an "overwhelm-

ingly positive attitude towards the foreign monarchy" in the Jewish Diaspora and could "particularly among young Jews of the aristocracy" in Judea give rise to the wish "to seek their fortunes far from the narrowness of their homeland in the service of the Hellenistic kings, whether as soldiers or as officials."[24] They also show, however, the difficulties that await a Jew in a "pagan" court and the conflicts of loyalty into which one may fall there (cf. also Sir 7:4ff.; 10:1ff.; 36:1ff.; 39:4). Qoheleth 8:6-9 not only names such "practical" problems but also fundamentally calls into question the self-understanding of courtly wisdom.

■ 6-9 Verses 6-9 take up the themes "knowledge" (v. 7) and "power" (vv. 8-9) from vv. 1-5; they no longer speak, however, of the "wise man" and the "king" (nor of God, either) but only of a "man" (אָדָם ʾādām: vv. 6b, 8a, 9b; cf. v. 1). Verses 6-9 ignore the fact that different people have at their disposal different degrees of knowledge and power. In addition, the theme of "time," which was already addressed at the end of vv. 1-5 in v. 5b, comes to the fore here.[25] The themes of vv. 1-5 are thereby illuminated from a new point of view that was presented in more detail earlier in the book of Qoheleth, above all in chap. 3. Some statements in vv. 6-7 have the effect of "citations from his own text that refer back to earlier argumentation" (Lohfink; cf. v. 6a with 3:1, 17; v. 6b with 6:1; v. 7 with 3:22; 6:12), and the examples of "wind," "death," and "war" named in v. 8 recall the poems in 1:3-11 (v. 6) and 3:1-9 (vv. 2, 8: the beginning and end of the list of various "times"!).

■ 6 Verse 6 begins a series of four clauses introduced with כִּי kî (vv. 6-7), which are followed in v. 8 by four

22 𝔊 (καιρὸν κρίσεως) and some Hebrew mss. (עֵת מִשְׁפָּט ʿēt mišpāṭ) apparently see here a reference to a future "judgment" of God, of which the wise man has knowledge (cf. Crenshaw). On the scope of the meaning of מִשְׁפָּט mišpāṭ cf. G. Liedke, "שׁפט šp̄ṭ to judge," *TLOT* 3:1395–97. As examples of the use of מִשְׁפָּט mišpāṭ in the sense of "order" Liedke (ibid., 1396) names Gen 40:13; 1 Kgs 5:8; 2 Kgs 11:14; Jer 8:7. Cf. also Backhaus, *Zeit und Zufall,* 247.

23 Cf. further Sir 1:23-24; 4:20, 23; 20:1, 6, 20; 38:13, as well as "the mention of chᵃkhāmîm at the court of the Persian king (Est 1:13a) . . . the added phrase yodhᵉꜥê hāꜥittîm, 'who knew the times,' may indicate more specifically that astrologers are meant, as the Targum assumes in the case of the other passages

where the express occurs, 1 Chr 12:33(32)" (H.-P. Müller, "חָכַם chākham," *TDOT* 4:377).

24 Hengel, *Judaism and Hellenism,* 1:29 and 31.

25 This is indicated not only by the key word עֵת ʿēt, "time" in vv. 6a and 9b (= beginning and end of the section) but also through the expressions מַה־שֶּׁיִּהְיֶה mah-šeyyihyeh, "what will happen" (v. 7a), כַּאֲשֶׁר יִהְיֶה kaʾăšer yihyeh, "what [or: how it] will be" (v. 7b), and יוֹם yôm, "day" (v. 8aβ).

clauses that each begins with a negation. Verse 6a expressly confirms what v. 5b presupposes implicitly: indeed, for every matter and every plan there is "time and judgment" (cf. 3:1, 17). If that is so, however, v. 3b (as statement about the human king) becomes problematic: can he really do what he wants (חֵפֶץ ḥps), if the realization of every plan (חֵפֶץ ḥēpeṣ) is dependent on a favorable time? Thus v. 6a can be read as a critique of an ideological raising of the power of the king.

Verse 6b can then be understood initially as a new, independent statement about the "misfortune" or "troubles" (thus, e.g., Longman, Whybray) or the "badness" (thus, e.g., Gordis) of a person; the echo of Gen 6:5 suggests the second interpretation of רָעָה rāʿâ.[26] In consideration of the magnitude of this evil, the assertion of v. 5a must, in retrospect, seem questionable—both in the sense that the wise man "knows no bad thing," that is, always acts in an ethically impeccable way, and in the sense that the wise man "experiences no bad thing," that is, remains protected from misfortune.[27]

The comments in 3:16-21, however, suggest connecting v. 6b, as substantiation, with 6a. Qoheleth 3:17-18 holds the view that in the time-bound nature of every matter or plan (that is, in the contingency of life and in its finite nature) the "judgment" of God is accomplished, which, because of the general guilt of all people, affects the "righteous" and the "evildoer" alike. In the sense of this conception, then, 8:6 also means that the time-bound nature of all events and actions (v. 6a) is a consequence of the "evil" of human beings and to this extent is properly loaded on them as "misfortune" (v. 6b), because in it the "judgment" (מִשְׁפָּט mišpāṭ) of God is carried out on people. With these presuppositions, however, it must seem completely improbable that the wise man, who is naturally also a human being, can make use of the time-bound nature of all events and actions for the pursuit of his interests at court, as v. 5 asserts. Thus from the standpoint of v. 6, both the statements about the power of the king and the statements about the abil-

ity of the wise man in vv. 1-5 must in retrospect seem questionable.

■ **7** Verse 7 strengthens this insight even further: no one can know "what will happen" and "how it will be." The question of who could give him this information can, according to 3:10-15, 22 and 6:10-12, only be understood as a rhetorical question. It perhaps contains another allusion to the image of a "courtly" wise man in the manner of Joseph or Daniel: each imparts to his king insights, provided by God, into the future (cf. Gen 41:25, 28; Dan 2:28-29).

■ **8** Whereas vv. 6-7 disputed above all the abilities of the wise man that are vaunted in vv. 1 and 5, v. 8 now questions the power of the king emphasized in vv. 3b-4 (at least in one possible and obvious understanding): if no one has power over the wind and over the day of one's death, then neither does a king. The tendency to deify him in vv. 3b-4 is rejected here.

In regard to the constellation wise man–king in vv. 1-5, the statements in v. 8a can be concretized in different ways: a king has no power over the "wind" or over his own "spirit" (cf. 10:4) or "life spirit" or over the "(life) spirit" of his subjects; he cannot determine his own "day of death" or that of his subjects; he cannot remove himself from an ongoing battle, nor can he simply leave his army in war. Thus the relative independence of the external and internal world, "fate," and "constraints" set limits on his possibilities for action and what is at his disposal. Moreover, with the reference to 3:2-8 through the key words "death" and "war," the reader is reminded of the whole "catalog" presented there of "times" that are only in a limited way at human disposal. Yet as statements about "human beings," the clauses in v. 8aα-γ are applicable not only to the king but also to the wise man of vv. 1-5: even with his ever so clever tactics at court, he cannot eliminate the named contingencies and limitations on what is at his disposal.

The introduction of the category of "injustice" (רֶשַׁע rešaʿ) in v. 8b is a little surprising and in the literature

---

26 Cf. C. C. Forman, "Koheleth's Use of Genesis," *JSS* 5 (1960) 258–59; Thomas Krüger, "Die Rezeption der Tora im Buch Kohelet," in idem, *Kritische Weisheit*, 189.

27 Gordis understands v. 6b as the substantiation of v. 5: "A wise courtier will find an opportunity to execute his designs, because human weakness is wide-spread, and an opening is sure to appear." If "human weakness is widespread," however, the "wise courtier" is not excepted from it.

has given rise to various proposals for correction (cf., e.g., Lauha; Crenshaw). Perhaps, after the determination of the "evil" of a person in v. 6b, it is supposed to establish that its consequences are also not to be eliminated through conscious "injustice." Verse 8b, however, can also be related back to vv. 2-3a, understood as an exhortation to unlimited obedience to the king even in cases in which his demands contradict one's religious loyalty toward God: even that kind of extreme opportunistic behavior cannot in the long run "save" a person from misfortune.

■ **9** Verse 9 summarizes the result of the preceding reflections and places it on the broader horizon of "everything that is done under the sun." If one understands v. 9b as the temporal accusative of v. 9a, then the formulation here is a sharp critique of contemporary government: they turn out "to the detriment of the dominated ones" (Lohfink). In the context of these conditions, however, even a wise man in the court cannot escape personal misfortune in the long run. The same is true (with less clear reference to present conditions) if one interprets v. 9b as a statement about existence ("There is a time . . ."). If, however, one interprets v. 9b as a prepositional clause (x–ל *l*–y), this clause formulates a general critique of any form of the rule of one human being over another (cf. Judg 8:23; 9:8-15), in which the perfect שָׁלַט *šālaṭ* points the reader to negative historical experiences with human rule—and raises the question whether there were ever times in which people did not rule over people. In any case, v. 9b makes opportunistic behavior seem questionable and with little promise of success.

In *Ep. Arist.* 262–63 the Jewish wise men answer King Ptolemy's question regarding "how he can avoid arrogance": "If he preserves equality and always remembers that he governs human beings as a human being."[28] This contradicts a "deification" of the king (cf. also Deut 17:20). Qoheleth 8:9 goes even a step further: if the knowledge and power of a human being are fundamentally limited (vv. 6-8), the rule of people over people is, as such, already questionable. With this, the content of the text connects with the OT traditions of the criticism of royalty and rulers[29]—yet without offering an alternative to the "rule of people over people."

■ **1-9** Verses 1-9 cannot be so clearly divided into a "quotation" of a foreign opinion in vv. 1-5 and a "commentary" of Qoheleth in vv. 6-9, as Michel, for example, proposes.[30] For, on the one hand, vv. 1-5 themselves are so ambiguous that this section practically "deconstructs" and criticizes itself. On the other hand, the advice of vv. 1-5 is not rendered completely obsolete by vv. 6-9: also according to v. 9b, it remains advisable to act with care in relation to a king! With its ambiguity and internal contradictions, the text seems rather to challenge its readers to repeated reading, in which vv. 1-5 are critically examined and revisited by what is said in vv. 6-9 (and for its part substantiated by chap. 3).

28 After the translation of N. Meisner, *JSHRZ* II.1.
29 Cf., e.g., Antonius H. J. Gunneweg and Walter Schmithals, *Authority* (Biblical Encounters; Nashville: Abingdon, 1982) 54–87.
30 Cf. Michel, *Untersuchungen*, 92ff.; similarly Schwienhorst-Schönberger, *Nicht im Menschen*, 181ff. Contra Lohfink, who regards v. 1b and v. 5 as "quotations" that are critically "commented" on in vv. 2-4 and vv. 6-12a.

10 Then[a] I saw how wicked people were buried and went in to rest;[b] but those who had done right had to leave a holy place[c] and were forgotten[d] in the city.[e] That also is futile.

11 Because [a] the sentence against the evil deed[b] is not executed immediately, the desire[c] to do evil grows within people. 12 For a sinner[a] does evil a hundred times[b] and still lives a long time. I know, however, that it is good for the God-fearers that they fear God.[c] 13 And it is not good for the wicked man, and like a shadow he will not live long when he does not fear God.[a]

14 There is something futile that takes place on earth: there are righteous people who are treated as if they had acted like the wicked, and there are wicked people who are treated as if they had acted like the righteous.[a] I thought: this too is futile.

15 So I praised pleasure: there is nothing good for people under the sun except to eat and to drink and to enjoy oneself. This can go with them in their toil in the time of their lives, which the Deity has given them under the sun.

10a On וּבְכֵן *ûbĕkēn* cf. Esth 4:16; Sir 13:7; Whitley, *Koheleth*, 74.

10b Thus could the difficult 𝔐 (רְשָׁעִים קְבֻרִים וָבָאוּ *rĕšāʿîm qĕburîm wābāʾû*) be understood (cf. Delitzsch). Often this is emended according to 𝔊 (εἰς τάφους εἰσαχθέντας) to read קְבָרִים מוּבָאִים *qĕbārîm mûbāʾîm* (". . . how wicked people were brought into [their] graves"; cf. *BHS* or קְבֻרִים *qĕburîm* is corrected to קְרֵבִים *qĕrēbîm* (and וָבָאוּ *wābāʾû* to וּבָאִים *ûbāʾîm*) (". . . how wicked people approached and entered [sc. into the holy place]"). Cf. Schoors, *Preacher*, 209.

10c Instead of וּמִמְּקוֹם קָדוֹשׁ *ûmimmĕqôm qādôš* one should read, with numerous Hebrew mss., וּמִמָּקוֹם קָדוֹשׁ *ûmimmāqôm qādôš*.

10d Instead of וְיִשְׁתַּכְּחוּ *wĕyištakkĕḥû* many Hebrew mss. read וְיִשְׁתַּבְּחוּ *wĕyištabbĕḥû* ("and boasted"; cf. 𝔊 α' ϑ' σ').

10e The recommended translation tries to follow as closely as possible the—in many respects—difficult 𝔐 (cf. here, e.g., Backhaus, *Zeit und Zufall*, 251–52). With some smaller corrections (cf. the foregoing text notes) the following interpretation would also be possible: "Then I saw how wicked people 'approached' and entered and went away (again) from the holy place and 'boasted' in the city that they had acted thus (כֵּן *kēn*)" (cf. Backhaus, *Zeit und Zufall*, 252).

11a It would also be possible to connect v. 11 with the preceding: "This too is futile: that the sentence . . ." (thus, e.g., Fox).

11b The way the Masoretic punctuation pulls the construct connection apart is hardly appropriate (cf. *BHS*).

11c Literally: "the heart of people is full."

12a Or: "Whoever sins" (cf. 𝔊).

12b Cf. Hier (*centies*). Vocalized as a construct from 𝔐, מְאַת *mĕʾat* perhaps tacitly presupposes a following פְּעָמִים *pĕʿāmîm* ("times"). Or perhaps one should read rather the pl. מֵאֹת *mĕʾōt*. 𝔊 𝔖[h] 𝔄 presuppose מֵאָז *mĕʾāz*; α' σ' ϑ', מֵת *mēt*.

12c Literally: "It is good for those who fear the Deity that they fear him."

13a On the problem of translating vv. 12b-13 see the commentary.

14a Literally: "in accordance with the actions of the wicked/the righteous."

The introduction in v. 10 ("then I saw . . .") connects (as does v. 16) with what precedes it and at the same time marks a relatively new beginning. In terms of form (introductions in vv. 10, 12b, 14, 15; closing הֶבֶל *hebel* statements in vv. 10 and 14) and content, vv. 10-15 are rather clearly divided. There are experiences that contradict the postulate of a "deed-result connection" (v. 10). Yet such experiences—as well as a "deed-result connection" that allows some time to pass between the evil deed and its punishment and that permits exceptions—promote human evil (vv. 11-12a). For human beings, however, the fear of God and wickedness are something good or bad in themselves, and not only on the basis of their good or bad later consequences (vv. 12b-13). Knowledge of this does not let the unrighteous deeds in the world appear any less offensive (v. 14; cf. v. 10). Yet they are more easily endured if a person does not expect his happiness from the future consequences of his present deeds, but rather in the present seizes the possibilities given him for enjoying his life (v. 15).

■ **10** Verse 10 is among the most difficult verses to understand in the book of Qoheleth. If the translation proposed above is correct, then we have here an observation that, like those in 7:15 and 8:14, contradicts the postulate of the "deed-result connection," which asserts that—at least in the long view—things will go well in life for a "righteous person" but bad for an "evildoer."[1] Under the presupposition that death is the definitive end for a human being, the processes described in v. 10 are finished and no longer correctable: the wicked have already gone to their grave with honor,[2] but the righteous (no doubt likewise dead) have been forgotten in the city. Thus, even a just compensation on the day of death, as it is postulated in Sir 11:26 (ה = 28 ⑥; cf. 11:26 ⑥), is no longer possible here. It seems especially offensive that the righteous must leave a "holy place." Here one would most likely think of the temple (thus, e.g., Crenshaw) or a synagogue (thus, e.g., Seow). If proper behavior is no longer promoted in such a "holy place" (cf., e.g., Psalms 15; 24:3-5), then the righteousness of world and social order is threatened from its center (cf. 3:16 and, e.g., Isa 1:10-17; Amos 4:4-5; 5:21-24).

■ **11-12a** Verses 11-12a describe the consequences that the experience of unrighteousness in life has for the moral consciousness of people: since they believe that doing evil will not be punished—or in any case not

quickly—their courage and their desire to do evil grows (v. 11b, lit.: "their heart is full of doing evil"). Verse 11a does not dispute the postulate of a "deed-result connection" entirely, but it presupposes that in life a "righteousness" corresponding to this postulate will in any case prevail *in the long run*. Yet only a *quick* punishment of evil deeds would have a deterrent effect on people. If, however, "no man on earth is so just that he does only good and never sins" (7:20), such quick punishment of evil deeds would, in the long run, necessarily lead to the eradication of humankind.

Perhaps 8:11—like 7:20, 29; 8:6; and 9:3—refers to the primal history in Genesis 1-11 (esp. Gen 6:5; 8:21).[3] Here the paradise story in Genesis 2-3 can be read as an illustration of the fact that "the sentence against the evil deed is not executed immediately": God had warned the man that he must die *as soon as* he eats from the tree of knowledge (Gen 2:17). After the man did this, he lived more than eight hundred years longer (cf. Gen 5:3-5). If God had executed the sentence immediately, there would be no humankind.

Verse 12a also does not necessarily have to be understood as a basic disagreement with the postulate of a "deed-result connection" in view of the reality of experience.[4] It can also be interpreted in the sense that the rule of the "deed-result connection" allows *exceptions*: not *every*, but *many a* "sinner does evil a hundred times and still lives a long time." Yet as the kind of rule with exceptions (v. 12a) that, in addition, works only in the long run (v. 11a), the "deed-result connection" loses its effect of holding people back from evil deeds (v. 11b)—apart from whether it basically describes experienced reality correctly.

---

1   Cf. Bernd Janowski, "Die Tat kehrt zum Täter zurück; Offene Fragen im Umkreis des 'Tun-Ergehen-Zusammenhangs,'" *ZThK* 91 (1994) 247–71.

2   "In addition to the institutionalization of a commemorative service connected with burial, the statement can perhaps also be understood especially against the background of the magnificent burial plots in Hellenistic style that were newly coming into vogue in Judea in Hellenistic times" (Schwienhorst-Schönberger, *Nicht im Menschen*, 188, with references to the literature).

3   Cf. Thomas Krüger, "Die Rezeption der Tora im Buch Kohelet," in idem, *Kritische Weisheit*, 188–91.

4   Cf., e.g., Mal 2:17; 3:14-15; Pss 10:4; 73:11. With Lohfink one can wonder whether v. 12a takes up a contemporary "proverb."

■ **12b-13** With their (in any case, apparent) reinforcement of a "deed-result connection," verses 12b-13 do not necessarily contradict the preceding. Nevertheless, v. 13a, with its assertion that the "wicked man" will not live long, stands in contradiction, by all appearances, with v. 12a, where the opposite is asserted of the "sinner."[5]

Based on this tension, vv. 12b-13 are often regarded as an "orthodox" gloss that, against the intention of the original text, tries to hold fast to the concept of a "deed-result connection."[6] Then, however, one must explain why this gloss is inserted before and not after v. 14: for the present text gives the impression that with vv. 12b-13 the final and definitive word on the "deed-result connection" has not been said.

Another attempt to clarify the tension between vv. 12b-13 and vv. 11-12a (as well as v. 14) has been proposed by, for example, Gordis, Lohfink, Loader, and Michel.[7] They understand vv. 12b-13 as a "quotation" of an "orthodox" doctrinal opinion that is critically "commented on" in the context. Thus Lohfink translates the beginning of v. 12b: "Of course, I recall the saying: . . ." and makes the beginning of the "commentary" known in his translation of v. 14 through an introductory "However, . . ." There is, however, no such signal in the Hebrew text of v. 14, which follows the preceding text asyndetically.

Thus it seems advisable initially to make an attempt to understand 8:10-15 as a unified text whose statements are to be ascribed to a single speaker. In this spirit Hertzberg and Zimmerli, for example, interpret vv. 12b-13 and v. 14 as an "it-is-true-but statement": "Qoheleth knows, to be sure, that it will go well for God-fearers if they fear God, and not well for the godless . . . if they do not fear God" (vv. 12b-13); but the individual cases named in v. 14 show "that precisely that which, according to the believed (Qoheleth says: known) rule would have to happen," at least occasionally "does not happen" (Zimmerli). That is, *it is true* that as a rule a "deed-result connection" functions, *but* there are exceptions to it in individual cases.[8] This understanding of the text appears essentially plausible, but then 8:12b-13 would be the only place in the book of Qoheleth in which "a clear causal link between the fear of God and well-being and long life" (Lohfink).

It is normally assumed that the expressions יִהְיֶה־טּוֹב *yihyeh-ṭôb* and (וְ)טּוֹב לֹא־יִהְיֶה (*wĕ)ṭôb lōʾ-yihyeh* in vv. 12b-13 mean "it will go well" or "not go well" or something similar.[9] If one follows this interpretation, the doublings in v. 12b and v. 13 are striking and in need of clarification: "It will go well for the God-fearers *who* [or: *if* they?] fear God. And it will not go well for the wicked man . . . , *who* [or: *if* he?] does not fear God." Are the "God-fearers" supposed to be thereby more precisely defined as

---

5   This tension would be understandable and explicable if v. 12a quoted a contemporary "proverb" (thus Lohfink) that showed a *possible* conclusion from v. 11a, without asserting that this conclusion was *correct*—if, that is, vv. 11-12a were to be paraphrased, for example, as follows: "Because the sentence against the evil deed is not executed immediately, the desire to do evil grows within people. For *they believe* a sinner can do evil a hundred times and still live a long time." Verse 13a would then show that *this* conclusion is *not* to be drawn from v. 11a. Speaking against this interpretation, nonetheless, is the fact that v. 12a is in no way set apart from the context as a "quotation" of a "foreign opinion."

6   So, e.g., Ellermeier, *Qohelet*, I/1, 127; Galling; Lauha; Crenshaw, 48 (yet Crenshaw, in loc., is more reserved); cf. McNeile; Barton; Podechard, who ascribes vv. 11-13 to the (second) reworking of the book of Qoheleth by a "Hasid."

7   Cf. also Backhaus, *Zeit und Zufall*, 254ff.; Schwienhorst-Schönberger, *Nicht im Menschen*, 189–90.

8   Fox interprets vv. 12-13 in this sense: "Verse 12 says: 'It is a fact that . . . although I also know that. . . .'" Although Qohelet 'knows' the principle of retribution and nowhere denies it, he *also* knows there are cases that violate the rule. It is because Qohelet generally maintains the axioms of Wisdom that he is shocked by their violation and finds the aberrations absurd." N. H. Tur-Sinai interprets 8:10-14 in the sense that vv. 12b-13 name exceptions to the rule described in vv. 10-12a, 14 by translating: "Although I also know (cases) in which it goes well for God-fearers . . ." (*Die Heilige Schrift ins Deutsche übertragen* [2d ed.; Neuhausen-Stuttgart: Hänssler, 1995] 1191).

9   Cf., e.g., Num 11:18; Deut 5:33; 15:16; 19:13; 1 Sam 16:16, 23.

"those who (really) stand in fear *before* God" (cf. 3:14)? Or is the expectation that things will go well for the God-fearers limited by saying: "*if* they (really) stand in fear before God"? In both cases the doublings in vv. 12b-13 could be understood as an indication that the labeling of a person as "God-fearing" or "wicked" does not always agree with one's actual behavior. Moreover, there may also be an allusion here to the general fallibility of human beings ascertained in 7:20. What is said there about the "just" man is also true analogously for the "God-fearer": no one succeeds in maintaining the "fear of God" in one's life constantly and without limitation. Something similar is then also validated in v. 13b mutatis mutandis for the "wicked man."

It is by no means clear, however, that the expressions יִהְיֶה־טּוֹב *yihyeh-ṭôb* and (וְ)טוֹב לֹא־יִהְיֶה *(wĕ)ṭôb lōʾ-yihyeh* in vv. 12b-13 are to be understood in the sense of "it will go well" or "not go well" or something similar, and in view of analogous formulations in the book of Qoheleth, it is rather unlikely.[10] They suggest instead the translation "it is (not) good," recommended above: "It is good for the God-fearers that they fear God. And it is not good for the wicked man . . . , when he does not fear God." Thus understood, vv. 12b-13 do not establish "a causal link between the fear of God and well-being" (Lohfink). Rather, in the view of the text, the fear of God does not have its value (and wickedness its negative value) in itself; people are to fear God not because they expect something from it, but because this behavior is appropriate for them as creatures of God (cf. 3:14).[11] With this, the motivation of moral action through its consequences for the actors (corresponding to the "deed-result connection") is critically overcome. Consequently, one may con-

cede that experiential reality does not (always) correspond to the postulate of the "deed-result connection" (vv. 10-12a, 14), without calling into question the ethical value of the fear of God and righteousness.

If, according to v. 12a, a sinner "lives a long time" (וּמַאֲרִיךְ לוֹ *ûmaʾărîk lô*), but according to v. 13, the wicked man, "like a shadow . . . will not live long" (וְלֹא־יַאֲרִיךְ יָמִים כַּצֵּל *wĕlōʾ-yaʾărîk yāmîm kaṣṣēl*), there is, upon closer examination, no contradiction between these two statements. According to 6:12a, namely, a person's life is in any case short and fleeting, "like a shadow." Similarly, v. 13 can be understood as an ironic "commentary" on v. 12a:[12] even if the sinner or the wicked man "lives a long time," his life is still "short like a shadow." Injustice can preserve a person from contingency and transitoriness no better than righteousness and piety (cf. 8:8; 9:2).

■ 14 Verse 14 relates again to vv. 10-12a and states that a "deed-result connection" is valid in experiential reality— if at all—only as a rule with exceptions. The idea that God repays "all according to their work" (Ps 62:13)[13] is, at any rate, not always the case. Even if this does not diminish the value of the fear of God and righteousness, according to vv. 12b-13, it is still extremely disagreeable from the human point of view (הֶבֶל *hebel*; cf. v. 10 and רַע *rāʿ* in 9:3).

If this "futility . . . takes place on earth," according to v. 14a (and not "under the sun"), this formulation, which in the book of Qoheleth occurs only here and in 8:16, perhaps indicates that for the deplorable situation lamented in v. 14 (as well as in v. 10) it is not God but human beings who are responsible (cf. 3:16—4:12). For

---

10 Cf. esp. 2:3 (. . . אֵי־זֶה טוֹב לִבְנֵי הָאָדָם אֲשֶׁר יַעֲשׂוּ *ʾê-zeh ṭôb libnê hāʾādām ʾăšer yaʿăśû* . . . , "what is good for people, that they should do it . . ."), as well as 2:24; 3:22; 5:4; 6:12; 7:18; 8:15; 11:7.

11 Cf. Antigonus of Socho, who, according to *Pirqe Abot* 1:3, "used to say: Do not be like the servants who serve the master in order to receive a wage; rather, be like the servants who serve the master with no intention of receiving a wage; and may the fear of God be on you" (after the translation of Hermann L. Strack, *Pirqê Aboth; Die Sprüche der Väter* [4th ed.; Leipzig: Hinrichs, 1915] 2). Cf. also Luke 17:7-10.

12 Cf. also the critical discussion of the ideal of a long life in Qoh 6:3ff.

13 Cf. Prov 24:12; Job 34:11; Sir 16:12; Jer 17:10; 32:19; Ezek 18:30; 33:20 as well as Ps 28:4; 2 Sam 3:39.

in 8:16a the expression הָעִנְיָן אֲשֶׁר נַעֲשָׂה עַל־הָאָרֶץ *hāʿinyān ʾăšer naʿăśâ ʿal-hāʾāreṣ* is clearly related to human activity, which is juxtaposed to the "work of the Deity" in v. 17.

■ **15** With "so I praised pleasure," v. 15 connects antithetically with v. 14b ("I thought [or: said]: this too is futile"). If in v. 15a (as already in v. 11b) the topic is simply "people," the juxtaposition in vv. 10-14 of "doing right," "God-fearers," and the "righteous," on the one hand, and the "wicked" and "sinners," on the other, is critically relativized. The designation of eating, drinking, and enjoyment as the highest or only good takes up the corresponding statements in 3:12-13, 22; 5:17-18. It is not supposed to contradict the qualification of the fear of God as "good" in vv. 12b-13. Rather, the fear of God and the enjoyment of life seem here, as already in 3:12-14, to be seen as closely connected (cf. also 7:14; 11:9—12:1). In the view of the book of Qoheleth, the fear of God leads also, and in the first place, to the enjoyment of the gifts of God in the present, instead of waiting to be rewarded by God in the future for one's presumed righteousness and piety.

Verse 15b states that the good exhibited in v. 15a can "go with, accompany" (לוה *lwh* qal[14]) people "in their toil." Thus it is not a question here of a result of "good" behavior to be expected only in the future, but rather of an experience that is possible at any time in the present (even if it is not absolutely at one's disposal). The closing qualification "in the time of their lives, which the Deity has given them under the sun," contains perhaps a final polemical point against the discussion of whether the

"sinner" or "wicked person" lives a long time (v. 12a) or not (v. 13a): anyone who takes on and enjoys as a gift of God what is good in the allotted time of one's life, as well as life itself, no longer has to strive for an "extension" of one's life (cf. 6:3ff.).

■ **10-15** This section basically does not criticize the assumption of a "deed-result connection" but rather the function of this concept as the motivation for ethics and piety. For human beings, fear of God and righteousness have their value in themselves and not in the fact that they guarantee prosperity. With this, however, the text is not juxtaposing a "eudemonistic" ethic with an "ethic of duty." Pleasure and enjoyment remain the only good ultimately to be striven for by human beings. Fear of God and righteousness can help make it possible for the doer, as well as one's fellow human beings, to enjoy this good. But since pleasure and enjoyment are not subject to human disposition and are available only in the present, they cannot represent the guiding goal of human activity. Yet they can "accompany" a person in one's activity—and thereby also shape it in an ethically relevant way.

With its exhortation to pleasure in the present (v. 15), 8:10-15 refers back to 7:1-14 (cf. 7:14); with the reference to experiences that do not correspond to a "deed-result connection" (8:10-12a, 14; cf. 7:15) and with the recommendation of fear of God (8:12b-13; cf. 7:18), it refers to 7:15-22. The following section 8:16-17 then completes the circle back to 6:10-12.

---

14   The qal is attested only here in the OT and then also in Sir 41:12. The niphal in the OT means "join"; the piel in Middle Hebrew means "accompany" (see *HALOT* s.v.; Whitley, *Koheleth*, 76–77). From this standpoint, Lohfink's assumption that the verb has the "original meaning of 'bind [a wreath],' or 'crown' (cf. Arabic *lawāʲ*, "wind, turn") and refers here perhaps to the "custom of crowning with flowers the participants in a festivity" seems rather improbable.

8

16 When I intended[a] to understand wisdom and to consider all that was done[b] on earth—day and night one grants[c] one's eyes no sleep—17 then I saw the whole work of the Deity: that human beings cannot comprehend[a] what is done under the sun[b].[c] Even when[d] humans work hard to research[e] (it), they still do not comprehend (it). And if the wise man claims to understand (it), he still cannot comprehend (it).

16a Literally: "when I gave [= directed] my heart (toward)."

16b Literally: "the activity that is/was done."

16c Literally: "one sees with."

17a Literally: "find" (thus also in the remainder of the verse).

17b Literally: "the doing/work that is done/accomplished under the sun."

17c On this understanding of the beginning of v. 17 cf. Schoors, *Preacher*, 215. By contrast, it is often assumed that "the whole doing/work of God" is anticipated from the following object clause ("that human beings cannot comprehend") as *casus pendens* and taken up there again through "what is happening under the sun": "there I saw (in regard to) the whole activity of God that human beings cannot comprehend the [= this] activity" (cf. Schoors, ibid.). In terms of syntax, as well as content, however, the understanding presupposed above is more apparent.

17d On the problem of the interpretation of בְּשֶׁל אֲשֶׁר *běšel ʾăšer* ("the doing . . . *about which* human beings work hard . . ."; "*as hard as* human beings might work . . ."; "*because* human beings work hard . . . [*but do not find* . . .]"?) cf. Schoors, *Preacher*, 145–46).

17e Literally: "seek."

Verses 16-17 form a relatively closed small unit,[1] but they show links with their immediate and broader contexts. Therefore commentators have connected them at times with what goes before, but more often with what follows.[2] The theme "limits of knowledge" is taken up again in the following texts (cf. 9:1, 5, 11-12, etc.), but it also already played an important role in the preceding context (cf. 6:10-12; 7:13-14, 23-29; 8:7-8).[3] Here v. 17, like 6:11, speaks against claims to knowledge that do not respect the human limits of knowledge that are ultimately based on the actions of God (cf. 3:11).

■ **16** Verse 16 exhibits terminological similarities to the royal travesty in 1:12—2:26 and its critical reflection in 3:1—4:12.[4] Verse 16b is probably supposed to illustrate the "professional zeal found among wisdom teachers" (Lohfink; cf. the image of the Torah scholar in Ps 1:2).

■ **17** The pointlessness of this endeavor is made clear by v. 17, which refers back terminologically to 7:23-29 (בקש *bqš* piel— מצא *mṣʾ*) and in terms of content to 3:10-11: Since the limits of human knowledge go back to the actions of God (v. 17aα; cf. 3:11), they are insurmountable for human beings, despite all toil and endeavor

---

1 The key words לָדַעַת חָכְמָה *lādaʿat ḥokmâ* in v. 16a and הֶחָכָם לָדַעַת *heḥākām lādaʿat* in v. 17b make a kind of frame.

2 For the former, see, e.g., Crenshaw: 8:10-17; Murphy: 8:1-17. For the latter see, e.g., Lohfink: 8:16—9:6; Galling: 8:16—9:10; Zimmerli: 8:16—9:12.

3 The expressions "on earth" (vv. 16/14) and "under the sun" (vv. 17/15) have also already occurred in the immediately preceding context.

4 Cf. 8:16aα: כַּאֲשֶׁר נָתַתִּי אֶת־לִבִּי לָדַעַת חָכְמָה *kaʾăšer nātattî ʾet-libbî lādaʿat ḥokmâ* with 1:17aα: וָאֶתְּנָה לִבִּי

וָאֶתְּנָה לִבִּי לָדַעַת חָכְמָה *wāʾettěnâ libbî lādaʿat ḥokmâ*; 8:16aβ: וְלִרְאוֹת אֶת־הָעִנְיָן *wělirʾôt ʾet-hāʿinyān* with 3:10: רָאִיתִי אֶת־הָעִנְיָן *rāʾîtî ʾet-hāʿinyān* and 1:13b: הוּא עִנְיָן רָע *hûʾ ʿinyan rāʿ*; 8:16b: כִּי גַם בַּיּוֹם וּבַלַּיְלָה שֵׁנָה בְּעֵינָיו אֵינֶנּוּ רֹאֶה *kî gam bayyôm ûballaylâ šēnâ běʿênāyw ʾênennû rōʾeh* with 2:23aβ: גַּם־בַּלַּיְלָה לֹא־שָׁכַב לִבּוֹ *gam-ballaylâ lōʾ-šākab libbô*.

163

(v. 17αβ)—even for the wise man (v. 17b with adoption of לֹא יוּכַל [. . .] לִמְצוֹא *lōʾ yûkal [. . .] limṣôʾ* from v. 17aα). Verse 17b also polemicizes against the claims of "theoreticians" to "possess authentic knowledge of the whole of the world event" (thus, e.g., Lohfink): such knowledge is withheld even from the "wise."

Lohfink notes on 8:17: "This verse is very important in understanding the whole book, because it makes the action of God equivalent to the activity 'that is carried on under the sun'—something that was to be surmised in any case from the use of passive formulations in many other texts. What is especially meant is all human activity. This then is at the same time always divine activity." Yet this very assumption seems in 8:16-17, as well as in 3:11ff., to be avoided through highly precise differentiating terminology: "all that is done on earth" (הָעִנְיָן אֲשֶׁר נַעֲשָׂה עַל־הָאָרֶץ *hāʿinyān ʾăšer naʿăśâ ʿal-hāʾāreṣ*: v. 16a) obviously refers to human activity, including the striving of human beings for knowledge. Clearly distinguished from this is "the whole work [or: activity] of God [or: the Deity]" (כָּל־מַעֲשֵׂה הָאֱלֹהִים *kol-maʿăśēh hāʾĕlōhîm*: v. 17a). The relationship of the following "what is happening under the sun" in v. 17a (הַמַּעֲשֶׂה אֲשֶׁר נַעֲשָׂה תַּחַת־הַשֶּׁמֶשׁ *hammaʿăśeh ʾăšer naʿăśâ taḥat-haššemeš*) to this "whole activity/work of God/the Deity" depends on how one relates the clause כִּי לֹא יוּכַל הָאָדָם לִמְצוֹא אֶת־הַמַּעֲשֶׂה אֲשֶׁר נַעֲשָׂה תַּחַת־הַשֶּׁמֶשׁ *kî lōʾ yûkal hāʾādām limṣôʾ ʾet-hammaʿăśeh ʾăšer naʿăśâ taḥat-haššemeš* to the preceding clause, וְרָאִיתִי אֶת־כָּל־מַעֲשֵׂה הָאֱלֹהִים *wĕrāʾîtî ʾet-kol-maʿăśēh hāʾĕlōhîm* (cf. n. 17c on the translation).

1. If one understands it as a new, independent main clause ("Yes, human beings cannot find . . ."), one can relate הַמַּעֲשֶׂה אֲשֶׁר נַעֲשָׂה תַּחַת־הַשֶּׁמֶשׁ *hammaʿăśeh ʾăšer naʿăśâ taḥat-haššemeš* both to human (v. 16a: הָעִנְיָן אֲשֶׁר נַעֲשָׂה עַל־הָאָרֶץ *hāʿinyān ʾăšer naʿăśâ ʿal-hāʾāreṣ*) and divine activity (v. 17a: כָּל־מַעֲשֵׂה הָאֱלֹהִים *kol-maʿăśeh hāʾĕlōhîm*).

This does not mean, however, that divine and human activity coincide and are the same. Rather, the text can also be understood in the sense that within the framework of "what is done under the sun," both human and divine activity occur without the difference between the two being erased: because the realm of "what is done under the sun" comprises, among other things, divine activity that (at least in part) escapes human knowledge (cf. 3:11; 11:5), this realm is not completely transparent for human beings.

2. If, however, one understands the clause . . . כִּי לֹא יוּכַל הָאָדָם לִמְצוֹא *kî lōʾ yûkal hāʾādām limṣôʾ* . . . as in the translation proposed above, as an explication of כָּל־מַעֲשֵׂה הָאֱלֹהִים *kol-maʿăśēh hāʾĕlōhîm* ("the whole work of the Deity that humans cannot find . . ."), then v. 17a is aimed at the situation, named in 3:11, that the limits of human knowledge go back to the actions of God. Then, however, the activity of God does not coincide with that of human beings, but rather sets its limits.

■ **16-17** With the statement that human beings cannot comprehend what is done under the sun, 8:16-17 contradicts not only the postulate of a "deed-result connection" as a law without exceptions (cf. 7:15ff.; 8:10ff.) but also "pessimistic" (cf. 7:1ff.), "optimistic" (7:8ff.), or quite simply "opportunistic" (cf. 8:1ff.) concepts of human conduct that promise other and presumably better goods than enjoyment of life in the present. The texts following in 9:1—12:7 will attempt to show how a meaningful conduct of life is possible, in that account is taken of both the contingency of reality, which is transparent in only limited ways, and the unavoidable transitoriness of human life.

Qoheleth 9:1–12:7 shows a clear framework through which this section is connected to a larger unit:[1]

9:1-6 Death as the unavoidable end of human beings
9:7-10 Exhortation to pleasure and enjoyment in the present
9:11-12 Success not at one's disposal / uncertainty of the future

11:1-6 Success not at one's disposal / uncertainty of the future
11:7-10 Exhortation to pleasure and enjoyment in the present
12:1-7 Death as the unavoidable end of human beings

Within this framework 9:13–10:20 contains a number of smaller units in which the strengths and weaknesses of wisdom are pondered. Thus 9:1–12:7 as a whole can be divided as follows:

9:1-12 Exhortation to pleasure and to vigorous action in view of death and chance
9:13–10:20 Strengths and weaknesses of wisdom
11:1–12:7 Advice for life in view of the uncertainty of the future and the certainty of death

After eating, drinking, and pleasure were defined in 1:3–8:17 as the highest and only good for human beings to strive for (3:12-13, 22; 5:17-19; 7:14; 8:15), 9:1-12 and 11:1–12:7 emphatically exhort the readers of the book of Qoheleth to orient their lives according to this insight. Here the exhortation to pleasure is linked with the exhortation to vigorous action. Death and chance are not displaced by pleasure and enjoyment, but rather are taken seriously in their unavoidability and integrated into the conduct of life.

Qoheleth 9:13–10:20 recalls the limits of wisdom vis-à-vis power and dominion—which were already demonstrated more than once in the preceding sections (9:13–10:1; 10:4-7, 18-20; cf., e.g., 4:13-16; 5:7-8; 8:1-9)—and vis-à-vis foolishness. Here foolishness and fools not only now form a contrast foil for wisdom and the wise, as in the foregoing (cf., e.g., 4:5, 13, 17; 5:3; 7:17), but in direct encounter also represent a present danger (10:2-3, 12-15; cf. also 10:1, 6). In addition to the limits of wisdom, 10:8-11 now also points expressly to its relative worth (יִתְרוֹן *yitrôn*).

---

1 Cf. Backhaus, *Zeit und Zufall*, 263–317; Schwien-horst-Schönberger, *Nicht im Menschen*, 194–95.

9

1 All this I took to heart and examined[a] all this: the righteous and the wise and their works[b] are in the hand of God. Whether it is love, whether it is hate, human beings cannot know everything that lies before them[c].[d] **2** Everyone gets what they deserve:[a] the same fate awaits the righteous and the wicked, the good[b] and pure and the impure, those who sacrifice and those who do not sacrifice, the good as well as sinners, those who swear as well as those who shy away from swearing. **3** This is bad in all that is done under the sun, that the same fate befalls everyone. But the heart of human beings is also full of evil, and blindness is in their heart as long as they live, and afterward[a]—to the dead. **4** Yet those who "belong"[a] to the living have hope;[b] for a living dog is better than a dead lion. **5** The living know that they will die, but the dead know nothing at all, and they have no more wage, for the remembrance of them has disappeared.[a] **6** Their love, their hate, and their jealousy are long gone, and never again will they have any portion in all that is done under the sun.

7 Go, eat your bread with pleasure, and drink your wine with a merry heart; for long ago God already approved this[a] activity. **8** Let your clothing always be white, and do not let oil be lacking on your head. **9** Enjoy life with a woman whom you love all the days of your fleeting life, which he has given you under the sun, all your fleeting days. That is your share in life and in your work and toil[a] under the sun. **10** Whatever you can do, do it.[a] For there is neither doing nor planning, neither knowledge nor wisdom in the realm of the dead, to which you are going.

11 Again I saw[a] under the sun: the swift do not win the race, nor heroes the battle; the wise do not get bread, nor the intelligent wealth nor those with understanding favor. For time and chance affect them all. **12** Nor do human beings know their time: like the fish that fall into a treacherous net,[a] like birds that are caught,[b] so are human beings ensnared in a time of disaster, when it suddenly strikes them.

1a Like the inf. abs. in 8:9; 9:11, the inf. cs. (with ל *l*) seems here also to be used in the sense of a finite verb; cf. Schoors, *Preacher*, 180–81. 𝕲 (καὶ καρδία μου σὺν πᾶν εἶδεν τοῦτο, "and my heart has seen/regarded all this"; cf. 𝕲 Syh 𝔎) already offers "an interpretative translation of the difficult Hebrew text" (Schoors, *Preacher*, 28; cf. 27-28, and Whitley, *Koheleth*, 78).

1b The Aramaic loanword עֲבָד *ʿābād* ("deed, work") is attested only here in the OT (cf. Whitley. *Koheleth*, 78; Schoors, *Preacher*, 60-61). It stands out here especially because in the immediately preceding verse, 8:17, the regular Hebrew noun מַעֲשֶׂה *maʿăśeh* was used twice. If the terminological variation is not accidental and does not betray the writer's Aramaic linguistic background (cf. Fox), it could indicate that in 9:1 there is an allusion to a contemporary saying.

1c The suffix of the third person m. pl. in לִפְנֵיהֶם *lipnêhem* can refer back to "human beings" (הָאָדָם *hāʾādām*—with incongruence of number), to "love and hate" (with incongruence of gender), or to "the righteous and the wise." "Before" (לִפְנֵי *lipnê*) can point either (temporally) to the past (but hardly to the future, contra 𝔅 and, e.g., Michel) or (spatially) to what is present (perhaps especially in the sense of accessible, at one's disposal; see Gordis).

1d On the numerous problems of interpretation in v. 1b cf., in addition to the commentaries, esp. Whitley, *Koheleth*, 78–79; Michel, *Untersuchungen*, 167ff.; Backhaus, *Zeit und Zufall*, 262–63; Pahk, *Canto*, 143ff. "Whether it is love, whether it is hate" could also be linked with the preceding sentence. It would also be possible in v. 1b to set the sentence boundaries as follows: "Whether it is love, whether it is hate—human beings cannot know. Everything lies before them." In emulation of 𝕲 (cf. σ' 𝔅), which, instead of the הַכֹּל *hakkōl* that follows in v. 2, has הֶבֶל *hebel*, many have proposed the following correction: "everything that lies before them is futile/fleeting" (thus 𝕲, which, however, still reads הַכֹּל *hakkōl* in v. 2); cf. also the following note.

2a Literally: "everything is just as it is (appropriate) for everyone." Cf., e.g., Delitzsch: "All is the same which comes to all." Also possible is the interpretation: "All is (thus) as it happens to all; i.e., there is no distinction of their experiences nor of their persons; all of every sort happens in the same way to all men of every sort" (Delitzsch). Cf. also Michel, *Untersuchungen*, 175, who interprets the syntax of v. 2 as follows: "Everything, as it comes to everyone, is one kind of destiny. . . ." The variant reading of 𝕲 (ματαιότης ἐν τοῖς πᾶσιν) probably represents an attempt to smooth out a difficult text.

2b The versions add: "and the evil." Numerous commentators, by contrast, eliminate "the good," since it occurs again in what follows (opposite "sinners") (cf. *BHK*; *BHS*).

3a Literally: "after him" (where the suffix of the third person m. sg. is to be related to each one of the previously named "human beings"). The different readings of the versions (see *BHK*; *BHS*) do not essentially change the meaning of the text.

4a   Thus with Q, numerous mss., and the versions (יְחֻבַּר *yĕḥubbar*). Lohfink, however, follows K (יִבָּחֵר *yibbāḥēr*) and translates: ". . . and afterward, as they are about to join the dead, which one would be exempted? For all the living, there happens to remain trust . . ." (similarly, Murphy). In this interpretation, nonetheless, both the translation of בחר *bḥr* niphal with "be exempted" and the interpretation of the expression אֶל כָּל־הַחַיִּים *ʾel kol-haḥayyîm* as "for all the living" appear problematic.

4b   Or: "certainty" (namely, the certainty of having to die, v. 5). "Lohfink's . . . suggestion that *biṭṭāḥôn* in Eccl. 9:4 has its later sense of trust, perhaps in God, has nothing to commend it" (Crenshaw).

5a   Literally: "has been forgotten."

7a   Literally: "your."

9a   Literally: "in your work with which you toil."

10a   Literally: "Everything that your hand finds to do with your strength, do!"

11a   On the inf. abs. instead of a finite verb, cf. 8:9, as well as the inf. cs. in 9:1; see GKC §113z.

12a   Literally: "that are caught in a net of misfortune."

12b   Literally: "are caught in a trap."

The three sections 9:1-6, 7-10, and 11-12 are distinguished by the introductory expressions in v. 1 and v. 11, as well as by the change to direct address to the reader in vv. 7-10 (second person m. sg.). In terms of content and argumentation, however, they are very closely connected. The exhortation to pleasure and to vigorous action in the present in vv. 7-10 is substantiated and underlined by the considerations in vv. 1-6 and vv. 11-12. Whereas vv. 1-6 show that after death a human being can expect nothing more worth striving for, vv. 11-12 remind the reader that even in life the success of human action is never guaranteed. The theme revisits the conclusion from 1:3—3:9: through their actions human beings can achieve neither a "gain" that *lasts* nor one that is *at their disposal*.

■ **1-6** Verses 1-6 relativize the distinctions between different people in life through the juxtaposition of the living and the dead: in view of death, which strikes all people in the same way, distinctions between the wise and fools, the righteous and the wicked, and so forth, are invalidated. This does not mean that they lose any significance for the limited realm of life, but they are not to be overvalued.

■ **1** The main problems in the interpretation of 9:1-6 lie in v. 1. What is meant by the assertion that "the righteous and the wise and their works [or: deeds] are in the hand of God" (v. 1aβ)? Michel assumes that this formulates "the expectation of a recompense for good deeds after death," which is dealt with critically in the following text.[1] For comparison he points to Wis 3:1ff.:

1   But the souls of the righteous are in the hand of God

    and no torment can touch them.

  2   In the eyes of fools they seem to have died,

     and their end is regarded as a failure

   3   and their separation from us as destruction;

     and yet they are at peace. . . .[2]

Now, vv. 4-6 do indeed exclude "the expectation of a recompense of good deeds after death." In contrast to 3:16-22, nonetheless, this theme seems at least not to be the center of interest in 9:1-6. For, in opposition to Wis 3:1, Qoh 9:1aβ contains no indication that it is a question here of the destiny of the "righteous" and the "wise" *after death*.[3]

---

1   *Untersuchungen*, 166ff., esp. 179ff. For a critique see Backhaus, *Zeit und Zufall*, 405ff.

2   Translation after Johannes Fichtner, *Die Weisheit Salomos* (HAT 2.6; Tübingen: Mohr [Siebeck], 1938) 18, quoted by Michel, *Untersuchungen*, 180.

☆   In Wis 7:16, where the expression "in the hand of God" also occurs, it clearly refers to the life of the wise *before death*: (15) ". . . [God] himself is the guide of wisdom and the corrector of the wise. (16) Both we and our words are in his hand, as are all understanding and knowledge in crafts" (translation after Dieter Georgi, *JSHRZ* III.4).

Yet even if one understands v. 1aβ as a statement about "the righteous and the wise and their works" before their death, the sense of the expression "in the hand of God" is not clear: does it refer to the actions "of the righteous and the wise" or to their destiny?[4] And does it emphasize the beneficially protective care of God for them or his power of disposition over them?[5] Perhaps the ambiguity of v. 1aβ is explained by the fact that the text here takes up or refers to a judgment from contemporary discussion and gives it a new meaning in the present context.[6]

The continuation in v. 1b clearly accentuates the viewpoint of the limited nature of human possibilities for knowledge and action (אֵין יוֹדֵעַ הָאָדָם ʾên yôdēaʿ hāʾādām),[7] but it can be read equally well both as a statement about the actions of "the righteous and the wise" and as a statement about their destiny. In the first case, "love and hate" could be regarded as attitudes of the "righteous and wise": "Not even here does a person understand his own deeds" (Zimmerli).[8] In the second case, by contrast,

"love and hate" are considered attitudes of God toward the "righteous and wise": "You cannot know whom or what God loves and hates—until you see the effects of his attitude" (Fox).[9] That "human beings cannot know everything that lies before them"[10] can agree with both possibilities if one interprets הַכֹּל לִפְנֵיהֶם hakkōl lipnêhem spatially ("everything before their eyes") and relates the suffix to הָאָדָם hāʾādām: human beings understand neither their own doing nor God's behavior in regard to them. If, however, one interprets הַכֹּל לִפְנֵיהֶם hakkōl lipnêhem temporally and relates the suffix to "love and hate" ("everything that was before them"; cf. 7:24), v. 1b could imply that human beings do not know what went before God's "love" or "hate"—and therefore also cannot allow themselves any judgment regarding their justification.[11]

Perhaps v. 1 intentionally leaves open whether the topic is the deed or the result of the "righteous and wise," in order thereby to point up the questionable nature of a perceivable "deed-result connection":[12] if

---

4   For the former see, e.g., Zimmerli: 9:1 shows "how all that is seemingly so properly and cleverly done by people themselves is in reality work effected by the hand of God, and over it the righteous and the wise have no power of disposition at all." Cf. Prov 16:9; 20:24; Jer 10:23, as well as Prov 19:21; 16:1. For the latter see, e.g., Lohfink: 9:1 makes clear that "even people who seem to be in the best position, the conscientious and educated, have no control over their fate, but rather God controls it." Cf. 2 Sam 24:14 = Sir 2:18; Ps 31:16; Job 12:9ff.

5   For the former see Levy, who understands 9:1aβ in the sense "that the pious enjoy God's special favor and are in his protective hand." Cf. Ezra 7:6, 9; 8:22; Neh 2:8, 18; Deut 33:3(?); Pss 31:6, 16; 139:5, 10; 2 Sam 24:14 = Sir 2:18, as well as Ps 37:23; Sir 37:15, and the conviction brought to expression by the Jewish wise men in the "symposium" of the *Letter of Aristeas* "that God rules everything and we in our noblest deeds do not carry out decisions from our own strength, but rather God in his power accomplishes and guides everything" (*Ep. Arist.* 195; cf. 193, 199, 216, 227, 231, 237–40, 243, 247, 251–52, 255, 264, etc.). For the latter see, e.g., Zimmerli and Lohfink (see above).

6   The idea that v. 1aβ is a "quotation" that is critically "commented on" in what follows is assumed by, e.g., Levy and Michel. Yet if one notes the ambiguity of this statement, one can hardly say that the following

text contradicts it; rather, its meaning is made more precise by the following reflections. On the possible tradition-historical background of v. 1aβ see the passages for comparison named in the above notes.

7   It should be noted "that yḏʿ does not merely indicate a theoretical relation, a pure act of thought, but that knowledge, as yḏʿ intends it, is realized through practical involvement with the obj[ect] of knowledge" (W. Schottroff, "ידע yḏʿ to perceive, know," *TLOT* 2:514).

8   Similarly, e.g., Ewald; Hitzig; Delitzsch; Hertzberg (see Michel, *Untersuchungen*, 172–73).

9   Similarly, e.g., Barton; Gordis; Galling; Scott; Lohfink (see Michel, *Untersuchungen*, 173).

10   This is the "weaker" interpretation of the Hebrew expression. The "stronger" interpretation (that "everything that lies before them cannot be known by human beings"; i.e., they can know nothing at all that lies before them) would not do justice to the otherwise very precise determination of limits of human knowledge in the book of Qoheleth (cf., e.g., 1:9-11; 3:11). contrast w/ ↗

11   Cf. Prov 16:2; 21:2; 24:12.

12   Cf. Bernd Janowski, "Die Tat kehrt zum Täter zurück: Offene Fragen im Umkreis des 'Tun-Ergehen-Zusammenhangs,'" *ZThK* 91 (1994) 247–71.

human beings neither fully understand their own actions nor have them completely at their disposal, the function of the "deed-result connection" as an action-guiding concept becomes problematic. (At the same time, however, the indication of the limits of knowledge about divine activity also calls into question the assertion that God deals with people arbitrarily and unfairly.)

■ **2** Verse 2 now turns clearly to human "destiny" (מִקְרֶה *miqreh*). Here the introductory הַכֹּל כַּאֲשֶׁר לַכֹּל *hakkōl ka'ăšer lakkōl* seems not (only) to say that this is "the same for everyone" but (also and especially) that "everything [that people encounter] is what is appropriate for them." This in no way disputes the correspondence between human "deed" and "result," but rather abides by and reinforces it.

In its generality and its high degree of abstraction, the clause הַכֹּל כַּאֲשֶׁר לַכֹּל *hakkōl ka'ăšer lakkōl* is comparable to statements in the book of Sirach that are significant for the "theodicy" developed there.[13] The starting point is the perception of polar opposites in experienced reality; cf. Sir 33:14-15:

14 [Opposite evil] stands good
    and opposite life stands death;
    opposite the good man stands the evil one,
    and opposite the light stands the [darkness].
15 Look at every work of God:
    They are all in pairs, one corresponding to the
        other
    (כולם שנים שנים זה לעומת זה *kwlm šnym šnym zh kʿwmt zh*).[14]

It is also true, however, that "[The works] of the Lord are all good" (Sir 39:16). For "everything is created for its purpose," and "everything has its meaning in its time" (39:21; cf. vv. 33-34). Under this directive the polarity of experienced reality is preserved and neutralized in a correspondence of "deed" and "result": "All this proves good for the good, but for the evil ones it turns into evil" (39:27; cf. vv. 25, 28ff.; 40:10).

The clause הַכֹּל כַּאֲשֶׁר לַכֹּל *hakkōl ka'ăšer lakkōl* in Qoh 9:2 can first be understood simply in the sense: "Everything is [or: happens] just as it comes to each person." The following מִקְרֶה אֶחָד *miqreh 'eḥād* then makes clear, however, that *the same thing* comes *to everyone*, and here מִקְרֶה *miqreh* has in view the same thing as in 2:14-15 and 3:19, namely, the destiny of death: since all people are guilty (cf. vv. 3b; 7:20, 29; 8:6b, 20), the result, based on the concept of a "deed-result connection," is not, as in Sir 39:27, a differentiation between the destiny of the "good" and that of the "bad," but rather a relativization of this differentiation. In individual cases this is already indicated before death (cf. Qoh 7:15; 8:14) and becomes perfectly clear in the destiny of death that strikes all in like manner. Thus the interpretation of chance and death as the "judgment" of God over human beings, which is developed in 3:16ff. and 11:9ff., is adopted here.

The enumeration in v. 2 of "opposed groups whose lot is death" illustrates this relativization of ethical differences: "The categories are drawn from religion: conformity or nonconformity to the various expectations of Jewish society in regard to religion." The focus here is probably less on "loners" than on "slowly forming" opposing groups, "perhaps even groups among whose new mentors Qoheleth was numbered. The counsels regarding religion in 4:17–5:6, in any case, might well suggest that people in his circles would take a rather cautious stand regarding the offering of sacrifice and the swearing of oaths" (Lohfink).[15]

■ **3** When v. 3a designates the fact that "the same fate

---

13 Cf., e.g., Preuss, *Einführung*, 145; G. L. Prato, *Il problema della teodicea in Ben Sira: Composizione dei contrari e richiamo alle origini* (AnBib 65; Rome: Biblical Institute Press, 1975); O. Kaiser, "Gottesgewißheit und Weltbewußtsein in der frühhellenistischen jüdischen Weisheit," in Trutz Rendtorff, ed., *Glaube und Toleranz: Das theologische Erbe der Aufklärung* (Gütersloh: Gütersloher, 1982) 85ff.

14 After the translation of Sauer, *JSHRZ* III.5.

15 The two opposing pairs "who sacrifice/do not sacrifice" and "who swear/shy away from swearing"

stand out in the series through the fact that their second member does not consist of only one word. It is hardly accidental that precisely behind these two antitheses current disagreements are to be presumed. Thus Zimmerli, for example, wonders whether in the juxtaposition of "sacrificing and nonsacrificing we are to think of a temple- and sacrifice-free 'pietism' in the sense of Pss 40:7; 50:13; 51:18-19" (cf. above on 4:17–5:6). And Lauha holds that "behind the swearing and nonswearing individuals one (must) presume two groups with religiously opposite attitudes toward the oath, although it is

befalls everyone" (כִּי־מִקְרֶה אֶחָד לַכֹּל *kî miqreh ʾeḥād lakkōl*) as something "bad" (זֶה רָע *zeh rāʿ*), it thereby nips in the bud any program of "theodicy" as a "cosmodicy," as developed, for example, in the book of Sirach:[16] the works of God are by no means all "very good," as asserted in Sir 39:16. Yet this does not speak against the "goodness" and "righteousness" of God, for it is also true that "the heart of human beings is full of evil (רָע *rāʿ*), and blindness is in their heart as long as they live." Apparently this statement alludes to Gen 6:5: "Yahweh saw that the wickedness of humankind was great on earth, and that every product of the thoughts of their hearts was only evil continually" (cf. Gen 8:21).[17] In any case, here (as already in 7:20, 29; 8:6, 11) the conception of the primal history in Genesis 1–11 (with emphasis on the accents placed by the non-Priestly texts[18]) is taken up: God has made the world "good" (Genesis 1–2), but because of human wickedness it now contains "good" and "evil" (Genesis 3ff.); in both God's work remains "beautiful" or "appropriate" (Qoh 3:11)—even and especially death, which, as the common "destiny" of all people, represents God's judgment over their wickedness (cf. Gen 3:19, 22ff.; Qoh 3:16ff.).

■ **4** Verses 4-6 relate to vv. 1-3:[19] if the destiny of death that is common to all negatively marks a limit on human possibilities (v. 3bβ: "and afterward—to the dead"), the life that is common[20] to all before death includes, con-

versely, positive possibilities for all people (v. 4a: "those who 'belong' to the living have hope"). Here "hope" (בִּטָּחוֹן *biṭṭāḥôn*) goes beyond the "certainty" of having to die (cf. v. 5a) to the "hope" of possibilities of pleasure and enjoyment that life offers (cf. vv. 7-10).[21] For understanding v. 4b, which perhaps takes up a contemporary "proverb," we must note "that in the ancient Near East the dog was one of the most despised of animals, while the lion was held to be king of the beasts" (Lohfink). If even a dog has it better than a dead lion solely on the basis of his being alive, then this underlines the positive value of life, rather than "ironically" demonstrating "what questionable luck it is to be alive" (thus Lauha).

■ **5-6** Even if v. 5 cites as a privilege of the living vis-à-vis the dead the fact that the former "know that they will die," whereas the latter "know nothing (more) at all," what is meant here does not have to be "ironically" the opposite of what is said.[22] Rather, this asserts that it is not the driving out or playing down of death, but only the consciousness of having to die, that "enables one to live properly. One can take hold of joy as the God-given lot in life, then, when occasion arises, take powerful action" (Lohfink). Moreover, the knowledge of the living about the death that faces them (v. 5a), in contrast to the total ignorance of the dead (v. 5b), shows in exemplary fashion that emphasis on the boundaries of human knowledge (v. 1b) in no way denies its possibilities.

not known which circles of Judaism may be involved that, like the later Essenes, already rejected swearing in Qoheleth's time (Josephus *Bell.* 2.8.6; *Ant.* 15.10.4; Sir 23:9ff.)" (cf. also above on 8:2-3).

16 Cf. Preuss, *Einführung*, 145: "In order to be able to hold fast to the divine righteousness vis-à-vis the unrighteousness in the world, [Sirach] takes refuge in a special kind of creation theology. According to it, God created the whole world both with wisdom and in and according to his order. Thus, God's righteousness can and should be perceived in and from the world as a whole, rather than from the life and fate of the individual."

17 Cf. C. C. Forman, "Koheleth's Use of Genesis," *JSS* 5 (1960) 258–59; T. Krüger, "Die Rezeption der Tora im Buch Kohelet," in idem, *Kritische Weisheit*, 190–91.

18 Gen 6:5 and 8:21 may belong to the post-Priestly reworking of the flood story; cf. T. Krüger, "Das menschliche Herz und die Weisung Gottes," in Reinhard Gregor Kratz and Thomas Krüger, eds.,

Rezeption und Auslegung im Alten Testament und in seinem Umfeld (OBO 153; Fribourg, Switzerland: University Press; Göttingen: Vandenhoeck & Ruprecht, 1997) 65–92.

19 The juxtaposition of "the living" and "the dead" in vv. 4-5 is anticipated in v. 3b (אֶל־הַמֵּתִים . . . בְּחַיֵּיהֶם *bĕḥayyêhem ... ʾel-hammētîm*): טוֹב *ṭôb* in v. 4b contrasts with the double רָע *rāʿ* in v. 3, יוֹדְעִים אֵינָם *ʾênām yôdĕʿîm* (v. 5) takes up אֵין יוֹדֵעַ הָאָדָם *ʾên yôdēaʿ hāʾādām* (v. 1b), אַהֲבָתָם גַּם־שִׂנְאָתָם גַּם *gam ʾahăbātām gam-śinʾâ* (v. 6a) corresponds to גַּם־אַהֲבָה גַם־שִׂנְאָה *gam-ʾahăbâ gam-śinʾâ* (v. 1b), and v. 6bβ repeats בְּכֹל אֲשֶׁר־נַעֲשָׂה תַּחַת הַשָּׁמֶשׁ *bĕkōl ʾăser-naʿăśâ taḥat haššemeš* from v. 3aα.

20 The verb חבר *ḥbr* here, like חָבֵר *ḥābēr* in 4:10, indicates the elementary "solidarity" that is created precisely by the common threats of chance and death.

21 Cf. the motive "parallels" to vv. 4-6 cited by Braun, *Kohelet*, 103–4, from the Greek world, esp. Euripides, *Troad.* 635: "Whoever still lives can hope."

22 Thus, e.g., Crenshaw: "Qohelet's words appear

The idea that the advantages of life should be recognizable in the negative description of the existence of the dead becomes clear in the key words "wage" (שָׂכָר *śākār*) and "portion" (חֵלֶק *ḥēleq*) in vv. 5b-6. Whereas the dead, after the fading of the "remembrance" (זֵכֶר *zēker*) of them (at the latest), have no more "wage" (שָׂכָר *śākār*), as v. 5b states with a beautiful play on words, the living, according to 4:9, have the prospect of a "good wage" (שָׂכָר טוֹב *śākār ṭôb*) for their work done in solidarity with their comrades. And whereas the dead will "never again . . . have any portion in all that is done under the sun" (v. 6b), the living can look forward to their "portion" of pleasure and enjoyment (3:22; 5:17-18; 9:9). If it is somewhat negative not to be able to participate "in all that is done under the sun," this realm apparently has not only its bad side (v. 3aα) but also its good aspects. If, finally, with "love," "hate," and "jealousy" (v. 6a) "the whole complexity of interpersonal dealing" has been lost by the dead, this makes clear the relative value that "interpersonal communication" (Lohfink) has, independent of its ambivalences (v. 1b).[23]

■ **1-6** Even more clearly than 7:15-22 and 8:10-15, in the critical discussion of an ethic that is based on the concept of a "deed-result connection" 9:1-6 takes as its starting point the interpretation, developed in 3:16ff. and 11:9ff., of chance and death as the "judgment" of God on human beings: in view of the general guiltiness of all humanity (v. 3bβ), it is consistent with the postulate of a "deed-result connection" if there is in the end no difference between the destiny of the "good" and the "bad" (v. 2). The differentiation between good and bad "deeds" is thus, in view of death, relativized in the same way as the differentiation between good and bad "results": in comparison with the dead, all those who are alive basically have it "good" (vv. 4-6). The ethical consequences of this insight are made clear in 9:7-10.

■ **7-10** Verses 7-10 connect with the previous sayings in the book of Qoheleth on pleasure and enjoyment as the "highest good" (3:12-13, 22; 5:17-18; 8:15). After the "praise" of pleasure in 8:15 we have here a further augmentation with a direct exhortation to the reader in the second person masculine singular (as later in 11:9ff.; cf. already—with other terminology—7:14) and a broader development of the theme (Whybray). The linking of the invitation to pleasure (vv. 7-9) with exhortation to vigorous action (v. 10) corresponds to 3:12 and 11:1–12:7.

■ **7-9** With "pleasure," "eat," and "drink," v. 7a already contains the key words used in 3:12-13; 5:17-18; and 8:15 to describe pleasure and enjoyment. בְּלֶב־טוֹב *běleb-ṭôb* can simply mean "with glad heart, happy, of good cheer"; similar to 11:9 (וְיטִיבְךָ לִבְּךָ *wîṭîběkā libběkā*), however, here we can also hear: "with good understanding," that is, in a reasonable way. This would indicate that pleasure and enjoyment are in no way supposed to serve as an "anesthetic" that helps "people forget the wretchedness of their lives" (Lauha).[24] Since according to 3:11ff. pleasure and enjoyment are the behavior appropriate to human beings, they can trust that this activity is "approved" by God (v. 7b).[25] If one relates 9:1 to the insecurity of human beings over God's "love" or "hate" toward them, here the way is shown to overcome it.

Verses 7-9 seem to have in view relatively "modest" pleasures that for the addressees of the text were rela-

---

ironic. No comfort derives from knowing that the dead have already received their rewards and are completely forgotten, for the living will experience the same oblivion. Awareness of such grim prospects can hardly form a basis for hope. In this instance, ignorance is preferable." The opposition of "optimistic" and "pessimistic" interpretations of the text in the secondary literature shows that the (pragmatic) effect of the "hope" for all the "living" exhibited in the book of Qoheleth is decisively influenced by the expectations or claims of life that the recipient has—a state of affairs that is strikingly presented by the royal travesty in 1:12–2:26.

23 Whereas "love" and "hate" in v. 1b stand in antithesis to each other (cf. 3:8), in v. 6a their opposition is relativized by the addition of "jealousy" (cf. 4:4).

24 Cf., e.g., Theognis 877–78 (quoted according to Braun, *Kohelet*, 137 n. 443): "Drink wine . . . then you will chase away pressing cares. Only in drunkenness will things seem a lot lighter to you."

25 Cf. van der Ploeg: "Wat God 'bij voorbaat' goedkeurt is het door Hem als gave aan de mensen geschonken genieten van het leven; God verlangt dat de mensen zijn goede gaven ook zullen gebruiken." ["What God approves of 'in advance' is the gift of enjoying the life that he gave to human beings; God requires that human beings use his good gift."]

tively easily available "always" (בְּכָל־עֵת *bĕkol-ʿēt*: v. 8a):[26] "Bread and wine represent everyday needs of life (Gen 14:18; Judg 19:19; Lam 2:12; Ps 104:14-15); wine is also a bringer of joy (Qoh 2:3; 10:19; Amos 9:14; Pss 4:8; 104:15; Sir 40:20)" (Lauha). "The value of white clothes in a hot climate was widely known, and the frequent application of oils to combat the deleterious effect of dry heat on skin was widely practiced by those who could afford it" (Crenshaw).[27]

The exhortation to enjoy life "with a woman whom you love" in v. 9a contradicts the (superficially) derogatory judgment of women in 7:26ff. The idea that אִשָּׁה *ʾiššâ* means "the wife of the one admonished" (thus, e.g., Lauha) is not to be derived from the text (as Lohfink correctly notes). The repeated reference to the whole length of life in v. 9a ("*all* the days of your fleeting life . . . *all* your fleeting days") could suggest understanding v. 9a as an exhortation to loyalty in partnership (which would then, to be sure, be substantiated quite differently than in texts like Prov 5:15-23 and Mal 2:13-16). If one relates Qoh 9:1 to the fact that people's own feelings of "love" and "hate" are uncertain and not at their disposal, then v. 9a would show one way to "overcome contingency."

When v. 9bα designates the possibilities of pleasure and enjoyment just named as "your share in life" (or "with the living"?) or "your portion in life" (cf. 2:10; 3:22; 5:17-18), this recalls the juxtaposition of "living" and "dead" in vv. 4-6 (cf. v. 6b: "never again will they have any portion . . ."): because *after* life there is no longer any "portion" for human beings, they are supposed to enjoy their "portion" *in* life. Verse 9bβγ, with its reference to "work and toil" (עָמָל *ʿāmāl*), makes clear that enjoyment and activity are not mutually exclusive and thereby leads to the exhortation to vigorous action in v. 10.

■ **10** Verse 10a encourages one to do whatever is necessary and possible.[28] Human action is not supposed to be oriented (in accordance with the concept of a "deed-result connection") toward the expectation of future benefits for the one acting but toward the exigencies of the present (cf. 11:1-6). With the use of the expressions יָדְךָ *yādĕkā* ("your hand") and בְּכֹחֲךָ *bĕkōḥăkā* ("with your strength") in v. 10a, it becomes clear that 9:1 ("in God's hand": בְּיַד הָאֱלֹהִים *bĕyad hāʾĕlōhîm*) is not to be understood in the sense of a total lack of human freedom of action. Verse 10b takes up once again the juxtaposition of "living" and "dead" from vv. 4-6: in view of the destiny of death facing everyone, the exhortation to pleasure and vigorous action in the present takes on more urgency (cf. 11:9ff.).[29]

■ **7-10** Like 8:15, 9:7-10 shows an alternative to an ethic that is based on the concept of a "deed-result connection": if human beings accept death as a destiny that (with justification!) affects everyone in like manner (9:1-6), they gain the freedom to actively shape and enjoy their lives in the present.

It is often assumed that 9:7-9 alludes to then extant texts or quotes such texts or reworks them literarily. Parallel motives are to be found especially in an Old Babylonian fragment of the Gilgamesh Epic (or an Old Babylonian Gilgamesh tradition), in Egyptian harpers' songs, and grave inscriptions, as well as in various Greek texts.

The so-called Meissner-Millard Tablet (ca. 1800 B.C.E.) offers an Old Babylonian variant of the episode of the visit of Gilgamesh with the taverner before his journey over the waters of death to Utnapishtim, as described in tablet X of the Ninevite version of the Gilgamesh Epic. Here in col. iii the taverner speaks to Gilgamesh:

26 Contra, e.g., Lohfink: "Qoheleth is no believer in the 'small joys of everyday,' as many moralists would recommend. He envisions great banquets."

27 On the use of oil as a "part of daily hygiene" cf. also, e.g., Ulrich Luz, *Matthew 1–7* (CC; Minneapolis: Fortress Press, 1989) 361 (on Matt 6:17-18).

28 Cf. Fox: "The hand 'finding' or 'reaching' signifies metaphorically the concept of *ability* (most clearly in Lev 12:8; 25:28; Isa 10:10). Nowhere does it mean 'happen to do (something)' without also implying the *ability* to do it."

29 On v. 10b Lauha writes: "Just as enjoyment is futile against this background, so all striving to do justice to earthly duties—worthy in and of itself—also dissolves into nothing in death." Thus in Lauha's view it is clear "between the lines" that Qoheleth "himself holds this motto (scil. v. 10a) to be illusory." But this is precisely what the text *does not say*!

O Gilgamesh, where are you wandering?
The life that you seek you never will find:
when the gods created mankind,
death they dispensed to mankind,
life they kept for themselves.
But you, Gilgamesh, let your belly be full,
enjoy yourself always by day and by night!
Make merry each day,
dance and play day and night!
Let your clothes be clean,
let your head be washed, may you bathe in water!
Gaze on the child who holds your hand,
let your wife enjoy your repeated embrace!
For such is the destiny [of mortal men].[30]

In the present state of our knowledge of the tradition history of the Gilgamesh Epic, a literary connection between this text and Qoh 9:7-9 must be excluded, since this speech of the taverner was not incorporated into the "canonical" version of the twelve-tablet epic, and only this "'canonical' version was handed down into the late period."[31] It is possible, at most, that the advice of the taverner goes back to a drinking song that (passed on via Old Syriac variants?) also gained entrance into the book of Qoheleth,[32] but this is nothing more than pure hypothetical speculation.

The Egyptian "Harpers' Song of Antef (or: Intef)," "which, according to its title . . . is supposed to stem from the time of the early 11th Dynasty (21st/20th century B.C.E.) but in reality probably did not originate until the late Amarna period,"[33] exhorts one to the enjoyment of life in view of human mortality:

A generation passes,
Another stays,
Since the time of the ancestors . . .
None comes from there,
To tell of their state,
To tell of their needs,
To calm our hearts,
Until we go where they have gone!
Hence rejoice in your heart!
Forgetfulness profits you,
Follow your heart as long as you live!
Put myrrh on your head,
Dress in fine linen,
Anoint yourself with oils fit for a god.
Heap up your joys,
Let your heart not sink!
Follow your heart and your happiness,
Do your things on earth as your heart commands!
When there comes to you that day of mourning,
The weary-hearted hears not their mourning,
Wailing saves no man from the pit!
Refrain: Make holiday,
Do not weary of it!
Lo, none is allowed to take his goods with him,
Lo, none who departs comes back again![34]

30 Translation by Andrew George, *The Epic of Gilgamesh* (New York: Barnes & Noble, 1999) 124.
31 Uehlinger, "Qohelet im Horizont," 188; see 183ff. Cf., e.g., Loretz, *Qohelet,* 116ff.; B. W. Jones, "From Gilgamesh to Qoheleth," in W. W. Hallo, B. W. Jones, and G. L. Mattingly, eds., *The Bible in the Light of Cuneiform Literature* (Scripture in Context 3; ANETS 8; Lewiston, N.Y.: Mellen, 1990) 349–79; J. H. Tigay, "On Evaluating Claims of Literary Borrowing," in M. E. Cohen, D. C. Snell, and D. B. Weisberg, eds., *The Tablet and the Scroll: Near Eastern Studies in Honor of W. W. Hallo* (Bethesda: CDL, 1993) 250–55; J. Y.-S. Pahk, "A Syntactical and Contextual Consideration of ʾšh in Qoh ix 9," *VT* 51 (2001) 370–80; idem, *Canto.*
32 See Tzvi Abusch, "Gilgamesh's Request and Siduri's Denial, Part I," in Cohen, Snell, and Weisberg, eds., *The Tablet and the Scroll,* 8. Cf. O. Loretz, "Altorientalische und kanaanäische Topoi im Buche Koheleth," *UF* 12 (1980) 268ff.; somewhat different is idem, "'Frau' und griechisch-jüdische Philosophie im Buch Qohelet (Qoh 7,23–8,1 und 9,6-10)," *UF* 23 (1991)" 257–58; Fischer, *Skepsis,* 137ff.; also Uehlinger, "Qohelet im Horizont," 188ff.
33 Uehlinger, "Qohelet im Horizont," 210–11.
34 Translation by Miriam Lichtheim in William W. Hallo and K. Lawson Younger, eds., *The Context of Scripture,* vol. 1 (Leiden: Brill, 1997) 49. On tradition history and history of influence see Uehlinger, "Qohelet im Horizont," 210ff.

"There is certainly no reason to assume a direct literary dependence of Qoheleth on particular harpers' songs. The connecting lines are too weak, especially when we consider that the harpers' songs known to us are all recorded in the graves of the new kingdom—more precisely, from the late Amarna period until into the Twentieth Dynasty, that is, barely a thousand years from the book of Qoheleth."[35] Again, we can speculate at most whether Qoh 9:7-9 "quotes a song whose original *Sitz im Leben* could be the symposium."[36] That at such banquets the remembrance of death can be the basis for a call to enjoyment is shown by the Egyptian custom attested by Herodotus (*Hist.* 2.78): "At a banquet, as they are held by the rich, after the meal a man carries around a wooden picture of a corpse lying in a casket. It is very well formed and painted, and one or two cubits long. He holds it in front of every drinking companion and says: 'Look at this and drink and be happy! When you are dead, you will be what he is.' Such are the customs that they have at their feasts."[37]

Yet the close connection of "*memento mori*" and "*carpe diem*" is also attested, for example, in biographical grave inscriptions from Egypt, as well as in various Greek texts; and thus the assumption that the book of Qoheleth "is to be understood in the least forced way against the background of the symposium (as the real *Sitz im Leben* and/or as a fictive-ideal constellation)" remains purely hypothetical.[38] In any case, the book of Qoheleth nowhere expressly calls readers to the celebration of festivals or feasts (cf. by contrast 7:2; 10:16ff.) and, in comparison to the named texts, seems to have in mind a rather "modest" enjoyment of life.[39]

■ **11-12** Qoheleth 9:1-6 relativizes the concept of a recognizable "deed-result connection" with a reference to death as the common destiny of all human beings (which, with the presupposition of a "deed-result connection" in regard to the general guiltiness of all people, is also deserved). Verses 11-12 place beside this the experience of contingency in life. "The key word is 'time' in the sense of *kairos* (see 3:1), in one case further determined by 'chance' (which can be open to the good as well as to the bad), and in the other by 'evil' (which leads only in one direction). 'Evil time' (already expressed in the artificial wording 'evil net') does not necessarily mean immediate death" (Lohfink).[40]

The examples in v. 11a are hardly supposed to show that in no case do the swift(est) win the race and so forth. The meaning is that they "have no guarantee."[41] Thus here, as in 7:15 and 8:1, is a reference to individual cases in which the expected success of human action

35 Uehlinger, "Qohelet im Horizont," 219.
36 Ibid., 220. Cf. also, e.g., Jan Assmann, "Der schöne Tag: Sinnlichkeit und Vergänglichkeit im altägyptischen Fest," *Stein und Zeit: Mensch und Gesellschaft im alten Ägypten* (Munich: Fink, 1991) 221–22. Contrary to Uehlinger, "Qohelet im Horizont," 220, however, "the sudden shift from reflection on the fate of the dead (third person pl.), which defines the preceding verses, into direct address and exhortation to celebrate (imperative)" is hardly an indication that Qoh "9:7ff. . . . was obviously not written ad hoc for its Qoheleth text"; cf. similar "sudden shifts" in 4:16/17; 7:8/9; 7:15/16; 7:20/21; 8:1/2; 10:3/4; 10:19/20.
37 Translation after *Herodot, Historien: Deutsche Gesamtausgabe*, trans. A. Horneffer, newly edited and clarified by H. W. Haussig, with an introduction by W. F. Otto (4th ed.; Stuttgart: Kröner, 1971) 132–33.
38 Uehlinger, "Qohelet im Horizont," 234; see 230ff. On Egypt see ibid., 208 (Petosiris), 209–10 (Taimhotep), 221 (Nebneteru). On Greek texts see Hengel, *Judaism and Hellenism*, 1:123–24; Braun, *Kohelet*, 137–38; Otto Kaiser, "Judentum und Hellenismus," *VF* 27 (1982) 73.
39 Cf. also, e.g., Whybray, "Qoheleth the Immoralist?": "Ranston's comment (1925, p. 146, quoted by Hertzberg) about the supposed relationship with *Gilgamesh* is valid for all the texts in question: Ec. 9:7-10 contains 'nothing which could not just as naturally have been written by one knowing nothing of the Babylonian poem'" (with reference to H. Ranston, *Ecclesiastes and the Early Greek Wisdom Literature* [London: Epworth, 1925]).
40 It is clear in the context that עֵת וָפֶגַע *ʿēt wāpegaʿ* in v. 11 cannot point toward death (thus, however, Ginsberg, for example): "the fact that everyone dies does not explain why the swift do not necessarily win the race, and so on" (Fox). Against this, v. 12 could be related to the destiny of death (thus, e.g., Fox, with reference to עִתֶּךָ *ʿittekā* in 7:17; cf. the corresponding images in Homer, *Odyssey* 22.383ff., 468ff.; see Braun, *Kohelet*, 87 n. 254). Yet it is just as possible to understand (רָעָה) עֵת *ʿēt (rāʿâ)* here in the sense of "time (of misfortune)" in life (cf. 3:1-8; 7:14; 8:9).
41 See Ellermeier, *Qoheletm* I/1, 245.

does not take place. Yet here, in contrast to the previously mentioned cases, it is not a question of the *effect* of the action on the one acting, in accordance with the concept of a "deed-result connection," but of the *immediate success* of the action: the "righteous" are distinguished precisely by the fact that their action is *not* aimed directly toward their own prosperity. By contrast, the "swift" run and "heroes" fight with the direct intention of winning the race or battle.

With a threefold וְגַם *wĕgam* v. 11a draws an analogy from the "swift" and the "heroes" to the "wise," the "intelligent," and the "understanding": just like the former, the latter also have no guarantee of success. Here it is presupposed that for the latter it is ultimately a matter of "bread," "wealth," and "favor."[42] Precisely this prospect was placed before the student by the teacher in the "professional self-praise of the educational industry" (Lohfink); cf., e.g., Sir 51:23ff.:

23 Turn to me, you who are uneducated,
   and lodge in the house of my teaching!
24 How long do you still want to lack this and that,
   and do you want to remain so thirsty?

. . . .

28 Many were those who heard my teaching in my
   youth;
   silver and gold will you also acquire through me.
29 I take pleasure in my house of learning,
   and you too will never be ashamed of my song.[43]

In contrast to this, v. 11b maintains that the contingency of "time and chance" (עֵת וָפֶגַע *ʿēt wāpegaʿ*), which "affect" (יִקְרֶה *yiqreh*; cf. מִקְרֶה *miqreh* in 9:2-3) everyone, cannot be completely eliminated through training and education. The immediate success of expert action is no more guaranteed than the positive effects of good deeds on the doers (in accordance with the "deed-result connection")—especially since human beings cannot foresee future misfortune (v. 12; cf. 11:1-6). In this respect as well, human beings are not distinguished from the animals ("fish" and "birds")—which they also treat in the same way (with "net" and "snare") as they themselves are treated by "time and chance" (cf. 3:18ff.). The following reflections in 9:13—10:20 show, nonetheless, that properly understood "wisdom" can offer a person a relative "advantage" over chance (10:10).

---

42 With Lohfink we may wonder whether "the whole series" in v. 11a designates "the biographical ideal of a young Greek": "success in sports as a youth, then a military career, eventually setting up a family, accumulation of wealth, public influence in the polis."

43 Translation after Sauer, *JSHRZ* III.5. Cf. also Prov 3:13ff.; 4:5ff.; 8:12ff.; Sir 39:9ff.

13 I have also seen this example of wisdom[a] under the sun, and it seemed to me significant.[b] **14** There was once a small city with few people in it, and against it came a great king, who surrounded it and erected mighty "siege towers"[a] against it. **15** Then he found in it a poor wise man who, through his wisdom, saved the city. But no one had thought about that poor man.[a] **16** Then I thought: wisdom is better than might, yet the wisdom of the poor is despised, and no one listens to their words. **17** One listens to the quiet words of the wise[a] rather than[b] to the cry of a ruler among[c] the fools. **18** Wisdom is better than the apparatus of war, but one person who goes astray can destroy much good. **10:1** Dead flies make the perfumer's oil stink and ferment.[a] More valuable than wisdom "and"[b] honor is little[c] folly.

2 The wise man has understanding on his right; the fool has understanding on his left. **3** And when the fool is underway,[a] he lacks understanding. But he thinks[b] every person is a fool.[c]

4 If the ruler's displeasure rises against you, do not give up your place! For calmness[a] covers up great shortcomings.[b] **5** There is an evil that I saw under the sun, an error like those committed by a ruler: **6** folly[a] is set in highest dignity,[b] and the rich sit below. **7** I saw slaves on their high horses and princes who had to go on foot like slaves.

8 Whoever digs a pit can fall in, and whoever breaks through a wall can be bit by a snake. **9** Whoever breaks stones can get hurt; whoever[a] splits wood puts himself in danger.[b] **10** If the iron is dull and one does not sharpen it, more strength is needed. But wisdom is the advantage[a] of the expert.[b] **11** If the snake bites before it is charmed, then the charmer has no gain.[a]

12 The words of the wise man's mouth bring him favor, but the lips of the fool swallow[a] him. **13** He begins to talk with foolishness; he ends his talk with wicked blindness.[a] **14** And the fool multiplies words. No man knows what will happen. And who can tell him what will be in the future?[a] **15** The fool is

13a Literally: "this too I saw as (a) wisdom." On ראה *rᵓh* with double accusative in the sense of "see that someone or something is such and such," cf. Gen 7:1; Ps 37:25; Job 5:3 (see *HALOT* s.v. 3.c).

13b On גָּדוֹל *gādôl* in the sense of "significant" cf., e.g., Gordis; Crenshaw; Whitley, *Koheleth*, 81.

14a Instead of מְצוֹדִים *mĕṣôdîm* ("snare, net" [cf. 7:26] or "great towers"?–cf. *HALOT* s.v.) one should read with two Heb. mss. 𝔊 σ' 𝔖 𝔙 מְצוּרִים *mĕṣûrîm* ("siegeworks"; cf. Deut 20:20); cf. *BHK*; *BHS*.

15a Or: "no one remembered that poor man (later)."

17a Literally: "words of wise men in calmness."

17b On the comparative understanding of נִשְׁמָעִים *nišmāʿîm* + מִן *min* cf. 𝔊 (ἀκούονται ὑπὲρ . . .) and 𝔙 (*audiuntur . . . plus quam . . .*).

17c Or: "over" (thus 𝔖 𝔗).

10:1a

The verb יַבִּיעַ *yabbîaʿ* is not attested by σ' 𝔗 𝔙 and therefore often stricken as a clarifying gloss. Fox recommends a correction to גְּבִיעַ *gābîaʿ* ("tumbler, cup") (cf. 𝔊 𝔖 Syh; see *BHS*).

1b With numerous Heb. mss. (cf. 𝔖 Hier 𝔙) one should read here וּמִכָּבוֹד *ûmikkābôd* (instead of מִכָּבוֹד *mikkābôd*; cf. *BHK*; *BHS*). 𝔐 can be understood in the sense of "more costly than wisdom, than esteem . . ." or "more costly than wisdom without esteem. . . ."

1c Usually מְעָט *mĕʿāṭ* is translated here with "a little" and יָקָר *yāqār* interpreted in the sense of "important" and the like (cf. 𝔖); cf., e.g., Zimmerli, who translates: "Heavier than wisdom, than honor is a little folly" and interprets: "So endangered is wisdom that even a little folly can take away all its fruit." The translation "(only) little folly" (i.e., as little folly as possible) is, however, likewise possible (cf. 5:1; 9:14) and is more likely in the context (see the commentary and T. Krüger, "Wertvoller als Weisheit und Ehre ist wenig Torheit' [Kohelet 10,1]," *BN* [1997] 62–75). 𝔊 (τίμιον ὀλίγον σοφίας ὑπὲρ δόξαν ἀφροσύνης μεγάλης) and 𝔙 (*pretiosior est sapientia et gloria parva ad tempus stultitia*) correct 𝔐 which appears offensive to them.

3a Literally: "on the way, when/as the fool goes" (K: כְּשֶׁהַסָּכָל הֹלֵךְ *kĕšehassākāl hōlēk*; Q: כְּשֶׂכָל הֹלֵךְ *kĕšessākāl hōlēk*). Perhaps K combines the variants כְּשֶׂכָל *kĕšessākāl* and כְּהַסָּכָל *kĕhassākāl* (see *BHS*).

3b Or: "says." Instead of וְאָמַר *wĕʾāmar* one should probably read וְאֹמֵר *wĕʾōmēr*.

3c Cf. 𝔙 (*omnes stultos aestimat*). The translation "and so he makes it clear to all [lit.: says to all] that he is a fool" (thus, e.g., Michel) is syntactically likewise possible but seems less sensible in the context. 𝔊 (ἃ λογιεῖται πάντα ἀφροσύνη ἐστίν) does not have to go back to a Hebrew text that varies from 𝔐.

4a מַרְפֵּא *marpēʾ* II ("calmness"); see *HALOT* s.v. 𝔊 (ἴαμα), 𝔖 (ܐܣܝܘܬܐ *ʾsywt*) and 𝔙 (*curatio*) assume מַרְפֵּא *marpēʾ* I ("healing").

16 tired by his effort;[a] he does not find his way to the city.[b]

Woe to you, O land, whose king is a boy[a] and whose princes feast in the morning. 17 Happy are you, O land, whose king is a nobleman and whose princes feast at the proper time—like heroes and not like drinkers. 18 Where sloth lives,[a] the roof beams fall, and where hands are idle, it rains into the house.[b] 19 Meals are made for enjoyment, and wine makes life joyful, and money makes everything possible.[a] 20 Even in your thoughts[a] do not curse the king; even in your bedroom do not curse the rich! For the birds of the sky could carry away the sound, and what has wings[b] could betray the saying.

4b   Or: "prevents great shortcomings," or: "makes room for great shortcomings"; see the commentary.

6a   Or (with the versions): "the fool/fools" (הַסָּכָל hassākāl instead of הַסֶּכֶל hassekel).

6b   Literally: "great heights." It is also possible to connect רַבִּים rabbîm with v. 6b: "The powerful [or: old?] and the rich sit below" (see BHK; Whitley, Koheleth, 85–86; Crenshaw).

9a   Or (with numerous mss.; cf. 𝔊 𝔙; see BHK; BHS): "and whoever splits wood. . . ."

9b   According to I. Kottsieper, "Die Bedeutung der Wz. ʿṣb und skn in Koh 10,9: Ein Beitrag zum hebr. Lexikon," UF 18 (1986) 213–22, the two finite verbs could be translated more concretely with "stab oneself" (עצב ʿṣb IV) and "cut oneself" (סכן skn II).

10a   Or: "gain."

10b   Thus with a change of the vocalization from הַכְשִׁיר hakšêr (K: הכשיר hkšyr, Q: הַכְשֵׁר hakšēr) to הַכַּשִׁיר hakkāšêr ("the capable one"; cf. Aramaic כַּשִּׁירָא kaššîrāʾ), following 𝔊 σ' 𝔊 (cf. BHS; Fox). 𝔐 (וְיִתְרוֹן הַכְשִׁיר חָכְמָה wĕyitrôn hakšêr ḥokmâ) is hard to understand. Attested only here in the OT, כשר kšr hiphil could mean "make suitable." Then one could translate: "the advantage of putting in working order is wisdom"; that is, "the advantage that a timely putting of tools in working order brings is a proof of wisdom" (thus Lauha). Whitley, Koheleth, 86, recommends interpreting הַכְשִׁיר hakšêr, in correspondence to כשר kšr aphel in Talmudic Hebrew, as "to improve, grow better," and (against the Masoretic accents) connecting it with חָכְמָה ḥokmâ: "but the development of skill is an advantage."

11a   Or: "advantage."

12a   Or: "confuse" (בלע blʿ III, thus, e.g., Lohfink).

13a   Literally: "The beginning of the words of his mouth is foolishness, and the end of his mouth is wicked blindness."

14a   Literally: "after him."

15a   Thus with the correction of 𝔐 (עֲמַל הַכְּסִילִים תְּיַגְּעֶנּוּ ʿămal hakkĕsîlîm tĕyaggĕʿennû) to עֲמַל הַכְּסִיל מְיַגְּעֶנּוּ ʿămal hakkāsîl mĕyaggĕʿennû (cf., e.g., Fox; on הַכְּסִיל hakkāsîl cf. also some Heb. mss., as well as 𝔊^SA 𝔗). 𝔐 would be understandable in the same sense at best with the assumption of a gender and number incongruence. The frequent conjecture עֲמַל הַכְּסִיל מָתַי יְיַגְּעֶנּוּ ʿămal hakkāsîl mātay yĕyaggĕʿennû ("when is the fool tired by his effort"; see BHK; BHS) makes little sense in the context.

15b   Literally: "he does not understand how to go to a city."

16a   Or: "servant."

18a   Literally: "through sloth." The dual בַּעֲצַלְתַּיִם baʿăṣaltayim (𝔐) is problematic and perhaps to be corrected in יָדִים בְּעַצְלָה bĕʿaṣlut yādayim ("through sloth of the hands") (cf. BHK and, e.g., Zimmerli; Crenshaw).

18b   Literally: "through hanging hands, the house becomes leaking."

19a Cf. *HALOT* s.v. ענה *ʿnh* I qal 3.a ("to satisfy"). Or: "money occupies everyone" (ענה *ʿnh* II hiphil; cf. 5:19; thus, e.g., Fox).

20a A change from בְּמַדָּעֲךָ *bĕmaddāʿăkā* into בְּמַצָּעֲךָ *bĕmaṣṣāʿăkā* ("in your night quarters"; cf. *BHK*; *BHS*; thus, e.g., Galling; Zimmerli) is not necessary.

20b With Q we should read וּבַעַל כְּנָפַיִם *ûbaʿal kĕnāpayim* instead of וּבַעַל הַכְּנָפַיִם *ûbaʿal hakkĕnāpayim* (K).

In the present context, 9:13–10:20 is framed and bound into a text unit by the mutually corresponding sections 9:1-12 and 11:1–12:7. The sayings and reflections gathered here are rather loosely connected, in terms of form and content, but they are thoroughly related to each other in terms of substance. The obvious assumption is that already formulated material has in part been incorporated here.

From the viewpoint of content, we may—without claiming thereby to describe *the* intended division of the text—observe that the sections in which the theme "power and dominion" plays a role (9:13–10:1; 10:4-7, 16-20) stand apart from those in which the juxtaposition of "wise man/fool" is prominent (10:2-3, 12-15). The question of the opportunities and limits of wisdom, which in these sections is considered in regard to the confrontation of the wise man with the powerful and with fools, is fundamentally explored in 10:8-11 in regard to the risks of human action. The result is the following possible division for the unit 9:13–10:20:

9:13–10:1	wisdom and power/dominion
10:2-3	wisdom and foolishness
10:4-7	wisdom and power/dominion
10:8-11	wisdom and the risks of human action
10:12-15	wisdom and foolishness
10:18-20	wisdom and power/dominion

This section begins with an illustrative story (9:13-15) in which the possibilities and limits of wisdom become clear. Verse 16 draws a "moral" from this example. Yet v. 17 (key word: "ruler") and v. 18 (key word: "apparatus of war") also point back to the story in vv. 13-15. One can read 10:1a as an illustration of 9:18b and 10:1b as a consequence thereof.

■ **9:13-15** Verse 13 introduces the story in vv. 14-15 as a "significant" example of wisdom. Where its "significance" lies for the evaluation of the opportunities and limits of wisdom is made clear by the reflections in vv. 16ff. The didactic wisdom tale in vv. 14-15 is often understood in the sense that in a small city besieged by a great king there was a "poor wise man" who *could have* saved his city, *if* someone had only thought of him.[1] This presupposes an impersonal understanding of the verb וּמָצָא *(û)māṣāʾ* ("and there was") and an interpretation of the verb וּמִלַּט *(û)millaṭ* as possibility ("and he could have saved").[2] Both are grammatically possible, yet in the present context they seem rather improbable (cf. Fox): וּמָצָא *ûmāṣāʾ* continues without interruption the series of verbs וּבָא *ûbāʾ*, וְסָבַב *wĕsābab*, and וּבָנָה *ûbānâ* whose subject is the "great king."[3] In v. 15aβ the change of subjects is marked by the postpositive הוּא *hûʾ* (וּמִלַּט־הוּא *ûmillaṭ-hûʾ*). The idea that in the city there was a "poor wise man," who did not get a chance, could have been expressed unambiguously with יֵשׁ *yēš* (instead of מָצָא *māṣāʾ*). If, however, the "great king" actually found the "poor wise man," nothing suggests that the latter could not have really saved his city.

The first point of the story, then, lies precisely in the idea that a "poor wise man" (cf. 4:13) could save his city from a "great king" and, indeed, that he could do it "through his wisdom" and not, say (like Archimedes),

---

1   Thus, e.g., Hertzberg; Galling; Crenshaw. On the didactic wisdom tale see Hans-Peter Müller, "Die weisheitliche Lehrerzählung im Alten Testament und in seiner Umwelt," *WO* 9 (1977) 77–98, reprinted in idem, *Mensch, Umwelt, Eigenwelt: Gesammelte Aufsätze zur Weisheit Israels* (Stuttgart: Kohlhammer, 1992) 22–43.

2   See respectively, GKC §§144d, 106p.
3   Cf. Ehrlich; Delitzsch.

through the construction of the weapons of war (cf. vv. 16, 18). "We are . . . to picture the king capturing an impoverished citizen, who proved able by persuasion or guile to get the king to spare the city" (Fox). Up to this point vv. 14-15 can be read as an illustration of the strength of wisdom (cf. 7:19; Prov 16:32; 21:22; 24:5), which can make even a poor man superior to a king. It is possible that this section takes up a "story of the school tradition"[4] that is supposed to make clear the true power of the wise man.

Yet in the background, vv. 14-15a already indicate a "flaw in the efficacy of the intellect" (Lohfink on v. 16): for the "poor wise man" got a chance only because the "great king" found him in the city. Whether this was a fortunate coincidence or the result of the king's systematic search for "wise men,"[5] it was, in any case, *not solely* his wisdom that enabled the poor man to save his city. Verse 15b underlines this "weakness" of wisdom—whether as an indication that none of the fellow citizens of the "poor wise man" had thought about him (so that he could have a chance only after the king had discovered him), or in the sense that later on, none of his fellow citizens still remembered him (so that his social position was probably not improved by his saving deed).

■ **16** This verse draws an initial moral from the story: *it is true* that wisdom is better than strength (v. 16αβ; cf. vv. 13b-15a), *but* the wisdom of the poor is [or: was] disparaged (v. 16bα; cf. v. 15b). Thus the assertion of a special "strength" of wisdom is *at the same time* both confirmed *and* critically relativized through an observation that is also by no means foreign to the book of Proverbs, for example (cf. Prov 14:20; 18:23; 19:7); there, however, vis-à-vis the emphasis on the strengths of wisdom, it is strongly pushed into the background—especially in the programmatic introductory chapters Proverbs 1–9. The

critical potential of the simultaneous emphasis of the strengths *and* weaknesses of wisdom in Qoh 9:13-16 becomes clear in comparison with the statements of the book of Sirach on this theme. Sirach 13:21-22[22-23] formulates an observation whose content corresponds to Qoh 9:16b:

21 [22] If a rich man speaks, there are many who
  support him,
   and his words, which are loathsome, they
    declare to be beautiful;
   the poor man totters, and they call: "Accident,
    accident!"
   And if he speaks reasonably, there is no place
    for him.
22 [23] A rich man speaks, and all are silent;
   and his brilliance is extolled up to the clouds;
   a poor man speaks, and they say: "Who is he?"
   And if he stumbles, they even push him down.[6]

Yet in other passages the book of Sirach also holds out to those of low social standing the prospect of advancement through wisdom: "free citizens will serve a wise servant" (10:25a); "there are poor people who are honored because of their insight" (10:30a); "the wisdom of the poor lifts their heads high and lets them sit among the prominent" (11:1); "many who were humiliated sat on royal thrones, and those who never came to mind have put on a crown" (11:5). Thus the strength and weakness of wisdom's assertiveness seem, according to the book of Sirach, to be related to the social position of the wise in just the opposite way from that in Qoh

---

4   Kurt Galling, "Kohelet-Studien," *ZAW* 50 (1932) 286. "It is precisely when there is not an allusion here to a known event that readers can imagine so much more easily a Hellenistic king of their own epoch" (Norbert Lohfink, "*melek, šallîṭ* und *môšēl* bei Kohelet und die Abfassungszeit des Buches," *Bib* 62 [1982] 539). On attempts to demonstrate a "historical reference" in the story (e.g., 2 Sam 20:15ff.; Themistocles; Archimedes) see, e.g., Delitzsch (s.v. and 212–13); Gordis; critical thereof is Aarre Lauha, "Kohelets Verhältnis zur Geschichte," in Jörg Jeremias and Lothar Perlitt, eds., *Die Botschaft*

und die Boten: FS H. W. Wolff (Neukirchen-Vluyn: Neukirchener Verlag, 1981) 397–98.
5   Cf., e.g., Dan 1:3ff.; on the promotion of wisdom and science by Hellenistic rulers cf., e.g., Walbank, *Hellenistische Welt*, 181ff.
6   Translation after Sauer, *JSHRZ* III.5.

9:16: *it is true* that the wisdom of the poor is (often) disparaged, *but* ultimately it is still superior in political and economic strength (and will help the wise man to improve his social position).

■ **17** The statements in vv. 16bβ-17 seem at first to contradict both what precedes and one another. In opposition to v. 16bβ, were not the words of the poor man heard *nevertheless* (at least by the king)? And *if*, as v. 16bβ asserts, they were *not* heard, is not the assertion of v. 17a—that words of the wise are heard—untenable in this kind of generality, since the poor man was also a wise man (v. 15a)?

Now, one can relate v. 16bβ, as well as v. 16bα, to the attitude of fellow citizens to the "poor wise man" (v. 15b): in spite of his success, as a poor man he is not heard (later). In contrast to this, v. 17 could then point to the hearing that the "poor wise man" received with the "great king." The term "ruler" (מוֹשֵׁל *môšēl*) in v. 17b by no means has to designate the "great king" of the example story of vv. 14-15: "*môšēl* and *šallîṭ* are broad concepts that would fit the widest variety of high officials, civil officeholders (such as tax leaseholders), military officers, and even religious authorities."[7] If one considers further that זְעָקָה *ze'āqâ* in particular also designates a "cry for *help*" and a "cry of *alarm*" (for calling out the army),[8] v. 17 could be juxtaposing the "quiet" procedure of the "poor wise man" for saving his city with the excited efforts of the "ruler" in the besieged city (cf. Crenshaw).

Understood in this way, the tension between v. 16b and v. 17a would point to the real tension between wisdom's strength and weakness. Wisdom can prevail only if it gets a hearing, and that depends not only on the wise man but also on his "public." This is the moral to be drawn from vv. 14-15.

■ **18** This verse refines this "weakness" of wisdom even further. It is true that wisdom is better (טוֹבָה *ṭôbâ*) than war apparatus (v. 18a; cf. v. 16aβ), but even one individual who makes a mistake can destroy much good (טוֹבָה *ṭôbâ*) (v. 18b). Thus the wise man is not only dependent on the support of others if his wisdom is going to have a chance (vv. 16-17); he is also threatened by the mistakes of others.

The commentaries mostly connect v. 17 with v. 18a as an "it is true" statement [or: quotation] that is followed in v. 18b (and 10:1) by a "but" statement [or: the "commentary"].[9] Yet this seems rather improbable, based on the structure of the text, for if one connects v. 17 with v. 16, then 9:16-17 and 9:18—10:1 form two analogously structured sections:

"it is true . . ." (טוֹב מִן *ṭôb min* saying)	9:16aβ	9:18a
"but . . ." (וְ *we . . .*)	9:16b	9:18b (10:1a)
comparison (without טוֹב *ṭôb*)	9:17	10:1b

Moreover, v. 18a also refers back to v. 16aβ in terms of content, which rather suggests a (relatively) new beginning.

■ **10:1a** Verse 10:1a obviously serves to illustrate 9:18b with an example from "the craft of the perfumer (1 Sam 8:13; Neh 3:8), in which something small—after all, what is a dead fly!—can bring to naught any large and lavish expense" (Zimmerli). Then v. 1b draws the conclusion from the previously illustrated "weakness" of wisdom: if social acceptance is crucial for the effectiveness of wisdom, and even one mistake can bring it to naught, then little folly (of the broad masses) is indeed more valuable than (great) wisdom and honor (of the individual "wise man"). A realistic appraisal of the strengths *and* weaknesses of wisdom, as presented in 9:13ff., supports the program of an "extensive broad education" instead of an "intensive" education for a few "elite."[10]

■ **2-3** If the text is arguing in this sense, 10:2-3 becomes understandable as a reasonable continuation. "Right" and "left" often stand for "good luck" and "misfortune" in the OT (cf. Zimmerli). Correspondingly, v. 2 is initially to be understood in the sense that the wise man has a good understanding ("heart"), but the fool a bad understanding. If v. 3 then speaks of the "way" of the fool ("underway" = "on the way"), v. 2 can be further interpreted that the wise man is well and correctly ("rightly") guided by his understanding, whereas the fool

---

7   Lohfink, "*melek, šallîṭ* und *môšēl* bei Kohelet," 542.

8   See R. Albertz, "צעק *ṣ'q* to cry out," *TLOT* 3:1090–91.

9   Cf., e.g., Zimmerli; Lohfink; Michel; Murphy.

10   See Krüger, "Wertvoller."

goes ("left-handed") onto a bad and wrong way. In the context of an "elite" conception of education, the conclusion can be drawn that the fool needs guidance by the wise man who shows him the right way and leads him to correct behavior. Against this, v. 3 raises two objections.[11] It is not enough to tell the "fool" what he should do and where he should go, because even "on the way" to the goal given him from the outside, "he lacks understanding" (v. 3a). And the "fool" will not let himself be "led" at all by a wise man, because he recognizes absolutely no one else as a "wise man" (v. 3b).[12] Thus an "elite" concept of education proves once again to be unrealistic.

■ **9:13—10:3** If one interprets 9:13—10:3 in this sense, as a contribution to a discussion of "broad education" (cf. 12:9) or "elite education," the text develops a consistent argument for the former concept. That there actually was such a discussion at the time of origin of the book of Qoheleth is shown by relevant texts of the late OT and early Jewish wisdom literature.[13] The problem is already easily recognized in the first chapter of Proverbs; it offers as the goal of that book: "to teach shrewdness to the simple, knowledge and prudence to the young. Let the wise also hear and gain in learning, and the discerning acquire skill" (1:4-5). At first glance the concepts of "extensive" (v. 4) and "intensive" (v. 5) education seem to be bound together programmatically. When, however,

v. 7 states: "fools despise wisdom and instruction," this draws clear boundaries for the program of a "broad education."

The book of Sirach also expresses skepticism regarding an "extensive" educational concept: "One who is free of work can devote himself to wisdom. How can anyone who holds the plow devote himself to wisdom" (Sir 38:24ff.). But the "intensively" educated wise man (cf. 38:34ff.) is supposed to apply his wisdom "for the people" (37:23; cf. 39:8ff.; 51:23ff.). Here one can recognize the concept of an "educational elite" that makes the claim of representing the interests of the people but, at the same time, also keeps the people in their minority: farmers and craftsmen remain excluded from political and religious office (38:33); the uneducated are exhorted to bend their necks under the "yoke" of wisdom (51:26).[14] Then a short time later the Pharisaic program of an "intensive instruction of the whole people in the law" led to the development of a "new 'plebeian' form of school" in "opposition" to the exclusive education program of the "aristocratic priestly tradition."[15]

When Qoh 9:13—10:3 confronts the program of an "elite" education with the real weaknesses of wisdom, the text reveals this concept of wisdom as ideological—even and precisely when it makes the claim of representing wisdom "for the people"!

---

11 Cf., e.g., Schwienhorst-Schönberger, *Nicht im Menschen*, 213, who interprets v. 2 as a traditional proverb and v. 3 as critical commentary by Qoheleth. In v. 3, just as in v. 2, it may also be a question of an already traditional proverb; on the type of the one "who lacks understanding" (חֲסַר־לֵב *ḥăsar-lēb*), cf. Prov 6:32; 7:7; 9:4, 16; 10:13, 21; 11:12; 12:11; 15:21; 17:18; 24:30.

12 Speaking against Lohfink's assumption that vv. 2-3 ascertain a "distinction between a lack of education and stupidity" (כְּסִיל *kĕsîl* and סָכָל *sākāl*) is, for one, the fact that the determined כְּשֶׁ(ה)סָּכָל *kĕše(has)sākāl* in v. 3a is most simply explained as a return to כְּסִל *kĕsîl* in v. 2b; and, second, that the word order in v. 3a emphasizes "the way" and not "the סָכָל *sākāl*," as would be expected in a differentiation between כְּסִיל *kĕsîl* and סָכָל *sākāl*. See also above on 7:25b.

13 In the Greek world Plato in particular, in his *Politeia*, developed a decidedly "elitist" concept of education; cf., e.g., Friedo Ricken, *Philosophie der*

Antike (Grundkurs Philosophie 6; Stuttgart: Kohlhammer, 1988) 96ff.

14 According to Hengel, *Judaism and Hellenism*, 2:54 n. 168, Sirach "may stand at a point of transition," since on the one hand he, "as a scribe conscious of tradition, wanted to exclude peasants and craftsmen from the study of wisdom," but on the other hand already emphasizes "that the true wise are wise for their people" (ibid., 1:180, with reference to Sir 38:25ff. on the one hand and 37:23; 51:23ff. on the other). Yet for Sirach, being "wise for the people" seems to mean precisely *not* conveying education to the people but rather employing his wisdom for "leadership" and for the (presumed) use of the people.

15 Ibid., 1:79-80 (in part with added emphasis in the original).

■ **10:4** With the use of direct address to the reader (second person m. sg., vetitive), v. 4 distinguishes itself from the preceding (and following) context. The circumstance given in v. 4aα could describe a variety of concrete situations: the expression "ruler" (מוֹשֵׁל *môšēl*) can be applied both to the king (in Alexandria) and to "locally available high officials, who were more significant for those addressed by this book,"[16] a representative of the high priest in Jerusalem, or of the Jewish gerousia. Also open is the reason for the "displeasure" of the ruler with the addressee and its justification.

In view of the ambiguity of v. 4aα, the exact sense of the exhortation "do not give up your place (מָקוֹם *māqôm*)" in v. 4aβ is not very clear. Is the addressee supposed to persist in his "viewpoint" even in a conflict with a more powerful person (cf. Daniel 3; 6)? Is he supposed to be ready for constructive criticism and cooperation in the political system, even if it brings him trouble?[17] Or should he, in a case of conflict, first think about how not to lose his (social) position[18] and opportunistically adapt himself accordingly to the superior power of the "ruler"? Like 8:2-3a, 10:4a is open to a

number of interpretive possibilities, whose breadth ranges from an exhortation to "civil courage" to a call for purely "opportunistic" behavior. In contrast to 8:2-3a, however, 10:4a clearly votes against a withdrawal from the company of the ruler.[19]

Verse 4b is mostly understood to mean that quiet and calmness vis-à-vis the wrath of the ruler (v. 4a) can "deter" or "make right" "great shortcomings" or "bad mistakes" (חֲטָאִים גְּדוֹלִים *ḥăṭāʾîm gĕdôlîm*) (cf. 𝔊 𝔖 𝔙).[20] חֲטָאִים *ḥăṭāʾîm* can then be related both to errors of the ruler—say, "actions he would take were his last good counselor to leave him" (Lohfink)—and to shortcomings of the one addressed, which then aroused the displeasure of the ruler regarding him. Read in that way, v. 4b would make sense as the rationale for v. 4a (understood as a call to opportunistic behavior): whoever remains calm toward the ruler can keep his position.[21] Moreover, in view of a statement like Sir 20:28b ("those who please the great atone for injustice"), v. 4b could also be understood as a reference to the fact that an individual's good relationship with the ruler can also be advantageous for the larger group (cf. Esther). Yet in this understanding

16 Lohfink; cf. idem, "*melek, šallîṭ* und *môšēl* bei Kohelet," 542: "*môšēl* and *šallîṭ* are broad concepts that would fit the most varied high officials, civil officeholders (such as tax leaseholders), and military officers, and even sacral authorities." Thus the reader of Qoh 10:4 could think of quite different concrete "figures who exercised real power in Judea or in 'Syria and Phoenicia' and thereby held 'court'" (ibid.)—for example, "the Tobiad Joseph" or "Ptolemy, son of Thraseas, who, at the end of the Ptolemaic and the beginning of the Seleucid hegemony, presumably lived as a strategos in Ptolemy (=Akko) and had at his disposal entire villages in the Megiddo plain as private property and royal fief" (ibid., 543).

17 Cf. Lohfink: "The leading class, to whom Qoheleth is speaking, must have constantly faced the question whether they should continue to seek political influence or retreat to commerce and trade and dedicate themselves only to enriching themselves and enjoying life."

18 For the comparison of מָקוֹם *māqôm* in the sense of "post, official position" Gordis refers to 1 Kgs 20:24.

19 Fox concludes from this that "Qohelet distinguishes behavior before a *melek* (8:2) from behavior before a *môšēl*, probably meaning a local authority. When a

king is angry, one should get away as soon as possible, presumably in silence and with permission. When a lesser authority is angry, one can remain in his presence and attempt to calm him down, an act that requires a certain familiarity with him." Yet the understanding of 8:2-3a presupposed here is in no way convincing (see above on this passage).

20 On the first possibility cf., e.g., *EÜ*: "Gelassenheit bewahrt vor großen Fehlern" (calmness protects against great errors); on the second possibility cf., e.g., the *ZB*: "Gelassenheit macht große Verfehlungen wett" (calmness makes up for great shortcomings).

21 For comparison one may refer to Prov 16:14 ("The king's wrath is a messenger of death, and whoever is wise will appease it"), as well as to the instructions for behavior toward rulers in Prov 14:35; 19:12; 20:2; 25:15; Sir 4:26-27; 8:1; 9:13; 20:27-28; Ahiqar 100ff. (see Loretz, *Qohelet*, 206); and the advice for dealing with superiors from Egyptian wisdom literature mentioned by Michel (*Untersuchungen*, 94–95). On the high estimation of "calmness" (מַרְפֵּא *marpēʾ*) cf. Prov 14:30; 15:4, as well as the "central conceptual antithesis of the 'silent one' and the 'hot one'" in Egyptian wisdom literature (Brunner, *Altägyptische Weisheit*, 26).

v. 4b would also support v. 4a as an exhortation to "civil courage": whoever calmly persists in his viewpoint, even in the face of the ruler's displeasure, can thereby prevent erroneous decisions.

The verb יַנִּיחַ *yannîaḥ*, however, allows for still other possible understandings.[22] *HALOT* gives for נוח *nwḥ* I hiphil B the following meanings: "place somewhere, set, lay . . . leave somewhere . . . leave behind . . . allow to stay, leave untouched . . . allow to act" (Qoh 10:4a: "give up one's place"; 10:4b: "undo"). On this basis it does not seem erroneous at all to interpret v. 4b in the sense that calmness *allows* great shortcomings—and here we can think again of both mistakes of the ruler and those of the one addressed: whoever calmly suffers displeasure over his own mistakes, or remains calm when the ruler makes a mistake, makes room for shortcomings through this attitude. Thus understood, v. 4b can be read as ironically critical commentary on v. 4a as a call for opportunistic behavior.

Thus, on the whole, v. 4 is ambiguous. It can be read (1) as a call for opportunistic behavior toward the ruler *and* (2) as a critique of such an attitude—*or* (3) as a call for "civil courage":

(1) If the ruler's displeasure rises against you, do not give up your place! For calmness covers up great shortcomings (that is, undoes them or prevents them).

(2) "If the ruler's displeasure rises against you, do not give up your place!" Indeed, calmness allows room for great shortcomings.

(3) (Even) if the ruler's displeasure rises against you, do not give up your viewpoint! Your calmness can prevent great shortcomings.

Like 8:1-9, through its ambiguity 10:4 provokes the readers to multiple readings that stimulate them to reflect critically on the advice of the text, instead of following it without question.

■ **5-7** Verses 5-7 can then be understood as the logical continuation and expansion of v. 4. The key words "highest dignity" (lit.: "great heights," מְרוֹמִים רַבִּים *měrômîm rabbîm*) and "below" (lit.: "lowness," שֵׁפֶל *šēpel*) in v. 6 take

up "place" (מָקוֹם *māqôm*) from v. 4a—in the sense of (social) "position." Here too it is a matter of "position" in relation to a representative of political power (v. 4a: "the ruler," הַמּוֹשֵׁל *hammôšēl*; v. 5b: "the ruler," הַשַּׁלִּיט *haššallîṭ*), in which possible "errors" again play a role (v. 4b: חֲטָאִים *ḥăṭā'îm*; v. 5b: שְׁגָגָה *šěgāgâ*). Here v. 4—understood as a call to "opportunistic" behavior—is placed on a broader horizon by vv. 5-7: if in v. 4 "position" in relation to the "ruler" was something given beforehand that needed to be preserved, vv. 5-7 now focus on the *presuppositions* under which social positions in general first come into being.

■ **5** When the experienceable evil (v. 5a) of a false division of social positions (vv. 6-7) is designated in v. 5b as an "error" or an "oversight" (שְׁגָגָה *šěgāgâ*) of the ruler, the irony of this statement lies not only in the fact that with שְׁגָגָה *šěgāgâ* a "cultic term" is used (cf. 5:5; Lohfink), but also in the contrast to v. 4b. Not only a "great error" but even a small "oversight" of the ruler can bring down the whole structure of social positions *within* which the addressees of v. 4—understood as a call to opportunistic behavior—assert themselves and prevent or correct "great errors." In this sense vv. 5-7 can be read as critical "commentary" to v. 4.[23] Yet in this way the criticism is directed at only *one* possible understanding of v. 4. If one interprets v. 4 as a call for "civil courage," it is reinforced by vv. 5-7: if the success of opportunistic behavior is nevertheless questionable on the basis of a possible "oversight" of the ruler, one can, in a case of conflict, remain true to one's viewpoint, even without consideration of one's "position." Verses 5-7 can thus be understood as a reflection on the themes of v. 4 on a broader horizon and from a new point of view (cf. 8:1-5, 6-9). It suggests to the reader a "second reading" in the course of which this verse is interpreted as a call for "civil courage" instead of as an exhortation to "opportunistic" behavior. Yet vv. 5-7 themselves also seem to run into a similar process of reflection.

■ **6** An indication of this is the fact that v. 6 names, in opposition to "folly,"[24] "surprisingly, not the cultured

---

22   The correction to יַנִּא *yānî'* (from נוא *nw'* hiphil: "prevent"), recommended by, e.g., *BHK* and *BHS,* has no basis in the text tradition.

23   Cf. Levy; Kroeber; Michel; Schwienhorst-Schön-berger, *Nicht im Menschen,* 214–15.

24   Schwienhorst-Schönberger, *Nicht im Menschen,*

214–15 sees in "folly" (sg.!) a cipher for the ruler of vv. 4-5: "As the personification of folly, he himself is the holder of power who decides the allocation of all offices" (ibid., 215). Yet vv. 5-6 seem intended,

but the rich" (Lohfink). The identification of wealth and wisdom presupposed here is contradicted more than once in other places in the book of Qoheleth (cf. esp. 4:13; 9:15-16).[25] It betrays an "aristocratic mind-set" (Lauha)[26] and interest in protection of the "advantages of privilege" (Crenshaw), which are called into question and threatened by processes of social upheaval.[27]

■ **7** This verse can initially be read as a continuation of the lament over upheaval processes like those in vv. 5-6. Yet closer examination reveals several signals in the text that indicate that the lament of vv. 5-6 is here relativized and ironized. Thus through the introductory "I saw" (cf. v. 5aβ), v. 7 is set apart from what precedes it. The opposition "in highest dignity"/"below" from v. 6 is taken up in v. 7 with "on their high horses"/"on foot" (lit.: "on the ground") and at the same time corrected in its dimensions: the difference in status between the riders and the walkers,[28] as measured in physical height, proves to be minimal. "On the ground" (v. 7b) is, nonetheless, the appropriate place for *all* people (cf. 5:1b)—especially since the upheaval processes lamented in vv. 5-6 take place, in any case, "under the sun" (v. 5aβ). Finally, v. 7 can also be read as an (ironic) reference to the everyday "observation" that slaves (also occasionally) ride on horses and princes go on foot. Moreover, if the reader sees in the verb הלך *hlk* the connotation "die,"[29] she or he can understand v. 7 as a reference to the power of death that levels all social differentiations (cf. 2:16; 3:19; 9:2-3).

■ Verse 7, with this relativization and ironization of the lament over upheaval processes in vv. 5-6, reveals the concept of an aristocratic or oligarchic social order as an arbitrary construct that stands in blatant disproportion to the actual realities of human life. In this respect the text is, on the level of contemporary discussion in the Greek-Hellenistic realm, comparable above all to positions of Cynicism, the older Stoa, and political utopias.[30] A corresponding confrontation between claim and reality is also shown in 8:1-5, 6-9.

■ **5-7** If this understanding of the text is correct, it in no way regards the "standards of value" of the Jerusalem gerousia—according to which "only the rich could be both knowledgeable and also therefore politically competent"—as the "only right" ones (thus Lohfink). Rather, the process "of the political disempowerment of a former upper stratum" by "a more powerful social stratum"[31] loses its terrors in view of the "natural" boundary conditions of human existence "under the sun": it only demonstrates *in concreto* the general "uncertainty of human beings in every situation and in every time" (Zimmerli).

■ **4-7** These verses show an argumentative strategy similar to that in 8:1-9. Against the background of wisdom traditions with an "opportunistic" tendency that are a component of his experiential knowledge, a contemporary reader would initially resolve the uncertainties and ambiguities in v. 4 by understanding the verse as an exhortation to opportunistic behavior vis-à-vis the

---

rather, to be understood in the sense that "folly" owes its position to the ruler, who is then not identical with it.

25   See F. Piotti, "Il rapporto tra ricchi, stolti e principi in Qoh. 10,6-7 alla luce della letteratura sapienziale," *ScC* 102 (1974) 328–33.

26   According to Aristotle (*Pol.* 1279a, b) "aristocracy" is the rule of the few, in which these "few" are "the best" or govern the state "for the best"; its degeneration is the "oligarchy," in which the few rule for the benefit of the rich. In the sense of these definitions, the "mind-set" that seems to lie behind Qoh 10:5-7 can be called more "oligarchic" than "aristocratic."

27   On the negative evaluation of such upheaval processes (from the perspective of a threatened upper class), cf. Prov 19:10; 30:21-22 and the Egyptian Admonitions of Ipuwer, often quoted by the commentators (see, e.g., Crenshaw), as well as the

"parallels . . . from lyric and drama from the Greek-Hellenistic realm" named by Braun, *Kohelet*, 98–99 n. 297. By contrast, Sir 10:25 and 11:5-6 (cf. Prov 17:2) see in such processes thoroughly positive opportunities for social climbing.

28   Lauha assumes that the thought here is of "the conditions in an army at war": "the people on foot were the great masses vis-à-vis the few fighters in chariots and later on horses."

29   Cf. 1:4; 3:20; 6:4, 6; 9:10; G. Sauer, "הלך *hlk* to go," *TLOT* 1:368.

30   On "dissent from the existing order" see G. J. D. Aalders, *Political Thought in Hellenistic Times* (Amsterdam: Hakkert, 1975) 39ff.

31   Hans-Peter Müller, "Neige der althebräischen 'Weisheit'; Zum Denken Qohäläts," *ZAW* 90 (1978) 258, 257; the latter "group in 10:6-7 must mean the upwardly mobile fools and slaves" (ibid., 257).

"ruler." The observations of vv. 5-7, however, call critically into question a fundamental presupposition of this interpretation (and the experiential knowledge that underlies it), namely, the possibility of safeguarding one's (social) position through "calmness." Thus the reader is challenged to a second reading of v. 4, in the wake of which he can interpret the verse as a call to "civil courage" and at the same time critically distance himself from the "opportunistic" traditions that determined his first reading. Within vv. 5-7, then, v. 7 again contains signals for a relativization and ironization of vv. 5-6, which again suggest to the reader a renewed reading of this section. In the process of reflection thereby encountered, the aristocratic or oligarchic status thinking evoked initially by vv. 5-6 (and v. 4a) is critically relativized. When we then read in the following v. 8: "Whoever digs a pit can fall in," this can also be read as a further commentary on vv. 4-7: perhaps the "fall" of the "rich" and "princes" also has something to do with their questionable political practices.[32]

■ 8-11 While the context discusses the strengths and weaknesses of wisdom in the confrontation of the wise with the powerful and fools, vv. 8-11 reflect fundamentally on the possibilities and limited success of wise action in the dealings of the wise man with the outside world, which for him is not completely accessible and controllable. Here the critique of the concept of a "deed-result connection"[33] in Qoheleth 7–8 (and 9:1-3) is taken up again and carried further.

■ 8-9 Verse 8 seems at first to reinforce the concept of a "deed-result connection," for which the situation in which one digs a pit (for others), but then falls in oneself, is an often cited example (cf. Prov 28:10; Pss 7:16; 9:16; 35:7-8; 57:7):

> Whoever digs a pit will fall into it,
> And whoever rolls a stone up will have it roll back
>   on him. (Prov 26:27)

Whoever throws a stone in the air throws it on his
    own head,
and a malicious blow causes wounds (on oneself).
Whoever digs a pit will fall into it,
and whoever sets a snare will be caught in it.
Whoever does injustice will have it roll back on him,
and he will not know where it came from. (Sir
    27:25-27).[34]

By v. 9 at the latest, however, it becomes clear that we are dealing here not ("metaphorically") with (later) repercussions of a bad action on the actor but with dangers that immediately threaten him in the carrying out of his action—quite apart from the question of whether it is a (morally) "good" or "bad" deed. Since at least v. 8a (on v. 8b cf. Amos 5:19) doubtless alludes to contemporary tradition, we must have here an intentional parody of the concept of a "deed-result connection," which is thereby "brought down to the level of fact."[35]

■ 10 Verse 10 continues the "game" begun in v. 8 with the building up of reader expectations and their disappointment in the ongoing text. After v. 9b calls attention to the dangers of splitting wood, one expects, after v. 10aα, a statement about the increased dangers that can arise from a poorly maintained tool in the working of stone or wood (v. 9). What follows in v. 10aβ, however, is a reference to the greater strength and effort required by the work in this case. For avoiding this (and not the unavoidable risks; cf. 9:11-12), the wisdom of the expert is to his advantage (v. 10b). Here "wisdom" clearly refers to the practical knowledge and skills of the expert worker, not to the "professional" knowledge of a "class" of "wise men."[36] In Qoheleth's view, only this kind of "wisdom"—and only in this regard (avoidance of unnecessary effort in work)—offers an "advantage" (יִתְרוֹן

Müller also identifies the attitude of "Qoheleth" with the political disempowerment of the rich.

32   Cf. Levy, who sees in 10:8-11 hidden warnings against the "dangers of associating with the powerful."

33   Cf. Bernd Janowski, "Die Tat kehrt zum Täter zurück: Offene Fragen im Umkreis des 'Tun-Ergehen-Zusammenhangs,'" *ZThK* 91 (1994) 247–71.

34   Translation after Sauer, *JSHRZ* III.5.

35   Contra, e.g., Crenshaw, who assumes that in v. 8 "Qohelet endorses the view that misconduct bears its own fruit, although elsewhere he calls this dogma into question" (similarly, e.g., Fox on vv. 8-9).

36   On the ambiguity of the concept "wisdom" in the OT cf., e.g., Preuss, *Einführung*, 10ff. (lit.).

yitrôn).[37] With this the text stands diametrically opposed to an "elite" conception of wisdom such as that represented by Sir 38:24—39:11,[38] according to which wisdom and work done by hand are mutually exclusive.

■ **11** Formulated with "biting" irony, v. 11 demonstrates that even the practical knowledge and skills of the expert do not totally eliminate dangers or guarantee success. One can initially read v. 11 in the sense that the snake bites the charmer before he has begun his charming; then here as well as in vv. 8-9 we have a reference to the unavoidable "occupational risk" of the expert, which relativizes the "advantage" of his "wisdom" mentioned in v. 10 (cf. Jer 8:17; Ps 58:5-6; and Sir 12:13: "Who pities a snake charmer when he is bitten, or all those who go near wild animals?"). Yet v. 11 can also be understood in the sense that the snake bit the one who commissioned the charmer before the latter could begin his charming, and thus in the end he has no "gain" from his activity; in this case not even the expert's wisdom can help him.[39]

■ **12-15** These verses take up again the juxtaposition of wise man and fool in vv. 2-3 but also show connections with vv. 8-11. Thus the theme "words" in vv. 12-14 is anticipated by "lord of the tongue" (thus literally for "charmer") in v. 11b (Fox), and in v. 15 we again have the juxtaposition of wisdom and toilsome work from v. 10. This indicates that vv. 8-11 and vv. 12-15 were intentionally placed together or formulated from the beginning as a coherent text.

■ **12-14** Verse 12 addresses the ("professional"?) "wise man" as opposed to the "fool." The two are compared with respect to their speech. Just like v(v). 8(-9), v. 12 can also be understood initially in the sense of the concept of a "deed-result connection" (thus, e.g., Crenshaw). The saying then corresponds to statements of traditional wisdom.[40] Then, however, v. 12a stands (at least) in tension

with 9:11a, according to which "those with understanding" have, in any case, no guarantee of "favor" (חֵן *ḥēn*). And in this understanding v. 12b is (at least) relativized by vv. 13-14a: the speech of the "fool" does not, in any case, lead immediately to his self-destruction. The nonsense that he speaks grows with the length of his talk (v. 13)—and he talks a long time (v. 14a).

Lohfink attempts to explain this tension between v. 12b and v. 14a with the assumption that in vv. 12-13 there is a "citation" that "has a full-dress commentary in Qoheleth's style" in v. 14.[41] Yet v. 12 (like vv. 8-9) already seems to contain an underlying critique of traditional wisdom, to which the present passage apparently alludes. That is, the suffix of the third person masculine singular in תְּבַלְּעֶנּוּ *tĕballĕʿennû* ("[the lips of the fool] swallow him": v. 12b) can be related both to the "fool" of v. 12b and to the "favor" of the "wise man" in v. 12a or to the wise man himself. After the weaknesses of the "wise" are repeatedly pointed out in the earlier context (9:13—10:3), this understanding of v. 12 hardly appears erroneous: the words of a wise man can lose their effect through the speech of a fool.

Verse 14b is against "the foolish, now degraded to the ignorant, with combined citations from 8:7 and 6:12. These were originally directed not against the ignorant, but rather against the traditional knowledge and its claim to explain the world. The thought may be that this is true, a fortiori, of the ignorant" (Lohfink; cf. also 3:11; 7:14; 8:17; 9:12; 11:2, 5-6): because the "fool" speaks of things of which he can understand nothing (v. 14b), his talk is nonsense (v. 13). Here too, however, we must, in the context, reckon with further possibilities of understanding. In view of the critique of wisdom's claims to knowledge presented in the preceding sections (esp. in 8:17), the "words of the wise man's mouth"

---

37 Both limitations of the "advantage" of "wisdom" by the context in 10:10b are overlooked by Michel, *Untersuchungen*, 107–8, and therefore he regards vv. 8-10 as a "quotation" that expresses the traditional conception of wisdom and is critically "commented" on by a further "quotation" appended in v. 11. Similar is Schwienhorst-Schönberger, *Nicht im Menschen*, 215–16, who, however, interprets v. 11 as a "commentary" formulated by Qoheleth himself.

38 Cf. Johannes Marböck, "Sir. 38,24—39,11: Der schriftgelehrte Weise: Ein Beitrag zu Gestalt und

Werk Ben Siras," in Gilbert, *Sagesse*, 293–316, esp. 299–300.

39 The idea that Qoh 10:11 presents a snake charmer who "in the marketplace takes a snake out of the basket and makes a show of his art before a curious public" is not quite as "obvious" as Schwienhorst-Schönberger, *Nicht im Menschen*, 216, believes.

40 Cf., e.g., Prov 10:21, 32; 15:2, 7; Sir 20:13; 21:15-17.

41 Similarly Michel, *Untersuchungen*, 266; Schwienhorst-Schönberger, *Nicht im Menschen*, 217.

(v. 12a) must, from the standpoint of v. 14b, also seem questionable[42]—at least to the extent that they contain any kind of prognosis. Yet this is precisely the case with the words of v. 12: they predict for the "wise man" and the "fool" an outcome that corresponds to the concept of a "deed-result connection." With them, v. 14b also critically calls this concept into question.

■ **15** If one understands the expression "not find one's way to the city" (lit.: "not understand how to go to a city") in v. 15b in the sense of "not reach one's goal,"[43] one can interpret v. 15 as the closing modified reformulation of v. 12 in consideration of the critical discussion of the concept of a "deed-result connection" in the book of Qoheleth and of the (only) "advantage" of "wisdom" indicated in 10:10. Since the "fool" must compensate for his lack of "wisdom" through greater "work and toil" (עָמָל ʿāmāl) (cf. v. 10), there remains the well-grounded prospect (but certainly no guarantee!) that he will tire before he reaches his goal.[44]

■ **16-20** These verses return to the theme of "dominion" and take up again the related key words from 9:13-18 and 10:4-7 ("king": 10:16-17, 20 [cf. 9:14]; "princes": 10:16-17 [cf. 10:7]; "the rich": 10:20 [cf. 10:6] "heroes/strength" [גְּבוּרָה gĕbûrâ]: 10:17 [cf. 9:16]). The argumentative connection between vv. 16-17, 18, 19, and 20 is not clear at first glance but is revealed with a closer reading.

■ **16-17** Just like 10:5-6, vv. 16-17 expresses a carefully critical conformism toward the system of monarchic rule. If in that passage, in spite of individual, "inadvertent" errors of the ruler, his power was not basically called into question (this direction is not followed until v. 7), here the concrete form of monarchic rule is tested for its quality, without this form of rule as such being rejected. The ideal king, as "nobleman" (בֶּן־חוֹרִים ben-ḥôrîm: "one who belongs to the free/prominent"), shows an "aristocratic" behavior (cf. Prov 31:4-5) that shines on his princes.[45] Verses 16b and 17bα serve as antithetical illustrations of exaggerated and appropriate expenditure and luxury in the royal court.[46] Whoever speaks thus "has in principle nothing against the luxurious life of the aristocracy, as long as it has its order" (Lauha, with reference to Jer 22:15).

The fact that the question of the appropriate class background of a king was a theme of contemporary political discussion[47] is shown by *Ep. Arist.* 288ff. In the context of the symposium in the Alexandrian court, the Ptolemy king asks a Jewish wise man here: "What is better for the people: when their ruler is of lowly background or when he is of royal blood?" The latter answers him: "When it is the best by nature! For even rulers of royal origin are at times inconsiderate and harsh toward their subjects; it is more likely, however, that those of lowly origin who have (themselves) known misery and

---

42 The antithesis "wise man/fool" (vv. 12-14a) is eliminated in v. 14b in "no man"!

43 Thus Fox with reference to "the Egyptian phrase, 'does not reach the city,' which means 'does not attain its goal'; e.g., *Eloquent Peasant*, B1, 326–27, where the idiom stands in antithesis to 'reach land,' an Egyptian cliché for succeeding." Cf. the translation of Erik Hornung, *Altägyptische Dichtung* (Stuttgart: Reclam, 1996) 25: "ein schlechtes Tun kann das Ziel nicht erreichen [a bad deed cannot reach the goal (lit.: does not reach the city—T.K.)], nur der Hilfreiche kommt an Land [only the helpful reach land]."

44 Another possible understanding of v. 15 is indicated by, e.g., Lohfink in his alternative translation: "Whoever does not understand how to go into the city wears himself out like an unlearned worker." Even in this interpretation, the concept of a "deed-result connection" in v. 15 would be called back to the ground of (social) fact. Schwienhorst-Schönberger, *Nicht im Menschen*, 219, understands 10:15

as an introduction to vv. 16-20 and sees in it the "following sense: through their many sayings the wise have proven themselves to be fools (10:12-14). They tire those who are not even in a position to go into the city and find their way in an urban milieu with advice about behavior in the royal court" (10:16-20).

45 Cf. Sir 10:2: "As the ruler of the people is, so are his officials." According to *Ep. Arist.* 280, the governor (στρατηγοί) is supposed to imitate the conduct of the king.

46 Cf. the warning against useless expense, extravagance, and opulence in *Ep. Arist.* 205 and 278, as well as the exhortation to the ruler to "be sober most of the time of his life" (*Ep. Arist.* 209). Cf. also the repeated exhortations to self-control and moderation (*Ep. Arist.* 211, 222–23, 245, 256) and the instructions for the holding of banquets (*Ep. Arist.* 286–87).

47 Cf. also L. Wickert, PW 20:2205ff. (N. Meisner, *JSHRZ* II.1, 82 [note on *Ep. Arist.* 289]).

poverty will prove themselves as rulers to be more cruel than godless tyrants. As said, however: a good and educated character equips one for ruling."[48] While the ideal of an aristocratic [or: oligarchic] background of the king is already critically relativized here as the criterion of the judgment of his rule through the criterion of character formation, it is expressed in comparatively unbroken form in Qoh 10:16-17.

If one interprets vv. 16-17 in this sense as a more "theoretical" contribution to the political discussion, one is led to interpret נַעַר *na'ar* in v. 16a as "servant." If, however, one understands this term in the sense of "boy, child," vv. 16-17 could formulate a very concrete political position in the contemporary historical context. Namely, v. 16 could then be directed at Ptolemy V ("Epiphanes"), "who ascended the throne in 205 B.C.E. at five years of age, while his guardian, Agathocles, and the latter's sister Agathoclea were creating an uproar by their mismanagement and debauchery. . . . There was a revolt in 203 B.C.E., and the hated brother and sister were slaughtered by the people of Alexandria. In this interpretation the 'king from noble stock' would be identified as Antiochus III, who during these years in Antioch was preparing himself to conquer Palestine" (Lohfink; see above on 4:13-16). Verses 16-17 could then express the opinion of the "Jerusalem party supporters" of Antiochus III.[49]

The juxtaposition of the eating and drinking customs of "princes" in v. 16b and v. 17b perhaps alludes to the reproaches in Isa 5:11, 22: "Woe to those who rise early in the morning in pursuit of strong drink, who linger in the evening to be inflamed by wine!" (v. 11). "Woe to those who are heroes in drinking wine (גִּבּוֹרִים לִשְׁתּוֹת יָיִן *gibbôrîm lištôt yāyin*) and valiant in mixing drink!" (v. 22). The curious expression in v. 17bβ[50] (בִּגְבוּרָה וְלֹא בַשֶּׁתִי *bigĕbûrâ wĕlōʾ baššĕtî*) could then possibly already indicate a background of ironic criticism of the aristocratic ideal brought to expression in vv. 16-17.

■ **18** The statement against laziness[51] in v. 18 is also easily imaginable in the mouth of rich aristocrats. It could connect with the critique of v. 16; then the writer here could have been thinking "about the lazy celebration of feasts in the court" (Zimmerli). And "house" may "be an image of the state, especially where the Ptolemaic Kingdom ideology considered the state as the *oikia*, the household, of the king" (Lohfink; contra Gordis).[52]

■ **19** This verse clearly relates to the eating and drinking customs of princes mentioned in vv. 16b, 17b. Which of the two types of princes named there is the topic here, however, is not made known—apparently what is said here is true of both. Thus in a way comparable to 8:1-5, 6-9, the statement in vv. 16-17, defined by an antithesis (good vs. bad kings with their princes), is abolished in v. 19 in a general, antithesis-leveling statement—and thereby critically relativized and commented on. The "appropriate" expense in the royal court, according to v. 16, serves enjoyment in the same way as that criticized in v. 17 as "inappropriate"—and naturally wine is also drunk in the process![53] By contrast, there is nothing to object to from the standpoint of the ethic of the book of Qoheleth, which, indeed, values eating, drinking, and pleasure quite positively (see 3:12-13, 22; 5:17-19; 8:15; 9:7)—yet as provided by *God* and not by *money*! Thus

---

48 Translation after Meisner, *JSHRZ* II.1.
49 Cf. also Hitzig; K. D. Schunck, "Drei Seleukiden im Buche Kohelet?" *VT* 9 (1959) 192–201, repr. in idem, *Altes Testament und Heiliges Land: Gesammelte Studien*, vol. 1 (BEAT; Frankfurt am Main: Lang, 1989) 9–18. If (as will be shown) vv. 16-17 are reflected on critically in the continued text, the "veiled declaration" to Antiochus III can be identified neither as the "main point of this part of the text" nor as the position of "Qoheleth," as Lohfink holds.
50 The clause is often excluded as a gloss (thus, e.g., Michel; Lauha; Zimmerli); Galling places it before v. 17bα.
51 Cf. Prov 6:6, 9; 10:26; 13:4; 19:15; 31:27 (Loretz, *Qohelet*, 207); on the image of the leaky roof cf. Prov 19:13; 27:15 (Zimmerli).

52 Or does v. 18 illustrate with critical irony the "strong food" of v. 17bβ? Then perhaps a "whimsical toast" is quoted or parodied here, with which the guests at the meal are encouraged to begin eating.
53 *Ep. Arist.* 187–294 (see above) also develops its teaching on the kingdom within the framework of a banquet. Here at the end of each of the seven dialogues, the transition to the "enjoyable part of the evening" is expressly noted; e.g., *Ep. Arist.* 274: "then he [the king] opened the feast by copiously drinking to each individual, and he conversed happily and very enjoyably with the men" (cf. 198, 202, 235, 247, 261, 294).

behind v. 19b one may suspect a "satirical intention."[54] In this way the statements of vv. 16-18 are stripped of their ideological dimensions and reduced to a realistic size. The conditions of dominion described in v. 17 have their (relative) advantage over that described in v. 16 and are not disputed by v. 19; rather, it is disputed that v. 17 describes an ideal condition: in each case the rulers think first of their own welfare—and their financial income and expense.

■ 20 The understanding of 10:16-19 as a critical discussion of superficially positive attitudes toward the monarchy on the basis of an aristocratic or oligarchic standpoint is supported by v. 20. The admonition to curse neither a king nor a rich man (v. 20a; cf. Exod 22:27) presupposes that the reader is equally poorly disposed toward both. Yet with all the criticism of the reigning order, v. 20 still seems to definitely call for a conformist and opportunistic quietism in political practice: "The king and the wealthy, whose incorporation into the apparatus of the state is shown here more clearly than anywhere else, must be exempted from any criticism. One must always be ready to side with the ruling order."[55]

Nevertheless, the admonition of v. 20a is already thwarted by the immediately preceding context. It is true that vv. 16-17 "are formally a cry of woe and weal over the land"; in terms of content, however, they—just like v. 19—are directed against "king and princes" (Lohfink). Thus v. 20a can be understood as "an ironic warning directed against Qohelet's own words in the opening verse of this passage, perhaps implying that he has just insulted actual people" (Fox). Yet this seems to be con-

tradicted by the reasoning behind the admonition in v. 20b, which seems to point to the endangerment, to be taken quite seriously, through "information sources" and "denunciations" (Lohfink).[56]

Quite serious advice comparable to v. 20 is found in the Aramaic Ahiqar sayings (10.2-4):

2 [My] son, do not [curse] the day until you see [its end].
3 May [this] come to your attention, that in every place their [i.e., the gods'] [eyes] and their ears are near to your mouth. Take care that it does not destroy [your] advantages.
4 Before all others mind your mouth, and [against] those who [ask], harden ‹your› heart; for a [b]ird is a word, and whoever releases it is a man without understanding.[57]

This text illustrates the image of Qoh 10:20b.[58] The comparison also makes clear, however, that this image is distorted here into a caricature. In 10:20 the word is not compared to a bird, but the bird is declared the transmitter of a word—and indeed a word spoken "in your bedroom," even an unexpressed thought! Consequently, v. 20a advises not only caution in speaking but also caution in thinking. Thus the text seems to propagate less a conformist-opportunist quietism than to make this attitude look ridiculous as the fruit of exaggerated anxiety. If 11:1-6 and similar passages polemicize against excessive caution, then this can also be related back to 10:20.

54 Braun, *Kohelet*, 99 (on v. 19 as a whole); cf. the statements mentioned in ibid., n. 300, from the "Greek realm . . . that exhibit an equally gnomic-satirically colored background."
55 Frank Crüsemann, "The Unchangeable World: The 'Crisis of Wisdom' in Koheleth," in Willy Schottroff and Wolfgang Stegemann, eds., *God of the Lowly: Socio-Historical Interpretations of the Bible* (Maryknoll, N.Y.: Orbis, 1984) 71.
56 "If the historicizing interpretation of v. 16 [see above] is correct, then v. 20 fits in, because Agathocles worked especially hard with information sources and in taking account of denunciations" (Lohfink).
57 Translation after Ingo Kottsieper, *TUAT* 3:336.
58 Cf. in German: "The sparrows sing it from the rooftops" and in German and English: "Walls have ears." Crenshaw points further to Aristophanes, *Birds* 49–50, 601; Juvenal, *Satires* 60, 95–96, where likewise "the motif of a communicative bird" appears.

1 Cast your bread into[a] the water
    after many days you can find it again.

2 Share with[a] seven or eight.
    You do not know what disaster may
        come on earth.

3 When the clouds are heavy,[a]
    they pour rain on the earth.[b]
    And if a piece of wood[c] falls to the
        south or to the north,
    wherever the wood falls, there it will
        lie.[d]

4 Whoever regards the wind will not sow,
    and whoever looks to the clouds will
        not reap.

5 As you do not know the way of the
        wind,
    nor[a] the child[b] in the womb of the
        pregnant one,
    so also you do not know the work of
        the Deity,
    who creates all this.

6 In the morning sow your seed,
    and in the evening do not let your hand
        rest!
    For you do not know what will
        prosper,
    Whether this or that,
    or whether both alike will turn out
        well.

7 But the light is sweet,
    and it is good for the eyes
    to see the sun.

8 When a man lives many years,
    he rejoices over that[a]
    but also thinks about the dark days,[b]
    for they are numerous.[c]
    All that comes is fleeting.

9 Rejoice, young man, in your youth,
    and let your heart cheer you in the
        days of your youth.
    Go your way with understanding[a] and
        with open eyes.[b]
    And know that regarding all this God
        will go with you into judgment.
    10 Let your heart be free from
        vexation,
    and keep your body far from evil.
    For youth and black hair[a] are fleeting.

12:1 So think about your creator[a] in the days
        of your youth,
    before the bad days come
    and years draw near of which you will
        say:
    "They do not please me."

1a   Literally: "upon."
2a   Literally: "give a portion to."
3a   Literally: "full."
3b   Or according to the Masoretic accents: "When the clouds
     are full of rain, they pour (it) on the earth."
3c   Or: "tree."
3d   On the verb form יְהוּא *yĕhûʾ* (= יְהִי *yĕhî* in the sense of יִהְיֶה
     yihyeh) see Schoors, *Preacher*, 42–43.
5a   Thus with 𝔐 כַּעֲצָמִים (*kaʿăṣāmîm*). Some mss. (cf. 𝔗) read
     בַּעֲצָמִים *baʿăṣāmîm*: "As you do not know the way of the
     breath of life into the child in the body of the pregnant
     one" (i.e., as you do not know how the breath of life
     comes into the child).
5b   Literally: "the bones."
8a   Or: "he is supposed to rejoice over that."
8b   Or: "but is also supposed to think about the dark days."
8c   Or: "they will be numerous."
9a   Literally: "Go on the ways of your heart."
9b   Instead of וּבמראי *wbmrʾy* one may read וּבמראה *wbmrʾh*
     (וּבְמַרְאֵה עֵינֶיךָ *ûbĕmarʾēh ʿênêkā*) with Q, several mss., and
     the versions. מַרְאֵה עֵינָים *marʾēh ʿênayim* can designate
     both the seeing of the eyes and what the eyes see (cf.
     HALOT s.v. מַרְאֶה *marʾeh*).
10a The meaning of the *hapax legomenon* שַׁחֲרוּת *šaḥărût* is
     uncertain; cf. *HALOT* s.v. 𝔊 (ἡ ἄνοια) and 𝔖 (ܐܠܒܬ
     lʾ ydʿt) interpret the noun in the sense of "ignorance"; 𝔙
     (*voluptas*) in the sense of "desire"; 𝔗 in the sense of the
     translation proposed above.

12:1a
     Instead of בּוֹרְאֶיךָ *bôrĕʾêkā*, which could also be inter-
     preted, if need be, as an orthographic variant of the sin-
     gular form or as a royal plural analogous to אֱלֹהִים
     ʾĕlōhîm, one could read, with some mss. and the versions,
     the sg. בּוֹרְאךָ *bôreʾkā*. Since the versions clearly read "your
     creator," the numerous proposed conjectures are hardly
     justified (e.g., בּוֹרְךָ *bôrĕkā*, "your cistern" = "your grave"
     or "your wife" [cf. Prov 5:15], בְּאֵרֶךָ *bĕʾērĕkā*, "your well"
     = "your origin, provenance"; cf., e.g., Lauha; Crenshaw).
3a   Or: "rich."
4a   Literally: "daughters of song," which could mean tones
     or songs or even female singers or songbirds (cf., e.g.,
     Gordis).
4b   The three verbs שפל *špl* ("subside, become quiet"), קום
     qwm ("rise"), and שחח *šḥḥ* niphal ("humble oneself,
     become subdued") are often corrected (see, e.g., Gordis)
     but may have been intentionally chosen to indicate a
     down-up-down movement (cf. H. Witzenrath, *"Süss ist das
     Licht . . ." Eine Literaturwissenschaftliche Untersuchung zu
     Koh 11,7—12,7* [ATSAT 11; St. Ottilien: Eos, 1979] 2
     [n. 5] and 24).
5a   יְרָאוּ *yirāʾû* is probably a defective writing of יִירָאוּ *yîrāʾû*;
     cf. 𝔖 𝔙 and Whitley, *Koheleth*, 97; contra 𝔊, which
     derives the verb from ראה *rʾh* ("see").
5b   Literally: "loads itself"(?). The probable meaning is that

2   **Before the sun goes dark, and the light**
       and the moon and the stars,
       and the clouds return after the rain.

3   **When the guards of the house tremble**
       and the strong[a] men are bent,
       the women who grind rest, because
          they are only a few,
       and those who look out the windows
          are darkened,
    4 **the doors to the street are shut.**
    When the sound of the mill becomes soft
       and high like the chirping of the birds,
       and all songs[a] fade away.[b]

5   **One is even afraid[a] of heights,**
       and terrors lie on the way.
    And the almond tree blossoms,
       and the grasshopper becomes heavy,[b]
       and the caper bursts open.[c]
    For a man goes to his eternal house,
       and mourners move through the
          streets.

6   **Before the silver cord "breaks"[a]**
       and the golden bowl is shattered[b]
       and the pitcher is smashed at the
          fountain
       and the wheel falls broken[c] into the
          cistern
    7 **and the dust returns[a] to the earth as**
       it was,
    and the spirit of life returns to the
       Deity that gave it.

the grasshopper "loads itself (with food)," i.e., gorges (thus, e.g., Loretz, *Qohelet*, 190; the versions also interpret in this direction; cf. Whitley, *Koheleth*, 98). It could also mean, however, that the grasshopper "drags itself away (weakly)" (see Gordis).

5c 𝔐 vocalizes וְתָפֵר *wtpr* as hiphil from פרר *prr* (I) (וְתָפֵר *wĕtāpēr*), which is otherwise always used transitively ("breaks"). In the context it is better to read the hophal (וְתֻפַּר *wĕtupar*) (cf. 𝔊 𝔖 σ') or to derive the form from פרה *prh* / פרא *pr'* or to correct to וְתִפְרֶה *wĕtipreh* ("brings fruit"; cf. α'); cf. *BHS* and *BHK*.

6a Thus with the correction of יֵרָחֵק *yērāḥēq* ("is removed") to יִנָּתֵק *yinnātēq* with 𝔊 𝔖 𝔙 α'. Q and numerous Heb. mss. (cf. 𝔗) read יֵרָתֵק *yērātēq* ("be joined or bound together"?—cf. pual "be fettered," Nah 3:10).

6b Instead of the otherwise always transitively used qal וְתָרֻץ *wĕtārūṣ* one could read here the niphal וְתֵרֹץ *wĕtērōṣ*.

6c Syntactically, וְנָרֹץ *wĕnārōṣ* does not fit well with the foregoing imperfects coordinated with ו *w* and could be corrected to וְיָרֻץ *wĕyārūṣ* (cf. 𝔊 𝔖 𝔗). Literally: "and the wheel breaks apart into the cistern."

7a Instead of the jussive וְיָשֹׁב *wĕyāšōb* one should read the indicative וְיָשֻׁב *wĕyāšub*.

This section can be read as the closing summary of the "teachings" of the book of Qoheleth and its consequences for the life one leads. The substantiated exhortations in 11:1-2, 6, 9-10, and 12:1 form the framework of the text. The reflectively or poetically descriptive passages in 11:3-5, 7-8, and 12:1-7 give them further emphasis. In terms of content, the call to spirited action in view of the unpredictability of the future in 11:1-6 can be distinguished from the exhortation to pleasure in the present in view of transitoriness and death in 11:7—12:7. Thus the themes of 9:1-9, 10 (11-12) are taken up here again in reverse order.[1]

■ **11:1-6** These verses can be subdivided into five sections: vv. 1-2, 3, 4, 5, and 6. Verses 1-2, 3, and 4 each

consists of two parts that are essentially constructed in parallel fashion. Verse 6, in closing, takes up again the form of the substantiated exhortation of vv. 1-2. Whereas vv. 1-2 and 5-6 directly address the reader in the second person singular, vv. 3-4 are formulated in the third person singular. Between the individual sections there are numerous key-word connections (e.g., "clouds" in vv. 3 and 4, "wind" in vv. 4 and 5, "sow" in vv. 4 and 6), among which the repeated reference to human ignorance is especially significant ("you do not know"; in Hebrew לֹא תֵדַע *lō' tēda'* in vv. 2 and 5 and אֵינְךָ יוֹדֵעַ *'ênĕkā yôdēa'* in vv. 5 and 6).

■ **1-2** Verses 1-2 are interpreted in various ways.[2] Essentially, three understandings can be distinguished:

---

1   Cf. the close connection between pleasure and activity in 3:12-13, 22; 5:17-19; 8:15.
2   Cf., e.g., Schoors, *Preacher*, 109–10; Fox; Murphy.

1. The two exhortations are related to dealing with one's own wealth in business activity. Whereas v. 1 encourages one to engage in risky businesses such as shipping (cf. Isa 18:2; Prov 31:14), v. 2 counsels investing in various businesses, in order not to lose everything all at once in one disaster.[3] Against this interpretation are, above all, the fact that "(your) bread" as a metaphor for trade goods is not otherwise attested, the point that in shipping one does not expect to "find again" what one has sent off on a voyage but rather to receive other goods for it and if possible make a profit thereby, and the fact that "giving a portion" (נתן חֵלֶק *ntn ḥēleq*) seems to mean not "investing one's capital (in various businesses)" but rather turning over a share of one's goods (to other people)" (cf. 2:21).

2. The two verses juxtapose the paradoxes that a foolish action can be successful, whereas wise actions can fail. "Although one ventures something unwisely, one may find success in it (v. 1), and, vice versa, when someone cautiously divides the risks, disaster can come and wipe out all of one's successes (v. 2)" (Zimmerli). This would presuppose, however, that the introductory כִּי *kî* in v. 1b and v. 2b is to be understood adversatively ("nevertheless, even so"), which seems rather unlikely both in regard to the lexical spectrum of meaning of *kî* and in consideration of the form of vv. 1 and 2 (imperative + כִּי *kî* + indicative), which suggests interpretation as an exhortation with following justification (cf., e.g., 4:17— 5:6; 11:6, 9-10).

3. Thus the traditional interpretation of vv. 1-2 as a call to generosity and charity (cf., e.g., 𝔗, Rashi, and Ibn Ezra)[4] seems to come the closest to doing justice to the text. A calculating and profit-oriented "rationality" makes charity seem as senseless as throwing one's bread into the water. With a similar image *Pseudo-Phocylides*

(152) warns against charity toward "evil" people: "Do nothing good for the evil person; you are only sowing your seed in the ocean."[5] Like Qoh 11:1, the Egyptian Teaching of Ankh-Sheshonq (301) states fundamentally that charity is by no means senseless: even if it is done without any expectation of "gain," it can still over the long term return to the benefactor: "Do a good deed and throw it into the flood; when the water recedes, you will find it again."[6]

Qoheleth 11:1-2 does not assert that charity assures the prosperity of the benefactor. The idea that after a long time one will again find the bread that one has thrown into the water (v. 1) is at first glance not what one would expect. Since, however, in view of the unpredictability of the future (v. 2; cf. 7:12, 14; 8:7; 9:12; 10:14), everyone must take into account the possibility of falling victim to misfortune, it is quite reasonable, and in one's own interest, to display generosity toward people who are in need. For within the context of a "community of solidarity" ("seven or eight"; cf. "two" and "three" in 4:9-12) there is at least the possibility of receiving the help of others if one should fall into misfortune oneself. Not even charity can eliminate the uncertainty of the future; nonetheless, it offers a reasonable strategy for taking into account this uncertainty in life. For "not even the outcome of insecurity can be taken for granted!"[7]

In contemporary early Jewish literature, charity in the form of "almsgiving" was considered a sign of piety.[8] According to Sir 35:3-4 alms were regarded as "sacrifice." To refuse to give them was regarded as "sin" according to Prov 14:21. Charity toward others can be connected with the expectation of one's own prosperity (Prov 28:27; Dan 4:24) and divine "blessing" (Deut 15:7ff.; 24:19). According to Tob 2:15-18; 4:11; 12:9,

---

3   Cf., e.g., Hesiod's comments on sailing (*Works and Days* 618ff.) and its risks (682ff.): "Do not place all your possessions in bulbous ships; leave most of them at home; you may ship the smaller portion" (689–90).

4   Cf. also Goethe (*Westöstlicher Diwan*): "Why do you want to investigate where charity goes? Throw your cakes into the water—who knows who will enjoy them."

5   Translation after Dietrich Ebener, *Griechische Lyrik* (Bayreuth: Gondrom, 1985) 446.

6   Translation after Brunner, *Altägyptische Weisheit*,

283. Cf. also Ankh-Sheshonq 189 ("If you do good for a hundred people and only one of them acknowledges it, then not a bit of it has gone to waste") and 204–5 ("Do not say: 'I did this man a good deed, but he did not acknowledge it to me'— there is no good deed except the one that one does for someone who [really] needs it."). Cf. also Lichtheim, *Late Egyptian Wisdom Literature*, 42.

7   Gerhard von Rad, *Old Testament Theology*, vol. 1 (New York: Harper & Row, 1962) 456–57.

8   Cf. Dan 4:24; Tob 1:3; 2:15; 4:7-12; 12:9; 14:11; Sir 3:30—4:10; 7:10; 29:1-20; 35:5-6, as well as Deut

alms even lead to "eternal life." In the context of reflections on alms, lending, and surety, one finds in Sir 29:1-20 (𝔊) the exhortation:

8 . . . show generosity to the humble
  and practice compassion and do not press them!
9 For the sake of the commandment, look after the poor,
  and in their need do not send them away empty-handed.
10 Give away your silver for the sake of a brother and a friend,
  and do not let it rust under a stone and be ruined.
11 Use your treasure according to the commandment of the Most High,
  and it will bring you more than gold.
12 Include compassion in your treasure,
  and this will rescue you from every evil.
13 Better than a strong shield and better than a mighty lance,
  it will fight for you against the enemy.

Regarding the risks of lending (vv. 4ff.) and surety (vv. 16ff.), however, there are also limits to generosity: "Look after your neighbor to the best of your ability, but be careful not to fall yourself!" (v. 20).

In comparison with this text, the peculiarities of the exhortation to generosity and charity in Qoh 11:1-2 become clear. Sirach 29:10 also seems to presuppose that there are people who hold the view that alms are like money thrown away and "lost" silver. Whereas Qoh 11:1-2, by contrast, only points to the *possibility* that charity can pay off for the giver (v. 1) but expressly refers to the uncertainty of the future (v. 2), Sir 29:11-13 expresses a much more confident *expectation*. If the

prospect for the giver consists, according to Qoh 11:1-2, in the idea that he himself may find "bread" in case of misfortune, according to Sir 29:11 it lies in a genuine "gain." If in Qoh 11:1-2 it is a matter of dealing generously with one's own food ("bread"), in Sir 29:10-12 it is a question of property that is not immediately essential ("silver," "treasure"). The motivation of charity by religious norms (cf. Sir 29:9, 11) is lacking in Qoh 11:1-2 (as also in Qoh 4:1-12). While the designation of charity as "giving a portion" (נתן חלק *ntn ḥēleq*) perhaps points in this direction, according to 5:17 every person has a "claim" to his "portion" (חלק *ḥēleq*) of the goods that are at the community's disposal.

■ **3** This verse formulates two seemingly trivial statements: when the clouds are heavy ("full"), there is rain, and a wood [or: tree] falls right where it falls. These statements are interpreted as a reference to "the immutable conformity of events to the laws of nature" (Lauha) and the inability of human beings to influence such events: "Mankind cannot control the difficulties of life, (i) even when he anticipates them, and (ii) because often there are totally unexpected events" (Eaton; similarly, e.g., Lohfink). It is also possible, however, that the text here is treating ironically prognosticating techniques that claim to draw indications of the future from the clouds and from the falling of a tree or perhaps a divining rod:[9] from the clouds one can tell no more than whether there will be rain, and from the falling of a tree or wood, one can learn nothing at all about the future.

Astrology and divination made progress "in the Hellenistic era. After the end of the third century it became more and more the spiritually dominant force among the educated. The collapse of old Greek religion in the fifth and fourth centuries B.C. . . . and its relegation to a mere belief in fate had inevitably to culminate in astrol-

15:7-11; 24:19; Prov 14:21; 19:17; 22:9; 28:27; Ps 112:9. Also, "It belonged to the philosophy of those seeking prosperity in the Hellenistic world to distribute gifts and considerations widely on all sides. Perhaps one day it would pay off" (Lohfink). This—well calculated—generosity, however, especially benefited those who did not need it; cf. Josephus, *Ant.* 12.4.5 on the Tobiad Joseph: "When he had then assembled a large quantity of money, he was still left, after paying the lease price, with a considerable profit, which he applied to consolidating his power, for he felt it was clever and advantageous to use his

wealth to secure his happiness. Thus he secretly sent gifts to the king, as well as to his wife, friends, and favorites, in order to obtain their goodwill."

9 Crenshaw speculates as to whether it is a question here of "a divining rod" (cf. Hos 4:12). 𝔊 and 𝔙 perhaps leave this possible understanding open with their translation of עץ *ʿēṣ* with ξύλον or *lignum*. 𝔗 interprets "tree" here as a cipher for "king" (cf. Ezekiel 31; Daniel 4). Is Qoh 11:3b perhaps alluding here cryptically to the disagreement between the Ptolemies (in the south) and the Seleucids (in the north)?

ogy, for here there was apparently a possibility of gaining a glimpse into the mysterious working of fate."[10] The fact that Judaism did not remain uninfluenced by this development is shown, for example, by the astrological and magical-mantic texts found in Qumran.[11]

The observation of the clouds (esp. in agriculture) served for the forecasting of weather. In his *Phaenomena*, which in the Greek gymnasia of the second century and later formed the foundation for the teaching of astronomy,[12] Aratus enumerated various meteorological phenomena (including clouds) as signs of weather (778ff.). Accordingly, certain kinds of clouds can announce showers (938ff., 1018ff.) or beautiful weather (988ff.). Now, Aratus "does not want to teach his urbanized contemporaries the signs of the stars and the weather in order to distinguish summer and winter and to avoid occasional downpours; he teaches, rather, that through observation and research into the physical world as a whole, a person communicates with God himself, in order not only to master one's personal fate but also to progressively cultivate the world."[13] "For we still do not know everything about Zeus; rather, much is still hidden from us that in the future Zeus will give us, if he will; indeed, as seen from all sides, he helps humankind visibly, showing his signs" (768ff.). "Therefore we should make an effort in regard to them. . . . The effort is small, but it is immediately and a thousandfold the blessing of prudence for the ever watchful man. First, he himself is more certain, and he has also helped others with good advice" (758ff.; cf. 1142ff.).

■ **4** Against such a position v. 4 holds polemically that the effort to learn something about the future keeps a person from acting in the present. 𝔗 interprets v. 4 as a polemic against magical-mantic and astrological practices: "A man who looks to sorcerers and charmers will never do good, and he who watches the planets will not reap a reward."[14] By contrast, 𝔐 simply has in view the farmer's search for the right time for sowing and harvesting: it is completely justified but can never lead to certain results—and can also actually cause him to miss the right time. In view of the basic unpredictability of the future, human action always remains risky.

■ **5** This verse underlines the basic unpredictability of the future for human beings through an exemplary demonstration of the boundaries of human knowledge and through a theological substantiation of these limits of knowledge. The unpredictability of the wind (cf. v. 4a) served already in 1:6 and 8:8 as a sign of the uncontrollability and unpredictability of the external world for human beings. Added here is the mystery of the origin of a human being in the womb (cf. Ps 139:13-16; Job 10:11-12; 2 Macc 7:22; *Qoh. Rab.* 5:10; Crenshaw) and the still simpler fact that (under conditions of that day) one knows only after birth what kind of child has developed in the womb. With the reference to the unpredictability of the work of God, 11:5 takes up the comments in 3:10-15 (esp. v. 11; cf. also 8:17) in terms of content and language: God's work can be known by human beings only in a limited way, and God wants it this way. Therefore, one cannot expect that God, who alone can convey to people a knowledge of the future, will do this (cf. 6:12; 7:7; 10:14). Contrary to Aratus, according to Qoheleth God gives no "signs" of the future. Therefore any human effort to protect oneself through prognostication is hopeless.

■ **6** Finally, v. 6 makes clear that "ignorance of God's actions in the future leaves people unrestricted in their activity"[15] and, instead, can even motivate them to activity. With the verb "sow" the focus here is primarily on agricultural activity. It is probably not supposed to be

10   Hengel, *Judaism and Hellenism,* 1:236; cf. H. Koester, *Introduction to the New Testament* (2d ed.; New York: de Gruyter, 1995) 1:150ff.; M. Grant, *From Alexander to Cleopatra* (New York: Scribner's, 1982) 219ff.; Gehrke, *Geschichte des Hellenismus,* 81–82.

11   Cf. Hengel, *Judaism and Hellenism,* 1:237ff.; Küchler, *Frühjüdische Weisheitstraditionen,* 108–9.

12   See Aratus, *Phaenomena: Sternbilder und Wetterzeichen* (Greek-German; ed. Manfred Erren; Munich: Heimeran, 1971) 115 (epilogue).

13   Aratus, *Phaenomena* 122 (epilogue by M. Erren); on the sources of Aratus see ibid., 123ff.

14   Translated by E. Levine, *The Aramaic Version of Qohelet* (New York: Sepher-Hermon, 1978) 45.

15   Loretz, *Qohelet,* 257.

carried out from morning "until evening" without interruption (as the Hebrew text could also be understood). Speaking against this is that in what follows "this and that" obviously refers to two different actions. The text does not dispute that human beings can know basically when it is time to sow, but it warns against trying to determine this time too exactly in order to exclude any uncertainty. 𝔗 interprets the "sowing of the seed" as a cipher for sexual activity and the procreation of children, and "morning" and "evening" as images for youth and old age, and it establishes thereby a connection with vv. 7ff.

"The structure and the message of 11:6 are the same as in vv. 1-2, and thus this verse rounds out the unit with its central teaching: compensate for your ignorance by preparing for multiple eventualities" (Fox). Thus, v. 6, like v. 1, presents the chances for successful action that lie in the uncertainty of the future.

■ **11:7—12:7** This section immediately relativizes the difference between success and failure in life through the juxtaposition of life and death (cf. 9:4). In the face of certain death, the value of life, with all its uncertainties, becomes clear. Qoheleth 11:1-6 and 11:7—12:7 are linked together by the copula ו w in 11:7. Qoheleth 11:9—12:1 is formally connected to the imperatives of 11:1-2, 6. A number of key words from 11:1-6 are found again in 11:7—12:7 (e.g., "good," "many days," "clouds," "rain"; cf. also 11:7: "see the sun" with 11:4: "look to the clouds").

In terms of context 11:7—12:7 can be divided into four (formally rather different) sections:

■ 11:7 states in a basic and unlimited way the value of *life* for human beings.
■ 11:8 emphasizes the value of a *long life*.
■ 11:9—12:1a adds to this the exhortation to young people to enjoy life already in their *youth*.
■ 12:1b-7 underlines this exhortation with a vivid poetic description of the "bad days" that face one until one's *death*.

The difference between youth and old age is thus overcome and relativized by the difference between life and death.

■ **7** This verse formulates an unrestricted affirmation of life. "Light" and "see the sun" are easily understandable as metaphors for "life" (cf. 6:5; 7:11; and, e.g., Euripides, *Iph. aul.* 1218). With this fundamentally and unreservedly positive appraisal of life 11:7 matches the comments in 9:4-10 and contradicts the life-negating "pessimism" of the "king" in 2:17, with which 4:2-3 already disagreed in an ironically critical way. In the context of 11:1—12:7, 11:7 makes clear that life is worthwhile *apart from* the success of human work (11:6) and of the possibilities and limits of various phases of life (11:8ff.). This is to be observed in the following juxtaposition of old age and youth.

■ **8** The understanding of this verse depends to a large degree on the sense in which one interprets the verb forms יִשְׂמָח *yiśmāḥ* and וְיִזְכֹּר *wĕyizkōr*.

1. Both verbs are usually interpreted as jussive. Thus Zimmerli, for example, translates: "For when a man also lives many years, he should enjoy them all and think of the days of darkness and that there will be many of them. . . ."

2. By contrast, Lauha, for example, takes יִשְׂמָח *yiśmāḥ* to be indicative and וְיִזְכֹּר *wĕyizkōr* to be jussive (cf. already 𝔙) and translates: "Yes, when a man lives many years, he rejoices over all of them—yet he should remember that the dark days will be many. . . ."

3. Galling, finally, understands both verbs indicatively (cf. already 𝔊): "For if a man also lives many years, he enjoys them all, yet he thinks of the days of darkness and their length. . . ."

According to the first interpretation, 11:8 exhorts one equally to enjoy life (in old age) *and* to be mindful of the coming days. According to the second interpretation, the text ascertains that an old man rejoices over his long life and recalls as a "counterweight to this general attitude . . . that everyone must die" (Lauha). According to the third interpretation, finally, 11:8 states that an old man enjoys his long life, *because* he remembers that "the hereafter is an empty darkness" (Galling).

In the context, the second interpretation is not very likely. As the critique of "an optimistic affirmation of life" (Lauha), 11:8 would be in contradiction to the immediately preceding v. 7. And as the relativization of the pleasure of life through the idea of approaching death, v. 8 would contradict the statements following in vv. 9ff., which motivate the call to pleasure in precisely the opposite way with a reference to approaching death. The first and third interpretations, however, can be easily harmonized, in terms of content, with the immediate and the broader contexts: even, and precisely, in old age, a person can and should enjoy life, because he or she faces death.

Yet one problem with all three interpretations consists in that they must relate "the dark days" to the duration of death. Then it is strange that the "many *years*" of life are juxtaposed with the "numerous *days*" of death. For apart from the fact that the doubtless longer time span of death (cf. 9:6) would be described with the shorter time unit "day" and the shorter time span of life, by contrast, with the longer time unit "year," it is hard to see what difference it can make to a person *how long* he will be dead.

Verse 8 is, in my view, easier to understand if one assumes that the "dark days" are times that an old man thinks back on in his life (cf. 5:16; 7:14; 12:1). The verse then determines that an old man rejoices over his long life *and* in accordance with the length of his life also remembers numerous "dark days" that he has experienced. Then v. 8 contradicts neither the basic evaluation of life expressed in v. 7 nor the call to pleasure expressed in vv. 9ff. especially for the young man. Rather, it reinforces v. 7: if there is in life a certain portion of "dark days" (cf. 7:14), then its worth does not grow with its length. Therefore, it is not a long life but life at any time (even in old age!) that is "sweet" and "good." Then, however, even for a young man, there is no reason to expect happiness only from a long life: he can and should enjoy life already in his youth (vv. 9ff.).

Thus understood, with a reference to the experience of the old man, 11:8, like 3:22 and 9:7-10, supports the call to pleasure and enjoyment in the present: "All that comes is fleeting!" The ideal of a long life (cf. already 6:3-6) is thereby relativized (v. 8b), as well as a basically negative evaluation of old age (v. 8a).[16]

■ **9a** The idea of the exhortation to the young man to enjoy himself in his youth is taken up from 3:12–13, 22; 5:17-19; 8:15; and above all 9:7-10. The advice to follow one's understanding ("heart") and what one's eyes see has the effect of a provocative allusion to Num 15:39: according to it, the "fringes" of their garments were supposed to remind the Israelites that they may *not* follow their hearts and eyes, which would lead them into "whoring," but rather that they are to obey all the commandments of Yahweh. Correspondingly, Sir 5:2 (𝔊) warns: "Do not follow your heart and your eyes, so that you wander in evil desires!" (This part of the verse is missing in a number of Greek mss. and was perhaps added secondarily as a critique of Qoh 11:9a; cf. Fox.)

According to all that precedes in the book of Qoheleth, it is clear in Qoh 11:9a that following his "heart" and "what his eyes see" is not the same as "walking in his desires," as Sir 5:2 presupposes. The application of the "understanding" ("heart") and the critical "observation" of situations and opinions were characteristic for the "method" of reflections presented here.[17] And in 6:9 "what one has in sight" (מַרְאֵה עֵינַיִם *marʾēh ʿênayim*) designates "realistic expectations" in contrast to the ("unrealistic") "appetite" (נֶפֶשׁ *nepeš*). Thus Qoh 11:9a can be understood as a summary of the ethic of the book of Qoheleth in the sense that "it urges for realism, striving for what is attainable" (Ogden): "Enjoy yourself—but with understanding and within the framework of what is realistically possible!"

■ **9b** This verse is often regarded as an "orthodox" gloss that is intended to correct the presumed "libertinism" of v. 9a with the reference to God's "judgment."[18] As an argument for a literary-critical exclusion of this half verse, we may cite (with Zimmerli) the following:

1. Verse 9b interrupts the series of short admonitions in vv. 9a-10a.
2. The expression used here, בוא *bwʾ* hiphil + בְּמִשְׁפָּט *bĕmišpāṭ*, is also found in 12:14 in the (second) "epilogue" to the book of Qoheleth, usually regarded as secondary (otherwise only in Job 14:3).[19]

---

16   Cf., e.g., J. L. Crenshaw, "Youth and Old Age in Qoheleth," *HAR* 10 (1986) 1–13, repr. in idem, *Urgent Advice and Probing Questions: Collected Writings on Old Testament Wisdom* (Macon, Ga.: Mercer Univ. Press, 1995) 535–47.

17   Cf. G. S. Ogden, "Qoheleth XI 7–XII 8: Qoheleth's Summons to Enjoyment and Reflection," *VT* 34 (1984) 31.

18   Cf., e.g., Zimmerli; Lohfink; Crenshaw.

19   Cf. בוא *bwʾ* qal + בְּמִשְׁפָּט *bĕmišpāṭ* in Isa 3:14; Ps 143:2; Job 9:32; 22:4.

3. Verse 9b reveals the "intention" to "tone down the unguarded admonition to enjoyment that Qoheleth addresses to youth" (Zimmerli) or to "protect the text from a libertine interpretation" (Lohfink).

In consideration of the formal complexity of 11:7–12:7 and the possibility that 12:14 takes up a formulation already given in 11:9b, the content argument (3) acquires decisive importance. As a correcting gloss to the preceding call to pleasure and enjoyment in v. 9a, however, v. 9b is, in my opinion, understandable only with difficulty. Would it not have been more likely to correct this call itself, as done by some Greek manuscripts, which read "walk *irreproachably* in the ways of your heart" or "walk . . . *not* in the sight of your eyes"? And how would one have had to imagine the "judgment" of God announced here? That "a next-worldly judgment is thought of . . . is rather unlikely. For in that case the book's statements about death as the radical end for each person would similarly have required an appropriate correction" (Lohfink). The same is also true, however, of a "judgment" before death (cf. 9:2-3!).

By contrast, the interpretation of v. 9b as reinforcement of the exhortation in v. 9a, recommended by Graetz, Levy, and Gordis, among others, is more enlightening: "A man must render account for everything he saw but did not enjoy" (*b. Ned.* 10a). Then the point is hardly a special time of judgment in this world or beyond it. Rather, the "judgment" of God over human beings consists precisely in their transitoriness (11:10b).[20] It is accomplished in the contingency of "time" (cf. 3:17; 8:6), which confronts people with "good" as well as with "bad days" (11:8; 12:1b).[21] No one can escape this "judgment of God" because no one is completely innocent (cf. 3:18; 7:29; 8:6; 9:3). Yet the man who in "good times" failed to rejoice and enjoy his life is struck harder than the one who followed the advice of v. 9a.

As in 3:17 and 8:6, so also in 11:9b the traditional concept of divine "judgment" seems to be reinterpreted. This no doubt happens with a certain irony—especially if in the formulation of v. 9a the author had in mind Num 15:39: the experience of contingency and transitoriness

supports the idea of enjoying the "good days"—and nothing indicates that God judges the matter differently (cf. 9:7b).

■ **10a** This verse takes up the call to pleasure in v. 9a and takes it further with the exhortation to avoid "vexation" (כַּעַס *kaʿas*) and "evil" (רָעָה *rāʿâ*). On the theme of "vexation" there are various statements in the foregoing context of the book of Qoheleth. The "king" regarded "vexation" as something negative (1:18) but unavoidable for human beings (2:23). Qoheleth 7:3 valued "vexation" positively and based this on the fact that things are going well for a man "internally" (in his "heart") when they are going badly for him "externally" (on his "face"). By contrast, 5:16, like 7:9, presents "vexation" as something negative that (within limits) is completely avoidable. In this discussion, finally, 11:10a takes a stance in the sense of 5:16 and 7:9 but against 1:18; 2:23; and 7:3: "vexation" and "evil" are negative experiences that, within limits (cf. 12:1b), are avoidable and should, if possible, be avoided—both "internally" ("heart") *and* "externally" ("body" or "flesh").

■ **10b** With its reference to the transitoriness of youth, v. 10b underlines the call to the young man to enjoy life. That the time of youth is just as "fleeting" (הֶבֶל *hebel*) as "all that comes [later in life]" (v. 8b) shows that in the text it is not a question of the favoring of youth over old age but of the exhortation to enjoy life in the present (v. 7) and not to postpone pleasure and enjoyment until an uncertain future.

■ **12:1a** This verse is the only time when the book of Qoheleth speaks of God as the "creator" (בּוֹרֵא *bôrēʾ*) of humankind. In the Hebrew term, one is perhaps intentionally reminded of the graphically and phonetically similar noun בּוֹר *bôr* ("cistern" = "grave"?). It is possible that "both words could be recognized at the same time. The reader of v. 1 expects 'death' but hears at first 'crater,' then realizes that 'Creator' was what was said. At the end of the poem, this 'Creator' is doubly recalled: through 'crater' (v. 6) and 'God' (v. 7)" (Lohfink). "To think about one's Creator" would then mean initially and above all to be conscious of one's own "creatureliness" and thus also of one's transitoriness (cf. 12:7).[22]

20 Cf. C. Dell'Aversano, "משפט in Qoh. 11:9c," in A. Vivian, ed., *Biblische und Judaistische Studien: FS Paolo Sacchi* (JudUm 29; Frankfurt: Lang, 1990) 121–34.

21 Cf. P. Sacchi, *Ecclesiaste* (NVB 30; Rome: Pauline, 1971) in loc.

22 Cf. M. Gilbert, "La description de la vieillesse en Qohelet XII 1-7 est-elle allégorique?" in J. A. Emer-

At the end of the book of Qoheleth, however, the reference to the "Creator" in 12:1a also recalls the whole breadth of "theological" statements in the preceding context. The statements that come closest to the designation of God as "your Creator" are those that say that God made *human beings* "right" (7:29) and gave them their lives (5:17; 8:15; 9:9) as well as possessions (5:18; 6:2) and the possibility of pleasure (5:18-19; 9:8). In this respect 12:1a can be understood not only as an exhortation to be conscious of one's transitoriness but also as a call to seize the opportunities granted by God for pleasure and enjoyment. Yet God is also "Creator" in that he has made *everything* "beautiful" (3:11; cf. 7:14), and his "work" is enduring, immutable (3:14-15; 7:13), and ultimately incomprehensible for human beings (3:11; 8:17; 11:5). In the contingency and unpredictability of the future they experience God's "judgment" (3:17-18; 11:9b). In view of the distance between God and humankind (5:1) the appropriate attitude of human beings toward God is "fear" (3:14; 5:6; 7:18; 8:12-13) and taking religious obligations seriously (5:3).

Thus 12:1a, together with 11:9b, summarizes the theological foundations of the ethic of the book of Qoheleth briefly and concisely: the proper attitude toward life grows out of the fact that one receives and accepts "good" as a "gift" and "bad" as the "judgment" of God (cf. 7:14). Hence, 12:1a in no way revokes or restricts the exhortation to pleasure in 11:9a, 10a.

Therefore there is, in my opinion, no literary-critical reason from the standpoint of content to exclude 12:1a as an "orthodox" gloss (thus, e.g., Galling; Lauha; Michel). This would also require a striking of 11:10b, since 12:1b cannot be connected with 11:10b. Speaking against this is the fact that both verses are firmly anchored in their context by various key-word relationships. The key words "rejoice" (שמח *śmḥ*) and "think about" (זכר *zkr*) from 11:8 are taken up again in 11:9a ("rejoice") and 12:1a ("think about"). Verses 11:10b (הֶבֶל *hebel*, "fleeting") and 12:1b (בוא *bwʾ*, "approach, come") hark back to 11:8b ("all that comes is fleeting"). And 11:10b (יַלְדוּת *yaldût*, "youth") and 12:1a (יְמֵי בְחוּרֹתֶיךָ *yĕmê bĕḥûrōtêkā*, "days of your youth") pick up the corresponding key words from 11:9a. This web of key words, which

can hardly have arisen by pure accident, would be destroyed by the exclusion of 11:10b—12:1a.

■ **1b-7** These verses direct attention to the time *after* "youth" (v. 1a). Do the "days" and "years" addressed here (cf. 11:8) thus qualify old age as a completely "bad" time? Then 11:9—12:7 would be in tension with 11:7-8. Lohfink assumes such a tension and tries to explain it in terms of redaction history. "In contrast with the poem from v. 9 on, which begins with joy during one's youth, v. 8 speaks of joy throughout life. Verses 7-8 thus open up, by an anticipatory interpretation, the immediately upcoming poem of closure—at least its opening position, which is modified later within the poem as well. Humans should be joyful as long as they can!" The (presumed) tension between 11:8 and 11:9—12:7 is resolved, however, if one assumes that 12:1b-7 does not qualify old age as such as a "bad" time. Rather, as 11:8 already states, the number of "dark" or "bad days" that a person experiences grows with increasing life span. The call to enjoy oneself *already* in one's youth, *before* the "bad days" come, is then based not on the idea that pleasure is no longer possible in old age, but rather on the fact that the "time of youth" as the present time of possible enjoyment is then irretrievably past (cf. 11:10b) and that one must always reckon with "bad" things in the future (cf. 11:2b, 8b). The young man should enjoy his life already in his youth, not because he can no longer do so in old age, but because in old age he can never make up for the pleasures missed in his youth—and because it is by no means certain that he will get old at all.

To be sure, this understanding of 11:9—12:1 seems to be contradicted by the fact that, according to the general view, there follows in 12:2-7 a "description of the toil of old age" that with the help of "various images" is "drawn as a dark future" that "everyone expects" (Lauha, 206). This interpretation of 12:2ff., however, is by no means indisputable. Both the question, What theme is treated in this section? and the question, In what manner does this take place? are debated in the literature.

An allegorizing interpretation of 12:2ff. as the presentation of bodily affliction in old age is found already in the Targum, Talmud (*b. Shab.* 131b–132a), Midrash,

ton, ed., *Congress Volume, Vienna 1980* (VTSup 32; Leiden: Brill, 1981) 101.

and, e.g., in Ibn Ezra.[23] Thus the Targum "translates" 12:2-7 as follows:

> Before the glorious brightness which is like the sun be changed, and before the light of thy eyes be darkened, and before the beauty of your cheeks becomes black, and before the centers of your eyes, which are like stars, be dim, your eyelids drip tears like clouds after rain. In the day when your knees tremble, and your arms shake, and the grinders of your mouth cease till they cannot chew food, and your eyes which look through the openings of your head darken, and your feet be fettered from going into the street, and the appetite for food leaves you. And you shall awake from sleep at the sound of a bird, as thieves that prowl at night. And your lips shall cease song. You shall even be afraid to remember the works which have been before now, and a little rising will be to you like a great mountain, when you walk on the road. And the top of your hip bone shall come out from leanness like the almond, and the ankles of your feet shall be swelled, and you shall be hindered from rest. For man tarries to go to the place of his burial. And the angels that seek your judgment walk about like mourners, walking about the street, to write the account of the judgment. Before your tongue is dumb from speaking, and your head dashed in pieces, and the gall at the liver emptied, and the body hastens into the grave, and the flesh which is created of dust returns into the earth as it was, and your breathing spirit returns to stand in judgment before the Lord who gave it to you.[24]

A thoroughly allegorical interpretation of 12:2-6 is also proposed, for example, by Delitzsch (for v. 2, for example, sun = spirit, light = thinking, moon = soul, stars = five senses, clouds = illness).

The diversity of detail in the proposed interpretations already shows the questionable nature of a thoroughly allegorical interpretation of 12:2-7. In more recent research, therefore, it is often assumed that in this section there are, in addition to "allegorical" statements (esp. in vv. 3-4 and 5aβγ), also "images" (in vv. 2 and 6) and nonfigurative "direct" statements (in v. 5aα, b and perhaps in v. 4bα). Thus Michel, for example, interprets vv. 3-4a allegorically: "guards = the arms; strong men = legs; the women who grind = teeth; those who look out the window = eyes; doors to the outside = ears; sound of the mill = voice." For v. 4bα Michel ventures both an allegorical interpretation (the voice "grows high like the voice of a bird") and a nonfigurative direct understanding ("one already arises early in the morning"). Likewise, in reference to v. 5aβγ he leaves open whether "almond tree = white hair; grasshopper = shuffling gait; caper = sexual desire (caper was regarded as an aphrodisiac)," or whether we have here "images of nature full of vitality in antithesis to the frail old man."[25]

Whereas the defenders of a completely or partially allegorical interpretation of 12:2-7 recognize here statements about a person's old age, the theme of the section is more strongly disputed by opponents of an "allegorical" interpretation. Thus, according to Loretz, for example, in vv. 2-5aα a bad winter day[26] is presented as an image of a person's old age, whereas vv. 5aβ-7 juxtaposes the death of a man (vv. 5b-7) with the blooming of nature in spring (v. 5aβγ). According to Gilbert, vv. 2-5 present in images of winter (v. 2), evening (vv. 3-4a), and morning (vv. 4b-5) the loneliness of people in old age, which precedes their death (vv. 6-7).[27] And Witzenrath interprets vv. 2-6 as "images of passing away" (27; cf. 20ff.) that, in addition to death, also relate to the "deterioration of an aging person" (vv. 3-4aα).[28]

---

23 See M. Gómez Aranda, "Ecl 12,1-7 interpretado por Abraham Ibn 'Ezra," *Sef* 52 (1992) 113-21.

24 Translation by Levine, *Aramaic Version,* 46-47.

25 Similarly, e.g., J. Scharbert, "Die Altersbeschwerden in der ägyptischen, babylonischen und biblischen Weisheit," in R. Schulz and M. Görg, eds., *Lingua restitua orientalis: FS Julius Assfalg* (ÄAT 20; Wiesbaden: Harrassowitz, 1990) 294ff.

26 Loretz, *Qohelet,* 191ff. Cf. Ginsburg and M. Leahy, "The Meaning of Ecclesiastes 12,1-5," *ITQ* 19 (1952) 297-300, repr. in Zuck, ed., *Reflecting with Solomon,*

375–79, who interpret vv. 2-5 as the representation of a thunderstorm.

27 Gilbert, "Description."

28 Witzenrath, *Süss ist das Licht.*

By contrast, according to Taylor and Anath, vv. 2-5 describe the situation of general sadness and lamentation at a burial and thus, just like vv. 6-7, relate not to old age but to death.[29] Ogden interprets vv. 2-7 as "speaking of the minimal existence which one enjoys in Sheol" and thus as a representation of human destiny after death.[30] And according to Sawyer, vv. 2-7 (in an original form reconstructed by him through literary criticism) speak *neither* of old age *nor* of death, but of "situations . . . which may at any time interrupt the young man's progress towards achieving success and fulfillment."[31]

Fox has proposed a more strongly differentiating interpretation that combines various explications.[32] He assumes that the text has several levels of meaning. On the level of a "literal meaning" he presents a burial and the related context of sadness. This state of affairs is placed on a second level of meaning ("symbolism") in a broader context: "While the poem describes the death and funeral of an individual, some of its imagery concurrently suggests a disaster of cosmic magnitude." Verses 2-3 in particular are "reminiscent of prophetic descriptions of the national and universal desolation awaiting humanity and nature at the end of this age."[33] Finally, some passages suggest a third level of meaning ("allegory and figuration"): "A few of the images in Qoh. 12:2-8 lend themselves naturally to interpretation as figures for the infirmities of aging" (esp. v. 3) or "of death" (v. 6), yet the "images that do work as figures do not add up to an allegory."[34] Fox describes the function of this multilevel presentation of old age and death as follows:

> the poem's purpose is not to convey information; it is to create an attitude toward aging and, more importantly, death. A reader, especially a young one like the youth ostensibly addressed in this unit, may not be aware of the fear, loneliness, and nostalgia for an earlier reality irretrievably lost, which are the lot of many (and to some extent, perhaps all) of the aged, Qohelet undoubtedly among them. They might not know of the prospective mourning for a vanished existence. This awareness is engendered by the interaction of the literal and symbolic types of meaning.[35]

On the basis of various introductory terms, the different tense structures, and the content addressed, 12:1b-7 can be divided as follows:[36]

---

29   C. Taylor, "The Dirge of Coheleth," *JQR* 4 (1892) 533–49; idem, *The Dirge of Coheleth in Ecclesiastes XII: Discussesd and Literally Interpreted* (Edinburgh: Williams & Norgate, 1874); M. E. Anath, "The Lament over the Death of Human Beings in the Book of Qoheleth" (Heb.), *BethM* 15 (1970) 375–80.

30   Ogden, "Qoheleth XI 7–XII 8," 34.

31   J. F. A. Sawyer, "The Ruined House in Ecclesiastes 12: A Reconstruction of the Original Parable," *JBL* 94 (1975) 523.

32   M. V. Fox, "Aging and Death in Qoheleth 12," *JSOT* 42 (1988) 55–77 (repr. in Zuck, ed., *Reflecting with Solomon*, 381–99; and in Clines, ed., *Poetical Books*, 199–221.

33   Ibid., 64. Cf. also, e.g., H. A. J. Kruger, "Old Age Frailty versus Cosmic Deterioration? A Few Remarks on the Interpretation of Qohelet 11,7–12,8," in Schoors, ed., *Qohelet in Context*, 399–411; T. K. Beal, "C(ha)osmopolis: Qohelet's Last Words," in T. Linafelt and T. K. Beal, eds., *God in the Fray: A Tribute to Walter Brueggemann* (Minneapolis: Fortress Press, 1998) 290–304. S. Leanza reminds us "che l'interpretazione escatologica di questa pericope . . . fi diffusissima nel periodo patristico e per tutto il Medio Evo" [that the eschatological interpretation of this pericope . . . was extremely diffuse in the patristic period and throughout the whole Middle Ages] ("Eccl 12,1-7: L'interpretazione escatologica dei Padri e degli esegeti medievali," *Aug* 18 [1978] 205). Cf., e.g., the paraphrase of Gregory Thaumaturgus (ed. Jarick).

34   Fox, "Aging," 69, 70.

35   Ibid., 71.

36   Witzenrath, *Süss ist das Licht*, 10ff., 21ff.

Section	Introduction	Tense structure	Theme
v. 1b	*ʿad ʾăšer lô,* "before"	*yiqtol – weqatal*	Bad days/years
v. 2	*ʿad ʾăšer lô,* "before"	*yiqtol – weqatal*	Darkening of heaven
vv. 3-4aα	*bayyôm še-,* "when"	*yiqtol – weqatal*	Fear of the residents, destruction of the house
v. 4aβb	*b- +* inf. cs., "when"	*b- +* inf. cs. *-, we-yiqtol*	Quiet
v. 5aα	*gam,* "even"	*yiqtol–NS*	Fear and terrors on the way
v. 5aβγ	*(w-,* "and")	*we-yiqtol*	Blooming of nature (in an overgrown garden?)
v. 5b	*kî,* "for (or: when)"	*qotel – weqatal*	Burial
v. 6	*ʿad ʾăšer lô,* "before"	*yiqtol – we-yiqtol*	Destruction of costly and essential items
v. 7	*(w-,* "and")	*we-yiqtol – we-x-yiqtol*	Human destruction in death

Because of the erratic and irregular change in form and content, 12:1b-7 has more the effect of a "collage" than that of a regular "poem" (by contrast, cf. 1:3-11 and 3:1-9). The text evokes a series of images for "bad times" that in the future await the "young man" addressed in 11:9—12:1.

■ **1b** This verse, however, begins by speaking still without image of the "bad days" and unpleasant "years" that come to him. The key words "days" and "years" refer back to 11:8. On this basis 12:1b-7 is not to be understood in the sense that after one's youth *only* bad days and years await, but rather that with increasing age one can *also* expect, as a rule, an increasing number of such unpleasant days and years.

■ **2** This verse can be read initially as presenting the darkening of the sky by day ("sun" and "light") and by night ("moon" and "stars"), as it is to be observed in rainy weather ("clouds" and "rain")—be it in winter or with an unusual storm. In the context, however, v. 2 takes up the key words "sun," "light," and "dark" from 11:7-8. There "sun" and "light" stand for "life," but "dark" for unpleasant experiences. Under this sign 12:2 can be understood as an image of death, old age, or a misfortune in life.[37] After 11:9b has already spoken of the "judgment" of God, 12:2 can then evoke further corresponding associations. Here one can think first of the "judgment" of God on an individual human being (cf., e.g., Prov 4:18-19; 13:9; Job 18:5-6, 18; 38:15). The numerous statements in the realm of "the prophetic proclamation of judgment," which "transforms the light of salvation into the darkness of approaching catastrophe,"[38] suggest, nonetheless, an understanding of v. 2 as the description of a universal cosmic catastrophe, which overturns one's usual experience of reality ("rain, then

---

37 Cf. M. Saebø, "אור *ʾôr* light," *TLOT* 1:66.

38 Ibid., 89, with reference to Amos 5:18, 20; 8:9; Isa 5:30; 13:10; Jer 4:23; 25:10; Ezek 32:7-8, as well as Jer 13:16 and Lam 3:2; cf. also Fox, "Aging," 64–65, who in addition cites Zeph 1:15; Joel 2:2, 6, 10 for comparison.

clouds," instead of "clouds, then rain," as in 11:3) and revokes the foundations of creation (cf. Gen 1:3; Jer 4:23). Here one may compare especially Isa 13:10 and Joel 2:10, where the "day of Yahweh" comes in with a darkening of "sun, moon, and stars."[39] An admonition to a certain behavior *before* an announced disaster that is comparable to Qoh 12:1-2 is found in Jer 13:16: "Give Yahweh your God the honor, *before* (בְּטֶרֶם *běṭerem*) it gets dark and *before* your feet stumble on the mountains at twilight. Then you hope for light, yet he makes it darkness and changes it into the darkness of clouds."

In the context of Qoheleth 11–12 and on the level of the topic of prophetic eschatology, 12:2 can thus be read on more than one level of meaning:

1. "cosmology" [or: "meteorology"]: winter—storm
2. "anthropology": misfortune—old age—death
3. "theology": judgment of God
   a. individual: destruction of an "evildoer"
   b. collective or universal: "world judgment"— "world destruction"

■ **12:3-4aα** These verses are likewise understandable on many levels. The passage can be read first with v. 2 as a "description of hopeless life in the formerly lively city" because of the "darkening of the winter sky by day and night during a rainstorm. . . . On such a stormy day or evening the men are afraid, and the usual life of work and the bustling activity and life of nature die out."[40] Independent of v. 2, vv. 3-4aα can also be understood as a description of a household in a situation of mourning.[41] If one assumes that "house" stands for human beings and their transitoriness (cf. Job 4:19; Isa 38:12), one could understand vv. 3-4aα further as an image of the death of an individual person.[42] The indication that

the women who grind "are only a few" (v. 3bα) points rather to an extraordinary catastrophe that can be interpreted as the judgment of God—be it the fall of the house of an individual "evildoer" or the destruction of all houses, whose comprehensive size is then named here through the naming of socially higher and lower positions, as well as of men and women.[43]

■ **4aβb-5aα** In one understanding of the text, these verses are usually interpreted as an "allegory of aging," mostly as images of the older person's hardness of hearing and reduced mobility. After vv. 2-4aα, however, they can be read at least as well as a continuation of the description of the fall of a house or a city. Here too, then, the presentation is again transparent to the announcements of prophetic judgment. Thus in Jer 25:10, for example, Yahweh announces: "I will banish from them [Judah and its neighbors] the sound of mirth and the sound of gladness, the voice of the bridegroom and the voice of the bride, the sound of the millstones and the light of the lamp" (cf. v. 4aβb).[44] And "fear" and "terror" (cf. v. 5aα) are announced as punishment both for the individual "evildoer" and for the people as a whole.[45]

■ **5aβγ-5b** These lines, however, now clearly limit again the room for interpretation opened by the foregoing. The blooming of "nature" (v. 5aβγ) can at most be understood as the consequence of a divine "judgment" on an individual "evildoer" (and his "house": his garden grows wild)[46] but no longer fits the image of a universal "end of the world," as evoked especially by v. 2. Thus in v. 5b the "catastrophic scenario" developed in vv. 2-5aα is further limited with the unambiguous portrayal of the

39   Cf. also Joel 3:4; Ezek 32:7-8, as well as, on clouds, Isa 5:30; Jer 13:16; Zeph 1:15; Joel 2:2.

40   Loretz, *Qohelet,* 191, 192.

41   Cf. Taylor, *Dirge,* iii–iv; Fox, "Aging," 60

42   See Braun, *Kohelet,* 105 n. 318; cf. Witzenrath, *Süss ist das Licht,* 47.

43   Cf. Sawyer, "Ruined House," 525. In particular, on v. 3aα cf. Jer 15:4; 24:9; 29:18; 34:17; Isa 28:19; Ezek 23:46, as well as Isa 32:10-11; 33:14; Nah 2:11; on v. 3aβ cf. Isa 2:9, 11, 17; 5:15 (on the verbs used here, שׁחה *šḥh* and שׁפל *špl*, cf. Qoh 12:4); on v. 3bα cf. Jer 25:10; on v. 3bβ cf. Ps 69:24 (cf. also Lam 4:8;

5:17); on v. 4aα cf. Isa 24:10. On the individual see, e.g., Prov 14:11; 15:25; Job 18:5-21; 27:13-23. On all houses see, e.g., Isa 5:9; 6:11; 13:16; Jer 6:12; 17:27; Amos 3:15; Zeph 1:13; Ezek 26:12.

44   Cf. further Jer 7:34; 16:9; Bar 2:23, as well as Isa 16:10; 24:8-9; Ezek 26:13.

45   For the individual see Prov 1:26-27; Job 15:20-21, 24; 18:11; 27:20. For the people as a whole see Isa 8:22; 31:9; Zeph 1:15; Jer 6:25; 20:3-4, 10; 46:5; 49:24.

46   Supporting this understanding of the text is the fact that the grasshopper can eat itself full and the

funeral of a man[47] and the mourning over him. Here v. 5aβγ and v. 5b can be understood as contrasting images: "Whereas nature knows a return to life, a man must go his way relentlessly to death."[48] Yet v. 5b itself also juxtaposes the dead and buried man with the mourners, who live on (cf. 1:4a). The death of a human being is thus presented as a "limited catastrophe": "Life goes on!"

■ **6** The destruction of costly and essential objects and apparatus[49] described in v. 6 can, like v. 5aβγ, be connected with the fall of a "house" presented in vv. 3-4aα: like its garden, its equipment also goes to ruin. Here, however, there is probably also a "figurative" meaning, "though it is unclear whether the components of the image each have a specific referent, and also whether the images represent death or burial or both."[50] Once again the destruction of human utensils (v. 6) forms a contrast to the flourishing of nonhuman nature (v. 5aβγ).[51]

■ **7** Finally, v. 7 describes the disintegration of a person

in death, in accordance with an anthropology that was already recognizable in 3:19ff. (cf. also 1:4 and Ps 104:29-30). Human beings are dust (עָפָר *ʿāpār*), which God has enlivened with the spirit of life (רוּחַ *rûaḥ*; cf. Gen 2:7: נְשָׁמָה *nĕšāmâ*). In death the dust returns to earth (cf. Gen 3:19) and the (impersonal!) spirit of life to its creator (cf. Qoh 12:1a). For the individual human being, therefore, death means the definitive end; for humankind, the possibility of the beginning of new life (cf. 1:4).[52]

■ **12:1-7** If one looks over 12:1-7 as a whole, it is apparent that vv. 2-5aα show strong echoes of "the apocalyptic topos of end-time catastrophes" (Lohfink), whereas vv. 5aβ-7 clearly speaks of the death of a man and its accompanying circumstances. If one considers this "slant" of the text, it is improbable in my view that its intention consists in "loading up symbolically" the experience or expectation of death.[53] Rather, its intention lies, conversely, in reducing the expectation (as hope or

---

caper bud, which would actually have to be harvested, can burst open (if the text is to be understood in this way). Cf. Sawyer, "Ruined House," 529: "The author, just like the author of Prov 24:31, has selected three common features of a neglected garden."

47 "The designtion of the grave as 'eternal house,' which ultimately goes back to Egypt, is found in Hellenistic times on Punic and Palmyran grave inscriptions (cf. *ZAW* 64 [1952] 211–17; cf. also Ps 49:12; Tob 3:6). In contracts from Murrabaʿat (DJD II, 20:7; 21:12) dying is paraphrased as a going into the house of eternity" (Galling). By contrast, the "eternal house" in 2 Cor 5:1ff. is a person's new heavenly body after death; on this understanding of death as "moving" in the sense of a transformation, cf. the texts in M. Eugene Boring, Klaus Berger, and Carsten Colpe, eds., *Hellenistic Commentary to the New Testament* (Nashville: Abingdon, 1995) 451–52.

48 Loretz, *Qohelet*, 19; cf. Job 14:1-2, 7ff., as well as Qoh 1:4ff.

49 Verse 6a perhaps describes the destruction of a golden lamp that is hung on a silver chain (cf., e.g., Delitzsch; Galling; Lohfink; and גֻּלָּה *gullâ* in Zech 4:2-3); contra, e.g., Lauha, who holds that here, just as in v. 6b, "aids for scooping water from the well" are intended (cf. Loader)—but did one use silver and golden utensils for this purpose? With the "wheel" in v. 6b "we must see a wheel over a well, upon which runs a rope with a bucket. These technical novelties were introduced in Palestine only in

the third century" (Lohfink; cf. Galling; A. Dalman, *Arbeit und Sitte in Palästina* [Gütersloh: Gütersloher, 1964] 1:645; 2:222ff.; Walbank, *Hellenistische Welt*, 165, 195–96). In Fox's view, however: "The verse seems to picture three vessels suspended by a cord over a well."

50 Fox, "Aging," 69.

51 The placing of v. 6 after v. 2, proposed by Galling and Lauha, for example, is completely arbitrary.

52 Galling excludes 12:7 as a secondary gloss, since here there is a "separation into what is decomposable and what is not," which stands in contradiction to 3:21 (cf., e.g., Michel). Yet 3:21 presupposes this very "separation"; the only thing called into question here is whether the human "spirit of life" is different from that of animals (not "that the life-spirit raises at death"—thus Fox on 12:7). Like 3:19-22, Qoh 12:7 underlines the idea that death really is the "end" of human life (Lohfink; cf. Crenshaw). Cf. also A. Schoors, "Koheleth: A Perspective of Life after Death?" *EThL* 61 (1985) 295–303; Witzenrath, *Süss ist das Licht*, 40ff.

53 Cf. in this sense Fox: "the poem's purpose is . . . to create an attitude toward aging and, more importantly, death" ("Aging," 71): "In one sense it . . . is the extinction of an individual life; in another, the extinction of a universe" (66). Just as questionable, then, are Fox's further conclusions: "Qohelet reveals an obsession with death . . . he reveals no consciousness of himself as part of a nation or a community. . . . This individualism imposes itself

fear) of an "end of the world" to the expectation of individual death: under the presuppositions of the anthropology of the book of Qoheleth (cf. 12:7), a possible "end of the world" could mean nothing other than death for the individual human being. (To be sure, v. 12:5aβγ makes clear that it is not a question of such a cosmic catastrophe; cf. 1:3-11; 3:15.) Death is "loaded up symbolically" by vv. 2-5aα at most in the sense that through the echoes of prophetic announcements of judgment, death is interpreted as the "judgment" of God on a human being (cf. 11:9b).

Thus an eschatology oriented on the end of the world and judgment of the world is critically "deconstructed" in 12:1-7 in a way similar to that in 1:9-11. In the text, however, it is also immediately critically "reconstructed" in a reasonable way: what the prophets (or their traditions) say (or write) about the universal judgment of God—properly understood—can be experienced at any time in the universal basic conditions of human life, namely, in the fact that all human beings are subject to contingency and death (cf. 3:16-21). If this understanding of the text is correct, then we have here a case of the "demythologizing" reinterpretation of religious traditions in the OT.

An understanding of 12:2-7 or of parts of this text as a description of old age is suggested by neither the text itself nor the level of traditional concepts evoked by it. On the basis of the preceding context, vv. 2-5aα can, admittedly, be indirectly related to old age: if a person must always reckon with future misfortune, increasing old age raises the probability of experiencing misfortune (cf. 11:8). Verses 2-5aα can be read (superficially) as the presentation of such misfortune (cf. v. 1b).

In this way 12:2-7 underlines the call to "pleasure" in youth of 11:9—12:1, without—in contradiction to 11:7-8—threatening with the "burden of old age." A young man, just like an old one, should enjoy himself in the present, because the future will bring him unforeseeable misfortune and ultimately certain (and final) death. In both, God's "judgment" on him is performed. Even if faced with an ("apocalyptic") "end of the world," it contains no

more "terrors"—but also no more hopes!— for the individual than does his "natural" death.

■ **11:1—12:7** At the close of the book of Qoheleth, 11:1—12:7 summarizes, in the form of instructions for behavior, what was developed "theoretically" in chaps. 1-4: in the center of ethics stand (charitable) activity and enjoyment (11:1-6 and 11:7—12:7) as the "highest good" (cf. 3:12). Only "in life" can human beings realize both (cf. 3:12), and in this temporal framework of their actions and indulgences, they should concentrate on the present ("before . . .": 12:1bff.). For the future is as unpredictable for them as God's actions are opaque (11:2b, 5, 6b; cf. 3:11); death alone faces every person as the certain end (12:5b, 7; cf. 3:20-22); and in both—the future that is equally contingent for all people and the destiny of death common to all—God's judgment on human beings is accomplished (11:9b; 12:2-5aα; cf. 3:17).

Like chaps. 1-4, 11:1—12:7 is probably also making critical reference to contrary positions in the contemporary discussion. Thus 11:3-4 is perhaps aimed against attempts to make the future predictable with the help of prognostic techniques, and when 12:2-5aα combines the death of a person (vv. 5b, 7) with an "apocalyptic" catastrophe scenario, the related hopes or fears are reduced to a realistic level of expectation for individual death. Both directions of the polemic turn against conceptions that orient the actions and enjoyment of human beings toward the expected future instead of toward the experienceable present.

A call to charity *and* enjoyment *before* death that is comparable to 11:1—12:7 is found in Sir 14:11ff. (ה):

11 My son, if you own something, make use of it,
    and if you own something, do something good for
        yourself;
    and according to the power of your wealth, take
        care of yourself.
12 Remember that in the realm of the dead there is
        no joy,
    and death does not tarry,

---

on his attitude toward death. Every death is an unmitigated loss, for its shock cannot be buffered by communal continuity" (67; cf., however, Qoh 12:5b).

and what is decreed in relation to the underworld
    is not shown to you.
13 Before you die, be good to your friend,
    and what your hand acquires, give to him.
14 Do not deny yourself the happiness of a day,
    and do not forgo your share of pleasure.
15 Will you not leave your wealth to another,
    and what you have acquired to those who cast
      lots?
16 Give to the brother, and give to (?) and indulge
    yourself;
  for it is not possible to seek joy in the underworld;
  and everything that is beautiful to do,
  do it before God.[54]

It is possible that this text was influenced by the statements on pleasure and enjoyment in the book of Qoheleth (esp. 9:4-10).[55] In contrast to the book of Qoheleth, however, the call for charity *and* enjoyment in the book of Sirach in no way grows logically from an overall conception that is also recognizable in other passages in the book. Here it gives, rather, "the impression of a chance quotation tossed in for the occasion. In Sirach the sentence can be deleted; in Qoheleth it is essential."[56] In other places Sirach warns against carefree enjoyment in the present (cf. Sir 11:21ff.; 18:25-26). And the admonition of Sir 7:36, which recalls Qoh 12:1a: "In all your deeds, remember the end [זכור אחרית *zkwr ʾḥryt*]," has a sense in Sirach that is different from that in Qoheleth, as the continuation shows: "and in eternity you will not sin." For Sirach, as for Qoheleth, death means both the end of a person and the judgment of God on that person: "By his end is a man known" (Sir 11:26 [28]).[57] For Sirach, however, this also means that death meets human beings in different ways, each according to his or her behavior in life. The only relevant difference that Qoheleth would concede in this regard would probably be whether death meets a person who has enjoyed the God-given "good days" or one who has not.

---

54 Translation after G. Sauer, *JSHRZ* III.5.
55 Thus, e.g., Preuss, *Weisheitsliteratur*, 145: "Sirach . . . takes up the carpe diem of Qoheleth"; cf. also Levy, 26; Kroeber, 65; more cautious are Hertzberg, 48, and T. Middendorp, *Die Stellung Jesu Ben Siras zwischen Judentum und Hellenismus* (Leiden: Brill, 1973) 88.
56 Levy, 26.
57 𝔊 interprets this sentence in the sense of a divine retribution in (or after?) death.

12

8   **Fleeting and futile, said Qoheleth;**
     all that is fleeting.

Qoheleth 12:8 repeats (in somewhat abbreviated form) the "motto" of the book from 1:2 (cf. the textual notes and commentary there). After the reading of 1:3—12:7 and in connection with the immediately preceding text, the clause הַכֹּל הֶבֶל *hakkōl hebel* can now be understood more precisely. Human beings and all that they do are transitory and "fleeting." And all convictions and wishes that do not do justice to this transitoriness of humankind are untenable and "futile." This in no way

means that life is completely "meaningless" and "absurd," as the "king" holds in 1:12—2:26. Rather, the meaning of human life consists in affording oneself and others the enjoyment of good things within the context of the possibilities and limits set by God (cf. 3:10—12:7). As a reference back to the beginning of the book, 12:8 exhorts readers at the end to read the book again and anew from this viewpoint.

12

9 Qoheleth was not only a wise man but also taught the people knowledge.[a] He heard[b] and examined[c] (and[d]) corrected[e] many proverbs. **10** Qoheleth sought to find pleasing words and to correctly record[a] true words. **11** The words of the wise are like goads, and like nails driven home are collected proverbs.[a] They were given by *one* shepherd. **12** And beyond these—my son, be warned!—many books are made,[a] without end, yet much study[b] tires the body. **13** At the end of a talk we[a] hear all this: fear the Deity and keep his commandments! For everyone is to do that.[b] **14** The Deity brings every deed into a judgment of everything hidden, whether good or evil.

9a In addition to this interpretation of the construction . . . וְיֹתֵר שֶׁ . . . עוֹד . . . *wĕyōtēr še . . . ʿôd . . .* (lit.: "in addition to [Qoheleth being a wise man, he taught] also [or: always] . . ."), the following understanding is also syntactically possible: *"And it remains (to be said) that* [Qoheleth was a wise man;] *also* [or: *always*] [he taught . . .]"; cf. in detail Lohfink, "Zu einigen Satzeröffnungen im Epilog des Koheletbuches," in Diesel et al., eds., *Jedes Ding,* 131–47.

9b Thus with the interpretation of the verb וְאִזֵּן *wĕʾizzēn* as אזן *ʾzn* piel (cf. the ancient versions). *HALOT* assumes here a verb אזן *ʾzn* II piel "balance," derived from the noun מֹאזְנַיִם *môzĕnayim,* "scale"; see, however, Seow.

9c Or: "researched." The meaning "search out," assumed by *HALOT* for the piel of חקר *ḥqr,* which is attested only here, seems less likely in view of the qal ("research, find out") and the niphal ("be discovered") of this root.

9d The conjunction is found in some Heb. mss., ϭ, and α'.

9e תקן *tqn* piel (cf. also 7:13 and Sir 47:9; qal: 1:15) is interpreted here mostly in the sense of "put into a good order, arrange a collection of proverbs" (thus *HALOT*); cf. Fishbane, *Biblical Interpretation in Ancient Israel* (2d ed.; Oxford: Clarendon, 1988) 32 ("to edit"). Yet the assumption of a meaning of "correct, put right" seems less forced; cf. 7:13, as well as the (later) תִּקּוּנֵי סוֹפְרִים *tiqqûnê sôpĕrîm* ("copyist corrections"), Murphy; N. Lohfink, "Les épilogues du livre de Qohélet et les débuts du Canon," in P. Bovati and R. Meynet, eds., *Ouvrir les écritures: Mélanges offerts à Paul Beauchamp* (LD 162; Paris: Cerf, 1995) 87–88. The *NJPSV* interprets תִּקֵּן *tiqqēn* as a noun ("propriety") and translates: "He listened to and tested the soundness of many maxims."

10a 𝔐 reads וכתוב *wktwb* as pass. ptc. וְכָתוּב *wĕkātûb* "(it is) written" (cf. ϭ). Some Heb. mss. read a finite verb וְכָתַב *wĕkātab,* "he wrote"; likewise α' σ' Hier 𝔙, which, however, could also have interpreted an inf. abs. וְכָתוֹב *wĕkātôb* as a finite verb (cf. 4:2; 8:9). The translation proposed above assumes that וכתוב *wktwb* as inf. abs. (וְכָתוֹב *wĕkātôb*), just like לִמְצֹא *limṣōʾ,* is dependent on בִּקֵּשׁ *biqqēš* (cf. 7:25).

11a בַּעֲלֵי אֲסֻפּוֹת *baʿălê ʾăsuppôt* can designate not only (personally) "masters = leaders of [or: participants in?] assemblies" (or also "authors of collections [of sayings]"?) but also (impersonally) "elements of the class 'gathered (words/sayings)'" = "gathered sayings" (cf. Isa 41:15; Prov 1:17; Qoh 10:20; Dan 8:6, 20), which more closely parallels "words."

12a Or: "And beyond this there is still more (to say): My son, be warned! Many books are made . . ." or: "And it remains (to be said): Against them [scil. the words and sayings named in v. 11], my son, be warned! . . ."; cf. above n. 9a.

12b Instead of the *hapax legomenon* לַהַג *lahag* ("study") one should perhaps read לְהֶגוֹ *lĕhāgô* (from הגה *hgh* qal) ("read half out loud, consider while mumbling").

13a Thus with the interpretation of נִשְׁמָע *nišmāʿ* as 1st person pl. impf. of שׁמע *šmʿ* qal (cf. 𝕭). The form could also be read as niphal ptc.: "(all this has been) heard," without essentially changing the meaning of the statement. 𝕲 and 𝕾 presuppose the impv. m. sg. (שְׁמַע *šĕmaʿ*).

13b For this usual but not entirely certain interpretation of the sentence, Seow refers for comparison to Pss 110:3; 109:4; 120:7; Job 8:9.

Verses 9-14 correspond to the title in 1:1. As there (and in 1:2; 12:8, as well as 7:27), here too we find the words of the "editor" of the book in addition to those of "Qoheleth"—which does not exclude the possibility that concealed behind the two voices is one and the same author.[1] In the literature, however, it is mostly assumed that the "epilogue" of 12:9-14 goes back to one or more (according to Jastrow, more than eight) authors who are different from the author of the corpus of the book in 1:(2)3–12:7(8).

Thus Lohfink (12–13), for example, presumes that the book of Qoheleth was introduced with the (secondary) framework in 1:1 and 12:9-11 as a text book in the Jerusalem temple school in addition to Proverbs (and Canticles?); 12:12-14 was then added somewhat later in order to counter the attempt to replace the "Corpus Salomonicum" (Proverbs + Qohelet [+ Canticles?]) with the book of Sirach as a new (and more comprehensive!) textbook; at the same time the "orthodoxy" of Qoheleth is defended here vis-à-vis the more strongly tradition-oriented book of Sirach. Finally, according to Lohfink, the book of Qoheleth as a textbook, like other writings common to the Jerusalem temple and the synagogues, "fell automatically, as it were, into the canon" (see Introduction above under "Influence").

Yet when following and further developing observations and hypotheses of Sheppard, Wilson, Dohmen/

Oeming, and Koenen, one could also assume that 12:9-14 already had in mind the embedding of the book of Qoheleth in a larger context of "(proto)canonical" writings: first, the ("Solomonic"?) wisdom literature (v. 11: "sayings of the wise"), then (in one or more further steps?) also the "Torah" (v. 13: "commandments" of God) and the "prophets" (v. 14: "judgment" of God).[2] Then one might ask further whether vv. 12-14 express a more critical attitude toward the book of Qoheleth (and the "words of the wise") than that in vv. 9-11 (thus, e.g., Lauha).

A closer examination of the text, however, reveals that its statements and admonitions contain a number of underlying ironical allusions that make it seem possible to understand the epilogue of the book of Qoheleth as its original literary conclusion through which it is once again pointedly inscribed in the context of contemporary theological discussion.[3] At the same time, for the reader the "teaching authority" of Qoheleth is again critically relativized here at the end of the book, as it was already at its beginning (see above on 1:1): its observations deserve attention because of their underlying experiences and reflections (vv. 9-10). For this very reason, however, they are also to be tested critically by the readers through their own reflection and in view of their own experiences—especially since there are in addition further "sayings of the wise" (v. 11), as well as other rele-

1   Cf. M. V. Fox, "Frame Narrative and Composition in the Book of Qohelet," *HUCA* 48 (1977) 83–106.

2   G. T. Sheppard, "The Epilogue to Qoheleth as Theological Commentary," *CBQ* 39 (1977) 182–89; idem, *Wisdom as a Hermeneutical Construct* (BZAW 180; Berlin: de Gruyter, 1980) 120–29; G. H. Wilson, "'The Words of the Wise': The Intent and Significance of Qohelet 12:9-14," *JBL* 103 (1984) 175–92; C. Dohmen, "Das viele Büchermachen hat kein Ende (Koh 12,12): Wachstumsspuren in der Heiligen Schrift," in Dohmen and M. Oeming, *Biblischer Kanon warum und wozu? Eine Kanontheo-*

logie (QD 137; Freiburg: Herder, 1992) 30–54; K. Koenen, "Zu den Epilogen des Buches Qohelet," *BN* 72 (1994) 24–27.

3   Fox, "Frame Narrative."

vant books (v. 12) and pertinent cultural traditions
(vv. 13-14: "commandments" of God, expectation of a
divine "judgment").

Regarding structure, 12:9-14 is especially comparable
to Sir 50:27-29:[4]

27 Instruction, insight, and proverbial writings on
      (various) life situations
   by Simon, the son of Jesus, the son of Eleazar,
      the son of Sirach,
   which poured forth from the seeking of his heart,
   and which he let pour forth in insight.
28 Happy are those who ponder (יהגה yhgh) them,
   and those who take them to heart will become
      wise.
29 For the fear of the Lord means life.

In both cases a presentation of the "author" and the
production of his writing (Qoh 12:9-10; Sir 50:27) is followed by a closing "parenesis" with an admonition to the
reader (Qoh 12:12-13; implicit in Sir 50:28) and a look
into the future (Qoh 12:14; Sir 50:29). Moreover, there
are also content parallels between the two texts (Qoh
12:12: (ה)נה(ל?) lhg(hî)/Sir 50:28: יהגה yhgh; "fear of God"
in Qoh 12:13 and Sir 50:29). The parallels in structure
could indicate that both texts were conceived according
to a conventional pattern for the conclusion of a "wisdom teaching"[5] (which is not a compelling argument for
the literary unity of Qoh 12:9-14 but makes this possibility worth considering).

These verses describe the work of Qoheleth out of
which the present book arose.

■ **9abα** Verse 9a designates Qoheleth as "wise" or as a
"wise man" (חָכָם ḥākām). In 1:3–12:7 the "editor" of the

book interprets and clarifies the ambivalent "self-"portrait of "Qoheleth": if "Qoheleth" initially presents himself in the role of a "king" as unsurpassed "wise man"
(1:16; cf. 2:15), later in 7:23, after giving up this role, he
points to the failure of his search for wisdom (cf. also
8:16-17). Nonetheless, statements like 4:13; 7:16-17;
9:13ff.; and 10:10 reveal a relative valuation of wisdom
by "Qoheleth." In that the "editor" now in closing designates "Qoheleth" as a "wise man," he defines with the
help of his "persona" *his* understanding of "wisdom": a
"wise man" is precisely one who—like "Qoheleth" and
not like the "king"—is conscious of the limits of his "wisdom" (cf. Socrates). The fact that in the epilogue of the
book Qoheleth is no longer given the title "king" is a
final indication that in 1:1 and 1:12–2:26 it is a question
of a fictive travesty.

Because of the ambiguity of the construction of v. 9a
and 9bα it must remain open whether the text sees in the
instruction of the people an aspect of Qoheleth's
"being (a) wise (man)" or an additional activity that
could not yet be taken for granted.[6] For comparison
Lohfink points to "the call of wisdom through the
streets and marketplaces in Proverbs 1–9." In addition,
one may mention the presentation of various types of
"wise men" in Sir 37:22ff.:

22 There is also a wise man who is wise for himself;
   the fruits of his knowledge will be to his
      advantage.
23 There is also a wise man who is wise for his
      people;
   the fruits of his knowledge will be to their
      advantage.

4   Translation after G. Sauer, *JSHRZ* III.5; on the var-
     ied text tradition of Sir 50:20 see Sauer on this pas-
     sage.
5   On the "parenetic" conclusion cf., e.g., the Egyptian
     teaching of Amenemope (Brunner, *Altägyptische
     Weisheit*, no. 14, 540ff.): "Look at these thirty chap-
     ters; they delight and they teach; they stand at the
     head of all books; they bring the unknowing knowl-
     edge. Whoever reads them to the unknowing man
     makes him a pure man. Fill yourself with them; put
     them in your heart; indeed, become a man who can
     interpret them by explaining them as a teacher. A
     writer who is experienced in his office is found wor-
     thy of being in the court."
6   For the former see, e.g., Fox: "public instruction is
     an aspect of being a *ḥākām*." For the latter see, e.g.,
     Lohfink: "An attempt to make education available
     to simple folk, or even the unrestricted offering of
     teaching to the general public, must have been
     something new or unusual—otherwise it would not
     have been so emphasized."

24 One who is wise for himself is filled with
    enjoyment,
  and all who see him call him happy.
25 The life of a person lasts numerable days,
  yet the days of the life of the people Israel are
    without number.
26 One who is wise for the people gains esteem,
  and his name stands fast in eternal life.[7]

If at first glance Qoh 12:9 and Sir 37:23 seem to
exhibit the same type of "wise man," a closer examination reveals, nonetheless, a crucial difference. The "wise
man" of Sir 37:23 applies "*his* knowledge" (דעתו *d⁽tw*) for
the benefit of the people (גוי *gwy*). "Qoheleth," by contrast, *conveys* to the "people" (הָעָם *hā⁽ām*) *their own*
"knowledge" (דַעַת *da⁽at*). Here one sees the contrast
between the concept of an "elite" education of a "leading class" *for* the people (cf. Sir 38:24ff.) and the concept
of an "education *of* the people." When in 12:9 the "editor" presents "Qoheleth" as a "wise man" in the sense of
the second concept, he is reinforcing the vote for a
"broad education" developed in 9:13–10:3.

■ **9bβ-10** With his representation of the production of
the book by "Qoheleth" in vv. 9bβ-10 the writer reinforces the fiction of "Qoheleth" as "author" of the
book and stylizes himself as its "editor." Verse 9bβγ ("he
heard and examined [and] corrected many proverbs") is
often interpreted as a description of the production
(and composition) of proverbs by "Qoheleth": "He pondered and searched out and set in order many proverbs"
(*NIV*).[8] Yet a comparison with the prologue of Proverbs
and the presentation of the wise man in Sir 39:1ff.
makes it more likely that the topic here is "Qoheleth's"
dealing with traditional "proverbs" already available—
and that the writer did not have in mind (only) "com-

pletely new (i.e., Greek) cultural tradition" (Lohfink). In
the context of describing the purpose of the book of
Proverbs, Prov 1:5-6 states:

5 Let the wise man hear and increase (his) education
  and let the understanding man acquire ideas,
6 to understand a proverb and a parable,
  words of the wise and their riddles.

And Sir 39:1-3 says of the "wise man":

1 He seeks out (ἐκζητήσει) the wisdom of all the
    ancients
  and is concerned with prophecies.
2 He observes the speeches of famous men,
  and he penetrates the expressions of the proverbs
    (παραβολῶν).
3 He seeks out (ἐκζητήσει) the mysteries of parables,
  and he is concerned with the riddles of proverbs
    (παραβολῶν).[9]

At first, Qoh 12:9bβγ also seems to deal with the
adaptation of traditional "wisdom" ("hear"). Then, however, there is a critical testing and *correction*. Wisdom is
accordingly defined here no longer primarily by a material tradition but by a capacity for critical reflection on
tradition in view of one's own experiences.[10] Corresponding to this is the sequence of "seeking," "finding,"
and "recording" in v. 10—in which it is not entirely clear
whether "pleasing words" (דִּבְרֵי־חֵפֶץ *dibrê-ḥēpeṣ*) and
"true words" (דִּבְרֵי אֱמֶת *dibrê ʾĕmet*) are used here synony-
mously, or whether *from* the "pleasing words" that he
found "Qoheleth" *selected* (and wrote down "directly"—
that is, without regard to "aesthetics"?) "true/reliable
words." Also in this characteristic, the presentation of

---

7 Translation after Sauer, *JSHRZ* III.5. Cf. also Sir
  24:34: "Observe that I did not labor for myself
  alone but for all who seek her [i.e., wisdom]"; contra Prov 9:12: "If you are wise, you are wise for your
  own benefit." That Sirach too was not a "wise man"
  entirely unselfishly is shown by 51:27-28, in addition
  to 37:26.
8 Cf. also Whybray: תקן *tqn* "may mean 'arrange'
  (. . .); but in rabbinic Hebrew it can mean 'set in
  order' or 'establish, ordain.' In Sir. 47:9 (Hebrew
  text) it may mean 'compose (music).' Taken
  together, these three verbs may refer to the stages in

the process of literary composition: experimenting
with, working on, and shaping proverbs."
9 Translation after Sauer, *JSHRZ* III.5.
10 If v. 9(ff.), as Fishbane, *Biblical Interpretation*, 29–32,
  presumes, was shaped after the model of a scribal
  colophon (cf., however, Fox's critical notes [on
  12:9]), this could be a carrying over of the model of
  "correct writing" (v. 10b) from the form to the content of a text.

"Qoheleth" by the "editor" agrees with his "self"-portrayal in 1:3–12:7, for he often carries on or encourages a critical engagement with "words" (cf. 1:10; 5:6; 6:11; 7:21; 10:12ff.).

■ **11** Beginning with v. 11, the talk is no longer directly of Qoheleth; to the extent that he was a "wise man" (v. 9) and worked with "words" (v. 10), however, what is said in v. 11 about the "sayings of the wise" applies both to the "words" of traditional wisdom, with which Qoheleth has dealt critically, and to his own "words" (cf. 1:1). The comparison in v. 11a between "words of the wise" and "collected proverbs," on the one hand, and "goads" and "nails driven home," on the other, presents several puzzles.[11] In any case, however, it is clear that here educational activity and agriculture (as well as handiwork?) are placed in parallel. One possible point of this statement is shown by the comparison with the juxtaposition of the "wise man" (Sir 39:1ff.; see above) and those who are active in agriculture (38:25-26) and handiwork (v. 27: worker, artisan; v. 28: smith; vv. 29-30: potter) in 38:24–39:11: "How can one who holds the plow become wise, and one who glories in the shaft of the goad, who drives cattle and turns the oxen?" (38:25)[12] By contrast, Qoh 12:11 states: as the farmer busies himself with ox goads and the craftsman with nails, so the wise man with words. At the same time, this recognizes the activity of the "wise man" as an independent "occupation" and rejects an elitist distinction regarding the worth of "head" and "hand" work, "white collar" and "blue collar" jobs.

Moreover, the juxtaposition of "words of the wise" (דִּבְרֵי חֲכָמִים dibrê ḥăkāmîm) and "collected proverbs" (בַּעֲלֵי אֲסֻפּוֹת ba'ălê 'ăsuppôt) in v. 11 perhaps "justifies the gathering of the sayings of teachers in books" (Lohfink). Then the comparison with "ox goads" and "nails" could emphasize the varied functions of (oral) "words" and (written) "collections." Whereas the former above all provoke, stimulate thinking, and give instructions for action, the latter offer security and support in the form of a comprehensive orientation. Yet the comparison would be quite ambivalent. Like "ox goads," the "words of the wise" can also incapacitate and injure hearers,[13] and like "nails," "collected proverbs" can also lead to "dogmatic" hardening and inflexibility.

Verse 11b ("they were given by *one* shepherd") is often understood in the sense that the "words of the wise" and the "collected proverbs" were "given" by God or by King Solomon.[14] Probably, however, the statement simply continues the comparison of v. 11a (cf. Fox): as one and the same shepherd employs in his work both "ox goads" and "nails" (say, in the building of a shelter or a fence), so one and the same wise man works with both (oral) "words" and (written) "collections." This again justifies "the gathering of the sayings of teachers in books" (Loh-

---

11 Cf. Lauha: "דָּרְבָן [dārbān] (only here and in 1 Sam 13:21; Ugar. *drb*) is the barb with which one drives and leads a draft animal. . . . The image comes from farm life. The comparison tries to convince one that the instruction of the wise can give to listeners or readers stimulating impulses and useful suggestions. . . . מַשְׂמְרָה [maśmērâ] 'nail' occurs only here and in Jer 10:4 (cf. מַשְׂמֵר [masmēr] Isa 41:7; 1 Chr 22:3; 2 Chr 3:9). נטע [nṭ'] (3:2) 'to plant' has here the specific meaning 'drive nails.' Either the farm image is continued here (nails = barbs), or the image passes into the realm of the craftsman: as nails give a building solidity, the teacher of wisdom helps a person stand fast." M. Rose, "Verba sapientium sicut stimuli," in D. Knoepfler, ed., *Nomen Latinum: Mélanges . . . offerts au professeur André Schneider* (Neuchâtel: Faculté de lettres; Geneva: Droz, 1997) 209–18, attempts to make the text more understandable with the help of conjectures.

12 Translation after Sauer, *JSHRZ* III.5.

13 Cf. Fox: "The goad prods one on to thought and better behavior, but it also hurts. . . . The words of the sages, in other words, are a bit dangerous. Compare the far more emphatic warning of R. Eliezer b. Hyrkanus to beware of the words of *ḥakamim*, for 'they burn like fiery coals, bite like jackals, sting like scorpions' (Avot 2:15)"; cf. also Ogden.

14 For the former see, e.g., Lauha; Dohmen, "Das viele Büchermachen"; idem, "Der Weisheit letzter Schluss? Anmerkungen zur Übersetzung und Bedeutung von Koh 12,9-14," *BN* 63 (1992) 12–18. For the latter see, e.g., Delitzsch. Lohfink and Crenshaw leave both possibilities open. Galling recommends vocalizing מרעה אחד *mr'h 'ḥd* as מֵרֵעֶה אֶחָד *mērē'eh 'eḥād* ("from a friend"): "The words of the wise and thus *also* and especially the words of Qoheleth are handed down" by a "pupil and friend of the deceased who remains anonymous." Speaking against this, however, is the fact that v. 11 does not speak especially of the "words of Qoheleth."

fink) but, at the same time, it is relativized: it represents only *one* realm of activity of the "wise man."

■ **12** Like the comparisons in v. 11, the warning (הִזָּהֵר *hizzāhēr*, cf. 4:13) against the "making" and "studying" of "books" in v. 12, introduced by the conventional addressing of a student or reader as "my son" (cf. esp. Proverbs 1–9; Sir 2:1; 3:8, 12, 17; 4:1, 20; and elsewhere), is ambivalent.[15] It can be read as "a warning to avoid the writing of more books and endless study . . . (cf. Gordis, Lohfink)" or as "a solemn counsel to any who would follow the sage that such a decision calls for a sincere commitment to an endless and all-consuming task" (Ogden).[16] In this ambivalence v. 12—especially in comparison with Sir 50:28: "Happy are those who ponder (יהגה *yhgh*) them [sc. the teachings of Sirach] . . . !" (cf. Josh 1:8; Pss 1:2; 37:30)—has the effect of a parody of the final parenesis in a wisdom teaching text.

Depending on how one interprets the syntax and semantics of the text (cf. the note on the translation), the warning of v. 12 can be related to the book of Qoheleth (vv. 9-10) and other wisdom writings and traditions (v. 11) or to "books" that come from other traditions and conceptual contexts ("beyond these [words of the wise and collected proverbs]"). This ambiguity of the text (cf., e.g., 5:7-8; 8:2-5) gives expression to an irony—which is also thoroughly self-critical.

■ **13-14** Verse 13a (סוֹף דָּבָר הַכֹּל נִשְׁמָע *sôp dābār hakkōl nišmāʿ*) is usually interpreted as a signal for the closing of the book of Qoheleth.[17] The exhortation "Fear the Deity and keep his commandments!" in v. 13b can then be understood either as an additional, complementary admonition of the "editor" or as a summary of the teachings of "Qoheleth." Quite the same can be said about the expectation of a divine judgment in v. 14. The undetermined סוֹף דָּבָר *sôp dābār* ("end of a talk") could, naturally, indicate that v. 13 does not refer at all to the book of Qoheleth but rather to the other kinds of writings mentioned in v. 12—which then are apparently (in the view of the "editor") a matter of boring and monotonous "pious" treatises. Verse 14 would then likewise be understood as a stereotypical assertion of this "religious" literature—or as another statement of the "editor" that subjects this literature (not without irony) to the final judgment of God (cf. v. 14: כָּל־מַעֲשֶׂה *kol-maʿăśeh* with v. 12: עֲשׂוֹת סְפָרִים *ʿăśôt sĕpārîm*).

---

15   Deviating from the usual linguistic usage (כתב *ktb* + סֵפֶר *sēper*), עֲשׂוֹת סְפָרִים *ʿăśôt sĕpārîm* has given rise to the assumption that עשה *ʿśh* here means "use" books (Loretz, *Qohelet*, 139), "working at books" (P. A. H. de Boer, "A Note on Ecclesiastes 12,12a," in R. H. Fischer, ed., *A Tribute to Arthur Vööbus* [Chicago: Lutheran School of Theology, 1977] 85–88, repr. in de Boer, *Selected Studies in Old Testament Exegesis* [ed. C. van Duin; OTS 27; Leiden: Brill, 1991] 168–71), or "compare," "compile" (Fishbane, *Biblical Interpretation*, 31). Perhaps the whole spectrum of dealing with books should be held open. Nevertheless, עשה *ʿśh* is probably used here to make clear that the production of books is also subject to divine judgment over human activity (מַעֲשֶׂה *maʿăśeh*) (v. 14). In any case, the text does not expressly say that it is a question here of *new text*books (thus, e.g., Lohfink) or of *foreign* (say, Greek) literature (thus, e.g., Barton).

16   Ogden favors the second meaning. The prologue to the Greek translation of the book of Sirach shows that the reference to an "endless production of books" in no way has to be automatically valued negatively:

   1 Because of the many and great traditions that were given to us through the law and the prophets 2 and the others who followed them . . . 4 and since not only those who can read [these writings] should receive understanding 5 but those eager to learn should be in a position also to be of service to those who find themselves on the outside, 6 through words and through writings (καὶ λέγοντας καὶ γρά-φοντας), 7 my grandfather Jesus, who even toiled greatly 8 over the knowledge of the law 9 and the prophets 10 and the other books of the fathers 11 and had gained from them a sufficient knowledge, undertook 12 also to write down something himself. . . .

   This would be even more valid if in v. 14 one could, with Loretz (*Qohelet*, 142), understand ἐπιπροσθῶσιν in the sense of "add": ". . . 13 so that the scholars, hereby enriched, 14 in the course of their lives faithful to the law added still much more" (contra Sauer, *JSHRZ* III.5: ". . . 13 so that those who strive for learning and constantly hold fast to it 14 could more easily make progress in regard to life according to the law").

17   Cf. Dan 7:28 and, e.g., the conclusion of the Egyptian Instruction of the Papyrus Insinger (Brunner, *Altägyptische Weisheit*, no. 17): "End of the teaching" (followed by a blessing for the author) or the close of the Teaching of Ankh-Sheshonq (Brunner, *Alt-*

Because of this ambiguity vv. 13-14 can be read in different senses:

- as a critique of an overflowing production of religious or theological literature that, however, only repeats and varies a few stereotypical statements and admonitions,
- as an (ironic) attempt to acknowledge the religious and theological "correctness" of the book of Qoheleth,[18] or
- as an (ironic) reinforcement of the "essentials" of traditional piety and theology vis-à-vis the irritating and provocative ideas of the book of Qoheleth.[19]

The formulations in vv. 13-14 show similarities and differences both in regard to comparable statements in the corpus of the book of Qoheleth and in regard to other contemporary texts and theological concepts. Like the ambiguities of the text, these allusions also call for readers to accept the responsibility of receiving the book of Qoheleth in the context of the contemporary discussion. The text confronts its readers not simply with the decision to reject either "Qoheleth" or the religious convictions criticized by him; with its formulations the text (in a way similar to 12:1-7 concerning eschatological expectations) raises the possibility of a critical reception and new interpretation of religious traditions.

In his analysis of vv. 13-14, Sheppard comes to the conclusion that "only Sirach has exactly the same ideology as Qoh. 12:13-14, a perspective not expressed in the body of Qoheleth itself. It is, therefore, probable that the redactor of Qoh. 12:13-14 either knew of the book of Sirach or shared fully in a similar, pervasive estimate of sacred wisdom."[20] On closer examination, however, it is apparent that Sheppard's observations need to be refined and his conclusions corrected accordingly:

1. The "ideology" and "perspective" of vv. 13-14 is in no way totally foreign to the rest of the book of Qoheleth. The admonition to fear God in v. 13b corresponds word for word with 5:6b. The keeping of the commandments is not otherwise expressly called for in the book of Qoheleth (on the formulation cf. 8:5); but 5:3 quotes almost word for word the commandment in Deut 23:22, and at no point in the book is the keeping of the commandments of God criticized. Thus both imperatives in 12:13 could be understood as a—like 1:2 and 12:8, highly selective!—résumé of the "words of Qoheleth." Just like 1:2 and 12:8, however, 12:13 is then also to be interpreted from the standpoint of 1:3–12:7. Then "fear of God" here not only means—as frequently in the Psalms and in the OT wisdom literature—"piety" and "moral behavior" in a rather unspecific sense,[21] but also includes the numinous element of fear before God (cf. 3:14; 8:12-13) and is in any case not identical with "wisdom" and "righteousness" (cf. 7:15-18). And the "keeping of the commandments," according to statements like 7:15; 8:14; and 9:2, cannot in any event be linked with an expectation of prosperity thereby guaranteed.

The same is true of 12:14: the expectation of a "judgment" of God on a man and his actions (v. 14a) is also formulated in comparable terminology in 11:9b, which is therefore often excluded as a gloss. In the context (11:7–12:7), however, this "judgment" of God is redefined here in the sense that it consists in the accidents and "strokes of fate" to which life subjects a person and, finally, in death. In a similar way 3:17 identifies the "judging" of God with the change of time. On this basis, then, 12:14 also does not have to be read as a reference to an "eschatological" judgment of God. In addition, the judgment of God on human actions is, according to v. 14, expressly based on points of view that are "hid-

---

ägyptische Weisheit, no. 15): "(It is) written." By all appearances, סוֹף *sôp* does not mean "sum" or "result" but simply "end" (cf. 3:11; 7:2; Hitzig; Sheppard, *Wisdom*, 122 n. 6). Cf., however, also Sir 43:27: "More of this sort we do not want to add, and the end of the talk (וקץ דבר *wqṣ dbr*): he [God] is everything/the universe."

18   Thus, e.g., Lohfink (13): 12:12-14 "defended the orthodoxy of the book."

19   Thus, e.g., Dohmen and Oeming, "Das viele Büchermachen," 51: 12:12-14 attempts "to immunize the book of Qoheleth . . . by declaring that . . . its study is superfluous in regard to the only important thing: living a life pleasing to God."

20   Sheppard, *Wisdom*, 127.

21   Cf. H.-P. Stähli, "ירא *yrʾ* to fear," *TLOT* 2:575–77.

den" from human beings (cf. 9:1). This, however, makes it unpredictable for human beings.[22] To this extent, the reference to the coming "judgment" of God here contains no promise for those who "fear God" and are "faithful to the law" (v. 13); rather, it substantiates a "fear of God" in the sense of awe before God.

2. A close connection between "fear of God" and "keeping the commandments" corresponding to Qoh 12:13 is otherwise found in contemporary literature only in Sirach. It is already anticipated, however, in "a few wisdom psalms" in which "the concept of the 'fear of God' becomes a 'nomistic' concept and refers exclusively to the law: yr⁾ designates those who have pleasure in Yahweh's commandments (Ps 112:1), those faithful to the law (Ps 119:63) who walks in his paths (Ps 128:1). In Ps 19:10 *yir⁾at yhwh* signifies the 'law' itself."[23] In the book of Sirach one may compare Qoh 12:13-14 especially to Sir 1:26ff., where, in addition to the parallelism of "fear of the Lord" and "keeping the commandments"[24] that corresponds to Qoh 12:13, one also finds a reference to God's judging activity in the future, which is comparable to Qoh 12:14:

26 If you desire wisdom, keep the commandments,
    and the Lord will lavish her upon you.
27 For wisdom and learning lie in the fear of the lord,
    and fidelity and humility are his delight.
28 Do not be hypocritical in the fear of the Lord,
    and do not approach it with a doubting heart,
29 Do not be a hypocrite before others,
    and keep watch over your lips.
30 Do not exalt yourself, so that you will not fall
    and thereby bring dishonor on yourself;
    the Lord will reveal your secret thoughts,
    and cast you down in the midst of the
      community.[25]

A comparison of this text with Qoh 12:13-14, however, shows considerable differences in "ideology" and "perspective"—especially if one interprets Qoh 12:13-14 in the sense of the comments of 1:3—12:7: in contrast to Sir 1:26ff., this passage lacks a direct connection between "fear of God" and "keeping the commandments," on the one hand, and "wisdom," on the other.[26] In any case, the "fear of God" here is not the *"beginning of wisdom"* (Sir 1:14; Prov 1:7; 9:10; 15:33; Ps 111:10); it stands rather at its *"end"* (v. 13a): "wisdom" does not lead to a higher form of "piety" and "morality" but, on the contrary, to an insight into the value of elementary "piety" and "morality." "Fear of God" and the "keeping of the commandments" in no way guarantees a person divine "delight." And the judgment of God of "everything hidden" has as its object not only "secret thoughts," which the "hypocrite" hides inside but otherwise knows well, but also the "unconscious," which remain inaccessible to *every* person. If every person is obligated by the "fear of God" and "keeping the commandments" (v. 13b), this nips in the bud a functionalization of "piety" and" religion" for the educational process, as discernible in exemplary fashion in Sir 1:26-30.

In a way similar to Qoh 12:13, Job 28:28 also reduces the wisdom accessible to human beings to "pious" and "moral" behavior. Wisdom is "hidden from the eyes of all living" (vv. 21-22); God alone knows the way to her" (vv. 23ff.); "he saw her and counted her; he established her and searched her out (v. 27); then he said to humankind: 'See! The fear of the Lord [read ‹Yahweh›?] is wisdom, and staying away from evil is understanding'" (v. 28). Here the previously established inaccessibility of "wisdom" for humankind is in no way taken back: "Fear of God" is, according to v. 28 not the *"beginning* of wisdom"; it *"is* wisdom" and, together with "staying away from evil," the *whole* of wisdom that is accessible to humankind.

3. If v. 13 designates the fear of God and the keeping of the divine commandments as the duty of every person, this can be understood first to mean that indeed all

---

22 On the possibility—foreseen, according to Lev 4:13ff.—of atoning for "hidden" guilt as "oversight," cf. the polemic in Qoh 5:5.
23 Stähli, *TLOT* 2:577–78.
24 Cf. further Sir 10:19 ("an esteemed race is the one that fears the Lord . . . a despised race is the one that breaks the commandment"); 23:27 ("nothing is dearer than the fear of the Lord, and nothing is sweeter than the fulfillment of the commandments of the Lord"); 32:22–33:1.
25 Translation after Sauer, *JSHRZ* III.5.
26 Cf. Fox, 320. Indirectly, there is naturally such a connection if one reads vv. 13b-14 as a "summary" of the "words of Qoheleth," who was indeed, according to v. 9, a "wise man."

people should worship the Deity Yahweh and obey the Mosaic Torah[27] (to which then "Israel"—in contrast to Bar 3:9—4:4—could, in any case, make no exclusive claim). One can, however, also interpret v. 13 with its final clause as a purely pragmatic recommendation to all people in daily life to hold "undogmatically" to the religious and cultural norms that they find in their particular living environment.[28] That would correspond to a skeptical way of life as described by Sextus Empiricus in his "Outline of Pyrrhonist Skepticism" (1.23-24): "We hold on . . . to phenomena and live undogmatically according to the everyday experience of life"; that includes, among other things, the "tradition of laws and customs" from which "we accept for everyday life the idea that we regard the fear of God as a good, and godlessness as an evil. . . . Yet we mean all of this undogmatically."[29]

Delitzsch remarks on v. 13 in his commentary: "It is a great thought that is thereby expressed, viz., the reduction of the Israelitish law to its common human essence." Instead of a "reduction," however, one should perhaps speak rather of a "relativization" of the Torah, which is more nearly reduced to its "common human core" by the ethical maxims of fearing God and keeping away from evil, as advocated in the book of Job (cf. Job 1:1, 8; 2:3; 28:28). These maxims presuppose that human beings can themselves autonomously determine what is good and what is evil (cf. Job 31:1[ff.]). Qoheleth 12:13, by contrast, does justice to the fact that in their ethical judgments and decisions human beings are already confronted by traditional directives (cf. the close connection of "fear of God" and "instruction" in Prov 1:7ff. and 9:1ff.) that they can consider critically (and must; cf. Qoh 6:11ff.) but from which they cannot fully liberate themselves, and which therefore retain a relative validity.

■ **9-14** The observations sketched regarding 12:9-14 in the context of the book of Qoheleth and of the contemporary discussion of various "wisdom" or "learning" concepts, as they are discernible above all in comparison with texts for the book of Sirach, show that it is possible, as recommended by Fox, to interpret this text as an integral component of the "original" book of Qoheleth.[30] By appearing in the role of the "editor" behind his protagonist "Qoheleth," the author creates distance between himself and "Qoheleth." *In* this distance he *reinforces* the "words of Qoheleth" by stylizing "Qoheleth" as a type of a "critical wise man" (vv. 9-10). At the same time, however, he also *relativizes* them by classifying them in the realm of wise "words" and "writings," and he shows their possibilities and their limits (vv. 11-12). In this way he makes clear that the critical wisdom represented by "Qoheleth" is also self-critical. As such it cannot lead beyond an elementary piety and ethic, but it can contribute to their critical self-clarification—without basically calling them into question (vv. 13-14 in light of the conceptions of the "fear of God" and a "judgment" of God developed in 1:3—12:7). Thus, in a thoroughgoing disputation with conceptions of a tradition-bound, elite, and religious wisdom, as they become perceivable especially in the book of Sirach, 12:9-14 defends *both* freedom of thought vis-à-vis an imposition of will by traditions, expert knowledge, or forced profession *and* the independence of simple piety vis-à-vis (presumed) theological wisdom.

Qoheleth 12:9-14 could also have these functions, however, if this section—perhaps divided into two stages (vv. 9-11, 12-14)—was added secondarily. Then it would not necessarily have to be interpreted as an "orthodox" correction or as a "pious" misunderstanding of the "words of Qoheleth" but could rather be understood as a defense of the critical wisdom of Qoheleth vis-à-vis competing orientation possibilities. If, however, the epilogue (in part or in whole) was written with the intention of criticizing and neutralizing the reflections of Qoheleth from an "orthodox" standpoint, the apparent failure of this effort in the present text would have ultimately and unintentionally confirmed the critical wisdom of Qoheleth.

---

27   Cf., e.g., Deut 4:6-8 (but also v. 19); Isa 2:3-4; 42:3-4; 51:4-5; Mic 4:2-3 (but also v. 5).

28   On model "piety" outside of Israel (and without the Torah), cf., e.g., Genesis 20 (v. 11!); Jonah 1; 3; Mal 1:11, 14; Ruth; and Job.

29   Sextus Empiricus, *Grundriss der pyrrhonischen Skepsis*

(introduced and translated by Malte Hossenfelder; Frankfurt on Main: Suhrkamp, 1985) 99.

30   Fox, "Frame Narrative."

Bibliography

Sources: Text Editions and Translations

(See also under: "Introduction: Text and Versions")

𝔊 = A. Rahlfs, ed., *Septuaginta* (vol. 2; Stuttgart: Württembergische Bibelanstalt, 1935).

𝔐 = *Codex Leningradensis* (see *BHK, BHS*).

𝔖 = D. J. Lane, ed., "Qoheleth," in *The Old Testament in Syriac*, vol. 2/5 (Leiden: Brill, 1979).

𝔗 = Alexander Sperber, ed., *The Bible in Aramaic*, vol. 4A (2d ed.; Leiden: Brill, 1992).

𝔙 = R. Weber, ed., *Biblia Sacra iuxta Vulgatam Versionem*, vol. 2 (3d ed.; Stuttgart: Deutsche Bibelgesellschaft, 1983).

Austin, M. M.
  The Hellenistic World from Alexander to the Roman Conquest: A Selection of Ancient Sources in Translation (Cambridge and New York: Cambridge Univ. Press, 1981).

Berger, Klaus
  Die Weisheitsschrift aus der Kairoer Geniza: Erstedition, Kommentar und Übersetzung (TANZ 1; Tübingen: Francke, 1989).

Beyerlin, Walter, ed.
  Religionsgeschichtliches Textbuch zum Alten Testament (GAT 1; Göttingen: Vandenhoeck & Ruprecht, 1975).

Brunner, Hellmut
  Altägyptische Weisheit: Lehren für das Leben (BAW.AO; Zurich: Artemis, 1988).

Diogenes Laertius
  Leben und Meinungen berühmter Philosophen (trans. O. Apelt; ed. K. Reich; 2d ed.; Philosophische Bibliothek 53/54; Hamburg: Meiner, 1967).

Effe, Bernd, ed.
  Hellenismus (Die griechische Literatur in Text und Darstellung 4; Stuttgart: Reclam, 1985).

Elliger, K., and W. Rudolph, eds.
  Biblia Hebraica Stuttgartensia (5th ed.; Stuttgart: Deutsche Bibelgesellschaft, 1997).

Gressmann, Hugo, ed.
  Altorientalische Texte zum Alten Testament (2d ed. 1926; repr. Berlin: de Gruyter, 1970).

Kaiser, Otto, et al., eds.
  Texte aus der Umwelt des Alten Testaments (3 vols.; Gütersloh: Gütersloher Verlagshaus, 1982–97).

Jerusalemer Bibel
  Die Bibel: Deutsche Ausgabe mit den Erläuterungen der Jerusalemer Bibel (ed. Diego Arenhoevel, Alfons Deissler, and Anton Vögtle; Freiburg: Herder, 1968).

Kittel, Rudolf, ed.
  Biblia Hebraica (16th ed.; Stuttgart: Württembergische Bibelanstalt, 1971).

Luther, Martin
  Die Bibel nach der Übersetzung Martin Luthers (Stuttgart: Deutsche Bibelgesellschaft, 1985).

Maier, Johann
  Die Qumran-Essener: Die Texte vom Toten Meer (3 vols.; Munich: Reinhardt, 1995–1996).

Pritchard, James B., ed.
  Ancient Near Eastern Texts Relating to the Old Testament (3d ed.; Princeton: Princeton Univ. Press, 1969).

Lexica and Grammars

Bartelmus, Rüdiger
  Einführung in das biblische Hebräisch (Zurich: Theologischer Verlag, 1994).

Dalman, Gustav H.
  Aramäisch-Neuhebräisches Handwörterbuch zu Targum, Talmud und Midrasch (3d ed.; Göttingen: Pfeiffer, 1938).

Gesenius, Wilhelm
  Hebräisches und Aramäisches Handwörterbuch über das Alte Testament . . . bearbeitet von Dr. Frants Buhl (17th ed. [1915]; repr. Berlin: Springer, 1962).

Gesenius, Wilhelm
  Hebräisches und Aramäisches Handwörterbuch über das Alte Testament . . . bearbeitet und herausgegeben von D. Rudolf Meyer und Dr. Dr. Herbert Donner (18th ed.; Berlin: Springer, 1987ff.).

Gesenius, Wilhelm
  Hebräische Grammatik, völlig umgearbeitet von E. Kautzsch (28th ed. 1909; repr. Hildesheim: Olms, 1985).

Jastrow, Marcus
  A Dictionary of the Targumim, the Talmud Babli and Yerushalmi, and the Midrashic Literature (2 vols.; New York: Pardes, 1950).

Jenni, Ernst
  Die hebräischen Präpositionen, vol. 1: *Die Präposition Beth* (Stuttgart: Kohlhammer, 1992).

Jenni, Ernst
  Die hebräischen Präpositionen, vol. 2: *Die Präposition Kaph* (Stuttgart: Kohlhammer, 1994).

Joüon, Paul, and Takamitsu Muraoka
  A Grammar of Biblical Hebrew (2 vols.; Subsidia Biblica 14/1-2; Rome: Pontifical Biblical Institute Press, 1993).

Koehler, Ludwig, and Walter Baumgartner
  Lexicon in Veteris Testamenti Libros (2d ed.; Leiden: Brill, 1958).

Koehler, Ludwig, Walter Baumgartner, J. J. Stamm, and Benedikt Hartmann
  The Hebrew and Aramaic Lexicon of the Old Testament (trans. and ed. M. E. J. Richardson et al.; 5 vols.; Leiden: Brill, 1994–1999).

Commentaries on the Book of Qoheleth (cited by author's name)

Aalders, Gerhard Charles
 Het Boek De Prediker vertaald en verklaard (Commentaar op het Oude Testament; Kampen: Kok, 1948).

Abrego-de Lacy, José Maria
 Lamentaciones, Cantar de los Cantares, Eclesiastés, Sabiduría (El mensaje del Antiguo Testamento 21; Salamanca: Sigueme, 1992).

Alfrink, Bernard
 Het Boek Prediker (Brugge: Beyaert, 1932).

Allgeier, Arthur
 Das Buch des Predigers oder Koheleth (HSAT 6.2; Bonn: Hanstein, 1925).

Alonso Schökel, Luis
 Eclesiastes y Sabiduria (LiSa V.17; Madrid: Ediciones Cristianidad, 1974).

Barton, George A.
 A Critical and Exegetical Commentary on the Book of Ecclesiastes (ICC 17; Edinburgh: T. & T. Clark, 1908).

Barucq, André
 Ecclésiaste–Qohéleth: traduction et commentaire (Verbum salutis 3; Paris: Beauchesne, 1968).

Barylko, Jaime
 El Eclesiastés (Kohélet) (Biblioteca popular judía. Colección: Hechos de la historia judía 34; Buenos Aires: Ejecutivo Sudamericano del Congreso Judio Mundial, 1970).

Baum, Alice
 Worte der Skepsis–Lieder der Liebe: Prediger, Hoheslied (SKK 21; Stuttgart: Katholisches Bibelwerk, 1971).

Bea, Augustin
 Liber Ecclesiastae qui ab Hebraeis appellatur Qohelet nova e textu primigenio interpretatio latina cum notis criticis et exegeticis (SPIB 100; Rome: Pontifical Biblical Institute Press, 1950).

Beek, Martinus Adrianus
 Prediker, Hooglied (POT; Nijkerk: Callenbach, 1984).

Bergant, Dianne
 Job and Ecclesiastes (OTMes 18; 1982; repr. Collegeville, Minn.: Liturgical Press, 1990).

Bettan, Israel
 The Five Scrolls: A Commentary (Cincinnati: Hebrew Union College Press, 1950).

Bickell, Gustav
 Der Prediger über den Wert des Daseins: Wiederherstellung des bisher zerstückelten Textes, Übersetzung und Erklärung (Innsbruck: Wagner'sche Universitätsbuchhandlung, 1884).

Boileau, M.-J.
 Le Livre de l'Ecclésiaste, ou le Discours inspiré du roi Salomon sur le Souverain bien, paraphrasé (Paris: 1892).

Bondt, A. de
 Paraphrase van het boek der Prediker (Franeker: Wever, 1940).

Bonora, Antonio
 Il libro di Qoèlet (Guide Spirituali all'Antico Testamento; Rome: Città Nuova, 1992).

Bonora, Antonio
 Qohelet: La gioia e la Fatica di vivere (LoB.AT 15; Brescia: Queriniana, 1987).

Bridges, Charles
 An Exposition of the Book of Ecclesiastes (1860; repr. Geneva Commentaries; Edinburgh: Banner of Truth, 1992).

Bright, Laurence, ed.
 Scripture Discussion Commentary, vol. 6: *Psalms and Wisdom* (London: Sheed & Ward, 1972).

Broch, Yitzhak L.
 Koheleth: The Book of Ecclesiastes in Hebrew and English with a Midrashic Commentary (New York: Feldheim, 1982).

Brown, William P.
 Ecclesiastes (Interpretation; Louisville: Westminster John Knox, 2000).

Buck, F.
 "Ecclesiastes," in R. C. Fuller, ed., *A New Catholic Commentary on Holy Scripture* (New York: Nelson, 1969) 512–20.

Budde, Karl
 "Der Prediger," in E. Kautzsch and A. Bertholet, eds., *Die Heilige Schrift des Alten Testaments* (4th ed.; 2 vols.; Tübingen: Mohr [Siebeck], 1923) 2:421–42.

Burkitt, F. Crawford
 Ecclesiastes Rendered into English Verse (2d ed.; London: 1922).

Buzy, Denis
 "L'Ecclésiaste traduit et commenté," in Louis Pirot and Albert Clamer, eds., *La Sainte Bible*, vol. 6 (Paris: Letouzey et Ané, 1946) 189–280.

Campos, Haroldo de
 Qohélet = O-que-sabe = Eclesiastes: Poema sapiencial (Coleção Signos 13; São Paulo: Perspectiva, 1990).

Cantalausa, Joan de
 Lo libre de Jòb (presentacion e causidas), Qohelèt (revirada integrala) (Rodès: Culturà d'òc, 1983).

Castelli, David
 Il libro del Cohelet, volgarmente detto Ecclesiaste (Pisa: 1866).

Ceronetti, Guido
 L'Ecclésiaste–Qohélet (Paris: Samuel Tastet, 1987), trans. *Qohélet o l'Ecclesiaste* (Torino: Einaudi, 1988).

Cheyne, Thomas Kelly
 Job and Solomon: Or the Wisdom of the Old Testament (London: Kegan Paul, Trench, 1887).

Cohen, A., and V. E. Reichert
 The Five Megilloth (3d ed.; SBBS 12; New York: Soncino, 1990).

Cox, Samuel
 The Book of Ecclesiastes (London: Hodder & Stoughton, 1891).

Crenshaw, James Lee
 Ecclesiastes: A Commentary (OTL; Philadelphia: Westminster, 1987).

Crenshaw, James Lee
"Ecclesiastes," in James L. Mays, ed., *Harper's Bible Commentary* (San Francisco: HarperCollins, 1999) 518–24.

Dale, Thomas Pelham
A Commentary on Ecclesiastes (London: Rivingtons, 1873).

Davidson, Robert
Ecclesiastes and the Song of Solomon (Daily Study Bible; Philadelphia: Westminster, 1986).

Deane, William John
Ecclesiastes (Pulpit Commentary 21; London: Funk & Wagnalls, 1893).

Delitzsch, Franz
Commentary on the Song of Songs and Eccesiastes (Edinburgh: T. & T. Clark, 1877), trans. of *Hoheslied und Koheleth* (Biblische Commentar IV.4; Leipzig: Dörffling und Franke, 1875).

Dietelmair, J. A.
"Der Prediger Salomo, sonst Ecclesiastes genannt," in *Die Heilige Schrift des Alten und Neuen Testaments, nebst einer . . . Erklärung . . . aus den auserlesensten Anmerkungen verschiedener Engländischen Schriftsteller . . .* , vol. 7 (Leipzig: 1856) 435–650.

Duesberg, Hilaire, and Irénée Fransen
Ecclesiastico (La Sacra Bibbia; Torino: Marietti, 1966) 11–353.

Eaton, Michael A.
Ecclesiastes (TOTC 16; Downers Grove, Ill.: Inter-Varsity Press, 1983).

Edman, Irwin
Ecclesiastes (New York: Odyssey, 1946).

Ehrlich, Arnold B.
Randglossen zur hebräischen Bibel, vol. VII (1914; repr. Hildesheim: Olms, 1968) 55–108.

Eichhorn, David Max
Musings of the Old Professor: The Meaning of Koheleth: A New Translation of and Commentary on the Book of Ecclesiastes (New York: David, 1963).

Ewald, Heinrich
Die Dichter des Alten Bundes erklärt: Die Salomonischen Schriften (2d ed.; Göttingen: Vandenhoeck & Ruprecht, 1867).

Farmer, Kathleen Anne
Who Knows What Is Good? A Commentary on the Books of Proverbs and Ecclesiastes (ITC; Grand Rapids: Eerdmans, 1991).

Figueras, Antoni M.
Ecclesiastès (La Biblia XI; Montserrat: Monestir de Montserrat, 1966).

Finlayson, Thomas Campbell
The Meditations and Maxims of Koheleth: A Practical Exposition of the Book of Ecclesiastes (London: Unwin, 1887).

Fischer, James A.
Song of Songs, Ruth, Lamentations, Ecclesiastes, Esther (Collegeville Bible Commentary 24; Collegeville, Minn.: Liturgical Press, 1986).

Fonzo, Lorenzo di
Ecclesiaste (La Sacra Bibbia, AT; Turin: Marietti, 1967).

Fox, Michael V.
Qohelet and his Contradictions (JSOTSup 71; Bible and Literature Series 18; Sheffield: Sheffield Academic Press, 1989).

Fuerst, Wesley J.
The Five Scrolls (CBC 8; Cambridge: Cambridge Univ. Press, 1975).

Galantî, M.
ספר קהלת: *Book of the Congregation of Jacob: Commentary on Qohelet* (Israel Hebrew Press Pioneers 2; Jerusalem: 1977) (Heb.).

Galling, Kurt
"Der Prediger," in Ernst Würthwein, Kurt Galling and Otto Plöger, *Die Fünf Megilloth* (2d ed.; HAT 1.18; Tübingen: Mohr [Siebeck], 1969) 73–125.

Garrett, Duane A.
Proverbs, Ecclesiastes, Song of Songs (New American Commentary 14; Nashville: Broadman, 1993).

Gemser, Berend
Spreuken II, Prediker en Hooglied van Salomo (Tekst en Uitleg 1; Groningen: Wolters, 1931).

Gentilini, B.
El Eclesiastés (Santiago de Chile: 1926).

Genung, J. F.
Ecclesiastes, Words of Koheleth, Son of David, King in Jerusalem (Boston: Houghton, 1904).

Gerson, Adolf
Der Chacham Kohelet als Philosoph und Politiker: Ein Kommentar zum biblischen Buche Kohelet, zugleich eine Studie zur religiösen und politischen Entwicklung des Volkes Israel im Zeitalter Herodes des Grossen (Frankfurt am Main: Kauffmann, 1905).

Gietman, Gerard
Commentarius in Ecclesiasten et Canticum Canticorum (Paris: 1890).

Ginsberg, Harold Louis
Koheleth Interpreted (New Commentary on the Torah, the Prophets, and the Holy Writings; Tel Aviv: Newman, 1961) (Heb.).

Ginsburg, Christian David
The Song of Songs and Coheleth: Translated from the Original Hebrew, with a Commentary, Historical and Critical (1861; repr. New York: Ktav, 1970).

Glasser, Étienne
Le Procès du Bonheur par Qohelet (LD 61; Paris: Cerf, 1970).

Glenn, Donald R.
"Ecclesiastes," in John F. Walvoord and Roy B. Zuck, eds., *The Bible Knowledge Commentary, Old Testament* (Wheaton, Ill.: Victor, 1985).

Goldberg, Louis
Ecclesiastes (Bible Study Commentary; Grand Rapids: Zondervan, 1983).

Gordis, Robert
Koheleth: The Man and His World: A Study of Ecclesiastes (1951; 3d ed.; TSJTSA 19; New York: Schocken, 1968) (cited as "Gordis").

Gordis, Robert
  The Wisdom of Koheleth: A New Translation with a Commentary and an Introductory Essay (East and West Library; London: Horovitz, 1950) (cited as "Gordis, *Wisdom of Koheleth*").
Graetz, Heinrich
  Kohélet קהלת *oder der salomonische Prediger* (Leipzig: Winter, 1871).
Hahn, H. A.
  Commentar über das Predigerbuch Salomos (Leipzig: 1860).
Haupt, Paul
  Koheleth oder Weltschmerz in der Bibel: Ein Lieblingsbuch Friedrichs des Grossen, verdeutscht und erklärt (Leipzig: Hinrichs, 1905).
Haupt, Paul
  The Book of Ecclesiastes: A New Metrical Translation with an Introduction and Explanatory Notes (Baltimore: Johns Hopkins Univ. Press, 1905).
Hendry, George Stuart
  "Ecclesiastes," in D. Guthrie and J. Motyer, eds., *New Bible Commentary Revised* (Grand Rapids: Eerdmans, 1970) 570–78.
Hengstenberg, Ernst Wilhelm
  Commentary on the Book of Ecclesiastes (Clark's Foreign Theological Library III.6; 1860; repr. Minneapolis: James & Klock, 1977), trans. of *Der Prediger Salomo ausgelegt* (Berlin: Oehmigke, 1859).
Hertzberg, Hans Wilhelm
  Der Prediger (2d ed.; KAT XVII.4; Gütersloh: Gütersloher Verlagshaus, 1963).
Herzfeld, L.
  קהלת *übersetzt und erläutert* (Braunschweig: Leibrock, 1838).
Hitzig, Ferdinand
  "Der Prediger Salomo's," in E. Bertheau and F. Hitzig, *Die Sprüche Salomo's–Der Prediger Salomo's* (KEH 7; Leipzig: Hirzel, 1847) 113–222 (2d ed. 1883 [ed. W. Nowack] 181–314) (1st ed. cited as "Hitzig"; 2d ed. as "Nowack").
Hubbard, David Allen
  Ecclesiastes, Song of Songs (Word Communicators Commentary 15B; Dallas: Word, 1991).
Huwiler, Elizabeth, and Roland E. Murphy
  Proverbs, Ecclesiastes, Song of Songs (NIBCOT 12; Peabody, Mass.: Hendrickson, 1999).
Jastrow, Morris
  A Gentle Cynic (1919; repr. New York: Oriole, 1972).
Jones, Edgar
  Proverbs and Ecclesiastes (TBC; New York: Macmillan, 1961).
Jong, P. de
  De Prediker vertaald en verklaart (Leuven: 1861).
Kaiser, Walter C.
  Ecclesiastes: Total Life (Chicago: Moody Press, 1979).
Kidner, Derek
  A Time to Mourn and a Time to Dance: Ecclesiastes and the Way of the World (Downers Grove, Ill.: Inter-Varsity Press, 1976).
Kleinert, Paul
  Der Prediger Salomo: Uebersetzung, sprachliche Bemerkungen und Erörterungen zum Verständniss (Berlin: 1864).
Knobel, August
  Commentar über das Buch Koheleth (Leipzig: 1836).
Kroeber, Rudi
  Der Prediger hebräisch und deutsch (SPAW 13; Berlin: Akademie-Verlag, 1963).
Kroeze, Jan Hendrik
  Die Woorde van die Prediker (Kampen: Kole, 1961).
Kuhn, Gottfried
  Erklärung des Buches Koheleth (BZAW 43; Giessen: Töpelmann, 1926).
Lamparter, Helmut
  Das Buch der Weisheit: Prediger und Sprüche (2d ed.; BAT 16; Stuttgart: Calwer, 1959).
Lange, Gerson
  Sefer Kohelet: Das Buch Koheleth, übersetzt und erklärt (Frankfurt am Main: 1910).
Lattes, Dante
  Il Qohéleth o l'Ecclesiaste (Rome: Unione delle comunità israelitiche italiane, 1964).
Lauha, Aarre
  Kohelet (BKAT 19; Neukirchen-Vluyn: Neukirchener Verlag, 1978).
Leiman, Harold I.
  Koheleth: Life and Its Meaning: A Modern Translation and Interpretation of the Book of Ecclesiastes (New York: Feldheim, 1978).
Leimdörfer, David
  "Der Prediger Salomonis" in historischer Beleuchtung: Neue Forschung über Ecclesiastes nebst Text, Übersetzung und Erklärung (2d ed; Hamburg: Fritzsche, 1892).
Lepre, Cesare
  Qoheleth: Traduzione ritmica dall'originale ebraico e note (Bologna: Libreria antiquaria Palma-Verde, 1975).
Leupold, Herbert Carl
  Exposition of Ecclesiastes (1952; repr. Grand Rapids: Baker, 1968).
Levy, Ludwig
  Das Buch Qoheleth: Ein Beitrag zur Geschichte des Sadduzäismus (Leipzig: Hinrichs, 1912).
Loader, James A.
  Ecclesiastes (Text and Interpretation; Grand Rapids: Eerdmans, 1986).
Lohfink, Norbert
  Kohelet (4th ed.; NEchtB 1; Würzburg: Echter, 1993), trans. *Qoheleth* (CC; Minneapolis: Fortress Press, 2003).
Longman, Tremper
  The Book of Ecclesiastes (NICOT; Grand Rapids: Eerdmans, 1998).

Loretz, Oswald
  Gotteswort und menschliche Erfahrung: Eine Aus-legung der Bücher Jona, Rut, Hoheslied und Qohelet (Freiburg: Herder, 1963).
Maggioni, Bruno
  Giobbe e Qohelet: La contestazione sapienziale nella Bibbia (Bibbia per tutti; Assisi: Cittadella, 1989).
Maillot, Alphonse
  La contestation: Commentaire de l'Ecclésiaste (2d ed.; Paris: Bergers et Mages, 1987).
Manresa, Ruperto M. de
  Libros sapienciales II. Eclesiastés: Versión segun el texto hebreo (Barcelona: 1935).
McNeile, Alan Hugh
  An Introduction to Ecclesiastes (Cambridge: Cambridge Univ. Press, 1904).
Meschonnic, Henri
  Les Cinq Rouleaux: Le Chant des chants, Ruth, Comme ou les Lamentations, Paroles du Sage, Esther: Traduit de l'Hébreu (Paris: Gallimard, 1970).
Michel, Diethelm
  Qohelet (EdF 258; Darmstadt: Wissenschaftliche Buchgesellschaft, 1988).
Mildenberger, Friedrich
  Der Prediger Salomo (Erlangen: Mildenberger, 1988).
Moulton, Richard G.
  Ecclesiastes and the Wisdom of Solomon (New York: Macmillan, 1896, repr. 1899 and 1903).
Murphy, Roland E.
  Ecclesiastes (WBC 23A; Dallas: Word, 1992).
Negenman, Johan
  Prediker (Belichting BB) (Brugge-Boxtel: Tabor-Kath. BS, 1988).
Nicolangelo, M.
  Il libro dell'Ecclesiaste (Naples: 1938).
Nötscher, Friedrich
  "Das Buch Kohelet: Ecclesiastes oder Prediger," in Friedrich Nötscher, ed., *Echter Bibel: Das Alte Testament*, vol. 4 (Würzburg: Echter, 1959) 535–67.
Nowack: see Hitzig, Ferdinand.
Odeberg, Hugo
  Kohælæth: A Commentary on the Book of Ecclesiastes (Uppsala: Almquist & Wiksells, 1929).
Ogden, Graham S.
  Qoheleth (Readings; Sheffield: JSOT Press, 1987).
Oort, Henricus Lucas
  Job, Spreuken en Prediker (Leiden: Brill, 1903).
Pautrel, Raymond
  L'Ecclésiaste (3d ed.; SB [J]; Paris: Cerf, 1958).
Perry, Theodore Anthony
  Dialogues with Kohelet: The Book of Ecclesiastes: Translation and Commentary (University Park: Pennsylvania State Univ. Press, 1993).
Ploeg, J. van der
  Prediker uit de grondtekst vertaald en uitgelegd (BOT VIII,2; Roermond: Romen, 1953).
Plumptre, E. H.
  Ecclesiastes or the Preacher, with Notes and Introduction (Cambridge: Cambridge Univ. Press, 1881).

Podechard, Emmanuel
  L'Ecclésiaste (EtB; Paris: Gabalda, 1912).
Power, A. D.
  Ecclesiastes or The Preacher: A New Translation with Introduction, Notes, Glossary, Index (London: Longmans, Green, 1952).
Rankin, Oliver S., and Gaius Glenn Atkins
  "The Book of Ecclesiastes," in *The Interpreter's Bible*, vol. 5 (Nashville: Abingdon, 1956) 3–88.
Ravasi, Gianfranco
  Qohelet (2d ed.; La Parola di Dio; Milano: Edizioni Paoline, 1991).
Renan, Ernest
  L'Ecclésiaste: Traduit de l'Hébreu avec une étude sur l'âge et le caractère du livre (Paris: Calmann Lévy, 1882 [3d ed. 1890, repr. 1922]), repr. *Un temps pour tout: L'Ecclésiaste, traduit de l'hébreu et commenté par Ernest Renan* (Retour aux grands textes 4; Paris: Arléa, 1990).
Reuss, Eduard Wilhelm Eugen
  Philosophie religieuse et morale des Hébreux: Job, les Proverbs, l'Ecclésiaste, la Sapience, Contes moraux, Baruch, Manassé (La Bible: Ancien Testament 6; Paris: Sandoz et Fischbacher, 1878).
Rosenberg, A. J.
  The Five Megilloth: A New English Translation, vol. 2: *Lamentations, Ecclesiastes* (New York: Judaica, 1992).
Rougemont, Frédéric de
  Explication du livre de l'Ecclésiaste (Neuchâtel: Michaud, 1844).
Ryder, E. T.
  "Ecclesiastes," in Matthew Black, ed., *Peake's Commentary on the Bible* (1962; repr. Sunbray-on-Thames: Nelson, 1977) 458–67.
Rylaarsdam, J. Coert
  The Proverbs, Ecclesiastes, the Song of Solomon (Layman's Bible Commentary 10; 1964, repr. Atlanta: John Knox, 1982).
Sacchi, Paolo
  Ecclesiaste (NVB 30; Rome: Paoline, 1971).
Scholz, Anton von
  Kommentar über den Prediger (Leipzig: 1901).
Scott, Robert Balgarnie Young
  Proverbs, Ecclesiastes (AB 18; Garden City, N.Y.: Doubleday, 1965).
Seow, Choon-Leong
  Ecclesiastes (AB 18C; New York: Doubleday, 1997).
Siegfried, Carl
  Prediger und Hoheslied (HKAT II 3,2; Göttingen: Vandenhoeck & Ruprecht, 1898).
Spangenberg, Izak J. J.
  Die boek Prediker (Kaapstad: NG Kerk, 1993).
Steinmann, Jean
  Ainsi parlait Qohélet (LiBi 38; Paris: Cerf, 1973).
Strobel, Albert
  Das Buch Prediger (WB.KK 9; Düsseldorf: Patmos, 1967).

Thilo, Martin

Der Prediger Salomo neu übersetzt und auf seinen Gedankengang untersucht (Bonn: Marcus und Weber, 1923).

Torrey, Charles C., and Ernesto Trenchard

Ecclesiastes: Una exposición breve (Cursos de estudio bíblico; Madrid: 1980).

Towner, W. Sibley

"The Book of Ecclesiastes," in *The New Interpreter's Bible,* vol. 5 (Nashville: Abingdon, 1997) 265–360.

Tyler, Thomas

Ecclesiastes: An Introduction to the Book, an Exegetical Analysis, and a Translation with Notes (2d ed.; London: 1899).

Vílchez Líndez, José

Sapienciales III: Eclesiastés o Qohélet (Nueva Biblia Española; Estella, Navarra: Editorial Verbo Divino, 1994).

Vischer, Wilhelm

Der Prediger Salomo: Übersetzt mit einem Nachwort und Anmerkungen (Munich: Kaiser, 1926).

Volck, Wilhelm

"Prediger Salomo," in Wilhelm Volck and Samuel Oettli, *Die poetischen Hagiographen (Buch Hiob, Prediger Salomo, Hohelied und Klagelieder)* (Kurzgefasster Kommentar 7; Nördlingen: Beck, 1889).

Volz, Paul

Hiob und Weisheit (Das Buch Hiob, Sprüche und Jesus Sirach, Prediger) (2d ed.; SAT 3.2; Göttingen: Vandenhoeck & Ruprecht, 1921).

Weber, Jean-Julien

Le livre de Job–L'Ecclésiaste: Texte et commentaire (Paris: Tournai, 1947).

Whybray, Roger Norman

Ecclesiastes (NCB; Grand Rapids: Eerdmans, 1989).

Wildeboer, Gerrit

"Der Prediger," in *Die fünf Megillot* (KHC XVII; Tübingen: Mohr, 1898) 109–68.

Wright, Addison G.

"Ecclesiastes (Qoheleth)," in R. E. Brown et al., eds., *The New Jerome Biblical Commentary* (Englewood Cliffs, N.J.: Prentice-Hall, 1990) 489–95.

Wright, C. H. H.

The Book of Koheleth (London: Hodder & Stoughton, 1883).

Wright, J. Stafford

"Ecclesiastes," in A. William van Gemeren et al., *Psalms–Song of Songs* (Expositor's Bible Commentary 5; Grand Rapids: Zondervan, 1991) 1137–97.

Zapletal, Vincenz

Das Buch Kohelet: Kritisch und metrisch untersucht, übersetzt und erklärt (Freiburg: Gschwend, 1905, 2d ed. 1911).

Zimmerli, Walther

"Das Buch des Predigers Salomo," in Helmer Ringgren and Walther Zimmerli, *Sprüche/Prediger* (3d ed.; ATD 16/1; Göttingen: Vandenhoeck & Ruprecht, 1980) 123–253.

Zlotowitz, Meir, and Nosson Scherman

מגילת קהלת — *Ecclesiastes: A New Translation with a Commentary Anthologized from Talmudic, Midrashic, and Rabbinic Sources* (2d ed.; Art Scroll Tanach Series; Brooklyn, New York: Mesorah, 1983).

Zorn, C. M.

Gottestrost: Der Prediger Salomo kurz ausgelegt (Zwickau: 1922).

Monographs and Anthologies on the Book of Qoheleth (cited by author's name and short title)

Anderson, Don

Ecclesiastes: The Mid-Life Crisis (Neptune, N.J.: Loizeaux, 1987).

Anderson, William H. U.

Qoheleth and Its Pessimistic Theology: Hermeneutical Struggles in Wisdom Literature (Mellen Biblical Press Series 54; Lewiston, N.Y.: Mellen, 1997).

Backhaus, Franz Josef

"Denn Zeit und Zufall trifft sie alle": Studien zur Komposition und zum Gottesbild im Buch Qohelet (BBB 83; Frankfurt am Main: Anton Hain, 1993).

Backhaus, Franz Josef

"Es gibt nichts Besseres für den Menschen" (Koh 3,22): Studien zur Komposition und zur Weisheitskritik im Buch Kohelet (BBB 121; Bodenheim: Philo, 1998).

Barsotti, Divo

Meditazione sul libro di Qoèlet (Bibbia e liturgia 23; Brescia: Queriniana, 1979).

Barthauer, Wilhelm

Optimismus und Pessimismus im Buche Koheleth (Halle: 1900).

Bartholomew, Craig G.

Reading Ecclesiastes: Old Testament Exegesis and Hermeneutical Theory (AnBib 139; Rome: Pontifical Biblical Institute Press, 1998).

Bellia, Giuseppe, and Angelo Passaro, eds.

Il Libro del Qohelet: Tradizione, Redazione, Teologia (Cammini Nello Spirito. Biblica 44; Milano: Paoline, 2001).

Bidder, Roderich

Über Koheleths Stellung zum Unsterblichkeitsglauben: Ein Beitrag zu gerechter Beurtheilung des Buches Koheleth (Erlangen: 1875).

Blieffert, Hans-Jürgen

Weltanschauung und Gottesglaube im Buch Kohelet: Darstellung und Kritik ([1938] Rostock: Beckmann, 1958).

Born, E. Th. van den

De wijsheid van den Prediker (Kampen: 1939).

Bottoms, Lawrence

Ecclesiastes Speaks to Us Today (Atlanta: John Knox, 1979).

Bradley, George Granville

Lectures on Ecclesiastes (Oxford: Clarendon, 1898).

Brandscheidt, Renate

Weltbegeisterung und Offenbarungsglaube: Literar-, form- und traditionsgeschichtliche Untersuchung zum Buch Kohelet (Trierer theologische Studien 64; Trier: Paulinus, 1999).

Braun, Rainer
Kohelet und die frühhellenistische Popularphilosophie (BZAW 130; Berlin: de Gruyter, 1973).

Bruno, Arvid
Sprüche, Prediger, Klagelieder, Esther, Daniel: Eine rhytmische und textkritische Untersuchung (Stockholm: Almquist & Wiksell, 1958).

Bühlmann, Walter, and Vreni Merz
Kohelet–Der Prediger: Impulse und Hilfen zum Bibel- und Religionsunterricht (Luzern: Rex, 1988).

Burkes, Shannon
Death in Qoheleth and Egyptian Biographies of the Late Period (SBLDS 170; Atlanta: Scholars Press, 1999).

Bush, Barbara
Walking in Wisdom: A Woman's Workshop on Ecclesiastes (Grand Rapids: Zondervan, 1982).

Cannizzo, Antonio
L'enigma della sfinge: La sapienza del Qohelet e l'interrogare di Giobbe (Rdt books 9; Rome: AVE, 1995).

Carlebach, J.
Das Buch Koheleth: Ein Deutungsversuch (Frankfurt: Hermon, 1936).

Christianson, Eric S.
A Time to Tell: Narrative Strategies in Ecclesiastes (JSOTSup 280; Sheffield: Sheffield Academic Press, 1998).

D'Alario, Vittoria
Il libro del Qohelet: Struttura letteraria e retorica (SRivB 27; Bologna: Dehoniane, 1992).

Devine, Minos
Ecclesiastes or the Confessions of an Adventurous Soul (London: MacMillan, 1916).

Dillon, Emile Joseph
The Sceptics of the Old Testament: Job, Koheleth, Agur (London: Isbister, 1895).

Dörsing, Frauke
Lehre mich doch, dass es ein Ende mit mir haben muss: Die Sicht des Menschen im Buch des Predigers Salomo (Frankfurt: Fischer, 1997).

Drijvers, Pius, and Pé Hawinkels
De mens heet mens: Het boek Prediker: Nieuwe vertaling en verklarende essays (Utrecht: Ambo, 1969).

Durandeaux, Jacques
Une foi sans névrose? Ou l'actualité de Qohéleth (Paris: Cerf, 1987).

Ellermeier, Friedrich
Qohelet, I/1: Untersuchungen zum Buche Qohelet (Herzberg: Jungfer, 1967).

Ellul, Jacques
Reason for Being: A Meditation on Ecclesiastes (Grand Rapids: Eerdmans, 1990), trans. of *La raison d'être: Méditation sur l'Ecclésiaste* (Paris: Seuil, 1987).

Elyo'enay, M.
Studies in Qohelet and Proverbs (Jerusalem: ha-Hevrah le-heker ha-Mikra be-Yisra'el, 1977) (Heb.).

Fischer, Alexander Achilles
Skepsis oder Furcht Gottes? Studien zur Komposition und Theologie des Buches Kohelet (BZAW 247; Berlin: de Gruyter, 1997).

Fischer, Stefan
Die Aufforderung zur Lebensfreude im Buch Kohelet und seine Rezeption der ägyptischen Harfnerlieder (Wiener alttestamentliche Studien 2; Frankfurt am Main: Lang, 1999).

Fox, Michael V.
A Time to Build and a Time to Tear Down: A Rereading of Ecclesiastes (Grand Rapids: Eerdmans, 1999).

Fredericks, Daniel C.
Coping with Transience: Ecclesiastes on Brevity in Life (BiSe 18; Sheffield: Sheffield Academic Press, 1993).

Fredericks, Daniel C.
Qoheleth's Language: Re-Evaluating Its Nature and Date (ANETS 3; Lewiston, N.Y.: Mellen, 1988).

Gangel, Kenneth O.
Thus Speaks Qoheleth: A Study Guide Based on an Exposition of Ecclesiastes (Christian Life and Ministry Series; Camp Hill, Pa.: Christian Publications, 1983).

Ginsberg, Harold Louis
Studies in Koheleth (TSJTSA 17; New York: Jewish Theological Seminary of America, 1950).

Gordis, Robert
The Wisdom of Ecclesiastes (New York: Behrman, 1945).

Gorssen, Leo
Breuk tussen God en Mens: Onderzoek naar de sammenhang en de originaliteit van de hoofdthema's uit het boek Prediker (Brugge: Desclée de Brouwer, 1970).

Hubbard, David Allen
Beyond Futility: Messages of Hope from the Book of Ecclesiastes (Grand Rapids: Eerdmans, 1976).

Hungs, F.-J.
Ist das Leben sinnlos? Bibelarbeit mit dem Buch Kohelet (Prediger) (Zurich: Benziger, 1980).

Isaksson, Bo
Studies in the Language of Qohelet with Special Emphasis on the Verbal System (AUU, SSU 10; Uppsala: Almqvist & Wiksell, 1987).

Johnston, David
A Treatise on the Authorship of Ecclesiastes (London: Macmillan, 1880).

Kamano, Naoto
Cosmology and Character: Qoheleth's Pedagogy from a Rhetorical Critical Perspective (BZAW 312; Berlin: de Gruyter, 2002).

Keddie, Gordon J.
Looking for the Good Life: The Search for Fulfillment in the Light of Ecclesiastes (Phillipsburg, N.J.: Presbyterian & Reformed, 1991).

Klein, Christian
Kohelet und die Weisheit Israels: Eine formgeschichtliche Studie (BWANT 132; Stuttgart: Kohlhammer, 1994).

Köhler, August
Über die Grundanschauungen des Buches Koheleth (Erlangen: 1885).

Kreeft, Peter

Three Philosophies of Life: Ecclesiastes: Life as Vanity; Job: Life as Suffering; Song of Songs: Life as Love (San Francisco: Ignatius, 1989).

Krüger, Thomas

"Theologische Gegenwartsdeutung im Koheleth-Buch" (Habil. Theol., Universität Munich, 1990).

Kushner, Harold S.

Le désir infini de trouver un sens à la vie: La quête de l'Ecclésiaste (Montréal: Roseau, 1987).

Lamorte, A.

Le livre de Qoheleth: Étude critique et philosophique de l'Ecclésiaste (Paris: Montauban, 1932).

Lang, Bernhard

Ist der Mensch hilflos? Zum Buch Kohelet (Theologische Meditationen 53; Zurich: Benziger, 1979).

Lange, Armin

Weisheit und Torheit bei Kohelet und in seiner Umwelt: Eine Untersuchung ihrer theologischen Implikationen (Europäische Hochschulschriften, Theologie Reihe 433; Frankfurt: Lang, 1991).

Laue, L.

Das Buch Koheleth und die Interpolationshypothese Siegfrieds (Wittenberg: 1900).

Lavoie, Jean-Jacques

La pensée du Qohélet: Étude exégétique et intertextuelle (Collection de théologie heritage et projet 49; Québec: Fides, 1992).

Lavoie, Jean-Jacques

Qohélet: Une critique moderne de la Bible (Parole d'actualité, 2; Montréal and Paris: Médiaspaul, 1995).

Loader, James A.

Polar Structures in the Book of Qohelet (BZAW 152; Berlin: de Gruyter, 1979).

Lods, Adolphe

L'Ecclésiaste et la philosophie grecque (Paris: Jouve, 1890).

Lohfink, Norbert

Studien zu Kohelet (SBAB 26; Stuttgart: Katholisches Bibelwerk, 1998).

Löhr, Max

Seelenkämpfe und Glaubensnöte vor 2000 Jahren (RV II.14; Tübingen: Gebauer-Schwetschke, 1906).

Loretz, Oswald

Qohelet und der Alte Orient: Untersuchungen zu Stil und theologischer Thematik des Buches Qohelet (Freiburg: Herder, 1964).

Lüthi, Walter

Der Prediger Salomo lebt das Leben: Eine Auslegung für die Gemeinde (Basel: Reinhardt, 1952).

Lys, Daniel

Des contresens du bonheur ou l' implacable lucidité de Qohéleth (Poliez-le-Grand: Moulin, 1998).

Lys, Daniel

L'Ecclésiaste ou Que vaut la vie? Traduction, Introduction générale, Commentaire de 1,1 à 4,3 (Paris: Letouzey et Ané, 1977).

Mandry, Stephen A.

There Is No God! A Study of the Fool in the Old Testament, Particularly in Proverbs and Qohelet (Rome: Officium Libri Catholici, 1972).

Michaud, Robert

Qohélet et l'hellénisme: La littérature de sagesse: Histoire et théologie II (LiBi 77; Paris: Cerf, 1987).

Michel

Qohelet.

Michel, Diethelm

Untersuchungen zur Eigenart des Buches Qohelet: Mit einem Anhang von Reinhard G. Lehmann: Bibliographie zu Qohelet (BZAW 183; New York: de Gruyter, 1989).

Motais, A.

Salomon et l'Ecclésiaste (Paris: Berche et Tralin, 1876).

Neher, André,

Notes sur Qohélét (L'Ecclésiaste) (2d ed.; Paris: Minuit, 1994).

Pahk, Johan Yeong Sik

Il canto della gioia in Dio: L'itinerario sapienziale espresso dall'unità letteraria in Qohelet 8,16–9,10 e il parallelo di Gilgameš Me. iii (SMDSA 52; Naples: Istituto Universitario Orientale, 1996).

Ranston, Harry

Ecclesiastes and the Early Greek Wisdom Literature (London: Epworth, 1925).

Ravasi, Gianfranco

Il Libro del Qohelet: Ciclo di conferenze (Conversazione bibliche; Bologna: Dehoniane, 1988).

Reimer, P. B.

A Time to Keep Silence–and a Time to Build: A Study of Ecclesiastes (Toronto: Institute for Christian Studies, 1987).

Rodrigues, Jecy

Vivenças do povo de Deus: O Eclesiastes (Petrópolis: 1976).

Roe, George

Koheleth: A Metrical Paraphrase of the Canonical Book of Ecclesiastes (New York: Dodge, 1912).

Roller, E.

Lichtstrahlen über den Prediger Salomo (Krakau: 1895).

Rose, Martin, ed.

Situer Qohélet: Regards croisés sur une livre biblique (Publications de la Faculté de Théologie de l'Université de Neuchâtel 21; Neuchâtel: Secrétariat de l'Université, 1999), repr. of *RThPh* 131 (1999) 97–215.

Rose, Martin

Rien de nouveau: Nouvelles approches du livre de Qohélet: Avec une bibliographie (1988–1998) élaborée par Béatrice Perregaux Allison (OBO 168; Fribourg: Editions Universitaires; Göttingen: Vandenhoeck & Ruprecht, 1999).

Rudman, Dominic

Determinism in the Book of Ecclesiastes (JSOTSup 316; Sheffield: JSOT Press, 2001).

Rudolph, Wilhelm

Vom Buch Kohelet (Münster: Aschendorff, 1959).

Salyer, Gary D.

Vain Rhetoric: Private Insight and Public Debate in Ecclesiastes (JSOTSup 327; Sheffield: JSOT Press, 2001).

Sargent, L. G.
　Ecclesiastes and Other Studies (Birmingham: 1965).
Schiffer, Sinai
　*Das Buch Kohelet: Nach der Auffassung der Weisen des
　Talmud und Midrasch und der jüdischen Erklärer des
　Mittelalters: Theil 1: Von der Mischna bis zum
　Abschluss des babyl. Talmud* (Frankfurt: Kauffmann,
　1884).
Schoors, Antoon
　*The Preacher Sought to Find Pleasing Words: A Study
　of the Language of Qoheleth* (OLA 41; Leuven:
　Departement Orientalistiek/Peeters, 1992).
Schoors, Antoon, ed.
　Qohelet in the Context of Wisdom (BEThL 136; Leu-
　ven: Univ. Press and Peeters, 1998).
Schubert, Mathias
　Schöpfungstheologie bei Kohelet (BEAT 15; Frankfurt
　am Main: Lang, 1989).
Schwienhorst-Schönberger, Ludger
　*"Nicht im Menschen gründet das Glück" (Koh 2,24):
　Kohelet im Spannungsfeld jüdischer Weisheit und hel-
　lenistischer Philosophie* (HBS 2; Freiburg: Herder,
　1994).
Schwienhorst-Schönberger, Ludger, ed.
　*Das Buch Kohelet: Studien zur Struktur, Geschichte,
　Rezeption und Theologie* (BZAW 254; Berlin: de
　Gruyter, 1997).
Scott, David Russell
　*Pessimism and Love in Ecclesiastes and the Song of
　Songs* (London: James Clarke, 1915).
Shaw, Jean
　The Better Half of Life: Meditations from Ecclesiastes
　(Grand Rapids: Zondervan, 1983).
Short, Robert L.
　*A Time to Be Born–A Time to Die: The Images and
　Insights of Ecclesiastes for Today* (New York: Harper
　& Row, 1973).
Spaller, Christina
　*"Die Geschichte des Buches ist die Geschichte seiner Aus-
　löschung . . .": Die Lektüre von Koh 1,3-11 in vier aus-
　gewählten Kommentaren* (Exegese in unserer Zeit 7;
　Münster: Lit, 2001).
Storniolo, Ivo, and Euclides M. Balancin
　Como ler o livro do Ecclesiastes: Trabalho e felicidade
　(Sao Paulo: Paulinas, 1990).
Támez, Elsa
　*Da hasste ich das Leben: Eine Lektüre des Buches
　Kohelet* (Luzern: Exodus, 2001).
Támez, Elsa
　When the Horizons Close: Rereading Ecclesiastes
　(Maryknoll, N.Y.: Orbis, 2000).
Vallet, Odon
　*Menus propos de Qohélet ou l'art de mourir un peu
　moins selon l'Ecclésiaste* (Limoges: Droguet et
　Ardant, 1976).
Vílchez Líndez, José
　Qohélet, maestro de Sabidura (Granada: Facultad de
　Teologia, 1990).
Vonach, Andreas
　*Nähere dich um zu hören: Gottesvorstellungen und
　Glaubensvermittlung im Koheletbuch* (BBB 125;
　Berlin: Philo, 1999).
Whitley, Charles F.
　Koheleth: His Language and Thought (BZAW 148;
　Berlin: de Gruyter, 1979).
Whybray, Roger Norman
　Ecclesiastes (OTG; Sheffield: JSOT Press, 1989).
Whybray, Roger Norman
　Two Jewish Theologies: Job and Ecclesiastes (Hull:
　1980).
Willmes, Bernd
　*Menschliches Schicksal und ironische Weisheitskritik im
　Koheletbuch: Kohelets Ironie und die Grenzen der
　Exegese* (BThSt 39; Neukirchen-Vluyn: Neukirche-
　ner Verlag, 2000).
Zimmer, Tilmann
　*Zwischen Tod und Lebensglück: Eine Untersuchung zur
　Anthropologie Kohelets* (BZAW 286; Berlin: de
　Gruyter, 1999).
Zimmerli, Walther
　Die Weisheit des Predigers Salomo (Aus der Welt der
　Religion–Biblische Reihe 11; Berlin: Töpelmann,
　1936).
Zimmermann, Frank
　*The Inner World of Qohelet (with Translation and
　Commentary)* (New York: Ktav, 1973).
Zuck, Roy B., ed.
　*Reflecting with Solomon: Selected Studies on the Book of
　Ecclesiastes* (Grand Rapids: Baker, 1994).
Zuckermann, A.
　The Treasure of Ecclesiastes Reopened (New York:
　1933).

**Additional Monographs and
Anthologies** (cited by author's or
editor's name and short title)

Aalders, Gerhard J. D.
　Political Thought in Hellenistic Times (Amsterdam:
　Hakkert, 1975).
Barton, John
　Reading the Old Testament: Method in Biblical Study
　(2d ed.; Louisville: Westminster John Knox, 1996).
Bickerman, Elias
　*Four Strange Books of the Bible: Jonah, Daniel,
　Koheleth, Esther* (New York: Schocken, 1967).
Blenkinsopp, Joseph
　*Wisdom and Law in the Old Testament: The Ordering
　of Life in Israel and Early Judaism* (2d ed.; New York:
　Oxford Univ. Press, 1995).
Brenner, Athalya, ed.
　A Feminist Companion to Wisdom Literature (FCB 9;
　Sheffield: Sheffield Academic Press, 1995).
Brown, William P.
　*Character in Crisis: A Fresh Approach to the Wisdom
　Literature of the Old Testament* (Grand Rapids: Eerd-
　mans, 1996).

Butting, Klara
  "Das Buch Kohelet," in *Die Buchstaben werden sich noch wundern: Innerbiblische Kritik als Wegweisung feministischer Hermeneutik* (Berlin: Alektor, 1994) 87–116.

Ceresko, Anthony R.
  Psalmists and Sages: Studies in Old Testament Poetry and Religion (ITSSup 2; Bangalore: St. Peter's Institute, 1994).

Clines, David J. A., ed.
  The Poetical Books: A Sheffield Reader (BiSe 41; Sheffield: Sheffield Academic Press, 1997).

Crenshaw, James Lee
  Urgent Advice and Probing Questions: Collected Writings on Old Testament Wisdom (Macon, Ga.: Mercer Univ. Press, 1995).

Crenshaw, James Lee, ed.
  Studies in Ancient Israelite Wisdom (New York: Ktav, 1976).

Diesel, Anja A., Reinhard G. Lehmann, Eckart Otto, and Andreas Wagner, eds.
  "Jedes Ding hat seine Zeit . . .": Studien zur israelitischen und altorientalischen Weisheit: FS Diethelm Michel (BZAW 241; Berlin: de Gruyter, 1996).

Dubarle, André-Marie
  Les Sages d'Israël (Paris: Cerf, 1946).

Duesberg, Hilaire, and Irénée Fransen
  Les scribes inspirés: Introduction aux livres sapientiaux de la Bible (Maredsous: Maredsous, 1966).

Enns, Peter
  Poetry & Wisdom (Institute for Biblical Research Bibliographies 3; Grand Rapids: Baker, 1997).

Fisch, Harold
  "Qohelet: A Hebrew Ironist," in *Poetry with a Purpose: Biblical Poetics and Interpretation* (Indiana Studies in Biblical Literature; repr. Bloomington: Indiana Univ. Press, 1990) 158–78.

Friedländer, M.
  Griechische Philosophie im Alten Testament: Eine Einleitung in die Psalmen- und Weisheitsliteratur (Berlin: Reimer, 1904).

Galling, Kurt
  Die Krise der Aufklärung in Israel (Mainzer Universitäts-Reden 19; Mainz: 1940).

Gammie, John G., Walter A. Brueggemann, W. Lee Humphreys, and James M. Ward, eds.
  Israelite Wisdom: FS Samuel Terrien (New York: Union Theological Seminary; Missoula: Scholars Press, 1978).

Gammie, John G., and Leo G. Perdue, eds.
  The Sage in Israel and the Ancient Near East (Winona Lake, Ind.: Eisenbrauns, 1990).

Gehrke, Hans-Joachim
  Geschichte des Hellenismus (Oldenbourg Grundriss der Geschichte 1A; Munich: Oldenbourg, 1990).

Gilbert, Maurice, ed.
  La Sagesse de l'Ancien Testament (BEThL 51; 2d ed.; Leuven: Leuven Univ. Press and Peeters, 1990).

Glasser, Étienne
  Le Procès du Bonheur par Qohelet (LD 61; Paris: Cerf, 1970).

Good, Edwin Marshall
  Irony in the Old Testament (1965; repr. Sheffield: Almond, 1981) 168–95.

Gordis, Robert
  The Word and the Book: Studies in Biblical Language and Literature (New York: Ktav, 1976).

Grant, Michael
  Von Alexander bis Kleopatra: Die hellenistische Welt (Bergisch Gladbach: Lübbe, 1984).

Hengel, Martin
  Judaism and Hellenism (2 vols. in 1; Philadelphia: Fortress Press, 1974).

Hölbl, Günther
  Geschichte des Ptolemäerreiches (Darmstadt: Wissenschaftliche Buchgesellschaft, 1994).

Hossenfelder, Malte
  Die Philosophie der Antike 3: Stoa, Epikureismus und Skepsis (Munich: Beck, 1985).

Humbert, Paul
  Recherches sur les sources égyptiennes de la littérature sapientiale d'Israël (MUN 7; Neuchâtel: Secrétariat de l'Université, 1929).

Kaiser, Otto
  Der Mensch unter dem Schicksal: Studien zur Geschichte, Theologie und Gegenwartsbedeutung der Weisheit (BZAW 161; Berlin: de Gruyter, 1985).

Kautzsch, Karl
  Die Philosophie des Alten Testaments (RV V1.6; Tübingen: Mohr, 1914).

Kidner, Derek
  Wisdom to Live By: An Introduction to the Old Testament's Wisdom Books of Proverbs, Job, and Ecclesiastes (Leicester: Inter-Varsity, 1985).

Kippenberg, Hans G.
  Religion und Klassenbildung in antiken Judäa (2d ed.; SUNT 14; Göttingen: Vandenhoeck & Ruprecht, 1982).

Koester, Helmut
  Introduction to the New Testament (2d ed.; 2 vols.; Berlin: de Gruyter, 1995).

Krüger, Thomas
  Kritische Weisheit: Studien zur weisheitlichen Traditionskritik im Alten Testament (Zurich: Pano, 1997).

Küchler, Max
  Frühjüdische Weisheitstraditionen (OBO 26; Freiburg, Switzerland: Universitätsverlag; Göttingen: Vandenhoeck & Ruprecht, 1979).

Lichtheim, Miriam
  Late Egyptian Wisdom Literature in the International Context (OBO 52; Freiburg, Switzerland: Universitätsverlag; Göttingen: Vandenhoeck & Ruprecht, 1983).

MacDonald, Duncan Black
  The Hebrew Philosophical Genius: A Vindication (1936; repr. New York: Russel & Russel, 1965).

McKay, Heather A., and David J. A. Clines, eds.
  Of Prophets' Visions and the Wisdom of Sages: Essays in Honour of R. Norman Whybray (JSOTSup 162; Sheffield: JSOT Press, 1993).

Müller, Hans-Peter
Mensch–Umwelt–Eigenwelt: Gesammelte Aufsätze zur Weisheit Israels (Stuttgart: Kohlhammer, 1992).

Murphy, Roland E.
The Tree of Life: An Exploration of Biblical Wisdom Literature (2d ed.; Grand Rapids: Eerdmans, 1996).

Murphy, Roland E.
Wisdom Literature: Job, Proverbs, Ruth, Canticles, Ecclesiastes and Esther (2d ed.; FOTL 13; Grand Rapids: Eerdmans, 1988).

Perdue, Leo G., Bernard B. Scott, and William J. Wiseman, eds.
In Search of Wisdom: Essays in Memory of John G. Gammie (Louisville: Westminster John Knox, 1993).

Preuss, Horst Dietrich
Einführung in die alttestamentliche Weisheitsliteratur (Stuttgart: Kohlhammer, 1987).

Rad, Gerhard von
Wisdom in Israel (Nashville: Abingdon, 1972).

Ricken, Friedo
Philosophie der Antike (Grundkurs Philosophie 6; Stuttgart: Kohlhammer, 1988).

Römer, Thomas
La sagesse dans l'Ancien Testament (Cahiers bibliques 3; Aubonne: Moulin, 1991).

Rostovtzeff, Michael I.
A Social and Economic History of the Hellenistic World (Oxford: Clarendon, 1941).

Sanchez-Prieto Borja, Pedro, and Bautista Horcajada Diezma
Alfonso El Sabio, General estoria Parte 3: Libros de Salomón: Cantar de los Cantares, Proverbios, Sabiduría y Ecclesiastés (Bibliotheca Románica Hispánica 4; Textos 23; Madrid: Gredos, 1994).

Schmid, Hans Heinrich
Wesen und Geschichte der Weisheit (BZAW 101; Berlin: Töpelmann, 1966).

Schulz, A.
Traurigkeit und Gottgeborgenheit im Alten Testament: Die Bücher Kohaelet und Habakuk und eine Auswahl aus den Psalmen (Warendorf: 1947).

Sellin, Ernst
Die Spuren griechischer Philosophie im A.T. (Leipzig: Deichert, 1905).

Sheppard, G. T.
Wisdom as a Hermeneutical Construct (BZAW 180; Berlin: de Gruyter, 1980).

Walbank, Frank W.
Die hellenistische Welt (3d ed.; Munich: Deutscher Taschenbuch, 1989), trans. of *The Hellenistic World* (3d ed.; Cambridge: Harvard Univ. Press, 1993).

Weeks, Stuart
Early Israelite Wisdom (Oxford: Clarendon, 1993).

Westermann, Claus
Forschungsgeschichte zur Weisheitsliteratur: 1950–1990 (AzTh 71; Stuttgart: Calwer, 1991).

Whybray, Roger Norman
The Intellectual Tradition in the Old Testament (BZAW 135; Berlin: de Gruyter, 1974).

Literature on Individual Sections of the Commentary

Introduction
Research Reports

Beentjes, Pancratius C.
"Recente visies op Qohelet," *Bijdr* 41 (1980) 436–44.

Bellia, Giuseppe, and Angelo Passaro
"Proverbi e Qohelet: Eredità e prospettive di ricerca," *Ho Theológos* 19 (2001) 115–32.

Bons, Eberhard
"Ausgewählte Literatur zum Buch Kohelet," *BK* 45 (1990) 36–42.

Bretón, Santiago
"Qohelet: Recent Studies," *TD* 28 (1980) 147–51.

Bretón, Santiago
"Qoheleth Studies," *BTB* 3 (1973) 22–50.

Chopineau, Jacques
"L'Image de Qohelet dans l'Exégèse Contemporaine," *RHPhR* 59 (1979) 595–603.

Chopineau, Jacques
"Le Livre de Qohelet et son Image dans l'Exégèse Contemporaine," *Analecta Bruxellensia* 6 (2001) 105–13.

Crenshaw, James Lee
"Qoheleth in Current Research," in R. Aharoni, ed., *Biblical and Other Studies: FS Robert Gordis* (HAR 7; Columbus: Ohio State Univ. Press, 1983) 41–56, repr. in Crenshaw, *Urgent Advice*, 520–34.

Galling, Kurt
"Stand und Aufgabe der Kohelet-Forschung," *ThR* 6 (1934) 355–73.

Kaiser, Otto
"Beiträge zur Kohelet-Forschung: Eine Nachlese," *ThR* 60 (1995) 1–31, 233–53.

Kaiser, Otto
"Judentum und Hellenismus: Ein Beitrag zur Frage nach dem hellenistischen Einfluss auf Kohelet und Jesus Sirach," *VF* 27 (1982) 68–88, repr. in Kaiser, *Der Mensch unter dem Schicksal*, 135–53.

Kottsieper, Ingo
"Alttestamentliche Weisheit: Proverbia und Kohelet," *ThR* 67 (2002) 1–34, 201–37.

Lavoie, Jean-Jacques
"Les livres de Job, Qohélet et Proverbes: Les enjeux méthodologiques dans l'histoire de la recherche depuis 1980," in Michel Gourgues and Léo Laberge, eds., *De bien des manières: La recherche biblique aux abords di XXIe siècle* (LD 163; Montréal: Fides; Paris: Cerf, 1995) 147–80.

Michel
Qohelet.

Murphy, Roland E.
"Recent Research on Proverbs and Qoheleth," *Currents in Research: Biblical Studies* 1 (1993) 119–39.

Pakala, J. C.
"A Librarian's Comments on Commentaries: 12 (Ecclesiastes)," *Presbyterion* 27 (2001) 147–49.

Palm, August

Die Qohelet-Literatur: Ein Beitrag zur Geschichte der Exegese des Alten Testaments (Mannheim: 1886).

Schwienhorst-Schönberger, Ludger

"Kohelet: Stand und Perspektiven der Forschung," in Schwienhorst-Schönberger, ed., Das Buch Kohelet, 5–38.

Schwienhorst-Schönberger, Ludger

"Neues unter der Sonne: Zehn Jahre Kohelet-Forschung (1987–1997)," TRev 94 (1998) 363–76.

Spangenberg, Izak J. J.

"A Century of Wrestling with Qohelet: The Research History of the Book Illustrated with a Discussion of Qoh 4,17–5,6," in Schoors, ed., Qohelet in Context, 61–91.

Themes and Overall Understanding

Allevi, L.

"Il messagio spirituale dell'Ecclesiaste," ScC 60 (1932) 143–54.

Anath, Moshe E.

"The Contemplative Method of Qohelet: Fearing God," in B. Z. Luria, ed., FS Baruch Ben-Yehuda (Jerusalem: 1981) 377–85 (Heb.).

Anderson, William H. U.

"A Critique of the Standard Interpretations of the Joy Statements in Qoheleth," JNSL 27 (2001) 57–75.

Anderson, William H. U.

"The Curse of Work in Qoheleth: An Exposé of Genesis 3,17-19 in Ecclesiastes," EvQ 70 (1998) 99–113.

Anderson, William H. U.

"Historical Criticism and the Value of Qohelet's Pessimistic Theology for Postmodern Christianity Through a Canonical Approach," OTE 13 (2000) 143–55.

Aquino, Ranhilio Callangan

"The Believing Pessimist: A Philosophical Reading of Qoheleth," PhilipSac 16 (1981) 207–61.

Armstrong, James F.

"Ecclesiastes in Old Testament Theology," PSB 94 (1983) 16–25.

Auwers, Jean-Marie

"La condition humaine entre sens et non-sens: Le bilan de Qohèlèth," in Aristide Théodoridès, Paul Naster, and Alois van Tongerloo, eds., Humana condici–La condition humaine (Acta Orientalia Belgica 6; Bruxelles: Société Belge d'Études Orientales, 1991) 193–211.

Azize, Joseph

"Considering the Book of Qohelet Afresh," Ancient Near Eastern Studies 37 (2000) 183–214.

Backhaus, Franz Josef

"Qohelet und der sogenannte Tun-Ergehen-Zusammenhang," BN 89 (1997) 30–61.

Backhaus

"Qohelet und der Tod," in Zeit und Zufall, 390–411.

Backhaus

"Zum Gottesbild in Qohelet," in Zeit und Zufall, 352–89.

Bakon, Shimon

"Koheleth," JBQ 26 (1998) 168–76.

Bartelmus, Rüdiger

"Haben oder Sein: Anmerkungen zur Anthropologie des Buches Kohelet," BN 53 (1990) 38–67.

Barrett, Michael P. V.

"Theology for Life," BV 31 (1997) 11–18.

Barucq, André

"Question sur le sens du travail: Qo 1,2; 2,21-23," AsSeign 49 (1971) 66–71.

Beaucamp, Évode

"L'Ecclésiaste et son message: A propos d'un commentaire récent," LTP 27 (1971) 191–94.

Beauchamp, Paul

"Entendre Qohéleth," Christus 16 (1969) 339–51.

Beek, Martinus Adrianus

"Prediker en de balans van het leven," in Schrift en Uitleg: FS W. H. Gispen (Kampen: Kok, 1970) 21–30.

Bell, Robert D.

"Structure and Themes of Ecclesiastes," BV 31 (1997) 3–9.

Bellia, Giuseppe, and Angelo Passaro

"Qohelet, ovvero la fatica di conoscere," in Bellia and Passaro, eds., Qohelet, 357–90.

Bergant, Dianne

"What's the Point of It All?" TBT 22 (1984) 75–78.

Berger, Benjamin Lyle

"Qohelet and the Exigencies of the Absurd," BibInt 9 (2001) 141–79.

Bianchi, Francesco

"'Un fantasma al banchetto della sapienza?' Qohelet e il libro dei Proverbi a confronto," in Bellia and Passaro, eds., Qohelet, 40–68.

Bishop, Eric F. F.

"A Pessimist in Palestine," PEQ 100 (1968) 33–41.

Blumenthal, Elhanan

"Introduction to a New Kohelet Commentary," Dor le-Dor 9 (1980) 46–52.

Blumenthal, Elhanan

"The Process in Qohelet (An Overview of the Book)," BethM 33 (1987/88) 397–401 (Heb.).

Bohlen, Reinhold

"Kritische Individualität und wache Skepsis: Auf dem Weg zu einer religiösen Grunderfahrung im Buch Kohelet," TThZ 106 (1997) 22–38.

Bojorge, H.

"Verkenning in de Gedachtenwereld van het boek Prediker," Bijdr 28 (1967) 118–45.

Bonora, Antonio

"Il piacere di vivere in Qohelet," Servitium 40 (1985) 93–99.

Bonora, Antonio

"Esperienza e timor di Dio in Qohelet," Teol(Br) 6 (1981) 171–82.

Bottéro, Jean

"L'Ecclésiaste et le Problème du Mal," NC 7-9 (1955–57) 133–59, repr. in Naissance de Dieu: La Bible et l'historien (2d ed.; Paris: Gallimard, 1992) 292–329.

Botterweck, Gerhard J.

"An die Resignierten—Kritische Reflexionen Kohelets," in Ludwig Bertsch and Karl-Heinz Rentmeister, eds., *Zielgruppen: FS Karl Delahaye* (Frankfurt am Main: Knecht, 1977) 61–75.

Bourget, D.

"Daniel Lys au miroir de l'Ecclésiaste," *EThR* 53 (1978) 402–9.

Bream, Howard N.

"Life without Resurrection: Two Perspectives from Qoheleth," in Howard N. Bream, Ralph D. Heim, and Carey A. Moore, eds., *A Light unto My Path: FS Jacob M. Myers* (Gettysburg Theological Studies 4; Philadelphia: Temple Univ. Press, 1974) 49–65.

Bretón, Santiago

"Ecclesiastés: Anotaciones exegéticas," *Revista teológica limense* 11 (1977) 375–92.

Brink, E.

"Het werk Gods in Prediker," in R. ter Beek et al., eds., *Een sprekend begin: FS H. M. Ohmann* (Kampen: van den Berg, 1993) 107–15.

Brown, William P.

"'Whatever your hand finds to do': Qoheleth's Work Ethic," *Int* 55 (2001) 271–84.

Brzegowy, Tadeusz

"La critique de la sapience traditionelle dans le Livre de Qohéleth," *ACra* 25 (1993) 21–42.

Buchholz, W.

"Kleiner Kommentar zum Buche des Predigers," *Judaica* 5 (1949) 41–49.

Buhl, Frants

"Ueber den Prediger Salomo's," *Saat auf Hoffnung* 27 (1890) 249–54; 28 (1891) 100–138.

Buss, Martin J.

"A Projection for Israelite Historiography: With a Comparison between Qohelet and Nagarjuna," in J. Andrew Dearman, ed., *The Land that I Will Show You: Essays on the History and Archaeology of the Ancient Near East in Honor of J. Maxwell Miller* (JSOTSup 343; Sheffield: Sheffield Academic Press, 2001) 61–68.

Buzy, Denis

"La notion du bonheur dans l'Ecclésiaste," *RB* 43 (1934) 494–511.

Caneday, Ardel B.

"Qohelet: Enigmatic Pessimist or Godly Sage?" *GTJ* 7 (1986) 21–56, repr. in Zuck, ed., *Reflecting with Solomon*, 81–113.

Carny, Pinhas

"Theodicy in the Book of Qohelet," in Henning Graf Reventlow, ed., *Justice and Righteousness: Biblical Themes and Their Influence* (JSOTSup 137; Sheffield: Sheffield Academic Press, 1992) 71–81.

Carrière, Jean-Marie

"'Tout est vanité': L'un des concepts de Qohélet," *EstBib* 55 (1997) 297–311, 463–77.

Castellino, George R.

"Qohelet and his Wisdom," *CBQ* 30 (1968) 15–28, repr. in Zuck, ed., *Reflecting with Solomon*, 31–43.

Celada, B.

"Pensamiento radical en un libro sagrado: El Qohélet o Eclesiastés," *CuBi* 23 (1966) 177–84.

Ceresko, Anthony R.

"Commerce and Calculation: The Strategy of the Book of Qoheleth (Ecclesiastes)," *ITS* 30 (1993) 205–19, repr. in Anthony R. Ceresko, *Psalmists and Sages: Studies in Old Testament Poetry and Religion* (ITSSup 2; Bangalore: St. Peter's Institute, 1994).

Chamakkala, Jacob

"Qoheleth's Reflections on Time," *Jeevadhara* 7 (1977) 117–31.

Chia, Philip P.

"Wisdom, Yahwism, Creation: In Quest of Qoheleth's Theological Thought," *Jan Dao* 3 (1995) 1–32.

Christianson, Eric S.

"Qohelet and the/His Self among the Deconstructed," in Schoors, ed., *Qohelet in Context*, 425–33.

Christianson, Eric S.

"Qoheleth the 'Old Boy' and Qoheleth the 'New Man': Misogynism, the Womb and a Paradox in Ecclesiastes," in Athalya Brenner and Carole R. Fontaine, eds., *Wisdom and Psalms* (FCB 2/2; Sheffield: Sheffield Academic Press, 1998) 109–36.

Cimosa, Mario

"La contestazione sapienziale di Giobbe e Qoèlet," *PaVi* 30 (1985) 280–85.

Clark, D. C.

"Between Prophet and Philosopher," *New Blackfriars* 58 (1977) 267–73.

Clemens, David Murray

"The Law of Sin and Death: Ecclesiastes and Genesis 1–3," *Themelios* 19 (1994) 5–8.

Cochrane, Arthur C.

"Joy to the World: The Message of Ecclesiastes," *ChrCent* 85 (1968) 27–35.

Condamin, Albert

"Études sur l'Ecclésiaste," *RB* 8 (1899) 493–509; 9 (1900) 30–44, 354–77.

Conradie, E. M.

"Is alles regtig tervergeefs en 'n gejaag na wind?" *NGTT* 37 (1996) 578–88.

Cosser, William

"The Meaning of 'Life' in Proverbs, Job, and Ecclesiastes," *TGUOS* 15 (1953/54) 48–53.

Crenshaw, James Lee

"Qoheleth's Understanding of Intellectual Inquiry," in Schoors, ed., *Qohelet in Context*, 205–24.

Crenshaw, James Lee

"The Shadow of Death in Qoheleth," in Gammie and Brueggemann, eds., *Israelite Wisdom*, 205–16, repr. in Crenshaw, *Urgent Advice*, 573–85.

Crenshaw, James Lee

"Youth and Old Age in Qoheleth," *HAR* 10 (1986) 1–13, repr. in Crenshaw, *Urgent Advice*, 535–47.

Crüsemann, Frank

"The Unchangeable World: The 'Crisis of Wisdom' in Koheleth," in W. Schottroff and W. Stegemann, eds., *God of the Lowly: Socio-Historical Interpretations of the Bible* (Maryknoll, N.Y.: Orbis, 1984) 57–77.

Cruveilher, P.
"La doctrine essentielle de l'Écclesiaste (Qohélet): La vie et le bonheur," *Revue Apologétique* 40 (1929) 404–26, 542–67.

D'Alario, Vittoria
"L'Assurdità del Male nella Teodicea del Qohelet," in Rinaldo Fabris, ed., *Initium Sapientiae: Scritti in Onore di Franco Festorazzi nel suo 70. Compleanno: FS Franco Festorazzi* (SRivB 36; Bologna: EDB, 2000) 179–97.

D'Alario, Vittoria
"Liberté de Dieu ou destin? Un autre dilemme dans l'interprétation du Qohélet," in Schoors, ed., *Qohelet in Context*, 457–63.

Dacquino, P.
"Significatio e dottrina del libro dell'Ecclesiaste," *PaVi* 11 (1966) 161–64.

Danker, Frederick
"The Pessimism of Ecclesiastes," *CTM* 22 (1951) 9–32.

Dattler, Federico
"Introducción a Qohelet," *RevistB* 30 (1968) 146–48.

Derenbourg, J.
"Notes détachées sur l'Ecclésiaste," *REJ* 1 (1880) 1–21.

Dewey, Rosemary
"Qoheleth and Job: Diverse Responses to the Enigma of Evil," *SpTo* 37 (1985) 314–25.

Donald, Trevor
"The Semantic Field of 'Folly' in Proverbs, Job, Psalms, and Ecclesiastes," *VT* 13 (1963) 285–92.

Dornseiff, F.
"Das Buch Prediger," *ZDMG* 89 (1935) 243–49.

Doré, Daniel
Qohélet, Le Siracide: Ou l'Ecclésiaste et l'Ecclésiastique (CEv 91; Paris: Cerf, 1995).

Dreese, J. J.
"The Theology of Qoheleth," *TBT* 56 (1971) 513–18.

Dubarle, André-Marie
"Qohéleth ou les déceptions de l'expérience," in André-Marie Dubarle, *Les Sages d'Israël* (Paris: Cerf, 1946) 95–128.

Duesberg, Hilaire
"Ecclésiaste," *Dictionnaire de spiritualité* 4 (1960) 40–52.

Ellul, Jacques
"Le statut de la philosophie dans Qohelet," *AF* 53 (1985) 151–64.

Farmer, Kathleen A.
"The Wisdom Books (Job, Proverbs, Ecclesiastes)," in Steven L. McKenzie and M. Patrick Graham, eds., *The Hebrew Bible Today: An Introduction to Critical Issues* (Louisville: Westminster John Knox, 1998) 129–51.

Felton, Jacob
"Koheleth: A Re-interpretation," *Dor le Dor* 5 (1976/77) 29–34, 143–47.

Fernández, Victor M.
"El valor de la vida presente en Qohelet," *RevistB* 52 (1990) 99–113.

Ferreira, Valério Paulo
"O papel do conselheiro na literatura sapiencial: Um sábio pessimista? O livro do Eclesiastes," *EstBib* 37 (1993) 18–24.

Festorazzi, Franco
"Il Qohelet: Un sapiente di Israele alla ricerca di Dio: Ragione-fede in rapporto dialettico," in *Quaerere Deum: Atti della XXV Settimana Biblica* (Brescia: Paideia and Associazione Biblica Italiana, 1980) 173–90.

Festorazzi, Franco
"In margine a un libro su Qoelet," *RivB* 36 (1988) 67–72.

Festorazzi, Franco
"La dimensione salvifica del binomio morte-vita (Qohelet e Sapienza)," *RivB* 30 (1982) 91–109.

Flowers, H. J.
"Ecclesiastes: A Translation and Commentary," *RevExp* 27 (1930) 421–37.

Flowers, H. J.
"The Book of Ecclesiastes: Second Section: III,1–V,20," *RevExp* 28 (1931) 52–74.

Fontaine, Carole R.
"Ecclesiastes," in Carol A. Newsom, ed., *The Women's Bible Commentary* (Louisville: Westminster John Knox, 1992) 145–55.

Foresti, Fabrizio
"*ʿāmāl* in Koheleth: 'Toil' or 'Profit,'" *ECarm* 31 (1980) 415–30.

Forman, Charles C.
"Koheleth's Use of Genesis," *JSS* 5 (1960) 256–63.

Forman, Charles C.
"The Pessimism of Ecclesiastes," *JSS* 3 (1958) 336–43.

Fox, Michael V.
"Qohelet's Epistemology," *HUCA* 58 (1987) 137–55.

Fox, Michael V.
"The Inner Structure of Qohelet's Thought," in Schoors, ed., *Qohelet in Context*, 225–38.

Fox, Michael V.
"Wisdom in Qoheleth," in Perdue et al., eds., *In Search of Wisdom*, 115–31.

Gallazzi, Ana Maria Rizzante, and Sandro Gallazzi
"La preuba de los ojos, la preuba de la casa, la preuba del sepulcro: Una clave de lectura del libro de Qohélet," *RIBLA* 14 (1993) 61–85.

Galling, Kurt
"Kohelet-Studien," *ZAW* 50 (1932) 276–99.

Galling, Kurt
"Weltanschauung und Gottesglaube im 'Prediger,'" in Otto Eissfeldt, ed. *Theologische Gegenwartsfragen* (Halle: Gebauer-Schwetschke, 1940) 36–46.

Garrett, Duane A.
"Qoheleth on the Use and Abuse of Political Power," *TJ* 8 (1987) 159–77.

George, Mark K.
"Death as the Beginning of Life in the Book of Ecclesiastes," in Tod Linafelt, ed., *Strange Fire: Reading the Bible after the Holocaust* (BiSe 71; Sheffield: Sheffield Academic Press, 2000) 280–93.

Gese, Hartmut
"Die Krisis der Weisheit bei Koheleth," in Maurice Gilbert, ed., *Les sagesses du Proche Orient Ancien* (Paris: Presses Universitaires de France, 1963) 139–51, repr. in Hartmut Gese, *Vom Sinai zum Zion* (BEvTh 64; Munich: Kaiser, 1964) 168–79, trans. as "The Crisis of Wisdom in Koheleth," in James Lee Crenshaw, ed., *Theodicy in the Old Testament* (IRT 4; Philadelphia: Fortress Press, 1983) 141–53.

Gese, Harmut
"Zur Komposition des Koheletbuches," in Hubert Cancik, Hermann Lichtenberger, and Peter Schäfer, eds., *Geschichte-Tradition-Reflexion: FS für Martin Hengel zum 70. Geburtstag,* vol. 1: *Judentum* (Tübingen: Mohr [Siebeck], 1996) 69–98.

Gianto, Agustinus
"Human Destiny in Emar and Qohelet," in Schoors, ed., *Qohelet in Context,* 473–79.

Gianto, Agustinus
"The Theme of Enjoyment in Qoheleth," *Bib* 73 (1992) 528–32.

Gilbert, Maurice
"Il Concetto di Tempo (T) in Qohelet e Ben Sira," in Bellia and Passaro, eds., *Qohelet,* 69–89.

Ginsberg, Harold Louis
"Qoheleth," *EstBib* 13 (1954) 434–39.

Ginsberg, Harold Louis
"Supplementary Studies in Koheleth," *PAAJR* 21 (1952) 35–62.

Ginsberg, Harold Louis
"The Quintessence of Koheleth," in Alexander Altmann, ed., *Biblical and Other Studies* (STLI 1; Cambridge: Harvard Univ. Press, 1963) 47–59.

Ginsberg, Harold Louis
"The Structure and Contents of the Book of Koheleth," in Martin Noth and D. Winton Thomas, eds., *Wisdom in Israel and in the Ancient Near East: FS H. H. Rowley* (VTSup 3; Leiden: Brill, 1955) 138–49.

Gire, Pierre
"Qohélet: L'espérance mendiante," *LumVie* 221 (1995) 41–54.

Glender, Shabbatai
"On the Book of Ecclesiastes: A Collection Containing 'Diverse' Sayings or a Unified and Consistent World-View?" *BethM* 26 (1981) 378–87 (Heb.).

Gordis, Robert
"The Wisdom of Koheleth," in *Poets, Prophets, and Sages: Essays in Biblical Interpretation* (Bloomington: Indiana Univ. Press, 1971).

Gorssen, Leo
"La cohérence de la conception de Dieu dans l'Ecclésiaste," *EThL* 46 (1970) 282–324.

Gossmann, Hans-Christoph
"תחת השמש – תחת השמיﬦ: Anmerkungen zum Ort des Menschen bei Qohälät," in Matthias Albani and Timotheus Arndt, eds., *Gottes Ehre erzählen: FS Hans Seidel* (Leipzig: Thomas, 1994) 221–23.

Graetz, Heinrich
"Schreiben an Master Th . . . in Triest über Kohelet," *MGWJ* 34 (1885) 74–92, 127–34.

Gramlich, Miriam Louise
"Qoheleth: Poet-Philosopher of Everyday Living," *TBT* 84 (1976) 805–12.

Grech, Prosper
"Il drama del povero in Qohelet," in Bernardo Antonini et al., eds., *Evangelizare Pauperibus: Atti della XXIV Settimana Biblica* (Associazione Biblica Italiana; Brescia: Paideia, 1978).

Griffiths, William
"Ecclesiastes: An Appreciation," *ExpT* 16 (1904) 44–48.

Gros Louis, Kenneth R. R.
"Ecclesiastes," in Kenneth R. R. Gros Louis, James S. Ackerman, and Thayer S. Warshaw, eds., *Literary Interpretations of Biblical Narratives* (Nashville: Abingdon, 1974) 208–82.

Gurlitt, J. F. K.
"Zur Erklärung des Buches Koheleth," *ThStK* 38 (1865) 321–43.

Gutridge, Coralie A.
"The Sacrifice of Fools and the Wisdom of Silence: Qoheleth, Job and the Presence of God," in Ada Rapoport-Albert and Gillian Greenberg, eds., *Biblical Hebrew, Biblical Texts: Essays in Memory of Michael P. Weitzman* (JSOTSup 333; The Hebrew Bible and Its Versions 2; Sheffield: Sheffield Academic Press, 2001) 83–99.

Guttiérrez, Jorge L.
"A lei, a fadiga e o vazio no livro de Eclesiastes," *EstBib* 51 (1996) 32–43.

Haden, N. Karl
"Qoheleth and the Problem of Alienation," *Christian Scholar's Review* 17 (1988) 52–66.

Hart, Thomas M.
"Advice on Marriage," *TBT* 32 (1994) 349–52.

Haupt, Paul
"Die religiösen Anschauungen des Buches Koheleth," in *Verhandlungen des 2. internationalen Kongresses für Allgemeine Religionsgeschichte 1904* (International Conference for the History of Religions; Basel: Helbing und Lichtenhahn, 1905) 120–23.

Hessler, Bertram
"Der verhüllte Gott: Der heilstheologische Sinn des Buches Ecclesiastes (Kohelet)," *ThGl* 43 (1953) 347–59, trans. "Kohelet: The Veiled God," *Bridge* 1 (1955) 191–206.

Hitzig, Ferdinand
"Zur Exegese und Kritik des Buches Kohelet," *ZWTh* 14 (1871) 566–75.

Höffken, Peter
"Die Stimme Qohelets vernehmen: Startpunkt für eine Reise durch die hebräische Bibel," *LM* 19 (1980) 666–67.

Holm-Nielsen, Svend
"Die Verteidigung für die Gerechtigkeit Gottes," *SJOT* 2 (1987) 69–89.

Hossfeld, Frank-Lothar
"Die theologische Relevanz des Buches Kohelet," in Schwienhorst-Schönberger, ed., *Das Buch Kohelet*, 377–89.

Humbert, Paul
"Qohéleth," *RThPh* 3 (1915) 253–77.

Jaeggli, J. Randolph
"Seven Reasons in Ecclesiastes for Enjoying life," *BV* 31 (1997) 25–33.

Johnston, Robert K.
"'Confessions of a Workaholic': A Reappraisal of Qoheleth," *CBQ* 38 (1976) 14–28, repr. in Zuck, ed., *Reflecting with Solomon*, 133–47.

Johnstone, William
"'The Preacher' as Scientist," *SJT* 20 (1967) 210–21.

Jong, Stephen de
"A Book on Labour: The Structuring Principles and the Main Themes of the Book of Qohelet," *JSOT* 54 (1992) 107–16, repr. in Clines, ed., *Poetical Books*, 222–30.

Jong, Stephen de
"God in the Book of Qohelet: A Reappraisal of Qohelet's Place in Old Testament Theology," *VT* 47 (1997) 154–67.

Junker, H.
"Kohelet, ein alttestamentlicher Wahrheitssucher," *Bonner Zeitschrift für Theologie und Seelsorge* 7 (1930) 297–306.

Kaiser, Otto
"Die Botschaft des Buches Kohelet," *EThL* 71 (1995) 48–70.

Kaiser, Otto
"Die Sinnkrise bei Kohelet," in Gotthold Müller, ed., *Rechtfertigung, Realismus, Universalismus in Biblischer Sicht: FS A. Köberle* (Darmstadt: Wissenschaftliche Buchgesellschaft, 1978) 3–21, repr. in Kaiser, *Der Mensch unter dem Schicksal*, 91–109.

Kaiser, Otto
"Qoheleth," in John Day, Robert P. Gordon, and H. G. M. Williamson, eds., *Wisdom in Ancient Israel: Essays in Honour of J. A.Emerton* (Cambridge: Cambridge Univ. Press, 1995) 83–93.

Kaiser, Otto
"Schicksal, Leid und Gott: Ein Gespräch mit dem Kohelet, Prediger Salomo," in Manfred Oeming and Axel Graupner, eds., *Altes Testament und christliche Verkündigung: FS Antonius H. J. Gunneweg* (Stuttgart: Kohlhammer, 1987) 30–51.

Kato, Kumiko
"Das Buch Kohelet: Der Mensch allein, ohne Frau," in Luise Schottroff and Marie-Theres Wacker, eds., *Kompendium Feministische Bibelauslegung* (Gütersloh: Kaiser and Gütersloher Verlagshaus, 1998) 221–32.

Kelly, James
"Qoheleth and the Mystery of Life," *ScrC* 14 (1984) 343–47.

Klausner, Max Albert
"Koheleth," *Israelitische Wochenschrift* 11:33–35 (1903) 526–28, 541–44, 557–59.

Klopfenstein, Martin A.
"Die Skepsis des Qohelet," *ThZ* 28 (1972) 97–109, repr. in idem, *Leben aus dem Wort: Beiträge zum Alten Testament* (BEAT 40; Bern: Lang, 1996) 13–26.

Klopfenstein, Martin A.
"Kohelet und die Freude am Dasein," *ThZ* 47 (1991) 97–107, repr. in H. Obst, ed., *Ueberlieferung und Geschichte: FS Gerhard Wallis* (Halle: Martin Luther Universität, 1990) 93–103, repr. in Martin A. Klopfenstein, *Leben aus dem Wort: Beiträge zum Alten Testament* (BEAT 40; Bern: Lang, 1996), 27–39.

Knopf, Carl S.
"The Optimism of Koheleth," *JBL* 49 (1930) 195–99.

Komlosh, Yehuda
"Is the Book of Qoheleth a Feminist Work?" in C. Rabin, D. Patterson, B.-Z. Luria, and Y. Avishur, eds., *Studies in the Bible and the Hebrew Language: FS M. Wallenstein* (Jerusalem: 1979) 250–55 (Heb.).

Köstlin, F.
"Kohelet-Studien," *Theologische Studien aus Württemberg* 3 (1882) 110–34.

Kroeber, Rudi
"'Der Prediger': Ein Werk der altjüdischen Weisheitsliteratur," *Altertum* 11 (1965) 195–209.

Krüger, Thomas
"Alles Nichts? Zur Theologie des Buches Qohelet," *ThZ* 57 (2001) 184–95.

Krüger, Thomas
"Dekonstruktion und Rekonstruktion prophetischer Eschatologie im Qohelet-Buch," in Diesel et al., eds., *Jedes Ding*, 107–29, repr. in Krüger, *Kritische Weisheit*, 151–72.

Krüger, Thomas
"Die Rezeption der Tora im Buch Kohelet," in Schwienhorst-Schönberger, ed., *Das Buch Kohelet*, 303–25, repr. in Krüger, *Kritische Weisheit*, 173–93.

Kuenen, Abraham
"Qoheleth," *Theologisch tijdschrift* 17 (1883) 1–32.

Kugel, James L.
"Qohelet and Money," *CBQ* 51 (1989) 32–49.

Kutschera, Franz
"Kohelet: Leben im Angesicht des Todes," in Schwienhorst-Schönberger, ed., *Das Buch Kohelet*, 363–76.

L'Hour, Jean
"Qohéleth: Le dur métier de l'homme," in *Si je savais comment l'atteindre* (Lectures bibliques; Paris: Centurion, 1978) 115–27.

Lacan, M.-F.
"L'Ecclésiaste ou le coeur insatisfait," *CEv* 31 (1958) 59–66.

Lang, Bernhard
"Ein hilfloser Mensch: Zum biblischen Buch Kohelet," *Dienender Glaube* 56 (1980) 96–100.

Lang, Bernhard

"Ist der Mensch hilflos? Das biblische Buch Kohelet, neu und kritisch gelesen," *ThQ* 159 (1979) 109–24, repr. in Bernhard Lang, *Wie wird man Prophet in Israel?* (Düsseldorf: Patmos, 1980) 120–36.

Lapide, Pinchas

"Eine Lektion der Vergänglichkeit: Kohelet bricht alle Konventionen der Verkündigung," *LM* 18 (1979) 590–92.

Lauha, Aarre

"Die Krise des religiösen Glaubens bei Kohelet," in Martin Noth and D. Winton Thomas, eds., *Wisdom in Israel and in the Ancient Near East: FS H. H. Rowley* (VTSup 3; Leiden: Brill, 1955) 183–91.

Lauha, Aarre

"Kohelets Verhältnis zur Geschichte," in Jörg Jeremias and Lothar Perlitt, eds., *Die Botschaft und die Boten: FS Hans Walter Wolff* (Neukirchen-Vluyn: Neukirchener Verlag, 1981) 393–402.

Lavoie, Jean-Jacques

"A quoi sert-il de perdre sa vie à la gagner? Le repos dans le Qohelet," *ScEs* 44 (1992) 331–47.

Lawrie, Douglas G.

"The Dialectical Grammar of Job and Qoheleth: A Burkean Analysis," *Scriptura* 66 (1998) 217–34.

Lawrie, Douglas G.

"Wat beteken dit om Kohelet ernstig op te neem?" *NGTT* 38 (1997) 268–83.

Leenhardt, F. J.

"Notes sur l'Ecclésiaste," *EThR* 4 (1926) 305–22.

Levine, Étan

"Qohelet's Fool: A Composite Portrait," in Yehuda T. Radday, ed., *On Humour and the Comic in the Hebrew Bible* (JSOTSup 92; Bible and Literature Series 2; Sheffield: Almond, 1990) 277–94.

Levine, Étan

"The Humor in Qohelet," *ZAW* 109 (1997) 71–83.

Lohfink, Norbert

"Von Windhauch, Gottesfurcht und Gottes Antwort in der Freude," *BK* 45 (1990) 26–32.

Loretz, Oswald

"Gleiches Los trifft alle! Die Antwort des Buches Qohelet," *BK* 20 (1965) 6–8.

Loretz, Oswald

"Jüdischer Gott und griechische Philosophie (ḥokmat yevanit) im Qohelet-Buch," *MARG* 8 (1994) 151–76.

Luder, Ernst

"Gott und Welt nach dem Prediger Salomo," *Schweizerische theologische Umschau* 28 (1958) 105–14.

Lux, Rüdiger

"'Denn es ist kein Mensch so gerecht auf Erden, dass er Gutes tue . . .': Recht und Gerechtigkeit aus der Sicht des Predigers Salomo," *ZThK* 94 (1997) 263–87.

Lux, Rüdiger

"'Ein jegliches hat seine Zeit . . .': Des Menschen Zeit nach dem Buch des Predigers Salomo," in *Vom*

Menschen: Die letzte Ringvorlesung der Kirchlichen Hochschule Naumburg (Naumburg: Naumburger Verlagsanstalt, 1993) 51–61.

Luzzatto, Aldo

"Il pensiero e la dottrina morale dell'Ecclesiaste," *RasIsr* 20 (1954) 25–31.

Lys, Daniel

"L'Etre et le Temps: Communication de Qohèlèth," in Gilbert, ed., *Sagesse*, 249–58.

Lys, Daniel

"Qohélet ou le destin de la perte de sens," *LumVie* 221 (1995) 9–17.

Machinist, Peter

"Fate, *miqreh*, and Reason: Some Reflections on Qohelet and Biblical Thought," in Ziony Zevit, Seymour Gitin, and Michael Sokoloff, eds., *Solving Riddles and Untying Knots: Biblical, Epigraphic, and Semitic Studies in Honor of Jonas C. Greenfield* (Winona Lake, Ind.: Eisenbrauns, 1995) 159–75.

Maltby, Arthur

"The Book of Ecclesiastes and the After-Life," *EvQ* 35 (1963) 39–44.

Manfredi, Silvana

"Qohelet in Dialogo: Una Sfida Intertestuale," in Bellia and Passaro, eds., *Qohelet*, 293–313.

Margalit, Shlomoh

"Qohelet," *BetM* 34 (1988/89) 176–81 (Heb.).

Mathew, Jakob

"Terrestrial Realities in Qoheleth's Teaching," *Jeevadhara* 8 (1978) 121–36.

McCabe, Robert V.

"The Message of Ecclesiastes," *Detroit Baptist Seminary Journal* 1 (1996) 85–112.

Michel, Diethelm

"Ein skeptischer Philosoph: Prediger Salomo (Qohelet)," in *Universität im Rathaus 7* (Mainz: Johannes Gutenberg-Universität, 1987) 1–31.

Michel, Diethelm

"Gott bei Kohelet: Anmerkungen zu Kohelets Reden von Gott," *BK* 45 (1990) 32–36.

Michel, Diethelm

"Kohelet und die Krise der Weisheit," *BK* 45 (1990) 2–6.

Michel, Diethelm

"Probleme der Koheletauslegung heute," *BK* 45 (1990) 6–11.

Michel, Diethelm

"'Unter der Sonne': Zur Immanenz bei Qohelet," in Schoors, ed., *Qohelet in Context*, 93–111.

Michel, Diethelm

"Vom Gott, der im Himmel ist (Reden von Gott bei Qohelet)," *ThViat* 12 (1973/74) 87–100.

Miller, Athanasius

"Aufbau und Grundproblem des Predigers," *SPIB Miscellanea Biblica* 2 (1934) 104–22.

Miller, Douglas B.

"What the Preacher Forgot: The Rhetoric of Ecclesiastes," *CBQ* 62 (2000) 215–35.

Mitchell, Hinckley G.

"'Work' in Ecclesiastes," *JBL* 32 (1913) 123–38.

Molina, Jean-Pierre
"Vanité des vanités: La leçon de l'Ecclésiaste," *Christus* 157 (1993) 29–38.

Mulder, J. S. M.
"Qoheleth's Division and Also Its Main Point," in W. C. Delsman and J. T. Nelis, eds., *Von Kanaan bis Kerala: FS J. P. M. van der Ploeg 1979* (AOAT 211; Kevelaer: Butzon & Bercker; Neukirchen-Vluyn: Neukirchener Verlag, 1982) 149–59.

Müller, Hans-Peter
"Das Ganze und seine Teile: Anschlusserörterungen zum Wirklichkeitsverständnis Kohelets," *ZThK* 97 (2000) 147–63.

Müller, Hans-Peter
"Der unheimliche Gast: Zum Denken Kohelets," *ZThK* 84 (1987) 440–64, repr. in Müller, *Mensch–Umwelt–Eigenwelt,* 169–93.

Müller, Hans-Peter
"Die Wirklichkeit und das Ich bei Kohelet angesichts des Ausbleibens göttlicher Gerechtigkeit und Barmherzigkeit," in Ruth Scoralick, ed., *Das Drama der Barmherzigkeit Gottes: Studien zur biblischen Gottesrede und ihrer Wirkungsgeschichte in Judentum und Christentum* (Stuttgarter Bibelstudien 183; Stuttgart: Katholisches Bibelwerk, 2000) 125–44.

Müller, Hans-Peter
"Neige der althebräischen 'Weisheit': Zum Denken Qohäläts," *ZAW* 90 (1978) 238–64, repr. in Müller, *Mensch–Umwelt–Eigenwelt,* 143–68.

Müller, Hans-Peter
"Plausibilitätsverlust herkömmlicher Religion bei Kohelet und den Vorsokratikern," in Beate Ego, Armin Lange, and Peter Pilhofer, eds., *Gemeinde ohne Tempel / Community Without Temple: Zur Substituierung und Transformation des Jerusalemer Tempels und seines Kults im Alten Testament, antiken Judentum und frühen Christentum* (WUNT 118; Tübingen: Mohr [Siebeck], 1999) 99–113.

Müller, Hans-Peter
"Wie sprach Qohälät von Gott?" *VT* 18 (1968) 507–21.

Muntingh, L. M.
"Fear of Yahweh and Fear of the Gods According to the Books of Qohelet and Isaiah," in Wouter C. van Wyk, ed., *Studies in Isaiah* (OTWSA 22/23; Pretoria: NAW, 1981) 143–58.

Murphy, Roland E.
"Kohelet, der Skeptiker," *Concilium (Deutsch)* 12 (1976) 567–70.

Murphy, Roland E.
"Qoheleth and Theology," *BTB* 21 (1991) 30–33.

Murphy, Roland E.
"Qoheleth's 'Quarrel' with the Fathers," in Dikran Y. Hadidian, ed., *From Faith to Faith: FS D. G. Miller* (Pittsburgh Theological Monograph Series 31; Pittsburgh: Pickwick, 1979) 235–45.

Murphy, Roland E.
"The Faith of Qoheleth," *Word & World* 7 (1987) 253–60.

Murphy, Roland E.
"The 'Pensées' of Coheleth," *CBQ* 17 (1955) 184–94, 304–14.

Murphy, Roland E.
"The Sage in Ecclesiastes and Qoheleth the Sage," in Gammie and Perdue, eds., *Sage,* 263–71.

Nembach, Ulrich
"Das weise Bekenntnis des Predigers," *LM* 25 (1986) 484–85.

Newsom, Carol A.
"Job and Ecclesiastes," in James Luther Mays, David L. Petersen, and Kent Harold Richards, eds., *Old Testament Interpretation: Past, Present, and Future: Essays in Honor of Gene M. Tucker* (Nashville: Abingdon, 1995) 177–94.

Niekerk, M. J. H. van
"Response to J. A. Loader's 'Different Reactions of Job and Qoheleth to the Doctrine of Retribution,'" *OTE* 4 (1991) 97–105.

Nishimura, Toshiaki
"Quelques réflexions sémiologiques à propos de 'la crainte de dieu' de Qohelet," *AJBI* 5 (1979) 67–87.

Oberholzer, J. P.
"Die Boek Prediker: 'N Smartkreet om die gevalle mens," *HvTSt* 27 (1971) 1–7.

Okorie, A. M.
"Vanidad de vanidades! Todo es vanidad: El veredicto del Ecclesiastés," *RevistB* 59 (1997) 129–33.

Palma, Gaetano di
"Il Giudizio di Dio nel libro del Qohelet," *Asprenas* 40 (1993) 349–72.

Papone, Paolo
"La presenza misteriosa di Dio (Kohelet)," *PSV* 30 (1994) 93–102.

Pazera, Woiciech
"De santione morali in Qohelet," in Stanislav Grzybek and Jerzy Chmiel, eds., *Studium Scripturae anima theologiae* (Kraków: Polskie Towarzystowo Teologiczne, 1990) 218–24.

Pennacchini, Bruno
"Qohelet ovvero il libro degli assurdi," *Euntes docete* 30 (1977) 491–510.

Perry, Theodore Anthony
"Kohelet's Minimalist Theology," in Schoors, ed., *Qohelet in Context,* 451–56.

Pfeiffer, Egon
"Die Gottesfurcht im Buche Kohelet," in Henning Graf Reventlow, ed., *Gottes Wort und Gottes Land: FS Hans-Wilhelm Hertzberg* (Göttingen: Vandenhoeck & Ruprecht, 1965) 133–58.

Pfeiffer, Robert H.
"The Peculiar Skepticism of Ecclesiastes," *JBL* 53 (1934) 100–109.

Pick, Bernhard
"Ecclesiastes or the Sphinx of Hebrew Literature," *Open Court* 17 (1903) 361–71.

Pinto, Carlos Osvaldo
"Ecclesiastes: Una análise introdutória," *Vox Scripturae* 4 (1994) 151–66.

Porter, L. B.
"Bankruptcy: The Words of Qoheleth, Son of David, King in Jerusalem," *TBT* 44 (1969) 341–46.

Poulssen, N.
"Een zinnige brief over de Prediker?" *Ons geestelijk leven* 57 (1980) 177–84.

Power, John
"A Surprisingly Successful Preacher," *ScrC* 18 (1988) 470–74.

Prior, John M.
"'When All the Singing Has Stopped': Ecclesiastes, a Modest Mission in Unpredictable Times," *International Review of Mission* 91 (2002) 7–23.

Pury, Albert de
"Qohélet, Noé et le bonheur," *LumVie* 221 (1995) 33–40.

Rad, Gerhard von
"Erwägungen zum Prediger Salomo: Im Anschluss an den Kommentar von K. Galling," *VF* 2 (1941) 1–7.

Rainey, Anson F.
"A Study of Ecclesiastes," *CTM* 35 (1964) 148–57.

Raurell, Frederick
"Qohèlet: Una visío diferent i provocadora de Déo," *Revista catalana de teologia* 20 (1995) 237–67.

Ravasi, Gianfranco
"Le lacrime da nessuno consolate: Il giusto sofferente in Giobbe e Qohelet," *PSV* 34 (1996) 85–95.

Reines, Ch. W.
"Koheleth on Wisdom and Wealth," *JJS* 5 (1954) 80–84.

Richards, Hubert
"What's It All About? A New Look at the Book of Ecclesiastes," *Scripture Bulletin* 6 (1975) 7–11.

Richter, Hans-Friedemann
"Kohelet: Philosoph und Poet," in Schoors, ed., *Qohelet in Context*, 435–49.

Robertson, D.
"Job and Ecclesiastes," *Soundings* 73 (1990) 257–72.

Rochettes, Jacqueline des
"Qohélet ou l'humour noir à la recherche de Dieu dans un contexte hébraico-hellénique," in Alain Marchadour, ed., *L'évangile exploré* (LD 166; Paris: Cerf, 1996) 49–71.

Rose, Martin
"Qohelet als Philosoph und Theologe: Ein biblisches Votum für universitas," in Matthias Krieg and Martin Rose, eds., *Universitas in theologia–theologia in universitate: FS Hans Heinrich Schmid* (Zurich: Theologischer Verlag, 1997) 177–99.

Rose, Martin
"Querdenken mit und über Qohelet," *ThZ* 53 (1997) 83–96.

Rowley, H. H.
"The Problems of Ecclesiastes," *JQR* (1951/52) 87–90.

Rude, Terry
"The Alleged Epicurean Passages," *BV* 31 (1997) 19–24.

Rudman, Dominic
"The Anatomy of the Wise Man: Wisdom, Sorrow and Joy in the Book of Ecclesiastes," in Schoors, ed., *Qohelet in Context*, 465–71.

Salters, Robert B.
"Exegetical Problems in Qoheleth," *Irish Biblical Studies* 10 (1988) 44–59.

Saracino, Francesco
"Qohelet, il vino e la morte," *PaVi* 31 (1986) 186–90.

Savignac, Jean de
"La sagesse du Qôhélét et l'épopée de Gilgamesh," *VT* 28 (1978) 318–23.

Schabl, R.
"Ein Buch der Bibel und das Nichts," *Seelsorge* 31 (1960/61) 503–11.

Scheffler, Eben H.
"Qohelet's Positive Advice," *OTWSA* 6 (1993) 248–71.

Scheid, Edward G.
"Qoheleth: Criticism of Values," *TBT* 25 (1987) 244–51.

Schmitt, Armin
"Zwischen Anfechtung, Kritik und Lebensbewältigung: Zur theologischen Thematik des Buches Kohelet," *TThZ* 88 (1977) 114–31.

Schoors, Antoon
"L'ambiguità della gioia in Qohelet," in Bellia and Passaro, eds., *Qohelet*, 276–92.

Schoors, Antoon
"Qohelet: Perspektief op een Leven hierna?" in *Vie et Survie dans les Civilisations Orientales* (Acta Orientalia Belgica 3; Leuven: Peeters, 1983) 149–57; trans. "Koheleth: A Perspective of Life after Death?" *EThL* 61 (1985) 295–303.

Schwienhorst-Schönberger, Ludger
"Gottes Antwort in der Freude: Zur Theologie göttlicher Gegenwart im Buch Kohelet," *BK* 54 (1999) 156–63.

Scibona, Rocco
"Il libro del Qohelet," *Rassegna di teologia* 34 (1993) 709–13.

Sciumbata, M. Patrizia
"Peculiartà e motivazioni della struttura lessicale dei verbi della 'conoscenza' in Qohelet: Abbozzo di una storia dell'epistemologia ebraico-biblica," *Hen* 18 (1996) 235–49.

Seguineau, R.
"Pas à pas avec la Bible: L'Ecclésiaste ou Qohelet," *LumVie* 41 (1958) 23–29; 42 (1959) 24–29; 43 (1959) 12–21; 44 (1959) 17–24; 45 (1959) 16–23.

Sekine, Seizo
"Qohelet als Nihilist," *AJBI* 17 (1991) 3–54; trans. "Qohelet as a Nihilist," in Seizo Sekine, *Transcendency and Symbols in the Old Testament* (BZAW 275; Berlin: de Gruyter, 1999) 91–128.

Seow, Choon-Leong
"Theology When Everything Is Out of Control," *Int* 55 (2001) 237–49.

Serrano, J. J.

"Qohélet o Eclesiastés," *Biblioteca de autores cristianos* 293 (1969) 527–82.

Shank, H. Carl

"Qoheleth's World and Life View as Seen in His Recurring Phrases," *WTJ* 37 (1974) 57–73, repr. in Zuck, ed., *Reflecting with Solomon*, 67–80.

Shead, Andrew G.

"Ecclesiastes from the Outside in," *Reformed Theological Journal* 55 (1996) 24–37.

Shead, Andrew G.

"Reading Ecclesiastes 'Epilogically,'" *TynBul* 48 (1997) 67–92.

Siméon, Jean-Pierre

"Le don du vivre: Qohélet," *LumVie* 38 (1989) 17–36.

Simian-Yofre, Horacio

"Conoscere la sapienza: Qohelet e Genesi 2–3," in Bellia and Passaro, eds., *Qohelet*, 314–36.

Smend, Rudolf

"Der Prediger Salomo," *Kirchenblatt für die reformierte Schweiz* 45 (1889) 1–23.

Smith, David L.

"The Concept of Death in Job and Ecclesiastes," *Didascalia* 4 (1992) 2–14.

Smith, L.

"A Critical Evaluation of the Book of Ecclesiastes," *JBR* 21 (1953) 100–105.

Sneed, Mark

"Qoheleth as 'Deconstructionist': 'It is I, the Lord, Your Redeemer . . . Who Turns Sages Back and Makes Their Knowledge Nonsense' (Is 44:24-25)," *OTE* 10 (1997) 303–11.

Spangenberg, Izak J. J.

"Die Prediker se uitsprake oor en uitkyk op die dood," *Scriptura* 27 (1988) 29–37.

Spangenberg, Izak J. J.

"Irony in the Book of Qohelet," *JSOT* 72 (1996) 57–69.

Spangenberg, Izak J. J.

"Jonah and Qohelet: Satire versus Irony," *OTE* 9 (1996) 495–511.

Spangenberg, Izak J. J.

"Psalm 49 and the Book of Qohelet," *SK* 18 (1997) 328–44.

Spieckermann, Hermann

"Suchen und Finden: Kohelets kritische Reflexionen," *Bib* 79 (1998) 305–32.

Spina, Frank Anthony

"Qoheleth and the Reformation of Wisdom," in H. B. Huffmon, F. A. Spina, and A. R. W. Green, eds., *The Quest for the Kingdom of God: FS George E. Mendenhall* (Winona Lake, Ind.: Eisenbrauns, 1983) 267–79.

Steveson, Pete

"The Vanity of Success," *BV* 31 (1997) 35–40.

Stiglmair, Arnold

"Weisheit und Jahweglaube im Buch Qohelet," *TThZ* 83 (1974) 257–83, 339–68.

Stock, George

"Nochmals Koheleths Pessimismus," in *Schopenhauer-Jahrbuch 43* (Frankfurt am Main: Kramer, 1962) 107–10.

Stockhammer, Morris

"Koheleths Pessimismus," in *Schopenhauer-Jahrbuch 41* (Frankfurt am Main: Kramer, 1960) 52–81.

Stone, E.

"Old Man Koheleth," *JBR* 10 (1942) 98–102.

Swain, L.

"The Message of Ecclesiastes," *Clergy Review* 51 (1966) 862–68.

Támez, Elsa

"Ecclesiastes: A Reading from the Periphery," *Int* 55 (2001) 250–59.

Támez, Elsa

"Überlegungen zur utopischen Vernunft bei Qohelet," in Carmen Krieg, Thomas Kucharz, and Miroslav Volf, eds., *Die Theologie auf dem Weg in das dritte Jahrtausend: FS Jürgen Moltmann* (Gütersloh: Kaiser, 1996) 284–99.

Taylor, J. Patton

"A Time to Dance: Reflections on the Book of Ecclesiastes," *IBS* 18 (1996) 114–35.

Torta, Giorgio

"Il figura dello stolto," *PaVi* 38 (1993) 33–39.

Trible, Phyllis

"Ecclesiastes," in Bernhard W. Anderson, ed., *The Books of the Bible*, vol. 1: *The Old Testament, the Hebrew Bible* (New York: Scribner's, 1989) 231–39.

Vattioni, Francesco

"Due note sull' Ecclesiaste," *AION* 17 (1967) 157–63.

Vattioni, Francesco

"Niente di nuovo sotto il sole," *RivB* 7 (1959) 64–67.

Vischer, Wilhelm

"Der Prediger Salomo," *ZZ* 4 (1926) 187–193.

Viviano, Pauline A.

"The Book of Ecclesiastes: A Literary Approach," *TBT* 22 (1984) 79–84.

Vogels, Walter P. B.

"Performance vaine et performance saine chez Qohélet," *NRTh* 113 (1991) 363–85.

Vonach, Andreas

"Bibelauslegung als Wertvermittlung: Religiös motivierte Gesellschaftskritik am Beispiel des Buches Kohelet," in Christian Kanzian, ed., *Gott finden in allen Dingen: Theologie und Spiritualität* (Thaur: Druck- und Verlagshaus Thaur, 1998) 228–41.

Wallis, Gerhard

"Das Zeitverständnis des Predigers Salomo," in Manfred Weippert and Stefan Timm, eds., *Meilenstein: Festgabe für Herbert Donner* (ÄAT 30; Wiesbaden: Harrassowitz, 1995) 316–23.

Walsh, Jerome T.

"Despair as a Theological Virtue in the Spirituality of Ecclesiastes," *BTB* 12 (1982) 46–49.

Weill, R.

"Le livre du 'Désespéré': Le sens, l'intention et la composition de l'ouvrage," *BIFAO* 45 (1947) 89–154.

Whybray, Roger Norman

"Conservatisme et radicalisme dans Qohélet," in E. Jacob, ed., *Sagesse et religion: Colloque de Strasbourg (Octobre 1976)* (Paris: Presses Universitaires de Strasbourg, 1979) 65–81.

Whybray, Roger Norman

"Qoheleth as a Theologian," in Schoors, ed., *Qohelet in Context*, 239–65.

Whybray, Roger Norman

"Qoheleth, Preacher of Joy," *JSOT* 23 (1982) 87–98, repr. in Zuck, ed., *Reflecting with Solomon*, 203–212, repr. in Clines, ed., *Poetical Books*, 188–97.

Williams, James G.

"Proverbs and Ecclesiastes," in Robert Alter and Frank Kermode, eds., *The Literary Guide to the Bible* (Cambridge: Harvard Univ. Press, 1987) 263–82.

Williams, James G.

"What Does It Profit a Man? The Wisdom of Koheleth," *Judaism* 20 (1971) 179–93, repr. in Crenshaw, ed., *Studies*, 375–89.

Wisdom, Thurman

"The Preacher in the 'House of Mourning,'" *BV* 31 (1997) 41–46.

Wright, J. Stafford

"Interpréter l'Ecclésiaste," *Hokhma* 13 (1980) 50–64.

Wright, J. Stafford

"The Interpretation of Ecclesiastes," *EvQ* 18 (1946) 18–23, repr. in Walter C. Kaiser Jr., ed., *Classical Evangelical Essays in Old Testament Interpretation* (Grand Rapids: Baker, 1973) 133–50, repr. in Zuck, ed., *Reflecting with Solomon*, 17–30.

Wyse, R. R., and W. S. Prinsloo

"Faith Development and Proverbial Wisom," *OTE* 9 (1996) 129–43.

Yancey, Philip

"Ecclesiastes: Telling It Like It Is," *Reformed Journal* 40 (1990) 14–19.

Zapletal, Vincenz

"Der Unsterblichkeitsglaube Kohelets," *Kath.* 84 (1905) 321–26.

Zapletal, Vincenz

"Die vermeintlichen Irrlehren Qohelets," *Schweizerische Rundschau* 4 (1903/04) 463–68.

Zapletal, Vincenz

"Ueber den Unsterblichkeitsglauben Kohelets," in *Verhandlungen des 2. internationalen Kongresses für allgemeine Religionsgeschichte 1904* (Basel: 1905) 216–17.

Zer Kavod, Mordechai

"Ecclesiastes," *BethM* 58 (1974) 360–62 (Heb.).

Zer Kavod, Mordechai

"God, Man, Toil, and the Wise Man in the Book of Qoheleth," *Sinai* 64 (1968) 1–8 (Heb.).

Zer Kavod, Mordechai

"Qoheleth Draws Conclusions in a Circular Argument," in B. Z. Luria, ed., *Zer li'gevurot: FS Z. Shazar* (Publications of the Israel Society for Biblical Research 28; Jerusalem: Kiriat Sefer, 1973) 346–50 (Heb.).

Zer Kavod, Mordechai

"Studies in Qohelet," *BethM* 53 (1973) 183–91 (Heb.).

Zuck, Roy B.

"God and Man in Ecclesiastes," *BSac* 148 (1991) 46–56, repr. in Zuck, ed., *Reflecting with Solomon*, 213–22.

Structure

Backhaus

Zeit und Zufall.

Bell, Robert, D.

"Structure and Themes of Ecclesiastes," *BV* 31 (1997) 3–9.

Brown, Stephen G.

"The Structure of Ecclesiastes," *Evangelical Quarterly Review* 14 (1990) 195–208.

Castellino, George R.

"Qohelet and His Wisdom," *CBQ* 30 (1968) 15–28.

Coppens, Joseph

"La structure de l'Ecclésiaste," in Gilbert, ed., *Sagesse*, 288–92.

D'Alario

Il libro del Qohelet.

D'Alario, Vittoria

"Struttura e Teologia del Libro del Qohelet," in Bellia and Passaro, eds., *Qohelet*, 256–75.

Fischer

Skepsis.

Fox, Michael V.

"Frame Narrative and Composition in the Book of Qohelet," *HUCA* 48 (1977) 83–106.

Gese, Harmut

"Zur Komposition des Koheletbuches," in Hubert Cancik, Hermann Lichtenberger, and Peter Schäfer, eds., *Geschichte–Tradition–Reflexion: FS Martin Hengel*, vol. 1: *Judentum* (Tübingen: Mohr [Siebeck], 1996) 69–98.

Ginsberg, Harold Louis

"The Structure and Contents of the Book of Koheleth," in Martin Noth and D. Winton Thomas, eds., *Wisdom in Israel and in the Ancient Near East: FS H. H. Rowley* (VTSup 3; Leiden: Brill, 1955) 138–49, repr. in Alexander Altmann, ed., *Biblical and Other Studies* (STLI 1; Cambridge: Harvard Univ. Press, 1963) 47–59.

Jong, Stephen de

"A Book on Labour: The Structuring Principles and the Main Themes of the Book of Qohelet," *JSOT* 54 (1992) 107–16, repr. in Clines, ed., *Poetical Books*, 222–30.

Lohfink, Norbert

"Das Koheletbuch: Strukturen und Struktur," in Schwienhorst-Schönberger, ed., *Das Buch Kohelet*, 39–121.

Miller, Athanasius
"Aufbau und Grundproblem des Predigers," *SPIB Miscellanea Biblica* 2 (1934) 104–22.

Mulder, J. S. M.
"Qoheleth's Division and Also Its Main Point," in W. C. Delsman and J. T. Nelis, eds., *Von Kanaan bis Kerala: FS J. P. M. van der Ploeg 1979* (AOAT 211; Kevelaer: Butzon & Bercker; Neukirchen-Vluyn: Neukirchener Verlag, 1982) 149–59.

Reich, Rachel
"Word Chains in Ecclesiastes," *BethM* 36 (1990–91) 94–96 (Heb.).

Reitman, James S.
"The Structure and Unity of Ecclesiastes," *BSac* 154 (1997) 297–319.

Rousseau, François
"Structure de Qohelet i 4-11 et plan du livre," *VT* 31 (1981) 200–217.

Schoors, Antoon
"La structure littéraire de Qohéleth," *OLP* 13 (1982) 91–116.

Schwienhorst-Schönberger
Nicht im Menschen.

Vaihinger, J. G.
"Plan Koheleths," *ThStK* 21 (1848) 442–78.

Waard, Jan de
"The Structure of Qohelet," in *Proceedings of the Eighth World Congress of Jewish Studies, Division A: The Bible and its World* (Jerusalem: World Union of Jewish Studies, 1982) 57–64.

Wright, Addison G.
"Additional Numerical Patterns in Qoheleth," *CBQ* 45 (1983) 32–43.

Wright, Addison G.
"The Riddle of the Sphinx Revisited: Numerical Patterns in the Book of Qoheleth," *CBQ* 42 (1980) 38–51.

Wright, Addison G.
"The Riddle of the Sphinx: The Structure of the Book of Qoheleth," *CBQ* 30 (1968) 313–34, repr. in Crenshaw, ed., *Studies*, 245–66, repr. in Zuck, ed., *Reflecting with Solomon*, 45–65.

Zimmerli, Walther
"Das Buch Kohelet: Traktat oder Sentenzensammlung?" *VT* 24 (1974) 221–30.

Genres

Anderson, William H. U.
"Ironic Correlations and Scepticism in the Joy Statements of Qoheleth?" *SJOT* 14 (2000) 67–100.

Anderson, William H. U.
"Philosophical Considerations in a Genre Analysis of Qoheleth," *VT* 48 (1998) 289–300.

Ausejo, Serafín de
"El género literario del Eclesiastés," *EstBib* 6 (1947) 451; *EstBib* 7 (1948) 369–406.

Backhaus, Franz Josef
"Kohelet und die 'Diatribe': Hermeneutische und methodologische Überlegungen zu einem noch ausstehenden Stilvergleich," *BZ* 42 (1998) 248–56.

Berger, Klaus
"Hellenistische Gattungen im Neuen Testament," *ANRW* 25.2 (1984) 1031–1885.

Christianson
A Time to Tell.

Crenshaw, James Lee
"Prohibitions in Proverbs and Qoheleth," in Eugene Ulrich, John W. Wright, Robert P. Carroll, and Philip R. Davies, eds., *Priests, Prophets and Scribes: Essays on the Formation and Heritage of Second Temple Judaism in Honour of Joseph Blenkinsopp* (JSOTSup 149; Sheffield: JSOT Press, 1992) 115–24, repr. in Crenshaw, *Urgent Advice*, 417–25.

Ellermeier
Qohelet, I/1, 53ff.

Fox, Michael V.
"Frame Narrative and Composition in the Book of Qohelet," *HUCA* 48 (1977) 83–106.

Greenstein, Edward L.
"Sages with a Sense of Humor: The Babylonian Dialogue between the Master and His Servant and the Book of Qohelet," *BethM* 157 (1999) 97–106, 192 (Heb.).

Höffken, Peter
"Das EGO des Weisen: Subjektivierungsprozesse in der Weisheitsliteratur," *ThZ* 41 (1985) 121–34.

Johnson, Raymond Eugene
"The Rhetorical Question as a Literary Device in Ecclesiastes" (Th.D. diss., Southern Baptist Theological Seminary, 1986).

Johnson, Robert Franklin
"A Form-Critical Analysis of the Sayings in the Book of Ecclesiastes" (Th.D. diss., Emory University, 1973).

Klein
Kohelet.

Loader
Polar Structures, 18ff.

Lohfink, Norbert
"Das 'Poikilometron': Kohelet und Menippos von Gadara," *BK* 45 (1990) 19.

Longman, Tremper
Fictional Akkadian Autobiography: A Generic and Comparative Study (Winona Lake, Ind.: Eisenbrauns, 1991).

Loretz, Oswald
"Zur Darbietungsform der 'Ich-Erzählung' im Buche Qohelet," *CBQ* 25 (1963) 46–59.

Meade, David G.
Pseudonymity and Canon: An Investigation into the Relationship of Authorship and Authority in Jewish and Earliest Christian Tradition (WUNT 39; Tübingen: Mohr [Siebeck], 1986).

Müller, Hans-Peter
"Kohelet und Amminadab," in Diesel et al., eds., *Jedes Ding,* 149–65.

Murphy
Wisdom Literature.

Ogden, Graham S.
"Qoheleth's Use of the 'Nothing is Better'-Form," *JBL* 98 (1979) 339-50.

Ogden, Graham S.
"The 'Better'-Proverb (Tôb-Spruch), Rhetorical Criticism, and Qoheleth," *JBL* 96 (1977) 489-505.

Rosendal, Bent
"Popular Wisdom in Qohelet," in Knud Jeppesen, Kirsten Nielsen, and Bent Rosendal, eds., *In the Last Days: On Jewish and Christian Apocalyptic and Its Period* (Aarhus: Aarhus Univ. Press, 1994) 121-27.

Schubert, Mathias
"Die Selbstbetrachtungen Kohelets: Ein Beitrag zu Gattungsforschung," *ThV* 17 (1989) 23-34.

Schwienhorst-Schönberger, Ludger
"Kohelet: Stand und Perspektiven der Forschung," in Schwienhorst-Schönberger, ed., *Das Buch Kohelet*, 20-24.

Seow, Choon-Leong
"Qohelet's Autobiography," in Astrid B. Beck et al., eds., *Fortunate the Eyes That See: Essays in Honor of David Noel Freedman* (Grand Rapids: Eerdmans, 1995) 275-87.

Uehlinger, Christoph
"Qohelet im Horizont mesopotamischer, levantinischer und ägyptischer Weisheitsliteratur der persischen und hellenistischen Zeit," in Schwienhorst-Schönberger, ed., *Das Buch Kohelet*, 155-247.

Tensions and Contradictions

Backhaus, Franz Josef
"Kohelet und die Ironie: Vom Umgang mit Widersprüchen durch die Kunst der Ironie," *BN* 101 (2000) 29-55.

Backhaus, Franz Josef
"Widersprüche und Spannungen im Buch Qohelet: Zu einem neueren Versuch, Spannungen und Widersprüche literarkritisch zu lösen," in Schwienhorst-Schönberger, ed., *Das Buch Kohelet*, 123-54.

Coppens, Joseph
"La structure de l'Ecclésiaste," in Gilbert, ed., *Sagesse*, 288-92.

Fischer
Skepsis.

Fox, Michael V.
"Frame Narrative and Composition in the Book of Qohelet," *HUCA* 48 (1977) 83-106.

Fox, Michael V.
"The Identification of Quotations in Biblical Literature," *ZAW* 92 (1980) 416-31.

Fox
Qohelet.

Gese, Harmut
"Zur Komposition des Koheletbuches," in Hubert Cancik, Hermann Lichtenberger, and Peter Schäfer, eds., *Geschichte–Tradition–Reflexion: FS Martin Hengel*, vol. 1: *Judentum* (Tübingen: Mohr [Siebeck], 1996) 69-98.

Glender, Shabbatai
"On the Book of Ecclesiastes: A Collection Containing 'Diverse' Sayings or a Unified and Consistent Worldview?" *BethM* 26 (1981) 378-87 (Heb.).

Gordis, Robert
"Quotations as a Literary Usage in Biblical, Oriental, and Rabbinic Literature," *HUCA* 22 (1949) 157-219.

Gordis, Robert
"Quotations in Wisdom Literature," *JQR* 30 (1939/40) 123-47.

Haupt, Paul
"On the Book of Ecclesiastes: With Special Reference to the Closing Section," *John Hopkins University Circulars* 10 (1891) 115-17.

Horton, Ernest
"Koheleth's Concept of Opposites as Compared to Samples of Greek Philosophy and Near and Far Eastern Wisdom Classics," *Numen* 19 (1972) 1-21, repr. in *TD* 23 (1975) 265-67.

Lepore, Luciano
"Un Qohelet o più Qohelet? Un problema che ritorna," *BeO* 41 (1999) 229-49.

Loader
Polar Structures.

Lohfink, Norbert
"War Kohelet ein Frauenfeind? Ein Versuch, die Logik und den Gegenstand von Koh. 7,23–8,1a herauszufinden," in Gilbert, ed., *Sagesse*, 259-87, 417-20, repr. in Lohfink, *Studien*, 31-69.

Loretz, Oswald
"Altorientalische und kanaanäische Topoi im Buche Koheleth," *UF* 12 (1980) 267-78.

Loretz, Oswald
"Anfänge jüdischer Philosophie nach Qohelet 1,1-11 und 3,1-15," *UF* 23 (1991) 223-44.

Loretz, Oswald
"'Frau' und griechisch-jüdische Philosophie im Buch Qohelet (Qoh 7,23–8,1 und 9,6-10)," *UF* 23 (1991) 245-64.

Loretz, Oswald
"Jüdischer Gott und griechische Philosophie (ḥokmat yevanit) im Qohelet-Buch," *MARG* 8 (1994) 151-76.

Loretz, Oswald
"Poetry and Prose in the Book of Qoheleth (1:1–3:22; 7:23–8:1; 9:6-10; 12:8-14)," in Johannes C. de Moor and Wilfred G. E. Watson, eds., *Verse in Ancient Near Eastern Prose* (AOAT 42; Kevelaer: Butzon & Bercker; Neukirchen-Vluyn: Neukirchener Verlag, 1993) 155-89.

Meyer, Ivo, and Martin Rose
"Sprüche und Widersprüche im Qohelet-Buch," *Variations herméneutiques* 6 (1997) 71-86.

Michel
Untersuchungen.

Munk, A.
"Går Praedikeren på Kompromis med 'Tomheden'?" ["Does the Preacher make a compromise with 'vanity'?"], in Niels Peter Lemche and Mogens Müller, eds., *Fra Dybet: FS John Strange* (Forum for Bibelsk Eksegese 5; Copenhagen: Museum Tusculanum, 1994) 157-79.

Podechard, Emmanuel
"La composition du livre de l'Ecclésiaste," *RB* 21 (1912) 161–91.

Rose, Martin
"De la 'crise de la sagesse' à la 'sagesse de la crise,'" *RThPh* 131 (1999) 115–34, repr. in Rose, ed., *Situer Qohélet*, 27–46.

Rose, Martin
"Qohéleth, le Maître: Compréhension de l'univers et compréhension de soi," *Variations herméneutiques* 3 (1995) 3–22.

Schoors, Antoon
"(Mis)use of Intertextuality in Qoheleth Exegesis," in André Lemaire and M. Sæbø, eds., *International Organization for the Study of the Old Testament: Congress Volume, Oslo 1998* (VTSup 80; Leiden: Brill, 2000) 45–59.

Schwienhorst-Schönberger, Ludger
"Kohelet: Stand und Perspektiven der Forschung," in Schwienhorst-Schönberger, ed., *Das Buch Kohelet*, 14–20.

Spangenberg, Izak J. J.
"Quotations in Ecclesiastes: An Appraisal," *OTE* 4 (1991) 19–35.

Umbreit, F. W. C.
"Die Einheit des Buches Koheleth," *ThStK* 30 (1857) 7–56.

Vignolo, Roberto
"La poetica ironica di Qohelet: Contributo allo svilupo di un orientamento critico," *Teol(Br)* 25 (2000) 217–40.

Wahl, Harald Martin
"Zweifel, Freude und Gottesfurcht als Glaubensgewissheit: Zum aspektivischen Denken Kohelets," *ThZ* 56 (2000) 1–20.

Whybray, Roger Norman
"The Identification and Use of Quotations in Ecclesiastes," J. A. Emerton, ed., *Congress Volume, Vienna 1980* (VTSup 32; Leiden: Brill, 1981) 435–51, repr. in Zuck, ed., *Reflecting with Solomon*, 185–99.

Origin and Historical Context

Abel, F.-M.
"Hellénisme et orientalisme en Palestine au déclin de la periode Seleucide," *RB* 53 (1946) 385–402.

Albertz, Rainer
A History of Israelite Religion in the Old Testament Period (OTL; Louisville: Westminster John Knox, 1994) 493–544.

Amir, Yehoshua
"Doch ein griechischer Einfluss auf das Buch Kohelet?" in *Studien zum antiken Judentum* (BEAT 2; Frankfurt am Main: Lang, 1985) 35–50, Hebrew original: *BethM* 10 (1965) 36–42.

Anderson, William H. U.
"The Curse of Work in Qoheleth: An Exposé of Genesis 3,17-19 in Ecclesiastes," *EvQ* 70 (1998) 99–113.

Anderson, William H. U.
"The Problematics of the *Sitz im Leben* of Qoheleth," *OTE* 12 (1999) 233–48.

Archer, Gleason L.
"The Linguistic Evidence for the Date of 'Ecclesiastes,'" *JETS* 12 (1969) 167–81.

Backhaus, Franz Josef
"Qohelet und Sirach," *BN* 69 (1993) 32–55.

Backhaus
"Zur Spätdatierung Qohelets durch C. F. Whitley," in *Zeit und Zufall*, 412–20.

Barnes, Jonathan
"L'Ecclésiaste et le scepticisme grec," *RThPh* 131 (1999) 103–14, repr. in Rose, ed., *Situer Qohélet*, 15–26.

Bellia, Giuseppe
"Il Libro del Qohelet e il suo Contesto Storico-Antropologico," in Bellia and Passaro, eds., *Qohelet*, 171–216.

Berlin, Andrea M.
"Between Large Forces: Palestine in the Hellenistic Period," *BA* 60 (1997) 2–51.

Blenkinsopp, Joseph
Wisdom and Law in the Old Testament: The Ordering of Life in Israel and Early Judaism (rev. ed.; Oxford Bible Series; New York: Oxford Univ. Press, 1995).

Boccaccini, Gabriele
Middle Judaism: Jewish Thought 300 B.C.E. to 200 C.E. (Minneapolis: Fortress Press, 1991).

Bohlen, Reinhold
"Kohelet im Kontext hellenistischer Kultur," in Schwienhorst-Schönberger, ed., *Das Buch Kohelet*, 249–73.

Braun
Kohelet.

Brown, John Pairman
Israel and Hellas (BZAW 231; New York: de Gruyter, 1995).

Brzegowy, Tadeusz
"La critique de la sapience traditionelle dans le Livre de Qohéleth," *ACra* 25 (1993) 21–42.

Bühlmann, Walter
Gott in einer kritischen Welt? Ein Schlüssel zu den Spätschriften des Alten Testaments (Luzern: Rex, 1991).

Buzy, Denis
"Les Auteurs de l'Ecclésiaste," *L'année théologique* 11 (1950) 317–36.

Cimosa, Mario
"La contestazione sapienziale di Giobbe e Qoèlet," *PaVi* 30 (1985) 280–85.

Collins, John J.
Jewish Wisdom in the Hellenistic Age (OTL; Louisville: Westminster John Knox, 1997).

Cosser, William
"The Meaning of 'Life' in Proverbs, Job, and Ecclesiastes," *TGUOS* 15 (1953/54) 48–53.

Crenshaw, James Lee
"The Birth of Skepticism in Ancient Israel," in idem and Samuel Sandmel, eds., *The Divine Helmsman: Studies on God's Control of Human Events: FS L. H. Silberman* (New York: Ktav, 1980) 1–19, repr. in Crenshaw, *Urgent Advice*, 548–72.

Crüsemann, Frank
"Hiob und Kohelet: Ein Beitrag zum Verständnis des Hiobbuches," in Rainer Albertz et al., eds., *Werden und Wirken des Alten Testaments: FS Claus Westermann* (Göttingen: Vandenhoeck & Ruprecht, 1980) 373–93.

Crüsemann, Frank
"The Unchangeable World: The 'Crisis of Wisdom' in Koheleth," in W. Schottroff and W. Stegemann, eds., *God of the Lowly: Socio-Historical Interpretations of the Bible* (Maryknoll, N.Y.: Orbis, 1984) 57–77.

D'Alario, Vittoria
"Chi può conoscere il disegno di Dio? Problematica e prospettive della sapienza critica," in Massimo Lorenzani, ed., *La volontà di Dio nella Bibbia* (Studi Biblici; L'Aquila: ISSRA, 1994) 87–111.

Dewey, Rosemary
"Qoheleth and Job: Diverse Responses to the Enigma of Evil," *SpTo* 37 (1985) 314–25.

Dhorme, P.
"Ecclésiaste ou Job?" *RB* 32 (1923) 5–27.

Donner, Herbert
Geschichte des Volkes Israel und seiner Nachbarn in Grundzügen, vol. 2 (2d ed.; Göttingen: Vandenhoeck & Ruprecht, 1995) 474–82.

Festorazzi, Franco
"Giobbe e Qohelet: Crisi della Sapienza," in Rinaldo Fabris, ed., *Problemi e prospettive di scienze bibliche* (Brescia: Queriniana, 1982) 233–58.

Forman, Charles C.
"Koheleth's Use of Genesis," *JSS* 5 (1960) 256–63.

Forster, A. H.
"The Date of Ecclesiastes," *Anglican Theological Review* 41 (1959) 1–9.

Galling, Kurt
Die Krise der Aufklärung in Israel (Mainz: Gutenburg, 1952).

Gammie, John G.
"Stoicism and Anti-Stoicism in Qoheleth," *HAR* 9 (1985) 169–87.

Gese, Hartmut
"Die Krisis der Weisheit bei Koheleth," in Maurice Gilbert, ed., *Les sagesses du Proche Orient Ancien* (Paris: Presses Universitaires de France, 1963) 139–51, repr. in Hartmut Gese, *Vom Sinai zum Zion* (BEvTh 64; Munich: Kaiser, 1964) 168–79, trans. as "The Crisis of Wisdom in Koheleth," in James Lee Crenshaw, ed., *Theodicy in the Old Testament* (IRT 4; Philadelphia: Fortress Press, 1983) 141–53.

Gese, Harmut
"Zur Komposition des Koheletbuches," in Hubert Cancik, Hermann Lichtenberger, and Peter Schäfer, eds., *Geschichte-Tradition-Reflexion; FS für Martin Hengel zum 70. Geburtstag,* vol. 1: *Judentum* (Tübingen: Mohr [Siebeck], 1996) 69–98.

Gilbert, Maurice
"Qohelet et Ben Sira," in Schoors, ed., *Qohelet in Context,* 161–79.

Grimme, Hubert
"Babel und Koheleth-Jojakhin," *OLZ* 8 (1905) 432–33.

Grootaert, A.
"L'Ecclésiastique est-il antérieur à l'Ecclésiaste?" *RB* 14 (1905) 67–73.

Harrington, Daniel J.
Wisdom Texts from Qumran (Literature of the Dead Sea Scrolls; London: Routledge, 1996).

Harrison, C. Robert
"Hellenization in Syria-Palestine: The Case of Judea in the Third Century BCE," *BA* 57 (1994) 98–108.

Harrison, C. Robert
"Qoheleth among the Sociologists," *BibInt* 5 (1997) 160–80.

Harrison, C. Robert
"Qoheleth in Socio-historical Perspective" (diss., Duke University, 1991).

Hengel
Judaism and Hellenism.

Hertzberg, Hans Wilhelm
"Palästinische Bezüge im Buche Kohelet," *ZDPV* 73 (1957) 113–24; repr. in Johannes Herrmann, ed., *Festschrift Friedrich Baumgärtel* (Erlanger Forschungen, series A 10; Erlangen: Universitätsbund Erlangen, 1959) 63–73.

Höffken, Peter
"Das EGO des Weisen: Subjektivierungsprozesse in der Weisheitsliteratur," *ThZ* 41 (1985) 121–34.

Hölbl
Geschichte des Ptolemäerreiches.

Horbury, W.
"Jewish Inscriptions and Jewish Literature in Egypt, with Special Reference to Ecclesiasticus," in Jan Willem van Henten and Pieter Willem van der Horst, eds., *Studies in Early Jewish Epigraphy* (AGJU 21; Leiden: Brill, 1994) 9–43.

Jagersma, Hendrik
"Prediker in het kader van zijn tijd," in Hendrik Jagersma, *Tekst & Interpretatie: Studies over getallen, teksten, verhalen en geschiedenis in het Oude Testament* (Nijkerk: Callenbach, 1990) 62–67.

Johnston, David
A Treatise on the Authorship of Ecclesiastes (London: 1880).

Jones, Bruce William
"From Gilgamesh to Qoheleth," in W. W. Hallo, B. W. Jones, and G. L. Mattingly, eds., *The Bible in the Light of Cuneiform Literature* (Scripture in Context 3; ANETS 8; Lewiston, N.Y.: Mellen, 1990) 349–79.

Jong, Stephen de
"'Quitate de mi Sol!' Eclesiastés y la Tecnocracia Helenística," *RIBLA* 11 (1992) 75–85.

Jong, Stephen de
"Qohelet and the Ambitious Spirit of the Ptolemaic Period," *JSOT* 61 (1994) 85–96.

Kaiser, Otto
"Anknüpfung und Widerspruch: Die Antwort der jüdischen Weisheit auf die Herausforderung durch den Hellenismus," in Joachim Mehlhausen, ed., *Pluralismus und Identität* (Veröffentlichungen

wissenschaftlichen Gesellschaft für Theologie 8; Gütersloh: Gütersloher Verlagshaus, 1995) 54–69.

Kaiser, Otto
"Determination und Freiheit beim Kohelet / Prediger Salomo und in der Frühen Stoa," *NZSTh* 31 (1989) 251–70.

Kaiser, Otto
"Gottesgewissheit und Weltbewusstsein in der früh-hellenistischen jüdischen Weisheit," in Trutz Rendtorff, ed., *Glaube und Toleranz* (Gütersloh: Gütersloher Verlagshaus, 1982) 76–88.

Kaiser, Otto
"Judentum und Hellenismus: Ein Beitrag zur Frage nach dem hellenistischen Einfluss auf Kohelet und Jesus Sirach," *VF* 27 (1982) 68–88, repr. in Kaiser, *Der Mensch unter dem Schicksal*, 135–53.

King, Nicholas
"'The Hand of the Lord Has Touched Me': Job, Qoheleth, and the Wisdom of Solomon," *Way* 22 (1982) 235–44.

Kleinert, Paul
"Sind im Buche Kohelet ausserhebräische Einflüsse anzuerkennen?" *ThStK* 56 (1883) 761–82.

Kleinert, Paul
"Zur religions- und kulturgeschichtlichen Stellung des Buches Koheleth," *ThStK* 82 (1909) 493–529.

Koester
Introduction.

Kratz, Reinhard G.
"Die Gnade des täglichen Brots: Späte Psalmen auf dem Weg zum Vaterunser," *ZThK* 89 (1992) 1–40.

Krüger, Thomas
"Dekonstruktion und Rekonstruktion prophetischer Eschatologie im Qohelet-Buch," in Diesel et al., eds., *Jedes Ding*, 107–29, repr. in Krüger, *Kritische Weisheit*, 151–72.

Krüger, Thomas
"Die Rezeption der Tora im Buch Kohelet," in Schwienhorst-Schönberger, ed., *Das Buch Kohelet*, 303–25, repr. in Krüger, *Kritische Weisheit*, 173–93.

Krüger, Thomas
"Le livre de Qohélet dans le contexte de la littérature juive du IIIe et IIe siècles avant Jésus-Christ," *RThPh* 131 (1999) 135–62, repr. in Rose, ed., *Situer Qohélet*, 47–74.

Krüger, Thomas
"Qoh 2,24-26 und die Frage nach dem 'Guten' im Qohelet-Buch," *BN* 72 (1994) 70–84, repr. in Krüger, *Kritische Weisheit*, 131–49.

Küchler
Frühjüdische Weisheitstraditionen.

Lange, Armin
"In Diskussion mit dem Tempel: Zur Auseinandersetzung zwischen Kohelet und weisheitlichen Kreisen am Jerusalemer Tempel," in Schoors, ed., *Qohelet in Context*, 113–59.

Lichtheim
Late Egyptian Wisdom Literature.

Loader, James A.
"Different Reactions of Job and Qoheleth to the Doctrine of Retribution," *OTWSA* 15/16 (1972/73) 43–48.

Loader, James A.
"Relativity in Near Eastern Wisdom," *OTWSA* 15/16 (1972/73) 49–58.

Loewenclau, Ilse von
"Kohelet und Sokrates: Versuch eines Vergleiches," *ZAW* 98 (1986) 327–38.

Lohfink, Norbert
"Das 'Poikilometron': Kohelet und Menippos von Gadara," *BK* 45 (1990) 19.

Lohfink, Norbert
"Der Bibel skeptische Hintertür: Versuch, den Ort des Buchs Kohelet neu zu bestimmen," *StZ* 198 (1980) 17–31; repr. in idem, *Kohelet* (4th ed.), 5–17; repr. in Lohfink, *Studien*, 11–30.

Lohfink, Norbert
"*melek, šallît* und *mošel* bei Kohelet und die Abfassungszeit des Buches," *Bib* 62 (1981) 535–43, repr. in Lohfink, *Studien*, 71–82.

Loretz, Oswald
"Jüdischer Gott und griechische Philosophie (ḥokmat yevanit) im Qohelet-Buch," *MARG* 8 (1994) 151–76.

Lys, Daniel
"Qohélet ou le destin de la perte de sens," *LumVie* 41 (1995) 9–17.

Magnanini, Pietro
"Sull'origine letteraria dell'Ecclesiaste," *AION* 28 (1968) 363–84.

Maier
Die Qumran-Essener.

Marböck, Johannes
Gottes Weisheit unter uns: Zur Theologie des Buches Sirach (ed. Irmtraud Fischer; HBS 6; Freiburg im Breisgau: Herder, 1995).

Marböck, Johannes
"Kohelet und Sirach: Eine vielschichtige Beziehung," in Schwienhorst-Schönberger, ed., *Das Buch Kohelet*, 275–301.

Marböck, Johannes
Weisheit im Wandel: Untersuchungen zur Weisheitstheologie bei Ben Sira (2d ed.; BZAW 272; Berlin: de Gruyter, 1999).

Margoliouth, David Samuel
"Ecclesiastes and Ecclesiasticus," *Exp.* 7,5 (1908) 118–26.

Michel, Diethelm
"Weisheit und Apokalyptik," in Adam S. van der Woude, ed., *The Book of Daniel in the Light of New Findings* (BEThL 106; Leuven: Leuven Univ. Press and Peeters, 1993) 413–34.

Middendorp, Th.
Die Stellung Jesu Ben Siras zwischen Judentum und Hellenismus (Leiden: Brill, 1972).

Müller, Hans-Peter
"Travestien und geistige Landschaften: Zum Hintergrund einiger Motive bei Kohelet und im Hohenlied," *ZAW* 109 (1997) 557–74.

Pahk, Johan Yeong Sik
"Qohelet e le tradizioni sapienziali del vicino oriente antico," in Bellia and Passaro, eds., *Qohelet*, 117–43.

Papone, Paolo
"Il Qohelet nel contesto della letteratura sapienziale: Novità e apertura al confronto culturale," *RStB* 10 (1998) 199–216.

Pedersen, Johannes
"Scepticisme israélite," *RHPhR* 10 (1930) 317–70.

Peters, Norbert
"Ecclesiastes und Ekklesiastikus," *BZ* 1 (1903) 47–54, 129–50.

Pfleiderer, Edmund
Die Philosophie des Heraklit von Ephesus im Lichte der Mysterienidee: Nebst einem Anhang über die heraklitischen Einflüsse im alttestamentlichen Koheleth und besonders im Buche der Weisheit, sowie in der ersten christlichen Literatur (Berlin: Reimer, 1866).

Raalte, J. van
"Het auteurschap van het boek Prediker," *Gereformeerd theologisch tijdschrift* 35 (1934) 497–531.

Reif, Stefan C.
"A Reply to Dr. C. F. Whitley," *VT* 32 (1982) 346–48.

Rizzante Galazzi, A. M. and S. Gallazzi
"La preuba de los ojos, la preuba de la casa, la preuba del sepulcro: Una clave de lectura del libro de Qohélet," *RIBLA* 14 (1993) 61–85.

Rochettes, Jacqueline des
"Qohélet ou l'humour noir à la recherche de dieu dans un contexte hébraico-hellénique," in Alain Marchadour, ed., *L'évangile exploré* (LD 166; Paris: Cerf, 1996) 49–71.

Rosso Ubigli, Liliana
"Qohelet di fronte all'apocalittica," *Hen* 5 (1983) 209–34.

Rudman, Dominic
"A Note on the Dating of Ecclesiastes," *CBQ* 61 (1999) 47–52.

Salters, Robert B.
"Scepticism in the Old Testament," *OTE* 2 (1989) 96–105.

Schoors, Antoon
"Qoheleth: A Book in a Changing Society," *OTE* 9 (1996) 68–87.

Schwienhorst-Schönberger, Ludger
"Kohelet: Stand und Perspektiven der Forschung," in Schwienhorst-Schönberger, ed., *Das Buch Kohelet*, 24–29.

Schwienhorst-Schönberger
Nicht im Menschen.

Schwienhorst-Schönberger, Ludger
"Via media: Koh 7,15-18 und die griechisch-hellenistische Philosophie," in Schoors, ed., *Qohelet in Context*, 181–203.

Seow, Choon-Leong
"Linguistic Evidence and the Dating of Qohelet," *JBL* 115 (1996) 643–66.

Seow, Choon-Leong
"The Socioeconomic Context of 'The Preacher's' Hermeneutic," *PSB* 17 (1996) 168–95.

Sheppard
Wisdom as a Hermeneutical Construct.

Silva Carvalho da, José Carlos
"A susposta influêcia grega em Qohelet," *Didaskalia* 28 (1998) 137–56.

Steck, Odil Hannes
Der Abschluss der Prophetie im Alten Testament: Ein Versuch zur Frage der Vorgeschichte des Kanons (BThSt 17; Neukirchen-Vluyn: Neukirchener Verlag, 1991).

Towner, W. Sibley
"Proverbs and Its Successors," in James Luther Mays et al., eds., *Old Testament Interpretation: Past, Present and Future: Essays in Honor of Gene M. Tucker* (Nashville: Abingdon: 1995) 367–85.

Uehlinger, Christoph
"Qohelet im Horizont mesopotamischer, levantinischer und ägyptischer Weisheitsliteratur der persischen und hellenistischen Zeit," in Schwienhorst-Schönberger, ed., *Das Buch Kohelet*, 155–247.

van der Toorn, Karel
"Did Ecclesiastes Copy Gilgamesh?" *Bible Review* 16 (2000) 22–30.

Vriezen, Theodor Christian
"Prediker en de achtergrond van zijn wijzheid," *NedThT* 1 (1946/47) 3–14, 65–84.

Walbank
Die hellenistische Welt.

Whitley, Charles F.
"A Reply to Dr. S. C. Reif," *VT* 32 (1982) 344–46.

Whitley
Koheleth.

Winckler, Hugo
"Zeit und Verfasser des Kohelet," in Hugo Winckler, *Altorientalische Forschungen,* vol. 2 (Leipzig: Pfeiffer, 1901) 143–59.

Winckler, Hugo
"Zum Kohelet," in Hugo Winckler, *Altorientalische Forschungen,* vol. 1 (Leipzig: Pfeiffer, 1897) 351–55.

Wischmeyer, Oda
Die Kultur des Buches Jesus Sirach (BZNW 77; New York: de Gruyter, 1995).

Zapletal, Vincenz
"Die vermeintlichen Einflüsse der griechischen Philosophie im Buche Kohelet," *BZ* 3 (1905) 32–39, 128–39.

Zenger, Erich, et al.
Einleitung in das Alte Testament (3d ed.; Kohlhammer Studienbücher Theologie 1.1; Stuttgart: Kohlhammer, 1998).

Zimmerli, Walther
"Das Buch Kohelet: Traktat oder Sentenzensammlung?" *VT* 24 (1974) 221–30.

Influence (See also the references below under "Text")

Aalders, W.
Luther en de angst van het Westen: Een pleidooi voor de rechtsstaat (The Hague: Voorhoeve, 1982).

Adriaen, Marcus, ed.
"S. Hieronymi Presbyteri Commentarius in Ecclesiasten," in *S. Hieronymi Presbyteri Opera, Pars I/1: Opera exegetica* (CChrSL 72; Turnhout: Brepols, 1959) 247–361.

Alshich, Moshe
The Book of Koheleth קהלת מגלת: *In Pursuit of Perfection* (trans. Ravi Shahar; Jerusalem: Feldheim, 1992).

Amigo Espada, Lorenzo
"Las glosas de Mosé Arraguel de Guadalajara al Eclesiastés," in J. Carreira das Neves, V. Collado Bertomeu, and V. Vilar Hueso, eds., *III simposio bíblico español [17–20 sept. 1989]* (Valencia–Lisboa: Fundación Bíblica Española, 1991) 649–65.

Aquino, Ranhilio Callangan
"The Believing Pessimist: A Philosophical Reading of Qoheleth," *PhilipSac* 16 (1981) 207–61.

Armstrong, James F.
"Ecclesiastes in Old Testament Theology," *PSB* 94 (1983) 16–25.

Asmussen, Jes P.
"Bemerkungen zu einer 'neuen' Jüdisch-Persischen Qohälät-Uebersetzung," in C. H. Fouchécour and P. Gignoux, eds., *Etudes irano-aryennes offertes à Gilbert Lazard* (Studia Iranica 7; Paris: Association pour l'avancement des Etudes iraniennes, 1989) 1–4.

Asmussen, Jes P.
"Some Textual Problems in the Hebrew Bible and Their Treatment in Judaeo-Persian Versions," in J. Duchesne-Guillemin et al., *Studia Iranica: Papers in Honour of Mary Boyce* (Hommages 10; Leuven: Brill, 1985).

Bardski, Krzysztof, *Il Commentarius in Ecclesiasten di Girolamo: Dall' intenzione del testo alle tradizioni interpretative* (Estratto della dissertazione per il dottorato in scienze bibliche al Pontifico Istituto Biblico; Rome: Pontifical Biblical Institute Press, 1997).

Bardski, Krzysztof
"'Vanità delle Vanità, tutto è Vanità': Il hebel dell'Ecclesiaste nell'interpretazione di Girolamo," *CoTh* 68 (1998) 39–81.

Beauchamp, Paul
"Entendre Qohéleth," *Christus* 16 (1969) 339–51.

Beckwith, Roger
The Old Testament Canon of the New Testament Church and Its Background in Early Judaism (Grand Rapids: Eerdmans, 1985).

Ben David, Israel
"Some Notes on the Text of Midrash Ecclesiastes Rabba," *Leš* 53 (1988/89) 135–40 (Heb.).

Bergada, M. M.
"La crítica a la esclavitud en la 'Homilía IV sobre el Eclesiastés' de Gregorio de Nyssa," *Patristica et Mediaevalia* 11 (1990) 69–78.

Berger, Klaus
"Die Bedeutung der wiederentdeckten Weisheitsschrift aus der Kairoer Geniza für das Alte Testament," *ZAW* 103 (1991) 113–21.

Berndt, Rainer
"Skizze zur Auslegungsgeschichte der Bücher Proverbia und Ecclesiastes in der abendländischen Kirche," *Sacrit erudiri* 34 (1994) 5–32.

Berndt, Rainer, ed.
[Andreas de Sancto Victore] Expositiones historicas in libros Salomonis (Andreae de Sancto Victore opera 3; CChrCM 53B; Turnhout: Brepols, 1986).

Boira Sales, José, and Abdón Moreno García
"Concepción jeronimiana de los sentidos bíblicos en el commentario a Qohélet," *EstBib* 55 (1997) 239–62.

Boira Sales, José, and Abdón Moreno García
"Fuentes y contenido teológico del commentario a Qohélet de S. Jerónimo," *ASEs* 14 (1997) 443–75.

Bons, Eberhard
"Das Buch Kohelet in jüdischer und christlicher Interpretation," in Schwienhorst-Schönberger, ed., *Das Buch Kohelet*, 327–61.

Bons, Eberhard
"Le livre de Qohélet: Les 'paradigmes' de l'histoire de son interprétation chrétienne," *RThPh* 131 (1999) 199–215, repr. in Rose, ed., *Situer Qohélet*, 111–27.

Botterweck, Gerhard J.
"An die Resignierten—Kritische Reflexionen Kohelets," in Ludwig Bertsch and Karl-Heinz Rentmeister, eds., *Zielgruppen: FS Karl Delahaye* (Frankfurt am Main: Knecht, 1977) 61–75.

Bottoms, Lawrence
Ecclesiastes Speaks to Us Today (Atlanta: John Knox, 1979).

Brenz, Johannes
Der Prediger Salomo: Faksimile-Neudruck der ersten Ausgabe Hagenau 1528 (ed. Martin Brecht; Stuttgart: Frommann, 1970).

Broyde, M. J.
"Defilement of the Hands, Canonization of the Bible, and the Special Status of Esther, Ecclesiastes, and Song of Songs," *Judaism* 44 (1995) 65–79.

Bruns, J. Edgar
"Some Reflections on Coheleth and John," *CBQ* 25 (1963) 414–16.

Buchanan, Alastair
The Essence of Ecclesiastes in the metre of Omar Khayyám (London: 1904).

Bunge, Gabriel
"'Der mystische Sinn der Schrift': Anlässlich der Veröffentlichung der Scholien zum Ecclesiasten des Evagrios Pontikos," *Studia Monastica* 36 (1994) 135–46.

Burkitt, F. Crawford
Ecclesiastes Rendered into English Verse (2d ed.; London: 1922).

Burrows, Millar
"Kuhn and Koheleth," *JBL* 46 (1927) 90–97.

Calandra, Gregorius
De historica Andreae Victorini expositione in Ecclesiasten (Panormi: 1948).

Cervera, Jordi
"Una lectura postmoderna de l'Eclesiastès," *Estudios franciscana* 91 (1990) 297–340.

Chomarat, Jacques
Desiderius Erasmus: Ecclesiastes (2 vols.; New York: North-Holland, 1991–1994).

Chopineau, Jacques
"Qoheleth's Modernity," *TD* 29 (1981) 117–18.

Christianson, Eric S.
"Qoheleth and the Existential Legacy of the Holocaust," *HeyJ* 38 (1997) 35–50.

Craigie, Peter C.
"Biblical Wisdom in the Modern World II: Ecclesiastes," *Crux* 16 (1980) 8–10.

Crenshaw, James Lee
"Ecclesiastes: Odd Book In," *BRev* 6 (1990) 28–33.

Curpratrick, Stephan
"A Disciple for Our Time: A Conversation," *Int* 55 (2001) 285–91.

Custer, John S.
"Qoheleth and the Canon: The Dissenting Voice in Dialogue," *Josephinum Journal of Theology* 1 (1994) 15–24.

Defélix, Chantal
"Qohélet dans la tradition juive," *LumVie* 221 (1995) 19–31.

Dell, Katharine J.
"Ecclesiastes as Wisdom: Consulting Early Interpreters," *VT* 44 (1994) 301–29.

Deppe, Klaus, ed.
Kohelet in der syrischen Dichtung: Drei Gedichte über das Kohelet-Buch von Afrēm, Jakob von Sarug und Johannes von Mossul (GOF.S 6; Wiesbaden: Harrassowitz, 1975).

Didymus the Blind
Kommentar zum Ecclesiastes (Tura-Papyrus): Kommentar zu Eccl. Kap. 1,1–2,14: Einleitung, Text, Übersetzung, Indices (ed. Gerhard Binder and Leo Liesenborghs; PTA 25; Bonn: Habelt, 1979); *Kommentar zu Eccl. Kap. 1,1–2,14: Erläuterungen* (ed. Gerhard Binder; PTA 26; Bonn: Habelt, 1983); *Kommentar zu Eccl. Kap. 3,1–4,12* (ed. Michael Gronewald; PTA 22; Bonn: Habelt, 1977); *Kommentar zu Eccl. Kap. 5 und 6* (ed. Johannes Kramer; PTA 13; Bonn: Habelt, 1970); *Kommentar zu Eccl. Kap. 7,1–8,8* (ed. Johannes Kramer and Bärbel Krebber; PTA 16; Bonn: Habelt, 1972); *Kommentar zu Eccl. Kap. 9,8–10,12* (ed. Michael Gronewald; PTA 9; Bonn: Habelt, 1979); *Kommentar zu Eccl. Kap. 11–12* (ed. Gerhard Binder and Leo Liesenborghs; PTA 24; Bonn: Habelt, 1969).

Diego Sánchez, Manuel
"El 'Comentario al Eclesiastés' de Didimo Alejandrino," *Teresianum* 41 (1990) 231–42.

Diego Sánchez, Manuel
El 'Comentario al Eclesiastés' de Dídimo Alejandrino: Exégesis y espiritualidad (Studia theologica Teresianum 9; Rome: Teresianum, 1991).

Dillmann, Rainer
"Hat Leben Sinn? Exegetische Überlegungen zu Kohelet—Aktualisierungsmöglichkeiten," *KatBl* 113 (1988) 561–69.

Doré, Daniel
"Qohélet: Le Siracide ou l'Ecclésiaste et l'Ecclésiastique," *Cahiers Evangile* 91 (1995).

Droz, Eugénie
"L'Ecclésiaste de Théodore de Bèze et ses éditions allemandes (1599 et 1605)," *RHPhR* 47 (1967) 338–46.

Durandeaux, Jacques
Une foi sans névrose? Ou l'actualité de Qohéleth (Paris: Cerf, 1987).

Einstein, Bertold, ed.
R. Josef Kara und sein Commentar zu Kohelet: Aus dem Ms. 104 der Bibliothek des Jüdisch-Theologischen Seminars zu Breslau (Berlin: Mampe, 1886).

Ellermeier, Friedrich
"Randbemerkung zur Kunst des Zitierens," *ZAW* 77 (1965) 93–94.

Ellul
Reason for Being.

Ellul, Jacques
"Le statut de la philosophie dans Qohelet," *AF* 53 (1985) 151–64.

Eppenstein, Simon
Aus dem Kohelet-Kommentar des Tanchum Jerushalmi (Berlin: 1888).

Erdrich, Louise
"The Preacher," in Christina Büchmann and Celina Spiegel, eds., *Out of the Garden: Women Writers on the Bible* (London: Pandora, 1995) 234–37.

Etlinger, Gerhard, H.
"The Form and Method of the Commentary on Ecclesiastes by Gregory of Agrigentum," in Elizabeth A. Livingstone, ed., *Papers of the Ninth International Conference on Patristic Studies: Oxford 1983* (StPatr 18/1; Leuven: Peeters, 1985) 317–20.

Eybers, Ian Heinrich
"The 'Canonization' of the Song of Solomon, Ecclesiastes and Esther," in Wouter Cornelus van Wyk, ed., *Aspects of the Exegetical Process* (OTWSA 20/21; Pretoria: NHW, 1979) 33–52.

Felton, Jacob
"Koheleth—A Re-interpretation," *Dor le Dor* 5 (1976/77) 29–34, 143–47.

Ferguson, Everett
"Some Aspects of Gregory of Nyssa's Interpretation of Scripture Exemplified in his *Homilies on Ecclesiastes*," in Elizabeth A. Livingstone, ed., *11th International Conference on Patristic Studies: Oxford 1991* (StPatr 27; Leuven: Peeters, 1993) 29–33.

Festorazzi, Franco
"La dimensione salvifica del binomio morte-vita (Qohelet e Sapienza)," *RivB* 30 (1982) 91–109.

Forbush, William Byron
Ecclesiastes in the Metre of Omar: With an Introductory Essay on Ecclesiastes and the Rubáiyát (Boston: Houghton, Mifflin, 1906).

Géhin, Paul, ed.
Évagre le Pontique, Scholies à l'Ecclésiaste (SC 397; Paris: Cerf, 1993).

Géhin, Paul
"Un nouvel inédit d'Evagre le Pontique: Son commentaire de l'Ecclésiaste," *Byz.* 49 (1979) 188–98.

Geier, Martin
In Salomonis Regis Israel Ecclesiasten Commentarius (2d ed.; Lipsiae: 1668).

Gire, Pierre
"Qohélet: L'espérance mendiante," *LumVie* 221 (1995) 41–54.

Gómez Aranda, Mariano
"Ecl 12,1–7 interpretado por Abraham Ibn 'Ezra," *Sef* 52 (1992) 113–21.

Gómez Aranda, Mariano
El comentario de Abraham ibn Ezra al libro del Eclesiastés (TECC 56; Madrid: CSIC, 1994).

Gómez Aranda, Mariano
"Grammatical Remarks in the Commentary of Abraham Ibn Ezra on Qohelet," *Sef* 56 (1996) 62–82.

Gómez Aranda, Mariano
"Teorias astronómicas y astrológicas en el Comentario de Abraham Ibn Ezra al libro del Eclesiastés," *Sef* 55 (1995) 257–72.

Gregorio, Domenico de
Gli insegnamenti teologici di S. Gregorio di Agrigento nel suo 'Commento all'Ecclesiaste' (Rome: Pontificio Ateno "Antonianum," 1989).

Guillod-Reymond, Daphné
"Echo à Qohéleth 3,18-22 dans le Nouveau Testament: Avec 2 Corinthiens 4,7-15," *Lire et Dire* 32 (1997) 12–14.

Guillod-Reymond, Daphné
"Echo à Qohéleth 4,17–5,6 dans le Nouveau Testament: Avec Matthieu 7,7-11," *Lire et Dire* 32 (1997) 24–26.

Guillod-Reymond, Daphné
"Echo à Qohéleth 5,9-17 dans le Nouveau Testament: Avec Luc 18,18-30," *Lire et Dire* 32 (1997) 32–34.

Guillod-Reymond, Daphné
"Echo à Qohéleth 8,16-17 dans le Nouveau Testament: Avec Marc 4,10-13," *Lire et Dire* 32 (1997) 41–43.

Hall, Joseph
Solomon's divine arts: Joseph Hall's representation of Proverbs, Ecclesiastes, and Song of Songs (1609) (Pilgrim Classic Commentaries; Cleveland: Pilgrim 1991).

Hall, Stuart G., ed.
Gregory of Nyssa: Homilies on Ecclesiastes: An English Version with Supporting Studies (New York: de Gruyter, 1993).

Hart, Thomas M.
"Advice on Marriage," *TBT* 32 (1994) 349–52.

Hayman, Allison Peter
"Qohelet and the Book of Creation," *JSOT* 50 (1991) 93–111.

Hayman, Allison Peter
"Qohelet, the Rabbis and the Wisdom Text from the Cairo Geniza," in A. Graeme Auld, ed., *Understanding Poets and Prophets: Essays in Honour of George Wishart Anderson* (JSOTSup 152; Sheffield: Sheffield Academic Press, 1993) 149–65.

Heard, R. Christopher
"The Dao of Qoheleth: An Intertextual Reading of the Daode Jing and the Book of Ecclesiastes," *Jian Dao* 5 (1996) 65–93.

Heer, Josef
"Ein Buch, doch viele Deutungen: Drei Interpretationsrichtungen des Buches Kohelet," *BiHe* 21 (1985) 52–53.

Heinen, Karl
"Kohelet: Ein Aussenseiter des Jahweglaubens," *BiHe* 21 (1985) 54–56.

Heinisch, P.
"Prediger und Weisheit Salomos," *Kath.* 90 (1910) 32–54.

Hessler, Bertram
"Der verhüllte Gott: Der heilstheologische Sinn des Buches Ecclesiastes (Kohelet)," *ThGl* 43 (1953) 347–359, trans. "Kohelet: The Veiled God," *Bridge* 1 (1955) 191–206.

Hirshman, M.
"The Greek Fathers and the Aggada on Ecclesiastes: Formats of Exegesis in Late Antiquity," *HUCA* 59 (1988) 137–65.

Holm-Nielsen, Svend
"On the Interpretation of Qoheleth in Early Christianity," *VT* 24 (1974) 168–77.

Holm-Nielsen, Svend
"The Book of Ecclesiastes and the Interpretation of It in Jewish and Christian Theology," *ASTI* 10 (1975/76) 38–96.

Hungs, F.-J.
Ist das Leben sinnlos? Bibelarbeit mit dem Buch Kohelet (Prediger) (Zurich: Benziger, 1980).

Iovino, Paolo
"'Omnia vanitas': Da Qohelet a Paolo," in Bellia and Passaro, eds., *Qohelet*, 337–56.

James, Kenneth W.
"Ecclesiastes: Precursor of Existentialists," *TBT* 22 (1984) 85–90.

Janecko, Benedict
"The Wisdom Tradition and Mid-Life," *TBT* 30 (1992) 213–17.

Japhet, S., and R. B. Salters, eds.
The Commentary of R. Samuel ben Meir, Rashbam, on Qoheleth (Jerusalem: Magnes; Leiden: Brill, 1985).

Jarick, John
"Gregory Thaumaturgos' Paraphrase of Ecclesiastes," *AbrN* 27 (1989) 37–57.

Jarick, John
Gregory Thaumaturgos' Paraphrase of Ecclesiastes
(SBLSCS 29; Atlanta: Scholars Press, 1990).

Jarick, John
"Theodore of Mopsuestia and the Interpretation
of Ecclesiastes," in M. Daniel, R. Carroll, et al.,
eds., *The Bible in Human Society: Essays in Honour of
John Rogerson* (JSOTSup 200; Sheffield: Sheffield
Academic Press, 1995) 306–16, repr. in Leonard J.
Greenspoon and Olivier Munnich, eds., *VIII Con-
gress of the International Organization for Septuagint
and Cognate Studies: Paris 1992* (SBLSCS 41;
Atlanta: Scholars Press, 1995) 367–85.

Jasper, F. N.
"Ecclesiastes: A Note for Our Time," *Int* 21 (1967)
259–73.

Keller, Rudolf
"Die Versuchung der Hirten—August Vilmar über
Kohelet," *Lutherische Kirche in der Welt* 37 (1990)
13–24.

Kern, Udo
" '. . . dass ein Mensch fröhlich sei in seiner
Arbeit' (Prediger 3,22): Theologische Überlegungen zur Arbeit," *ThLZ* 119 (1994) 209–22.

King, Nicholas
" 'The Hand of the Lord Has Touched Me': Job,
Qoheleth, and the Wisdom of Solomon," *Way* 22
(1982) 235–44.

Kleinhans, Robert G.
"Ecclesiastes sive de Ratione Concionandi," in
Richard L. De Molen, ed., *Essays on the Works of
Erasmus: FS Craig R. Thompson* (New Haven: Yale
Univ. Press, 1978) 253–66.

Kraus, Matthew
"Christians, Jews and Pagans in Dialogue: Jerome
on Ecclesiastes 12:1-7," *HUCA* 70–71 (1999–2000)
183–231.

Kreitzer, Larry J.
*The Old Testament in Fiction and Film: On Reversing
the Hermeneutical Flow* (BiSe 24; Sheffield:
Sheffield Academic Press, 1994).

Labate, Antonio
*Catena Hauniensis in Ecclesiasten in qua saepe exege-
sis servatur Dionysii Alexandrini* (CChrSG 24; Tourn-
hout: Brepols, 1992).

Labate, Antonio
"Il recupero del 'Commentario all' Ecclesiaste' die
Dionisi Alessandrino attraverso le catene bizan-
tine," *Koinonia* 16 (1992) 53–74.

Labate, Antonio
"L'apporto della catena Hauniensis sull'Ecclesiaste
per il testo delle versioni greche di Simmaco e
della LXX," *RivB* 35 (1987) 57–61.

Labate, Antonio
"La catena sull'Ecclesiaste del cod. Barb. gr. 388,"
Aug 19 (1979) 333–39.

Labate, Antonio
"Nuove catene esegetiche sull'Ecclesiaste," in
ANTIDWRON: FS Maurits Geerard (Wetteren: Cul-
tura, 1984) 241–63.

Labate, Antonio
"Sui due frammenti di Ippolito all' Ecclesiaste,"
VetChr 23 (1986) 177–81.

Labate, Antonio
"Sulla catena all' Ecclesiaste die Policronio," in
Elizabeth A. Livingstone, ed., *Papers of the 1983
Oxford Patristics Conference,* vol. 1 (StPatr 18.2; Kala-
mazoo: Cistercian, 1989) 21–35.

Lange, Armin
"Eschatological Wisdom in the Book of Qoheleth
and the Dead Sea Scrolls," in Lawrence H. Schiff-
man, Emanuel Tov, and James C. VanderKam, eds.,
*The Dead Sea Scrolls: Fifty Years after Their Discovery:
Proceedings of the Jerusalem Congress, July 20–25,
1997* (Jerusalem: Israel Exploration Society, 2000)
817–25.

Leanza, Sandro
"A proposito di una recente edizione del presunto
'Commentario all' Ecclesiaste' di Evagrio Pontico,"
Rivista di storia e letteratura religiosa 33 (1997)
365–98.

Leanza, Sandro
"Due nuovi frammenti dionisiani sull' 'Ecclesiaste,' " *Orph.* 6 (1985) 156–61.

Leanza, Sandro
"Eccl 12,1-7: L'interpretazione escatologica dei
Padri e degli esegeti medievali," *Aug* 18 (1978)
191–208.

Leanza, Sandro, ed., *Gregorio di Nissa: Omelie sull'
Ecclesiaste* (Collana di testi patristici 86; Rome:
Città Nuova, 1990).

Leanza, Sandro
"I condizionamenti dell' esegesi patristica: Un caso
sintomatico: L' interpretazione di Qohelet," *RStB* 2
(1990) 25–50.

Leanza, Sandro
"L' atteggiamento della più antica esegesi cristiana
dinanzi all' epicureismo et edonismo di Qohelet,"
Orph. 3 (1982) 73–90.

Leanza, Sandro
L'esegesi di Origene al libro dell'Ecclesiaste (Reggio
Calabria: Parallelo, 1975).

Leanza, Sandro
"L' esegesi patristica di Qohelet da Melitone di
Sardi alle compilazioni catenarie," in Franco Bolgiani, ed., *Lettura cristiane dei Libri Sapienziali: XX
incontro di studiosi della antichità cristiana, 9–11
maggio 1991* (St. Eph. Aug. 37; Rome: Institutum
Patristicum Augustinianum, 1992) 237–50.

Leanza, Sandro
"Le catene esegetiche sull' Ecclesiaste," *Aug* 17
(1977) 545–52.

Leanza, Sandro
"Le tre versioni geronimiane dell' Ecclesiaste,"
ASEs 4 (1987) 87–108.

Leanza, Sandro
"Pour une réédition des Scolies à l' Ecclésiaste de
Denys d' Alexandrie," in Jean Pouilloux, ed., *ALE-
CANDRINA: Hellénisme, judaisme et christianisme à
Alexandrie: FS P. Claude Mondésert* (Paris: Cerf,
1987) 239–46.

Leanza, Sandro
  "Sul Commentario all' Ecclesiaste di Girolamo: Il
  problema esegetico," in Yves-Marie Duval, ed.,
  *Jérôme entre l' Occident et l' Orient (Actes du colloque
  de Chantilly, septembre 1986)* (EtAug 34; Paris:
  Études Augustiniennes, 1988) 267–82.

Leanza, Sandro
  "Sull' autenticità degli scolii origeniani della 'Catena sull' Ecclesiaste' di Procopio di Gaza," in Henri
  Crouzel and Antonio Quacquarelli, eds., *Origeni-
  ana Secunda: Second colloque international des études
  origéniennes (Bari, 20–23 septembre 1977)* (Quaderni
  di VetChr 15; Rome: Edizioni dell' Ateneo, 1980)
  363–69.

Leanza, Sandro
  "Sulle fonti del commentario all' Ecclesiaste di
  Girolamo," *ASEs* 3 (1985/86) 173–99.

Leanza, Sandro
  "Un capitolo sulla fortuna del 'Commentario all'
  Ecclesiaste' di Girolamo," *Civiltà classica e cristiana*
  6 (1985) 357–89.

Leanza, Sandro
  *Un nuovo testimone della Catena sull' Ecclesiaste di
  Procopio di Gaza: Il Cod. Vindob. Theol. Gr. 147*
  (CChrSG 4 Sup; Turnhout: Brepols; Leuven:
  Leuven Univ. Press, 1983).

Lee, Archie C. C.
  "Death and the Perception of the Divine in Qohelet and Zhuang Zi," *Ching Feng* 38 (1995) 69–81.

Lehmann, T.
  "'Der Prediger' als Prediger für die Gegenwart,"
  Magazin für evangelische Theologie und Kirche 38
  (1910) 351–66.

Leimdörfer, David
  *Die Lösung des Koheleträtsels durch den Philosophen
  Baruch Ibn Baruch im 16. Jahrhundert* (Berlin: 1900).

Levine, Étan
  "Ecclesiastes in New England," *Journal of Reform
  Judaism* 28 (1981) 60–64.

Liesenborghs, Leo, ed.
  Didymus der Blinde: Kommentar zum Ecclesiastes
  (Cologne: Liesenborghs, 1965).

Lohfink, Norbert
  "Les épilogues du livre de Qohélet et les débuts
  du Canon," in Pietro Bovati et Roland Meynet,
  eds., *Ouvrir les écritures: Mélanges offerts à Paul
  Beauchamp* (LD 162; Paris: Cerf, 1995) 77–96.

Lucà, Santo, ed.
  *Anonymus in Ecclesiasten commentarius qui dicitur
  Catena trium patrum* (CChrSG 11; Turnhout:
  Brepols; Leuven: Leuven Univ. Press, 1983).

Lucà, Santo
  "Gli scolii sull'Ecclesiaste del Vallicelliano greco E
  21," *Aug* 19 (1979) 287–96.

Lucà, Santo
  "Nilo d' Ancira sull' Ecclesiaste: Dieci scolii
  sconosciuti," *Bib* 60 (1979) 237–46.

Lucchesi, Enzo
  "Les homélies sur l'Ecclésiaste de Gregoire de
  Nysse," *VC* 36 (1982) 292–93.

Luck, Ulrich
  "Das Weltverständnis in der jüdischen Apokalyptik," *ZThK* 73 (1976) 283–305.

Malchow, Bruce V.
  "Qoheleth and Jesus," *TBT* 31 (1993) 110–15.

Maly, Eugene
  "Qoheleth and Advent," *Worship* 35 (1960) 26–29.

Mangan, Céline
  "Some Similarities between Targum Job and
  Targum Qohelet," in D. R. G. Beattie and M. J.
  McNamara, eds., *The Aramaic Bible: Targums in
  Their Historical Context* (JSOTSup 166; Sheffield:
  Sheffield Academic Press, 1994) 349–53.

Mann, Jakob
  "Early Karaite Bible Commentaries," *JQR* 12
  (1921/22) 435–526.

Manns, Frédéric
  "Le Targum de Qohelet—Manuscrit Urbinati 1:
  Traduction et commentaire," *SBFLA* 42 (1992)
  145–98.

Marböck, Johannes
  "Kohelet und Sirach: Eine vielschichtige
  Beziehung," in Schwienhorst-Schönberger, ed., *Das
  Buch Kohelet*, 275–301.

Mateo Seco, Lucas F.
  "'ὁ εὔκαιρος θάνατος': Consideraciones en torno
  a la muerte en las homilias al Eclesiastés de Gregorio de Nisa," *Scripta theologica* 23 (1991) 921–37.

Mendelssohn, Moses
  *Der Prediger Salomo mit einer kurzen und zureichenden
  Erklärung . . .* (Ansbach: Jacob Christoph Posch,
  1771).

Merkin, Daphne
  "Ecclesiastes," in David Rosenberg, ed., *Congregation: Contemporary Writers Read the Jewish Bible* (San
  Diego: Harcourt, Brace and Jovanovich, 1987)
  393–405.

[Midrash] *Kohelet Rabbah*
  (Jerusalem: Makhon Midrash Rabbah ha-Mevoar,
  1992) (Heb.).

Molina, Jean-Pierre
  "Jésus ben Qohélet," in Olivier Abel and Françoise
  Smyth, eds., *Le Livre de traverse: De l'exégèse biblique
  à l'anthropologie* (Patrimoines; Paris: Cerf, 1992)
  237–56.

Molina, Jean-Pierre
  "L'Ecclésiaste et l'Ecclésioclaste," *LumVie* 211
  (1995) 55–67.

Moriarty, Rachel
  "Human Owners, Human Slaves: Gregory of
  Nyssa, Hom. Eccl. 4," in Elizabeth A. Livingstone,
  ed., *11th International Conference on Patristic Studies:
  Oxford 1991* (StPatr 27; Leuven: Peeters, 1993)
  62–69.

Moyise, Steve
  "Is life futile? Paul and Ecclesiastes," *ExpT* 108
  (1997) 178–79.

Murphy, Roland E.
  "Qohelet Interpreted: The Bearing of the Past on
  the Present," *VT* 32 (1982) 331–37.

Negele, Manfred

"Ein Skeptiker im Alten Testament: Das Buch Kohelet philosophisch gelesen," in Stefan Schreiber and Alois Stimpfle, eds., *Johannes aenigmaticus: Studien zum Johannesevangelium für Herbert Leroy* (Biblische Untersuchungen 29; Regensburg: Friedrich Pustet, 2000) 13–30.

Nerses of Lampron

Erklärung des "Versammlers" (armenisch), ed. and trans. Max Herzog von Sachsen (Leipzig: 1929).

Nichols, Francis W.

"Samuel Beckett and Ecclesiastes on the Borders of Belief," *Encounter* 45 (1984) 11–22.

Noakes, K. W.

"The Metaphrase on Ecclesiastes of Gregory Thaumaturgus," in Elizabeth A. Livingstone, ed., *Papers Presented to the Seventh International Conference on Patristic Studies: Oxford 1975* (StPatr 15; Leuven: Peeters, 1984) 196–99.

Opelt, I.

"Der Kommentar zum Ecclesiastes, der Salonius von Genf zugeschrieben wird," in Franco Bolgiani, ed., *Letture cristiane dei Libri Sapienziali: XX incontro di studiosi della antichità cristiana, 9–11 maggio 1991* (St. Eph. Aug. 37; Rome: Institutum Patristicum Augustinianum, 1992) 251–64.

Pampaloni, Massimo

"O gesto interrompido e o grão de trigo: Reflexões sobre a morte e sobre o morrer a partir do Qohelet e do mistério pascal," *Perspectiva Teológica* 33 (2001) 87–104.

Paulson, Gail N.

"The Use of Qoheleth in Bonhoeffer's 'Ethics,'" *Word & World* 18 (1998) 307–13.

Peter, C. B.

"In Defence of Existence: A Comparison Between Ecclesiastes and Albert Camus," *Bangalore Theological Forum* 12 (1978) 26–43.

Piras, Antonio

"A proposito di una citazione pregieronimiana di Qoh 3,15-16 in Lucifero di Cagliari, Ath. 1,35,19s," in Francesco Atzeni and Tonino Cabizzosu, eds., *Studi in onore di Ottorino Pietro Alberti* (Saggi e ricerche 1; Cagliari: Edizioni della Torre, 1998) 73–84.

Puech, Émile

"Qohelet a Qumran," in Bellia and Passaro, eds., *Qohelet*, 144–70.

Pury, Albert de

"Qohélet et le canon des *Ketubim*," *RThPh* 131 (1999) 163–98, repr. in Rose, ed., *Situer Qohélet*, 75–110.

Quacquarelli, Antonio

"La lettura patristica di Qoèlet," *VetChr* 29 (1992) 5–18.

Rabinovitch, Gérard, ed.

L'Ecclésiaste: Traduit de l'hébreu par Louis-Isaac Lemaître de Sacy (Paris: Mille et une Nuits, 1994).

Raurell, Frederic

"Dimensione etico-pedagogica della provocazione nel 'Qohelet,'" *Laur.* 33 (1992) 375–402.

Rosin, Robert

Reformers, The Preacher, and Skepticism: Luther, Brenz, Melanchthon, and Ecclesiastes (Mainz: von Zabern, 1997).

Rothuizen, G. Th.

Scherven brengen geluk: Het ethos van Prediker (Baarn: Ten Have, 1983).

Rottzoll, Dirk U.

Abraham Ibn Esras Kommentar zu den Büchern Kohelet, Ester und Rut (Studia Judaica 12; New York: de Gruyter, 1999) [on this cf. Hanna Liss, "Dirk U. Rottzoll, Abraham Ibn Esras Kommentar zu den Büchern Qohelet, Ester und Rut," *BN* 99 (1999) 14–19].

Ruler, A. A. van

Dwaasheden in het leven: Het boek Prediker in morgenwijdingen (2 vols.; Nijkerk: Callenbach, 1966).

Sacchi, Paolo

"Da Qohelet al tempo di Gesù: Alcune linee del pensiero giudaico," in Wolfgang Haase, ed., *Religion (Judentum: Allgemeines; Palästinisches Judentum)* (*ANRW* II.19.1; New York: de Gruyter, 1979) 3–32.

Salters, Robert B.

"A gloss in Rashbam on Qohelet," *JQR* 86 (1996) 407–08.

Salters, Robert B.

"L'Exégèse de Rashi et de Rashbam sur l'Ecclésiaste," *REJ* 149 (1990) 507–19.

Salters, Robert B.

"Notes on the History of Interpretation of Koh 5,5," *ZAW* 90 (1978) 95–101.

Salters, Robert B.

"Notes on the Interpretation of Qoh 6,2," *ZAW* 91 (1979) 282–89.

Salters, Robert B.

"Observations on the Commentary on Qoheleth by R. Samuel ben Meir," *Her.* 127 (1979) 51–62.

Salters, Robert B.

"Qoheleth and the Canon," *ExpT* 86 (1975) 339–42.

Salters, Robert B.

"The Mediaeval French Glosses of Rashbam on Qoheleth and Song of Songs," in Elizabeth Anne Livingstone, ed., *Studia Biblica 1978* (JSOTSup 11; Sheffield: JSOT Press, 1979) 249–52.

Sandberg, Ruth N.

Rabbinic Views of Qohelet (Lewiston, N.Y.: Mellen, 1999).

Savigni, Raffaele

"Il commentario di Alcuino al libro dell'Ecclesiaste e il suo significato nella cultura carolingia," in Franco Bolgiani, ed., *Letture cristiane dei Libri Sapienziali: XX incontro di studiosi della antichità cristiana, 9–11 maggio 1991* (St. Eph. Aug. 37; Rome: Institutum Patricicum Augustinianum, 1992) 275–303.

Sawicki, Franz

    Der Prediger, Schopenhauer und Ed. v. Hartmann oder Biblischer und moderner Pessimismus (Fulda: 1903).

Schwartz, Matthew

    "Koheleth and Camus: Two Views of Achievement," *Judaism* 35 (1986) 29–34.

Seidel, Martin

    "Was soll's? Gespräch mit dem Buch Kohelet angesichts der gegenwärtigen Sinnkrise," *Christenlehre* 48 (1995) 479–84.

Sen, Felipe

    "El pensamiento judío: Influencia de Qohelet," *CuBi* 37 (1980) 233–37.

Sheridan, Sybil

    "The Five Megilloth," in Stephen Bigger, ed., *Creating the Old Testament* (Oxford: Blackwell, 1989) 293–317.

Siclari, Alberto

    "La dottrina della 'doppia creazione' nelle Omelie sull'Ecclesiaste di Gregorio di Nissa," in Franco Bolgiani, ed., *Letture cristiane dei Libri Sapienziali: XX incontro di studiosi della antichità cristiana, 9–11 maggio 1991* (St. Eph. Aug. 37; Rome: Institutum Patristicum Augustinianum, 1992) 251–64.

Sitwell, G.

    "A Fourteenth-Century English Poem on Ecclesiastes," *Dominican Studies* 3 (1950) 285–90.

Smalley, Beryl

    Medieval Exegesis of Wisdom Literature (ed. Roland E. Murphy; Scholars Press Reprints and Translations Series; Atlanta: Scholars Press, 1987).

Spangenberg, Izak J. J.

    "Galileo Galilei en die boek Prediker: 'n les uit die kerksgeschiedenis," *Theologia evangelica* (Pretoria) 26 (1993) 121–31.

Steyn, J. J.

    "Die boek Prediker: Alles is nie sinnloos nie!" *SK* 21 (2000) 326–34.

Storr, R.

    "Anleitung zu Predigten aus dem Buche des Predigers," *Kirche und Kanzel* 6 (1923) 163–68.

Strauss, Hans

    "Erwägungen zur seelsorgerlichen Dimension von Kohelet 12,1-7," *ZThK* 78 (1981) 267–75.

Streza, Sergiu

    Storia dell'esegesi del libro dell'Ecclesiaste nei Padri (fino a Origene) (Rome: Pontificia Universita Gregoriana, 1992).

Strothmann, Werner

    "Der Kohelet-Kommentar des Theodor von Mopsuestia," in Manfred Görg, ed., *Religion im Erbe Ägyptens: FS Alexander Böhlig* (ÄAT 14; Wiesbaden: Harrassowitz, 1988) 186–96.

Strothmann, Werner, ed.

    Das syrische Fragment des Ecclesiastes-Kommentars von Theodor von Mopsuestia (GOF.S 28; Wiesbaden: Harrassowitz, 1988).

Strothmann, Werner, ed.

    Der Kohelet-Kommentar des Dionysius bar Salibi: Auslegung des Septuaginta-Textes (GOF.S 31; Wiesbaden: Harrassowitz, 1988).

Strothmann, Werner, ed.

    Der Kohelet-Kommentar des Johannes von Apamea (GOF.S 30; Wiesbaden: Harrassowitz, 1988).

Strothmann, Werner, ed.

    Syrische Katenen aus dem Ecclesiastes-Kommentar des Theodor von Mopsuestia (GOF.S 29; Wiesbaden: Harrassowitz, 1988).

Támez, Elsa

    "De silencios y gritos: Job y Qohólet en los noventa," *Pasos* 82 (1999) 1–6.

Taradach, Madeleine

    "La figure insolite de Salomon dans TgQo 1,12 dans les Talmuds et quelques Midrasim," in Frederic Raubell et al., eds., *Tradició i Traducció de la Paraula: Mischellània Guia Camps* (SDM 47; Monserrat: Associació Biblica de Catalunya–Publicacions del'Abadia de Montserrat, 1993) 325–35.

Templeton, Douglas A.

    "A 'Farced Epistol' to a Sinking Sun of David: Ecclesiastes and Finnnegans Wake," in Robert P. Carroll, ed., *Text as Pretext: Essays in Honour of Robert Davidson* (JSOTSup 138; Sheffield: JSOT Press, 1992) 282–90.

Thurn, Hans

    "Zum Text des Hieronymos-Kommentars zum Kohelet," *BZ* 33 (1989) 234–44.

Tidball, Derek

    That's Life! Realism and Hope for Today from Ecclesiastes (Leicester: Inter-Varsity, 1992).

Uricchio, Francesco

    "'Vanità delle vanità e tutto è vanità' (Eccle 12,8) nella lettura evangelica di S. Francesco (I Reg. 8,7)," *Miscellanea francescana* 84 (1984) 490–543.

Vajda, Georges

    Deux commentaires Karaïtes sur l'Ecclésiaste (Études sur la judaisme médiéval IV; Leiden: Brill, 1971).

Vajda, Georges

    "Ecclésiaste XII 2-7, interprété par un auteur juif d'Andalousie du XIᵉ siècle," *JSS* 27 (1982) 33–46.

Vignes, Jean

    "Paraphrase et appropriation: Les avatars poétiques de l' Ecclesiaste au temps des Guerres de Religion," *Bibliothèque d'humanisme et renaissance* 55 (1993) 503–26.

Vinel, F., ed.

    Grégoire de Nysse, Homélies sur L'Ecclésiaste (SC 416; Paris: Cerf, 1996).

Vischer, Wilhelm

    Der Prediger Salomo im Spiegel des Michel de Montaigne: Ein Brevier (Pfullingen: Neske, 1981).

Vischer, Wilhelm

    "Der Prediger Salomo im Spiegel Michel de Montaigne's," *Jahrbuch der Theologische Schule Bethel* 4 (1933) 27–124.

Vischer, Wilhelm

    "L'Ecclesiaste, testimone di Christo Gesú," *Protest* 9 (1954) 1–19.

Vocht, Constant de

    "Deux manuscrits perdus de la Catena Trium Patrum in Ecclesiasten (CPGC 100)," *Byz.* 59 (1989) 264–66.

Vogel, D.
"Koheleth and the Modern Temper," *Tradition* 2 (1959) 82–92.

Voltaire, F. M. A.
Précis de l'Ecclésiaste, et du Cantique des Cantiques (Liège: Bassompierre, 1759).

Vonach, Andreas
"Der Ton macht die Musik: Vorgaben und Normen der Exegese bei Hieronymus und in der rabbinischen Tradition," *BN* 97 (1999) 37–44.

Wachten, Johannes
Midrasch-Analyse: Strukturen im Midrasch Qohelet Rabba (Judaistische Texte und Studien 8; Hildesheim: Olms, 1978).

Weidmann, Franz
Anstössige Denker (Frankfurt am Main: Fischer-Taschenbuch, 1990) 26–42.

Weinberg, Zvi
"Jakob Barth's Notes to the Consolation Chapters in Isaiah, Song of Songs and Ecclesiastes," *BethM* 31 (1985/86) 78–87 (Heb.).

Weiss, James
"Ecclesiastes and Erasmus: The Mirror and the Image," *ARG* 65 (1974) 83–108.

White, Graham
"Luther on Ecclesiastes and the Limits of Human Ability," *NZSTh* 29 (1987) 180–94.

Wichern, Frank B.
"'All is Vanity' Saith the Exhausted Executive: Ecclesiastes Counsels the Workaholic," *Eternity* 32 (1981) 23–24.

Wilch, John Robert
"Laubhüttenfest und Prediger Salomos: Freud und Ernst," *Friede über Israel* 58 (1975) 99–107.

Windel, Karl Albert R.
Luther als Exeget des Predigers Salomo (Lat. Hauptsch. Halle: 1897).

Wölfel, Eberhard
Luther und die Skepsis: Eine Studie zur Kohelet-Exegese Luthers (FGLP X,12; Munich: Kaiser, 1958).

Wuckelt, Agnes
"Über Leben lehren—Überlebenslehren: Kohelet und das Musical 'Hair,'" *KatBl* 113 (1988) 570–75.

Wünsche, August
Der Midrasch Kohelet (Bibliotheca Rabbinica I; Leipzig: Otto Schulze, 1880).

Wyk, W. C. van
"Die teologiese relevansie van die boek Prediker," *HvTSt* 45 (1989) 557–72.

Wyngaarden, Martin F.
"The Interpretation of Ecclesiastes," *Calvin Forum* 20 (1953–55) 157–60.

Zimmerli, Walther
"'Unveränderbare Welt' oder 'Gott ist Gott'? Ein Plädoyer für die Unaufgebbarkeit des Predigerbuches in der Bibel," in Hans Georg Geyer et al., eds., *Wenn nicht jetzt, wann dann? FS H.-J. Kraus* (Neukirchen-Vluyn: Neukirchener Verlag, 1983) 103–14.

Zschoch, Hellmut
"Martin Luthers Argumentation mit Eccl 7,21 in der Auseinandersetzung mit Jacobus Latomus," *Luther-Jahrbuch* 60 (1993) 17–38.

Language

Archer, Gleason L.
"The Linguistic Evidence for the Date of 'Ecclesiastes,'" *JETS* 12 (1969) 167–81.

Backhaus, Franz Josef
"Die Pendenskonstruktion im Buch Qohelet," *ZAH* 8 (1995) 1–30.

Bianchi, Francesco
"The Language of Qohelet: A Bibliographical Survey," *ZAW* 105 (1993) 210–23.

Böhl, Eduard
"De Aramaismis libri Coheleth: Dissertatio historica et philological" (Th.D. diss., Erlangen University, 1860).

Burkitt, J.
"Is Ecclesiastes a Translation?" *JTS* 23 (1922) 22–26.

Cazelles, H.
"Conjonctions de subordination dans la langue de Qohelet," *GLECS* 8 (1957–60) 21–22.

Ceresko, Anthony R.
"The Function of Antanaclasis (*mṣ'* 'to find' // *mṣ'* 'to reach, overtake, grasp') in Hebrew Poetry, Especially in the Book of Qoheleth," *CBQ* 44 (1982) 551–69.

Dahood, Mitchell
"Canaanite Words in Qoheleth 10,20," *Bib* 46 (1965) 210–12.

Dahood, Mitchell
"Canaanite-Phoenician Influence in Qoheleth," *Bib* 33 (1952) 30–52, 191–221.

Dahood, Mitchell
"The Language of Qoheleth," *CBQ* 14 (1952) 227–32.

Dahood, Mitchell
"Northwest Semitic Philology and Three Biblical Texts," *JNSL* 2 (1972) 17–22.

Dahood, Mitchell
"The Phoenician Background of Qoheleth," *Bib* 47 (1966) 264–82.

Dahood, Mitchell
"Qoheleth and Northwest Semitic Philology," *Bib* 43 (1962) 349–65.

Dahood, Mitchell
"Qoheleth and Recent Discoveries," *Bib* 39 (1958) 302–18.

Dahood, Mitchell
"Scriptio Defectiva in Qoheleth 4,10a," *Bib* 49 (1968) 243.

Davila, James R.
"Qoheleth and Northern Hebrew," in Edward M. Cook, ed., *Sopher Mahir: Northwest Semitic Studies Presented to Stanislav Segert* (*Maarav* 5-6; 1990) 69–87.

Delsman, Wilhelmus C.

"Die Inkongruenz im Buch Qohelet," in Karel Jongeling et al., eds., *Studies in Hebrew and Aramaic Syntax: Presented to Professor J. Hoftijzer* (Studies in Semitic Language and Linguistics 17; Leiden: Brill, 1991) 27–37.

Delsman, Wilhelmus C.

"Zur Sprache des Buches Koheleth," in W. C. Delsman et al., eds., *Von Kanaan bis Kerala: FS J. P. M. van der Ploeg* (AOAT 211; Kevelaer: Butzon & Bercker; Neukirchen-Vluyn: Neukirchener Verlag, 1982) 341–65.

Du Plessis, S. J.

"Aspects of Morphological Peculiarities of the Language of Qoheleth," in I. H. Eybers et al., eds., *De fructu oris sui*: *FS A. van Selms* (Pretoria Oriental Studies 9; Leiden: Brill, 1971) 164–80.

Fernández, Andrés

"Es Ecclesiastes una Versión?" *Bib* 3 (1922) 45–50.

Fredericks

Language.

Gordis, Robert

"Koheleth: Hebrew or Aramaic?" *JBL* 71 (1952) 93–109, repr. in Gordis, *Word*, 263–79.

Gordis, Robert

"Qoheleth and Qumran: A Study of Style," *Bib* 41 (1960) 395–410, repr. in Gordis, *Word*, 292–307.

Gordis, Robert

"The Original Language of Qohelet," *JQR* 37 (1946/47) 67–84, repr. in Gordis, *Word*, 231–48.

Gordis, Robert

"The Translation-Theory of Qohelet Re-examined," *JQR* 40 (1949/50) 103–16, repr. in Gordis, *Word*, 249–62.

Gordis, Robert

"Was Koheleth a Phoenician? Some Observations on Methods in Research," *JBL* 74 (1955) 103–14, repr. in Gordis, *Word*, 280–91.

Hays, J. Daniel

"Verb Forms in the Expository Discourse Sections of Ecclesiastes," *Journal of Translation and Textlinguistics* 7 (1995) 9–18.

Hurvitz, Avi

"Qoheleth's Language: Re-Evaluation of its Nature and Date," *HS* 31 (1990) 144–54.

Isaksson

Studies.

Joüon, Paul

"Notes de syntaxe hébraïque 2: L'emploi du participe et du parfait dans l'Ecclésiaste," *Bib* 2 (1921) 225–26.

Joüon, Paul

"Notes philologiques sur le texte hébreu d'Ecclésiaste," *Bib* 11 (1930) 419–25.

Lavoie, Jean-Jacques

"Étude de Quelques Mots Obscurs du Qohélet à la Lumière de l'Histoire de l'Exégèse et des Manuscrits Judéo-Persans de la Bibliothèque Nationale de France," *SR* 29 (2000) 183–97.

Lohfink, Norbert

"Kohelet übersetzen: Berichte aus einer Übersetzerwerkstatt," in Lohfink, *Studien*, 259–90.

Piotti, Franco

"La Lingua dell'Ecclesiaste e lo sviluppo storico dell'Ebraico," *BeO* 15 (1973) 185–96.

Piotti, Franco

"Osservazioni su alcuni usi linguistici dell'Ecclesiaste," *BeO* 19 (1977) 49–56.

Rudman, Dominic

"A Note on the Dating of Ecclesiastes," *CBQ* 61 (1999) 47–52.

Rudman, Dominic

"Qohelet's Use of *lpny*," *JNSL* 23 (1997) 143–50.

Schoors, Antoon

"Emphatic and Asseverative *kî* in Koheleth," in Herman L. J. Vastophout et al., eds., *Scripta signa vocis: FS J. H. Hospers* (Groningen: Forsten, 1986) 209–15.

Schoors

Preacher.

Schoors, Antoon

"The Pronouns in Qohelet," *HS* 30 (1989) 71–87.

Schoors, Antoon

"The Use of Vowel Letters in Qoheleth," *UF* 20 (1988) 277–86.

Schoors, Antoon

"The Verb *hāyâ* in Qoheleth," in David Penchansky and Paul Redditt, eds., *Shall Not the Judge of All the Earth Do What Is Right? Studies on the Nature of God in Tribute to James L. Crenshaw* (Winona Lake, Ind.: Eisenbrauns, 2000) 229–38.

Schoors, Antoon

"The Verb ראה in the Book of Qohelet," in Diesel et al., eds., *Jedes Ding*, 227–41.

Schoors, Antoon

"The Word אדם in Qoheleth," in Karel van Lerberghe and Antoon Schoors, eds., *Immigration and Emigration within the Ancient Near East: FS E. Lipiński* (OLA 65; Leuven: Peeters, 1995) 299–304.

Schoors, Antoon

"The word טוב in the Book of Qoheleth," in Manfried Dietrich and Ingo Kottsieper, eds. *"Und Mose schrieb dieses Lied auf": Studien zum Alten Testament und zum Alten Orient: FS Oswald Loretz* (AOAT 250; Münster: Ugarit, 1998) 685–700.

Schoors, Antoon

"Words Typical of Qohelet," in Schoors, ed., *Qohelet in the Context of Wisdom*, 17–39.

Schwarzschild, Roger

"The Syntax of אשר in Biblical Hebrew with Special Reference to Qoheleth," *HS* 31 (1990) 7–39.

Seow, Choon-Leong

"Linguistic Evidence and the Dating of Qohelet," *JBL* 115 (1996) 643–66.

Torrey, Charles C.

"The Question of the Original Language of Kohelet," *JQR* 39 (1948/49) 151–60.

Vílchez Líndez, José
"Lengua original de Qohelet," *EstBib* 50 (1992) 553–64.

Whitley, Charles F.
"Koheleth and Ugaritic Parallels," *UF* 11 [FS Claude F. A. Schaffer] (1979) 811–24.

Whitley
Koheleth.

Zer Kavod, Mordechai
"The Expressions ואלו־היה and החוטא in the Book of Qoheleth," *Bar Ilan* 9 (1971/72) 7–17 (Heb.).

Zimmermann, Frank
"The Aramaic Provenance of Qohelet," *JQR* 36 (1945/46) 17–45.

Zimmermann, Frank
"The Question of Hebrew in Qohelet," *JQR* 40 (1949/50) 79–102.

Text and Versions

Asmussen, Jes Peter
"Bemerkungen zu einer 'neuen' jüdisch-persischen Qohälät-Uebersetzung," in C. H. Fouchécour and P. Gignoux, eds., *Études irano-aryennes offertes à Gilbert Lazard* (StIr 7; Paris: Association pour l'avancement des Études iraniennes, 1989) 1–4.

Asmussen, Jes Peter
"Some Textual Problems in the Hebrew Bible and Their Treatment in Judaeo-Persian Versions," in J. Duchesne-Guillemin et al., *Studia Iranica: Papers in Honour of Mary Boyce* (Hommages 10; Leiden: Brill, 1985).

Bardsky, Krzysztof
"Księga Koheleta w przekładach św Hieronima: Diachroniczne aspekty pracy translacyjney" [St. Jerome's translations of the book of Qoheleth: Diachronic aspects in the work of translation], *CoTh* 69 (1999) 33–46.

Barthélemy, Dominique
Les devanciers d'Aquila (VTSup 10; Leiden: Brill, 1963).

Beckwith, Roger
"The Four Greek Versions of Ecclesiastes in Origen's *Hexapla*," in *The Old Testament Canon of the New Testament Church and Its Background in Early Judaism* (Grand Rapids: Eerdmans, 1985) 472–77.

Bertram, Georg
"Hebräischer und griechischer Qohelet: Ein Beitrag zur Theologie der hellenistischen Bibel," *ZAW* 64 (1952) 26–49.

Bosson, Nathalie
"Un palimpseste du Musée Copte du Caire," *Mus* 104 (1991) 5–37.

Cannon, W. W.
"Jerome and Symmachus: Some Points in the Vulgate Translation of Koheleth," *ZAW* 45 (1927) 191–99.

Chamiel, Chaim
"Luck, Destination, and Prayer in the Targum of Qohelet," *BethM 39* (1994) 261–68 (Heb.).

Chilton, Bruce
"The Targum of Qohelet," *JBL* 112 (1993) 337–39.

Clarke, Ernest G.
"Reflections on the Preparation of a Critical Edition of the Targum of Koheleth," *Textus* 16 (1991) 79–94.

[*Codex Leningradensis*]
The Leningrad Codex: A Facsimile Edition (ed. David Noel Freedman, Astrid B. Beck, and Bruce E. Zuckerman; Grand Rapids: Eerdmans, 1998).

Cook, Johann
"Aspects of the Relationship between the Septuagint Versions of Kohelet and Proverbs," in Schoors, ed., *Qohelet in Context*, 481–92.

Diebner, Bernd Jørg
"Die biblischen Texte des Hamburger Papyrus Bilinguis 1 (Cant, Lam Co., Eccl Gr. et Co.) in ihrem Verhältnis zum Text der Septuaginta besonders des Kodex B (Vat. Gr. 1209): Beobachtungen und methodische Bemerkungen," in Tito Orlandi and Frederik Wisse, eds., *Acts of the Second International Congress of Coptic Studies* (Rome: C.I.M., 1985) 59–74.

Diebner, Bernd Jørg, and Rodolphe Kasser, eds.
Hamburger Papyrus Bil. 1: Die altestamentlichen Texte des Papyrus Bilinguis 1 der Staats- und Universitätsbibliothek Hamburg (Cahiers d'orientalisme 18; Geneva: Cramer, 1989).

Diez Merino, Luis
Targum de Qohelet: Edición Príncipe del Ms. Villa-Amil No. 5 de Alfonso de Zamora (Bibliotheca Hispanica biblica 13; Madrid: Consejo Superior de Investigaciones Cientificas, 1987).

Dillmann, August
"Über die griechische Übersetzung des Kohelet," *SPAW* (1892) 3–16.

Euringer, Sebastian
Der Masorahtext des Koheleth kritisch untersucht (Leipzig: Hinrichs, 1890).

Ferrer, Joan, and Madeleine Taradach
Un Targum de Qohélet: Ms. M-2 de Salamanca (MoBi 37; Geneva: Labor et Fides, 1998).

Gwynn, R. M.
"Notes on the Vocabulary of Ecclesiastes in Greek," *Her.* 42 (1920) 115–22.

Hyvärinen, Kyösti
Die Übersetzung von Aquila (ConBOT 10; Lund: Gleerup, 1977).

Janichs, G.
Animadversiones criticae in versionem syriacam peschitthonianam librorum Koheleth et Ruth (Vratislaviae: 1871).

Jarick, John, ed.
A Comprehensive Bilingual Concordance of the Hebrew and Greek Texts of Ecclesiastes (SBLSCS 36; Atlanta: Scholars Press, 1993).

Jarick, John
"Aquila's Kohelet," *Textus* 15 (1990) 131–39.

Kamenetzky, Abraham Schalom
"Die P'šita zu Ḳoheleth," *ZAW* 24 (1904) 181–239.

Klostermann, Erich
 "De libri Coheleth versione Alexandrina" (Ph.D. diss., Universität Kiel, 1892).

Knobel, P. S.
 "Targum Qoheleth: A Linguistic and Exegetical Inquiry" (Ph.D. diss., Yale University, 1976).

Knobel, Peter S.
 "The Targum of Qoheleth," in Céline Mangan, John F. Healey, and Peter S. Knobel, *The Targum of Job–The Targum of Proverbs–The Targum of Qohelet* (Aramaic Bible 15; Collegeville, Minn.: Liturgical Press, 1991).

Komlosh, Yehuda
 "The Manner of Interpretation of Targum Qohelet," *Sinai* 54 (1964) 169–79 (Heb.).

Lagarde, P. de, ed.
 Hagiographa Chaldaice (Osnabrück: Zeller, [1873] repr. 1967).

Lane, David J.
 "Peshitta Institute Communication XV: 'Lilies that Fester . . .': The Peshitta Text of Qoheleth," *VT* 29 (1979) 481–90.

Lange, Nicholas de
 "A Greek Translation of Kohelet [Ecclesiastes]," in *Greek Jewish Texts from the Cairo Genizah* (TSAJ 51; Tübingen: Mohr [Siebeck], 1996) 71–78.

Lange, N. R. M. de
 "Two Genizah Fragments in Hebrew and Greek," in J. A. Emerton and S. C. Reif, eds., *Interpreting the Hebrew Bible: FS E. I. J. Rosenthal* (University of Cambridge Oriental Publications 32; Cambridge: Cambridge Univ. Press, 1982) 61–83.

Lavoie, Jean-Jacques, and Minoo Mehramoz
 "Quelques remarques sur les manuscrits judéo-persans du Qohélet de la Bibliothèque nationale de France," *Religiologiques* 17 (1998) 195–215.

Levine, Étan
 The Aramaic Version of Qohelet (2d ed.; New York: Sepher-Hermon, 1981).

Levine, Étan, ed.
 Targum to the Five Megillot: Ruth, Ecclesiastes, Canticles, Lamentations, Esther: Codex Vatican Urbinati I (Jerusalem: Makor, 1977).

Levy, A., ed.
 Das Targum zu Kohelet nach südarabischen Handschriften (Breslau: Fleischmann, 1905).

Mainz, E.
 "L'Ecclésiaste en judéo-persan," *StIr* 3 (1974) 221–28.

Mercer, S. A. B., ed.
 The Ethiopic Text of the Book of Ecclesiastes (Oriental Society Research Series 6; London: Luzac, 1931).

Montaner, Luis Vegas
 "El texto hebreo de Qohelet en la Biblia Poliglota Complutense: Sus fuentes," *MEAH* 26–28 (1977/79) 271–82.

Mopsik, Charles
 L'Ecclésiaste et son double araméen: Qohélet et son Targoum (Les Dix Paroles) (Lagrasse: Verdier, 1990).

Muilenburg, James
 "A Qoheleth Scroll from Qumran," *BASOR* 135 (1954) 20–28, repr. in James Muilenburg, *Hearing and Speaking the Word* (Chico, Calif.: Scholars Press, 1984) 375–83.

Nebe, G. Wilhelm
 "Qumranica I: Zu unveröffentlichten Handschriften aus Höhle 4 von Qumran," *ZAW* 106 (1994) 307–322 (312–13).

O'Callaghan, José
 "Frammenti antologici dell'Ecclesiaste, del Cantico dei Cantici e dell'Ecclesiastico (P. Palau Rib. inv. 225r)," *Atti del XVII Congresso Internazionale di Papirologia 1983, II* (Neapel: 1984) 357–65.

Paper, Herbert H.
 "Ecclesiastes in Judeo-Persian," *Or* 42 (1973) 328–37.

Salters, Robert B.
 "Observations on the Peshitta of Ecclesiastes," *OTE* 8 (1995) 388–97.

Salters, Robert B.
 "Observations on the Septuagint of Ecclesiastes," *OTE* 6 (1992/93) 163–74.

Salters, Robert B.
 "Observations on the Targum to Qoheleth," *JNSL* 24 (1998) 13–24.

Salters, Robert B.
 "Textual Criticism and Qoheleth," *JNSL* 23 (1997) 53–71.

Salters, Robert B.
 "The Word for 'God' in the Peshitta of Koheleth," *VT* 21 (1971) 251–54.

Schoors, Antoon
 "Kethib-Qere in Ecclesiastes," in Jan Qaegebeur, ed., *Orientalia Antiqua: FS Paul Naster,* vol. 2 (OLA 13; Leuven: Peeters, 1982) 215–22.

Schoors, Antoon
 "The Peshitta of Koheleth and Its Relation to the Septuagint," in C. Laga, J. A. Munitiz, and L. van Rompay, eds., *After Chalcedon: Studies in Theology and Church History*: FS Albert van Roey (OLA 18; Leuven: Peeters, 1985) 347–57.

Stec, David M.
 "The Recent English Translation of the Targumim to Job, Proverbs and Qohelet: A Review," *JSS* 39 (1994) 161–81.

Strothmann, Werner
 Konkordanz des syrischen Koheletbuches nach der Peshitta und Syrohexapla (Wiesbaden: Harrassowitz, 1973).

Thompson, J. David
 A Critical Concordance to the Septuagint Ecclesiastes (Computer Bible Volume 71; Lewiston, N.Y.: Biblical Research Associates, 1999).

Ulrich, Eugene
"Ezra and Qoheleth Manuscripts from Qumran
(4QEzra, 4QQoh)," in Eugene Ulrich et al., eds.,
*Priests, Prophets and Scribes: Essays on the Formation
and Heritage of Second Temple Judaism in Honour of
Joseph Blenkinsopp* (JSOTSup 149; Sheffield: JSOT
Press, 1992) 139–57.

Vegas Montaner, Luis
"El texto hebreo de Qohelet en la Biblia Poliglota
Complutense: Sus fuentes," *MEAH* 26–28
(1977/79) 271–82.

Vinel, Françoise
"Accumulation de ôti dans l'Ecclésiaste: Brouillage
du sens ou force rhétorique?" in Bernard A. Taylor, ed., *IX. Congress of the International Organization
for Septuagint and Cognate Studies* (SBLSCS 45;
Atlanta: Scholars Press, 1997) 391–401.

Vinel, François
"Le livre de l'Ecclésiaste," in Marc d'Harmonville
et al., eds., *Autour des livres de la Septante: Proverbes,
Ecclésiaste, Nombres, 3ème Livre des Regnes* (Le
centre d'études du Saulchoir; Paris: Cerf, 1995)
27–45.

Vinel, Françoise
"Le texte grec de l'Ecclésiaste et ses caractéristiques: Une relecture critique de l'histoire de la
royauté," in Schoors, ed., *Qohelet in the Context of
Wisdom*, 283–302.

Vogt, Ernst
"Fragmentum Qohelet ex Qumran," *Bib* 36 (1955)
265–66.

Wahl, Otto
Der Proverbien- und Kohelet-Text der Sacra Parallela
(FB 51; Würzburg: Echter, 1985).

Zafrani, Haim, and André Caquot, eds.
*L'Ecclésiaste et son commentaire–Le Livre de L'Ascese–
La Version Arabe de la Bible de Sa'adya Gaon*
(Judaisme en terre d'Islam 4; Paris: Maisonneuve &
Larose, 1989).

Ziegler, Joseph
"Der Gebrauch des Artikels in der Septuaginta des
Ecclesiastes," in Detlef Fraenkel, Udo Quast, and
John W. Wevers, eds., *Studien zur Septuaginta: FS
Robert Hanhart* (Mitteilungen des Septuaginta-
Unternehmens 20; Abhandlungen der Akademie
der Wissenschaften in Göttingen, Philosophische-
historische Klasse 190; Göttingen: Vandenhoeck &
Ruprecht, 1990) 83–120.

Ziegler, Joseph
"Die Wiedergabe der nota accusativi ʾet, ʾaet- mit
syn," *ZAW* 100 (1988) 222–33.

Commentary
■ 1:1

Albright, William Foxwell
"Some Canaanite-Phoenician Sources of Hebrew
Wisdom," in Martin Noth and D. Winton Thomas,
eds., *Wisdom in Israel and in the Ancient Near East:
FS H. H. Rowley* (VTSup 3; Leiden: Brill, 1955)
1–15.

Bauer, H.
"Die hebräischen Eigennamen als sprachliche
Erkenntnisquelle," *ZAW* 48 (1930) 73–80.

Ellermeier
Qohelet, I/1, 161–66.

Fox, Michael V.
"Frame Narrative and Composition in the Book of
Qohelet," *HUCA* 48 (1977) 83–106.

Fox
Qohelet, 311–29.

Ginsberg
Studies, 33–35.

Höffken, Peter
"Das EGO des Weisen: Subjektivierungsprozesse
in der Weisheitsliteratur," *ThZ* 41 (1985) 121–34.

Joüon, Paul
"Sur le nom de Qohelet," *Bib* 2 (1921) 53–54.

Kamenetzky, Abraham Schalom
"Das Kohelet-Rätsel," *ZAW* 29 (1909) 63–69.

Kamenetzky, Abraham Schalom
"Der Rätselname Kohelet," *ZAW* 34 (1914) 225–28.

Kamenetzky, Abraham Schalom
"Die ursprünglich beabsichtigte Aussprache des
Pseudonyms קהלת," *OLZ* 34 (1921) 11–15.

Loretz, Oswald
"Zur Darbietungsform der 'Ich-Erzählung' im
Buche Qohelet," *CBQ* 25 (1963) 46–59.

Loretz
Qohelet, 146–48.

Michel
Qohelet, 1–8.

Noth, Martin
Die israelitischen Personennamen (Stuttgart:
Kohlhammer, 1928) 38–39.

Perrin, Nicholas
"Messianism in the Narrative Frame of Ecclesiastes?" *RB* 108 (2001) 37–60.

Tur-Sinai, Naftali Herz
"On the Question of the Meaning of QHLT,"
Tarbiz 21 (1949/50) 208 (Heb.).

Ullendorf, Edward
"The Meaning of קהלת," *VT* 12 (1962) 215.

Whitley
Koheleth, 4–6.

Zimmermann, Frank
"The Aramaic Provenance of Qohelet," *JQR* 36
(1945/46) 17–45.

■ 1:2

Amir, Yehoshua
"Doch ein griechischer Einfluss auf das Buch
Kohelet?" in *Studien zum antiken Judentum* (BEAT
2; Frankfurt am Main: Lang, 1985) 35–50, Hebrew
original: *BethM* 10 (1965) 36–42.

Anderson, William H. U.
"The Poetic Inclusio of Qoheleth in Relation to 1,2
and 12,8," *SJOT* 12 (1998) 203–13.

Anderson, William H. U.
"The Semantic Implications of הבל and ראה רוח in
the Hebrew Bible and for Qoheleth," *JNSL* 25
(1999) 59–73.

255

Barucq, André
"Question sur le sens du travail: Qo 1,2; 2,21-23," *AsSeign* 49 (1971) 66–71.

Bergant, Dianne
"Vanity (Hebel)," *TBT* 22 (1984) 91–92.

Bertram, Georg
"Hebräischer und griechischer Qohelet: Ein Beitrag zur Theologie der hellenistischen Bibel," *ZAW* 64 (1952) 26–49.

Braun
Kohelet, 45–46.

Conradie, E. M.
"Is alles regtig tervergeefs en 'n gejaag na wind [Is Everything Really in Vain and a Chasing after Wind?]?" *NGTT* 37 (1996) 578–88.

Ehlich, Konrad
"LBH—Metaphern der Nichtigkeit," in Diesel et al., eds., *Jedes Ding*, 49–64.

Fox, Michael V.
"The Meaning of *hebel* for Qohelet," *JBL* 105 (1986) 409–27.

Fox
Qohelet, 29–51.

Fransen, Irénée
"Vanité des Vanités, dit l'Ecclésiaste," *BVC* 75 (1967) 19–29.

Heemrood, J.
"Alles is ijdelheid," *Het heilig Land* 15 (1962) 65–68.

Ho, Kit-Ching
"Kohelet and 'futility' (*habel*)," *Collectanea theologica Universitatis Fujen* 84 (1990) 229–36.

Jarick, John
"The Hebrew Book of Changes: Reflections on *hakkol hebel* and *lakkol zeman* in Ecclesiastes," *JSOT* 90 (2000) 79–99.

Lauha, Aarre
"Omnia Vanitas: Die Bedeutung von הבל bei Kohelet," in Jarmo Kiilunen, Vilho Riekkinen, and Heikki Räisänen, eds., *Glaube und Gerechtigkeit: In Memoriam Rafael Gyllenberg* (SESJ 38; Helsinki: Suomen eksegeettise seura, 1983) 19–25.

Lohfink, Norbert
"Ist Kohelets הבל-Aussage erkenntnistheoretisch gemeint?" in Schoors, ed., *Qohelet in Context*, 41–59.

Lohfink, Norbert
"Koh 1,2 'alles ist Windhauch'—universale und anthropologische Aussage?" in Ruldolf Mosis and Lothar Ruppert, eds., *Der Weg zum Menschen: FS Alfons Deissler* (Freiburg im Breisgau: Herder, 1989) 201–16, repr. in Lohfink, *Studien zu Kohelet*, 125–42.

Lohfink, Norbert
"Zu חבל im Buch Kohelet," in Lohfink, *Studien*, 215–58.

Loretz
Qohelet, 218–34.

McKenna, John E.
"The Concept of *hebel* in the Book of Ecclesiastes," *SJT* 45 (1992) 19–28.

Meek, Theophile J.
"Translating the Hebrew Bible," *JBL* 79 (1960) 328–35.

Michel
Qohelet, 84–86.

Michel
Untersuchungen, 40–51.

Miller, Douglas B.
"Qohelet's Symbolic Use of הבל," *JBL* 117 (1998) 437–54.

Ogden, Graham S.
"'Vanity' It Certainly Is Not," *BT* 38 (1987) 301–7.

Polk, Timothy
"The Wisdom of Irony: A Study of *hebel* and Its Relation to Joy and the Fear of God in Ecclesiastes," *SBTh* 6 (1976) 3–17.

Seow, Choon-Leong
"Beyond Mortal Grasp: The Usage of *hebel* in Ecclesiastes," *Australian Biblical Review* 48 (2000) 1–16.

Staples, William E.
"The 'Vanity' of Ecclesiastes," *JNES* 2 (1943) 95–104.

Staples, William E.
"Vanity of Vanities," *CJT* 1 (1955) 141–56.

Whitley
Koheleth, 6–7.

Zer Kavod, Mordechai
"On the Problem of the Word *HBL* in the Book of Qoheleth," *Bar Ilan* 4 (1967) 50–59 (Heb.).

■ **1:3—4:12**

Backhaus
Zeit und Zufall, 87–158.

Brown, Stephen G.
"The Structure of Ecclesiastes," *Evangelical Quarterly Review* 14 (1990) 195–208.

Castellino, George R.
"Qohelet and His Wisdom," *CBQ* 30 (1968) 15–28.

Fischer, Alexander Achilles
"Beobachtungen zur Komposition von Kohelet 1,3–3,15," *ZAW* 103 (1991) 72–86.

Fischer
Skepsis, 183–250.

Ginsberg, Harold Louis
"The Structure and Contents of the Book of Koheleth," in Martin Noth and D. Winton Thomas, eds., *Wisdom in Israel and in the Ancient Near East: FS H. H. Rowley* (VTSup 3; Leiden: Brill, 1955) 138–49, repr. in Alexander Altmann, ed., *Biblical and Other Studies* (STLI 1; Cambridge: Harvard Univ. Press, 1963) 47–59.

Jong, Stephen de
"A Book on Labour: The Structuring Principles and the Main Themes of the Book of Qohelet," *JSOT* 54 (1992) 107–16, repr. in Clines, ed., *Poetical Books*, 222–30.

Kamano, Naoto
"Character and Cosmology: Rhetoric of Qoh 1,3–3,9," in Schoors, ed., *Qohelet in Context*, 419–24.

Krüger, Thomas

"Qoh 2,24-26 und die Frage nach dem 'Guten' im Qohelet-Buch," *BN* 72 (1994) 70–84, repr. in Krüger, *Kritische Weisheit*, 131–49.

Lohfink, Norbert

"Das Koheletbuch: Strukturen und Struktur," in Schwienhorst-Schönberger, ed., *Das Buch Kohelet*, 39–121.

Loretz, Oswald

"Poetry and Prose in the Book of Qoheleth (1:1–3:22; 7:23–8:1; 9:6-10; 12:8-14)," in Johannes C. de Moor and Wilfred G. E. Watson, eds., *Verse in Ancient Near Eastern Prose* (AOAT 42; Kevelaer: Butzon & Bercker; Neukirchen-Vluyn: Neukirchener Verlag, 1993) 155–89.

Lys, Daniel

"L'Etre et le Temps: Communication de Qohèlèth," in Gilbert, ed., *Sagesse*, 249–58.

Michel, Diethelm

"Humanität angesichts des Absurden: Qohelet (Prediger) 1,2–3,15," in Heinrich Foerster, ed., *Humanität Heute* (Berlin: Lutherisches Verlagshaus, 1970) 22–36.

Michel

Untersuchungen, 1–83.

Mulder, J. S. M.

"Qoheleth's Division and Also Its Main Point," in W. C. Delsman and J. T. Nelis, eds., *Von Kanaan bis Kerala: FS J. P. M. van der Ploeg 1979* (AOAT 211; Kevelaer: Butzon & Bercker; Neukirchen-Vluyn: Neukirchener Verlag, 1982) 149–59.

Müller, Hans-Peter

"Theonome Skepsis und Lebensfreude: Zu Koh 1,12–3,15," *BZ* 30 (1986) 1–19.

Schwienhorst-Schönberger

Nicht im Menschen, 12–125.

Wright, Addison G.

"The Riddle of the Sphinx Revisited: Numerical Patterns in the Book of Qoheleth," *CBQ* 42 (1980) 38–51.

Wright, Addison G.

"The Riddle of the Sphinx: The Structure of the Book of Qoheleth," *CBQ* 30 (1968) 313–34, repr. in Crenshaw, ed., *Studies*, 245–66, repr. in Zuck, ed., *Reflecting with Solomon*, 45–65.

Zimmerli, Walther

"Das Buch Kohelet: Traktat oder Sentenzensammlung?" *VT* 24 (1974) 221–30.

■ 1:3-11

Abramson, Shraga

"Biblical Explanation Based on Medieval Exegesis," *BethM* 32 (1986/87) 355–57 (Heb.).

Anderson, William H. U.

"A Note on יתר for Qoheleth," *JNSL* 26 (2000) 133–36.

Auffret, Pierre

"'Rien du tout de nouveau sous le soleil': Étude structurelle de Qo 1,4-11," *Folia Orientalia* 26 (1989) 145–66.

Backhaus

Zeit und Zufall, 3–56.

Braun

Kohelet, 56–66.

Döller, Johannes

"Altorientalisches Weltbild in Qoh. 1,5-7," *Kath.* 87 (1907) 361–65.

Ellermeier

Qohelet, I/1, 186–211.

Fischer, Alexander Achilles

"Beobachtungen zur Komposition von Kohelet 1,3–3,15," *ZAW* 103 (1991) 72–86.

Fischer

Skepsis, 186–202.

Foresti, Fabrizio

"ʿāmāl in Koheleth: 'Toil' or 'Profit,'" *ECarm* 31 (1980) 415–30.

Fox, Michael V.

"Qoheleth 1,4," *JSOT* 40 (1988) 109.

Good, Edwin Marshall

"The Unfilled Sea: Style and Meaning in Ecclesiastes 1:2-11," in Gammie et al., eds., *Israelite Wisdom*, 59–73.

Grossberg, Daniel

"Form and Content and Their Correspondence," *HS* 41 (2000) 47–52.

Holzer, Paul-Joseph

"Der Mensch und das Weltgeschehen nach Koh. 1,4-11: Eine Textanalyse" (Th.D. diss., University of Regensburg, 1981).

Japhet, Sara

"'Goes to the South and Turns to the North' (Ecclesiastes 1:6): The Sources and History of the Exegetical Traditions," *JSQ* 1 (1993/94) 289–322.

Jenni, Ernst

"Das Wort ʿōlām im Alten Testament," *ZAW* 64 (1952) 197–248; 65 (1953) 1–35.

Krüger, Thomas

"Dekonstruktion und Rekonstruktion prophetischer Eschatologie im Qohelet-Buch," in Diesel et al., eds., *Jedes Ding*, 107–29, repr. in Krüger, *Kritische Weisheit*, 151–72.

Lévy, Isidore

"Rien de nouveau sous le soleil," *NC* 5 (1953) 326–28.

Lohfink, Norbert

"Die Wiederkehr des immer Gleichen: Eine frühe Synthese zwischen griechischem und jüdischem Weltgefühl in Kohelet 1,4-11," *AF* 53 (1985) 125–49, repr. in Lohfink, *Studien*, 95–124.

Lohfink, Norbert

"The Present and Eternity: Time in Qoheleth," *TD* 34 (1987) 236–40, trans. of "Gegenwart und Ewigkeit: Die Zeit im Buch Kohelet," *GuL* 60 (1987) 2–12.

Loretz, Oswald

"Anfänge jüdischer Philosophie nach Qohelet 1,1-11 und 3,1-15," *UF* 23 (1991) 223–44.

Margoliouth, David Samuel
"The Prologue of Ecclesiastes," *Exempla Scripturarum* 8 (1911) 463–70.

Michel, Diethelm
"Humanität angesichts des Absurden: Qohelet (Prediger) 1,2–3,15," in Heinrich Foerster, ed., *Humanität Heute* (Berlin: Lutherisches Verlagshaus, 1970) 22–36.

Min, Young-Jin
"How Do the Rivers Flow? (Ecclesiastes 1.7)," *BT* 42 (1991) 226–31.

Mitchell, Hinckley G.
"'Work' in Ecclesiastes," *JBL* 32 (1913) 123–38.

Moss, Steven A.
"Ecclesiastes 1:4: A Proof Text for Reincarnation," *JBQ* 21 (1993) 28–30.

Müller, Hans-Peter
"Theonome Skepsis und Lebensfreude: Zu Koh 1,12–3,15," *BZ* 30 (1986) 1–19.

Nishimura, Toshiaki
"Un Mashal de Qohelet 1,2-11," *RHPhR* 59 (1979) 605–15.

Ogden, Graham S.
"The Interpretation of דור in Ecclesiastes 1.4," *JSOT* 34 (1986) 91–92.

Rainey, Anson F.
"A Second Look at Amal in Qoheleth," *CTM* 36 (1965) 805.

Rose, Martin
"'Der Früheren gedenkt man nicht mehr': Erinnern und Vergessen bei Qohelet und in der biblischen Literatur," in Roger Müller Farguell, ed., *Memoria* (Colloquium Helveticum 27; Bern: Lang, 1998) 83–103.

Rousseau, François
"Structure de Qohelet i 4-11 et plan du livre," *VT* 31 (1981) 200–217.

Spaller, Christina
"Die Geschichte des Buches . . .": Die Lektüre von Koh 1,3-11 in vier ausgewählten Kommentaren (Exegese in unserer Zeit 7; Münster: Lit, 2001).

Staples, William E.
"'Profit' in Ecclesiastes," *JNES* 4 (1945) 87–96.

Tin-Sheung, Wong
"Qohelet 1:3-11: Prose or Poetry?" *Jian Dao* 14 (2000) 25–47.

Verheij, Arian J. C.
"Words Speaking for Themselves: On the Poetics of Qohelet 1:4-7," in Janet Dyk, ed., *Give Ear to My Words: Psalms and Other Poetry in and around the Hebrew Bible: Essays in Honour of Professor N. A. van Uchelen* (Amsterdam: Societas Hebraica Amstelodamensis, 1996) 183–88.

Whybray, Roger Norman
"Ecclesiastes 1.5-7 and the Wonders of Nature," *JSOT* 41 (1988) 105–12, repr. in Zuck, ed., *Reflecting with Solomon*, 233–39.

Williams, James G.
"What Does It Profit a Man? The Wisdom of Koheleth," *Judaism* 20 (1971) 179–93, repr. in Crenshaw, ed., *Studies*, 375–89.

Wilson, Lindsay
"Artful Ambiguity in Ecclesiastes 1,1-11: A Wisdom Technique?" in Schoors, ed., *Qohelet in Context*, 357–65.

■ **1:12—2:26**

Anderson, William H. U.
"The Semantic Implications of הבל and ראה רוח in the Hebrew Bible and for Qoheleth," *JNSL* 25 (1999) 59–73.

Bartelmus, Rüdiger
"Haben oder Sein: Anmerkungen zur Anthropologie des Buches Kohelet," *BN* 53 (1990) 38–67.

Barucq, André
"Question sur le sens du travail: Qo 1,2; 2,21-23," *AsSeign* 49 (1971) 66–71.

Bons, Eberhard
"ʾiddā weʾiddōt: Überlegungen zum Verständnis eines Hapaxlegomenons," *BN* 36 (1987) 12–16.

Bons, Eberhard
"Zur Gliederung und Kohärenz von Koh 1,12–2,11," *BN* 24 (1984) 73–93.

Byargeon, Rick W.
"The Significance of Ambiguity in Ecclesiastes 2,24-26," in Schoors, ed., *Qohelet in Context*, 367–72.

Carr, David McLain, *From D to Q: A Study of Early Jewish Interpretations of Solomon's Dream at Gibeon* (SBLMS 44; Atlanta: Scholars Press, 1991).

Chopineau, Jacques
"Une image de l'homme: Sur Ecclésiaste 1/2," *EThR* 53 (1978) 366–70.

Corré, Alan D.
"A Reference to Epipasm in Koheleth," *VT* 4 (1954) 416–18.

Crocker, P. T.
"'I Made Gardens and Parks . . . ,'" *Buried History* 26 (1990) 20–23.

de Waard, Jan
"The Translator and Textual Criticism (with Particular Reference to Eccl 2,25)," *Bib* 60 (1979) 509–29.

Ellermeier, Friedrich
"Das Verbum חוש in Koh. 2,25: Eine exegetische, auslegungsgeschichtliche und semasiologische Untersuchung," *ZAW* 75 (1963) 197–217.

Ellermeier, Friedrich
"Der Harem Qohelet / Salomos—vorläufiges Warnsignal zu Qoh. 2,8," in Ellermeier, *Sibyllen–Musikanten–Haremsfrauen* (Theologische und orientalische Arbeiten 2; Herzberg: Jungfer, 1970) 22–27.

Ellermeier, Friedrich
Qohelet, I,2: *Einzelfrage Nr. 7: Das Verbum חוש in Qoh. 2,25* (2d ed.; Herzberg: Jungfer, 1970).

Fernández, Eleazar
"Bible Study IV, Wisdom from the Underside: Ecclesiastes 1:12-18," *Ministerial Formation* 80 (1998) 15–23.

Fischer, Alexander Achilles
"Beobachtungen zur Komposition von Kohelet 1,3–3,15," *ZAW* 103 (1991) 72–86.

Fischer
Skepsis, 203–17.

Fischer, Stefan
"Zur Uebersetzung von Kohelet 2,25: Wer isst und sorgt sich ohne mich?" *Fundamentum* 3 (1995) 217–23.

Giversen, Søren
"Solomon und die Dämonen," in Martin Krause, ed., *Essays on the Nag Hammadi Texts in Honour of A. Böhlig* (Nag Hammadi Studies 3; Leiden: Brill, 1972) 16–21.

Gordis, Robert
"Ecclesiastes 1,17: Its Text and Interpretation," *JBL* 56 (1937) 323–30, repr. in Gordis, *Word*, 365–72.

Görg, Manfred
"Zu einer bekannten Paronomasie in Koh 2,8," *BN* 90 (1997) 5–7.

Höffken, Peter
"Das EGO des Weisen: Subjektivierungsprozesse in der Weisheitsliteratur," *ThZ* 41 (1985) 121–34.

Krüger, Thomas
"Qoh 2,24-26 und die Frage nach dem 'Guten' im Qohelet-Buch," *BN* 72 (1994) 70–84, repr. in Krüger, *Kritische Weisheit*, 131–49.

Lavoie, Jean-Jacques
"Étude de Quelques Mots Obscurs du Qohélet à la Lumière de l'Histoire de l'Exégèse et des Manuscrits Judéo-Persans de la Biliothèque Nationale de France," *SR* 29 (2000) 183–97.

Lohfink, Norbert
"Technik und Tod nach Kohelet," in H. Schlier et al., eds., *Strukturen christlicher Existenz: FS F. Wulf* (Würzburg: Echter, 1989) 27–35.

Loretz, Oswald
"Zur Darbietungsform der 'Ich-Erzählung' im Buche Qohelet," *CBQ* 25 (1963) 46–59.

Lux, Rüdiger
"'Ich, Kohelet, bin König . . .': Die Fiktion als Schlüssel zur Wirklichkeit in Kohelet 1,12–2,26," *EvTh* 50 (1990) 331–42.

Michel, Diethelm
"Humanität angesichts des Absurden: Qohelet (Prediger) 1,2–3,15," in Heinrich Foerster, ed., *Humanität Heute* (Berlin: Lutherisches Verlagshaus, 1970) 22–36.

Montgomery, James A.
"Notes on Ecclesiastes," *JBL* 43 (1924) 241–44.

Müller, Hans-Peter
"Kohelet und Amminadab," in Diesel et al., eds., *Jedes Ding*, 149–65.

Müller, Hans-Peter
"Theonome Skepsis und Lebensfreude: Zu Koh 1,12–3,15," *BZ* 30 (1986) 1–19.

Müller, Hans-Peter
"Travestien und geistige Landschaften: Zum Hintergrund einiger Motive bei Kohelet und im Hohenlied," *ZAW* 109 (1997) 557–74.

Nida, Eugene A.
"Intelligibility and Acceptability in Bible Translating," *BT* 39 (1988) 301–8.

Schubert, Mathias
"Die Selbstbetrachtungen Kohelets: Ein Beitrag zu Gattungsforschung," *ThV* 17 (1989) 23–34.

Schwienhorst-Schönberger, Ludger
"'Zum Lachen sprach ich: Wie dumm! und zur Freude: Was bringt sie ein?' (Koh 2,2)," *Una Sancta* 52 (1997) 294–303.

Seow, Choon-Leong
"Qohelet's Autobiography," in Astrid B. Beck et al., eds., *Fortunate the Eyes That See: Essays in Honor of David Noel Freedman* (Grand Rapids: Eerdmans, 1995) 275–87.

Smelik, Klaas A. D.
"A Re-Interpretation of Ecclesiastes 2,12b," in Schoors, ed., *Qohelet in Context*, 385–89.

Smend, Rudolf
"Essen und Trinken—ein Stück Weltlichkeit des Alten Testaments," in *Die Mitte des Alten Testaments: Gesammelte Studien,* vol. 1 (Munich: Kaiser, 1986) 200–211.

Taradach, Madeleine
"La figure insolite de Salomon dans TgQo 1,12 dans les Talmuds et quelques Midrasim," in Frederic Raubell et al., eds., *Tradició i Traducció de la Paraula: Mischellània Guia Camps* (SDM 47; Monserrat: Associació Biblica de Catalunya—Publacions del'Abadia de Montserrat, 1993) 325–35.

Vaccari, A.
"'Stultorum infinitus est numerus' (Eccl. 1,15 Vulg.)," *VD* 8 (1928) 81–84.

Verheij, Arian J. C.
"Paradise Retried: On Qohelet 2:4-6," *JSOT* 50 (1991) 113–15.

Vignolo, Roberto
"Maschera e sindrome regale: Interpretazione ironico-psicanalitica di Qoh 1,12–2,26," *Teol(Br)* 26 (2001) 12–64.

Watson, Wilfred G. E.
"The Unnoticed Word Pair 'eye(s)' // 'heart,'" *ZAW* 101 (1989) 398–408.

Williams, James G.
"What Does It Profit a Man? The Wisdom of Koheleth," *Judaism* 20 (1971) 179–93, repr. in Crenshaw, ed., *Studies*, 375–89.

■ 3:1-9

Bannach, Horst
"Bemerkungen zu Prediger 3,1-9," in Horst Bannach, ed., *Glaube und öffentliche Meinung* (Stuttgart: Radius, 1970) 26–32.

Blenkinsopp, Joseph
"Ecclesiastes 3,1-15: Another Interpretation," *JSOT* 66 (1995) 55–64.

Brenner, Athalya
"M Text Authority in Biblical Love Lyrics: The Case of Qoheleth 3.1-9 and its Textual Relatives," in Athalya Brenner and Fokkelien van Dijk-Hemmes, *On Gendering Texts: Female and Male Voices in the Hebrew Bible* (Biblical Interpretation Series 1; New York: Brill, 1993) 133–63.

Brisson, E. Carson
"Ecclesiastes 3,1-8," *Int* 55 (2001) 292–95.

Carmichael, Calum M.
"A Time for War and a Time for Peace: The Influence of the Distinction upon Some Legal and Literary Material," in Bernard S. Jackson, ed., *Studies in Jewish Legal History: FS David Daube* (London: Jewish Chronicle Publications, 1974) 50–63.

Deist, F. E.
"'God met ons?' Prediker 3,1-9," in W. S. Vorster et al., *Hoe lees 'n mens die Bybel?* (Miscellanea Congregalia 33; Pretoria: Pretoria Univ. Press, 1988).

Ebach, Jürgen
". . . und Prediger 3 auslegen hat seine Zeit: Über Zusammenhänge von Exegese und Zeit, beobachtet beim Auslegen von Koh 3,1-15," in Friedrich-Wilhelm Marquard et al., eds., *Die Bibel gehört nicht uns* (Einwürfe 6; Munich: Kaiser, 1990) 95–123.

Eissfeldt, Otto
"Alles Ding währt seine Zeit," in *Kleine Schriften*, vol. 5 (ed. Rudolf Sellheim and Fritz Maass; Tübingen: Mohr, 1973) 174–78, repr. from Arnulf Kuschke and Ernst Kutsch, eds., *Archäologie und Altes Testament: FS Kurt Galling* (Tübingen: Mohr, 1970) 69–74.

Ellis, Robert
"'A Time to Weep and a Time to Laugh,'" *ExpT* 99 (1987/88) 176–77.

Fischer, Alexander Achilles
"Beobachtungen zur Komposition von Kohelet 1,3–3,15," *ZAW* 103 (1991) 72–86.

Fischer
Skepsis, 217–25.

Fox, Michael V.
"Time in Qohelet's 'Catalogue of Times,'" *JNSL* 24 (1998) 25–39.

Galling, Kurt
"Das Rätsel der Zeit im Urteil Kohelets (Koh. 3,1-15)," *ZThK* 58 (1961) 1–15.

Gilbert, Maurice
"Il Concetto di Tempo (עת) in Qohelet e Ben Sira," in Bellia and Passaro, eds., *Qohelet*, 69–89.

Helm, Lothar
"Prediger 3,1-8: Alles hat seine Zeit," in Eva Renate Schmidt et al., eds., *Feministisch gelesen: Ausgewählte Bibeltexte für Gruppen und Gemeinden . . . ,* vol. 2 (Stuttgart: Kreuz, 1989) 157–64.

Holland, Francis T.
"Heart of Darkness: A Study of Qohelet 3.1-15," *PIBA* 17 (1994) 81–101.

Horton, Ernest
"Koheleth's Concept of Opposites as Compared to Samples of Greek Philosophy and Near and Far

Eastern Wisdom Classics," *Numen* 19 (1972) 1–21, repr. in *TD* 23 (1975) 265–67.

Hutchinson, Henry
"Are You a Good Loser? 'There Is a Time to Lose,' Eccles 3,6," *ExpT* 90 (1978) 336–38.

Jarick, John
"The Hebrew Book of Changes: Reflections on *hakkol hebel* and *lakkol zeman* in Ecclesiastes," *JSOT* 90 (2000) 79–99.

Junod, Mireille
"Qohelet 3,1-15," *Lire et Dire* 1 (1989) 14–24.

Laumann, Maryta
"Qoheleth and Time," *TBT* 27 (1989) 305–10.

Lavoie, Jean-Jacques
"Il y a un temps pour tout, mais tout est pour rien: Quelques observations à partir de Qohéleth 3,1-9," *Revue des études et civilisations anciennes du Proche Orient* 6 (1997) 20–44.

Loader, James A.
"Qohelet 3,2-8: A 'Sonnet' in the Old Testament," *ZAW* 81 (1969) 240–42.

Lohfink, Norbert
"The Present and Eternity: Time in Qoheleth," *TD* 34 (1987) 236–40, trans. of "Gegenwart und Ewigkeit: Die Zeit im Buch Kohelet," *GuL* 60 (1987) 2–12.

Loretz, Oswald
"Anfänge jüdischer Philosophie nach Qohelet 1,1-11 und 3,1-15," *UF* 23 (1991) 223–44.

Maas, Jacques, and Jack Post
"Qohéleth et le savoir de Dieu: La modalité du croire dans Qohéleth à partir de Qo 3,1-15," *SémBib* 80 (1995) 34–50.

Maillot, Alphonse
"La contradiction Qohélet 3,1-8," *BVC* 96 (1970) 55–58.

Mathias, Dietmar
"Das Problem der Zeit in weisheitlichen Texten des Alten Testaments," in Dieter Vieweger and Ernst-Joachim Waschke, eds., *Von Gott reden: FS Siegfried Wagner* (Neukirchen-Vluyn: Neukirchener Verlag, 1995) 217–32.

Mettayer, Arthur
"De quel(le) mort s'agit-il?" *SR* 9 (1980) 339–43.

Michel, Diethelm
"Humanität angesichts des Absurden: Qohelet (Prediger) 1,2–3,15," in Heinrich Foerster, ed., *Humanität Heute* (Berlin: Lutherisches Verlagshaus, 1970) 22–36.

Müller, Hans-Peter
"Theonome Skepsis und Lebensfreude: Zu Koh 1,12–3,15," *BZ* 30 (1986) 1–19.

Peters, Norbert
"Miszelle zu Ekkle 3,5," *BZ* 1 (1903) 245.

Sauter, Gerhard
"'Sinn' und 'Wahrheit': Die 'Sinnfrage' in religions-theoretischer und theologischer Sicht," *EvTh* 40 (1980) 93–126.

Sauter, Gerhard

Was heisst: nach Sinn fragen? Eine theologisch-philosophische Orientierung (KT 53; Munich: Kaiser, 1982) 27–38.

Schwienhorst-Schönberger, Ludger

"Leben in der Gegenwart: Kohelet 3,1-9," *BL* 70 (1997) 285–89.

Shefi, Elisha

"Ecclesiastes' Treatment of the Concept of Time," *BethM* 36 (1990/91) 144–151 (Heb.)

Staples, William E.

"The Meaning of *ḥēpeṣ* in Ecclesiastes," *JNES* 24 (1965) 110–12.

Tamez, Elsa

"Ecclesiastes 3:1-8: A Latin American Perspective," in John R. Levison and Priscilla Pope-Levison, eds., *Return to Babel: Global Perspectives on the Bible* (Louisville: Westminster John Knox, 1999) 75–80.

Vílchez Líndez, José

"Poema sobre el tiempo (Ecle 3,1-8)," *Sal terrae* 81 (1993) 871–77.

Wallis, Gerhard

"Das Zeitverständnis des Predigers Salomo," in Manfred Weippert and Stefan Timm, eds., *Meilenstein: Festgabe für Herbert Donner* (ÄAT 30; Wiesbaden: Harrassowitz, 1995) 316–23.

Whybray, Roger Norman

"'A Time to Be Born and a Time to Die': Some Observations on Ecclesiastes 3:2-8," in Masao Mori, Hideo Ogawa, and Mamoru Yoshikawa, eds., *Near Eastern Studies: Dedicated to H. I. H. Prince Takahito Mikasa* (Wiesbaden: Harrassowitz, 1991) 469–83.

Wright, Addison G.

"'For Everything There Is a Season': The Structure and Meaning of the Fourteen Opposites (Ecclesiastes 3,2-8)," in Maurice Carrez, Joseph Doré, and Pierre Grelot, eds., *De la Tôra au Messie: Mélanges Henri Cazelles* (Paris: Desclée, 1981) 321–28.

■ 3:10—4:12

Aerts, Theo

"Two Are Better Than One (Qohelet 4:10)," *Point Series* 14 (1990) 11–48.

Bartelmus, Rüdiger

"Haben oder Sein: Anmerkungen zur Anthropologie des Buches Kohelet," *BN* 53 (1990) 38–67.

Bianchi, Francesco

"C'è una 'teologia della prova' in Qohelet? Osservazioni filologiche e bibliche su Qo 3,18," in Rinaldo Fabris, ed., *Initium sapientiae: Scritti in onore di Franco Festorazzi nel suo 70. Compleanno: FS Franco Festorazzi* (SRivB 36; Bologna: EDB, 2000) 163–78.

Bianchi, Francesco

"'Essi non hanno chi li consoli' (Qo 4,1)," *RivB* 40 (1992) 299–307.

Bianchi, Francesco

"'Ma Dio ricerca ci che è scomparso?' (Qo 3,15b): La storia, la memoria e il tempo nel libro di Qohelet," *RivB* 42 (1994) 59–73.

Blenkinsopp, Joseph

"Ecclesiastes 3,1-15: Another Interpretation," *JSOT* 66 (1995) 55–64.

Buhlman, Alain

"The Difficulty of Thinking in Greek and Speaking in Hebrew (Qoheleth 3,18; 4,13-16; 5,8)," *JSOT* 90 (2000) 101–8.

Burkhalter, Carmen

"Qohélet 3,18-22: La mort," *Lire et Dire* 32 (1997) 3–11.

Crenshaw, James Lee

"The Eternal Gospel (Eccl. 3:11)," in James Lee Crenshaw and John Thomas Willis, eds., *Essays in Old Testament Ethics: FS J. P. Hyatt* (New York: Ktav, 1974) 23–55, repr. in Crenshaw, *Urgent Advice*, 548–72.

Crenshaw, James Lee

"The Expression *mî yôdēaʿ* in the Hebrew Bible," *VT* 36 (1986) 274–88, repr. in Crenshaw, *Urgent Advice*, 279–91.

D'Alario, Vittoria

"'Chi sa se lo spirito dell'uomo sale in alto . . .?' (Qo 3,21): Un testo problematico sul tema dell'immortalità," in Giuseppe Lorizio, ed., *Morte e sopravvivenza: In dialogo con Xavier Tilliette* (Saggi 32; Rome: A.V.E., 1995) 211–22.

Dahood, Mitchell

"Scriptio Defectiva in Qoheleth 4,10a," *Bib* 49 (1968) 243.

Dondeyne, A.

"De animae immortalitate iuxta Eccl. 3,18-22," *Collationes Brugenses* 32 (1932) 10–15.

Duesberg, Hilaire

"Les animaux savent-ils parler? (Qoh. 3,21)," *BVC* 79 (1968) 3–9.

Ebach, Jürgen

". . . und Prediger 3 auslegen hat seine Zeit: Über Zusammenhänge von Exegese und Zeit, beobachtet beim Auslegen von Koh 3,1-15," in Friedrich-Wilhelm Marquard et al., eds., *Die Bibel gehört nicht uns* (Einwürfe 6; Munich: Kaiser, 1990) 95–123.

Fischer, Alexander Achilles

"Beobachtungen zur Komposition von Kohelet 1,3–3,15," *ZAW* 103 (1991) 72–86.

Fischer, Alexander Achilles

"Kohelet und die frühe Apokalyptik: Eine Auslegung von Koh 3,16-21," in Schoors, ed., *Qohelet in Context*, 339–56.

Fischer

Skepsis, 228–44.

Fonzo, Lorenzo di

"Ecclesiastes 3,21," *VD* 19 (1939) 257–68, 289–99; *VD* 20 (1940) 166–76.

Forman, Charles C.

"Koheleth's Use of Genesis," *JSS* 5 (1960) 256–63.

Galling, Kurt

"Das Rätsel der Zeit im Urteil Kohelets (Koh. 3,1-15)," *ZThK* 58 (1961) 1–15.

Garrett, Duane A.
"Qoheleth on the Use and Abuse of Political Power," *TJ 8* (1987) 159–77.

Guillod-Reymond, Daphné
"Echo à Qohéleth 3,18-22 dans le Nouveau Testament: Avec 2 Corinthiens 4,7-15," *Lire et Dire 32* (1997) 12–14.

Grimm, Willibald
"Ueber die Stelle Koheleth 3,11b," *ZWTh* 23 (1880) 274–79.

Günther, Johannes
"Der Zusammenhang in Koh 3,11-15," *ZAW* 51 (1933) 79–80.

Hart, Thomas M.
"Qoheleth Looks at Friendship," *TBT* 32 (1994) 74–78.

Hart, Thomas M.
"The Wise Man and the Absurd (Qoh. 4,2-3)," *TBT* 52 (1971) 236–39.

Herrman, Wolfram
"Zu Kohelet 3,14," *WZ(L).GS* 3 (1953/54) 293–95; repr. in William Foxwell Albright, ed., *Geschichte und Altes Testament: FS Albrecht Alt* (BHTh 16; Tübingen: Mohr [Siebeck], 1955) 163–65.

Hieke, Thomas
"'Geh zur Ameise, du Fauler . . .' (Spr 6,6): Zur Beurteilung der menschlichen Arbeit in den Psalmen und der biblischen Weisheitsliteratur," *Lebendiges Zeugnis* 53 (1998) 19–31.

Hitzig, Ferdinand
"Ueber die Stelle Prediger 3,11," *ThStK* 12 (1839) 513–18.

Holland, Francis T.
"Heart of Darkness: A Study of Qohelet 3.1-15," *PIBA* 17 (1994) 81–101.

Irwin, William A.
"Ecclesiastes 3,18," *AJSL* 56 (1939) 298–99.

Jenni, Ernst
"Das Wort ʿōlām im Alten Testament," *ZAW* 64 (1952) 197–248; 65 (1953) 1–35.

Junod, Mireille
"Qohelet 3,1-15," *Lire et Dire* 1 (1989) 14–24.

Kaiser, Walter C.
"Integrating Wisdom Theology into Old Testament Theology: Ecclesiastes 3:10-15," in Walter C. Kaiser and Ronald F. Youngblood, eds., *A Tribute to Gleason Archer: Essays on the Old Testament* (Chicago: Moody Press, 1986) 197–209.

Klopfenstein, Martin A.
"Kohelet und die Freude am Dasein," *ThZ* 47 (1991) 97–107, repr. in H. Obst, ed., *Ueberlieferung und Geschichte: FS Gerhard Wallis* (Halle: Martin Luther Universität, 1990) 93–103, repr. in Martin A. Klopfenstein, *Leben aus dem Wort: Beiträge zum Alten Testament* (BEAT 40; Bern: Lang, 1996), 27–39.

Kramer, Samuel N.
"Gilgamesh and the Land of the Living," *JCS* 1 (1947) 3–46.

Kroon, J.
"Mundum tradidit disputationi eorum (Eccl. 3,11)," *VD* 6 (1926) 357–59.

Krüger, Thomas
"Die Rezeption der Tora im Buch Kohelet," in Schwienhorst-Schönberger, ed., *Das Buch Kohelet*, 303–25, repr. in Krüger, *Kritische Weisheit*, 173–93.

Krüger, Thomas
"Qoh 2,24-26 und die Frage nach dem 'Guten' im Qohelet-Buch," *BN* 72 (1994) 70–84, repr. in Krüger, *Kritische Weisheit*, 131–49.

Laumann, Maryta
"Qoheleth and Time," *TBT* 27 (1989) 305–10.

Lavoie, Jean-Jacques
"De l'inconvénient d'être né: Étude de Qohélet 4,1-3," *SR* 24 (1995) 297–308.

Loader, James A.
"Sunt lacrimae rerum (et mentem mortalia tangunt): Qoh 4:1-3," *OTWSA* 20/21 (1977/78) 83–94.

Lohfink, Norbert
"Gegenwart und Ewigkeit: Die Zeit im Buch Kohelet," *GuL* 60 (1987) 2–12, trans. "The Present and Eternity: Time in Qoheleth," *TD* 34 (1987) 236–40.

Loretz, Oswald
"Anfänge jüdischer Philosophie nach Qohelet 1,1-11 und 3,1-15," *UF* 23 (1991) 223–44.

Löwenstein, D.
"'. . . that they are, for each other, only animals' (Qoh 3:18)," *BethM* 20,3 (1974) 415–16 (Heb.).

Maas, Jacques and Jack Post
"Qohéleth et le savoir de Dieu: La modalité du croire dans Qohéleth à partir de Qo 3,1-15," *SémBib* 80 (1995) 34–50.

MacDonald, Duncan Black
"Eccl. iii 11," *JBL* 18 (1899) 212–13.

Maltby, Arthur
"The Book of Ecclesiastes and the After-Life," *EvQ* 35 (1963) 39–44.

Mathias, Dietmar
"Das Problem der Zeit in weisheitlichen Texten des Alten Testaments," in Dieter Vieweger and Ernst-Joachim Waschke, eds., *Von Gott reden: FS Siegfried Wagner* (Neukirchen-Vluyn: Neukirchener Verlag, 1995) 217–32.

Mazzinghi, Luca
"Il mistero del tempo: Sul termine ʿôlām in Qoh 3,11," in Rinaldo Fabris, ed., *Initium Sapientiae: Scritti in Onore di Franco Festorazzi nel suo 70. Compleanno* (SRivB 36; Bologna: EDB, 2000) 147–61.

Michel, Diethelm
"Humanität angesichts des Absurden: Qohelet (Prediger) 1,2–3,15," in Heinrich Foerster, ed., *Humanität Heute* (Berlin: Lutherisches Verlagshaus, 1970) 22–36.

Müller, Hans-Peter
"Theonome Skepsis und Lebensfreude: Zu Koh 1,12–3,15," *BZ* 30 (1986) 1–19.

Müller, Hans-Peter
"Weisheitliche Deutungen der Sterblichkeit: Gen 3,19 und Pred 3,21; 12,7 im Licht antiker Parallelen," in Müller, *Mensch–Umwelt–Eigenwelt*, 69–100.

Murphy, Roland E.
"On Translating Ecclesiastes," *CBQ* 53 (1991) 571–79.

Nishimura, Toshiaki
"Quelques réflexions sémiologiques à propos de 'la crainte de dieu' de Qohelet," *AJBI* 5 (1979) 67–87.

Oeming, Manfred
"Biblische Funktion und altorientalische Ursprünge der Kanonformel," in Christoph Dohmen and Manfred Oeming, *Biblischer Kanon warum und wozu? Eine Kanontheologie* (QD 137; Freiburg: Herder, 1992) 68–89.

Ogden, Graham S.
"The Mathematics of Wisdom: Qoheleth IV 1-12," *VT* 34 (1984) 446–53.

Pahk, Johan Yeong Sik
Canto.

Pfeiffer, Egon
"Die Gottesfurcht im Buche Kohelet," in Henning Graf Reventlow, ed., *Gottes Wort und Gottes Land: FS Hans-Wilhelm Hertzberg* (Göttingen: Vandenhoeck & Ruprecht, 1965) 133–58.

Piotti, Franco
"Osservazioni su alcuni problemi esegetici nel libro dell' Ecclesiaste: Studio I," *BeO* 20 (1978) 169–81.

Reuter, Eleonore
"'Nimm nichts davon hinweg und füge nichts hinzu!' Dtn 13,1, seine alttestamentlichen Parallelen und seine altorientalischen Vorbilder," *BN* 47 (1989) 107–14.

Rodríguez Ochoa, J. M.
"Estudio de la dimensión temporal en Prov., Job y Qoh.: El eterno volver y comenzar en Qoh.," *EstBib* 22 (1963) 33–67.

Salters, Robert B.
"A Note on the Exegesis of Ecclesiastes 3,15b," *ZAW* 88 (1976) 419–22.

Sauter, Gerhard
"'Sinn' und 'Wahrheit': Die 'Sinnfrage' in religionstheoretischer und theologischer Sicht," *EvTh* 40 (1980) 93–126.

Sauter, Gerhard
Was heisst: nach Sinn fragen? Eine theologisch-philosophische Orientierung (KT 53; Munich: Kaiser, 1982) 27–38.

Shaffer, Aaron
"New Light on the 'Three-ply Cord,'" *ErIsr* 9 (1969) 159–60 (Heb.) 138–39*.

Shaffer, Aaron
"The Mesopotamian Background of Qohelet 4:9-12," *ErIsr* 8 (1967) 246–50 (Heb.) 75*.

Shefi, Elisha
"Ecclesiastes' Treatment of the Concept of Time," *BethM* 36 (1990/91) 144–51 (Heb.).

Smend, Rudolf
"Essen und Trinken—ein Stück Weltlichkeit des Alten Testaments," in *Die Mitte des Alten Testaments: Gesammelte Studien,* vol. 1 (Munich: Kaiser, 1986) 200–211.

Spangenberg, Izak J. J.
"Psalm 49 and the Book of Qohelet," *SK* 18 (1997) 328–44.

Spieckermann, Hermann
"Suchen und Finden: Kohelets kritische Reflexionen," *Bib* 79 (1998) 305–32.

Stolze, Jürgen
"'Die Schrift mit der Schrift auslegen': Ein Versuch zur Auslegung von Kohelet 3,16-22," *Theologie für die Praxis* 26 (2000) 42–61.

Uehlinger, Christoph
"Qohelet im Horizont mesopotamischer, levantinischer und ägyptischer Weisheitsliteratur der persischen und hellenistischen Zeit," in Schwienhorst-Schönberger, ed., *Das Buch Kohelet,* 155–247.

Umbreit, F. W. C.
"Gott hat den Menschen die Welt in ihr Herz gelegt: Bemerkungen zu Pred.Sal. Kap. 3,11," *ThStK* 19 (1846) 147–58.

Vonach, Andreas
"Gottes Souveränität anerkennen: Zum Verständnis der 'Kanonformel' in Koh 3,14," in Schoors, ed., *Qohelet in Context,* 391–97.

Wallis, Gerhard
"Das Zeitverständnis des Predigers Salomo," in Manfred Weippert and Stefan Timm, eds., *Meilenstein: Festgabe für Herbert Donner* (ÄAT 30; Wiesbaden: Harrassowitz, 1995) 316–23.

Zimmermann, Frank
"Notes on Some Difficult Old Testament Passages," *JBL* 55 (1936) 303–8.

Zimmermann, Frank
"On Eccles. 3:18," *AJSL* 58 (1941) 100–101.

■ **4:13-16**

Buhlman, Alain
"The Difficulty of Thinking in Greek and Speaking in Hebrew (Qoheleth 3,18; 4,13-16; 5,8)," *JSOT* 90 (2000) 101–8.

Garrett, Duane A.
"Qoheleth on the Use and Abuse of Political Power," *TJ* 8 (1987) 159–77.

Gevarjahu, H. M. I.
"On Clarifying the Identity of the 'Needy and Wise' Child and the 'Next Child' in Qoh 4:13-16," *BethM* 9 (1964) 198 (Heb.).

Irwin, William A.
"Eccles. 4:13-16," *JNES* 3 (1944) 255–57.

Ogden, Graham S.
"Historical Allusion in Qohelet IV 13-16?" *VT* 30 (1980) 309–15.

Rudman, Dominic
"A Contextual Reading of Ecclesiastes 4,13-16," *JBL* 116 (1997) 57–73.

Schlögel, Nivard
"Qoheleth 4,13-16," *WZKM* 33 (1927) 163–65.

Schunck, Klaus-Dietrich
"Drei Seleukiden im Buche Kohelet?" *VT* 9 (1959) 192–201, repr. in Schunck, *Altes Testament und Heiliges Land: Gesammelte Studien zum Alten Testament und zur biblischen Landeskunde,* vol. 1 (Frankfurt am Main: Lang, 1989) 9–18.

Torrey, Charles C.
"The Problem of Ecclesiastes IV, 13-16," *VT* 2 (1952) 175–77.

Tropper, Josef
"Hebräisch *zhr*$_2$ 'kundtun, warnen,'" *ZAH* 8 (1995) 144–48.

Weisman, Ze'ev
"Elements of Political Satire in Koheleth 4,13-16; 9,13-16," *ZAW* 111 (1999) 547–60.

Wright, Addison G.
"The Poor but Wise Youth and the Old but Foolish King (Qoh 4:13-16)," *CBQ* 29 (1997) 142–54.

■ 4:17—5:6

Cartledge, Tony W.
Vows in the Hebrew Bible and the Ancient Near East (JSOTSup 147; Sheffield: Sheffield Academic Press, 1992).

Ernst, Alexander B.
Weisheitliche Kultkritik: Zu Theologie und Ethik des Sprüchebuchs und der Prophetie des 8. Jahrhunderts (BThSt 23; Neukirchen-Vluyn: Neukirchener Verlag, 1994).

Fletcher, Douglas K.
"Ecclesiastes 5,1-7," *Int* 55 (2001) 296–98.

Guillod-Reymond, Daphné
"Echo à Qohéleth 4,17–5,6 dans le Nouveau Testament: Avec Matthieu 7,7-11," *Lire et Dire* 32 (1997) 24–26.

Habegger, Werner
"Qohéleth 4,17–5,6: La pratique religieuse comme expression de notre humanité," *Lire et Dire* 32 (1997) 15–23.

Hieke, Thomas
"Wie hast Du's mit der Religion? Sprechhandlungen und Wirkintentionen in Kohelet 4,17–5,6," in Schoors, ed., *Qohelet in Context,* 319–38.

Lavoie, Jean-Jacques
"Critique cultuelle et doute existentiel: Étude de Qoh 4,17–5,6," *SR* 26 (1997) 147–67.

Lohfink, Norbert
"Warum ist der Tor unfähig, böse zu handeln? (Koh 4,17)," in Fritz Steppat, ed., *XXI. Deutscher Orientalistentag vom 24. bis 29. März 1980 in Berlin: Ausgewählte Vorträge* (ZDMG Sup 5; Wiesbaden: Steiner, 1983) 113–20, repr. in Lohfink, *Studien,* 83–94.

Perdue, L. G.
Wisdom and Cult (SBLDS 30; Missoula, Mont.: Scholars Press, 1977).

Rofé, Alexander
"The 'Messenger' in Qoh 5:5 in Light of a Wisdom Discussion Formula," *ErIsr* 14 (1978) 105–9, 126 (Heb.).

Salters, Robert B.
"Notes on the History of Interpretation of Koh 5,5," *ZAW* 90 (1978) 95–101.

Schmidt, Johannes
"Koh 4,17," *ZAW* 58 (1940/41) 279–80.

Spangenberg, Izak J. J.
"A Century of Wrestling with Qohelet: The Research History of the Book Illustrated with a Discussion of Qoh 4,17–5,6," in Schoors, ed., *Qohelet in Context,* 61–91.

Spangenberg, Izak J. J.
"Die struktuur en strekking van Prediker 4:17–5:6," *NGTT* 30 (1989) 260–69.

Tita, Hubert
"Ist die thematische Einheit Koh 4,17–5,6 eine Anspielung auf die Salomoerzählung? Aporien der religionskritischen Interpretation," *BN* 84 (1996) 87–102.

■ 5:7-8

Anderlini, Gianpaolo
"Qohelet 5,7-8: Note linguistiche ed esegetiche," *BeO* 37 (1995) 13–32.

Buhlman, Alain
"The Difficulty of Thinking in Greek and Speaking in Hebrew (Qoheleth 3,18; 4,13-16; 5,8)," *JSOT* 90 (2000) 101–8.

Garrett, Duane A.
"Qoheleth on the Use and Abuse of Political Power," *TJ* 8 (1987) 159–77.

Kugel, James L.
"Qohelet and Money," *CBQ* 51 (1989) 32–49.

Schulte, Adalbert
"Zu Koh. 5,7 u. 8," *BZ* 8 (1910) 4.

Varela, A. T.
"A New Approach to Eccle 5:8-9," *BT* 27 (1976) 240–41.

■ 5:9—6:9

Ackroyd, Peter R.
"Two Hebrew Notes," *ASTI* 5 (1966/67) 82–86.

Baker, Phil
"Qohélet 5,9-17: L'argent et le bonheur," *Lire et Dire* 32 (1997) 27–32.

Barton, George Aaron
"The Text and Interpretation of Ecclesiastes 5,19," *JBL* 27 (1908) 65–66.

Dahood, Mitchell
"Hebrew-Ugaritic Lexicography VI," *Bib* 49 (1968) 355–69.

Dahood, Mitchell
"Hebrew-Ugaritic Lexicography VIII," *Bib* 51 (1970) 391–404.

Ellermeier, Friedrich
"Die Entmachtung der Weisheit im Denken Qohelets: Zu Text und Auslegung von Qoh. 6,7-9," *ZThK* 60 (1963) 1–20.

Fredericks, Daniel C.
"Chiasm and Parallel Structure in Qoheleth 5:9–6:9," *JBL* 108 (1989) 17–35.

Guillod-Reymond, Daphné
"Echo à Qohéleth 5,9-17 dans le Nouveau Testa-ment: Avec Luc 18,18-30," *Lire et Dire* 32 (1997) 32–34.

Krüger, Thomas
"Das Gute und die Güter: Erwägungen zur Bedeu-tung von טוב und טובה im Qoheletbuch," *ThZ* 53 [FS Ernst Jenni] (1997) 53–63.

Kugel, James L.
"Qohelet and Money," *CBQ* 51 (1989) 32–49.

Lange, Armin
"In Diskussion mit dem Tempel: Zur Auseinander-setzung zwischen Kohelet und weisheitlichen Kreisen am Jerusalemer Tempel," in Schoors, ed., *Qohelet in Context*, 113–59.

Lohfink, Norbert
"Kohelet und die Banken: Zur Übersetzung von Kohelet V 12-16," *VT* 39 (1989) 488–95, repr. in Lohfink, *Studien*, 143–50.

Lohfink, Norbert
"Qoheleth 5:17-19: Revelation by Joy," *CBQ* 52 (1990) 625–35; trans. of "Koh 5,17-19—Offen-barung durch Freude," in Lohfink, *Studien*, 151–65.

Michel
Untersuchungen, 138–59.

Murphy, Roland E.
"On Translating Ecclesiastes," *CBQ* 53 (1991) 571–79.

Ogden, Graham S.
"Translation Problems in Ecclesiastes 5.13-17," *BT* 39 (1989) 423–28.

Salters, Robert B.
"Notes on the Interpretation of Qoh 6,2," *ZAW* 91 (1979) 282–89.

■ 6:10-12

Crenshaw, James Lee
"The Expression *mî yôdēaʿ* in the Hebrew Bible," *VT* 36 (1986) 274–88, repr. in Crenshaw, *Urgent Advice*, 279–91.

Michel
Untersuchungen, 159–64.

Qimron, Elisha
"שהתקיף (Qoh 6,10)—An Unnoticed Aramaism," *Leš* 56 (1991) 117 (Heb.).

Wise, Michael O.
"A Calque from Aramaic in Qoheleth 6:12, 7:12, and 8:13," *JBL* 109 (1990) 249–57.

■ 7:1-14

Andrews, Susan R.
"Ecclesiastes 7,1-19," *Int* 55 (2001) 299–301.

Driver, Godfrey Rolles
"Problems and Solutions," *VT* 4 (1954) 225–45.

Garrett, Duane A.
"Qoheleth on the Use and Abuse of Political Power," *TJ* 8 (1987) 159–77.

Gelio, Roberto
"Osservazioni critiche sul *māšāl* di Qoh 7,5-7," *Lateranum* 54 (1988) 1–15.

Lavoie, Jean-Jacques
"La philosophie comme réflexion sur la mort: Étude de Qohélet 7,1-4," *LTP* 54 (1998) 91–107.

Lohfink, Norbert
"Zur Philosophie Kohelets: Eine Auslegung von Kohelet 7,1-10," *BK* 45 (1990) 20–25.

Margoliouth, David Samuel
"Ecclesiastes VII.10, and Incidentally Parts of VI.3 and VIII.9," *Exp.* 9,1 (1924) 94–102.

Margoliouth, David Samuel
"Qoheleth (Ecclesiastes) VII.7," *Theology* 8,2 (1924) 228–29.

Michel, Diethelm
"Qohelet-Probleme: Überlegungen zu Qoh 8,2-9 und 7,11-14," *ThViat* 15 (1979/80) 81–103.

Michel
Untersuchungen, 84–105.

Murphy, Roland E.
"A Form-Critical Consideration of Ecclesiastes VII," *SBLSP* 2 (1974) 77–85.

Murphy, Roland E.
"On Translating Ecclesiastes," *CBQ* 53 (1991) 571–79.

Osborn, Noel D.
"A Guide for Balanced Living: An Exegetical Study of Ecclesiastes 7:1-14," *BT* 21 (1970) 185–96.

Piotti, Franco
"Osservazioni su alcuni problemi esegetici nel libro dell'Ecclesiaste: Studio II: Il canto degli stolti (Qoh. 7,5)," *BeO* 21 (1979) 129–40.

Wise, Michael O.
"A Calque from Aramaic in Qoheleth 6:12, 7:12, and 8:13," *JBL* 109 (1990) 249–57.

■ 7:15-22

Andrews, Susan R.
"Ecclesiastes 7:1-19," *Int* 55 (2001) 299–301.

Brindle, Wayne A.
"Rigteousness and Wickedness in Ecclesiastes 7:15-18," *AUSS* 23 (1985) 243–57, repr. in Zuck, ed., *Reflecting with Solomon*, 301–13.

Lichtheim, Miriam
"Observations on Papyrus Insinger," in Erik Hor-nung and Othmar Keel, eds., *Studien zu altägypti-schen Lebenslehren* (OBO 28; Freiburg: Universitätsverlag; Göttingen: Vandenhoeck & Ruprecht, 1979) 283–305, esp. 301–2.

Lux, Rüdiger
"Der 'Lebenskompromiss'—ein Wesenszug im Denken Kohelets? Zur Auslegung von Koh 7,15-18," in Jutta Hausmann and Hans-Jürgen Zobel, eds., *Alttestamentlicher Glaube und Biblische Theolo-gie: FS Horst Dietrich Preuss* (Stuttgart: Kohlham-mer, 1992) 267–78.

Mazzinghi, Luca
"Qohelet tra Giudaismo ed Ellenismo: Un'Indagine a partire da Qo 7,15-18," in Bellia and Passaro, eds., *Qohelet*, 90–116.

Murphy, Roland E.
"A Form-Critical Consideration of Ecclesiastes VII," *SBLSP* 2 (1974) 77–85.

Murphy, Roland E.
"On Translating Ecclesiastes," *CBQ* 53 (1991) 571–79.

Piotti, Franco
"Osservazioni su alcuni problemi esegetici nel libro dell'Ecclesiaste: Studio III," *BeO* 22 (1980) 243–53.

Schwienhorst-Schönberger, Ludger
"Via media: Koh 7,15-18 und die griechisch-hellenistische Philosophie," in Schoors, ed., *Qohelet in Context*, 181–203.

Whybray, Roger Norman
"Qoheleth the Immoralist? (Qoh. 7:16-17)," in Gammie et al., eds., *Israelite Wisdom*, 191–204.

■ **7:23-29**

Amsler, Samuel
"La sagesse de la femme," in Amsler, *Le dernier et l'avant-dernier: Etudes sur l'Ancien Testament* (MoBi 28; Geneva: Labor et Fides, 1993) 282–87.

Backhaus
Zeit und Zufall, 234–44.

Baltzer, Klaus
"Women and War in Qohelet 7:23–8:1a," *HTR* 80 (1987) 127–32.

Bedenbender, Andreas
"Geschlechtertausch und Geschlechtsverlust (Lk 24,10 und Pred 7,27): Zur Funktion der Attribute 'männlich' und 'weiblich' im Lukasevangelium und im Prediger Salomo," *TeKo* 20 (1998) 17–34.

Brenner, Athalya
"Some Observations on the Figurations of Women in Wisdom Literature," in Heather A. McKay and David J. A. Clines, eds., *Of Prophets' Visions and the Wisdom of Sages: Essays in Honour of R. Norman Whybray* (JSOTSup 163; Sheffield: Sheffield Academic Press, 1993) 192–208.

Burns, John Barclay
"Some Personifications of Death in the Old Testament," *Irish Biblical Studies* 11 (1989) 23–34.

Butting, Klara
"Weibsbilder bei Kafka und Kohelet: Eine Auslegung von Prediger 7,23-29," *TeKo* 14 (1991) 2–15.

Ceresko, Anthony R.
"The Function of Antanaclasis (מצא 'to find' // מצא 'to reach, overtake, grasp') in Hebrew Poetry, Especially in the Book of Qoheleth," *CBQ* 44 (1982) 551–69.

D'Alario, Vittoria
"Qo 7,26-28: Un testo antifemminista?" in Donatella Abignente et al., *La Donna nella Chiesa e nel mondo* (Studi promossi dalla Facoltà Teologica dell'Italia Meridionale e dalla Commissione Diocesana Donna; Napoli: Dehoniane, 1988) 225–34.

Fontaine, Carole R.
"'Many Devices' (Qoheleth 7,23–8,1): Qoheleth, Misogyny and the Malleus Maleficarum," in Athalya Brenner and Carole R. Fontaine, eds., *Wisdom and Psalms* (FCB 2/2; Sheffield: Sheffield Academic Press, 1998) 137–68.

Fox, Michael V., and Bezalel Porten
"Unsought Discoveries: Qoheleth 7:23–8:1a," *HS* 19 (1978) 26–38.

Garrett, Duane A.
"Ecclesiastes 7:25-29 and the Feminist Hermeneutic," *Criswell Theological Review* 2 (1988) 309–21.

Jost, Renate
"Frau und Adam (hebr. אדם): Feministische Überlegungen zur Auslegung von Kohelet 7,23-29," in Erhard S. Gerstenberger and Ulrich Schoenborn, eds., *Hermeneutik – Sozialgeschichtlich: Kontextualität in den Bibelwissenschaften aus der Sicht (latein)amerikanischer und europäischer Exegetinnen und Exegeten* (Exegese in unserer Zeit 1; Münster: Lit, 1999) 59–67.

Kagan, Z.
"'And I find more bitter than death the woman' (Qoh 7:26) ," *Yedaᶜ ᶜAm* 11,30 (1965) 78–87 (Heb.).

Krüger, Thomas
"'Frau Weisheit' in Koh 7,26?" *Bib* 73 (1992) 394–403, repr. in Krüger, *Kritische Weisheit*, 121–30.

Lohfink, Norbert
"War Kohelet ein Frauenfeind? Ein Versuch, die Logik und den Gegenstand von Koh. 7,23–8,1a herauszufinden," in Gilbert, ed., *Sagesse*, 259–87, 417–20, repr. in Lohfink, *Studien*, 31–69.

Long, V. Philips
"One Man among a Thousand, but Not a Woman among Them All: A Note on the Use of *māṣāʾ* in Ecclesiastes vii 28," in Klaus Dietrich Schunck and Matthias Augustin, eds., *"Lasset uns Brücken bauen . . .": Collected Communications to the XVth Congress of the International Organization for the Study of the Old Testament, Cambridge 1995* (BEAT 42; Frankfurt am Main: Lang, 1998) 101–9.

Loretz, Oswald
"'Frau' und griechisch-jüdische Philosophie im Buch Qohelet (Qoh 7,23–8,1 und 9,6-10)," *UF* 23 (1991) 245–64.

Loretz, Oswald
"Poetry and Prose in the Book of Qoheleth (1:1–3:22; 7:23–8:1; 9:6-10; 12:8-14)," in Johannes C. de Moor and Wilfred G. E. Watson, eds., *Verse in Ancient Near Eastern Prose* (AOAT 42; Kevelaer: Butzon & Bercker; Neukirchen-Vluyn: Neukirchener Verlag, 1993) 155–89.

Meyer, Ivo, and Martin Rose
"Sprüche und Widersprüche im Qohelet-Buch," *Variations herméneutiques* 6 (1997) 71–86.

Michel
Untersuchungen, 225–38.

Murphy, Roland E.
"A Form-Critical Consideration of Ecclesiastes VII," *SBLSP* 2 (1974) 77–85.

Murphy, Roland E.
"On Translating Ecclesiastes," *CBQ* 53 (1991) 571–79.

Pahk, Johan Yeong-Sik

"The Significance of אשר in Qoh 7,26: 'More bitter than death is the woman, *if* she is a snare,'" in Schoors, ed., *Qohelet in Context*, 373–83.

Pahk, Johan Yeong-Sik

"Women as Snares: A Metaphor of Warning in Qoh 7,26 and Sir 9,3," in Núria Calduch-Benages and J. Vermeylen, eds., *Treasures of Wisdom: Studies in Ben Sira and the Book of Wisdom: FS Maurice Gilbert* (BEThL 143; Leuven: Peeters, 1999) 397–404.

Richter, Hans-Friedemann

"Kohelets Urteil über die Frauen: Zu Koh 7,26.28 und 9,9 in ihrem Kontext," *ZAW* 108 (1996) 584–93.

Riesener, Ingrid

"Frauenfeindschaft im Alten Testament? Zum Verständnis von Qoh 7,25-29," in Diesel et al., eds., *Jedes Ding*, 193–207.

Rudman, Dominic

"Woman as Divine Agent in Ecclesiastes," *JBL* 116 (1997) 411–27.

Schoors, Antoon

"Bitterder dan de Dood is de Vrouw (Koh 7,26)," *Bijdr* 54 (1992) 121–40.

Schwienhorst-Schönberger

Nicht im Menschen, 173–80.

Spieckermann, Hermann

"Suchen und Finden: Kohelets kritische Reflexionen," *Bib* 79 (1998) 305–32.

Stolze, Jürgen

"Kohelet und die Frauen: Ein Versuch zu Gedankengang und Sinn von Kohelet 7,23-29," *Theologie für die Praxis* 24 (1998) 51–63.

■ **8:1-9**

Beentjes, Panc

"'Who Is Like the Wise?' Some Notes on Qohelet 8,1-15," in Schoors, ed., *Qohelet in Context*, 303–15.

Garrett, Duane A.

"Qoheleth on the Use and Abuse of Political Power," *TJ 8* (1987) 159–77.

Hurvitz, Avi

"The History of a Legal Formula: *kōl ʾăšer ḥāpēṣ ʿāśāh* (Psalms CXV 3, CXXXV 6)," *VT* 32 (1982) 257–67.

Irwin, William A.

"Ecclesiastes 8:2-9," *JNES* 4 (1945) 130–31.

Michel, Diethelm

"Qohelet-Probleme: Überlegungen zu Qoh 8,2-9 und 7,11-14," *ThViat* 15 (1979/80) 81–103.

Waldman, Nahum M.

"The *dābār rāʿ* of Eccl 8:3," *JBL* 98 (1979) 407–8.

■ **8:10-15**

Beentjes, Panc

"'Who Is Like the Wise?' Some Notes on Qohelet 8,1-15," in Schoors, ed., *Qohelet in Context*, 303–15.

Garrett, Duane A.

"Qoheleth on the Use and Abuse of Political Power," *TJ 8* (1987) 159–77.

Homissen, Guy van

"Et je fais l'éloge de la joie (Qoh 8,15)," *LumVie* 43 (1988) 37–46.

Reines, Ch. W.

"Koheleth VIII,10," *JJS* 5 (1954) 86–87.

Serrano, J. J.

"I Saw the Wicked Buried (Eccl. 8,10)," *CBQ* 16 (1954) 168–70.

Wise, Michael O.

"A Calque from Aramaic in Qoheleth 6:12, 7:12, and 8:13," *JBL* 109 (1990) 249–57.

■ **8:16-17**

Cochand-Méan, Corinne

"Qohéleth 8,16-17: L'insaississable oeuvre de Dieu," *Lire et Dire* 32 (1997) 35–40.

Guillod-Reymond, Daphné

"Echo à Qohéleth 8,16-17 dans le Nouveau Testament: Avec Marc 4,10-13," *Lire et Dire* 32 (1997) 41–43.

Pahk

Canto.

Rudman, Dominic

"The Translation and Interpretation of Eccl 8:17A," *JNSL* 23 (1997) 109–16.

■ **9:1-12**

Brown, William P.

"'Whatever your hand finds to do': Qoheleth's Work Ethic," *Int* 55 (2001) 271–84.

Burns, John Barclay

"Some Personifications of Death in the Old Testament," *IBS* 11 (1989) 23–34.

Garrett, Duane A.

"Qoheleth on the Use and Abuse of Political Power," *TJ 8* (1987) 159–77.

Grimme, Hubert

"Babel und Koheleth-Jojakhin," *OLZ* 8 (1905) 432–33.

Jones, Bruce William

"From Gilgamesh to Qoheleth," in W. W. Hallo, B. W. Jones, and G. L. Mattingly, eds., *The Bible in the Light of Cuneiform Literature* (Scripture in Context 3; ANETS 8; Lewiston, N.Y.: Mellen, 1990) 349–79.

Kaiser, Otto

"Von der Schönheit des Menschen als Gabe Gottes," in Axel Graupner, Holger Delkurt, and Alexander B. Ernst, eds., *Verbindungslinien: FS für Werner H. Schmidt zum 65. Geburtstag* (Neukirchen-Vluyn: Neukirchener Verlag, 2000) 153–63.

Lavoie, Jean-Jacques

"Bonheur et finitude humaine: Étude de Qo 9,7-10," *ScEs* 45 (1993) 313–24.

Lavoie, Jean-Jacques

"Étude de Quelques Mots Obscurs du Qohélet à la Lumière de l'Histoire de l'Exégèse et des Manuscrits Judéo-Persans de la Bibliothèque Nationale de France," *SR* 29 (2000) 183–97.

Lavoie, Jean-Jacques

"Temps et finitude humaines: Étude de Qohéleth IX 11-12," *VT* 46 (1996) 430–47.

Lavoie, Jean-Jacques

"Vie, mort et finitude humaine en Qo 9,1-6," *ScEs* 47 (1995) 69–80.

Lichtheim, Miriam

"Observations on Papyrus Insinger," in Erik Hornung and Othmar Keel, eds., *Studien zu altägyptischen Lebenslehren* (OBO 28; Freiburg: Universitätsverlag; Göttingen: Vandenhoeck & Ruprecht, 1979) 283–305, esp. 301–2.

Loretz, Oswald

"Altorientalische und kanaanäische Topoi im Buche Koheleth," *UF* 12 (1980) 267–78.

Loretz, Oswald

"'Frau' und griechisch-jüdische Philosophie im Buch Qohelet (Qoh 7,23–8,1 und 9,6-10)," *UF* 23 (1991) 245–64.

Loretz, Oswald

"Poetry and Prose in the Book of Qoheleth (1:1–3:22; 7:23–8:1; 9:6-10; 12:8-14)," in Johannes C. de Moor and Wilfred G. E. Watson, eds., *Verse in Ancient Near Eastern Prose* (AOAT 42; Kevelaer: Butzon & Bercker; Neukirchen-Vluyn: Neukirchener Verlag, 1993) 155–89.

Ogden, Graham S.

"Qoheleth IX 1-16," *VT* 32 (1982) 158–69.

Pahk, Johan Yeong Sik

"A Syntactical and Contextual Consideration of *ʾšh* in Qoh ix 9," *VT* 51 (2001) 370–80.

Pahk

Canto.

Richter, Hans-Friedemann

"Kohelets Urteil über die Frauen: Zu Koh 7,26.28 und 9,9 in ihrem Kontext," *ZAW* 108 (1996) 584–93.

Rudman, Dominic

"Woman as Divine Agent in Ecclesiastes," *JBL* 116 (1997) 411–27.

Savignac, Jean de

"La sagesse du Qôhélét et l'épopée de Gilgamesh," *VT* 28 (1978) 318–23.

Schmid, Hans Heinrich

"Kohelet als Platzhalter des Evangeliums: Eine Predigt über Koh 9,11f," in Manfred Oeming and Axel Graupner, eds., *Altes Testament und christliche Verkündigung: FS für Antonius H. J. Gunneweg* (Stuttgart: Kohlhammer, 1987) 412–15.

Thompson, David L.

"The Godly and the Good Life: The Relationship between Character and Circumstance in Biblical Thought," *Asbury Seminarian* 34 (1979) 28–46.

Tigay, Jeffrey H.

"On Evaluating Claims of Literary Borrowing," in M. E. Cohen, D. C. Snell, and D. B. Weisberg, eds., *The Tablet and the Scroll: Near Eastern Studies in Honor of W. W. Hallo* (Bethesda, Md.: CDL, 1993) 250–55.

Uehlinger, Christoph

"Qohelet im Horizont mesopotamischer, levantinischer und ägyptischer Weisheitsliteratur der persischen und hellenistischen Zeit," in Schwienhorst-Schönberger, ed., *Das Buch Kohelet*, 155–247.

■ **9:13—10:20**

Bianchi, Francesco

"Qohelet 10,8-11 or the Misfortunes of Wisdom," *BeO* 40 (1998) 111–17.

Brawer, A. J.

"The Meaning of the Word מדע in the Book of Qoheleth," *BethM* 21 (1974) 158ff. (Heb.).

Chen, Chin-Wen

"A Study of Ecclesiastes 10:18-19," *Taiwan Journal of Theology* 11 (1989) 117–26.

Dahood, Mitchell

"Canaanite Words in Qoheleth 10,20," *Bib* 46 (1965) 210–12.

Dahood, Mitchell

"Three Parallel Pairs in Eccl. 10:18: A Reply to Prof. Gordis," *JQR* 62 (1971) 84–87.

Freedman, David Noel

"Caution: Bible Critic at Work," *BRev* 15 (1999) 42–43.

Frendo, Anthony

"The Broken Construct Chain in Qoh 10,10b," *Bib* 62 (1981) 544–45.

Keel, Othmar

Vögel als Boten (OBO 14; Freiburg: Universitätsverlag; Göttingen: Vandenhoeck & Ruprecht, 1977).

Kottsieper, Ingo

"Die Bedeutung der Wz. *ʿšb* und *skn* in Koh 10,9: Ein Beitrag zum hebr. Lexikon," *UF* 18 (1986) 213–22.

Krüger, Thomas

"'Wertvoller als Weisheit und Ehre ist wenig Torheit,' (Kohelet 10,1)," *BN* 89 (1997) 62–75.

Lavoie, Jean-Jacques

"La philosophie politique de Qohélet 9,13-16," *ScEs* 49 (1997) 315–28.

Leahy, Michael

"The Meaning of Ecclesiastes 10,15," *ITQ* 18 (1951) 288–95.

Ogden, Graham S.

"Qoheleth IX 1-16," *VT* 32 (1982) 158–69.

Ogden, Graham S.

"Qoheleth IX 17–X 20: Variations on the Theme of Wisdom's Strength and Vulnerability," *VT* 30 (1980) 27–37.

Piotti, Franco

"Il rapporto tra ricchi, stolti e principi in Qoh. 10,6-7 alla luce della letteratura sapienziale," *ScC* 102 (1974) 328–33.

Salters, Robert B.

"Text and Exegesis in Koh 10,19," *ZAW* 89 (1977) 423–26.

Saracino, Francesco

"Ras Ibn Hani 78/20 and Some Old Testament Connections," *VT* 32 (1982) 338–43.

Schunck, Klaus-Dietrich

"Drei Seleukiden im Buche Kohelet?" *VT* 9 (1959) 192–201, repr. in Klaus-Dietrich Schunck, *Altes Testament und Heiliges Land: Gesammelte Studien zum Alten Testament und zur biblischen Landeskunde,* vol. 1 (Frankfurt am Main: Lang, 1989) 9–18.

Staerk, Willy

"Zur Exegese von Koh 10,20 und 11,1," *ZAW* 59 (1942/43) 216–18.

Weisman, Ze'ev

"Elements of Political Satire in Koheleth 4,13-16; 9,13-16," *ZAW* 111 (1999) 547–60.

Winton Thomas, David

"A Note on בְּמַדָּעֲךָ in Eccles. X.20," *JTS* 50 (1949) 177.

■ 11:1—12:7

Anath, Moshe E.

"The Lament over the Death of Human Beings in the Book of Qoheleth," *BethM* 15 (1970) 375–80 (Heb.).

Anderson, Phyllis

"Credible Promises: Ecclesiastes 11:3-6," *Currents in Theology and Mission* 20 (1993) 265–67.

Beal, Timothy K.

"C(ha)osmopolis: Qohelet's Last Words," in Tod Linafelt and Timothy K. Beal, eds., *God in the Fray: A Tribute to Walter Brueggemann* (Minneapolis: Fortress Press, 1998) 290–304.

Bruns, J. Edgar

"The Imagery of Eccles 12:6a," *JBL* 84 (1965) 428–30.

Busto Saiz, José Ramón

"בוראיך (Qoh. 12,1), reconsiderado," *Sef* 46 (1986) 85–87.

Busto Saiz, José Ramón

"Estructura metrica y estrofica del 'poema sobre la juventud y la vejez': Qohelet 11,7-12," *Sef* 43 (1983) 17–25.

Buzy, Denis

"Le portrait de la vieillesse (Ecclésiaste XII, 1-7)," *RB* 41 (1932) 329–40.

Crenshaw, James Lee

"Youth and Old Age in Qoheleth," *HAR* 10 (1986) 1–13, repr. in idem, *Urgent Advice*, 535–47.

Davis, Barry C.

"Ecclesiastes 12:1-8: Death, an Impetus for Life," *BSac* 148 (1991) 298–318, repr. in Zuck, ed., *Reflecting with Solomon*, 347–66.

Dell'Aversano, C.

"משפט in Qoh. 11:9c," in Angelo Vivian, ed., *Biblische und Judaistische Studien: FS Paolo Sacchi* (JudUm 29; Frankfurt: Lang, 1990) 121–34.

Dulin, Rachel Z.

"'How Sweet Is the Light': Qoheleth's Age-Centered Teachings," *Int* 55 (2001) 260–70.

Fox, Michael V.

"Aging and Death in Qoheleth 12," *JSOT* 42 (1988) 55–77; repr. in Zuck, ed., *Reflecting with Solomon*, 381–99, repr. in Clines, ed., *Poetical Books*, 199–221.

Fredericks, Daniel C.

"Life's Storms and Structural Unity in Qoheleth 11.1–12.8," *JSOT* 52 (1991) 95–114.

Gilbert, Maurice

"La description de la vieillesse en Qohelet XII 1-7 est-elle allégorique?" in J. A. Emerton, ed., *Congress Volume, Vienna 1980* (VTSup 32; Leiden: Brill, 1981) 96–109.

Ginsberg, Harold Louis

"Koheleth 12:4 in the Light of Ugaritic," *Syria* 33 (1956) 99–101.

Glasson, T. Francis

"'You never know': The Message of Ecclesiastes 11:1-6," *EvQ* 60 (1983) 43–48.

Gómez Aranda, Mariano

"Ecl 12,1-7 interpretado por Abraham Ibn 'Ezra," *Sef* 52 (1992) 113–21.

Henslow, G.

"The Carob and the Locust," *ExpT* 15 (1904) 285–86.

Holtzhammer, Henri

"Réflexions sur le sens biologique du chapitre douze de l'Ecclésiaste," *Revue de l'histoire et de médecine hébraïque* 10 (1957) 77–86, 111–20, 161–69.

Jarick, John

"An 'Allegory of Age' as Apocalypse (Ecclesiastes 12:1-7)," *Colloquium* 22 (1990) 19–27.

Jirku, Anton

"Eine Laterne aus dem altorientalischen Palästina," *Forschungen und Fortschritte* 29 (1955) 157.

Kraus, Matthew

"Christians, Jews and Pagans in Dialogue: Jerome on Ecclesiastes 12:1-7," *HUCA* 70–71 (1999–2000) 183–231.

Kruger, H. A. J.

"Old Age Frailty versus Cosmic Deterioration? A Few Remarks on the Interpretation of Qohelet 11,7–12,8," in Schoors, ed., *Qohelet in Context*, 399–411.

Krüger, Thomas

"Dekonstruktion und Rekonstruktion prophetischer Eschatologie im Qohelet-Buch," in Diesel et al., eds., *Jedes Ding,* 107–129, repr. in Krüger, *Kritische Weisheit*, 151–72.

Kruse, Heinz

"'Da partem septem necnon et octo,'" *VD* 27 (1949) 164–69.

Lavoie, Jean-Jacques

"Étude de l'expression בֵּית עוֹלָמוֹ dans Qo 12,5 à la lumière des textes du Proche-Orient ancien," in Jean-Claude Petit et al., eds., *Où demeures-tu? La maison depuis le monde biblique: FS Guy Couturier* (Saint Laurent, Québec: Fides, 1994) 213–26.

Leahy, Michael
 "The Meaning of Ecclesiastes 12,1-5," *ITQ* 19 (1952) 297–300, repr. in Zuck, ed., *Reflecting with Solomon*, 375–79.

Leanza, Sandro
 "Eccl 12,1-7: L'interpretazione escatologica dei Padri e degli esegeti medievali," *Aug* 18 (1978) 191–208.

Lohfink, Norbert
 "'Freu dich, junger Mann . . .': Das Schlussgedicht des Koheletbuches (Koh 11,9–12,8)," *BK* 45 (1990) 12–19.

Lohfink, Norbert
 "'Freu dich, Jüngling—doch nicht, weil du jung bist': Zum Formproblem im Schlussgedicht Kohelets (Koh 11,9–12,8)," *BibInt* 3 (1995) 158–89, repr. in Lohfink, *Studien zu Kohelet*, 181–214.

Lohfink, Norbert
 "Grenzen und Einbindung des Kohelet-Schlussgedichts," in Peter Mommer and Winfried Thiel, eds., *Altes Testament–Forschung und Wirkung: FS Henning Graf Reventlow* (Frankfurt am Main: Lang, 1994) 33–46, repr. in Lohfink, *Studien*, 167–80.

Margalit, Shlomoh
 "Light on Obscurities," *BethM* 33 (1987/88) 68–71 (Heb.).

Moore, George F.
 "The Caper-Plant and Its Edible Products: With Reference to Eccles. XII.5," *JBL* 10 (1891) 55–64.

Müller, Hans-Peter
 "Weisheitliche Deutungen der Sterblichkeit: Gen 3,19 und Pred 3,21; 12,7 im Licht antiker Parallelen," in Müller, *Mensch–Umwelt–Eigenwelt*, 69–100.

Munnich, Olivier
 "Traduire la Septante: Ecclesiaste XII, 1–8," *Lalies* 3 (1984) 105–11.

Murison, R. G.
 "The Almond," *ExpT* 16 (1905) 334–35.

Murphy, Paul R.
 "Petronius 71,11 and Ecclesiastes 12:5-6," *Classical Weekly* 45 (1951/52) 120.

Niekerk, M. J. H. van
 "Qohelet's Advice to the Young of His Time—and to Ours Today? Chapter 11:7–12:8 as a Text of the Pre-Christian Era," *OTE* 7 (1994) 370–80.

Ogden, Graham S.
 "Qoheleth XI 1–6," *VT* 33 (1983) 222–30.

Ogden, Graham S.
 "Qoheleth XI 7–XII 8: Qoheleth's Summons to Enjoyment and Reflection," *VT* 34 (1984) 27–38.

Olinger, Danny
 "Is Wisdom Literature Eschatological?" *Kerux* 11 (1996) 14–22.

Piotti, Franco
 "Osservazioni su alcuni paralleli extrabiblici nell' 'allegoria della vecchiaia' (Qohelet 12,1-7)," *BeO* 19 (1977) 119–28.

Rodríguez, I.
 "Una antigua estampa otoñal: Ecl. 11,3 y paralelos clásicos," *Helmantica* 10 (1959) 383–90.

Salvaneschi, Enrica
 "Memento vivere (Qohélet 12,1-8)," *RasIsr* 56 (1990) 31–59.

Sawyer, John F. A.
 "The Ruined House in Ecclesiastes 12: A Reconstruction of the Original Parable," *JBL* 94 (1975) 519–31.

Scharbert, Josef
 "Die Altersbeschwerden in der ägyptischen, babylonischen und biblischen Weisheit," in R. Schulz and M. Görg, eds., *Lingua restitua orientalis: FS Julius Assfalg* (ÄAT 20; Wiesbaden: Harrassowitz, 1990) 289–98.

Seow, Choon-Leong
 "Qohelet's Eschatological Poem," *JBL* 118 (1999) 209–34.

Slemmons, Timothy Matthew
 "Ecclesiastes 12:1-13," *Int* 55 (2001) 302–4.

Staerk, Willy
 "Zur Exegese von Koh 10,20 und 11,1," *ZAW* 59 (1942/43) 216–18.

Stoute, P. P.
 "Bread upon the Waters," *BS* 107 (1950) 222–26.

Strauss, Hans
 "Erwägungen zur seelsorgerlichen Dimension von Kohelet 12,1-7," *ZThK* 78 (1981) 267–75.

Taylor, Charles
 "The Dirge of Coheleth," *JQR* 4 (1892) 533–49.

Taylor, Charles
 The Dirge of Coheleth in Ecclesiastes XII: Discussed and Literally Interpreted (Edinburgh: Williams & Norgate, 1874).

Tsukimoto, Akio
 "The Background of Qoh 11,1-6 and Qohelet's Agnosticism," *AJBI* 19 (1993) 34–52.

Vajda, Georges
 "Ecclésiaste XII 2-7, interprété par un auteur juif d'Andalousie du XIe siècle," *JSS* 27 (1982) 33–46.

Viviers, H.
 "Nie'n kans vat of'n kans vermy nie, maar alle kanse benut! 'n Sosio-retoriese waardering van Prediker 11,1-6," *SK* 18 (1997) 365–79.

Wal, A. J. O. van der
 "Qohelet 12,1a: A Relatively Unique Statement in Israel's Wisdom Tradition," in Schoors, ed., *Qohelet in Context*, 413–18.

Watson, Wilfred G. E.
 "The Unnoticed Word Pair 'eye(s)' // 'heart,'" *ZAW* 101 (1989) 398–408.

Witzenrath, Hagia
 "Süss ist das Licht . . .": Eine literaturwissenschaftliche Untersuchung zu Koh 11,7–12,7 (ATSAT 11; St. Ottilien: Eos, 1979).

Youngblood, Ronald F.
 "Qoheleth's 'Dark House' (Eccl. 12:5)," *JETS* 29 (1986) 397–410, repr. in Walter C. Kaiser and Ronald F. Youngblood, eds., *A Tribute to Gleason Archer: Essays on the Old Testament* (Chicago: Moody Press, 1986) 211–17.

◼ 12:8

See under 1:2.

◼ 12:9-14

Auwers, Jean-Marie
"Problèmes d'interprétation de l'épilogue de Qohèlèt," in Schoors, ed., *Qohelet in Context*, 267–82.

Backhaus, Franz Josef
"Der Weisheit letzter Schluss! Qoh 12,9–14 im Kontext von Traditionsgeschichte und beginnender Kanonisierung," *BN* 72 (1994) 28–59.

Backhaus
Zeit und Zufall, 344–51.

Baumgärtel, Friedrich
"Die Ochsenstachel und die Nägel in Koh 12,11," *ZAW* 81 (1969) 98.

Boer, Pieter Arie Hendrik de
"A Note on Ecclesiastes 12,12a," in Robert H. Fischer, ed., *A Tribute to Arthur Vööbus: Studies in Early Christian Literature and its Environment, Primarly in the Syrian East* (Chicago: Lutheran School of Theology, 1977) 85–88, repr. in P. A. H. de Boer, *Selected Studies in Old Testament Exegesis* (ed. C. van Duin; OTS 27; Leiden: Brill, 1991) 168–71.

Bronznik, Nahum M.
"The Making of Many Books Has No End," *BethM* 82 (1979/80) 213–18 (Heb.).

Dohmen, Christoph
"Das viele Büchermachen hat kein Ende (Koh 12,12): Wachstumsspuren in der Heiligen Schrift," in Christoph Dohmen and Manfred Oeming, *Biblischer Kanon warum und wozu? Eine Kanontheologie* (QD 137; Freiburg: Herder, 1992) 30–54.

Dohmen, Christoph
"Der Weisheit letzter Schluss? Anmerkungen zur Übersetzung und Bedeutung von Koh 12,9-14," *BN* 63 (1992) 12–18.

Fishbane, Michael
Biblical Interpretation in Ancient Israel (2d ed.; Oxford: Clarendon, 1988) 29–32.

Fox, Michael V.
"Frame Narrative and Composition in the Book of Qohelet," *HUCA* 48 (1977) 83–106.

Galling, Kurt
"The Scepter of Wisdom: A Note on the Gold Sheath of Zendjirli and Ecclesiastes 12:11," *BASOR* 119 (1950) 15–18.

Goldin, Judah
"The End of Ecclesiastes: Literal Exegesis and Its Transformation," in Alexander Altmann, ed., *Biblical Motifs: Origins and Transformations* (STLI 3; Cambridge: Harvard Univ. Press, 1966) 135–58, repr. in Barry Eichler and Jeffrey Tigay, eds., *Studies in Midrash and Related Literature* (JPS Scholars of Distinction Series; Philadelphia: Jewish Publication Society, 1988) 3–25.

Haupt, Paul
"On the Book of Ecclesiastes: With Special Reference to the Closing Section," *Johns Hopkins University Circulars* 10 (1891) 115–17.

Koenen, Klaus
"Zu den Epilogen des Buches Qohelet," *BN* 72 (1994) 24–27.

Lavoie, Jean-Jacques
"Étude de Quelques Mots Obscurs du Qohélet à la Lumière de l'Histoire de l'Exégèse et des Manuscrits Judéo-Persans de la Bibliothèque Nationale de France," *SR* 29 (2000) 183–97.

Lavoie, Jean-Jacques
"Un éloge à Qohélet: Étude de Qo 12,9-10," *LTP* 50 (1994) 145–70.

Lohfink, Norbert
"Der Weise und das Volk in Koh 12,9 und Sir 37,23," in Núria Calduch-Benages and J. Vermeylen, eds., *Treasures of Wisdom: Studies in Ben Sira and the Book of Wisdom: FS Maurice Gilbert* (BEThL 143; Leuven: Peeters, 1999) 405–10.

Lohfink, Norbert
"Les épilogues du livre de Qohélet et les débuts du Canon," in Pietro Bovati et Roland Meynet, eds., *Ouvrir les écritures: Mélanges offerts à Paul Beauchamp* (LD 162; Paris: Cerf, 1995) 77–96.

Lohfink, Norbert
"Zu einigen Satzeröffnungen im Epilog des Koheletbuches," in Diesel et al., eds., *Jedes Ding*, 131–47.

Loretz
Qohelet, 139–43, 290–97.

Loretz, Oswald
"Poetry and Prose in the Book of Qoheleth (1:1–3:22; 7:23–8:1; 9:6-10; 12:8-14)," in Johannes C. de Moor and Wilfred G. E. Watson, eds., *Verse in Ancient Near Eastern Prose* (AOAT 42; Kevelaer: Butzon & Bercker; Neukirchen-Vluyn: Neukirchener Verlag, 1993) 155–89.

Margoliouth, G.
"Ecclesiastes XII.8-14," *ExpT* 35 (1923/24) 121–24.

Mazzinghi, Luca
"'Date da un Solo Pastore' (Qo 12,11): L'Epilogo del Qohelet e il Problema dell'Ispirazione," *RStB* 12 (2000) 59–74.

Meek, Theophile J.
"Translating the Hebrew Bible," *JBL* 79 (1960) 328–35.

Murphy, Roland E.
"The Sage in Ecclesiastes and Qoheleth the Sage," in Gammie and Perdue, eds., *Sage*, 263–71.

Palma, Gaetano di
"Il Giudizio di Dio nel libro del Qohelet," *Asprenas* 40 (1993) 349–72.

Pautrel, Raymond
"Data sunt a pastore uno (Eccl. XII,11)," *Recherches de science religieuse* 41 (1953) 406–10.

Perrin, Nicholas
"Messianism in the Narrative Frame of Ecclesiastes?" *RB* 108 (2001) 37–60.

Rose, Martin
  "Verba sapientium sicut stimuli," in Denis Knoepfler, ed., *Nomen Latinum: Mélanges de langue, de littérature et de civilisation latines offerts au professeur Andé Schneider* (Neuchâtel: Faculté de lettres; Geneva: Droz, 1997) 209–18.

Schwienhorst-Schönberger
  Nicht im Menschen, 7–11.

Seow, Choon-Leong
  "'Beyond Them, My Son, Be Warned': The Epilogue of Qohelet Revisited," in Michael L. Barré, ed., *Wisdom, You Are My Sister: Studies in Honor of Roland E. Murphy* (CBQMS 29; Washington: Catholic Biblical Association of America, 1997) 125–41.

Sheppard, G. T.
  "The Epilogue to Qoheleth as Theological Commentary," *CBQ* 39 (1977) 182–89.

Sheppard, G. T.
  Wisdom as a Hermeneutical Construct, 120–29.

Shields, Martin A.
  "Ecclesiastes and the End of Wisdom," *TynBul* 50 (1999) 117–39.

Shields, Martin A.
  "Re-examining the Warning of Eccl. xii 12," *VT* 50 (2000) 123–27.

Skehan, Patrick W.
  "Staves and Nails, and Scribal Slips (Ben Sira 44:2-5)," *BASOR* 200 (1970) 66–71.

Slemmons, Timothy Matthew
  "Ecclesiastes 12:1-13," *Int* 55 (2001) 302–4.

Tropper, Josef
  "Hebräisch zhr_2 'kundtun, warnen,'" *ZAH* 8 (1995) 144–48.

Wilson, Gerald H.
  "'The Words of the Wise': The Intent and Significance of Qohelet 12:9-14," *JBL* 103 (1984) 175–92.

1. Texts

a / Hebrew Bible

Genesis

1–11	25, 100, 159, 170
1–9	92
1–6	100
1–3	92
1–2	25, 65, 170
1	86, 87, 88, 132
1:3-24	85
1:3	132, 202
1:4	83, 85
1:5	132
1:6	132
1:8	132
1:9	132
1:10	85, 132
1:11	65, 86, 93
1:12	85
1:18	85
1:21	85
1:25	85, 93
1:26-28	92
1:27	149
1:29	89
1:31	85, 86
2–3	87, 133, 159
2	92
2:6	65
2:7	92, 93, 203
2:8	65
2:9	65
2:16-17	89
2:17	87, 159
2:18-19	92, 93
2:18	99, 100, 133
2:19-20	132
2:20	92
2:23	132
3	25, 100, 149
3ff.	170
3:3	87
3:5	133
3:7	87
3:16	149
3:17-19	25, 89
3:19	93, 170, 203
3:20	132
3:22-24	88, 170
3:22	87, 133
4:7	92
4:17-22	149
4:25-26	92
5	126
5:1-2	149
5:2	132
5:3-5	159
5:3	149
5:22	92
5:24	92, 126
6	29
6:3	25, 93, 125
6:5	25, 86, 92, 141, 149, 156, 159, 170
6:9	92
6:11-12	86
6:12-13	92
6:17	93
7:1	92, 176
7:15	93
7:22	93
8	29
8:21	25, 141, 159, 170
8:22	55, 90
14:18-20	64
15:5	125
20:11	215
22:17	125
24:1	113
26:4	125
30:1	125
30:23	125
35:17	104
37:7	125
37:10	125
38:7	125
38:10	125
40–41	109
40:5	151
40:8	151, 152
40:13	155
40:16	151
40:22	151
41:8	151
41:11	151
41:12-13	151
41:15	151
41:16	151, 152
41:22	151
41:25	133, 156
41:28	156
41:38-39	151, 152
41:39	24
44:4	139
49:6	77

Exodus

1:8	48
9:8	83
9:29	139
9:33	139
10:25	106
15:25	25
18:12	107
18:13-27	25
20	25
22:10	153
22:27	189
22:28	101
23:8	137
23:15	108
31:3	24
34:20	108
35:25	24

Leviticus

1–7	27
4–5	109, 110
4:13ff.	214
12–16	27
12:8	172

16:12	83
22:14	109
25:28	172
26:10	48

Numbers

2:31	48
11:15	70
11:18	160
15:22-31	25, 109, 110
15:30-31	109
15:32ff.	25
15:37-41	24, 25
15:39	25, 196, 197
35:9ff.	110
35:11	109
35:15	109
36	25

Deuteronomy

1:9-18	25
4	24
4:2	89
4:6-8	24, 215
5	25
5:27	107
5:33	160
6:6-9	23
12:6-7	107
12:31	104
13:1	89
13:10	48
14:22-29	123
15:7-11	193
15:16	160
16:14	27, 123
16:16	108
16:19	137
17:15	125
17:18-20	24
17:20	157
18:15-19	24
19:13	160
20:5	48
20:19-20	77
20:20	176

23:22-24	25, 109, 111
23:22	213
24:5	48
24:12	123
24:19-22	123
24:19	193
25:1	91
25:18	51
26:11	27, 123
28:30-33	125
30:9-13	24
31:24-29	24
33:3	168
34:10-12	24

Joshua

1:7-8	24
1:8	212
11:6	77
11:9	77
20:3	109
20:9	109
24:25	25
24:26	25

Judges

8:23	157
8:32	125
9:8-15	157
19:19	172

1 Samuel

1:1-20	125
2:5	122
6:9	69
8:13	180
13:21	211
15:22	108
15:26	56
15:35	116
16:16	160
16:23	160
20:26	69
21:9	104
22:17	104
29:2	48

2 Samuel

2:11	56
2:26	48
3:39	161
4:2	104
6:13-23	125
8:4	77
11:1	78
11:6ff.	78
17:2	51
20:15ff.	179
21:7	153
23:3	141
24:14	168

1 Kings

1:1-4	98
1:31	70, 154
1:37	64, 66
1:47	64, 66
2:43	153
3	66
3:4-15	63
3:12	64, 68
3:13	64
4:20	66, 72
4:21ff.	66
4:25	66, 72
4:29ff.	66
5–7	66
5:8	155
7:14	24
8:1	39
8:11	137
8:27-30	109
8:27	27
8:31-32	91
8:46ff.	27, 141
9:15ff.	66
10	66
10:23	64
11:1ff.	66
11:37	56
12:14	68
17:13	48
19:4	70
20:24	182

2 Kings	
2:3	126
2:5	126
3:19	78
3:25	78
4:8-17	125

Isaiah	
1:10-17	159
1:10ff.	27, 108
1:19	108
2:2	87
2:3-4	215
2:9	202
2:11	202
2:16	202
3:14	196
5:9	202
5:15	202
5:11	188
5:21	64
5:22	188
5:30	201
6:11	202
8:22	202
9:5	103
10:5-15	62
10:10	172
11:2	103, 141
11:14	155
13:9-10	26
13:10	201, 202
13:16	202
14:5-21	62
16:10	202
18:2	192
19:21	109
24:8-9	202
24:10	202
26:12	104
28:19	202
28:21	125
28:23-29	79
29:15-16	63
29:16	133
30:12	95

31:2	152
31:9	202
32:10-11	202
33:6	141
33:14	202
33:15	95
34:1	107
35:10	90
38:10	125
38:12	202
40–66	24
40:8	90
40:26	85, 132
40:28	85
41:7	211
41:15	207
41:20	85
41:22-23	54, 87
41:26	54, 87, 133
42:3-4	215
42:5	85
42:9	54, 87, 133
43:9	54, 87
43:18-19	54, 87
44:7-8	54, 87
44:7	133
44:24	85
45:7	85
45:8	85
45:9	123
45:12	85
45:17	90
45:18	85
46:9-10	54, 87
47:8-9	125
48:1-11	54
48:3	87
49:4	121
51:4-5	215
51:6	43, 90
51:8	90
51:11	90
52:4	95
54:14	95
55:3	90
55:13	90

56:5	49, 136
57:1	141
59:4	141
59:13	95
59:16	95
60:15	90
60:19-21	90
62:2	54, 136
65–66	54, 100
65	26
65:13	26, 54
65:15	136
65:17ff.	25, 43, 54
65:20-25	54
65:20	125
65:22-23	125
65:22	125
65:23	121
66:1ff.	27, 108
66:3	108
66:22	54

Jeremiah	
1:1	39
4:23	201, 202
5:1	141
6:6	95
6:11	104
6:12	202
6:19-20	108
6:25	202
7	27
7:6	95
7:22	108
7:23	108
7:34	202
8:7	79
8:17	186
9:17	24
10:4	211
10:6f.	152
10:9	24
10:12	24
10:16	42
10:23	168
12:6	104

13:16	201, 202	20:25ff.	108	4:4-5	159		
14:5	104	20:38	92	5:13	79		
14:11-12	108	20:39	108	5:18	201		
14:18	104	22:7	95	5:19	185		
15:4	202	22:12	95	5:20	201		
16:19	202	22:29-30	95	5:21-24	159		
17:10	161	22:29	95	5:21ff.	27, 108		
17:27	202	23:46	202	8:9	201		
18:6	133	26:12	202	9:14	172		
20:3-4	202	26:13	202				
20:10	202	27:9	24	Jonah			
20:14-18	96	28	62	1	215		
20:14ff.	70	28:2	62	1:9	109		
21:12	95	28:6	62	1:16	109		
22:3	95	32:7-8	201, 202	3	215		
22:12	95	33:20	161				
22:15	187	36:26-27	54	Micah			
22:17	95	36:27	81	2:2	95		
23:5	103	38:16	87	4:2-3	215		
23:11	104			5:2	103		
23:20	87	Hosea		6:6ff.	27, 108		
24:9	202	3:5	87	6:8	65, 108		
25:10	201, 202	4:12	193	7:2	141		
29:18	202	5:11	95				
31:13	58	6:6	108	Nahum			
31:31	54	8:1ff.	108	2:11	202		
32:19	161	9:11-12	125	3:10	191		
34:17	202	9:12	104				
46:5	202	9:14	125	Zephaniah			
46:21	104	9:16	125	1:12	63		
48:34	104	12:8	95	1:13	202		
48:47	87			1:15	201, 202		
49:24	202	Joel		2:4	77		
49:39	87	2:2	202				
50:33	95	2:2	201	Zechariah			
51:12	104	2:6	201	4:2-3	203		
51:19	42	2:10-11	26	7:10	95		
		2:10	201, 202	8:4-5	125		
Ezekiel		3:4	202	9:9	103		
8:12	63						
9:9	63	Amos		Malachi			
11:19-20	54	1:1-2	42	1:7ff.	108		
16:8	79	1:1	39	1:11	215		
18:11	104	3:9	95	1:14	215		
18:18	95	3:15	202	2:7	109		
18:30	161	4:1	95	2:13-16	172		

2:13-14	108
2:17	159
3:14-15	63, 159

Psalms

1	24
1:2	163, 212
4:8	172
7:16	185
9:16	185
10:4	63, 159
10:11	63
14	32
14:1	63, 141
14:3	141
15	27
19	24
19:10	214
23:6	27
24	27
25:11	110
25:18	110
26:8	27
27:4	27
28:4	161
31:6	168
31:16	168
32:3ff.	110
33:6-9	154
35:7-8	185
37:1	96
37:23	168
37:25ff.	11, 23
37:25	176
37:30	212
37:35-36	11, 23
39:6-7	43
39:12	43
40:7ff.	27, 169
40:7-9	108
49	26
49:7	122
49:10-12	26
49:11	70
49:12	203
49:15	26

49:16	70
49:18	121
50	27
50:7-15	108
50:13	169
51	110
51:7	141
51:18-19	108, 169
53	32
53:2	63
57:7	185
58:5-6	186
62:10	43
62:11	95, 122
63:2	27
64:7	63
65:4	27
69:24	202
73	11, 23, 26
73:3	96
73:8	95
73:11	63, 159
73:22ff.	94
73:23ff.	70, 126
73:25	126, 127, 136
84	27
89:4	153
90:3	93
90:9-10	125
94:7	63
94:11	43
102	26
102:24-25	125
103:19	42
104:14-15	54, 89, 172
104:15	26
104:24	24, 144
104:27-30	26
104:27-28	54, 89
104:27	79
104:29-30	93, 203
109:4	203
110:3	208
110:4	64, 153
111:10	89, 214
112:1	214

112:6	49
112:9	193
115:3	154
119	24
119:63	214
119:91	42
120-134	27
120:7	208
127:1	121
127:3-5	125
128:1	214
128:3	125
130:3-4	110
132:15	26, 54
135:6	154
136:5	24
136:25	26, 54
139:5	168
139:6	51
139:10	168
139:13-16	194
139:16	31
143:2	141, 196
143:4	139
144:4	43
145:9	42
145:15-16	26, 54
145:15	79
146:4	93
146:7	26, 54
147:8-9	26, 54
147:14	26, 54
149	26

Job

1	129
1:1	141, 215
1:8	141, 215
1:21	32, 121, 122, 126
2:3	215
3	96
3:1ff.	70
3:11-16	126
3:17ff.	96
4-5	141

4:7ff.	140	22:13-14	63	1:20ff.	23, 147
4:8ff.	11, 23	22:15ff.	144	1:26-27	202
4:12ff.	108, 109	22:23ff.	110	1:29	141
4:16	141	25:4ff.	141	2:4-5	23, 28, 141,
4:17ff.	141	27:13-23	202		143
4:19	202	27:16-17	73	2:12ff.	23
4:20	82	28	23, 24, 64,	2:16ff.	23, 146
5:2	96, 137		89, 144	2:21-22	140
5:3ff.	11, 23, 176	28:28	141, 145,	3:1-2	125
5:8ff.	110		214, 215	3:3	23
5:26	79	29:5	125	3:7	64, 140, 141
6:8ff.	70	29:25	40	3:9-10	111
7:15ff.	70	31:1ff.	215	3:11-12	64
7:16	43	31:24ff.	122	3:13-26	23, 64
8:5-6	110	32	102	3:13	28, 137, 175
8:8ff.	23, 140	33:14ff.	108, 109	3:19-20	23, 24
8:9ff.	144, 208	33:18ff.	110	3:31ff.	23, 96
8:14ff.	133	33:23	148	3:33	140
8:30ff.	133	34:11	161	4	64
9:3	148	34:14-15	93	4:1ff.	23, 144
9:4	152	34:23	133	4:3-4	11
9:32	196	35:9	95	4:5-9	23
10:11-12	194	35:11	148	4:5ff.	175
10:18ff.	70	35:28	148	4:10, 13, 22-23	125
11:13ff.	110, 140	36:3	125	4:13	125
12:9ff.	168	36:13-14	125	4:14ff.	23
12:13	152	36:22-23	154	4:18-19	69, 201
12:24-25	69	38–42	111	4:19-20	140
13:3	133	38:15	201	4:22-23	125
14:1	203	42:17	125	4:22	28
14:2	203			4:27	107
14:3	196	Proverbs		5:3ff.	23, 146
14:4	141	1–31	42	5:15-23	172
14:7	203	1–9	22, 23, 24,	5:15	190
10:18-22	126		28, 29, 42,	5:18	58
15:5	148		141, 147, 179	5:20-23	146
15:14ff.	141	1:1	28, 39	5:22-23	146
15:17ff.	144	1:2-3	145	6:6	188
15:20ff.	140, 202	1:5-6	210	6:9-11	97
18:5-21	202	1:6	18	6:9	188
18:5ff.	69, 140, 201	1:7	89, 141, 214,	6:20ff.	23
18:17	136		215	6:23	69
18:18	201	1:8-9	23, 215	6:24ff.	23, 146
19:22	97	1:10ff.	23	6:32	181
20:4ff.	140, 144	1:15	107	7:2	125
22:4	196	1:17	207	7:3	23

7:4	24
7:5-17	146
7:5ff.	23
7:6ff.	11
7:7	181
7:15	28
8–9	23, 147
8:9	28
8:11ff.	137
8:12ff.	175
8:12	28
8:13	141
8:17	23, 28, 143
8:22ff.	23, 24, 144
8:35-36	23, 125
8:35	28
9	14
9:1ff.	215
9:4	181
9:8	136
9:10	89, 141, 214
9:11-12	64
9:12	210
9:13-18	147
9:16	181
10ff.	11, 18, 22, 24
10	145
10:1	28, 39
10:3	140
10:4-5	97
10:7	49, 136
10:13	181
10:21	181, 186
10:24-25	140
10:26	188
10:27-28	140
10:27	125, 141
10:30	140
10:32	186
11:5	140
11:8	140
11:12	181
11:21	140
11:28	122
12:3	140
12:7	140
12:11	97, 119, 181
12:12-13	140
12:16	137
12:21	140
12:24	97
12:27	97
13:1	64, 136
13:4	188
13:6	140
13:9	69, 140, 201
13:11	119
13:18	136
13:21	140
13:22	73, 122
13:24	64
13:25	140
14:6	23, 143
14:11	140, 202
14:13	136
14:20	96, 120, 179
14:21	192, 193
14:29	137
14:30	96, 182
14:31	95
14:32	140
14:35	182
15:2	186
15:4	182
15:6	122
15:7	186
15:8	27, 107, 111
15:12	136
15:16-17	22
15:18	137
15:21	181
15:23	47, 78, 79
15:25	202
15:29	111
15:32	136
15:33—16:15	101
15:33	89, 141, 214
16:1	22, 168
16:2	168
16:8	22
16:9	22, 168
16:14-15	152
16:14	182
16:16	137
16:32	137, 179
17:1	22, 97, 111
17:2	184
17:4	125
17:10	136
17:18	181
18:9	97
18:23	179
19:1	22
19:4	96, 120
19:6	120
19:7	96, 179
19:10	184
19:11	137
19:12	182
19:13	188
19:15	97, 188
19:16	125
19:17	193
19:18	64
19:21	22, 168
19:24	97
20:1	65
20:2	182
20:9	141
20:13	97
20:24	22, 168
20:25	109, 111
21:1	101
21:2	168
21:3	27, 107, 111
21:9	98
21:17	65, 107, 109
21:19	98
21:22	141, 179
21:27	27, 107, 111
21:30-31	22
22:1	49, 136
22:9	193
22:14	146
22:15	64
22:23	125
22:26	95
23:4-5	122

23:13-14	64	31:10	28	1:4	3
23:17	96	31:14	192	1:5	36
23:20-21	65, 97	31:27	188	1:8-11	30
23:26	62			1:8	38
23:27-28	146	Ruth		1:9-11	25, 26
23:29-35	65, 97	2:3	69	1:9	2, 16, 28
24:1	96	4:11-12	125	1:10-14	36
24:5	141, 179			1:10	3, 37
24:11ff.	95	Canticles		1:11	3
24:12	152, 161, 168	1:1	28	1:12—6:9	7
24:19	96	1:3	136	1:12—4:12	8
24:20	69	3:1-4	28, 149	1:12—3:15	8
24:21-22	22, 101	3:1-2	146	1:12—2:26	4, 5, 6, 7, 8,
24:28	116	4:4	147		9, 14, 17, 20,
24:30ff.	11, 23, 97,	5:6-8	28		22, 28
	119, 181	5:6	146, 149	1:12—2:11	10
24:31	203	6:1	28	1:12	6, 10, 33
25:1	28, 39	6:10	147	1:13	2, 3, 4, 9, 10,
25:2	101	7:5-6	147		33
25:11	79	8:1	28	1:14	2, 10, 16, 38
25:15	137, 182	8:6-7	28	1:15	9, 16, 37
25:17	107	8:9-10	147	1:16-17	10
25:24	98	8:11-12	28	1:16	37
26:12	140			1:17	16
26:14-15	97	Qoheleth (references from		1:18	5, 9, 14, 16
26:16	140	pages 1–38 only)		2	14
27:2	125	1–6	7	2:1	10, 14
27:15	188	1:1—2:26	11	2:2	9, 16
27:20	98	1:1-11	17	2:3	1, 3, 10, 16
27:23-27	119	1:1	5, 6, 7, 11,	2:7	4
28:3	95		15, 16, 28	2:8	4
28:6	22	1:2—3:15	8, 15	2:10-11	3, 4
28:8	73	1:2-11	7, 8	2:11-22	2
28:9	111	1:2-3	8, 33	2:11	3, 10, 16
28:10	185	1:2	3, 5, 6, 12,	2:12-17	10
28:11	140		15, 16	2:12	9, 10, 16
28:13	110	1:3—12:7	5	2:13-15	9
28:16-17	95	1:3—4:12	6, 8, 18	2:13-14	14, 16
28:19	119	1:3—3:22	9	2:13	3, 5, 9, 10
28:27	192, 193	1:3—3:15	15	2:14-15	3, 5
29:9	64	1:3—3:9	6	2:14	9, 10
29:15	64	1:3-11	5, 6, 7, 16,	2:15	9, 10, 14
30:10	142		30	2:16	3, 5, 9, 14
30:21-22	184	1:3	2, 3, 4, 6, 9	2:17	10, 16
31	28	1:4-11	8, 9, 10	2:18-24	4, 10, 16
31:4	65, 187	1:4-7	9, 16	2:18	9, 10

2:19	9, 36	3:21-22	2, 9	5:6	2, 9, 15, 27
2:20	10, 16	3:21	36	5:7—6:10	8
2:21	3, 9	3:22	1, 4, 9, 10	5:7—6:9	5
2:22	9	4:1—6:9	8	5:7-8	6, 15, 17, 21
2:23	3, 4	4:1-16	7	5:7	4, 9
2:24-26	1, 2, 10	4:1-12	21	5:8	3, 4, 14, 36
2:24	9	4:1-3	10	5:8—6:9	7
2:25	9	4:1	2, 4, 10, 21	5:9—6:9	5, 6, 15, 21, 32
2:26	4, 15	4:2-4	16	5:9-14	14
3	11, 26, 29, 30	4:2-3	9, 10	5:9-11	6, 9
3:1-22	7	4:2	36	5:9	9, 21
3:1-15	10	4:3	2	5:10-11	17
3:1-9	5, 6, 7, 8, 16	4:4-16	15	5:10	9, 36
3:1-8	3, 9, 32	4:4-8	1, 4	5:11	36
3:1-4	16	4:4-6	10	5:12—6:6	3, 9
3:1	3, 9	4:5-6	9	5:12-19	10
3:2	3	4:5	4, 5, 9, 17	5:12-16	4, 6
3:9-10	16	4:6	9	5:12-14	1, 4
3:9	3, 4, 9	4:7-8	4, 10	5:12	2, 4, 10
3:10—4:16	9	4:7	2	5:13-17	37
3:10—4:12	6, 8, 11, 17	4:8	4, 9, 36	5:13	4
3:10	2, 4, 10, 28	4:9-12	4, 6, 10, 21	5:14	4, 28, 32
3:11-18	2	4:9	3, 4, 9	5:15	3, 4, 9, 28, 36
3:11-15	25	4:10	9, 36	5:16	3, 4, 9
3:11	3, 16, 24, 25, 28, 30	4:11	9, 38	5:17-19	1, 4, 6, 28
3:12-13	1, 4	4:12	9, 21	5:17	2, 3, 4, 10, 37
3:12	9, 10, 16	4:13—12:7	6	5:18	2, 3, 4, 36
3:13-16	1	4:13—5:8	6, 8	5:19	3, 4
3:13	2, 3	4:13-16	4, 6, 10, 21	6:1-6	6, 10
3:14-16	2	4:13-14	17	6:1-5	1
3:14	3, 10	4:13	9, 19, 20	6:1	3, 10
3:15	6	4:15-16	10	6:2	2, 4, 10, 15, 21, 36
3:16—6:10	8	4:15	2	6:3-8	37
3:16—6:9	8, 15	4:16	15	6:3-6	28
3:16—4:16	8, 15	4:17—5:6	2, 6, 8, 9, 15, 25, 27, 30	6:3	3, 9, 10
3:16—4:3	15	4:17	2, 5, 9, 25, 27, 36	6:4	37
3:16-22	10, 25			6:5	9, 37
3:16	10, 17	5:1-7	7	6:6	3, 9
3:17	2, 3, 10, 15, 16, 30	5:1	2, 9, 32	6:7-9	5, 6, 9,10
3:18	2, 15, 16, 25	5:2	4, 5, 9	6:7	4, 9, 17, 37
3:19-22	3, 16	5:3	2, 3, 5, 9	6:8	3, 5, 9, 14
3:19-21	26	5:4	9	6:9	9, 15
3:19	9, 36	5:5	2, 3, 9, 25, 27, 38		
3:20b	9	5:6-7	6		

6:10—11:6	7	7:20	2, 25, 32	9:1—12:8	8, 15
6:10—8:17	6, 8	7:21	4, 9	9:1—12:7	6, 8
6:10—7:14	5, 7	7:22	36	9:1—11:6	7
6:10-12	6, 7, 10	7:23—8:1	10	9:1-12	1, 3, 5, 6, 7, 15
6:10	2, 9, 16, 31, 36	7:23-29	4, 6		
		7:23	9, 10, 15, 23	9:1-10	7, 14
6:11—9:6	8	7:24	9, 15, 28	9:1-3	16, 25
6:11—8:17	8, 15	7:25-29	15, 24	9:1	2, 10, 17
6:11	3, 9, 15	7:25	10	9:2	3, 27, 30
6:12—7:6	37	7:26-29	10	9:3	2, 3, 9, 15, 16, 25
6:12	2, 3, 9, 15	7:26	15, 17, 28		
7-8	7	7:27	36	9:4-6	26
7:1—8:17	7	7:28	9, 17	9:4	9, 36
7:1-22	15	7:29	2, 25	9:6	3
7:1-14	1, 6, 10, 16	8:1-17	7	9:7—12:8	8
7:1-6	17	8:1-9	4, 6, 10, 15, 16, 20	9:7—12:7	8
7:1-4	9			9:7-10	1, 9, 16, 28
7:1	3, 17	8:1-5	17	9:7	2, 3, 14
7:2	37	8:1	9, 14, 17, 18	9:8	3, 9
7:5-12	9	8:2-8	10	9:9	2, 3, 4, 28
7:5-7	10	8:2	2, 9, 36	9:10	3
7:5-6	17	8:3	9	9:11—10:15	7
7:5	37	8:4	9	9:11	3, 4, 5, 10, 16
7:6-7	9	8:5-6	2, 24		
7:6	37	8:5	3, 9, 15, 17	9:12	2, 3, 5, 16
7:7-10	37	8:6	3, 25, 28	9:13—19:13	15
7:8-9	17	8:7	2, 9, 28	9:13—10:20	5, 6
7:8	37	8:8	3, 9, 36	9:13-18	4
7:9	9, 32	8:9-15	10	9:13-16	10
7:10	3, 9	8:9	3, 4, 10, 16, 21, 36	9:13	3, 10
7:11-14	10			9:14-15	9, 20
7:11-12	17	8:10-15	1, 6, 15, 16	9:14	36
7:11	3, 9, 14	8:10-13	10	9:15-16	4
7:12	3, 9	8:10	10, 30, 36	9:16	9, 10, 14
7:13	9	8:11	2, 3, 25, 36	9:17	9, 17
7:14-15	1, 2, 3	8:12-13	15, 16, 17	9:18	9
7:14	9	8:12	2, 3, 36	10:1	5, 9, 14, 17, 36
7:15—10:7	9	8:13	2, 9		
7:15-22	6, 10	8:14	9, 10	10:2-4	9
7:15-18	24	8:15	2, 3, 4, 9, 10	10:2	17
7:15	10	8:16—9:10	10	10:3	36
7:16	3, 8, 9	8:16-17	6, 15, 24	10:4	4, 9, 17, 20
7:17	3, 5, 2, 9	8:16	3, 4, 10	10:5-7	4, 10, 20
7:18	2, 9	8:17	2, 3, 4, 10, 28	10:5	3
7:19-21	9			10:6	28
7:19	14, 17, 36	9-12	7	10:8-11	4, 5, 9, 24

10:8-10   17
10:10   3, 14, 36
10:11   3, 4, 9
10:12-15   5, 9, 10
10:12-13   17
10:12   14, 35
10:14   2, 9, 15
10:15   4, 15, 36
10:16—11:6   7
10:16-20   17
10:16-19   4, 9, 15
10:16-17   9, 19, 20
10:17   3
10:18   36
10:19   4
10:20   4, 9, 15, 36
11:1—12:7   3, 5, 6, 7, 9,
               15
11:1-10   1
11:1-6   2, 4, 10
11:1-4   9
11:1   3
11:2   3
11:3   9, 32, 35
11:4   9
11:5   2, 9
11:6   9
11:7—12:7   7, 10, 14, 16
11:7   9
11:8   3
11:9—12:7   25
11:9   2, 3, 9, 15,
               16, 25, 36
11:10   15
12   26
12:1-7   6
12:1   3, 15, 36
12:2-7   9
12:3   3
12:6   36
12:7   2, 3, 36
12:8   3, 5, 6, 8, 12,
               15, 16
12:9-14   5, 6, 7, 11,
               12, 15, 16,
               17, 28, 30

12:9-11   5, 29
12:9-10   16
12:9   3, 23, 28, 38
12:10   28, 36
12:11   16
12:12-14   16, 29
12:12   3, 36
12:13   2, 16, 25, 33
12:14   2, 16, 32, 33

Lamentations
1:2   95
1:9   95
1:17   95
1:21   95
2:12   172
3:2   201
4:8   202
5:17   202

Esther
1:13   79
3:11   56
4:16   158
8:11   56
9:27   79
9:31   79

Daniel
1–7   24
1–6   11
1   154
1:3ff.   179
2–7   30
2   54, 151
2:4-7   151
2:4   70, 154
2:9   151
2:10b   152
2:16   151
2:18-19   109, 152
2:20ff.   152
2:21-23   152
2:24-26   151
2:27-28   152
2:28-29   87, 123, 156

2:30   135, 151
2:36   151
2:44   90
2:45   87, 123, 151,
               156
2:46ff.   151, 152
2:47   152
3   154
3:9   70, 154
4   151
4:3-4   151
4:6   151
4:14   135
4:15-16   151
4:17   154
4:21   151
4:24   192
4:33   63
5   151
5:7-8   151
5:10   70, 154
5:12   151
5:15-17   151
5:16   151
5:26   151
6   154
6:7   70, 154
6:11   27
6:22   70, 154
7–12   11
7   54, 151
7:16   151
7:18   90
7:22   79
7:25   79
7:28   212
8:3   48
8:6   207
8:17   79
8:20   207
8:27   139
9:4-19   55
9:25   79
10:12   62
10:14   87
10:20   139

11:6	79
11:13	79
11:14	79
11:24	79
11:35	79
11:40	79
12:1-3	54
12:1	79
12:2	90
12:3	90, 94
12:4	79
12:9	79
12:11	79

Ezra

1:2	109
2:55-57	40
2:59-60	125
7	155
7:6	168
7:9	168
8:22	168
9	110

Nehemiah

1:1	39
1:4	109
1:5ff.	110
2:3	70, 154
2:8	168
2:18	168
3:8	180
5:4	115
5:18	92
9	55
9:8	143
9:36-37	115, 125
13:1-3	24, 25

1 Chronicles

7:40	92
9:22	92
12:33	155
16:41	92
18:4	77
22:3	211

22:15	24
22:19	62
25	66
27:27ff.	66
28:1-8	39
29:1	39
29:12	42
29:28	125

2 Chronicles

1	66
1:1-12	63
1:3	39
1:5	39
1:12	64, 68
1:13ff.	66
2-4	66
3:9	211
5:2	39
5:3	39
6:3	39
6:12	39
7:8	39
8:1ff.	66
10:14	68
11:16	62
20:10	56
24:15	125
26:15	143
36:23	109

**b / Apocrypha
(Deuterocanonical Books)**

1 Baruch

1:15—3:8	55, 110
2:23	202
3:9—4:4	24, 215

3 Ezra

3-5	155

Judith

8:13-14	32
8:15-17	32
8:18ff.	32

9:5-6	32

2 Maccabees

7:22	194
4:10-11	53

Sirach

1:1-10	31, 144
1:10	89
1:14ff.	145, 214
1:14	89
1:20	64
1:23-24	31, 78, 155
1:26-30	214
1:26	214
2:1	212
2:2	31
2:18	168
3:8	212
3:12	212
3:17	212
3:25	69
3:30—4:10	192
4:1	212
4:12-13	23, 64, 143
4:15-19	144
4:17	64
4:20	31, 79, 155, 212
4:23	31, 78, 79
4:26-27	182
4:26	110
5:1-2	127, 128
5:2	196
5:3	90
6:1-3	127, 128
6:5-17	99
6:6	148
6:8	79
6:13-15	99
6:18-37	24, 29, 64
6:24ff.	147
6:27	23, 143
7:4ff.	155
7:10	111, 192
7:14	108, 111

7:15	119	15:11	86	26:4	79
7:18	99	16:1-3	126	26:22	146
7:36	205	16:12	161	26:23	146
8:1	152, 182	16:24—17:14	55	27:12	31, 79
8:2	137	17:1ff.	29	27:13	136
8:5	141	17:2-4	92	27:14	154
8:9	31	17:6-10	87	27:16-21	99
9:1-9	146	17:8	89	29:1-20	193
9:3	152	17:11ff.	28	29:1-10	192
9:10	99	17:16-17a	29	29:2-3	18, 31
9:11-12	96	17:25	110, 111	29:2	79
9:13	182	18:1	42	29:8	79
10:1ff.	155	18:6	89	29:9-13	193
10:2	187	18:21	31	30:22-23	28
10:4	79	18:22-23	109, 111	30:24	79
10:19	214	18:25-26	78, 79, 124, 205	31:5	119
10:23-25	102			31:6	122
10:25	184	18:30—19:2	127	31:14	120
10:30-31	102	20:1	79, 155	31:28	31, 79
11:4-6	28	20:6-7	31, 78, 79, 155	32:4	79
11:5-6	184			33:6	99
11:9	79	20:7	155	33:7-19	23
11:10f.	122	20:13	186	33:14-15	169
11:11	51	20:20	31, 78, 79, 155	33:16ff.	11
11:14-26	124			33:25-32	142
11:15-26	29	20:27-28	182	34:1-7	109
11:18	129	20:28	119, 182	34:21—35:26	28, 111
11:19	70, 78	20:29	137	34:21ff.	27, 107
11:20	79	21:1	64	35:2-5	107
11:21-23	124, 205	21:15-17	186	35:3-4	192
11:25-26	124, 205	21:15	64	35:5-6	192
11:26	126, 136, 159	21:20	64	35:6-7	28
11:28	137, 205	22:6	31, 79	35:8ff.	27, 107
11:29-34	99	22:11	69	35:10-11	111
12:8—13:23	99	22:16	31, 79	36:1-22	28
12:13	186	22:19-26	99	36:1ff.	155
13:7	158	23:4-6	127	36:1	42
13:20	96	23:9-11	154, 170	36:10	154
13:24—14:19	123	24	24, 29, 144, 147	36:20-21	28
13:24-25	152			36:23-25	99
14:11-16	28, 70, 204	24:8	42	37:1-15	99
14:13ff.	119	24:23	28	37:15	168
14:15	70	24:30ff.	11	37:19-26	28
14:20—15:10	29, 147	24:34	210	37:22ff.	209
15:5	41	25:24	145	37:23	181, 210
15:11—16:23	29	26:3	146	37:26	49, 70

38:13	77, 79, 155
38:24—39:11	29, 186
38:24ff.	181, 210
38:25ff.	181
38:33	181
38:34ff.	181
39	29
39:1-3	210
39:1	144, 210
39:4	155
39:5-6	109, 110, 111
39:8ff.	181
39:9	70, 175
39:12-35	28, 29, 31, 87
39:16-35	79, 137
39:16	86, 169, 170
39:21	42, 169
39:25	86
39:27	86, 169
39:33-34	86
39:34	42, 169
40:5	96
40:8-10	87
40:10	86
40:11	93
40:20	172
40:23	31
41:1ff.	136
41:1-4	28
41:3-4	26
41:11	49, 70
41:12	162
42:13-14	145
42:15-25	23, 87, 144
42:21	89
43:24	139
43:27	42, 213
43:33	42
44ff.	144
45:6ff.	28
46:6ff.	108
47:9	207, 210
47:23	70
48–49	28
48:24-25	28, 87
48:25	133

49:1	136
50	27, 28
50:1ff.	108
50:20	209
50:27-29	11, 209
50:28	212
51:12	42
51:13ff.	11, 23, 29, 143, 147
51:23	30, 175, 181
51:26-27	23, 143
51:26	181
51:27-28	210
51:28	137
51:29	30

Tobit

1–12	31
1:3	192
2	136
2:11	31
2:15-18	192
3:1-6	110
3:6	70, 203
3:7	31
3:10	31
3:11	31
3:16	31
4:1	31
4:7-12	192
4:11	192
6:18	31
12:9	192
12:14	31
13	55
13–14	31
13:11-16	31
14	90
14:4-5	31, 79
14:11	192

Wisdom

1–6	30
1ff.	145
1:13-14	30
2	30
2:1-5	30

2:2-9	30
2:10-20	30
2:23-24	30
3:1—12:5	30
3:1ff.	126, 167
4:10ff.	126
4:12	118
6–9	11
7–10	30
7:10	69
7:16	167
7:17ff.	144
7:18	87
7:26	69
7:29	69
8:8	18
10ff.	144
11–19	30

c / New Testament

Matthew

6:7	32, 108
6:17-18	172
6:25ff.	32
11:17	32

Mark

2:18-20	32
13:32-33	32

Luke

1:25	125
1:53	122
8:1ff.	32
12:13ff.	32
17:7-10	161

John

3:8	32

Romans

3:10	32
3:21-26	32
5	32
8:29	132

2 Corinthians
5:1ff.	203
5:10	32

1 Thessalonians
5:1ff.	32
5:17	108

1 Timothy
6:6ff.	33
6:7	32

James
1:19	32
4:13-14	32

1 Peter
2:18-19	142

d / Ancient Near Eastern Sources

Admonitions of Ipuwer
184
Ahiqar
155, 182
Amenemhet I
39
Gilgamesh Epic
99, 172
Harpers' Song of Antef
173
Kagemni
11
Meissner-Millard Tablet
172
Proverbs of Ahiqar
11
Ptahhotep
11
Teaching of Ankh-Sheshonq
11, 98, 192, 212
Teaching of King Khety
11, 39
Teaching for Merikare
11, 39

Teaching of Prince Djedefhor
39

e / Pseudepigrapha

1 Enoch
1–36	25, 30, 79, 94
1:6-7	25
2–5	55
2:1	79
9:3	94
13:6	94
17–36	11, 25, 55
18:15	79
22	26, 54
22:3-4	94
22:5	94
72–82	11, 30, 55, 79
72:1	25, 79
72:7	79
75:3-4	79
78:15-16	79
79:2	79
79:4-5	79
80	54
80:1	79
81:2	87
82:10	79
98:5	125
103:4	94
104:2	94
104:4	94

Epistle of Aristeas
passim	19
92ff.	108
95	108
187–294	85, 188
193	168
195	168
198	188
199	168
202	188
205	187
209	187
211	187
216	168
222–23	187
227	168
235	188
237–40	168
243	168
245	187
247	168, 188
251–52	168
255	168
256	187
261	188
262-63	157
264	168
274	188
278	187
280	187
288	103
288ff.	187
289	187
294	188

Jubilees
1	87
4:18-19	87
10:17	87
23:31	94

Testaments of the Twelve Patriarchs
11

f / Early Jewish and Rabbinic Sources

BABYLONIAN TALMUD
Baba Batra 14b-15a
	39
Gittim 68b	62
Megillah 7a	14
Nedarim 10a	197
Shabbat 30b	14
Shabbat 131v-132a	198
Sanhedrin 2.6b	62

JERUSALEM TALMUD
Sanhedrin 2.7	61

Midrash Rabbah, Qoheleth
                        78, 248
    3:11   62
    5:10   194

MISHNAH
ʾAbot
    1:3   161
    2:15   211

TARGUM
Qoheleth 12:2-7   199

Dead Sea Scrolls
1QApGen
    20:12-13   42
1QIsaᵃ   37
4QEzra   36
4QQohᵃ (4Q109)   19, 37, 134,
                    139
4QQohᵇ (4Q110)   36
11QPsᵃ
    151:18:7-8   42

Josephus
    Antiquities
    12.1   153
    12.4   20, 66, 155
    12.4.4   125
    12.4.5   66, 193
    12.4.8   129
    12.4.11   66
    15.10.4   154, 170
    18.1.5   94
    Bellum Judaicum
    2.8.6   170
    2.8.11   94

g / Greek and Roman Authors

Aratus, Phaenomena
                    194
Archilochus   138
Aristophanes, Birds
                    189

Aristotle
    Nicomachean Ethics
    9.9   99
    1106-7a   140
    Politics   184
Axiochus   120
Bion of Borysthenes
                    12
Cleanthes, Hymn to Zeus
                    85
Crates   13, 74
Diogenes   145
Diogenes Laertius
                    217
    2.86   74
    6.12   151
    6.32   148
    6.50   119
    6.63   74
    6.66   136
    6.71   74
    6.73   112
    6.82-83   43
    6.86   74
    6.87   74
    7.62   52
Eratosthenes   103
Euripides   119, 120, 195
Herodotus   174
Hesiod
    Works and Days
    11–12   97
    20–24   97
    220ff.   90
    298–301   97
    308–9   97
    311–12   97
    383ff.   79
    617ff.   79
    618ff.   192
    765ff.   79
    Theogony
    226–27   97
Homer, Iliad
    10.222ff.   98
Juvenal, Satires   189

Menippos of Gadara
                    12
Megalopolis   103
Menander   43, 112, 119,
                    120, 121, 133
Monimos   43
Phylarchos   73, 103
Plato   93
    Menon   94
    Phaidon   94
    Phaidros   94
    Politeia   94, 181
Polybius   103, 153
Pseudo-Phocylides
                    192
Pythagoras   120
Sextus Empiricus   122, 215
Sophocles   119
Teles of Magara   12, 122
    1, 2, 3, 4A, 6 12
    2, 3, 4B, 5, 6, 13
Theocritus   120
Theognis   90, 153

h / Early Christian Authors

Bonaventure   33
Didymus the Blind
                    245
Gregory of Nyssa   33
Gregory Thaumaturgus
                    33, 42, 102
Gregory the Great
                    33
Jerome   33, 34, 41
Origen   34

i / Papyri

Chester Beatty IV   64
Harris 500   147
Insinger   212

2. Authors

Aalders, G. J. D.
112, 119, 123, 184,
218, 225

Aalders, W.
244

Abel, F.-M.
240

Abramson, Shraga
257

Abrego-de Lacy, José
218

Abusch, Tzvi
173

Ackroyd, Peter R.
127, 264

Adriaen, Marcus
244

Aerts, Theo
261

Aland, Barbara
32

Albertz, Rainer
42, 121, 180, 240

Albright, W. F.
40, 89, 255

Alfrink, Bernard
218

Allevi, L.
228

Allgeier, Arthur
145, 218

Allinson, F. G.
121

Alonso Schökel, Luis
218

Alshich, Moshe
244

Amigo Espada,
Lorenzo
244

Amir, Yehoshua
43, 240, 255

Amsler, Samuel
265

Anath, Moshe E.
200, 228, 268

Anderlini, Gianpaolo
264

Anderson, Don
222

Anderson, Phyllis
268

Anderson, William
H. U.
222, 228, 238, 240,
255, 257, 258

Andrews, Susan
265

Apelt, O.
74, 148, 217

Aquino, Ranhilio C.
228, 244

Aranda, M. Gómez
199

Archer, Gleason L.
240, 251

Arenhoevel, Diego
217

Armstrong, James F.
228, 240

Asmussen, Jes P.
244, 253

Assmann, Jan
25, 174

Atkins, Gaius G.
221

Auffret, Pierre
257

Augustin, M.
148

Ausejo, Serafin de
238

Austin, M. M.
53, 65, 114, 115,
123, 153, 217

Auwers, Jean-Marie
270

Azize, Joseph
228

Backhaus, Franz Josef
5, 12, 16, 19, 28, 43,
45, 47, 48, 51, 58,
59, 68, 81, 82, 89,
92, 93, 94, 102, 104,
106, 117, 131, 135,
146, 155, 158, 160,
165, 166, 167, 222,
228, 237, 238, 239,
240, 251, 256, 257,
265, 270

Bagnall, R. S.
114

Baker, Phil
264

Bakon, Shimon
228

Balancin, Euclides M.
225

Baltzer, Klaus
143, 145, 146, 147,
148, 265

Bannach, Horst
259

Bardski, Krzysztof
244, 253

Barnes, Jonathan
240

Barrett, Michael P. V.
228

Barsotti, Divo
222

Bartelmus, Rüdiger
67, 76, 92, 217, 228,
258, 261

Barthauer, Wilhelm
222

Barthélemy,
Dominique
253

Bartholomew, Craig C.
222

Barton, George A.
44, 73, 82, 97, 113,
135, 140, 141, 160,
218, 264, 268

Barton, John
225

Barucq, André
218, 228, 255, 258

Barylko, Jaime
218

Baum, Alice
218

Baumgärtel, Friedrich
270

Baumgartner, Walter
217

Baur, H.
255

Bea, Augustin
218

Beal, Timothy K.
200, 268

Beaucamp, Évode
228

Beauchamp, Paul
228, 244

Beck, Astrid B.
253

Beckwith, Roger
28, 33, 244, 253

Bedenbender, Andreas
265

Beek, Martinus
Adrianus
218, 228

Beentjes, Pancratius C.
150, 227, 266, 267

Begrich, Joachim
122

Bell, Robert D.
228, 237

Bellia, Giuseppe
222, 227, 228, 240

Ben David, Israel
244

Bergada, M. M.
244

Bergant, Dianne
218, 228, 255

Berger, Benjamin L.
228
Berger, Klaus
11, 13, 33, 203, 217,
238, 244
Berlin, Andrea M.
20, 240
Berndt, Rainer
244
Bertheau, E.
18
Bertram, Georg
38, 253, 255
Bettan, Israel
218
Beyerlin, Walter
217
Bianchi, Francesco
35, 228, 251, 261,
268
Bickell, Gustav
218
Bickerman, Elias
225
Bidder, Roderich
222
Billerbeck, P.
109
Bishop, Eric F. F.
228
Blenkinsopp, Joseph
77, 225, 240, 259,
261
Blieffert, Hans-Jürgen
222
Blumenthal, Elhanan
228
Blutting, Klara
226
Boccaccini, Gabriele
240
Boer, Pieter A. H. de
212, 270
Böhl, Eduard
251

Bohlen, Reinhold
20, 21, 228, 240
Böhme, Gernot
145, 147
Boileau, M.-J.
218
Boira Sales, José
244
Bojorge, H.
228
Bondt, A. de
218
Bonora Antonio
218, 228
Bons, Eberhard
57, 227, 244, 258
Borati, P.
29
Boring, M. Eugene
203
Born, E. Th. van den
222
Bosson, Nathalie
253
Bottéro, Jean
228
Botterweck, Gerhard J.
229, 244
Bottoms, Lawrence
222, 244
Bourget, D.
229
Bovati, P.
207
Bradley, George
Granville
222
Brandscheidt, Renate
222
Braun, Rainer
10, 50, 72, 74, 80,
81, 90, 96, 97, 98,
102, 112, 119, 121,
133, 136, 138, 140,
141, 145, 148, 151,
153, 170, 171, 174,

184, 189, 202, 223,
240, 255, 257
Brawer, A. J.
268
Bream, Howard N.
229
Brenner, Athalya
225, 259, 265
Brenz, Johannes
34, 244
Bretón, Santiago
227, 229
Bridges, Charles
218
Bright, Laurence
218
Brindle, Wayne A.
265
Brink, E.
229
Brisson, E. Carson
259
Broch, Yitzhak L.
218
Bronznik, Nahum M.
270
Brown, John P.
240
Brown, Raymond E.
76
Brown, Stephen G.
45, 111, 237, 256
Brown, William P.
218, 225, 229, 267
Broyde, M. J.
244
Brueggemann, Walter
226
Brunner, Hellmut
11, 39, 42, 63, 64,
70, 182, 208, 212,
217
Brunner-Traut, Emma
108
Bruno, Arvid
223

Bruns, J. Edgar
244, 268
Brzegowy, Tadeusz
229, 240
Buchanan, Alastair
244
Buchholz, W.
229
Buck, F.
218
Budde, Karl
124, 218
Buhl, Frants
229
Buhlman, Alain
261, 263, 264
Bühlmann, Walter
78, 108, 223, 240
Bultmann, Rudolf
32
Bunge, Gabriel
244
Burkes, Shannon
223
Burkitt, F. Crawford
218, 244
Burkitt, J.
35, 251
Burns, John Barclay
265, 267
Burrows, Millar
245
Bush, Barbara
223
Buss, Martin J.
229
Busto Saiz, José Ramón
268
Butting, Clara
265
Buzy, Denis
218, 229, 240, 268
Byargeon, Rick W.
258

Calandra, Gregorious
245

Campos, Haroldo de
218

Caneday, Ardel B.
229

Cannizzo, Antonio
223

Cannon, W. W.
253

Cantalausa, Joan de
218

Caquot, André
254

Carlebach, J.
223

Carmichael, Calum M.
259

Carny, Pinhas
229

Carr, David McLain
258

Carrez, M.
76, 261

Carriére, Jean-Marie
229

Cartledge, Tony
263

Castelli, David
218

Castellino, George R.
45, 140, 229, 237,
256

Cazelles, Henri
251

Celada, B.
229

Ceresko, Anthony R.
80, 144, 226, 229,
251, 266

Ceronetti, Guido
218

Cervera, Jordi
245

Chamakkala, J.
229

Chamiel, Chaim
253

Chen, Chin-Wen
268

Cheyne, Thomas Kelly
218

Chia, Philip P.
229

Chilton, Bruce
253

Chomarat, Jacques
245

Chopineau, Jacques
227, 245, 258

Christianson, Eric S.
223, 229, 238, 245

Cimosa, Mario
229, 240

Clark, D. C.
229

Clarke, Ernest G.
253

Clemens, David M.
229

Clines, David J. A.
45, 200, 226

Cochand-Méan,
Corinne
267

Cochrane, Arthur C.
229

Cohen, A.
218

Cohen, M. E.
104, 173

Collins, John J.
55, 108, 240

Colpe, Carsten
203

Condamin, Albert
229

Conradie, E. M.
229, 255

Cook, Johann
38, 253

Coppens, Joseph
16, 237, 239

Corré, Alan D.
258

Cosser, William
229, 240

Cox, Samuel
218

Crüsemann, Frank
54, 55, 95, 96, 153,
189, 229, 241

Craigie, Peter C.
245

Crenshaw, James L.
15, 45, 77, 80, 83,
91, 95, 97, 109, 120,
121, 126, 132, 139,
145, 146, 148, 150,
155, 157, 160, 163,
167, 172, 176, 177,
178, 184, 185, 189,
190, 196, 211, 218,
226, 227, 229, 238,
240, 245, 261, 264,
269

Cross, Frank Moore
55

Cruveilher, P.
230

Curpatrick, Stephan
245

Custer, John S.
245

Dacquino, P.
230

Dahood, Mitchell
35, 127, 146, 251,
261, 264, 268

D'Alario, Vittoria
45, 223, 230, 237,
241, 261, 266

Dale, Thomas Pelham
219

Dalman, A.
203, 211

Dalman, Gustav H.
217

Danker, Frederick W.
100, 230

Dattler, Federico
230

Davidson, Robert
219

Davila, James R.
251

Davis, Barry C.
269

Deane, William John
219

Defélix, Chantal
245

Deissler, Alfons
217

Deist, F. E.
259

Delitzsch, Franz
40, 50, 78, 82, 103,
106, 113, 114, 117,
118, 166, 168, 178,
179, 203, 211, 215,
219

Dell, Katharine J.
245

Dell'Aversano, C.
197, 269

Delsman, Wilhelmus C.
7, 45, 251

Deppe, Klaus
245

Derenbourg, J.
230

Devine, Minos
223

Dewey, Rosemary
230, 241

Dhorme, P.
241

Di Lella, Alexander A.
85, 90, 93, 99, 145

Diebner, Bernd Jørg
253

Diego Sánchez, Manuel
245

Diesel, Anja A.
54, 145, 207, 226

Dietelmair, J. A.
219

Diezma, Bautista
Horcajada
226

Diez Merino, Luis
253

Dillmann, August
253

Dillmann, Rainer
245

Dillon, Emile Joseph
223

Dohmen, Christoph
208, 211, 213, 270

Döller, Johannes
257

Donalt, Trevor
230

Dondeyne, A.
261

Donner, Herbert
20, 241

Doré, Daniel
230, 245

Doré, Joseph
76, 261

Dornseiff, F.
230

Dörsing, Frauke
223

Dreese, J. J.
230

Drijvers, Pius
223

Driver, G. R.
134, 265

Driver, S. R.
14

Droz, Eugénie
245

Du Plessis, S. J.
252

Dubarle, André-Marie
226, 230

Duesberg, Hilaire
219, 226, 230, 261

Duin, C. van
212

Dulin, Rachel Z.
269

Durandeaux, Jacques
223, 245

Eaton, Michael
45, 63, 193, 219

Ebach, Jürgen
259, 261

Ebener, Dietrich
192

Eco, Umberto
18

Edman, Irwin
219

Effe, Bernd
14, 18, 85, 120, 217

Ehlich, Konrad
255

Ehrlich, Arnold B.
139, 178, 219

Eichhorn, David Max
219

Einstein, Bertold
245

Eissfeldt, Otto
77, 259

Ellermeier, Friedrich
9, 10, 15, 39, 40, 44,
47, 57, 59, 69,
80, 120, 124, 134,
160, 174, 223, 238,
245, 255, 257, 258,
264

Elliger, Karl
217

Ellis, Robert
260

Ellul, Jacques
223, 230, 245

Elyo'enay, M.
223

Emerton, J. A.
64, 197f.

Enns, Peter
226

Eppenstein, Simon
245

Erdrich, Louise
245

Ernst, Alexander B.
107, 263

Erren, Manfred
194

Etlinger, Gerhard H.
245

Euringer, Sebastian
253

Ewald, Heinrich
168, 219

Eybers, Ian H.
245

Ezra, Abraham ibn
14, 102, 106, 199

Farmer, Kathleen A.
67, 219

Felton, Jacob
230, 245

Ferguson, Everett
245

Fernández, Andrés
252

Fernández, Eleazar
258

Fernandez, Victor M.
230

Ferreira, Valério P.
230

Ferrer, Joan
253

Festorazzi, Franco
230, 241, 245

Fichtner, Johannes
167

Figueras, Antoni M.
219

Finlayson, Thomas
Campbell
219

Fisch, Harold
113, 226

Fischer, Alexander A.
8, 15, 45, 60, 63, 93,
223, 237, 239, 256,
257, 258, 260, 261

Fischer, James A.
219

Fischer, Stefan
223, 258

Fishbane, Michael
207, 210, 212, 270

Fletcher, Douglas K.
263

Flowers, H. L.
230

Fontaine, Carole R.
230, 266

Fonzo, Lorenzo di
219, 261

Forbush, William B.
246

Foresti, Fabrizio
230, 257

Forman, Charles C.
55, 156, 170, 230,
241, 261

Forster, A. H.
241

Fox, Michael V.
11, 18, 40, 42, 43,
49, 51, 123, 134,
139, 146, 151, 158,
160, 172, 174, 177,
178, 185, 186, 187,
191, 200, 201, 202,
203, 208, 209, 210,
211, 214, 215, 223,
230, 237, 238, 239,

255, 257, 260, 266, 269, 270

Fransen, Irénée
219, 226, 256

Fredericks, Daniel C.
19, 83, 223, 252, 264, 269

Freedman, David Noel
253, 268

Frendo, Anthony
268

Friedländer, M.
226

Fromm, Erich
67

Fuerst, Wesley J.
219

Galanti, M.
219

Gallazzi, Ana Maria R.
230

Gallazzi, Sandro
230, 243

Galling, Kurt
47, 52, 57, 63, 68, 69, 77, 80, 81, 85, 86, 91, 118, 121, 124, 126, 132, 139, 148, 151, 160, 163, 168, 178, 179, 195, 203, 219, 226, 227, 230, 241, 260, 261, 270

Gammie, John G.
48, 51, 74, 139, 226, 241

Gangel, Kenneth O.
223

García, Abdón Moreno
244

Garrett, Duane A.
219, 230, 261, 263, 264, 265, 266, 267

Géhin, Paul
246

Gehrke, Hans-Joachim
62, 65, 68, 69, 154, 226

Geier, Martin
82, 246

Gelio, Roberto
265

Gemser, Berend
219

Gentilini, B.
219

Genung, J. F.
219

George, Andrew
173

George, Mark
231

Georgi, Dieter
30, 167

Gerleman, G.
50, 125

Gerson, Adolf
14, 15, 16, 17, 219

Gese, Hartmut
231, 237, 239, 241

Gesenius, Wilhelm
217

Gevaryahu, H. M. I.
263

Gianto, Agustinus
231

Gietman, Gerard
219

Gilbert, Maurice
16, 17, 45, 143, 186, 197, 199, 226, 231, 241, 260, 269

Ginsburg, Christian David
219

Ginzburg, H. L.
33, 35, 40, 41, 199, 219, 223, 231, 237, 255, 256, 269

Gire, Pierre
231, 246

Gitin, Seymour
233

Giversen, Søren
258

Glann, Donald R.
219

Glasser, Étienne
219, 226

Glasson, T. Francis
269

Glender, Shabbatai
231, 239

Glessmer, Uwe
92

Goethe, J. W. von
192

Goldberg, Louis
219

Goldin, Judah
271

Gómez Aranda, Mariano
246, 249

Good, Edwin Marshall
48, 226, 257

Gordis, Robert
41, 44, 49, 52, 57, 62, 68, 72, 76, 81, 82, 97, 103, 109, 113, 116, 117, 118, 121, 126, 139, 148, 151, 155, 156, 160, 168, 176, 182, 188, 190, 191, 212, 219, 220, 223, 226, 231, 239, 252, 258

Görg, Manfred
199, 258

Gorssen, Leo
223, 231

Gossmann, Hans-Christoph
231

Graetz, Heinrich
220, 231

Gramlich, Miriam L.
231

Grant, Michael
194, 226

Graupner, A.
51

Grech, Prosper
231

Greenstein, Edward L.
238

Gregorio, Domenico de
246

Grelot, Pierre
76, 261

Gressmann, Hugo
217

Griffiths, William
231

Grimm, Willibald
261

Grimme, Hubert
241, 267

Grootaert, A.
241

Gropp, D. M.
36

Gros Louis, Kenneth R. R.
231

Grossberg, Daniel
257

Grotius, Hugo
34

Guillod-Reymond, Daphné
246, 261, 263, 264, 267

Gunkel, Hermann
93, 122

Gunneweg, A. H. J.
40, 157

Günther, Johannes
261

Gurlitt, J. F. K.
231

Gutridge, Coralie A.
231

Guttiérrez, Jorge L.
231

Gwynn, R. M.
253

Habeger, Werner
263

Haden, N. Karl
231

Hahn, H. A.
220

Hall, Joseph
246

Hall, Stuart G.
246

Hallo, W. W.
173

Harrington, Daniel J.
241

Harrison, C. Robert
20, 21, 22, 241

Hart, Thomas M.
231, 246, 261

Hartmann, Benedikt
217

Haupt, Paul
220, 231, 239,
271

Hausmann, J.
141

Haussig, H. W.
174

Hawinkels, Pé
223

Hayman, Allison P.
246

Hays, J. Daniel
252

Heard, R. Christopher
246

Heemrood, J.
256

Heer, Josef
246

Heinen, Karl
246

Heinevetter,
Hans-Josef
120

Heinisch, Paul
246

Hellholm, David
52

Helm, Lothar
260

Hendry, George Stuart
220

Hengel, Martin
21, 42, 73, 74, 75,
76, 79, 87, 93, 100,
109, 111, 115, 119,
122, 155, 174, 181,
194, 226, 241

Hengstenberg,
Ernst W.
220

Henslow, G.
269

Herder, J. G. H.
16

Herrman, Wolfram
89, 261

Herrmann, Johannes
241

Hertzberg, Hans W.
63, 69, 97, 109, 126,
169, 168, 178, 220,
241

Herzfeld, L.
220

Hessler, Bertram
231, 246

Hieke, Thomas
261, 264

Hirshman, M.
246

Hitzig, F.
18, 19, 80, 103,
168, 188, 220, 231,
261

Höffken, Peter
231, 238, 241, 255,
258

Hölbl, Günther
103, 241, 226

Holland, Francis T.
260, 261

Holm-Nielsen, Svend
38, 232, 246

Holzer, Paul J.
47, 257

Holzhammer, Henri
269

Homissen, Guy van
267

Horbury, W.
241

Horneffer, A.
174

Hornung, Erik
108, 187

Horton, Ernest
17, 239, 260

Hossenfelder, Malte
22, 46, 51, 65, 73,
74, 85, 94, 99, 100,
112, 122, 127, 128,
226

Hossfeld, Frank-Lothar
232

Hubbard, David Allen
220, 223

Humbert, Paul
50, 226, 232

Humphreys, W. Lee
226

Hungs, F.-J.
223, 246

Hurvitz, Avi
252, 267

Hutchinson, Henry
260

Huwiler, Elizabeth
220

Hyvärinen, Kyösti
38, 253

Iovino, Paolo
246

Irwin, William A.
262, 263, 267

Isaksson, Bo
35, 61, 80, 223, 252

Ishida, Tomoo
64

Jaeggli, J. Randolph
232

Jagersma, Hendrik
241

James, Kenneth W.
246

Janecko, Benedict
246

Janichs, G.
253

Janowski, Bernd
50, 92, 140, 159,
168, 185

Japhet, Sara
48, 246, 257

Jarick, John
38, 42, 246, 247,
253, 256, 260, 269

Jasper, F. N.
247

Jastrow, Marcus
217

Jastrow, Morris
220

Jenni, Ernst
47, 56, 57, 59, 70,
76, 79, 80, 81, 82,
90, 92, 116, 140,
144, 217, 257, 262

Jeremias, Jörg
179

Jirku, Anton
269

Johnson, Raymond E.
238

Johnson, Robert F.
9, 238

Johnston, David
  223, 241
Johnston, Robert K.
  232
Johnstone, William
  232
Jones, Bruce W.
  173, 241, 267
Jones, Edgar
  220
Jong, P. de
  220
Jong, Stephen de
  45, 232, 237, 241,
  256
Jost, Renate
  266
Joüon, Paul
  41, 80, 217, 252, 255
Junker, H.
  232
Junod, Mireille
  260, 262

Kagan, Z.
  266
Kaiser, Otto
  8, 9, 15, 23, 24,
  39, 51, 53, 54, 55,
  74, 86, 94, 112,
  169, 174, 217, 226,
  227, 232, 241, 242,
  267
Kaiser, Walter
  220, 262
Kalugila, L.
  62
Kamano, Naoto
  45, 223, 256
Kamenetzky, Abraham
  S.
  38, 39, 41, 253, 255
Kasser, Rodolphe
  253
Kato, Kumiko
  232

Kautsch, Karl
  226
Keddie, Gordon J.
  223
Keel, Othmar
  50, 65, 108
Keller, C. A.
  139, 142
Keller, Rudolf
  247
Kellermann, Ulrich
  93
Kelly, James
  232
Kern, Udo
  247
Kidner, Derek
  220, 226
King, Nicholas
  242, 247
Kippenberg, Hans G.
  66, 122, 123, 125,
  226
Kittel, Rudolf
  217
Klausner, Max Albert
  232
Klein, Christian
  63, 64, 223, 238
Kleinart, Paul
  220, 242
Kleinhans, Robert G.
  247
Klopfenstein, Martin A.
  232, 262
Klostermann, Erich
  253
Knauf, Ernst Axel
  109
Knierim, Rolf
  72
Knobel, August
  220
Knobel, Peter S.
  253

Knoefler, D.
  211
Knopf, Carl S.
  232
Koch, Klaus
  55
Koehler, Ludwig
  217
Koenen, Klaus
  208, 271
Koester, Helmut
  100, 194, 226, 242
Köhler, August
  223
Komlosh, Yehuda
  232, 253
Köstlin, F.
  232
Kottsieper, Ingo
  152, 153, 177, 189,
  227, 268
Kramer, Samuel N.
  99, 262
Kratz, Reinhard Gregor
  26, 54, 170, 242
Kraus, Matthew
  247, 269
Kreeft, Peter
  224
Kreitzer, Larry J.
  247
Kroeber, Rudi
  40, 44, 53, 86, 108,
  126, 183, 205, 220,
  232
Kroeze, Jan H.
  220
Kronholm, T.
  66
Kroon, J.
  262
Kruger, H. A. J.
  200, 269
Krüger, Thomas
  11, 45, 54, 55, 59,
  73, 83, 92, 116, 123,

  145, 147, 156, 159,
  170, 176, 180, 224,
  226, 232, 242, 256,
  257, 258, 262, 264,
  266, 268, 269
Kruse, Heinz
  269
Küchler, Max
  194, 226, 242
Kuenen, Abraham
  232
Kugel, James L.
  114, 232, 264
Kuhn, Gottfried
  220
Külunen, V.
  42
Kushner, Harold
  67, 224
Kutscher, E. Y.
  35
Kutschera, Franz
  232

Labate, Antonio
  247
Lacan, M.-F.
  232
Laga, C.
  38
Lagarde, P. de
  254
Lamorte, A.
  224
Lamparter, Helmut
  220
Lane, David J.
  217, 254
Lang, Bernard
  224, 232, 233
Lange, Armin
  224, 242, 247, 264
Lange, Gerson
  220
Lange, Nicholas de
  254

Lapide, Pinchas
233

Lattes, Dante
220

Laue, L.
224

Lauha, Aarre
42, 52, 64, 69, 72,
73, 77, 78, 80, 85,
91, 97, 115, 121,
125, 126, 127, 132,
145, 146, 148, 149,
151, 157, 160, 169,
170, 172, 177, 179,
188, 190, 193, 195,
211, 220, 233, 256

Laumann, Maryta
260, 262

Lausberg, H.
8

Lavoie, Jean-Jacques
135, 224, 227, 233,
252, 254, 259, 260,
262, 264, 265, 267,
268, 269, 271

Lawrie, Douglas G.
233

Leahy, Michael
199, 268, 269

Leanza, Sandro
247, 248, 269

Lebram, J. C. H.
52, 55

Lee, Archie C. C.
248

Leenhardt, F. J.
233

Lehmann, Reinhard G.
226

Lehmann, T.
248

Leiman, Harold I.
220

Leimdörfer, David
220, 248

Lempke, Werner E.
55

Lepore, Luciano
239

Lepre, Cesare
220

Leuphold
113

Leupold, Herbert Carl
220

Levine, Étan
194, 199, 233, 248,
254

Levy, A.
254

Lévy, Isidore
257

Levy, Ludwig
19, 76, 126, 136,
168, 183, 185, 205,
220

L'Hour, Jean
232

Lichtheim, Miriam
22, 70, 96, 173, 192,
226, 242, 265, 267

Liedke, Gerhard
155

Liesenborghs, Leo
248

Linafelt, Tod
200

Loader, James A.
9, 43, 76, 77, 78, 86,
105, 109, 132, 160,
203, 220, 224, 238,
239, 242, 260, 262

Lods, Adolphe
224

Loewenclau, Ilse von
242

Lohfink, Norbert
6, 7, 8, 17, 20, 29,
39, 40, 42, 43, 44,
45, 47, 48, 50, 51,
54, 56, 63, 66, 72,
73, 75, 76, 83, 86,
97, 98, 105, 106,
109, 116, 117, 121,
127, 132, 135, 139,
143, 145, 146, 150,
151, 152, 154, 157,
160, 163, 164, 167,
168, 169, 170, 171,
172, 174, 175, 177,
179, 180, 181, 182,
183, 186, 187, 188,
189, 193, 196, 197,
198, 203, 207, 208,
211, 213, 224, 233,
237, 238, 239, 242,
248, 252, 256, 257,
259, 260, 262, 264,
265, 266, 269, 271

Löhr, Max
224

Lohse, Eduard
94

Long, V. Philips
266

Longman, Tremper
9, 11, 156, 220, 238

Loretz, Oswald
9, 14, 40, 41, 61, 64,
65, 72, 77, 145, 146,
173, 182, 190, 191,
194, 199, 202, 203,
212, 221, 224, 233,
238, 239, 242, 255,
256, 257, 259, 260,
262, 266, 267, 271

Löwenstein, D.
262

Lucà, Santo
248

Lucchesi, Enzo
248

Luck, C.
31

Luck, Ulrich
248

Luder, Ernst
233

Luther, Martin
34, 41, 217

Lüthi, Walter
224

Lux, Rüdiger
62, 141, 233, 259,
265

Luz, Ulrich
108, 154, 172

Luzzato, Aldo
233

Lys, Daniel
58, 224, 233, 242,
256

Maas, Jacques
260, 262

MacDonald, Duncan B.
226, 262

Machinist, Peter
233

Maggioni, Bruno
221

Magnanini, Pietro
242

Maier, Johann
217, 242

Maillot, Alphonse
221, 260

Mainz, E.
254

Malchow, Bruce V.
248

Malherbe, A.
74

Maltby, Arthur
233, 262

Maly, Eugene
248

Mandry, Stephen A.
224

Manfredi, Silvana
233

Mangan, Céline
248

Mann, Jakob
248

Manns, Frédéric
248

Manresa, Ruperto M. de
221

Marböck, Johannes
19, 28, 29, 186, 242, 248

Margalit, Shlomoh
233, 269

Margoliouth, David S.
242, 257, 265, 271

Martin-Achard, R.
125

Mateo Seco, Lucas F.
248

Mathew, Jakob
233

Mathias, Dietmar
260, 262

Mattingly, G. L.
173

Mazzinghi, Luca
262, 265, 271

McCabe, Robert V.
233

McKay, Heather A.
226

McKenna, John E.
256

McNeile, Alan H.
73, 97, 135, 141, 169, 221

Meade, David G.
39, 238

Meek, Theophile J.
256, 271

Mehramoz, Minoo
254

Meinhold, Arndt
147

Meisner, N.
85, 104, 157, 187, 188

Melanchthon, Philipp
34

Mendelssohn, Moses
248

Mercer, Samuel A. B.
254

Merkin, Daphne
248

Merz, Vreni
223

Meschonnic, Henri
221

Mettayer, Arthur
260

Meyer, Ivo
239, 266

Meynet, R.
29, 207

Michaud, Robert
66, 114, 224

Michel, Diethelm
14, 15, 16, 17, 40, 41, 42, 45, 48, 57, 62, 63, 64, 66, 68, 91, 93, 94, 95, 97, 110, 111, 115, 119, 121, 123, 124, 127, 128, 133, 134, 135, 136, 139, 140, 141, 145, 146, 148, 149, 150, 157, 160, 166, 167, 168, 176, 180, 182, 183, 186, 188, 203, 221, 224, 227, 233, 239, 242, 255, 256, 257, 259, 260, 262, 264, 265, 266, 267

Middendorp, Th.
205, 242

Mildenberger, Friedrich
221

Miller, Athanasius
233, 238

Miller, Douglas B.
256

Miller, Patrick D.
55

Min, Young-Jim
257

Mitchell, Hinckley G.
233, 257

Moffatt, James
113

Molina, Jean-Pierre
234, 248

Montaner, Luis Vegas
254

Montgomery, James A.
259

Moor, J. C. de
16, 146

Moore, George F.
269

Mopsik, Charles
254

Moriarty, Rachel
248

Mosis, R.
42, 43

Moss, Steven A.
257

Motais, A.
224

Moulton, Richard G.
221

Moyise, Steve
248

Muilenburg, James
37, 254

Mulder, J. S. M.
45, 234, 238, 257

Müller, Hans-Peter
14, 41, 45, 56, 57, 62, 65, 66, 72, 81, 85, 86, 89, 145, 152, 155, 178, 184, 185, 227, 234, 238, 242, 257, 259, 260, 262, 269

Munitiz, J. A.
38

Munk, A.
239

Munnich, Olivier
269

Muntingh, L. M.
234

Muraoka, Takamitsu
217

Murison, R. G.
269

Murphy, Paul R.
269

Murphy, Roland E.
7, 9, 33, 34, 38, 59, 62, 73, 77, 81, 97, 113, 114, 126, 132, 139, 145, 146, 151, 163, 167, 180, 191, 207, 220, 221, 227, 234, 238, 248, 262, 264, 265, 266, 271

Nebe, G. Wilhelm
36, 37, 254

Negele, Manfred
248

Negenman, Johan
221

Neher, André
224

Nelis, J. T.
7, 45

Nembach, Ulrich
234

Neumann-Gorsolke, Ute
92

Newsom, Carol A.
234

Nichols, Francis W.
249

Nickel, Rainer
12

Nicolangelo, M.
221

Nida, Eugene A.
259

Niekerk, M. J. H. van
234, 269

Nishimura, Toshiaki
234, 257, 262

Noakes, K. W.
249

North, R.
48

Noth, Martin
40, 255

Nötscher, Friedrich
221

Oberholzer, J. P.
234

O'Callaghan, José
254

Odeberg, Hugo
221

Oeming, Manfred
51, 208, 213, 262

Ogden, Graham S.
9, 42, 49, 104, 196,
200, 211, 221, 238,
239, 256, 257, 262,
263, 264, 267, 268,
270

Okorie, A. M.
234

Olinger, Danny
270

O'Neil, E. N.
12

Oort, Henricus Lucas
221

Opelt, I.
249

Osborn, Noel D.
135, 265

Otto, Eckart
226

Pahk, Johan Yeong Sik
99, 166, 173, 224,
243, 262, 266,
267

Pakala, J. C.
227

Palm, August
228

Palma, Gaetano di
234, 271

Pamploni, Massimo
249

Paper, Herbert H.
254

Papone, Paolo
234, 243

Passaro, Angelo
222, 227, 228

Paulson, Gail N.
249

Pautrel, Raymond
41, 221, 271

Pazera, Woiciech
234

Pedersen, Johannes
243

Pennacchini, Bruno
234

Perdue, Leo G.
107, 109, 110, 111,
226, 227, 264

Perlitt, Lothar
179

Perrin, Nicholas
255, 271

Perry, Theodore
Anthony
221, 234

Peter, C. B.
249

Peters, Norbert
28, 243, 260

Pfeiffer, Egon
234, 262

Pfeiffer, Robert H.
234

Pfleiderer, Edmund
243

Pick, Bernhard
234

Pinto, Carlos O.
234

Piotti, Franco
87, 184, 252, 262,
265, 268, 270

Piras, Antonio
249

Ploeg, J. van der
171, 221

Plumptre, E. H.
49, 113, 221

Podechard, Emmanuel
73, 97, 135, 139,
160, 221, 240

Polk, Timothy
42, 256

Polzin, R.
35

Porter, L. B.
235

Post, Jack
260, 262

Poulssen, N.
235

Power, John
235

Prato, G. L.
169

Preuss, Horst D.
169, 170, 185, 205,
227

Prinsloo, W. S.
237

Prior, John M.
235

Pritchard, James B.
217

Puech, Émile
249

Pury, Albert de
235, 249

Qaegebeur, J.
36

Qimron, Elisha
265

Quacquarelli, Antonio
249

Raalte, J. van
243

Rabinovitch, Gérard
249

Rad, Gerhard von
18, 31, 79, 192, 227,
235

Rahlfs, A.
139, 217

Rainey, Anson F.
235, 258

Räisänen, H.
42

Rankin, Oliver S.
221

Ranston, Harry
174, 224

Rashi
106

Raurell, Frederick
235, 249

Ravasi, Gianfranco
221, 224, 2353

Reich, K.
74, 217

Reich, Rachel
238

Reichert, V. E.
104, 218

Reif, Stefan C.
243

Reimer, P. B.
224

Reines, Ch. W.
235, 267

Reitman, James S.
238

Renan, Ernest
221

Rendtorff, Rolf
7

Rendtorff, Trutz
46, 169

Reuss, Eduard W. E.
221

Reuter, Eleonore
89, 262

Richards, Hubert
235

Richardson, M. E. J.
217

Richter, Hans-
Friedemann
235, 266, 267

Ricken, Friedo
112, 181, 227

Riekkinen, V.
42

Riesener, Ingrid
145, 146, 147, 148,
149, 266

Ringgren, Helmer
85

Rizzante Galazzi, A. M.
243

Robertson, D.
235

Rochettes, Jacqueline
des
243

Rodrigues, Jecy
224

Rodríguez, I.
270

Rodríguez Ochoa,
J. M.
263

Roe, George
224

Rofé, Alexander
264

Rohls, Jan
46

Roller, E.
224

Römer, Thomas
227

Römheld, K. F. D.
39

Rompay, L. van
38

Rose, Martin
16, 211, 224, 235,
239, 240, 258, 266,
271

Rosenberg, A. J.
221

Rosendal, Bent
239

Rosin, Robert
249

Rosso Ubigli, Liliana
243

Rostovtzeff, Michael
114, 115, 227

Rothuizen, G. Th.
249

Rougemont, Frédéric
de
221

Rousseau, François
238

Rowley, H. H.
235

Rude, Terry
235

Rudman, Dominic
224, 235, 243, 252,
263, 266, 267

Rudolph, Wilhelm
217, 224

Ruler, A. A. van
249

Ruppert, L.
42, 43

Ryder, E. T.
221

Rylaarsdam, J. Coert
221

Saadia Gaon
33

Sacchi, P.
197, 249

Sacchi, Paolo
221

Saebø, M.
201

Salters, Robert B.
38, 109, 235, 243,
246, 249, 254, 263,
264, 268

Salvaneschi, Enrica
270

Salyer, Gary D.
224

Sanchez-Prieto Borja,
Pedro
226

Sandberg, Ruth N.
249

Saracino, Francesco
235, 268

Sargent, L. G.
225

Sauer, Georg
96, 124, 127, 145,
147, 148, 152, 169,
175, 179, 205, 209,
210, 211, 212, 214,
269

Sauter, Gerhard
77, 263

Savignac, Jean de
235, 267

Savigni, Raffaele
249

Sawicki, Franz
249

Sawyer, John F. A.
200, 202, 203, 270

Schabl, R.
235

Schäfer, P.
114

Scharbert, Josef
199, 270

Scheffler, Eben H.
235

Scheid, Edward G.
235

Scherman, Nosson
222

Schiffer, Sinai
225

Schischkoff, Georgi
1

Schlögel, Nivard
263

Schmeller, Thomas
13

Schmid, Hans
Heinrich
66, 67, 123, 227,
268

Schmidt, Johannes
264

Schmithals, Walter
157

Schmitt, Armin
126, 235

Scholz, Anton von
221

Schoors, Anton
35, 36, 38, 42, 45,
47, 48, 49, 56, 57,
58, 59, 80, 81, 82,
83, 93, 102, 104,
106, 116, 117, 118,
132, 134, 143, 150,
151, 153, 158, 166,
190, 191, 200, 203,
225, 235, 238, 240,
243, 252, 254, 266

Schottroff, Willy
52, 54, 95, 111, 153,
189

Schubert, Mathias
9, 225, 239, 259

Schulte, Adalbert
264

Schulz, A.
227

Schulz, R.
199

Schunk, Klaus-Dietrich
103, 148, 188, 263,
268
Schwartz, Matthew
249
Schwarzchild, Roger
252
Schwertner, S.
49
Schwienhorst-
Schönberger, Ludger
5, 6, 7, 8, 14, 17, 18,
19, 21, 22, 25, 45,
83, 91, 93, 94, 96,
97, 98, 101, 104,
111, 115, 117, 119,
120, 126, 131, 135,
140, 141, 145, 146,
149, 152, 153, 157,
159, 160, 165, 181,
183, 186, 187, 225,
228, 235, 238, 239,
240, 243, 257, 259,
260, 265, 266, 271
Scibona, Rocco
235
Sciumbata, M. Patrizia
235
Scott, David Russell
168, 225
Scott, R. B. Y.
221
Seel, Othmar
50
Seguineau, R.
235
Seibert, P.
39
Seidel, Martin
250
Sekine, Seizo
235
Sen, Felipe
250
Seow, Choon-Leong
7, 19, 81, 208, 221,

235, 239, 243, 252,
256, 259, 270, 271
Serrano, J. J.
236, 267
Seybold, Klaus
42
Shaffer, Aaron
99, 263
Shank, H. Carl
236
Shaw, Jean
225
Shead, Andrew G.
236
Shefi, Elisha
260, 263
Sheppard, G. T.
208, 227, 243, 271
Sheridan, Sybil
250
Shields, Martin A.
271
Short, Robert L.
225
Siclari, Alberto
250
Siegfried, Carl
76, 91, 124, 221
Silva Carvalho da, José
Carlos
243
Siméon, Jean-Pierre
236
Simian-Yofre, Horacio
236
Sitwell, G.
250
Skehan, Patrick W.
85, 90, 93, 99, 145,
271
Slemmons, Timothy M.
270, 271
Smalley, Beryl
34, 250
Smelik, Klaas A. D.
58, 259

Smend, Rudolf
72, 236, 259, 263
Smith, David L.
236
Smith, L.
236
Sneed, Mark
236
Snell, D. C.
173
Soggin, J. A.
109
Sokoloff, Michael
233
Spaller, Christina
225, 258
Spangenberg, Izak J. J.
221, 228, 236, 240,
250, 263, 264
Sperber, Alexander
217
Spieckermann,
Hermann
236, 263, 266
Spina, Frank A.
236
Staerk, Willy
268, 270
Stähli, H.-P.
141, 213, 214
Stamm, J. J.
217
Staples, William E.
42, 256, 258, 260
Stec, David M.
254
Steck, Odil Hannes
16, 37, 52, 54, 55,
243
Stegemann, Wolfgang
54, 95, 111, 153,
189
Steinmann, Jean
221
Steppat, F.
109

Steyn, J. J.
250
Stiglmair, Arnold
236
Stock, George
236
Stockhammer, Morris
236
Stoebe, Hans Joachim
72, 85, 95
Stolze, Jürgen
263, 266
Stone, E.
236
Stone, Michael E.
55
Storniolo, Ivo
225
Storr, R.
250
Stoute, P. P.
270
Stowers, Stanley K.
13
Strack, Hermann L.
108, 161
Strauss, Hans
250, 270
Stresa, Sergiu
250
Strobel, Albert
221
Strothmann, Werner
250, 254
Swain, L.
236

Tàmez, Elsa
225, 236, 250, 260
Taradach, Madeleine
250, 253, 259
Taylor, Charles
200, 202, 270
Templeton, Douglas A.
250
Thilo, Martin
222

Thomas, D. Winton
40

Thompson, David L.
268

Thompson, J. David
254

Thurn, Hans
250

Tidball, Derek
250

Tigay, Jeffrey H.
173, 268

Tin-Sheung, Wong
258

Tita, Hubert
264

Toorn, Karel van der
243

Torrey, C. C.
35, 222, 252, 263

Torta, Giorgio
236

Towner, W. Sibley
222, 243

Tracy, David
25

Trenchard, Ernesto
222

Trible, Phyllis
236

Tropper, Josef
263, 271

Tsevat, M.
123

Tsukimoto, Akio
270

Tur-Sinai, Naftali Herz
160, 255

Tyler, Thomas
222

Uehlinger, Christoph
14, 173, 174, 239,
243, 263, 268

Ullendorf, Edward
41, 255

Ulrich, Eugene
36, 37, 254

Umbreit, F. W. C.
240, 263

Uricchio, Francesco
250

Vaccari, A.
259

Vaihinger, J. G.
238

Vajda, Georges
250, 270

Vallet, Odon
225

Vanderkam, James C.
126

Varela, A. T.
115, 264

Vattioni, Francesco
236

Vegas Montaner, Luis
254

Verheij, Arian J. C.
65, 258, 259

Vignolo, Roberto
240, 259

Vílchez Líndez, José
6, 222, 225, 252, 260

Vinel, François
38, 250, 254, 255

Vischer, Wilhelm
222, 236, 250

Viviano, Pauline A.
236

Vocht, Constant de
250

Vogel, D.
250

Vogels, Walter P. B.
236

Vogt, Ernst
255

Vögtle, Anton
217

Voltaire, F. M. A.
250

Volz, Paul
124, 141, 222

Vonach, Andreas
225, 236, 251, 263

Vriezen, Theodor C.
243

Waard, Jan de
59, 238, 258

Wachten, Johannes
251

Wagner, Andreas
226

Wahl, Harald M.
240

Wahl, Otto
255

Wal, A. J. O. van der
270

Walbank, Frank W.
100, 154, 179, 203,
227, 243

Waldman, Nahum M.
267

Wallis, Gerhard
236, 260, 263

Walsh, Jerome T.
236

Ward, James M.
226

Watson, Wilfred G. E.
16, 146, 259, 270

Weber, Jean-Julien
222

Weber, R.
217

Weeks, Stuart
227

Weidmann, Franz
251

Weill, R.
237

Weinberg, Zvi
251

Weinfeld, Moshe
100

Weisberg, D. B.
173

Weisman, Ze'ev
263, 268

Weiss, James
251

Wendland, P.
100

Westermann, Claus
48, 227

White, Graham
251

Whitley, Charles F.
28, 39, 40, 41, 57,
58, 77, 79, 80, 82,
96, 126, 132, 134,
139, 146, 153, 158,
162, 166, 176, 177,
190, 191, 225, 243,
252, 255, 256

Whybray, Roger N.
50, 51, 109, 113,
139, 140, 148, 156,
171, 174, 210, 222,
225, 227, 237, 240,
258, 260, 265

Wichern, Frank B.
251

Wickert, L.
187

Wilch, John Robert
251

Wildeboer, Gerrit
14, 222

Williams, James G.
66, 237, 258, 259

Willis, T.
80

Willmes, Bernd
225

Wilson, Gerald H.
208, 271

Wilson, Lindsay
258

Winckler, Hugo
243

Windel, Karl Albert R.
251

Winton Thomas, David
268

Wischmeyer, Oda
243

Wisdom, Thurman
237

Wise, Michael
265, 267

Witzenrath, Hagia
190, 199, 200, 202,
203, 270

Wölfel, Eberhard
140, 251

Wright, Addison G.
7, 76, 222, 238, 257,
261, 263

Wright, C. C.
222

Wright, J. Stafford
222, 237

Wuckelt, Agnes
251

Wünsche, August
251

Wyk, W. C. van
251

Wyngaarden, Martin E.
251

Wyse, R. R.
237

Yancey, Philip
237

Youngblood, Ronald F.
270

Younger, K. Lawson
173

Zafrani, Haim
254

Zapletal, Vincenz
15, 124, 222, 237,
243

Zenger, Erich
243

Zer Kavod, Mordecai
237, 252, 256

Zevit, Ziony
233

Ziegler, Joseph
254

Zimmer, Tilmann
225

Zimmerli, Walther
5, 11, 49, 63, 69, 70,
82, 85, 120, 126,
132, 142, 145, 146,
151, 160, 163, 168,
169, 176, 177, 180,
184, 188, 192, 195,
196, 197, 222, 225,
238, 243, 251, 257

Zimmermann, Frank
39, 225, 252, 253,
255, 263

Zlotowitz, Meir
113, 114, 222

Zobel, Hans-Jürgen
141

Zorn, C. M.
222

Zschoch, Hellmut
251

Zuck, Roy B.
45, 200, 225, 237

Zuckerman, Bruce E.
253

Zuckermann, A.
225

3. Subjects

Agur
39

Aleppo Codex
36

Animals
93, 170, 203

Antigonus of Socho
161

Antiochus II
103

Antiochus III
103, 188

Antisthenes
151

Aquila
38

Arabic version
38

Archimedes
178, 179

Arsinoe III
103

Bezalel
24

Chance
3

Charity
192–93

Contingency
6, 29, 68–69, 79

Coptic
38

Corpus Salomonicum
27–28, 30, 33–34,
38, 41, 208

Cynics
112, 119, 184

Death
25, 67–68, 70, 165,
167, 169–71, 191,
203, 204

Deuteronomic History
55

Diatribe (genre)
12–13

Diogenes of Sinope
148

Dionysos
103

Eating and drinking
1, 3, 26, 88, 127,
165, et passim

Eliezer ben Hyrcanus
211

Enoch
126

Envy
96

Epicurus, Epicureans
85, 94, 122

Essenes
17, 94, 100, 170

Ethics
46, 100, 162, et
passim

Ethiopic
38

Euripides
93

Folly
    personification of
    183

Futility (*hebel*)
3, 42–43, 61, 133,
136, 197, 206, et
passim

Gezer calendar
79

God
    anger of
    3
    and the good
    83–84
    and time
    84–85
    creator
    2, 25, 30, 75, 84,
    86–87, 90, 198
    fear of
    2, 10, 23, 27, 89,
    160–62, 214
    gifts of
    1, 3, et passim
    judgment of
    156
    justice of
    91

piety toward
106–12
Government, royal
221, 113–15, 125
Greed
98
Greek philosophy and
literature
1, 12, 17, 21–22,
93–94, 100, 128

Happiness
80–83
"Happy medium"
140
Hebel: See Futility
Hedonism
1
Hegesias
(Peisithanatos)
40
Herod
154
Hillel
33
History, concept of
52
Hyrcanus
20

Inheritance
70–71
Injustice
26, 95

Joseph ben Tobiah
20, 21, 66, 103,
129, 182, 193
Joshua
24

King (See also
Government)
4, 6, 14, 20, 21, 39,
58–75, 83, 101–8,
113–15, 150–54,
156–57, 177–80,
187–88

Lemuel
39
Leningrad Codex, the
36, 352

Meteorology
194
Midrash
38, 78, 198
Mishnah, the
35, 40, 59, 139
Moses
24, 25

Nebneteru
174
New Testament
32–33

Onias II
20
Onias
103

Parallelism of members
9, 76
Peshitta
38
Petosiris
174
Pharisees
17, 100, 181
Plato
93
Pleasure
1, 61, 64–66,
71–72, 94, 127,
165, 166–67,
171–73, et passim
Portion, right
3, 124
Poverty
4, 116–30
Power
4
Ptolemy Euergetes
16, 103

Ptolemy I
19, 20
Ptolemy II
Philadelphus
19, 65, 66, 73
Ptolemy III
65
Ptolemy IV
103
Ptolemy V
53, 65, 103, 154,
188
Pyrrho of Elis
112

Qoheleth, book of
as textbook
29, 30, 208, 211
contraditions in
14–19
eschatology of
25–27, 90
genres of
8–14
history of influence
27–34
language of
34–36
most difficult verse
in
159
motto of
42–44
origin of
19–27
structure
5–8, 209
text of
36–38
title of
39–41

Raphael
31
Reformers, Protestant
34

Rehoboam
33
Reward and justice
1, 3, 25, 30,
140–42, 160, 162,
171

Sadducees
17
Sara, wife of Tobias
31
School
13, 14, 15, 29, 30,
74, 128, 179, 181,
208
Seleucid II
103
Shammai
33
Sirach
28–29
Socrates
145
Solomon
11, 16, 29, 30, 33,
34, 40, 211
Soter
20
Stoics, Stoicism
74, 85, 184

Taimhotep
174
Targum
33, 38, 155, 198,
199
Teacher
17, 64, 148, 163,
175, 211
Temple and cult
27, 107–12
Themistocles
179
Time
3, 31, 75–79, 84
Tobit (book)
31

Torah
24–25, 163
Tyche
69

Vulgate
38

Wealth
4, 116–30
Wisdom of Solomon
(book)
30
Wisdom, human
5, 22–25, 60, 61,
64, 89, 131,

176–89, et passim
limits of
143–49
personification of
23–24, 125,
145–49
Work, toil
4, 49, 97, et passim

In the design of the visual aspects of *Hermeneia,* consideration has been given to relating the form to the content by symbolic means.

The letters of the logotype *Hermeneia* are a fusion of forms alluding simultaneously to Hebrew (dotted vowel markings) and Greek (geometric round shapes) letter forms. In their modern treatment they remind us of the electronic age as well, the vantage point from which this investigation of the past begins.

The Lion of Judah used as visual identification for the series is based on the Seal of Shema. The version for *Hermeneia* is again a fusion of Hebrew calligraphic forms, especially the legs of the lion, and Greek elements characterized by the geometric. In the sequence of arcs, which can be understood as scroll-like images, the first is the lion's mouth. It is reasserted and accelerated in the whorl and returns in the aggressively arched tail: tradition is passed from one age to the next, rediscovered and re-formed.

"Who is worthy to open the scroll and break its seals. . . ."
Then one of the elders said to me
"weep not; lo, the Lion of the tribe of David,
the Root of David, has conquered,
so that he can open the scroll and
its seven seals."
Rev. 5:2, 5

To celebrate the signal achievement in biblical scholarship which *Hermeneia* represents, the entire series will by its color constitute a signal on the theologian's bookshelf: the Old Testament will be bound in yellow and the New Testament in red, traceable to a commonly used color coding for synagogue and church in medieval painting; in pure color terms, varying degrees of intensity of the warm segment of the color spectrum. The colors interpenetrate when the binding color for the Old Testament is used to imprint volumes from the New and vice versa.

Wherever possible, a photograph of the oldest extant manuscript, or a historically significant document pertaining to the biblical sources, will be displayed on the end papers of each volume to give a feel for the tangible reality and beauty of the source material.

The title-page motifs are expressive derivations from the Hermeneia logotype, repeated seven times to form a matrix and debossed on the cover of each volume. These sifted-out elements will be seen to be in their exact positions within the parent matrix.

Horizontal markings at gradated levels on the spine will assist in grouping the volumes according to these conventional categories.

The type has been set with unjustified right margins so as to preserve the internal consistency of word spacing. This is a major factor in both legibility and aesthetic quality; the resultant uneven line endings are only slight impairments to legibility by comparison. In this respect the type resembles the handwritten manuscripts where the quality of the calligraphic writing is dependent on establishing and holding to integral spacing patterns.

All of the type faces in common use today have been designed between AD 1500 and the present. For the biblical text a face was chosen which does not arbitrarily date the text, but rather one which is uncompromisingly modern and unembellished so that its feel is of the universal. The type style is Univers 65 by Adrian Frutiger.

The expository texts and footnotes are set in Baskerville, chosen for its compatibility with the many brief Greek and Hebrew insertions. The double-column format and the shorter line length facilitate speed reading and the wide margins to the left of footnotes provide for the scholar's own notations.

Kenneth Hiebert

Category of biblical writing,
key symbolic characteristic,
and volumes so identified.

1
Law
(boundaries described)
  Genesis
  Exodus
  Leviticus
  Numbers
  Deuteronomy

2
History
(trek through time and space)
  Joshua
  Judges
  Ruth
  1 Samuel
  2 Samuel
  1 Kings
  2 Kings
  1 Chronicles
  2 Chronicles
  Ezra
  Nehemiah
  Esther

3
Poetry
(lyric emotional expression)
  Job
  Psalms
  Proverbs
  Ecclesiastes
  Song of Songs

4
Prophets
(inspired seers)
  Isaiah
  Jeremiah
  Lamentations
  Ezekiel
  Daniel
  Hosea
  Joel
  Amos
  Obadiah
  Jonah
  Micah
  Nahum
  Habakkuk
  Zephaniah
  Haggai
  Zechariah
  Malachi

5
New Testament Narrative
(focus on One)
  Matthew
  Mark
  Luke
  John
  Acts

6
Epistles
(directed instruction)
  Romans
  1 Corinthians
  2 Corinthians
  Galatians
  Ephesians
  Philippians
  Colossians
  1 Thessalonians
  2 Thessalonians
  1 Timothy
  2 Timothy
  Titus
  Philemon
  Hebrews
  James
  1 Peter
  2 Peter
  1 John
  2 John
  3 John
  Jude

7
Apocalypse
(vision of the future)
  Revelation

8
Extracanonical Writings
(peripheral records)